Canadian Edition

COMMUNICATION RESEARCH METHODS

Gerianne Merrigan, Carole L. Huston, and Russell Johnston

OXFORD

UNIVERSITY PRESS

OXFORD
UNIVERSITY PRESS

Oxford University Press is a department of the University of Oxford.
It furthers the University's objective of excellence in research, scholarship,
and education by publishing worldwide. Oxford is a registered trade mark of
Oxford University Press in the UK and in certain other countries.

Published in Canada by
Oxford University Press
8 Sampson Mews, Suite 204,
Don Mills, Ontario M3C 0H5 Canada

www.oupcanada.com

Library and Archives Canada Cataloguing in Publication

Merrigan, Gerianne
Communication research methods / Gerianne Merrigan, Carole L. Huston & Russell Johnston.
Canadian ed.

Includes bibliographical references and index.
ISBN 978–0–19–544279–3

1. Communication Research. 2. Communication Research Canada.
I. Huston, Carole Logan II. Johnston, Russell T. (Russell Todd), 1967– III. Title.

P91.3.M47 2012   302.2072   C2011-908056-7

Cover image: Thomas Lottermoser/Getty
Chapter opening photos: p. 2: Courtesy Louis Forsdale Estate. Library and Archives Canada/PA-172802;
p. 20: © iStockphoto.com/DNY59; p. 34: © iStockphoto.com/apomares; p. 48: © iStockphoto.com/Grafissimo;
p. 60: © iStockphoto.com/ideabug; p. 82: © iStockphoto.com/carlofranco; p. 104: © iStockphoto.com/wdstock;
p. 186: © iStockphoto.com/posteriori; p. 144: Library and Archives Canada/P.P.B./K-0000004; p. 174:
© iStockphoto.com/ArnoMassee; p. 200: © iStockphoto.com/sculpies; p. 222: © iStockphoto.com/erikreis;
p. 244: © iStockphoto.com/track5; p. 264: © iStockphoto.com/contour99

Printed and bound in Canada

7 8 9 — 21 20 19

Contents

Preface

This book started with two separate conversations, a continent apart, among teacher-scholars who have never met. As educators and researchers, however, we share a commitment to multiple ways of knowing and the idea that different research methodologies are useful for exploring different questions about communication and culture. This is the guiding insight that informs the structure and content of this text.

The first conversation took place in California. Since the early 1990s, Geri and Carole have taught research methods courses at San Francisco State University and the University of San Diego, respectively. Carole has taught both qualitative and quantitative methods courses for undergraduate students, and Geri has taught undergraduate and graduate courses in quantitative and multiple methods. They developed this book to reflect changing trends in communication and cultural research that had happened over the past 50 years, some of which they had witnessed first hand. The field, once dominated by studies of media effects and persuasion, had expanded into multiple areas using an array of methods such as surveys, content analyses, ethnographies, and textual deconstruction.

The second conversation took place in Ontario. Since the late 1990s, Russell has taught research methods courses at Brock University. As a scholar, he had trained in history but he was now conducting research and teaching in media studies. Russell was fascinated by the vast array of theories and methods available in communication and cultural studies, an observation brought very close to home since his department offered degrees in communication, popular culture, and film. Indeed, his department represented the changes seen by Geri and Carole. In discussions with his colleagues, he understood that his undergraduate course had to speak to these many interests, but it also had to reflect the Canadian experience of communication and culture.

This text is a result of those conversations. We view quantitative, qualitative, and critical research methods as equally important means to understand communication and culture in our world. We believe that each method has its place, and we highlight the role of different methodologies for making different types of research arguments. We hope to introduce undergraduate students to a wide range of communication and cultural research methods. Those students should be second- or third-year majors in communication or cultural studies who have completed an introductory course in their chosen discipline. However, no other prerequisite is assumed (e.g. communication theory, statistics, or specific computer programs).

Second, the Canadian edition of this text addresses issues pertinent to Canadian students. That makes this text somewhat unique. In the past, instructors who wanted to teach research methods with Canadian examples of research and regulation had to adapt British or American works to their needs. Generally, this is a cumbersome task since those texts do not reflect the research environment for Canadian academics, private sector researchers or the civil service (e.g. for issues as such as population demographics, research ethics, or publishing). Only recently the need for a domestic text was addressed for francophones with Bonneville, Grosjean, and Lagacé's *Introduction aux methods de recherché en communication* (2007). In English, Schrøder, Drotner, Kline, and Murray's *Researching Audiences* (2003) offers advanced instruction in one sub-field of research, but does not offer a broad introduction to communication and cultural studies. Hence, this volume tries to address this gap for Canadian undergraduate students who are taking their first course in methods.

In the pages that follow the methods discussed are illustrated with references to Canadian social situations and recent research. This research is drawn from the array of sub-fields in communication and cultural studies: organizational communication, media studies, film studies, digital culture, popular culture studies, and more. At the same time, we have sought examples from outside Canada where they offer useful insights into a particular research problem or where they offer intriguing points for discussion.

The *Research-as-Argument* Model

Because many programs in communication and cultural studies require a research methods course for their majors, this book treats communication and cultural research comprehensively. We've organized the book around three epistemological paradigms or responses to the question, 'How can we know about communication and culture?' These paradigms include discovery, interpretation, and criticism. If you are an experienced instructor of research methods, you will be familiar with the concepts used in this book. The term 'discovery' has been used in place of 'functionalist' to emphasize its investigative processes rather than its philosophical assumptions.

Part I of this book gives readers an overview of some essential questions in communication and cultural research. We have used Toulmin, Reike, and Janik's (1984) model of argument to talk about research as a way of making arguments. We believe that model is applicable to quite different research methodologies. The *research as argument* model is embraced by scholars in a variety of disciplines. This point has been made by Booth, Colomb, and Williams (1995) in the following passage:

> When you make a claim, give good reasons, and add qualifications, you acknowledge your readers' desire to work with you in developing and testing new ideas. In this light, the best kind of argument is not verbal coercion but an act of cooperation and respect. (p. 93)

This is equally relevant to quantitative analysis, as Abelson (1995) observes:

> Rather than mindlessly trashing any and all statements with numbers in them, a more mature response is to learn enough about statistics to distinguish honest, *useful* conclusions from skullduggery or foolishness.

. . . My central theme is that good statistics involves principled argument that conveys an interesting and credible point. (pp. 1–2)

In this book we are using the Toulmin model to show that research methodology is a process of making claims about communication and culture, and then supporting those claims with evidence and reasoning. The reasoning is always based on the values of a particular paradigm, whether that paradigm is discovery, interpretation, or criticism.

Part I of this book introduces students to 'The What and Why of Communication Research'. In chapter 1, we consider the links between communication theories and methods, the audiences for communication research, two types of manuscripts for reporting research, and the importance of the literature review. In chapter 2, we turn to research ethics by outlining its history, its regulation in Canada, and some ethical choices we face when we decide to conduct research. In chapter 3, we introduce our claim-data-warrant model and develop the three paradigms for communication research: discovery, interpretation, and criticism. In chapters 4–6, we outline the different kinds of claims made by researchers. We introduce students to research design and the most common sources, settings, and strategies for collecting and analyzing data or evidence; and we provide an extensive treatment of the ways that discovery, interpretive, and critical researchers warrant the value or worth of their studies.

Part 2 of this book consists of eight chapters, each concerned with how to conduct research using specific methodologies. Although hard-and-fast distinctions are impossible, this part is organized into three sections. Chapters 7 and 8 concern two methods most often associated with the discovery paradigm: survey research and content analysis.

Chapters 9, 10, and 11 concern three methods that are more often associated with the interpretive or critical paradigms. In chapter 9, we present issues pertinent to historical, policy, and case analysis. In chapter 10, we address the methodologies of conversation and discourse analysis. Then, in chapter 11, we discuss ethnographic research and present auto- and critical ethnographies. Although each of these methodologies began with roots in the discovery paradigm, we contend that many Canadian scholars using these methods adhere more closely to interpretive or critical values and assumptions.

All of the part 2 chapters on methodologies are organized in parallel fashion, using the elements of the *research-as-argument* model (i.e. claims, data or evidence, warrant). Additionally, each of these chapters gives special attention to the ethical issues involved in making claims, collecting data or evidence, and reporting those studies.

Finally, in chapters 12, 13, and 14, we present sets of concepts and tools which can further analysis in each of the methodologies described in the earlier chapters. Chapter 12 addresses a number of qualitative analytical insights and techniques typically grouped under the umbrella of critical studies, focusing upon various versions of structural and poststructural criticisms. By contrast, chapters 13 and 14 address quantitative analytical techniques. The first of these two chapters introduces student to the basics of descriptive statistics and hypotheses testing. The second chapter provides an overview of basic inferential statistics for testing significant differences and relationships.

Features of this Book

The style of presentation and writing in this book is similar to that modelled in other research methods texts currently available. Each chapter begins with a reader-friendly introduction, and each chapter concludes with a summary, often accompanied by a table, highlighting the key points. This summary is followed by a list of key terms, discussion questions, and suggested activities for students to try. Each chapter provides readers with extensive examples from published communication research on Canadian topics. Our reviewers have said that our examples are current, engaging, and cover a broad range of research fields in communication and cultural studies.

Acknowledgements

Geri and Carole wish to say that, to all our students and teachers, we have learned from you, and we will continue to learn from you. We are grateful for the support of our families and friends over the 10 years we now have worked together on this project. We appreciate and have benefited from the expertise of our reviewers, both the anonymous reviewers hired by Peter Labella at Oxford University Press and our colleagues, who read chapters, suggested resources, and encouraged us in the writing of this book. Finally, we value the contributions made by Brian Spitzberg, both as a reviewer and critic of this book.

Russell echoes these sentiments. The many students who have taken COMM 2P15 at Brock University have constantly pushed me to improve the course, and their thoughts have driven many of the decisions made in this text. The staff and reviewers at Oxford University Press were very generous with their faith, time, and suggestions; their reward is—I hope—a better book. My family has shown tremendous support for this project, and in particular my wife Sara and daughter Hannah have been endlessly patient while wondering if I would ever emerge from my basement office. The fresh-baked oatmeal cookies were really quite helpful.

Ultimately, however, any errors or omissions remain our own.

In memory of my father, James R. Merrigan, and to my mother and siblings, without whose continuous love and support I would not have attempted to write, let alone complete, this book project.

—Gerianne Merrigan

In memory of my mother, Arlene, and to my husband, Don, and my children, Sierra, Josh, and David. Their continued support and encouragement helped to make this project possible.

—Carole Huston

In memory of my mother, Florence, and to my dad, Russell, with special thanks to my wife, Sara, and daughter, Hannah, for their endless patience.

—Russell Johnston

Part I
The What and Why of Communication Research

1 Introduction to the Field of Communication

Introduction

In this chapter, we provide you with an overview of research in communication and cultural studies and offer ways to distinguish everyday ways of knowing about the world from the ways of knowing employed in academic research. We consider the relationships among theories and research methods and introduce you to the idea that research is a way of crafting arguments. Whether you conduct your own research in this class or not, you will benefit by learning how to read and understand scholarly research papers. Toward this end, we will also introduce you to the variety of venues in which they appear, including conferences, scholarly journals and the books published by academic presses, as well as the popular press where research is made accessible for lay audiences. We focus on the two most prominent forms of scholarly writing: research reports and critical essays.

Studying communication and culture is good preparation for life. Your degree should help you to become a more competent communicator, and to become more sensitive to the multi-faceted nature of culture in modern Canada. These skills will be useful no matter what you choose to do following university.

An ability to understand a wide range of research methods will increase your critical thinking abilities (Canary, 2003), and that can only have a positive impact on everything you do in life. It will start immediately as you will apply skills and insights learned in this course to all of your readings and assignments in your other courses. Beyond your university's walls you will also find that it is expected of intelligent citizens that they read research critically. This will apply in your role as a parent, homeowner, community member, voter, and consumer.

Graduates of communication and cultural studies programs pursue a wide variety of careers in Canada. We work in marketing, public relations and sales, human resources and management, research and consulting, and news and entertainment production, among many other fields. We find these careers in small family businesses and large corporations from a wide range of industries, as well as government institutions and non-profit organizations.

Maybe you chose this major because you do not want to work for a traditional business. Perhaps you are a committed social activist who seeks to advance a particular cause, such as the environment or electoral reform. With the skills developed through a communication or cultural studies program, you might work as a fundraiser, a policy analyst, or a spokesperson. If you plan to pursue a career in politics as a candidate, campaign manager, or media relations specialist, communication courses will be essential. If you aspire to a career that involves public speaking and interpersonal communication skills, such as journalism, education, hospitality, or sales, then once again a background in communication and culture will be an important asset.

Of course, you may want to become a researcher yourself. As a student, you already write papers that ask you to read and apply academic research to specific issues. Business people perform communication audits, manage organizational cultures and branding, and investigate new and existing markets, all activities heavily vested in research. Likewise, government officials depend on research to make decisions about public policies, grant funding, and public service campaigns. Finally, academic researchers embrace all arenas of communication and culture, and explore relationships between theories and methods.

Academic research is the focus of this text. As a recognized academic discipline, communication and cultural studies is relatively new in Canada. Nonetheless, Canadian scholars from a variety of backgrounds have researched communication and culture for decades. They have drawn upon insights, theories, and research methods from several other disciplines, most prominently psychology, sociology, political science, history, English, and film studies, as well as the professional insights provided through journalism schools. More recently, scholars in management studies, and particularly organizational behaviour and marketing, have added their expertise to the field.

The modern roots of communication and cultural studies can be traced to the Victorian era. As modern industrial society took hold, governments and businesses worldwide began to seek more efficient communication systems that could span continents and, indeed, oceans. In every community, newspapers carried stories ranging from local happenings to world events, and in the biggest cities these stories were supplied to thousands of readers on a daily basis. Big cities and small towns were linked by ever-expanding networks of telegraph and telephone cables. After

1900 these cables were joined by the advent of wireless communications. The growth of this communication infrastructure prompted governments worldwide to regulate their competitive practices and to ensure that they served some measure of public service. As legislators and corporations turned their attention to communication, their efforts sparked public debate over the nature and influence of mass communication.

In the United States academic study of communication began as scholars sought to enhance corporate productivity. In the 1890s psychologist Harlow Gale initiated a research program into the cognitive effects of advertising messages. By the 1910s his research had inspired a generation of psychologists and management scholars to investigate marketing practices and the desires of American consumers (Eighmey & Sar, 2007). Simultaneously, engineers like Frederick Winslow Taylor began studying factory labourers and their work routines in order to streamline production lines and increase outputs. The insights of these engineers led to the development of research into organizational behaviour and human relations, often within the confines of schools of business. By the 1930s scholars such as sociologist P.F. Lazarsfeld and political scientist Harold Lasswell built upon the work of these scholars and others to investigate the place of mass media in American society (Babe, 2000).

In Canada, the academic study of communication had two streams: speech communication and media studies. Although speech communication had longer roots here than media studies, by the mid-1970s it was scholars who were working in media studies who developed university communication programs (Tate, Osler, & Siegel 2000). In English-speaking Canada, this reflected the presence of American popular culture. Since the late 1800s writers and artists who have worked in cultural industries have lobbied the federal government to protect Canadian culture. In the 1920s, when the domestic film industry and then radio broadcasting appeared to be overwhelmed by their American rivals, the federal government sought means to reverse the trend. The government's actions have typically been grounded in commissioned research reports. The first research issued in the field of communication and culture was the Aird Report of 1928, an examination of radio broadcasting. In French-speaking Canada, there was a similar interest in the influence of mass media, though francophone policy-makers have often been more tightly focused on the preservation of a specifically French-language culture in Quebec (Lacroix & Levesque, 1985; Robinson, 2000). Since the Aird Report there have been dozens of studies commissioned by the federal government and its provincial counterparts, and these reports have examined the print media, broadcasting, film, telecommunications, and even the languages of everyday life.

Until the 1960s there was no university program in Canada dedicated to teaching in the areas we now associate with communication and cultural studies. There were, however, scholars interested in these fields. Most notable among them were political economist H.A. Innis and literary critics Northrop Frye and Marshall McLuhan. Then, in the mid-1960s, programs started at Loyola College (now Concordia University), Université de Montréal, Université Laval, University of Windsor, and University of Saskatchewan in Regina (Lacroix & Levesque, 1985; Tate, Osler, & Siegel 2000). Following their pioneering efforts the field has flourished. Although most programs once concentrated on the study of the mass media, they grew with the addition of insights from British cultural studies, French post-structural philosophy, and American advances in interpersonal communication. By the 1980s alliances with schools of business introduced organizational communication and promotional communication, while journalism programs provided professional training in print and broadcast news. This combination of theoretical and methodological approaches has produced programs that, in general, cast a critical eye on every topic and pragmatically draw upon the most efficient methods available to gather information (Babe, 2000; Hamilton, 2010).

Today academic research in communication and culture addresses this entire range of topic areas, and degree programs in communication and cultural studies are offered at most Canadian universities. Such programs mix courses on contemporary issues, theory, history, and research methods with courses in applied areas such as public policy, health communication, journalism, and media arts. If you wish to explore the broad range of programs offered in Canada, check out the webpage of the Canadian Communication Association

(www.acc-cca.ca). It maintains a list of communication and cultural studies programs across the country, with instruction offered in English and in French. Ultimately, as scholars of communication and culture, we believe our work is highly relevant to the challenges of contemporary society. The National Communication Association (NCA) (2002) identified four major challenges facing the United States that could benefit from the insights of our field. This list readily applies to Canada as well. It includes: 'revitalizing our political system, promoting physical and mental health, fostering emerging global organizations, and understanding basic human relationships.'

Again, because communication and cultural research investigates a wide range of topics from several perspectives, we employ a wide range of theories and methods. In this book, you will learn about a wide range of methods and how each one relates to communication theory. Before we embark on that journey let's consider: 'What is a theory?'

Communication and Cultural Theories

In simple terms, a **theory** is a description or explanation for what something means, how something works, or how something ought to work. In formal terms, a theory is a set of interrelated ideas and arguments that offer a general insight into some aspect of the world. These ideas and arguments should be logical and free from contradiction. For instance, majors in communication and cultural studies learn theories about the symbolic meaning of particular cultural trends, how advertising works, or how certain social groups within society dominate others (and how those situations might be changed). If you are studying communication and cultural studies, then your program probably includes a course dedicated to the major theories in these fields. You will also encounter theories in courses dedicated to interpersonal, organizational, and intercultural communication courses, as well as courses on media and technology.

Some theories are very detailed and use formal logic to construct their arguments. Those theories are made up of axioms and propositions. **Axioms** are statements about the relationships among two or more concepts, relationships that have been demonstrated in previous research. The term 'axiom' comes from mathematics in which it refers to a relationship that is incontestable and is accepted as law. In our field, axioms specify what we already know about communication or culture. **Propositions** predict what relationships are likely among two or more concepts given what we already know (i.e. that knowledge which is axiomatic). We can point to two major examples of communication theories based on formal logic. The first is Berger and Calabrese's (1975) uncertainty reduction theory. It deals with interpersonal communication. The second, uses and gratifications theory, addresses an audience's role in mass mediated communication (Palmgreen, 1984). Theories based on formal logic are often used to explain and predict how communication processes work. Uncertainty reduction theory has been used to show how interpersonal relationships develop and deteriorate, whereas uses and gratifications theory has been used to explain and predict how the general public engages with the mass media.

In contrast to theories structured by formal logic, some theories are metaphoric. Metaphoric theories use one idea or story rather than axioms and propositions to describe and explain a communication or cultural issue. For example, McLuhan (1964) described our engagement with technology using the terms 'hot' and 'cool'. Hot and cool operate in a dialectical relationship (i.e. they are opposite of each other) in which the advantages and disadvantages of heat are best realized in comparison with cold, and vice versa. McLuhan argued that the same was true of technology. Our level of engagement with any one medium, such as television, might not be fully realized unless that medium is compared to another medium, such as radio. In the relationship between radio and television, McLuhan believed radio was hot and television was cool; because television conveyed audio and visual data, it offered more sensual stimulation and demanded less participation from the viewer. In the relationship between radio and comic books, however, radio was cool and comic books were hot.

Whether formal or metaphorical, there are many theories of communication and culture, and most address some specific aspect of the communication process. For example, there are theories about communicators themselves, those individuals who create, disseminate, and interpret messages and meanings. By 'communicators', we can refer to anyone: family members, corporate employees, entertainers, media organizations, or anyone else who sends and receives information. Uses and gratifications theory is just one example of a theory that addresses communicators. There are also theories explaining messages. 'Messages' refers to any form of **text** by which we convey meaning, and there are theories addressing such forms as conversation, journalism, and digital culture, as well as the very nature of language and symbolism. There are also theories about our means of communication, those technologies that convey messages. McLuhan's concept of 'hot' and 'cool' provides one example of this field. Finally, there are multiple theories about culture that attempt to explain the nature of entire societies (Littlejohn & Foss, 2005). Remember, no matter what aspect of communication and culture is addressed by a **theory**, the job of that theory is to organize our thoughts and make an issue understandable.

You may think that we have all the theories we need to describe and explain everything about communication and culture. Or, you might think that we are replacing older, outdated theories with newer, better theories. In fact, theories are more fluid and flexible than you might imagine. Theories, like communicators themselves, change constantly (Philipsen, 1997). The topics we try to understand and explain, and the ways that we conduct research, are still evolving.

Theory and Research Methods

Just as there are many theories used to explain communication and culture, there are many research methods used by scholars in the field. You may think that theory is something distinct from method, and some researchers do try to keep their methods separate from the theories they wish to test. Nonetheless, theory and method are quite interconnected. Indeed, in some instances theory and method are one and the same thing, and they are taught as such in courses on media criticism, discourse analysis, and ethnography. These different approaches highlight the fact that there is no one uniform approach to research methods.

Why do we have so many theories and methods to study communication and culture? Part of the answer lies with the topics we study. The theories and methods we use to explore messages can be very different from those we use to study communicators or technologies. More profoundly, however, our theories and methods are shaped by how we think about 'knowledge' itself. Consider these three questions: 'How do I know what I know?', 'What is communication and culture?', and 'What is my goal as a researcher?' Your answers to these questions will give you a particular perspective on research. Among scholars in communication and cultural studies, there are three common perspectives that we will discuss in chapter 3 on the three paradigms of knowing. Here, we shall simply note that your perspective as a researcher will likely determine which theories you will use and will shape the methodology you select.

One final point on theory and method: When you select a methodology, you will also tap the theory or perspective that shaped it. You may believe that each method is a simple tool, like a shovel, that will dig up whatever information you need. However, this is not the case. Because every method is interconnected with a particular theory or is informed by a particular perspective, their means of collecting information contain biases towards particular kinds of information. Hence, it is worthwhile to consider the relative merits of each methodology.

In the next section, we consider some everyday ways of knowing, contrast them with a more rigorous way of knowing used in scholarly research, and introduce the idea of research as making an argument.

General Ways of Knowing

How do we know what we know? Philosopher Charles S. Peirce wanted to answer this question. He believed that the way most people know things—that is, through ordinary common sense—was categorically different from the more rigorous methods of knowing that scholars apply in philosophy and the sciences. He identified four basic ways of knowing: by tenacity, by authority, by *a priori* claim, and by the scientific method (Kerlinger, 1986).

Knowing by tenacity refers to customary knowledge: We believe something is true because it is commonly held to be true. For example, the people of Western Europe once believed the earth was flat and sat at the centre of the universe. Today, many individuals believe that the moon's phases affect human moods and behaviour (i.e. lunar influence), or that planetary alignment can forecast individual fates (i.e. astrology). There is no evidence to support these beliefs. However, the fact that these beliefs are commonplace convinces many people to accept them as true. Tenacity is the weakest way of knowing. It relies purely on a belief or a perception that something is true. Nonetheless, even when we are shown evidence contradicting such beliefs, we often prove unwilling to drop them. It may seem that knowledge grounded only in a perception of reality cannot be questioned or verified through any methodological means.

Your beliefs are influenced by what you experience, and this includes your experience of the media. For example, if you are a faithful follower of television news then you may think crime is more prevalent than it actually is. Studies by Gerbner and others (summarized in Gerbner et al., 1986) have tested the ways that media cultivate certain perceptions of reality, like those regarding crime. They found that the media can create a perception that certain beliefs are commonplace. Once a perception of reality is considered ordinary, it is accepted tenaciously. This can give the media tremendous influence and power within society.

The second way of knowing is **knowing by authority**. We embrace this kind of knowledge when we accept that an idea is true because someone we regard as an expert says it is true. We cannot possibly develop expertise in every area of specialized knowledge, so we rely heavily on experts such as physicians and druggists, lawyers and accountants, architects and engineers. Every time we ride public transit or drive a car, we accept the authority of automobile designers and urban planners to get us safely from one point to another.

Knowledge gained by authority is trustworthy if the experts are correct. What if they are wrong? In most debates concerning public policy, there are two sides supported by the expert opinions of lawyers, economists, and academics. In every one of these debates, presumably one set of experts is wrong. There are many examples of experts who were prosecuted for misleading those people who trusted them. The biggest scandal in Canadian financial history involved a mining company, Bre-X Minerals Limited, that misled thousands of stockholders who trusted its report of a major gold discovery. The report was false and greatly exaggerated the amount of gold at the site (Goold & Willis, 1997). Such scandals teach us that it is sometimes difficult to determine when the experts are wrong.

Sometimes we attribute greater weight to an individual's statements simply because of who he or she is. Hence, when we admire certain figures, we might accept their advice in areas where they have only customary or tenacious knowledge. For example, you may value the opinion of a favourite teacher or coach in their areas of expertise, and therefore accept their opinions on other topics as well. Many celebrities use their fame to advertise products of which they have no relevant knowledge. We must remember that an individual's expertise in one field does not mean that he or she is authoritative in any other field.

The third way of knowing is **knowing on *a priori* grounds**. To assert that a statement is true *a priori* is to assert that it is intuitively true, without any experience of the relevant facts. The truth of a statement known *a priori* rests on reasonableness. For example, let's say that you want to determine if a particular action is appropriate. You might establish criteria based on moral grounds and ask 'Is this action justifiable?'. Or, you might establish criteria based on aesthetic considerations, and ask 'Is this action beautiful?'. Whatever criteria you select, you will use your reason to deduce whether or not the action is appropriate.

There is one important problem with this way of knowing: the concept of reasonableness. It is very difficult to define the concept of reasonableness. Can you determine what is reasonable by using your mind alone, or do you need some sensory experiences (what you experience with touch or taste, for example) to confirm your thoughts? And if you need sensory experiences is the knowledge gained still known *a priori*? The issue here is assurance: How can you be sure that any statement you believe to be true *a priori* is, in fact, true? If you have no way to confirm your knowledge, then it is held purely on faith. It is possible, then, that most *a priori* knowledge is knowledge that is actually known by tenacity. Such knowledge may seem reasonable—that is, it may seem moral, beautiful, or

justifiable—because everyone else we know already believes that to be true.

The final way we know things is through the scientific method (Peirce, 1992). The **scientific method** requires us to establish criteria just like the *a priori* approach, and these criteria are used to assess the truth of any statement. However, the scientific method also insists that statements be tested through observation and experience. In the 1600s Sir Francis Bacon and René Descartes argued that scientific reasoning should be characterized by observation, experimentation, and generalization. Today, these terms are associated with one particular approach to science. It should be noted, however, that all research methodologies are based on some form of observation and reflection, though not all methodologies are based on experimentation and generalization.

For Pierce (1992), tenacity, authority, and *a priori* reasoning were ordinary ways of knowing. He believed the scientific method was superior because it relied on careful reasoning tested by experience. We agree with Pierce that researchers must reason carefully. We argue, however, that his understanding of the scientific method must include reflective methods of interpretation and evaluation as well as strictly **empirical methods**. Indeed, even our ordinary ways of knowing play a role in research. Researchers develop their own tenaciously held beliefs about communication and culture, and some of their criteria come from authority figures—usually other, perhaps more experienced, researchers. We bring all our ways of knowing into the research process, and even the most careful reasoning leads us to express a point of view. We call this point of view an argument. In the next section, we introduce you to the idea that research methods are ways of making arguments about what we know.

Research as Argument

Abelson contended that research 'should make an interesting claim; it should tell a story that an informed audience will care about, and it should do so by intelligent interpretation of appropriate evidence' (1995, p. 2). In other words, we should view research as a way to construct an engaging argument (Abelson, 1995; Jackson, Jacobs, Burrell, & Allen, 1986). To explain this contention, we refer you to a classic form of argument (Toulmin, 1972; Toulmin, Rieke, & Janik, 1984) that will help you to distinguish research from Peirce's ordinary ways of knowing. As presented by Figure 1.1, our *research as argument* model is a simplified version of a detailed form developed by Toulmin et al. (1984).

Whenever we make an argument, it is always based on some central assertion. We call this assertion the **claim**. For example, a very simple claim would be 'This is my bicycle.' As you will see in chapter 4, on claims, assertions in research programs take many different forms. They can be phrased as statements or as questions. A statement might describe an aspect of communication or culture, explain the relationship between two phenomena, or predict how something will behave in a given situation. A question might ask how we should describe an aspect of communication or culture, how we should explain the relationship between two phenomena, or how something will behave in a given situation. A claim can also articulate the general purpose or goal of a research program, as happens when a researcher claims that a study will help us to solve a problem in communication or to understand better some aspect of our culture. In part 2 of this book, you will learn about several methods that investigate the many types of research claims.

Data, the second element of our *research as argument* model, refers to the evidence or grounds that support a claim. Using our earlier example, you might claim 'This is my bicycle.' Your evidence might be a receipt that supports your claim. In chapter 5, on what counts as data, you will learn about many forms of evidence for research claims. For example, data can be recorded as numbers and statistics, as words and sentences, or as images and symbols. It may be gathered through careful measurement using specially designed

tools, or it may be gathered by taking extensive notes while reading rare texts or observing a public event. You will learn much more about data collection and analysis in of part 2 of this book.

The third element of an argument, the warrant, is the primary means of linking research claims to data or evidence. Researchers must explain their reasons for making particular claims with specific evidence. A **warrant**, then, is the standard the researcher applies to assess the merits of the data supporting a claim. The reasons themselves can take the form of rules, principles, laws, or formulas (Toulmin et al., 1984). **Rules** are informal but recognized guidelines that anyone in our society would be likely to accept as a basis for some action. Examples of communication and cultural rules might include the common courtesies of etiquette, or grammar—the rules of language itself. By contrast, **principles** refer to formal guidelines within our society such as statutes and government regulations, like those enforced by the Canadian Radio-television and Telecommunications Commission (CRTC). **Laws**, meanwhile, represent the immutable, physical laws of nature (e.g. gravity). Finally, **formulas** describe mathematical principles used in the physical and applied sciences (Toulmin et al., 1984, p. 50). All of these rules, principles, laws, and formulas are warrants that allow us to evaluate the merits of data used to support a claim.

To return to the bicycle example: you can claim your ownership of the bicycle based on the evidence you have provided, the receipt. Your receipt is warranted because of the 'receipt rule' that we recognize in our society. That is, a receipt documents your purchase and, therefore, establishes that you have obtained an item legally, and by extension the receipt rule is part of a broader set of rules governing legitimate ownership in our society. As this example suggests, every warrant depends on extensive background information that clarifies how specific rules are understood and applied (Toulmin et al., 1984, p. 26). In chapter 6, on warrants for research arguments, we present the different ways of establishing warrants for particular types of claims and data. Then, in part 2, we show you how those warrants are applied for specific methodologies.

The **claim-data-warrant model** is a useful way to distinguish ordinary ways of knowing from the reasoning we use to conduct research. Everyday thinking is

FIGURE 1.1 The *Research as Argument* Model based on Toulmin's Form of Argument

similar to the research process in many ways, but everyday thinking is not subjected to the same systematic tests. Moreover, everyday thinking frequently includes elements that are not used in research. To explore this idea more, let's talk about what makes a good argument.

Making Good Arguments

You know now that arguments include three elements: claims, data, and warrants. A good argument includes all three elements. However, not every argument that includes all three elements is good. One way to evaluate an argument is to ask yourself: 'Who am I?, Who do I represent?, How does this research affect us?, and Who benefits from this research?' This series of questions asks you to consider not just the internal logic of the argument, but the potential effects the argument will have on everyone who has a stake in it. For example, let's say that you hear a news report that coffee is good for you. If you drink coffee every day, you will be happy to find evidence that supports your habit. It may mean nothing to you that coffee producers are likely to benefit from the publication of this research. If you are a tea drinker, however, or a tea producer, you may feel less inclined to accept the report, even with evidence.

In this book we describe research as a process of making good arguments. We hope that you will learn to identify good claims, data, and warrants as they are used in different types of research methodologies. Because there are different methods, and different standards for evaluating them, a good way to learn about research arguments is to read the research articles found in scholarly journals. Those articles are written for particular audiences and in two formats: research reports and critical essays. The rest of this chapter profiles the audiences for communication and cultural research, and describes the first stage of all research: the literature review.

Audiences for Communication and Cultural Research

Research is usually made public. Even when a scholar completes a project in isolation, he or she wants to share the findings. And, typically, more than one community

of readers wants to know the findings. Such communities may consist of other researchers who share an interest in the subject; they may also consist of individuals who participated in the project, or they may consist of practitioners who use the knowledge produced by research and want to apply it to some aspect of their work in industry, the media, or government.

When presenting your arguments, then, you should consider your intended audience. Each audience reads a different set of publications and expects a different writing style; they do not all read the same publications or share the same criteria for effective writing (Childress, 1998). Whether you are writing a research manuscript for a class assignment, for presentation to a professional association, for publication, or for some other purpose, it is important to consider your readers and to adjust your style accordingly. Professional associations and scholarly journals are the most common outlets for research manuscripts written by communication and cultural scholars, whereas trade journals, popular press publications, and textbooks constitute a secondary but nonetheless important set of outlets. Let's consider each audience in turn.

Professional Associations

The primary audience for most research reports is a researcher's peer group, composed of fellow scholars who work in the same discipline or study the same field. Generally, scholars who share a discipline or field also share membership in the same professional association. A **professional association** is a voluntary organization that connects scholars with shared interests and disseminates research in their common field. Often, such associations also promote the work of their members to audiences outside of academia and lobby governments for policies that favour research in their field. The main way that associations make research findings available is through conferences. A conference is typically held in conjunction with the annual business meeting of a professional association. Once the business meeting is complete, additional sessions are held that allow members to describe their research to their peers through an oral presentation.

The meetings of professional associations help scholars to stay abreast of the most recent developments in their field. Such meetings can foster ongoing dialogues about issues of common interest and allow scholars to develop relationships with peers who share those interests. Professional associations also allow members to gain important feedback from their peers. Indeed, it is customary for original research reports to be presented at conferences before they are published. The feedback, which peers provide on conference presentations, can help a scholar to revise a written manuscript and to determine what other audiences, if any, should be sought.

Canadian scholars look to Canadian and international associations when seeking a venue for their research. They also look to associations that represent other disciplines but which take an interest in communication and cultural research. There are two reasons for this tendency. First, the theoretical, practical, and methodological issues that concern scholars in our discipline have no boundaries. Most research provides insights that can be readily transferred from one context to another, no matter how closely the data might be tied to one country or, for that matter, one academic discipline. Second, Canadian scholars working in communication and cultural studies represent only a small portion of the international community of researchers in the discipline. For example, the annual meeting of the Canadian Communication Association may attract 500 scholars and practitioners. By contrast, the National Communication Association in the United States usually attracts 5000 attendees each year. The relative size of our community means there are far fewer associations based in Canada itself, since there are fewer scholars available to administer them and fewer scholars available to support them financially. As such, by looking to other disciplinary associations in Canada, or other associations worldwide, Canadian scholars integrate themselves into an interdisciplinary and international discussion of issues that matter to them. The most prominent associations frequented by Canadian scholars of communication and cultural studies are listed in Exhibit 1.1.

Scholarly Journals and Academic Presses

Scholarly journals are essentially magazines that publish peer-reviewed research. Much like a professional association, each journal is dedicated to a single discipline or field and presents relevant new theories and research to a community of scholars with similar interests.

To ensure quality, each manuscript submitted to a scholarly journal for publication must pass through a process called 'peer review'. When the manuscript arrives, the journal's editor must establish a committee of two or more researchers to review it. These researchers must be the author's peers; that is, they must have expertise in the topic discussed in the manuscript. These researchers will consider every aspect of the manuscript, but especially its claims, data, and warrants. If the committee agrees that a manuscript is logical, compelling, and noteworthy, they will recommend it for publication. If the manuscript is noteworthy but suffers from some minor problems, then the editor can ask the author to revise it and resubmit it for reconsideration. If the manuscript has no merit, however, the committee and editor will reject it outright (Katzer, Cook, & Crouch, 1998). Ultimately, only a small percentage of research is ever published in a scholarly journal. Many of the papers presented at conferences are works in progress rather than completed projects, and therefore they may never be submitted to scholarly journals. Exhibit 1.2 lists some of the scholarly journals that publish communication and cultural research.

An **academic press** is a publishing company that specializes in books reporting new, peer-reviewed research. Not all research can be explained in 10 to 25 pages. When a scholar's work is too expansive or too complicated for a typical journal article, he or she will draft a book-length manuscript. Regardless of the length of the manuscript, however, the research must still pass through a peer-review process. Academic presses organize the production of scholarly books by acquiring manuscripts, by assessing their merits through peer review, by supervising their editing and revision, and ultimately by publishing and marketing them. Most academic presses have mandates that define which kinds of research they will handle by isolating individual disciplines and fields. Because the functions of an academic press parallel those of scholarly journals, some academic presses in fact publish journals on behalf of the associations or groups that produce them.

> **EXHIBIT 1.1**   Professional Associations of Interest to Canadian Scholars in Communication and Cultural Studies
>
> **CANADIAN DISCIPLINARY ASSOCIATIONS**
> Canadian Communication Association
> Canadian Association of Cultural Studies
>
> **OTHER ASSOCIATIONS OF INTEREST TO COMMUNICATION AND CULTURAL STUDIES**
> Association for Canadian and Quebec Literatures
> Association of Canadian Studies
> Canadian Anthropology Society
> Canadian Historical Association
> Canadian Political Science Association
> Canadian Sociological Association
> Film Studies Association of Canada
> Popular Culture Association of Canada
>
> **INTERNATIONAL ASSOCIATIONS**
> American Communication Association
> Association for Education in Journalism and Mass Communication (United States)
> Association of Cultural Studies
>
> Australia and New Zealand Communication Association
> Communication Association of Japan
> Cultural Studies Association (United States)
> Cultural Studies Association of Australia
> European Communication Research and Education Association
> European Communications Policy Research
> International Association for Intercultural Communication Studies
> International Association for Media and Communication Research
> International Association of Business Communicators
> International Communication Association
> Media, Culture and Communication Studies Association (United Kingdom)
> National Communication Association (United States)
> Popular Culture Association (United States)
> Société Française des Sciences de l'Information et de la Communication (France)

When we discussed professional associations, we noted that Canadians scholars look to both interdisciplinary and international associations to find venues for their work. The same observation is true of scholarly journals and academic presses, and the same reasons are relevant. Within Canada, there are five journals dedicated to communication research and two dedicated to cultural studies. Internationally, however, there are dozens of journals in both areas, and some of these journals are dedicated to highly specialized fields. Exhibit 1.2 lists some of the academic presses that publish communication and cultural research.

Trade Journals and the Popular Press

Traditionally, most researchers held scholarly journals and academic presses in higher esteem than **trade journals** and the popular press. This is often still the case, since our research peers are still the most desired audience when we wish to share our research findings.

However, today's researchers also recognize the interests of audiences other than our peers. For example, corporate managers may be the primary audience for researchers who study organizational communication and culture and who propose ways to improve how organizations function. Participants in research projects have come to constitute a primary audience for the findings of researchers who study particular cultures in context (Brodkey, 1987). And policy makers are often the primary audience for researchers whose work supports calls for social reform.

Given this interest in new audiences, it is now common to see research summaries presented in trade journals and quoted in the popular press. Trade journals are publications aimed at practitioners in a particular line of work. Just as scholarly journals are read by scholars who specialize in a common discipline or field of study, trade journals are produced for individuals who work in a single business or industry. Some examples of trade journals that report on communication and cultural research include *Broadcaster* (broadcastermagazine.com), *Marketing* (marketing-mag.ca), *Playback* (playbackonline.ca), *Masthead* (mast-headonline.com), and *Infopresse* (infopresse.com). By contrast, the **popular press** are those publications that target the general public by focusing on their readers' common interests more than their training or education. Think of the newspapers and magazines that you can purchase at a newsstand—most of these are popular press publications.

If you want your research to have an immediate impact outside of academia, then you may want to issue an executive summary. An **executive summary** is a brief one to two–page overview of a study's purpose, methods, and findings, and it is used to publicize research among audiences who do not regularly read scholarly publications. Executive summaries are typically sent to individuals who have some influence over public policy, such as elected officials and civil servants, government lobbyists, or industry standards boards (e.g. the Canadian Broadcast Standards Council or provincial film ratings boards). In some situations, however, a trade journal may provide the

---

EXHIBIT 1.2 Scholarly Journals and Academic Presses that Publish Research in Communication and Cultural Studies

CANADIAN JOURNALS
Canadian Journal of Communication
Canadian Journal of Film Studies
Canadian Journal of Media Studies
Canadian Journal of Popular Culture
Global Media Journal, Canadian Edition
Journal of Canadian Studies
Revue Communication
Revue internationale de communication sociale et publique
Topia: Canadian Journal of Cultural Studies

CANADIAN ACADEMIC PRESSES
McGill-Queen's University Press
Les Presses de l'Université Laval
Les Presses de l'Université du Québec
Wilfrid Laurier University Press
University of British Columbia Press
University of Ottawa Press
University of Toronto Press

INTERNATIONAL JOURNALS
American Communication Journal
Communication Monographs
Communication Quarterly
Communication Research
Communication Studies
Communication Theory
Cultural Studies
Cultural Studies Review
Discourse and Communication
Études de communication
European Journal of Communication
Historical Journal of Film, Radio & Television
International Journal of Cultural Studies
Journalism & Mass Communication Quarterly
Journal of Advertising Research
Journal of Broadcasting & Electronic Media
Journal of Business Communication
Journal of Communication
Journal of Computer-Mediated Communication

Journal of Film and Television
Journal of Popular Culture
Language and Society
Mass Communication & Society
Media, Culture & Society
Media History
New Media and Society
Popular Music
Revue Communication & Organisation
Sex Roles

INTERNATIONAL ACADEMIC PRESSES
Cambridge University Press
Duke University Press
Oxford University Press
Praeger
Routledge
Sage
University of Tennessee Press

best access to policy makers; authority figures may be more inclined to read a trusted journal rather than an unsolicited research report. Meanwhile, if your goal is simply to raise awareness of a problem, then the popular press may provide the best channel since it can expose your findings to the greatest number of readers. Ultimately, you need to select the medium that will deliver the audience you want to reach.

At this point in your education, you may wonder how you will ever write any manuscript, let alone the kinds of specialized reports we've just described. Spradley (1980) offers an encouraging word in this respect when he notes 'the only way to learn to write is *to write*' (p. 160, italics in the original). You cannot learn to write a research report simply by reading published research, although reading is very helpful! Learning to write is analogous to learning to swim (Spradley, 1980). We don't learn to swim by watching other people swim, or even reading books about swimming. Rather, we learn to swim by trying it and having someone coach us as we do it. Learning to write research manuscripts is quite similar. You may have trouble when writing your first manuscript, but with practice you will become much more confident and able. Writing is a highly personal yet skill-driven activity, one that becomes easier with practice. It helps to pursue a project that engages you intellectually and emotionally so that your passion for the topic keeps you motivated when the going gets tough.

Two Manuscripts: Research Reports and Critical Essays

In the next two sections, we compare and contrast two kinds of manuscripts, the **research report** and the **critical essay**. These are distinct types of writing. The term 'research report' refers to a written summary of a research project that includes some form of data collected by the author especially for that project. The term 'critical essay' refers to a manuscript based primarily on textual data, whether the texts being analyzed are speeches, artefacts, or the researcher's experiences as evidence and reasoning given in support of a claim. These two ways of writing reflect different ways

of thinking about research, something you will learn much more about in chapter 3.

Both research reports and critical essays typically begin with a title page and end with a reference list. For an unpublished paper, the title page includes the title of the paper, the writer's name and institutional affiliation, as well as contact information such as address, telephone number, and email address. Once published, the title of the paper, as well as the author name and affiliation, are listed on the first page. A **reference list** appears at the end of written research reports and critical essays, and it contains the full citations for all the works cited in your manuscript. Most of those citations will be the published works included in the literature review. The chief purpose of the reference list is to allow readers to locate and read all of the materials on which the author relied, so the list must be complete and accurate. In some reports and essays, this list is titled 'Works Cited'.

There are two style manuals that scholars in communication and cultural studies typically consult when formatting their source citations. One is the *Publication Manual of the American Psychological Association* (American Psychological Association, 2001), and it is usually preferred for research reports written in the style of the social sciences. The second is the *MLA Handbook for Writers of Research Papers* (Gibaldi, 1995), and it is usually preferred for critical essays written in the style of the humanities. A scholar may use either style manual depending on the kind of manuscript he or she is writing and its intended audience. However, a scholar should never use more than one style in any single manuscript. Ask your instructor which style manual you should consult for assignments in this class.

Research Reports

As we have already noted, the term 'research report' refers to a written summary of a research project that includes some form of data collected by the author especially for that project. Knowing something about the elements and characteristics of research reports will help you to read and to understand them. Remember, this is an important goal of this textbook. Even if you do not work as a researcher after graduation, we hope that you will have learned how to read and assess research on your own.

Research reports are written in 'a formal and objective style' (Dangle & Haussman, 1963, p. 10), and they have clearly identifiable elements. In this section, we give you an overview of each element of the research report that will help you to locate those elements in each report you read. Then, we shall outline some of the characteristics of research reports, such as their precise, detailed, and objective style of reporting. Knowing these characteristics will help you to develop your own 'voice' when writing your own research report.

There are six elements of a research report: (1) the abstract, (2) the introduction, (3) the literature review, (4) the methodology, (5) the findings, and (6) the discussion. The very first element of a research report, appearing right underneath the title and author's name is the **abstract**, a single paragraph of about 100 words that summarizes the entire study. In the first sentence, it should state the issue or problem addressed in the study. Then, it should briefly describe the data, theory, and analytical strategies that the researcher brought to the issue or problem. Finally, the key findings of the study should be outlined in the last sentence. Knowledgeable readers use abstracts to determine if a report is relevant or useful in their own search for information; that is, the abstract lets readers know whether or not they should invest their time in the details of the report.

Where an abstract can stand on its own as a summary of an entire research project, an **introduction** is an integral component of the report itself. The introduction serves as the author's formal opening statement regarding the topic, the topic's significance, and the author's approach to that topic (Pyrczak & Bruce, 1992, p. 33). The goal here is context. When the author describes the significance of the topic, he or she establishes a context for the research that reveals it to be relevant, novel, or useful to readers. Just as the abstract tells knowledgeable readers if a report is useful, the introduction can help less knowledgeable readers by explaining why the study is necessary or worthwhile.

A research project may be of personal, social, or theoretical significance, or it may be significant in all of these ways. To establish **personal significance**, a researcher will state why a topic is important to him or her as an individual. To establish **social significance**, a researcher will identify a common problem that the research is designed to address. Finally, to establish **theoretical significance**, a researcher will state how the study will contribute to communication and cultural theory either by developing a new theory or by testing, extending, or refuting an existing theory. You already know that research reports are written for particular audiences (e.g. academics, practitioners, policy makers, or the general public). Knowing this, a researcher must draft an introduction that includes an appropriate amount of detail for the intended audience's level of education and interest in the topic.

Immediately following the introduction is the next element of the research report, the literature review (Galvin, 1999). In a **literature review**, a researcher provides his or her summary of previously published studies on the same topic. Depending on the nature of the topic, this literature may be quite extensive or quite small. The studies included may be theoretical, empirical, or critical, or any combination of the three. The goal of the literature review is to demonstrate how the researcher's current study will be innovative and worthwhile by addressing or correcting issues overlooked in previous studies.

Conducting a literature review and writing a literature review are two very different, though related, tasks. To conduct a literature review, we locate and read everything we can on a given topic. Usually, this work occurs at the beginning of a research project. For scholars who devote their careers to research, locating and reading topic-relevant literature is an ongoing practice. If you are a beginning researcher, however, you will need to locate and read many studies on your topic before you can fully conceptualize your research project (i.e. what claims you want to make, the appropriate types of data to collect, and how you will analyze the data).

There are three good reasons to conduct a literature review. First, as researchers, we view ourselves as participants in a grand conversation about our discipline, our individual fields, and about our society. Adams and Schvaneveldt (1991) note that to become engaged in this conversation, you must conduct a thorough search of the literature to discover those ideas, methods, and arguments already circulating among the community of scholars and practitioners who share your passions and concerns. Knowing these things makes you a more articulate and effective researcher. Second, a literature review typically begins with the most recent work in the field. If your own study is founded on outdated data, discredited theories, or faulty critiques, then you set yourself up for potential failure. An effective literature review should alert you to the most recent data, the leading theories, and the most rigorous critiques. This leads into our final reason: knowing these aspects of the existing literature can spare you time and energy if you discover that another scholar has already completed a project similar to the one you have conceived. When this happens, you can continue with your own research to confirm the other scholar's results, or you can build upon the other scholar's work with innovations of your own (Adams & Schvaneveldt, 1991, pp. 50–52).

Most of the literature you will review will be scholarly and can be found in a research library like that at your university. As we have already noted, research reports are most frequently published in scholarly journals and the books produced by academic presses. Other scholarly sources exist, the main one being the minutes of conferences where new research is presented. Such publications are referred to as 'proceedings'. Research can also be found in government documents that contain commissioned studies, and consultant's reports drafted for private industry, non-governmental organizations (NGOs), or the voluntary sector. Most Canadian university libraries have all of these kinds of materials in their holdings. Additionally, most university libraries provide electronic access to many journals and books through online databases linked to their catalogues. We cannot provide you with instruction in library research strategies because every library and database is somewhat unique. If you want to learn more about research strategies and sources, ask your instructor for help or seek out workshops at your university library.

Once you have read the existing studies in your field, you are ready to write a literature review. It should be concise. When conducting a review, you will identify and critique the claims, data, and warrants for every study you find. Such attention to detail will give you tremendous breadth of knowledge about your topic. When writing the review, however, you

must distill this knowledge into a set of insights relevant to your immediate project. Therefore you will not share every detail you have gleaned, but will note the most important trends in the literature pertaining to your topic (Cooper, 1984). For example, you may gain insights into the type of data sought by other scholars in your field, the methods they use to collect that data, or the theories they apply to analyze their data. What you find worthy of inclusion will depend on the nature of your own study and its contribution to the field. Table 1.1 lists a variety of questions you may ask as you review each work.

The literature review typically closes with the researcher's own claim, which may be phrased in the form of a thesis, hypothesis, or research question. **Theses** are declarative sentences that succinctly outline the researcher's goal for the study. Generally, the goal is to establish the truth or viability of a particular assertion about the topic. **Hypotheses** are also declarative statements, but hypotheses predict specific relationships among variables (e.g. 'Males interrupt speakers more frequently than females.'). **Research questions** are interrogative statements that investigate processes or the relationships between variables (e.g. 'What makes a leader persuasive?' or 'What is the relationship between musical genres and clothing styles?').

Following the literature review, the next section of the research report is labelled 'Methodology'. This section provides detailed descriptions of the researcher's sources of data, the settings where these sources can be found, and the ways that the data were collected. You will learn much more about these topics in chapter 5, on data. For now, we will simply note that the methodology section of any research report will also usually include descriptions of the analytical procedures the researcher used to make sense of the data. Finally, the methodology section should provide the warrants for all these procedural choices.

The methodology section is closely followed by the researcher's findings and discussion. The findings section usually opens with a reminder of the study's purpose statement, hypothesis, or research question. From there, the researcher will profile the data collected using the method described in the methodology section. The discussion section will then offer the

TABLE 1.1 Criteria for Evaluating Literature

CRITERIA	QUESTIONS TO CONSIDER WHEN READING ANY ARTICLE, BOOK, OR WEBSITE
Authorship	• What do you know about the author? • What is the author's area of expertise, training, and institutional affiliation? • Does the author have sound credentials for research on this topic?
Publisher	• Who published the manuscript? • How credible is the publishing house or editor?
Peer review	• Was the manuscript submitted for consideration in a competitive process? • Was the manuscript invited by the publisher or editor? • Was the manuscript peer reviewed? • Was the author's name hidden from the peer reviewers?
Currency	• When was the manuscript published? • When were the data collected? • Has anything relevant changed since the data were collected, or since the manuscript was published? • If yes, then how does this affect the author's conclusions?
References	• Are the references from scholarly, peer-reviewed journals? • How current are the references?

researcher's analysis of this data, as it has been shaped by the analytical procedure outlined in the methodology section. The discussion section may also include the researcher's own conclusions with respect to the study, his or her qualifications regarding these conclusions, and proposals for future research on the same topic.

We must note that not all research reports separate their findings from the discussion. As we noted earlier in this chapter, some scholars maintain a strict separation between their means of collecting data and their means of interpreting data; that is, they distinguish between their methods and theories. As such, these scholars are inclined to present their findings as pure facts that are free of spin and bias. This allows readers to interpret the data for themselves before they read the author's analysis in the discussion section. This is particularly true of researchers whose data is comprised of statistics, all of which may be summarized and presented in tables.

By contrast, other scholars do not make this distinction between method and theory. Indeed, their method and theory may be one and the same thing. Such scholars argue that data cannot be presented as 'pure' facts since the simple act of describing the data imparts qualities to the data. For example, any given number may be large or small depending on your perspective. Similarly, any observation may be significant or insignificant depending on your priorities as a researcher. As such, these scholars are inclined to combine their findings and discussion into a single section, headed either 'Findings' or 'Findings and Discussion'. This is particularly true of researchers whose data is mainly qualitative, based on their readings of texts and artefacts, or their field observations of individual and group behaviours.

Critical Essays

The term 'critical essay' refers to a written summary of a research project based on data derived mainly from texts or artefacts. These texts may be any records of any spoken or printed word, and cultural artefacts are any objects that convey some meaning that is socially significant. By extension, we also include the researcher's beliefs and experiences of these texts and artefacts as data. As we noted with respect to research reports, knowing something about the elements and characteristics of critical essays will help you to read and to understand them.

All six elements of a research report also appear in a critical essay. That said, these elements are presented very differently in a critical essay than they are in a research report. Rather than repeat the prior section, we shall explain the significance of these differences and why they occur. There are four key differences between the two forms of scholarly writing: (1) conception of the writing process, (2) standardization of the manuscript, (3) the unit of analysis, and (4) findings and discussion.

The one major difference between the two forms is the researcher's conception of writing as a process. Most scholars who draft research reports conceive of writing as an activity to be completed after the research is complete. By contrast, most scholars who draft critical essays conceive writing as an emergent process. This means that they prefer to write as their research program is in progress so that they may determine what additional data is needed, when they have enough data, or when new questions must be addressed after considering the original data. Some scholars who write critical essays frame writing itself as a form of inquiry (e.g. Goodall, 2000).

The second difference concerns the standardization of all manuscripts. Critical writers tend to resist standardization or a formal structure because they believe that standardization always privileges some persons or values and oppresses others. As Sprague has argued: 'even a simple literature review runs the risk of privileging existing patterns of thought' (1992, p. 181). In other words, the critical essay is an act of representation and should itself be read critically. Thus you will see considerable variety in the ways that critical essays are organized. It is not always the case that the literature review, methodology, findings, and discussion appear in that sequence. Further, critical essays do not use headings in the body of the manuscript to identify each element as they are used in research reports (Foss, 1996, p. 16). However, critical essays open with introductions just like research reports. In a critical essay, the introduction usually describes what rhetorical 'artefact is being analyzed, the research question that is the impetus for analysis, and the contribution

to rhetorical theory that will result from the analysis' (Foss, 1996, p. 16).

The third difference between research reports and critical essays is the unit of analysis that concerns the researcher. A **unit of analysis** is that aspect of a thing that you wish to analyze. Put another way, each unit of analysis can be considered a single building block in the structure of your argument. For example, in most research reports that rely on data gathered from human beings, each participant is a single unit of analysis. In a critical essay, each block of evidence drawn from a text or artefact is a unit of analysis.

The terms 'text' and 'artefact' have become almost interchangeable in the research community, but they do refer to different things. A **text** is any spoken or written word, performance, or visual sign. These things can be ephemeral, like the spoken word or a live performance, or they can be recorded as in print, electronic media, or artistic media (i.e. music, sculpture, film, paint). By contrast, an **artefact** is any object made by humans and used within a group or society. Artefacts can be texts, but they are not limited to words or visual representations. An artefact may be a personal item, a technology, or an element of the landscape, among many other things. So long as an object conveys meaning that is socially significant, it is an artefact and can be read as a text.

A scholar drafting a critical essay should use the introduction to identify the text or artefact that will be analyzed. Next, the scholar should identify the precise unit of analysis central to the research, which places the study in context. For example, in a study of comic books, will the analysis focus on the narrative and dialogue, the portrayals of male and female characters, or the use of colour and framing techniques? Once the readers are fully oriented to the artefact and its context through the introduction, the scholar should describe the artefact. Because readers do not necessarily have access to the text or artefact this component of the essay is quite important. For instance, if the artefact was a film, the author might describe its plot as well as its characters and any significant technical features (Foss, 1996). This description should justify why the selected text or artefact was 'a particularly appropriate or useful one to analyze in order to answer the research question' (Foss, 1996, p. 17).

The findings and discussion comprise the largest part of most critical essays. The goal in a critical essay is not to discover some truth about a text or artefact but to substantiate a particular claim made by the author. The final paragraph or conclusion should let the reader know what contribution the author feels his or her analysis makes to our collective wisdom by addressing this text or artefact.

In writing a critical essay, then, you are creating another layer of text, another set of meanings that may be associated with the issue you have studied. Mumby believes that, 'In this sense, providing accounts of . . . phenomena is both a poetic and a political process' (1993, p. 20). The critical essay is poetic in that it gains credibility by adhering to the conventions or forms that are accepted by the researcher's **interpretive community** (i.e. the community of scholars who share an academic discipline or field). It is political because the process of analysis and writing usually separates researchers from their research participants, no matter how many experiences they may share during the research itself. Ultimately, the critical scholar believes there is no neutral representation of knowledge; a point of view must be adopted and a conclusion must be sought (Sprague, 1992).

Summary

After reading this chapter, you should have a sense of the broad scope of research in communication and cultural studies, as well as some of the career paths available to graduates in these areas. We described theories as descriptions and explanations for what things mean, how things work, or how they should work. Also, we noted that theories may be presented as formal logic or as metaphors to convey their ideas. Next, we introduced the idea that research programs are, in essence, ways to draft arguments. We believe that the *research as argument* model is useful because it is impossible to do research without representing a particular point of view. Thus, we stressed that good arguments include claims, data, and warrants. We also outlined three everyday ways of knowing (tenacity, authority, and *a priori*), and we contrasted them with the scientific method of knowing used in academic research. Last, we outlined the ways that research is made public through professional associations, scholarly journals, academic presses, and trade journals and the popular press. In noting these venues, we outlined the two forms of scholarly writing you will encounter: the research report and the critical essay.

Key Terms

Abstract	Knowing by authority	Rule
Artefact	Knowing by tenacity	Scholarly journal
Axiom	Knowing on a priori grounds	Scientific method
Claim	Law	Social significance
Claim-data-warrant model	Literature review	Text
Critical essay	Personal significance	Theory
Data	Popular press	Theoretical significance
Empirical methods	Principle	Thesis
Executive summary	Professional association	Trade journal
Formula	Proposition	Unit of analysis
Hypothesis	Reference list	Warrant
Interpretive community	Research question	
Introduction	Research report	

Discussion Questions

1. Think about your career plans. How might you use what you learn in *Communication Research Methods* after you graduate from university?
2. Identify theories that you already know from other courses you've taken. Which of those theories use formal logic, and which are more conceptual or metaphorical?
3. Consider the three everyday ways of knowing (i.e. tenacity, authority, *a priori*). What are the potential strengths and weaknesses of each?

Try It!

1. Find two or three issues of a scholarly journal of communication or cultural studies. It does not matter if the journal is available in a print or online edition. For each research report or critical essay, can you identify the elements outlined in this chapter?
2. Select one research report from the journals you reviewed. Either alone or in a group, consider the report using the following questions:
    (a) Did the report contain all six elements described in this chapter? How did each element contribute to the author's argument?
    (b) Was the report difficult to read? What made it difficult? What helped you to understand the author's purpose and conclusions?
    (c) How credible was the author's argument? Did your opinion of the author's analysis or conclusions change while you were reading the report?
    (d) Did this report have any impact on you? Will you think or act any differently because you have read this report? (Adapted from Buchmann, 1992)

    A suitable research report for this activity is H. M. Ahmad (2008), War in Iraq: Comparative Coverage of *The Toronto Star* and *The New York Times*. *Canadian Journal of Media Studies, 3*, 33–56.
3. Select one critical essay from the journals you reviewed. Either alone or in a group, consider the report using the following questions.
    (a) Did the essay contain all six elements described in this chapter? How did each element contribute to the author's argument?
    (b) Was the essay difficult to read? What made it difficult? What helped you to understand the author's purpose and conclusions?
    (c) How credible was the author's argument? Did your opinion of the author's analysis or conclusions change while you were reading the essay?
    (d) Did this essay have any impact on you? Will you think or act any differently because you have read this essay? (Adapted from Buchmann, 1992)

    A suitable critical essay for this activity is J. F. Cosgrave and P. Cormack (2008), Disenchanted wonder: Collecting Canadian identity through the CBC's 'Seven Wonders of Canada Project'. *Topia: Journal of Canadian Cultural Studies, 20*, 5–22.

2 Ethics and Research

Introduction

In this chapter, we provide a brief history of research ethics. We then outline some of the ethical choices that you will face whenever you select a topic for study, implement a methodology, report your findings, and evaluate other people's work. Even if you never become a researcher, studying research ethics will make you a more critical research consumer and help you participate in civic processes more reflectively (Gale & Bunton, 2005; Jaksa & Pritchard, 1994; Kienzler, 2001, 2004).

Despite a growing interest in ethics instruction, too often we find that ethics is the last topic to be addressed in a methods course. That is why we have placed this chapter near the front of this book. However, we also agree with Cheney (2004) who argued 'Discussions of ethics and values should be integrated across topics and issues. That is, the treatment of ethics should not be compartmentalized or ghettoized as it typically has been' (p. 38). Thus, we have addressed very specific ethical issues in each of the chapters included in part 2, which discusses various methods for conducting communication and cultural research.

This chapter describes the origins of our contemporary codes of ethical conduct for researchers. It also notes how recent changes in digital technologies can test our ability to apply these codes in all facets of our research work. We introduce you to a slew of ethical choices you will need to make at three phases of the research process: when selecting research topics and projects; when establishing and implementing rights and responsibilities for research participants; and when reporting or evaluating research ethically.

A Brief History of Communication Ethics

In ancient times, Greek and Roman scholars were concerned about how values translated into actions. Their concerns are still addressed today in many forms of critical communication and cultural analysis. As Andersen (2000) pointed out, 'For classical authors, the relationship between one's "character" and communication effectiveness was clear and direct' (p. 132). Contemporary scholars have expanded beyond the concept of character to consider equal opportunities for social action (Nakayama, 1997). Consider your own access to communication. If you own a personal computer, and have free wireless access on your campus, you can participate in global networks of communication and culture and can gain access to a wealth of resources. Meanwhile, individuals without either a computer or Internet access lack this ability completely. Hence, access to communication becomes a moral issue in a representative democracy, since you cannot fully participate in society if you cannot access information in a timely manner.

Furthermore, because all people don't participate in the public sphere in the same ways, the common good cannot be achieved simply by giving everyone simple technological or physical access to information and communication. Rather, ethical communication includes a range of socially and culturally constructed ways of speaking, writing, and performing communication. To that end, Granzberg & Steinbring (1980) identified an aboriginal understanding of communication by working with Algonkian communities in Manitoba (see also Bredin, 1993). Perez (1997) discussed the construction of communication ethics in a Latin American context, and Hsieh, Hsieh, and Lehman (2003) articulated some of the ethical conflicts that have arisen among Chinese and Western scholars who work together. Each of these studies challenged traditional assumptions about communication ethics by considering perspectives that were formerly marginalized. Although much of this scholarship is theoretical, there are plenty of studies that address practical issues in communication ethics. For example, can loyalty go too far among Public Relations practitioners (Stoker, 2005)? When do a company's efforts to reduce its environmental impact count as 'greening' versus 'greenwashing'—that is, adopting environmentally friendly policies only to improve the company's reputation (Munshi & Kurian, 2005)? What is the responsibility of the press towards identifiable social groups when journalists cover social trends such as teen pregnancy? Can journalists distinguish between objective 'information' and personal 'judgments' (Wong, 2000a)? These are just three examples of ethical issues in specific contexts. There are many other issues, including the ethical conduct of researchers who involve human participants.

With the rise of social science in the 19th and early 20th centuries, philosophers like C. S. Peirce and Karl Popper elaborated a unitary method of scientific research that was both amoral and neutral in its objectivity. According to Peirce (and other philosophers of social science like John Locke, John Stuart Mill, and Max Weber), ethical issues belonged to the realm of *a priori* knowledge and therefore were not the purview of science. Those philosophers envisioned the ideal scientist as dispassionate and detached from human values and norms. The true scientist approached research from a value-free perspective, they argued, and the true scientist searched for objective truth in empirical evidence. One alternative view, during the 18th century, was that ethical issues required a subjective investment in faith or a metaphysical trust in reasoning about morals. Thus, during the Age of Enlightenment, science and morality were seen as two fundamentally separate dimensions of thought (Christians, 2003).

There were social critics. Mary Shelley's novel about Dr. Frankenstein, first published in 1818, portrays a scientist who pursued knowledge irrespective of the harm it caused to his subjects. Some contemporary members of the scientific community argued for ethical guiding principles that would create the greatest good for the greatest number of people and for the right of researchers to exercise individual freedoms, so long as no harm was done to another person. Thus, an important implication of **utilitarian ethics** was balancing the potential benefits and harms of scientific research (Christians, 2003).

The First and Second World Wars prompted an increasing awareness among researchers that a code of ethics was needed to guide the treatment of research participants and the conduct of researchers. As a case in point, during the Second World War Nazi physicians conducted 'medical experiments' on thousands of concentration camp prisoners, 'injecting people with gasoline and live viruses, immersing people in ice water, and forcing people to ingest poisons' (National Institute of Health [NIH], 2002, p. 5). After the war, those responsible for conducting the experiments were tried at a series of military tribunals held in Nuremberg, Germany. Twenty-three physicians and administrators were subsequently convicted of 'crimes against humanity' of which 16 were found guilty and seven were sentenced to death. The verdict included a statement about 'Permissible medical experiments', which later became known as the *Nuremberg Code*.

Unfortunately, other examples of inhumane and unethical research are readily found. One infamous study was conducted in Tuskegee, Alabama, by the United States Public Health Service. From the early 1930s until 1972 more than 600 black men participated in a study of 'the natural history of untreated syphilis' (NIH, 2002, p. 6). They were recruited without being told the true purpose of the research, and even when the researchers knew that penicillin was an effective treatment for syphilis the men in the experiment were neither told about the antibiotic nor treated with it. When a report of the study was first published in 1972, public outrage brought pressure on government agencies to ensure that research institutions monitor researcher's motives, treatment of research participants (i.e. human subjects), and the consequences of the research (Veatch, 1996). In 1997, American President Bill Clinton acknowledged the American government's responsibility vis-à-vis the NIH study with an official apology to the surviving participants, and today the government continues to compensate them and their surviving family members (NIH, 2002, p. 7).

Revelations of unethical research influenced the development of ethical standards worldwide. The United Nations felt compelled by the Nuremberg evidence to craft a document that would articulate the most basic rights and freedoms of every individual on Earth, no matter where he or she lives. The result was the United Nations' *Universal Declaration of Human Rights* (1948) written under the direction of Canadian legal scholar John Peters Humphrey. Its preamble noted that 'disregard and contempt for human rights have resulted in barbarous acts which have outraged the conscience of mankind', and it charged all member states to embrace and promote the dignity of all people. This included the goal that 'No one shall be subjected to torture or to cruel, inhuman or degrading treatment or punishment' (United Nations, 1948, Article 5).

In the United States, the federal government established a national commission in 1974 to recommend guidelines for the protection of human participants in biomedical and behavioural research. The commissioners, most of whom were medical doctors and researchers, established three principles for ethical research: beneficence, respect for the autonomy of persons, and justice. Those principles were outlined in *The Belmont Report* (1979; see Simmerling, Schwegler, Sieber, & Lindgren, 2007, p. 838). Later that year, the United States' federal government mandated that any organization receiving federal funds to support research (e.g. universities, hospitals) set up **Institutional Review Boards** (IRBs); that is, working groups responsible for establishing and implementing formal research codes of conduct (Madison, 2005).

In Canada, the agencies that fund scholarly research also began to develop ethics guidelines in the 1970s. The first important document for scholars in the social sciences and humanities was a publication of the Canada Council titled *Ethics: Report of the Consultative Group on Ethics* (1977). The report sought a common code that all social scientists and humanists could follow and would balance the welfare of all individuals with the benefits derived from research. The fulcrum was the principle of **informed consent**—that is, that research participants must understand all of the potential risks associated with their participation and must be able to decide for themselves if they wish to participate. Attempts to withhold information from participants, mislead them, or coerce them into participating would not be tolerated as legitimate research procedures. When the federal government established the Social Sciences and Humanities Research Council (SSHRC) that same year, the new agency based its ethics guidelines upon the Canada Council report's recommendations (Owen, 2002).

At first, enforcement of the SSHRC guidelines was difficult as researchers were reluctant to embrace them. In the humanities, for example, many studies examine texts and behaviours readily available in the public realm. Historians and literary scholars found it difficult to believe that ethical concerns that arose in the scientific and medical communities were relevant when studying the arts, public policy, or national cultures (Owen, 2002; Janovicek, 2006). Perceptions began to change in the early 1990s, however, when Canadian medical researchers revised their ethics guidelines with two goals in mind: to create a common Canadian code for all research disciplines (both scientific and otherwise) and to ensure that the code's provisions kept pace with international developments. To achieve these goals, the medical researchers convinced the SSHRC and the National Science and Engineering Council of Canada (NSERC) to collaborate. The result was a single code endorsed by all three groups of researchers called the *Tri-Council Policy Statement* (Medical Research Council, 1998).

Since 1999, the **Tri-Council Policy Statement**—known as the TCPS—has been enforced using procedures and financial penalties like those found in the American system. Today, SSHRC, NSERC, and the Canadian Institutes of Health Research (CIHR) provide funding for academic research in Canada. In order to hold a research grant from any one of them, a researcher must abide by the ethical procedures in place at his or her university. In turn, each university must ensure that its researchers comply with the TCPS. The code has undergone regular reviews during the last decade and a second edition was published in 2010 (CIHR et al., 2010). Nonetheless, its core principles and enforcement procedures have remained essentially the same.

Compliance with the TCPS is achieved through the oversight of a **Research Ethics Board** (REB). Each university with active research programs must have an administrative unit, an REB, that is responsible for the establishment and implementation of formal clearance procedures for all research conducted by its faculty and staff. When a new research program is conceived, the researcher must submit details regarding the purpose of the study; who will be recruited to participate and why; how recruiting will take place; what risks the participants will face; and how personal identities will be protected both during and after the study. If any procedure described in the submission fails to meet the ethical standards of the TCPS, the program will not receive clearance to proceed. Failure to gain clearance has two unfortunate consequences. First, any research funds granted by one of the agencies to the researcher will be frozen and hence inaccessible for research expenses. Second, the researcher's university may withdraw its institutional insurance coverage from the project and thereby expose the researcher to personal liabilities if participants object to their treatment. Either consequence may render the researcher financially unable to continue his or her research.

The guidelines articulated by the TCPS are informed by one cardinal principle: a respect for human dignity. The code states 'Respect for human dignity requires that research involving humans be conducted in a manner that is sensitive to the inherent worth of all human beings and the respect and consideration that they are due' (CIHR et al., 2010, p. 8). This cardinal principle obligates researchers to be mindful of three areas of concern: respect for persons; concern for welfare; and justice. Since these guidelines govern universities' REB practices, we use them here as a framework for ethical communication and cultural research.

First, research should respect participants by preserving individual autonomy wherever possible. This value is addressed through the practice of informed consent. It is not enough that consent be informed, however; it must also be given freely and without coercion. Think here of children or those in emotional distress who may not be capable of understanding their own best interests. In situations where recruits are potentially vulnerable, the researcher is charged with the responsibility to protect his or her participants from manipulation or exploitation. We will discuss this in more detail later in this chapter.

Second, the researcher has a duty to consider how the research will affect each participant's experience of life, in all its aspects. The TCPS states that 'welfare' consists of 'the impact on individuals of factors such as their physical, mental and spiritual health, as well as their physical, economic and social circumstances' (CIHR et al., 2010, p. 9). Any use of human participants must be justified, and any potential harms they may face must be minimized and explained to them clearly. More importantly, the potential benefits of the research must outweigh the risks, both for the participants and for society at large.

Third, researchers should be concerned with justice. They should consider who will bear the costs of the research as well as who will benefit from it. The key is to treat every participant fairly and equitably. As it is described in the TCPS, 'Equity requires distributing the benefits and burdens of research participation in such a way that no segment of the population is unduly burdened by the harms of research or denied the benefits of the knowledge generated from it' (CIHR et al., 2010, p. 10). This concern for justice should be evident in the goals of the research as well as in the way that a researcher recruits participants.

Each of these three values has been interpreted in ways that emphasize scientific research. The way that REBs interpret beneficence (i.e. being kind or charitable), respect, and justice do not always fit SSHRC-funded research studies as well as they fit biomedical studies, for example. The following quotation neatly summarizes the problems faced by communication scholars:

> It is a major leap from not harming subjects of biomedical research in the process of curing a disease or benefiting society with new health-giving technologies, to issues of whether one may inconvenience or upset subjects of social, educational or behavioral research in return for learning something about human behavior for the sake of knowledge, or for policy purposes. (Simmerling et al., 2007, p. 844)

As you learn about the unique ethical issues that are associated with each research methodology, you will see why the TCPS is considered a problematic model for some types of research (Janovicek, 2006; Simmerling et al., 2007).

Returning to our discussion of REBs, all research that involves human participants and is homed at a university must be reviewed by an REB. Each REB must have members with varied backgrounds to ensure that multiple perspectives are brought to bear on every research program. The TCPS mandates further that each REB must consist of at least five members and that the REB must include the following: a mixture of men and women, at least two members with expertise in the method or research area to be considered, at least one member knowledgeable in ethics, and at least one member knowledgeable in any laws applicable to the research area to be considered. Most of these members may be employees of the university, and this fact raises the possibility of a conflict of interest. A scholar may feel reluctant to criticize or delay a colleague's research with ethics concerns. For this reason, each REB must include one community member with no affiliation with the university (CIHR et al., 2010, p. 70).

Based on the potential risks and benefits involved, an REB must first decide if a study poses **minimal**

risk or more than minimal risk. A study poses minimal risk if 'the probability and magnitude of possible harms implied by participation in the research is no greater than those encountered by participants in those aspects of their everyday life that relate to the research' (CIHR et al., 2010, p. 23). Studies that are deemed to pose a minimal risk to participants receive a **delegated review**. This means the research protocol can be approved by either a single member of the REB or another delegated individual with relevant qualifications. A research proposal deemed to pose more than minimal risk to participants must be reviewed by a full REB panel (CIHR et al., 2010, pp. 77–79).

When discussing issues related to 'risk' it is important to note three additional points. First, the 'risks' to participants can be economic, legal, physical, psychological, or social. Second, the 'minimal risk' category applies only to autonomous consenting persons. In addition to children, and to people with mental disabilities, people may be unable to consent to participate in research if they have 'circumstances that severely restrict individual liberty (e.g. incarceration, military service)' (Simmerling et al., 2007, p. 848). Furthermore, Madison (2005) pointed out that in some cultural contexts, even an adult of sound mind can be constrained from autonomous consent. For example, in some tribal or marriage contexts, a male member may be required to give consent for females to participate in research. If a situation such as this strikes you as either good or bad, you should acknowledge that your personal values are being challenged. Further, your values may not match the values that guide REB reviews.

Our third point concerning risk is that researchers must always protect the rights of participants regardless of the level of risk posed by the research. The TCPS fosters protection by requiring that women and minorities be included among the participants selected for biomedical research, so that the findings from those studies can be generalized to the entire population and everyone will be able to benefit from the research. According to the justice ethic, if any one social group is unlikely to benefit from the research, then its members should not be subjected to the risks of participating in it. This is the principle of **distributive justice**, which deems that the costs and benefits of a decision be distributed fairly. Other justice principles also exist (Simmerling et al., 2007). For example, **procedural justice** decrees that everyone has the opportunity to participate equally in the process, even though some might benefit more from it than others. **Corrective justice** (or restorative justice) ensures that those who have benefitted least in the past, or who have been harmed most by past practices, should benefit most from present decisions. Typically REBs operate on the principle of distributive justice.

In the next section, we outline some of the ways that you can attend to the values of respect, beneficence, and justice when conducting and reporting research. These choices begin when you start thinking about what to study and what not to study. We also make ethical choices as we go about conducting communication research and as we decide how to report our findings and evaluate other people's research.

Ethical Choices: Getting Started in Research

We have placed this chapter near the front of the book because we want you to start thinking about ethics right away by examining your motives for doing research and for selecting a particular research topic.

Motives for Research Projects and Topics

Every research program begins with a question. You may be a student, a pollster, a government policy analyst, or any other professional whose work depends on information. Whatever your position, the search for new information begins with a question to be answered or a problem to be solved (Halloran, 1998). Once that question is known, every conscientious researcher must consider two issues: 'Why am I doing this study?', and 'Can my question be answered with research?'

The first question concerns your motivation. As a student you may pursue research simply because it is a required component of a course assignment. It is more likely, however, that current issues in communication and culture pique your curiosity and demand your attention. You may want to help others by making their problems or issues visible to other people. Or

perhaps you want to collaborate with your research participants in solving a social problem (Miles & Huberman, 1994). When framing a research question you should understand your motives for doing the research and the ethical consequences that the research may have for yourself, for your research participants, and for society.

For example, let's imagine that you work in the private sector and must develop research to support a new product, or that you work for a political party and must organize a winning election campaign. In either scenario, you might be tempted to design a study that puts your product or candidate in the best light. If you think that academic research is free of questionable motives, think again. University careers are judged by a scholar's success at winning research grants and publishing reports. If you conduct research simply because you must to get tenure and to be promoted, are you necessarily serving the public good? Students and instructors, as well as private and public sector researchers, must consider their motives for doing research and their reasons for studying particular topics.

Every arena of communication and culture, from interpersonal relations to the public sphere, involves ethical issues. For example, let's say you want to contribute to the good of society by studying interpersonal romantic relationships. Will you limit your study to married persons and long-term dating relationships? Will gay and lesbian couples be included in your research? Will you share all of your findings with your participants, and if so, how might those findings affect their relationships? What if you end up documenting unethical or illegal behaviours in your study? How will you ensure that the benefits of your research study outweigh the potential costs to your research participants, or to you, the researcher?

The second question we face when considering our motives for research concerns practicality. There are several criteria for developing sound, researchable questions. Chapter 4, on claims, will help you to make sense of the research process as a way to build logical arguments. Before you can build a logical argument, however, you must determine whether or not your question can be answered with research. No matter your interest, your question should be broad enough to be socially significant. That is, the question should matter to other people beyond your own interests. At the same time, your question should be narrow enough to produce a satisfactory conclusion in one research study.

Good research questions can be answered by collecting the necessary empirical data. Even if a research question cannot be answered in full, it can be explored by considering the available evidence and comparing the possible interpretations of that evidence. However, some questions cannot be answered with empirical data, and hence such questions are not amenable to research as it is discussed in this text. Let's look at one simple example. The following question:

> 'What communication channels do university students value most?'

is answerable with research, and the empirical data would probably be collected by using an opinion poll. By contrast, the following question:

> 'What communication channels should university students value most?'

cannot be answered with empirical research. Values are intangible aspects of our culture. They are informed by our beliefs and attitudes regarding all aspects of life. A response to this question can be explored through discussion, and empirical data might describe the variety of different approaches taken by students themselves, but a satisfactory answer cannot be tested or proven with empirical research.

A final consideration when deciding upon a research question is your resources. You should think pragmatically about your relevant expertise, the time needed, and access to money. There may be questions that fascinate you, but you may lack the expertise needed to investigate them. Likewise, you may have the curiosity and the expertise, but lack the necessary time, funding, or other resources needed to conduct the work.

These are the basic ethical concerns raised by research. Let's move on from our discussion of motives for doing research to the specific actions you might take to honour the values of beneficence, respect for individual autonomy, and justice.

Rights and Responsibilities of Research Participants

Research participants and the research community have a right to be assured of treatment that is fair, just, and respectful, and researchers are responsible for acting with integrity and ensuring that participants' rights are protected (Jaksa & Pritchard, 1994; Scanlon, 1993). Notice that the word 'right' to things like informed choices about participating in research, privacy, justice, and respect derive from a theory of moral rights that goes beyond utilitarianism, arguing that human beings are moral agents whose rights cannot rightly be violated, regardless of the desirability of the outcome (Kant, 1785/1993; Nozick, 1974).

In fact, quite a few contemporary theorists have argued that our basic assumptions about ethics in social science research should be revisited (Bok, 1979; Gilligan, 1982; Johannesen, 2001; Perez, 1997). For example, Bok (1979) critiqued the use of deception as a research technique. Foucault (1979) argued that the research process cannot escape being value laden because the community of scholars exerts power over participants that is neither equal nor neutral. Denzin (1997) argued that social science research should include diverse perspectives and multiple voices and that it should also encourage critical thinking and 'promote social transformation' (Christians, 2003, pp. 228–229).

As you have probably gathered, then, a number of ethical tensions can develop among a researcher's goals, the participant's goals, and society's goals. As the researcher, it is your responsibility to consider the ethical implications of your actions for yourself, for your participants, and for society. In the next section, we introduce you to specific actions that are consistent with the TCPS values of respect, welfare, and justice, actions you can take to protect the rights of your research participants. In particular, you will learn to protect your participants' rights to (1) freely choose whether to participate in research, (2) maintain their privacy, and (3) be treated honestly.

Right to Freely Choose Research Participation

As we mentioned earlier, the TCPS requires academic researchers to protect the rights of those involved in research. The guiding principle of ethical research is a respect for human dignity. One mechanism that respects human dignity and protects the rights of participants is the requirement that they exercise their own free choice about whether to participate in your study.

We protect free choice by providing potential research participants the opportunity to give their **informed consent**. As previously noted, informed consent means that we, as researchers, communicate any potential risks and benefits of our research to potential study participants, in language that they can understand; answer questions if they have questions; and then secure their written permission to collect their responses, videotape their interactions, or observe them. Informed consent is a legal, ethical, and policy matter, and it must be voluntary, not coerced. Figure 2.1 contains a sample informed consent document.

The idea of obtaining a participant's informed consent to participate in research may seem simple at first, but, in fact, it can be quite complicated. As a case in point, Amason, Allen, and Holmes (1999) conducted interviews with employees in a multicultural organization about their experiences seeking social support at work. Some of the interviews were conducted with Hispanic employees who spoke in Spanish. As illustrated in the quotation below from Amason et al. (1999), the presence of translators had an enormous impact on the results that were obtained:

> When the interviews were conducted with Spanish speaking employees, a translator (not affiliated with the organization to protect employee confidentiality) was used. Translators were native Spanish speakers who either taught Spanish at the university level or provided translation services for the community through a local social service agency. (Amason et al., 1999, p. 316)

Thinking ethically, the researchers' use of translators ensured that everyone in the organization who wanted to participate in the study could have volunteered. Thinking practically, the use of translators also allowed the researchers to collect the widest breadth of data available from that organization.

Status differentials can also threaten participants' autonomous consent. Researchers and participants may vary in terms of financial means, time available, expert knowledge, skills, and so on. When one party to an agreement has more access to needed resources than the other, then differences in status can clear the way for potential abuses of power (Scanlon, 1993). For example, inducements to participate in research studies can threaten autonomous consent if participants really need whatever is being provided as an incentive, such as course credits or financial compensation. Likewise a researcher may use deception when testing the effects of a specific text (e.g. an advertisement or television pilot) on participants. To ensure that participants approach the text without prejudice, the researcher may not tell them the true nature of the study until after their participation is complete. Such treatment raises ethical concerns about autonomy. If participants think they are volunteering their time and efforts for one reason, and that reason is false, then their ability to provide informed consent is restricted. We must remember, however, that studies like these ones allow researchers to isolate competing explanations about causal relationships. We have all benefited from this type of research, not only in the field of communication but also in medical research (e.g. polio vaccine).

Right to Privacy

As researchers, we must also think about how we will protect our participants' privacy. In some cases, we protect participants' privacy by promising them **anonymity**, the assurance that neither the researcher, nor anyone who sees the research data and final report, will learn the names of the participants or other identifying information (e.g. telephone numbers, addresses, or photos). In other cases, it may be enough to protect participants' privacy by assuring them **confidentiality** (defined as when the researcher is the only person who knows the identities of participants and ensures that the participants' responses can never be connected to them individually). It is up to us as researchers, and to an REB, to weigh the potential risks and benefits of the ways that participants are treated and to decide what degree of privacy to provide to them.

That being said, the potential for privacy violations is sometime unavoidable. For example, the blurred boundary between work and home life can become an ethical minefield if research is conducted

FIGURE 2.1   Sample Informed Consent Document

BROCK UNIVERSITY

DEPARTMENT OF COMMUNICATION, POPULAR CULTURE, AND FILM

COMM 3000: ORGANIZATIONAL COMMUNICATION

Observational Research Consent Form

Title of Study: COMM 3000: Organizational Communication / Assignment #2

Professor: Declan McManus

Student Researchers: (main contact)   _____

_____   _____   _____

Name of Participant: _____

Title and Organization: _____

PURPOSE AND BACKGROUND

I understand that this study in will involve a communication audit of my organization. This audit will be conducted by student researchers, will identify current communications practices within my organization, and will assess these practices in relation to their speed, accuracy, and role in the development of organizational culture. This research will help the students to complete a course assignment. It may also help my organization to identify best practices and improvements.

PROCEDURES

To conduct the research, ___ student researcher(s) will be placed in my work area for ___ hours over ___ days. They will ask some questions with respect to my work but they will not interfere with my work.

I understand that my participation in this study is voluntary and that I may withdraw from the study at any time and for any reason without penalty.

CONFIDENTIALITY

I understand that all data collected will be kept strictly confidential. I understand that only the researchers and the professor named above will have access to the data. This data will be destroyed once the final grades for the course have been submitted (or, within four months of the date of this document).

RISKS

I understand that all data collected by the student researchers will be coded so that my name will not be associated with my comments and activities. However, I also acknowledge that any discussion of the organization in which job titles are relevant make it impossible to ensure absolute confidentiality in the final report.

[Please initial only one of the following two lines to indicate your preference].

_____   I have read the above statement, and accept it.

_____   My job title may not be used in connection with anything specific which I may
              say or do while the students are conducting their research in my work area.

COSTS AND COMPENSATION

I understand that there will be no cost to me for my participation, nor will I receive any payment.

QUESTIONS

This study has been received clearance from the Brock University Research Ethics Board (File # 00-111). If you have any questions or concerns about your participation in the study, you may contact Professor McManus at (222) 333-4444, ext. 666, or the Ethics Board at ext. 777.

FEEDBACK

The final report written by the student researchers will be made available to the organization within four months of the date of this document. The organization will make it available to me.

PARTICIPANT

The student researcher has explained the above procedures and I agree to participate.

Signature _____   Date _____

STUDENT RESEARCHER – MAIN CONTACT

I have fully explained the procedures of this study to the above volunteer.

Signature _____   Date _____

Contact Number _____

THANK YOU FOR YOUR HELP!

PLEASE RETAIN ONE COPY OF THIS FORM FOR FURTHER REFERENCE.

Copy 1: For Participant / Copy 2: For Research Team

in private spaces. For example, Ladner (2008) used in-home interviews to gather data on high-tech workers in Toronto. While the research setting allowed her to observe their work environment first-hand, it created other issues. As she notes:

> I drank cups of tea and munched cookies. I was served a full meal with a family. I sampled a new recipe of chicken and pears. I took a tour of a newly purchased house. I chatted with workers' partners and children. I played with pets. All the while, I observed where work and home intersected for these workers. (Ladner, 2008, p. 473)

Hence, in-home interviews provided Ladner with far richer data than she might have gained through telephone interviews or written questionnaires. However, her presence in homes also allowed her to collect data about individuals other than her participants, individuals who may not have consented to participate in the study.

Rapid changes in communications technology also bring with them new and unexpected ethical considerations, as 'web-based experiments, online focus groups, email questionnaires, and computerized assessments of face-to-face behaviors' relocate traditional research procedures into the electronic arena (Palomares & Flanagin, 2005, pp. 175–6). For example, there is still great debate about the public or private nature of information obtained and given online: When information is posted in a blog or on a newsgroup, do the rules of public domain and fair use govern ethical use of that information, or do REB guidelines govern its use? If you post your survey on the World Wide Web, with a hyperlink to an informed consent document, how will you ascertain that those who agree to participate in your study are autonomous, consenting adults (Palomares & Flanagin, 2005, p. 171)? Questions like these are still very much unanswered for researchers.

Every time we use the Internet, information is being collected about us, and we do not have the same guarantees to privacy online that we have in other areas of our lives. For instance, Chung and Grimes (2005) explored the process of 'data mining', the process of collecting information for marketing purposes,

when children play games online. Those kinds of technological advances suggest how difficult it can be to apply any ethical standards to protect the privacy of research participants, not to mention how hard it becomes to protect the confidentiality of informants and the researchers and reporters who protect informants' confidentiality (Kennamer, 2005). Some of the new media resources are prompting researchers to think in new ways about the ethical consequences of how violence is portrayed, often to vulnerable audiences (Dragga & Voss, 2003; Scharrer, 2001; Stern, 2003). These examples begin to suggest how the original TCPS, with its focus on biomedical research, failed to anticipate and account for some of the ethical issues inherent in studying human communication.

Some of the choices that you make as a researcher can simultaneously protect and threaten your participants' rights. For example, you may want to protect a recruit's free choice to participate in your research but, at the same time, you may not want to tell him or her your study's true purpose before his or her participation because you fear that knowledge would change the participant's responses. That dilemma brings us to the issues of deception and omission in research conduct.

Right to be Treated With Honesty

In all communication research, the protection of human rights for those involved in this research is paramount. 'The value of the best research is not likely to outweigh injury' to a person harmed by the project (Stake, 1998, p. 103). Omitting information and deceiving research participants may harm them, either directly or indirectly. REBs determine whether the benefits of gaining particular information and observations from participants merit omitting information from participants or even deceiving them. In some cases, information can be omitted or falsified so long as the researcher provides a **debriefing**, telling participants the full truth after their responses have been collected and giving them a chance to withdraw their participation or data from the study once they know about that omission or deception.

Reporting and Evaluating Research Ethically

The rights of research participants and of society, as well, to be treated with honesty leads us to your next ethical obligation as a researcher: the duty to report and evaluate research ethically. As researchers, just as we make choices about our motives, topics, and methodologies, we must also consider the ethical impact of sharing our findings and evaluating other people's research. You must always assess the potential consequences that the conduct and publication of your research study has for yourself and for others (Madison, 2005).

The right of research participants to free choice, privacy, and honesty continue to be important as we present our findings to audiences through public lectures, professional conferences, and publication. As members of a research community, we also must honour those rights when we evaluate other people's research.

Let's consider privacy. Pollach (2005) analyzed websites' privacy policies to see whether the online policy statements communicated 'clearly and unequivocally when, how and for what purpose data are collected, used or shared' (p. 221). In fact, Pollach found that the corporate policies she examined used persuasive appeals to increase the companies' perceived trustworthiness. In practice, however, the opposite was true as the language used in policy statements often disguised unethical data handling practices. Thus, her study showed how both the values articulated and actions performed demanded ethical choices.

The same link between values and actions holds true for researchers who are studying people's online discussions. For example, it may be more accurate to download digital chat room data than it is to record conversations in real time, in a face-to-face context, and then transcribe those conversations. In Canada, messages posted to an online chat room are considered part of the public domain and are treated no differently than letters to the editor published in a newspaper (Office of the Privacy Commissioner, 2004). In other jurisdictions, however, this is not the case. In the United States, for example, posters must know in advance that their online comments may be used for research purposes or published outside their original site; a researcher who fails to inform participants of this fact violates their right to privacy (Palomares & Flanagin, 2005). Similarly, 'data mining'—the practice of aggregating individuals' personal information from Internet commerce transactions for marketing purposes—can threaten individual rights to privacy and freedom from harm (Office of the

Privacy Commissioner, 2004; Chung & Grimes, 2005). That threat is no less real for communication researchers who aggregate electronic information—as they may do with information about their students, for example.

We cannot end this section without mentioning **plagiarism**, the act of representing another person's words, ideas, or work as your own. Plagiarism is a violation of professional codes of conduct and it violates your reader's right to be treated with honesty (e.g. your teacher). When presenting your research to an audience, in addition to citing your sources of information accurately in the literature review, you also must strive to avoid misrepresenting information in your research report or critical essay, to cite your sources fully and accurately, and to represent information as ethically as you can. For example, think about whether your representations of the participants and their communication are fair. Or, when you are presenting your findings to colleagues, would you do anything differently if your research participants were there in the room with you during the presentation? If so, chances are that you may be violating the rights of your research participants. Furthermore, conduct permitted by an REB may be legal conduct, but sometimes you must take extra precautions to be both legal and ethical.

As a matter of fact, your responsibility to protect the rights of participants and the research community extends beyond avoiding plagiarism or misrepresenting research participants in presentations and manuscripts. As Madison (2005) advocated, you must think about the effect of publicizing your research, too. For example, what are the likely policy implications of publishing your findings? If you report that a 'stop smoking' program is ineffective, is the funding for the program likely to be cut? Who would benefit and who would be harmed if that happened? For some very sensitive research topics (e.g. those involving criminal behaviour), we must be very cautious indeed. Informed consent forms are not entirely protected from legal subpoena in Canada. Police investigators have tried to open research files when they believed those files contained evidence that could be used for criminal prosecutions. Such police actions clearly undermine the promise of participant confidentiality, and may dissuade both researchers and participants from engaging in future work on controversial issues (Lowman and Palys, 2007).

Finally, you need to consider how researchers who come after you might be affected by your presentations or publications. Avoid burning bridges during data collection and analysis, and when presenting and publishing your research. If you do not respect your sources, other researchers may not have the same opportunity you had to learn from the people who contributed to your study (Madison, 2005).

Summary

After reading this chapter, you should have a sense of the long history of research ethics, and you should understand how actual instances of unethical research led to our current ideas about ethical research,

specifically to the REB review process and the values of beneficence, respect for autonomy of persons, and justice. You also should be able to articulate why your choice of a research topic is ethical as well as some of the ways that you can protect your research participants' privacy and autonomy, including informed consent procedures. You should be prepared to think about ethical issues in how you treat research participants as data sources as well ethical issues related to your analysis, use, and reporting of research data. We hope this chapter will help you appreciate the complexities of ethics in practice and learn to be an ethical scholar in your own research. Table 2.1 summarizes some of these ethical issues and choices at each phase of research conduct.

TABLE 2.1 Ethical Issues and Choices in Research

PHASE OF RESEARCH	ETHICAL ISSUES OR CHOICES
Motives for research projects and topics	• Why am I doing research? • What topics have I selected (or rejected) to study, and why? • Who will my research benefit or harm?
Protecting the rights of research participants	• Can my participants freely choose whether to participate in my study, and do they really understand what they are consenting to do? • How might status differentials threaten my participants' right to freely choose their own participation? • How might incentives threaten my participants' right to freely choose their own participation? • How will the participants' privacy be threatened or protected in my study? • How shall I treat myself, my participants, and the research community with honesty and integrity during data collection and analysis? • Is any type of deception or omission merited in my study? • What differences exist, if any, between legal and ethical treatment of people in my study?
Reporting and evaluating research ethically	• If I document illegal or unethical behaviour in my data collection, what will I do with that information? • How shall I treat myself, my participants, and the research community with honesty and integrity when I present or publish my research findings?

Key Terms

Anonymity

Confidentiality

Corrective justice

Debriefing

Distributive justice

Delegated review

Informed consent

Minimal risk

Plagiarism

Procedural justice

Research Ethics Board (REB)

Status differential

Tri-Council Policy Statement (TCPS)

Utilitarian ethics

Discussion Questions

1. Imagine that your roommate offers to edit your research manuscript if you perform a database search for articles she could use in her literature review. Would you agree to this exchange? If so, would you share that fact with your teacher? Why or why not?

2. When, if ever, is it ethical to cite an article or book that you have not read or have only partially skimmed?

3. Why do researchers need to be concerned about status differentials between researchers and participants (or even among participants), when conducting research?

4. Your school email address is owned by the university, just as your work email address is owned by your employer. Under what conditions is it ethical for researchers at the university to use your emails in a research study?

5. If you are in a class that uses a content-management system like Sakai CLE, WebCT or Blackboard CITL, when is it ethical for your teacher to use your comments or other contributions in a research study? Is it enough if the university's REB approves the study in advance of your enrollment in the class, or is individual informed consent required?

Try It!

This activity asks you to consider the ethical issues underlying five case studies. The activity can be completed by an individual, but it may be more interesting to work in a group with two or more other members on it. Depending on the size of your tutorial group, it may also be adapted as a tutorial exercise.

Identify at least one ethical dilemma in each situation given below. Consider the potential harms and benefits of this dilemma, and describe the ethical standards you, as a researcher or member of a research team, would uphold. Identify the ethical choices you would make in this case as well as the potential harms that could ensue if you do not behave ethically:

(a) You are collecting observational and interview research data at a clothing manufacturing company. You are given hundreds of dollars worth of free clothing during your data collection. You really like the clothes and wear them proudly, but you don't know whether to tell people they were free or keep that a secret.

(b) You discover information during data collection that could hurt the research participants if you disclose it (e.g. either the participants are engaging in illegal behaviours, like underage drinking or the use of controlled substances, or they are behaving in ways that will be called to moral account by others, like committing certain sexual acts or making racial slurs).

(c) You want to conduct research in a group of which you are a member but, for your own personal reasons, you don't want to disclose your membership status (e.g. HIV positive, incest survivor, recovering alcoholic, or drug addict).

(d) You are interested in studying cross-cultural interactions, particularly how members of one culture respond when their social codes or customs are broken by members of a different culture. You want to collect actual instances of rule violations and responses from several different cultural contexts.

(e) To ensure that your interpretations of certain field data are correct, you return to check your interpretations with your participants. However, they refuse to help. Should you publish your interpretations? And if you do, should you mention that you checked the interpretations with the participants?

(Source for 'Try It!': Adapted from Braithwaite, Dollar, Fitch, & Geist, 1996 and used with permission of the first author.)

3 Three Paradigms of Knowing

Introduction

In this chapter, we begin with an overview of three methodological ways of knowing about communication: discovery, interpretation, and criticism. Each of these paradigms is a response to the question 'How can we know about communication?' In the last section of this chapter, we outline the philosophical perspectives that contributed to each of the three epistemological paradigms.

In the first chapter, we introduced you to the concepts of theory and method. The most compelling and powerful theories are explanations. They can illustrate what things mean, or they can be assertions about what should be or should not be happening. They can be formal and contain rule-like propositions, or they can be in the form of a story. Theories are ideas we have about the way things are. They organize what and how we think.

When we do research, we adopt a method that we can use to test our theories. Sometimes the methods we use seem distinct from theories, and sometimes the theory and the method are thoroughly intertwined. In chapter 1, we introduced you to Toulmin's (1972) claim-data-warrant model to help you understand each method, because each method can be explained in terms of claims, data, and warrants. We explore each element separately in the remaining chapters of this first section. Before we do, however, we must consider how our assumptions about research influence the kinds of theories and methods we select to do research.

In the first chapter, we distinguished everyday common sense from the methods of knowing we apply more rigorously in the social sciences and humanities. The methods we use vary widely. These differences in methodologies come from profoundly different ways of thinking about what we know, how we view communication and culture, and what we do as researchers when we study them. Each perspective represents a particular set of assumptions. Frequently, when you are a researcher, you may simply come up with an idea for a study that answers a question you have, and you may never consider the merits of one particular method over another. Whenever you choose a method, however, you tap the underlying assumptions that go with it. And each set of assumptions represents a different way of knowing.

These different ways of knowing are called **paradigms**. Sometimes, researchers separate paradigms into two types: ontological and epistemological. Ontological paradigms address the question: 'What is the thing?' Epistemological paradigms address the question: 'How can a thing be known?' Because this is a methods book, we will focus on ways of knowing. We will emphasize the epistemological assumptions that underlay how and why we study communication and culture rather than focusing on the nature and substance of communication and culture.

Methodological Ways of Knowing

Think of any one thing that you know. Now consider: How do you know it? Do you have experiences of that thing? Do you have unique ideas about that thing which no one else shares? Or, do you have some insight into that thing which will make it better? However you may think about that one specific thing, it's wise to remember that, in general, your knowledge is your way of making sense of the world. The way that you acquire that knowledge can be quite different from other people you know, and consequently your ideas themselves can be quite distinctive. Even so, it is still possible to agree upon certain ideas.

Let's consider an example. Some people claim that violence in the media makes people more violent in everyday life. It's fair to ask: How do they know? Are their claims based on their own experiences witnessing the connection between mediated violence and actual behaviour? Have they gathered opinions from various media audiences about violence and its portrayal in popular culture? Do they view violent content in the media as a symptom of a larger social problem, such as increasing alienation? Do media critics think that social problems such as alienation and violence can be solved by consumer action or legislative reform?

With this one example, we can illustrate the three main epistemological paradigms in communication and cultural research. First, we may see media violence in terms of its observable properties, that is, those particular actions, statements, and situations that we encounter while watching a program, playing a video game, or listening to a song. When we focus on the observable aspects of an issue, we work within

the discovery paradigm. Second, we may see media violence as a symbolic text with several, equally valid interpretations. When we try to understand rival perspectives on an issue, we work within the interpretive paradigm. Or we may see the portrayal of media violence as a way to make violence appear to be a normal part of our society. When we focus on the cultural or ideological implications of an issue, we work within the critical paradigm. How we choose to study communication and culture depends on the assumptions that underlie each paradigm. What, then, do these assumptions entail? In the next section, we provide you with a thumbnail sketch of the three major paradigms operating in our field and their basic assumptions, and explain how they affect our research methods.

Knowing by Discovery

Some researchers believe that knowledge is obtained through a process of discovery. To **know by discovery** implies accepting several fundamental assumptions; these assumptions are identified in Table 3.1. The first is the belief that things or objects exist in reality separate from our perceptions of them. This reality is composed of the physical world of objects and the world of social interaction. Second, it is assumed that this reality is discoverable and that we may gain knowledge of it. A third assumption is that this knowledge of reality is testable through logical and empirical methods. Logical methods help us determine through rational means what is theoretically connected and free from contradiction, whereas empirical methods help us identify what is probable based on our observations. The fourth assumption is that rigorous standards for testing our observations will result in a shared system of evaluating our observations and our conclusions (Corman, 2005; Pavitt, 2004; Bostrom, 2004).

Within the discovery paradigm, we evaluate our observations against standards that test validity and reliability, and only observations that pass these tests are accepted as knowledge. Rigorous tests can be accomplished by making precise, systematic, and repetitive observations of some event or thing. When we use the term **precise**, we mean being careful for the purpose of ensuring accuracy. Being **systematic** means that we follow clear, known procedures. Most

TABLE 3.1 Defining Assumptions of the Epistemological Paradigms

	KNOWLEDGE BY DISCOVERY	KNOWLEDGE BY INTERPRETATION	KNOWLEDGE BY CRITICISM
Nature of reality	There is one knowable reality that can be discovered.	There are multiple realities that are socially constructed.	There are multiple realities that are socially constructed.
Role of knower	Reality can be known by any knower.	Each reality is interpreted from the standpoint of a knower.	Each reality is interpreted from the standpoint of a knower.
Role of context	The method of knowing is objective and decontextualized.	The method of knowing is subjective and contextualized within the participants' perspective.	The method of knowing is subjective and contextualized within two or more perspectives.
Process characteristics	The process of knowing is precise, systematic, and repetitive.	The process of interpretation is creative and value laden.	The process of interpretation is creative, value laden, and judgmental.
Purpose of research	The purpose of research is to represent reality accurately.	The purpose of research is to understand meaning and how it is created.	The purpose of research is to identify structures and instigate social change.
Nature of findings	Accurate representation is accomplished by classifying objects and identifying universal rules or laws.	Understanding meaning is accomplished by describing participants' perspective in context.	Instigating social change is accomplished by identifying historically and culturally situated structures, and assessing their utility.

discovery-based research begins with a claim constructed from the evidence collected in many previous studies. Out of past evidence, we develop a prediction that will be tested through a series of new observations, or the gathering of new evidence. Finally, when we use **repetitive** research methods, it means that we make precise, systematic observations, over and over, to ensure that our findings are verifiable.

When you conduct research, each of these properties is evident in the way you design your study. For example, Burleson, Holmstrom, and Gilstrap (2005) examined the role of gender differences in the care given by personal support workers to their distressed patients. The research team wrote a scripted conversation in which they could vary the genders of the support provider and a support receiver. Burleson et al. then asked survey participants to read one version of

the conversation and then to share their impressions of the support worker. Burleson et al. (2005) were precise in the way that they constructed their test, using the exact same conversation script and questionnaire format with all their participants. They were systematic in varying the gender of each role to isolate the effects of gender on their participants' impressions. The researchers also used repetitive research methods, conducting not just one but four separate experiments to confirm their findings. You will learn much more about these characteristics of research methods in later chapters dealing with content analysis, surveys, and historical research.

The discovery process also requires you to classify objects into categories based on observed similarities and differences. Grouping objects together based on their similarities allows you to generalize based on their common properties. Sorting objects by their differences allows you to discriminate. To illustrate how the process of **generalization** works, consider a study by Jansen and Koop (2005). The researchers followed two online discussion boards during a provincial election in British Columbia to assess the Internet's role in the democratic process. For the study, they coded every message or thread posted to the boards by individuals during the entire election campaign. They found that opinion leaders emerged on both boards who set the ideological character and conversational tone of the discussions. Subsequently, some people stopped posting messages and, ultimately, relatively few people participated in the online discussions. Jansen and Koop analyzed the behaviours of these two online boards to make generalizations about all similar boards. Although their findings tempered optimistic claims that the Internet encourages greater participation in the democratic process, they also supplied insights for anyone who wishes to improve the democratic potential of the Internet.

By contrast, the process of **discrimination** prompts you to discover and understand significant differences in your observations. In a study of televised sports, Hallmark and Armstrong (1999) wanted to see if the media represent women's and men's basketball games in different ways. Previous studies had shown that there were a variety of sex differences across broadcasts of men's and women's sports. Past observations revealed that men's sports generally occupied more airtime than women's sports, that women's team sports had been virtually ignored, and that announcers tended to make negative comments more frequently during women's games than during men's. Although they cited progressive changes in media coverage of women's sports, Hallmark and Armstrong (1999) wanted to explore whether some gender biases might be subtler, requiring a different level of discrimination. They focused on specific features of media presentation: camera shot variation, the length of a shot, and the type and frequency of graphics in each broadcast of women's and men's basketball games during a championship division playoff. By refining their conceptualizations of media presentation, Hallmark and Armstrong were able to make finer discriminations about the types of sex differences that exist in sports media coverage.

In the preceding examples, the researchers emphasize discovery as their way of knowing. Both begin by making claims, and both make multiple observations using precise, systematic, and repetitive procedures. Using the processes of generalization and discrimination, they explore what can be known or discovered from their observations. Finally, they draw conclusions from their observations, generalizations, and discriminations. The discovery paradigm assumes that knowledge is discoverable through logical and empirical methods (i.e. researchers who share the same standards of precision and systematic observation will observe the same patterns of results in repeated tests of the research claims). Knowledge is discovered and expanded through rational means that minimize the subjective viewpoint of the researcher.

Knowing by Interpretation

Knowing by interpretation is a very different epistemological process than knowing by discovery. One clear contrast emerges: this paradigm assumes that no one reality exists separate from our perceptions. Rather, the knower is inseparable from the known. Thus each person's perceptions and values affect what is seen and understood about the world. Since each person has his or her own perception of reality, there can be multiple, equally legitimate, interpretations of it. Therefore, the purpose of research is to understand how meaning is constructed in various social contexts. To be consistent, researchers working within the interpretive paradigm must acknowledge that their own values affect their perceptions of reality. As such, subjectivity is embraced wholeheartedly, and the researcher often becomes an active participant in the research setting. The process of knowing relies upon rich description. Rich description refers to the use of a broad range of data sources to show how communication occurs and what it means to participants in that context. Meanings may be categorized during the process of interpretation, but categorization is not the central point. Rather, rich description represents an attempt to understand the whole context in which meanings are constructed.

Within the interpretive paradigm, it is not important to determine which interpretations are more accurate. Instead, it is vital to reflect the full range of sensible interpretations and to show how these interpretations were constructed. This emphasis on reflecting the full range of interpretations is central to the interpretive paradigm of research, which you will learn much more about from the methods of historical research, discourse analysis, and ethnography later in this book (see chapters 9, 10, and 11 respectively).

To illustrate the interplay of multiple interpretations, Foster (2002) examined a public debate surrounding 'squeegee kids', those 'individuals who approach stopped cars at urban intersections and offer. . . to clean windshields' (p. 37). The article revealed how the debate became polarized around notions of what constitutes a legitimate use of public space. The Ontario provincial government argued that the activity was a nuisance conducted by disorderly teens, was potentially threatening to motorists, and hence represented an illegitimate use of public space. By contrast, supporters of the squeegee kids portrayed the activity as an enterprise conducted by law-abiding fellow citizens, with no malice intended, and hence represented a perfectly legitimate use of public space. Foster showed that the debate could be reduced to fear. The government wanted to reduce the perceived risks faced by drivers as they travelled through urban space, and the government did so by demonizing the squeegee kids rather than finding a mutually satisfactory solution. Ultimately, Foster's research demonstrated how the government and the kids' supporters constructed highly conflicted interpretations of everyday events and shared public space.

Knowing by interpretation also means that you wish to understand the meaning imparted to conversations, texts, and behaviours by the people you observe. Remember, the discovery researcher defines what will be observed, categorizes the observations, and then draws conclusions from them. Conversely, the interpretive researcher describes observations in rich detail, rather than simplifying them into categories. The researcher then interprets the patterns that emerge out of those descriptions. Again, interpretive researchers acknowledge that by observing, describing, and interpreting their research subjects, they become active participants in the research process.

Knowing by Criticism

Scholars who work within the critical paradigm share many of the interpretivists' assumptions. Both agree that individual perceptions and values affect what is seen and understood about the world, and that there can be multiple, equally legitimate, interpretations of reality. Researchers who work within the critical paradigm, however, differ from those who work within the interpretivist paradigm in one important respect. While the interpretivist tries to understand how meaning is constructed in a given context, he or she does not assess the quality or utility of that meaning. The critical scholar does. If we believe that everything we know is shaped by our values, then it is important to understand the source of those values. **Knowing by criticism**, then, means that the source of our values may be rooted in our experience of social practices, politics, economics, ethnicity, gender, sexual orientation, or individual abilities. Research may reveal that the dominant values in a given context allow one set of experiences to receive prominence over another. One example of this phenomenon is that, historically, the value of men's experience has been given more weight than that of women's experience in almost every realm of public endeavour, such as politics, commerce, religious life, the arts, and sports. The critical research agenda, then, has two goals. First, it seeks to make people aware of how specific values shape reality. Second, it seeks to foster social change when those values conflict with social ideals and goals. The critical research process relies upon rich description and critical reflection on the dominant values in a given context.

For instance, Tator, Henry, and Mattis (1998) examined the debate that surrounded a Toronto revival of the musical *Showboat*. The premise of the original story, written in 1926, was based upon racist portrayals of African Americans. Although the racist portrayals were clearly observable to many African Canadians, the producers of the musical argued that the offensive elements of the original story had been removed. Tator, Henry, and Mattis documented the claims of both groups, and described how the producers' access to local media ultimately overwhelmed the protests of anti-racist groups. By describing these events, the researchers hoped to reveal how racism is perpetuated in Canadian society and to illustrate that, by understanding such events, we can work to end racism in the future.

Knowing by criticism, then, means that the researcher not only reveals his or her subjective view, but also emphasizes that he or she has an obligation to expose social injustice and to become an advocate for social change. Critical scholars believe that if scholarship does not emphasize how dominance silences marginalized groups, then the research community is as guilty of perpetuating the existing hierarchy as the rest of society. Critical analysis, then, must focus on the historical, political, and economic contexts that continually reinforce a social structure, so that it can be revealed, understood, and changed.

In this section, you have learned about three epistemological paradigms: knowing by discovery, knowing by interpretation, and knowing by criticism. The next section provides an outline of the philosophical perspectives that contributed to each of these three epistemological paradigms. Exploring the philosophical bases of these paradigms will help you to understand why epistemological distinctions have occurred and how these have been applied to specific methods of research in our field. We should bear in mind, however, that researchers are developing an appreciation for multiple methods and perspectives. The boundaries between the various paradigms are becoming fuzzy with the growing number of research studies that bridge them.

Philosophical Bases of the Three Paradigms

Each way of knowing, or epistemological paradigm, is supported by its own philosophical traditions. Historically, the discovery paradigm emerged first and gave rise to the development of the other two paradigms. Historical pedigree, however, should have little influence on how you value each paradigm. Each paradigm stands on its own merit, and every philosophical perspective within each paradigm brings a new facet to our understanding of how we might study communication and culture. Table 3.2 provides an overview of the many philosophical perspectives that have contributed to each paradigm.

TABLE 3.2 Philosophical Traditions Associated With the Epistemological Paradigms

KNOWLEDGE BY DISCOVERY	KNOWLEDGE BY INTERPRETATION	KNOWLEDGE BY CRITICISM
Rationalism	Hermeneutics	Critical theory
Empiricism	Phenomenology	Semiotics
Logical positivism	Symbolic interactionism	Deconstruction
Behaviourism	Constructivism	Late structuralism
Early structuralism	Structuralism	Poststructuralism
Realism	Naturalism	Postmodernism
Modernism	Later modernism	Postcolonialism
Postpositivism		

Sources: General adaptations from R. C. Bogdan and S. K. Biklen (1982), A. Gill (1994), D. M. Mertens (1998), and M. J. Smith (1988).

The categorization of perspectives here leads us to mention one general problem associated with classifying schemes. The categories represented in Table 3.2 are not mutually exclusive, i.e. some philosophical perspectives can be placed in two categories because they offer bridges to the next paradigm. For example, the writings of modernists like Chaïm Perelman expressed more of the discovery paradigm assumptions, whereas other modernists like I. A. Richards, Warren Weaver, and Kenneth Burke expressed the assumptions of the interpretive paradigm (Gill, 1994). The problem of classification is especially acute in a field like ours that borrows from many philosophical traditions, such as classical philosophy, literary criticism, and the social sciences. As one tradition collides with another, it is easy to become confused about epistemological bases, their defining assumptions, and the methods of research associated with each.

Confusion, however, is no excuse for lumping together any combination of methods you favour in the name of fuzzy boundaries. As you will see, researchers working within each paradigm prefer certain research methods and environments over others. Discovery researchers favour controlled settings that limit the number of variables that will affect their data, while interpretivist and critical researchers favour natural settings. Instead of engaging in a theoretical battle over which school of thought is correct, we present you with all three points of view. We hope that, by understanding their differences, you will understand the advantages and disadvantages each paradigm offers in relation to its rivals. As students of communication and culture, we can benefit from all three kinds of research. That is precisely why we believe it is important to provide you with an overarching view of all the various approaches to research practised today. We provide only a thumbnail sketch of each philosophy, but you will gain a basic vocabulary to understand the contributions made by each perspective to our ways of studying communication and culture.

Discovery Paradigm

The first paradigm, knowledge by discovery, has been the dominant paradigm in philosophy and science for many years. The philosophies of empiricism and rationalism have deep roots and were advanced in the ancient Greek writings of Plato and Aristotle. **Empiricism** assumes that the only way to grasp objective reality is by observing and explaining sensory information. **Rationalism** insists that the mind can conceive a clear logic in objective reality. By combining these two perspectives, the scientific method of research became associated with the three emphases we identified earlier: (1) clarity or precision, (2) systematic inquiry, and (3) repetition for the purposes of verification (Mertens, 1998, pp. 6–10; Smith, 1988, pp. 307–309).

Behaviourism and **logical positivism** emerged as later developments of empiricism. Both of these philosophies embraced an objective reality knowable through observational or empirical processes rather than through rational thought alone. Behaviourists sought to discover causal links between external factors and an individual's responses. Logical positivists believed precision was better served as a goal if they identified *related* rather than *caused* events. They also believed they could increase precision by identifying how scientists should classify objects and procedures and what exactly would constitute empirical evidence.

Currently, many communication researchers working within the discovery paradigm adopt a 'postpositivist' view. **Postpositivism** advances the argument that human thought may be fallible, but that human reason can still aspire to map and understand objective reality. Corman (2005) identified several principles of postpositivist research. Among the most important are **falsification**, which prompts us to believe our claims are false until we can prove they are true; **naturalism**, which prompts us to study 'natural' settings for social interaction and culture; and **realism**, which prompts us to distinguish between objective reality and our perceptions of reality (pp. 22–30; see also Pavitt, 2004; Bostrom, 2004).

The philosophical perspectives of modernism and structuralism are also focused on a discoverable reality separate in some sense from that of the knower or perceiver. **Modernism** has been described as essentially 'positivistic, technocentric, and rationalistic' (Harvey as cited in Gill, 1994, p. 171). Modernism elevated science to the pursuit of a shared and objective truth. As Gill (1994) described this perspective: 'A key element in the modern worldview was belief in progress, of movement toward truth in all areas of life; knowledge could be standardized and social orders planned' (p. 171).

Structuralism represents the third perspective. Early structuralists like Ferdinand de Saussure, Gaston Bachelard, and Mikhail Bakhtin identified the discoverable reality in the patterns or relationships between objects, events, or people rather than in the truthfulness of the objects themselves (Lechte, 1994, pp. 3–12). They were interested in how form became manifested in observations. Structuralists attempted to identify the various forms of thought, language, and experience by finding evidence of rules for explaining human interaction. The goal of the early structuralists, then, was to discover the embedded *rules* or *laws* grounded in observation and experience (Denzin & Lincoln, 1998a, pp. 16–17). In its essence, this early form of structuralism became a means of combining rationalism (ideation) and empiricism (tangible experience). Later developments in structural theories and semiotics reappear in the interpretive and critical paradigms.

The philosophical perspectives informing the discovery paradigm contributed several defining assumptions. In brief: there is an objective reality that can be known by any observer; we come to know about this reality by testing our observations; we test our observations through precise, systematic, and repetitive procedures; and the purpose of research is to classify objects based on their similarities and differences and to identify something essential and useful about them. You may refer again to the defining assumptions for this paradigm that appear in Table 3.1.

The research methods most frequently associated with each paradigm are listed in Table 3.3. These methods were derived out of each paradigm's assumptions about what constitutes knowledge, claims, data, and warrants. Often, researchers do not consciously think about the assumptions associated with each paradigm when they adopt their methods, but the assumptions are present nonetheless. The assumptions of the discovery paradigm underlie studies such as surveys, content analyses, and conversational analyses. Often, the data collected through these methods is quantifiable. Whether the data is quantitative or qualitative, however, the grounding assumptions will be shared.

Not all studies using the same methodology come from the same paradigm. A growing number of scholars attempt to integrate several methods common to different paradigms. For instance, Ladner (2008) sought to understand how certain employees of advertising agencies use mobile devices at home. Ladner wanted to explore whether the employees could make a clear distinction between work and home life. Ladner stated that her research took a 'mixed-method' approach. First, she used ethnographic interviews to collect in-depth information from 20 participants. This method is usually associated with

TABLE 3.3 Research Methods Typically Affiliated with Each Paradigm

DISCOVERY	INTERPRETIVE	CRITICAL
Survey research	Survey research	Historical research
Content analysis	Historical research	Policy analysis
Historical research	Case analysis	Critical discourse analysis
Policy analysis	Discourse analysis	Critical ethnography
Case analysis	Ethnography	Marxist criticism
Conversation analysis	Narrative and mythic rhetorical criticism	Feminist criticism
Classical genre rhetorical criticism	Dramatism in rhetorical criticism	Postmodern and poststructural criticism
		Postcolonial criticism

the interpretive paradigm. Second, she used an online survey and descriptive statistical procedures to gather data from another 59 participants. These methods are usually associated with the discovery paradigm. Ladner's decision to combine these procedures resulted in a far richer set of data than she would have collected using a single methodology.

Interpretive Paradigm

The second paradigm of knowledge by interpretation is also associated with a number of philosophical traditions. The first of these, **hermeneutics**, has been defined as the 'study of interpretive understanding or meaning' (Mertens, 1998, p. 11). It began as the pursuit of several German phenomenologists—most prominently Edmund Husserl, Wilhelm Dilthey, and Max Weber—who emphasized '*Verstehen*' or understanding, a term that referred to interpretation as a process that grew out of a specific historical and cultural perspective. **Phenomenologists** believe that interpretation of experience is only possible by understanding the perspective of the participants whose experience you wish to study.

Symbolic interactionism is an approach to sociology initiated by Margaret Mead (1934) and advanced by the Canadian sociologist Erving Goffman (1959). Its claims were originally grounded in the discovery paradigm. Over the years, however, the main purpose of the approach changed to understand how people construct and interpret the meaning of their experiences. The process became increasingly interpretive because it was centred in the interaction each individual has with other people. New emphasis on the individual underlined a shift in understanding that what may be true in one context is not true in another. Philosophically, this new emphasis was articulated in **constructivism** and the principle of naturalism. Constructivism is rooted in the belief that there are multiple realities that are socially constructed. As we noted above, naturalism insists that individuals be studied in everyday settings. To understand meaning from the perspective of the participants selected for study means adopting their frame of reference (Bogdan & Biklen, 1982, pp. 10–14; Mertens, 1998, pp. 11–15; Smith, 1988, pp. 310–311).

Structuralism bridged the discovery paradigm and the interpretive paradigm. Saussure, a Swiss linguist, is credited as its founder, but other notable proponents include the philosophers C. S. Peirce, Roland Barthes, and Umberto Eco, the linguist Roman Jakobson, Claude Levi-Strauss in anthropology, and Jacques Lacan in psychoanalysis (Blanchard, 1980, p. 10; Gill, 1994, pp. 173–186; Sturrock, 2003). Many of these theorists were trained in both the sciences and humanities, and they were inclined to view the structure of human interaction as a system embedded in a sociocultural and historical context (Lechte, 1994, pp. 148–152). For Saussure, language was regarded as a malleable construct. He argued that linguistic codes have 'no necessary relation to an external reality and, thus, no relation to an absolute and abiding truth' and yet they are relatively stable structures, and so exert 'enormous influence over human action and understanding' (Gill, 1994, pp. 174–175).

The interpretivist paradigm is defined by the assumptions we explained earlier in this chapter. These include the belief that there are multiple realities, and these realities are socially constructed through each individual's interactions with others. The process of interpretation happens when the researcher tries to understand how participants construct meaning. It is critical that the researcher understands the participants' perspectives because all meaning and interaction is regarded as 'contextually situated' (Denzin & Lincoln, 1998a, pp. 16–17; Mertens, 1998, pp. 11–15).

Typical research studies associated with the interpretivist paradigm include ethnography, historical research (including case studies and oral history), and narrative analysis. You will learn about each of these methods in later chapters. As we noted with the discovery paradigm, however, one method does not ensure one paradigmatic view. A number of researchers in our field conduct critical ethnographies, using procedures identified originally with the interpretive paradigm, while maintaining a desire to reveal oppression and, in some cases, to instigate social change (e.g. Adelman & Frey, 1994; Conquergood, 1991; Harter, Berquist, Titsworth, Novak, & Brokaw, 2005). Generally speaking, however, studies using the methodologies identified in column two of Table 3.3 are most likely to work within the interpretive paradigm.

Critical Paradigm

The third paradigm, knowledge by criticism, has its origins in the philosophical traditions of critical theory, semiotics, late structuralism, poststructuralism, postmodernism, postcolonialism, and deconstruction.

Critical theory was inspired by Immanuel Kant's critique of rationalism. Its founders were scholars at the University of Frankfurt, Germany, who adapted Kant's ideas to modern life and incorporated insights from modernists such as G. W. F. Hegel, Karl Marx, Sigmund Freud, and Max Weber. The theory was systematized by Theodor Adorno, Max Horkheimer, and, later, Jürgen Habermas. As a critique of positivism and modernism, 'critical theory derives its basic insight from the idea that thought can transform itself through a process of reflection in history' (Rasmussen, 1996, p. 12). The purpose of critical theory is to liberate individuals who have become oppressed in modern society by increasing their awareness of the ideological structures of power and domination.

Critical theorists influenced the development of other important social philosophies, including semiotics and structuralism. **Semiotics** is the study of signs and their social significance. Early studies of semiotics concentrated primarily on discovering the hidden structure of signs through a systematic analysis of language, narrative, cultural rules, and the unconscious mind (Chandler, 1995). Those early studies aligned structuralism with the discovery and interpretive paradigms. However, the emphasis in late structuralism and semiotics has shifted from a search for structure toward the view that historical development is determined by economic or 'material' conditions. From this perspective, the significance of signs cannot be anything but ideological, especially as they are expressed by social institutions such as the mass media. Combining semiotics with economic philosophy, Jean Baudrillard (Lechte, 1994, pp. 233–237) argued that signs have value and are used primarily to convey social status; this symbolic function is separated from any utilitarian function they might serve. For an example, think of the modern wedding reception where parents may outspend their savings as a show of status for the benefit of their children.

Theorists of **poststructuralism** argue that the search for a foundational structure of language and society

should be abandoned. Two proponents of poststructuralism, Gilles Deleuze and Félix Guattari, contended that what we know is nothing but thought, discourse, and social interaction (Lechte, 1994). Another poststructuralist, Jacques Derrida, used **deconstruction** to question the very idea of 'structure' as a metaphor for philosophy (Sedgwick, 2001). He believed deconstruction was liberating because Western society had separated itself from all other cultures in which discourse is not regarded in the same way. Westerners tend to perceive truth within a word's meaning, regardless of who is using the word, but not all societies think about discourse in the same way. Derrida rejected any notion that language constituted a system of meaning separate from the users of that discourse. In other words, meaning is not located in discourse itself but in the meaning perceived by each of its individual users.

Postmodernism refers primarily to the works of Jean-François Lyotard and Michel Foucault, works based on Friedrich Nietzsche's theory of power (Sedgwick, 2001, pp. 251–281). Nietzsche contended that the modern world represented a complete restructuring of authority. Up to this point in history, individuals had relied on the church and state as dual and uncontestable sources of authority. In the modern world, industrialization led to the rise of science as the 'new faith', while religious and governmental institutions declined as sources of power. Lyotard believed that the basis of all knowledge was narrative and historical in character, insofar as telling stories can supply a compelling sense of order to the world. Nonetheless, he rejected the 'grand narratives of politics and history' that attempted to universalize human experience, such as those found in the philosophies of Marx and Nietzsche. Like Lyotard, Foucault also argued that discursive practice becomes the source of knowledge and power. The 'order' of history is created when the narrative of history is told, and power is dispersed throughout society through multiple narratives that explain or legitimize its existence (Lechte, 1994, p. 111).

The last 'ism' we shall consider from the critical paradigm is postcolonialism. **Postcolonialism** contends that the Western countries of the 'first world' oppress peoples of the 'third world' through their conceptions and representations of Third World countries. With increasing globalization, it is recognized that cultures cannot exist independently from the influences of other cultures. Instead, the postcolonial critic focuses on how cultural identities can be challenged and changed (Shome, 1999).

Common to the preceding philosophies is the understanding that evaluation and criticism are impossible to avoid and, in fact, they are desirable ends. Since the researcher cannot escape the subjective and interpretive view of reality, then this standpoint should be made explicit and clear. Otherwise, the researcher misrepresents research as objective when it simply reinforces the existing hierarchy of power. Research that is influenced by feminism, Marxism, and cultural studies relies on the critical paradigm to explain how privileged groups oppress marginalized groups (like women, targeted ethnicities, and politically disfavoured or economically disadvantaged groups).

Within the critical paradigm, research is designed to identify the ways that power is constructed and distributed in society. Critical researchers want to expose how power functions so that dominant social structures of power are revealed and so that real change in the sociocultural, political, and economic bases can be instigated. Some researchers may approach these social structures as material and verifiable and other researchers consider them experiential and subjective. Often, poststructural studies demonstrate that the mass media represent the dominant paradigm of thought and communication in ways that do not allow alternative ways of thinking and communicating to be represented fairly. Some feminist scholars, for example, have argued that ideological and methodological differences emerging from feminist scholarship must be given equal footing with the existing masculine paradigm (Blair, Brown, & Baxter, 1999, pp. 563–590; Gilligan, 1982). Likewise, some married people refer to their spouse as 'partner' (rather than 'husband' or 'wife'), because the word 'partner' can equitably include gay, lesbian, bisexual, and transgendered as well as heterosexual relationships. Critical scholars believe that by changing our language we can changes our thoughts, and by extension we can change the world.

As we noted with the discovery paradigm and the interpretive paradigm, it is possible for a research method to fit with the assumptions of more than one paradigm. With that in mind, the methods that tend to be associated most commonly with the critical paradigm in Canada are discourse analysis, historical research, policy analysis, and ethnography. Some such studies may have an interpretive emphasis and they may not adopt expressly political conclusions. Others may press overtly for radical social change.

It is worth noting that scholars in communication and cultural studies still debate the major tenets and assumptions common to all three paradigms. We are always in a state of flux as researchers, as theorists, and as students and teachers! The discussion in this section is meant to provide you with a brief overview of the major paradigms in communication research and of current trends in our methodological approaches. Whenever we do research, we select methods that have, at their core, basic assumptions about how we acquire knowledge.

Summary

This chapter began with an identification of the three paradigms of discovery, interpretation, and criticism and an explanation of these as methodological ways of knowing about communication and culture. The next section of this chapter provided a brief history of the philosophical perspectives that contributed to each of the three epistemological paradigms. Overall, this chapter was designed to help you identify the epistemological assumptions common to the research methods applied in communication and cultural studies. For a quick visual summary of the main points, it is useful to review the three tables included in this chapter, but particularly Table 3.1. The assumptions of each paradigm provide different answers to how researchers make claims (to be covered next in chapter 4), to what counts as data (chapter 5), and to how researchers should warrant their claims (chapter 6).

Key Terms

Behaviourism

Constructivism

Critical theory

Deconstruction

Discrimination

Empiricism

Falsification principle

Generalization

Hermeneutics

Knowing by criticism

Knowing by discovery

Knowing by interpretation

Logical positivism

Modernism

Naturalism principle

Paradigm

Phenomenology

Postcolonialism

Postmodernism

Postpositivism

Poststructuralism

Precise, systematic, and repetitive observations

Rationalism

Realism principle

Semiotics

Structuralism, early and late

Symbolic interactionism

Discussion Questions

1. At the beginning of this chapter, we asked you to identify one thing that you know. Write it down here. Try to identify which epistemological paradigm presented in this chapter best describes the way you came to know this.

2. Some people argue that you should not use a research method outside of its original paradigm. How would you counter this argument? What would make such research *bad*?

3. Review a study that investigates communication or culture as an observable and quantifiable phenomenon. By adopting an empirical and rational approach, researchers use methods common to the discovery paradigm. For example, you could explain how Westlund (2008) developed a typology of cellphone users based on their willingness to use their phones to supply news updates.

4. Review a study that describes communication within a specified cultural group for the purposes of understanding what is occurring from the perspectives of its members. This approach is central to the interpretation paradigm. For example, you could explain how Montemurro (2005) studied the phenomenon of wedding showers from various participant views.

5. Review a study that describes and critiques how marginal groups are either co-opted or marginalized by the dominant social group as one of the central assumptions of the critical paradigm. For example, you could explain how MacLeod (2002) shows that musician Ashley MacIsaac challenged the Canadian media's ability to construct 'stars' who are unconventional and exciting yet mainstream and safe.

Try It!

1. Using an Internet search engine, find the following two photographic images: an aerial view of your university (a satellite image may work), and a ground level view of your university. If you cannot find both photos of your university, then try to find both views of any prominent landmark in your area.

   Examine each photo, and answer the following questions:

   (a) What is visible and what is not in each photo?

   (b) What things can you know by looking at each photo? Or, what kinds of questions could you answer by examining each photo?

   (c) If you only had one kind of photo, how would this affect your ability to research this building or site?

   (d) How does this difference between visual perspectives compare with the difference between paradigm perspectives?

2. This activity asks you to consider a single case from each of the three paradigm perspectives. The activity can be completed by an individual, but it may be more interesting to work in a group with three or more other members. Depending on the size of your tutorial group, it may also be adapted as a tutorial exercise.

This chapter has described the three major research paradigms in communication and cultural research. In particular, it has drawn attention to the important differences that distinguish these paradigms from each other. Researchers who work within different paradigms will focus on different aspects of the exact same topic. It should not be surprising, then, that as these researchers collect data, assess their findings, and then draw conclusions, they may produce greatly different reports about the same topic. This activity reveals the importance of your own research paradigm by asking you to consider the same case from all three paradigm perspectives.

The following steps and questions will help you through the process:

(a) Select a written or video case for study, or ask your instructor for guidance. A suitable case for this activity is Case 46: Multi-Bake Corporation, found in Hoffman and Ruemper (2010).

(b) Summarize the case in your own words. This summary may include any one or more of the following things:

   • A list of the key individuals involved in the case, and their relationships

- A narrative account of key events which occur during the case
- A list of the key issues that arise.

3. Answer the following questions from each paradigm perspective. If you are working with a group or an entire tutorial, you may wish to divide yourselves into three groups and to assign each group one of the three paradigm perspectives. Table 3.1 may provide some help with these questions.

   (a) What are the key assumptions about reality from your paradigm perspective?
   (b) What is your purpose as a researcher?
   (c) What will be the nature of your findings?
   (d) From your perspective, which aspect of the case is most important?
   (e) From your perspective, how would you assess or interpret the issues that arise?
   (f) Is there anything you would like to know but which is not reported in the case? If yes, what is the nature of this information and how would it affect your assessment or interpretation?
   (g) What recommendations or conclusions would you offer to the individuals described in the case?

4. Compare the answers generated for each paradigm perspective. It may be useful to record your answers in a grid so that it is easy to compare the three paradigms perspectives.

5. Consider or discuss the following questions:

   (a) Did the three paradigm perspectives produce different answers to questions 3.d, 3.e, and 3.g?
   (b) How significant are the differences in their answers? How would you describe these differences?
   (c) Which perspective offers the most valuable insights into the case and its issues?
   (d) What makes a perspective valuable?

(Source for 'Try It!': Adapted from Braithwaite, Dollar, Fitch, & Geist, 1996 and used with permission of the first author.)

4 Making Claims

Introduction

In this chapter, we begin our discussion of the *research as argument* model that we identified in chapter 1 by examining its first component: the claim. The claim is the central assertion or premise on which a research analysis is based. We consider how claims are framed by the kinds of questions we ask as communication researchers. There are six different types of claims: descriptive, explanatory, predictive, interpretive, evaluative, and reformist. We describe each type and show you how each is applied to different communication research methodologies across our three epistemological paradigms: discovery, interpretive, and critical research. Often, we combine different types of claims into one analysis (i.e. a study may be premised on two or more kinds of claims). Moreover, we will note how we as researchers understand and use any one of these types of claims will depend on our paradigmatic assumptions.

The Process of Making Claims

As we noted in chapter 1, the research process usually begins with a problem or topic that piques your curiosity. Perhaps you wonder why some friends enjoy teasing one another as a part of their relationship, whereas others try to avoid it. Or you might want to understand what makes some political campaigns more persuasive than others. Or maybe you are concerned that violence in visual media is adversely affecting us as audience members.

Our interests guide our research decisions. From these interests, we form a claim, or central assertion of a research study. Let's be clear, however: scholars don't consciously decide to do a particular study because they possess a set of values as described in chapter 3. You wouldn't say, for instance: 'I want to assess the practical value of a CRTC policy because I believe there is a discoverable objective reality, that my purpose is to accurately represent reality, and that I will do so by precise, systematic, and repetitive methods.' Rather, you would think that the policy was significant or interesting and deserved your attention. Nevertheless, the process of thinking about communication, the nature of your questions, and how you study them, are all implicitly informed by one of the three paradigms whether you are aware of this or not.

To illustrate this point, let's imagine that you are working within the discovery paradigm. You will craft a research design that begins with a testable claim, requires precise procedures for measurement, and reports the results of testing those predictions. Butovsky (2007) offers a good example of this process in a study of the misuse of polls in the *National Post* newspaper. To begin, he summarized a previous report that found the newspaper had manipulated one poll's data in a way that suggested the newspaper's views were supported by Canadian popular opinion. This observation regarding the manipulation of poll data became Butovsky's claim. To test this claim, he reviewed the *Post*'s coverage of opinion polls for one full year. He looked to see if the poll's methods were described, how the results were interpreted, and how the results were portrayed in headlines. Hence, Butovsky established a claim about the newspaper, and then tested that claim against his observations. We have more to say about these types of studies in chapter 7, on survey research, and chapter 8, on content analysis.

If you value the assumptions of the interpretive paradigm, you will think of communication problems in a very different way. Frequently, you may not know what your claims will be until you explore a particular social group and then describe your observations, since your knowledge of the group will presumably be limited until you actually gather data. Examples of such social groups are found in Broad, Boyer, and Chataway's (2006) study of cultural renewal as an element of community building in a First Nation; DeSantis's (2003) study of rationalization in discussions of a cigar-smoking group of friends; and Elliott's (2009) study of children's thoughts about 'fun foods' (i.e. packaged foods that are marketed to them). We focus on studies like these in chapter 10, on conversation and discourse analysis, and in chapter 11, on ethnography.

If you value the assumptions of the critical paradigm, you might begin by looking for those political and social practices that reveal the oppression of marginalized social groups, and you might feel that you have an obligation to instigate some form of social change. For example, the central message in Calhoun's (2005) critique of Eminem's album, *The Marshall Mathers LP*, is that the popular rapper constructs 'whiteness' by negotiating a particular intersection of ethnicity, gender, class, and sexuality. Ice-T and 2 Live Crew used similar strategies in their lyrics, but while they were criticized for racist and sexist lyrics, Eminem did not face the same accusations. Calhoun believed this disparity reveals a strategy for silencing or marginalizing certain groups, in this case African American rap artists. We explore the many types of communication phenomena from the critical paradigm perspective in chapter 12, on critical studies.

By understanding how the three paradigms guide us in making claims, it becomes clear that we cannot tell you all research has the same, systematic set of practices, stages, or sequence of steps (Philipsen, 1977). Not all research begins with a claim, continues by testing that claim with data or evidence, and concludes by verifying that process with warrants. Some research begins with a claim, some begins with data, and some begins with a description of existing social warrants of specific social practices. Methods and their paradigm assumptions do not have strictly equivalent components and processes. We chose to start our explanation instead by considering how claims reflect paradigmatic assumptions.

Definition of 'Claim'

In the first chapter, we defined a **claim** as the central assertion of a research study. It often represents the study's purpose or goal as well, if only implicitly. Having distinct purposes or goals leads us to the identification of six types of claims made in research: descriptive, explanatory, predictive, interpretive, evaluative, and reformist claims (adapted from Smith, 1988, and Littlejohn, 1996). Not every type of claim is found in every paradigm, nor is every type mutually exclusive. Descriptive claims are found across all three types of paradigms. Explanatory and predictive claims are concentrated in the discovery paradigm. The interpretive paradigm emphasizes the claim as interpretation, obviously, and to some extent as evaluation. And the critical paradigm focuses on evaluation and social reform. The six types of claims are categorized by paradigm in Table 4.1. There are exceptions to these distinctions but generally each paradigm perspective emphasizes certain types of claims over others.

TABLE 4.1 Types of Claims Across the Paradigms

DISCOVERY PARADIGM	INTERPRETIVE PARADIGM	CRITICAL PARADIGM
Descriptive claims	Descriptive claims	Descriptive claims
Explanatory claims	Interpretive claims	Evaluative claims
Predictive claims	Evaluative claims	Reformist claims

Types of Claims

Descriptive Claims

If you want to define some particular communication or cultural phenomenon, you make a **descriptive claim**. Description is a process that appears across all three paradigms and across a variety of research methods. Its focus is on defining some aspect of communication, not explaining why it happens or whether it is valued positively or negatively. The specific types of descriptive claims you make and how you put them to work will depend on your paradigmatic assumptions. Exhibit 4.1 shows a clear distinction in how descriptive claims function across the three paradigms.

The purpose of descriptive research claims is to describe reality accurately (Exhibit 4.1). The goal of description remains the same throughout the discovery paradigm whether researchers are administering a survey, analyzing message content, or exploring the culture of a special social group. Surveys and

EXHIBIT 4.1 Characteristics of Descriptive Claims

General Function: Descriptive claims generally define what is occurring.

1. **Discovery Paradigm:** Function of descriptive claims is to represent reality accurately.
2. **Interpretive Paradigm:** Function of descriptive claims is to reveal the meanings of communication processes in specific contexts.
3. **Critical Paradigm:** Function of descriptive claims is to reveal the ideological framework for communication processes in a specific context.

content analyses are **empirical methods** that rely on measuring quantitative or numerical data, whereas ethnographic methods from within the discovery paradigm retain observational data that is qualitative or descriptive.

Description is essential in survey studies. Survey studies are a type of empirical research in which researchers construct conceptual measures to use in interviews or written questionnaires. To illustrate this process, Mongeau, Serewicz, and Therrien (2004) used open-ended survey questions to obtain descriptions of the goals university students are aware they have for first dates. The descriptions were analyzed and participants provided over 500 goals for their first dates! In subsequent studies reported in the same article, the researchers refined those goals into categories to explore how various contexts, such as the degree of intimacy and the availability of alcohol, might influence the relational goals.

Within the discovery paradigm, claims usually take the form of research questions or hypotheses (Smith, 1988; Mertens, 1998). **Research questions** ask how a concept chosen for study can be classified or what relationship exists between various types of communication variables. **Hypotheses** are considered more precise since hypotheses make specific predictions about relationships between communication variables. You will learn more about research questions and hypotheses in chapters 7 and 8, devoted to survey research and content analysis. Some examples of descriptive research questions from published communication research literature are shown in Exhibit 4.2.

Researchers who rely upon empirical data often separate descriptive claims from explanatory claims. Explanatory claims are described in detail in the next section but are introduced here for contrast. With a purely descriptive focus, a researcher 'begins with a

EXHIBIT 4.2 Discovery Paradigm:
Descriptive Research Questions

RQ1: What goals will college students report for first dates? (Mongeau, Serewicz, & Therrien, 2004)

RQ2: How have Canadian newspapers adapted their news operations to the Internet, to benefit from technological convergence? (Sparks, Young, & Darnell, 2006)

RQ3: How usable are wireless networks? (Potter, McIntyre, & Middleton, 2008)

Note: RQ = research question.

well-defined subject and conducts research to describe it accurately. The outcome of a descriptive study is a detailed picture of the subject' (Neuman, 1994, p. 19). Examples of descriptive claims can be found in articles describing how newspapers have adapted their news operations to the Internet (Sparks, Young, & Darnell, 2006) and how a government report on health care addressed issues related to health care communication (Balka, Rodje, & Bush, 2007). By contrast, explanatory claims are assertions about why one communication characteristic or behaviour influences another. In other words, an explanatory claim moves beyond what a descriptive claim is intended to do.

Descriptive claims often require the development of a **taxonomy**, or categorizing scheme, for communication behaviours, events, and messages. The study we cited earlier by Mongeau et al. (2004) found that romantic couples identified many different types of goals for their first dates. By using a statistical analysis to group the various reasons for going on a first date, five general categories of goals emerged: reduction of uncertainty, relational escalation, companionship, sexual activity, and having fun. They conducted their subsequent studies to verify their taxonomy or classification system of first date goals was accurate and useful.

If you view description as a preliminary stage prior to explanation and prediction, as many discovery paradigm researchers do, then your research will never end in description. Instead, you will adopt a deductive method of inquiry in which you will make a descriptive

claim and then test your claim against observations. Your ultimate goals are explanation and prediction. Descriptive studies are initial attempts to map out conceptual territory for empirical study. In our earlier example, Mongeau et al. (2004) used research questions to ask what types of goals university students have for first dates. Results from the first and second studies permitted them to construct an experiment for the third study to test specific hypotheses, such as the effects of sex, the availability of alcohol, and relationship type on relational goals for first dates. In empirical research, you will advance descriptive claims as a way of preparing to achieve more accurate and precise explanations and predictions.

Although scholars who adopt the discovery paradigm tend to view observation and description as preliminary stages in a research program, scholars who embrace the interpretive paradigm view description as a complete process. It is not meant to be part of the larger process of explanation and prediction. Interpretive researchers move back and forth between what they are observing and their descriptions, and modify their descriptions as they uncover patterns in human behaviour. For example, when conducting ethnographic research, your goal as an interpretive researcher is 'to discover the meanings communicators have in mind when they talk with others in particular contexts' (Smith, 1988, p. 9). Hence, your descriptive claims will emerge and change throughout the research process as meanings become apparent to you. Interpretive researchers tend to view description as an articulation of a socially constructed reality rather than as a physical, external reality as it is viewed by proponents of the discovery paradigm.

When using description in the interpretive paradigm, you will typically collect three sets of observational data. Each set of data reveals a distinct type of claim about your research topic, and these claims describe the observational domain, interpretive schemes, and relations between your observations (Smith, 1988, p. 9). With respect to the observational domain, you make a claim about what type of communication is occurring—verbal or nonverbal, face-to-face or mediated, formal or informal, and so forth. For example, Buddle (2005) investigated particular First Nations members' use of radio in Southern Ontario. She argued that their use of radio represented not their submission to a European technology (and by extension, a European culture), but instead their desire to construct a uniquely Aboriginal space within radio broadcasting. With the second set of data, you make descriptive claims about the interpretive schemes that communicators use to produce meaning. To illustrate, Buddle (2005) explained the concepts of 'kinship', 'place', and 'production of locality' to explain how members of First Nations can organize their experiences as Aboriginals in North America and maintain a coherent, rooted culture.

The third set of observations leads to descriptive claims about how the communication practices you observe become productive through the interpretive scheme shared by the participants. Buddle (2005) illustrated how certain radio hosts created programming that was rooted in Native cultural models such as powwows and 'teachings' (a discursive form reserved for elders in Aboriginal society). The radio shows produced new forms of community between listeners who could imagine their locality was Native as much as it was non-Native. These examples are drawn from case study analysis, but interpretivists use descriptive claims in a variety of methodologies. The main point here is that description via the interpretive paradigm is used to reveal the underlying structure of meaning within the communication practices of a social group.

Within the critical paradigm, you may still collect three sets of data but your purpose in using description is to provide a framework for understanding power inequalities and instigating social change. Your research should satisfy this basic purpose regardless of the theoretical framework you bring to your data, be it critical ethnography, feminist and cultural studies, or any other version of critical communication research (e.g. Marxist, postmodern, and semiotic criticism).

To illustrate this form of description, Thomas (1993) stated that critical ethnography deviates from conventional ethnography in that conventional ethnographers 'study culture for the purpose of describing it' whereas critical ethnographers 'do so to change it' (p. 4). Certainly, your first goal is to explain how members of a culture share their interpretations of reality, but your second goal is to give voice to and represent members who are otherwise marginalized (Thomas, 1993, p. 34). Description via the critical

paradigm can become a powerful tool for change if it can reveal the processes that marginalize either individuals or groups, and thereby lead to social reform. Schneider's (2003) study of individuals with schizophrenia revealed that the social effects of their diagnosis could be as debilitating as their physical symptoms. She found, through an ethnomethodological study, that individuals with schizophrenia could construct positive self-images for themselves by confronting stereotypes about the condition and reducing the stigma attached to it. By extension, Schneider argued that activists could use her findings to develop strategies to normalize perceptions of schizophrenia throughout society. We tell you more about evaluative and reformist goals in later sections of this chapter.

Remember that the use of description changes as we move from paradigm to paradigm. Refer again to Exhibit 4.1, where we note how descriptive claims function in each paradigm. Whatever we see as researchers is influenced by our existing beliefs. When studying an argument, for example, an ethnographer who embraces the interpretive paradigm will see a very different event than a content analyst who functions within the discovery paradigm. In the former instance, description may reveal the interpretive schemes that two individuals use during arguments. In the latter instance, description may classify behaviours as a first step in the development of a theory about arguments. We explore other paradigmatic changes in chapter 5, on data, and chapter 6, on warrants.

Explanatory and Predictive Claims

When they appear together, 'explanation' and 'prediction' are terms often associated with the discovery paradigm. As we noted in the previous section, **explanatory claims** explain the relationships between various phenomena, often by identifying reasons or causes for specific kinds of phenomena. Explanation and prediction are the means by which you can make causal arguments. If you share the view that knowledge is objective and that reality is discoverable, then it is causal arguments that make that reality intelligible and predictable. You would expect to find such claims in survey research, content analysis, and historical research, but you will not find them in interpretive and critical paradigm research (see, e.g. Madison, 2005; Silverman, 1993; Thomas, 1993).

In discovery paradigm research, you will attempt to discover what rules or laws explain whatever relationship you observe between one set of data and another. To do so, you will treat theorizing and data collection as two parts of a larger research process. In this context 'explanatory theories are composed of logically inter-related propositions' that allow you to make causal predictions (Jorgensen, 1989, p. 17). First you will develop theories about your topic. Next you will test your theories against available data and assess the merits of alternative explanations. Depending on the results of these tests, you may feel compelled to revise your theories. Finally, you will test your theories with new evidence that you collect (Kerlinger, 1986). Hence, you will see theories as explanatory claims 'aimed at explanation, prediction, and control of human phenomena,' and the role of data collection as testing these claims through a 'logic of verification' (Jorgensen, 1989, p. 17).

When the claim you construct *predicts* that a change in one phenomenon precedes and influences a change in the other, you have made a **causal claim**. Generally, we refer to the original or active phenomenon as the **independent variable**, and the secondary or reactive phenomenon as the **dependent variable**. We have more to say about variables and the nature of causality in chapter 6, on warrants, and chapter 7, on survey research. For now, it is important that you understand that explanatory claims are formulated as predictions in the discovery paradigm, rather than as separate types of claims.

As we said before, explanatory claims can be phrased as research questions or as hypotheses. Typically, you will use research questions when past research is limited in scope or when different studies contradict one another. This is particularly true when researchers try to understand new communication technologies as they develop. For example, in a study of urban Wi-Fi infrastructure, Potter, McIntyre, and Middleton (2008) asked 'How usable are wireless networks?' (p. 511). Although the technology is unregulated, relatively inexpensive, and has the potential to foster new community networks, Potter et al. noted that questions about the technology's practical limitations had not been asked. Hence, Potter et al. constructed their claim in question

format to address a perceived gap in knowledge. We should note that they selected three variables that they believed were most important to answer their question: the wireless devices used by community members, the natural environment, and the technological landscape. When we expect to find an association between variables, we call this an **associative claim**. While a claim of association is not sufficient to make a causal argument, it is one of the conditions of causality we discuss later in chapter 7, on survey research.

By contrast, some topics have been explored by many scholars. When that is the case there may be sufficient depth in the available knowledge that new research can begin with a specific hypothesis. An example of this can be found in a study by Barber and Rauhala (2005) where they review competing interpretations of how news is produced in television newsrooms. After comparing several studies that argue that economics, technology, and ownership structures affect the production of news content, Barber and Rauhala hypothesize that the personal perspectives of individual news directors and reporters cannot be dismissed. As they put it, quite simply, 'journalists matter' (p. 284). In this case, Barber and Rauhala constructed an associative claim to predict a relationship between the type of news produced and the demographic and ideological profiles of the journalists behind it.

One line of research that is undertaken solely for practical and applied outcomes rather than to develop theory or increase 'pure knowledge' is called **action research** (Taylor & Bogdan, 1998, pp. 260–261). Bogdan and Biklen (1982) defined action research as 'the systematic collection of information that is designed to bring about social change' (p. 215). It is used to evaluate a specific problem and to find a practical solution. When you conduct such research, you will collect data and analyze it for evidence of a negative relationship between two aspects of a current social situation. Then, when drafting your conclusions, you will propose ways to overcome or eliminate the effect of the negative relationship. Bogdan and Biklen cited numerous action research examples, which included studies designed to change the negative ways in which females are depicted in textbooks used by schools, to advocate for the rights of disabled students, and to expose the discriminatory practices of government institutions serving ethnic minorities. More examples of explanatory research questions and hypotheses can be found in Exhibit 4.3.

Even though action research may identify practical needs and their solutions, Bogdan and Biklen (1982) explained that it is frequently considered unacceptable because it violates two assumptions some discovery-paradigm scholars hold dear: (1) research should be conducted by academically trained personnel only and should not be pursued in applied contexts; and (2) research should always be non-partisan (p. 214). Because action research goes beyond purely descriptive and explanatory claims, it has been criticized by some scholars. Be that as it may, research that blurs paradigm boundaries is often research that engages us creatively and constructively, as you will see in many instances throughout this book.

EXHIBIT 4.3 Discovery Paradigm: Explanatory/Predictive Claims

CLAIMS FRAMED AS RESEARCH QUESTIONS

RQ1:   Do journalists' personal backgrounds and values affect their decision-making when producing newscasts? (Barber & Rauhala, 2005)

RQ2:   What is more important in the media-buying strategies of advertising agencies: a newspaper's editorial bias or its circulation figure? (Johnston, 2007)

RQ3:   To what extent do men and women use different types of macro argument structures? (Suzuki, 2006, p. 199)

CLAIMS FRAMED AS HYPOTHESES

H1:   Journalists' personal backgrounds and values affect their decision-making when producing newscasts. (Barber & Rauhala, 2005)

H2:   A newspaper's circulation figure is more important than its editorial bias in the media-buying strategies of advertising agencies. (Johnston, 2007)

H3:   Women use personal statements in arguments more frequently than men. (Suzuki, 2006, p. 199)

Note: RQ = research question; H = hypothesis.

For the most part, the ability to make accurate predictions is a major characteristic of empirical research within the discovery paradigm. However, if you work within the critical paradigm, you can still conduct research that is explanatory and predictive. Andrews, Leff, and Terrill (1998) claimed that some theories help us to understand patterns or principles that 'explain a complex set of facts or phenomena'. They suggested that the following was true of rhetorical studies:

> The more we learn about what happened in one particular situation—that is, the more information bits that can be adduced—the better able we will be to generalize a pattern of rhetorical behaviour. As these patterns are formed, and compared and contrasted with other patterns, a basis for predicting what will happen in similar cases is established. (pp. 19–20)

This statement is generally true, whether we are studying rhetoric or any other aspect of communicative behaviour. We should remember, however, that not all criticism is explicitly explanatory and predictive; that is, your intention may be not to develop a set of generalizations that allow us to predict certain results. Rather, you may wish simply to enhance our knowledge of a particular person, text, or culture. If this is your general purpose, your claims are likely to be more interpretive than explanatory.

Interpretive Claims

If you work within the interpretive paradigm, you will not assume your goals are driven by explanation and prediction. Instead, you will assume that your goal is interpretation. In so far as you wish to show how communicators create meaning, you are engaged in making **interpretive claims** that broaden understanding among all researchers. In ethnographic research, for example, you will achieve this goal by describing and interpreting how meaning is accomplished from the participants' perspectives, and those perspectives will be situated in the context of their lived experiences.

Interpretive claims are found in ethnographic studies, conversational and discourse analyses, and historical research. If you take an interpretive approach, your emphasis will be on interpreting meanings and identifying cultural patterns instead of on reporting behaviours and pursuing scientific laws as you would by taking the discovery approach (Hammersley, 1992, pp. 48–50). As Jorgensen noted, for example, 'descriptive ethnographies are marked by minimal interpretation and conceptualization. The researcher tells the story not through concepts but through descriptions of events. Readers are free to come to their own interpretations and draw their own generalizations' (1989, p. 135). By contrast, he argues that interpretive researchers 'try to paint a picture of what people say and how they act in their everyday lives' (p. 189).

In the normal course of interpretive scholarship, you will develop an initial claim using inductive reasoning, or 'induction'. Induction occurs when you make a generalization based on your knowledge of particular cases. By contrast, deduction involves 'moving from the general to the particular' (Bulmer, 1979, p. 660). Researchers engaged in interpretive research projects are more likely to use induction because inductive reasoning will help them 'to maintain faithfulness to the empirical data while abstracting and generalizing from a relatively small number of cases' (Bulmer, 1979, p. 661). Some scholars refer to this reasoning process as **analytic induction**. Jackson (1986) outlined the method of analytic induction as follows:

> The process of analytic induction begins with collection of a set of examples of the phenomenon being studied. The examples are used to build, inductively, a hypothesis. The hypothesis may be about the properties of a class, the rules that generate a pattern of interaction, the sequential characteristics of a kind of interaction, or some other empirical issue. An initial test of the hypothesis is its adequacy as an account of the examples. But this is only a preliminary step. . . .The method of analytic induction requires that empirical claims be tested through active, procedurally diverse search for counter-examples. (p. 129)

We will describe how adequacy and counterexamples provide warrants for interpretive research in chapter 6, on warrants.

Interpretive studies can also be used to move beyond description to develop theories. An approach similar to induction is the **grounded theory approach** developed by Glaser and Strauss (1967). We have more to say about this approach in chapter 11, on ethnography. To illustrate briefly, Tracy, Myers, and Scott (2006) explored how employees used humour to develop personal identities within an organization. Their primary research question asked: 'In what ways does humour assist employees in negotiating and affirming preferred identities?' (p. 284). The study employed Glaser and Strauss's method of constant comparison, a method that 'entails an iterative, reflective process that moves back and forth between the data and categories so that the findings are theoretically grounded within the data' (Pepper & Larson, 2006, p. 56). To ground the data, they used Weick's (1995) theory of 'sense-making'. Please refer to Exhibit 4.4 for examples of interpretive research questions from these and other studies.

Interpretive studies are not restricted to ethnographic and grounded theory research on communication issues and culture. Rather, interpretive studies can examine a wide variety of topics including the social uses of technology. The popularity and complexity of online networks provide a broad field for interpretive claims. For example, Soukup (2006) explored the designs of fansites, websites that are dedicated to individual celebrities and appeal to those celebrities' 'fan communities'. Soukup uncovered three themes during interviews with fansite designers: (1) they engage in a dialogue with the fan community, (2) their representations of the celebrity tend to be 'controlled', and (3) they feel a personal identification with the celebrity. In another recent study, Skovholt and Svennevig (2006) applied strategies from discourse analysis to investigate the potential impact of 'cc'ing' third parties in email conversations. You will learn more about discourse analysis in chapter 10 of this book.

In another interpretive study, Stroud (2001) explored the story of the hero quest in the movie *The Matrix*. In a complex web of interconnections revealed throughout the film, Stroud claimed that the hero, Neo, maintained his individuality because he could use his technological expertise to stay free from the technologically trapped members of a futuristic society. Stroud (2001) used narrative theory as support

EXHIBIT 4.4   Interpretive Paradigm: Descriptive and Interpretive Claims

1. In what ways does humour assist employees in negotiating and affirming preferred identities? (Tracy, Myers, & Scott, 2006, p. 284)

2. Via the identification processes associated with fansites, fans can significantly influence the meanings, uses, and even production-distribution of media texts and manipulate the complex iconography of celebrities to 'visibly' participate in public discourse (Soukup, 2006, p. 319).

3. This film [*The Matrix*] is shown to be a powerful myth for alienated and disempowered individuals in technologically driven communities, with potentially troubling consequences due to its theme of 'solitary enlightenment' (Stroud, 2001, p. 416).

for his claim that the film was 'shown to be a powerful myth for alienated and disempowered individuals in technologically driven communities' (p. 416).

The essays of Soukup (2006), Skovhold and Svennevig (2006), and Stroud (2001) offer unique interpretations or applications of existing theories. They do not argue that one explanation is more justified or accurate than another. When you adopt the perspective of an interpretive critic, you are 'not concerned with finding the one correct interpretation of the artifact because the critic recognizes the artifact does not constitute a reality that can be known and proved.' In other words, you can never 'know what the artifact "really" is' (Foss, 2004, p. 21). Instead, as an interpretive critic, you will argue for a new understanding of a theory as it is applied socially, culturally, or politically to a selected communication behaviour or text. Examples of these interpretive claims can be found in Exhibit 4.4. When you move beyond interpretation to make claims that are evaluative and reformist, your perspective on the significance of communication shifts from the interpretive paradigm to the critical paradigm.

Evaluative and Reformist Claims

When you make **evaluative claims**, you establish a set of standards and render judgments about how well or how poorly some communication phenomenon meets those standards. **Reformist claims** are not only evaluative; they identify negative consequences of the existing social system as a way of instigating change. Because evaluative and reformist claims require you to make explicit value judgments, they are associated only with the critical paradigm. By contrast, the underlying assumptions of the discovery paradigm require you to maintain an objective perspective when observing communication. When operating from the interpretive paradigm, you will value subjectivity, but you will observe and interpret your subject matter without assessing if it is effective or ineffective, constructive or destructive, nor will you advocate for social change. Many evaluative and reformist claims can be found in historical, ethnographic, and discourse analytic research, as well as critical studies.

As a critical researcher, you will make the general argument that no research can ever be value free. Indeed, you may argue further that scholars have an ethical obligation to improve social conditions through their efforts (Campbell, 1974; Foss & Foss, 1988; Madison, 2005; Thomas, 1993). In a recent study, Rinehart (2008) reviewed press coverage of child care issues during the 2006 Canadian general election. In her view, news organizations treat elections and party platforms as 'hard news', and typically assign male journalists to cover them. By contrast, child care is treated as 'soft news' and it is typically assigned to female journalists. When child care policy became an election issue in 2006, it was assigned to male reporters who had little familiarity with its nuances. Subsequently, Rinehart claims, their analysis of the issue lacked depth or insight, and the Canadian public was ill served. Rinehart uses this episode to reveal the inadequacies of sexist hiring and promotion practices at Canada's daily newspapers. Such private practices appear to have clear public consequences for Canadian society. By exposing this problem, she may raise general awareness and instigate social action.

When you work within the critical paradigm, you must decide not only whether your argument is logical but also whether it makes a positive contribution to society. Effectiveness becomes an ethical value judgment rather than a precise measure of a rational claim (Foss, 2004, p. 243). One strand of critical research, feminist criticism, is often based on the assumption that society must be reorganized 'on the basis of equality for the sexes in all areas of social relations' (Foss, Foss, & Griffin, 1999, p. 2). A prominent critical theorist, bell hooks, has argued that resisting dominance is a central part of learning to think and speak freely, and an essential quality of a truly democratic society (hooks, 1989, 1994, 2000). hooks refused to capitalize the letters of her name as a personal protest against all means of standardization and conformity in modern society. In chapter 12, on critical studies, we will discuss in greater detail how your focus as a critical researcher will be to determine how communication perpetuates the dominant social order, thereby marginalizing any voices in the minority, and how social texts can articulate forms of resistance and offer ways to construct a new society.

Evaluative claims and reformist claims do not always appear together in the same study. A scholar may choose to concentrate his or her research efforts on a single claim. That said, whenever one type of claim is made explicitly, generally the other type of claim is made implicitly through the scholar's analysis and conclusions. Rinehart (2008), for example, offered a clear critique of sexist hiring and promotion policies at Canadian newspapers, but she did not recommend any specific action to end them. Rather, a call for change was implicit in her conclusion. By contrast, Wilson (2008) advanced reformist claims when he argued that the development of broadband networks must be conceived as a public good. At present, broadband development is led by private companies like Bell Canada, Rogers Communications, and TELUS Canada who profit from selling access to the network. Wilson believed policy makers should intervene to ensure that public access—and hence, widespread social, cultural, and commercial interaction via the Internet—is available to everyone. So, in this case, Wilson did not make an explicit evaluative claim establishing the utility of the public good; rather, that claim was implicit in the logic of his article. Instead, he focused on his reformist claim by describing a new conception of broadband policy that was based on historical precedents. Additional examples of evaluative and reformist claims appear in Exhibit 4.5.

In brief, you can see that your research will always be multifaceted if you operate within the critical paradigm. Your claims will be descriptive and interpretive, and evaluative and reformist, with these goals thoroughly intertwined.

Summary

In this chapter, we defined and explained the first component of our *research as argument* model, the 'claim'. The 'claim' refers to the central assertion on which a specific analysis is based. It can be phrased as a statement, a research question, or a hypothesis. There are six different types of claims: descriptive, explanatory, predictive, interpretive, evaluative, and reformist. We illustrated each of these types of claims by describing actual studies, using a variety of research methods and spanning all three epistemological paradigms.

As researchers, we tend to construct claims in accordance with the assumptions of our paradigms.

EXHIBIT 4.5   Critical Paradigm: Evaluative and Reformist Claims

1. 'The *National Post* regularly misrepresents the results of public opinion polls.' Even '. . . unintentional obfuscations damage the ability of readers to understand the world and then to act within it effectively' (Butovsky, 2007, pp. 100–101).

2. The media failed to cover child care reform adequately as a policy issue due to the sexist hiring and advancement policies of news organizations (Rinehart, 2008, pp. 1–2).

3. The development of broadband networks in Canada must be overseen by a strong regulatory hand that takes the public good into consideration (Wilson, 2008, pp. 96–98).

TABLE 4.2 Typical Claims made by Researchers in Each Paradigm

DISCOVERY PARADIGM	INTERPRETIVE PARADIGM	CRITICAL PARADIGM
Descriptive claims that represent one objective reality	Descriptive claims that represent participants' meanings	Descriptive claims that represent ideology and hegemonic relations
Explanatory claims	Interpretive claims	Evaluative claims
Predictive claims	Evaluative claims	Reformist claims

Many empirical researchers, who see their studies as descriptive, explanatory, and predictive, do not share the same goals of or assumptions about research as rhetorical critics, who see their analyses as descriptive, interpretive, evaluative, and reformist. Thus, you would likely find explanatory and predictive claims presented together in research developed within the discovery paradigm, and evaluative and reformist claims combined in research developed within the critical paradigm. We present these differences here not to force you take sides but rather to help you understand why they exist as you begin to read through the different types of studies conducted in our field. You will have an opportunity to explore the differences in assumptions and goals in the 'Try It!' activity that appears at the end of this chapter.

Key Terms

Action research
Associative claim
Causal claim
Claim
Dependent variable
Descriptive claim

Empirical method
Evaluative claim
Explanatory claim
Grounded theory approach
Hypothesis
Independent variable

Interpretive claim
Reformist claim
Research question
Taxonomy

Discussion Questions

1. Why are descriptive claims found across all three paradigms? Do descriptive claims have the same function across all three paradigms?
2. What assumptions are made from within the discovery paradigm that make explanatory and predictive claims more likely than interpretive or evaluative claims?
3. In what ways are evaluative and reformist claims different than descriptive and interpretive claims?

Try It!

This activity asks you to consider a video case study from one or more of the three paradigm perspectives. It can be completed by an individual, but it is more interesting to complete the work in a group of three or more. Depending on the size of your tutorial group, it may be adapted for a tutorial activity.

In this chapter, we outlined how each epistemological paradigm and its perspective can shape your goals as a researcher. The assumptions and beliefs you have about research will shape the claims you make. To gain a better appreciation of how different these paradigms and perspectives are, we constructed this exercise to illustrate how they might be applied in a 'real world' setting. For the purpose of this activity, we will draw on the television program *The Office*. This situation comedy portrays the daily interactions of a group of idiosyncratic office employees at the regional sales office of a large paper manufacturer. The pilot episode introduces the manager and his staff to a film crew who are making a 'fly-on-the-wall' documentary about the company. The crew records interviews with the manager and three employees, and they record several events that occur during their first day on-site. These interviews and events convey a great deal about the manager's leadership strategies and staff morale. They are presented without a narrator (Gervais et al., 2001; Daniels et al., 2005).

For this activity, imagine that you are a member of the film crew and your responsibility is to write a narrative voiceover for the finished documentary. This voiceover should provide a thoughtful and consistent explanation of the organizational culture that is revealed during the film. And, this voiceover should be written from the perspective of one epistemological paradigm.

If you are a proponent of the discovery paradigm, you should remember that your research goals involve descriptive claims about the manager and staff as well as their operations. You should devise claims that describe, explain, and predict communication phenomena that occur within the office without interjecting your subjective point of view. As far as possible your claims should be based upon careful and systematic observations of the manager and staff and their behaviours.

If you are a proponent of the interpretive paradigm, you should remember that your research goals involve developing an understanding of the office culture from the manager and staff's point of view. This will involve careful observation and description of their conversations, texts, and behaviours. As an interpretive scholar, you should also remember that your personal perspective cannot be eliminated; its presence should be acknowledged while carefully allowing the perspectives of the manager and staff to be brought to the foreground. The goal of understanding can only be achieved when you enter the interpretive process with no pre-formulated or pre-constructed explanations or predictions about what you will see.

If you are a proponent of the critical paradigm, you should remember that your research goal is to assess how power is distributed and used within the office (but keep in mind that there are different kinds of power). As is the case with the interpretive scholar, this will involve careful observation and description of the manager and staff's conversations, texts, and behaviours. Likewise, you should remember that your personal perspective cannot be eliminated. However, rather than simply acknowledging your own views, you should engage with the manager and staff to evaluate the culture of the office and to judge whether or not some change or reform is necessary.

Here are a few questions you might consider regardless of the paradigm you choose to adopt:

1. What is the primary goal of the office?
2. What are the manager's leadership strategies?
3. Should the effectiveness of the manager's leadership strategies be assessed? If so, what factors would you take into consideration?
4. Is the organizational culture of the office productive? What factors should we consider to answer this question?
5. Can the answers to these questions help to foster more effective leadership strategies or a more productive organizational culture?

The television program *The Office* provides a rich and engaging video case study for analysis. That said, any episode of a television program that is set in the workplace may work for this activity if carefully selected. So, too, would any written case drawn from a case reader.

5 What Counts as Data?

Introduction

In this chapter, we will examine the second component of our *research as argument* model, the data. We first outline some typical sources, settings, and strategies for collecting data, and then we describe the relative value of each of these research factors for supporting particular types of claims. We then introduce the ideas of measurement, research design, and triangulation, focusing on how each of those processes are used somewhat differently from the perspective of the discovery, interpretive, and critical research paradigms.

In chapters 3 and 4, we outlined the three major epistemological paradigms and demonstrated how they shape our general goals as researchers. We also described claims, those statements that articulate our specific goals in any one research program. In this chapter we turn our attention to 'data'. Data are the empirical facts you gather to support your claims. The term 'data' is often used interchangeably with 'evidence'. Just as a prosecuting lawyer will present evidence in a courtroom to make a case, a researcher must present empirical data to support a claim.

By 'empirical' we mean any fact that is known through direct observation of the world at a particular place and time. Observation is not limited to the naked eye. We can detect facts through all of our five senses, and often we are aided by devices that measure or record observations for us. For example, a decibel meter may measure sound levels at a public event, while a video camera may create an audio-visual record of the event itself. Contrast this notion of empirical facts with abstract ideas. Where empirical data is concrete and reflects some tangible aspect of our experience, abstract ideas, such as cultural theories and analytical concepts, are inherently intangible. Such ideas help us to make sense of our experiences, but abstract ideas cannot, themselves, be experienced by our senses or recorded by any device (Bouma, Ling, & Wilkinson, 2009, p. 21).

Through this chapter, then, you will learn about sources of data, the settings in which data are collected, and the strategies that you can use to collect data. In addition, we introduce you to conceptual and operational definitions used in research studies, to levels of measurement, to basic structures of research design, and to triangulation. These concepts will help you to evaluate any research you read, and to develop your own research studies. Let's start with some basic definitions and examples of data sources, settings, and strategies.

Sources for Data Collection

Sources can be any individual, text, or artefact that supplies data or evidence that is relevant to your research. Four categories of sources are available for communication and cultural data: (1) existing texts; (2) direct observations of phenomena; (3) self-reports of behaviours, beliefs, and/or characteristics; and (4) other-reports of behaviours, beliefs, and/or characteristics. Let's briefly differentiate each category.

Texts

We usually think of **texts** as written or spoken words. However, when you think of textual data for research, you should also include texts that are symbolic, performed, and purely visual or pictorial (Bowman, 1996; Jarmon, 1996). Whenever we do a close reading of a text to collect evidence for a study, we are conducting **textual analysis**. All communication and cultural research includes textual evidence of some form.

Texts may be categorized as 'primary' or 'secondary' sources. These terms describe a source's relationship to the topic you wish to study. A **primary source** is one that supplies first-hand, direct, or unmediated facts about the behaviours you wish to study. For example, if you are researching a speech given by an important public figure, there are several sources that may be considered primary: the script of the speech, the actual speaker, an unedited audio or video recording of the speech, or your own eye-witness account if you were present when the speech was given. All of these sources are direct and tangible sources of the behaviour you wish to study. By contrast, a **secondary source** is one that supplies second-hand, indirect, or mediated facts about the behaviour you wish to study. Staying with the example of the speech, there are several sources that may be considered secondary: an edited sound bite aired on the evening news, the opinion of someone who was not present at the speech but spoke with someone who was, or a scholar's interpretation of the speech based on journalists' accounts.

These sources are tangible but indirect sources of the behaviour you wish to study. Put another way, secondary sources are dependent on primary sources for all of the information they have about the speech (Deacon, Pickering, Golding, & Murdock, 2007, pp. 32–33).

An endless variety of texts can be analyzed for communication and cultural studies. Typically, researchers first consult secondary texts when conducting a literature review. To collect new primary data, however, researchers may turn to any texts relevant to their topic, be they annual reports, census documents, chat room discourse, class notes, corporate balance sheets, diagrams, diaries, email messages, employee records, financial records, journals, maps, memos, magazine and newspaper articles, photographs, poetry, prose, policy statements, production records, or videos. This list can be extended by the inclusion of symbolic texts like architecture, gestures or signs, clothing, hairstyles, jewellery, and types of automobile or other possessions. The range of texts studied by communication and cultural scholars is, theoretically, endless. We will discuss this point in further detail in chapter 8, on content analysis, and in chapter 9, on historical research.

Direct Observations

If you collect **direct observations** of interactions between people, you can be sure you are studying communication or culture in action (Patterson, Neupauer, Burant, Koehn, & Reed, 1996). You may be interested in observing the verbal and nonverbal messages themselves, the individuals who construct and interpret those messages, or the channels through which their interaction occurs. Your choice of subjects and settings is endless; you might observe boardroom conversations or shop floor humour, children's facial expressions or the hand signals used by patrons in a noisy pub, or any other interaction in a setting where it occurs naturally.

Whatever behaviours or interactions you choose to observe, you'll want to take detailed notes about what you see. Depending on your research claim, you may also want to digitally record live interactions, since such recordings will provide the most exact replications of the original behaviour (Amidon, 1971). The specific decisions about what or whom to observe, how to observe, and when to observe are all important aspects of collecting observational data that you will learn more about in part two of this book, especially in chapters 10, on conversation and discourse analysis, and 11, on ethnography.

Recognizing physiological responses, like pupil dilation and blushing, provides another way to observe communicative behaviour. Early advertising researchers believed that pupil dilation indicated a desire to buy the product, and they used pupil dilation to evaluate packaging and advertising materials (Blackwell, Hensel, & Sternthal, 1970). Physiological symptoms like a queasy stomach or a shaky voice have been associated with anxiety in making sales calls (Verbeke & Bagozzi, 2000); and in at least one set of nonverbal experiments, blushing has been shown to contribute to an observer's perceptions that someone who has violated a social rule is trustworthy and less responsible than someone who does not blush (De Jong, 1999). Whether you observe participants' physiological responses, collect direct observations of communicative interactions, or use an archive of digitally recorded interactions, observations are an important source of data for communication research.

Self-reports

A third source of data for communication research is to ask people to **self-report**, or to disclose their own behaviours, beliefs, or characteristics. If you want to know what people feel and how they think, self-report data should be your data source. You collect self-report data in survey questionnaires and whenever you interview key informants.

From the point of view of the discovery researcher, self-report data is subject to some standard biases or to systematic sources of error. For example, humans tend to overestimate their own positive qualities and behaviours and to underestimate their negative qualities and behaviours. Depending on the research topic, their relationship with the researcher, and many other factors, people may not report all of their thoughts and feelings. Reported memories can be incomplete, inaccurate, and so on. Despite these well-known limitations, self-report data are quite prevalent in communication and cultural studies.

Other-reports

The fourth source of communication data is other-reports. **Other-reports** are collected by asking people to report their perceptions of another person's behaviours, beliefs, or characteristics. Researchers routinely use such data in three ways, each for a different purpose. First, other-reports are used when a researcher wants to know how a certain text or performance affects those who receive it. For example, researchers who study an audience's reaction to a speech or television show often rely on other-report data. Second, other-report data are used when a researcher wants to compare self-perceptions of a performance with other perceptions of the same performance. For example, scholars who study communication competency have learned that people typically think of themselves as more competent or attractive than others do (e.g. Spitzberg & Hecht, 1984). Finally, other-report data is sometimes used to verify other sources; other-reports are used to confirm or question the data provided by a text or self-report.

Settings for Data Collection

Settings for data collection are the places where observations, self-reports, other-reports, and communicative artefacts are found and gathered. There are three categories of settings. First, most texts are available in hard formats in libraries or archives, or in digital formats through databases or online websites. While a library tends to collect secondary materials, an **archive** is a pre-existing collection of primary textual data or evidence. Most archives are maintained by libraries and other public institutions. Examples include universities and the provincial and federal governments, but municipal offices tend to house important local records while some private companies maintain documents detailing their own operations. We will discuss these settings in greater detail in chapter 9, on historical research.

For non-archival data, data that are collected via direct and immediate observations, self-reports or other-reports, there are two possible settings: the field or the laboratory (Smith, 1988). Most interpretive communication research takes place in **field settings** where individuals interact naturally. By contrast, in

laboratory settings, the researcher selects and controls the environment in which individuals interact. Essentially, the laboratory setting allows the researcher to focus on specific aspects of interactions and to eliminate certain factors that might complicate both data collection and data analysis. Research laboratories are often designed to resemble the settings in which interactions occur (e.g. classrooms, living rooms, or waiting areas). Such laboratories sometimes have one-way mirrors so that interactions can be observed without participants' knowledge. Laboratories can also be equipped with hidden audio or video recording equipment. Nonetheless, laboratory settings are somewhat artificial, no matter how well they are designed. For this reason, the rigour provided by a laboratory setting often comes at a cost. Any research findings that are obtained in the laboratory may be less relevant than findings obtained in a field setting. With either setting, however, the fact that research participants may be aware of the researcher and may change their behaviours during data collection is a grave concern to researchers who intend to make explanatory and predictive claims.

Strategies for Data Collection

Data collection strategies deal with how the data for a study are gathered. For example, self-report data can be captured using oral interviews, written surveys, or written diaries. Other-report data can be collected using interviews, surveys, or existing texts (e.g. written performance appraisals). Behavioural observations can be gathered by taking field notes but may also be preserved by using digital recordings. Obviously, all self-reports, other reports, and direct observations can be stored in textual form and then used for similar or different purposes in subsequent research projects. Conversation analysts often maintain collections of interpersonal interactions and use those databases to test claims about interaction structures or functions across a variety of contexts (e.g. Loughborough University in England and the University of Texas in the United States maintain archives of interaction data).

We first discuss the process of data selection, which describes how researchers decide which individuals, behaviours, or texts to include in a particular study.

Selection is an issue that receives much more attention in some research methodologies (e.g. content analysis) than in others (e.g. rhetorical criticism). It all depends on the research claim you are pursuing.

Selecting Data Sources

How do researchers pick specific participants for study? Or, if their data consist of messages, how do researchers pick specific texts for study? These are issues of data selection. As a general rule, random selection methods are preferred by those who adopt the discovery paradigm, whereas non-random selection methods are preferred by those who adopt the interpretive paradigm. Critical researchers approach the issue of selection quite differently than do researchers who work from either the discovery or interpretive paradigms.

For those who conduct research from the perspective of the discovery paradigm, the issue of selection, referred to as data **sampling**, is 'the process of selecting a set of subjects for study from a larger population' (Fink & Gantz, 1996, p. 117). 'Sampling' is a term that we use whenever we select a small number of cases to represent an entire group of like cases. We refer to the entire group of like cases as the **population**, and we refer to the small number of selected cases as the **sample**. In technical terms, a research population is a 'comprehensive and well-defined group (a universal set) of the elements pertinent to a given research question or hypothesis' (Smith, 1988, p. 77). For example, the 'population' of Canada can be defined in a number of ways, such as all the persons residing within the country's borders (regardless of their citizenship), or all the persons who are Canadian citizens (regardless of where they live). Notice how these two definitions of the 'population' include slightly different groups of people. Research populations must always be carefully described to ensure that anyone reading your study knows exactly which cases you have considered. Of course, sampling is unnecessary if you choose to study a population that is very small, in which case you can simply study every case in the population. Regardless of the size of your population, however, if your sample's characteristics match up well with those of the population, then you have created a **representative sample**.

Researchers engaged in discovery research will try to select a sample that represents the population that they want to know. Generally, they will use **random selection methods**. These procedures represent samples that are most likely to represent a population within the limits of chance or random error (Smith, 1988). By introducing a random element to your data selection, you make an important trade-off. There is a chance that your sample will not be representative of the population, but you can reduce any conscious **bias** from creeping into your selection of data.

Random Selection Methods

In this section, we outline three types of random selection methods: (1) simple random sampling, (2) systematic sampling with a random start, and (3) stratified sampling. These methods are listed in Table 5.1.

Simple random sampling occurs when each participant or text in the population has an equal chance of being selected for inclusion in a study. You will begin with a **sample frame**. A sample frame is a list of all the members of the population that can be selected for inclusion in a study. For example, if you want a random sample of students from your university, the registrar may allow you to consult his or her list of currently enrolled students and that list is one possible sample frame for that population. Likewise, a telephone book provides a sample frame for the population of any given city. Notice, however, that any frame may include some members of the population and exclude others. Telephone books may include only one name per household, and exclude those with unlisted numbers or those with cellphones. In order to conduct sound research, you must ensure that your sample frame is sufficiently accurate, complete, and up-to-date if the participants

or texts selected from it are to represent the population well.

The second random selection method is **systematic sampling with a random start**. To conduct systematic sampling with a random start, select the first participant by chance, and select the remaining participants systematically by moving logically through the sample frame. For example, let's say that you are studying the population of students at your university and have been given the registrar's list to use as a sample frame. Let's also imagine that 10,000 students are currently enrolled at the university. If you want to create a sample of 1000 students, you could select the first student in the frame randomly (e.g. roll a die; if it lands on '5', begin with the fifth student listed). You could then select every tenth student from the registrar's list for inclusion in your study. It is fairly well established that simple random sampling and systematic sampling yield virtually identical samples, so most researchers choose systematic sampling as the easier of the two methods (Babbie, 2001).

There is one potential problem with systematic sampling, however, and that is periodicity. **Periodicity** is a recurring pattern or arrangement that exists naturally in the sample frame. For example, imagine that you want to obtain a random sample of students from a large co-ed residence, that your sample frame is a complete list of room numbers, and that you decide to select the students who live in every tenth room for inclusion in the study. The rooms might be arranged in such a way that every other room houses female students. If that is the case, then your sample will recruit only participants who are either male or female (adapted from Babbie, 2001). Obviously, such patterning would produce a biased sample, not a representative one.

Our third random selection method, **stratified sampling**, is more refined and complex than either

TABLE 5.1 Types of Data Sampling Methods

RANDOM SAMPLING METHODS	NON-RANDOM SAMPLING METHODS
• Simple random sampling • Systematic sampling with a random start • Stratified sampling	• Convenience sampling • Purposive sampling • Network or snowball sampling • Quota sampling

simple random sampling or systematic sampling with a random start. Stratified sampling organizes a population into subsets of similar participants so that we can then select participants from each subset using systematic or simple random sampling. As with the other types of random sampling methods, we must first obtain a sample frame. When using stratified sampling, however, we know that some groups in the population share common characteristics. For example, you may know that two-thirds of your university's student population is female and one-third is male. You can stratify that population by separating the sample frame into females and males and then randomly selecting a sample from each subset with the approximate proportions of the sexes designed to represent the population. Large research companies like Ipsos Canada frequently stratify voters to increase the representativeness of their public opinion polls. Research companies stratify voters in terms of gender, ethnicity, socioeconomic class, age, and language spoken in the home, as well as urban and rural settings. Generally, if you want to measure several variables in a large population, you will produce a more representative sample if you stratify the population than if you use simple random or systematic sampling (Babbie, 2001).

No matter which random selection method you use, you will have an interest in ensuring sample representativeness. If your sample adequately represents its population, then the results of your study will be generalizable to all other members of the targeted population. We call this ability to generalize findings to a parent population external validity. Since generalizability is a warrant for causal arguments, we develop this concept further in chapter 6, on warrants. For now, let's contrast random selection methods with non-random selection methods.

Non-random Selection Methods

Non-random selection occurs when we select participants or texts without ensuring that the sample represents some theoretical population. There are at least three reasons for choosing non-random selection methods. First, some aspect of your research question or data setting may make random selection methods impractical or unethical (Fink & Gantz, 1996; Stake,

1998). In such cases, you might want to use quota sampling, defined later in this section, as an alternative to random selection methods. Second, you may lack the required time or money to use one of the random selection methods. In that case, use of non-random selection methods will weaken your ability to generalize your sample results to the larger population.

A third reason for using non-random data selection methods is that you have chosen to rely on interpretive or critical paradigm–based assumptions and not on the discovery paradigm assumption of generalizability. Interpretive and critical researchers often prefer non-random selection methods because their research claims are more likely to be based on representing an issue within a specific context. In that case, you do not need to use a small sample of data to represent the larger population. If you want to preserve participants' subjective realities and describe in detail a specific communication context, you may prefer one of the non-random selection methods that we outline next.

There are four types of non-random selection: (1) convenience or volunteer sampling, (2) purposive sampling, (3) network or snowball sampling, and (4) quota sampling (listed in Table 5.1). The first non-random selection method is called convenience sampling. **Convenience samples** are comprised of whatever data is conveniently available to the researcher (e.g. people who volunteer to fill out a questionnaire, messages that are readily available, or behaviours that the researcher had already captured for other purposes). Unfortunately, convenience sampling is not a desirable method of data collection for most researchers. For example, imagine that you are a survey researcher who uses convenience sampling to recruit participants who are readily available. In academic contexts, your participants may be university students. The fact that they are students is irrelevant since they will be recruited only for their accessibility. Because your selection process is non-random, the sample will not represent the population of either university students or the general population. Factors like the type of introductory course you draw from, the time of day you draw your sample, and the geographic region of the university are all likely to introduce biases that could threaten your sample's likelihood of representing the population of interest.

Purposive samples 'intentionally focus on the target group to the exclusion of other groups' (Smith, 1988, p. 85). Purposive sampling methods lack representativeness, as do all other non-random selection methods, but randomization may not be a practical or desirable way to collect evidence about some research questions. To illustrate, Buddle (2005) studied Native Canadians' use of radio broadcasting to establish aboriginal cultural spaces in urban areas. Because she sought to understand the motives and strategies of the radio personalities who hosted the programs, her pool of research participants was extremely limited, especially given that few aboriginal radio programs exist in urban areas. Hence, she relied upon a purposive sample of these hosts to report their perceptions of their activities. Purposive sampling lets you access just the right people or texts for your study when you do not have the sample frame that would be required to use stratified random sampling.

For similar reasons, researchers often use network sampling (Lindlof, 1995). **Network sampling** is sometimes called **snowball sampling** because the data sample grows like a snowball when it is rolled. Just as a snowball picks up snowflakes, participants in a snowball sample solicit additional participants. For example, when Ladner (2008) sought participants for her study of workers in the digital marketing industry, she knew she had a limited pool of potential volunteers who would be difficult to identify. So she asked her participants to recruit their colleagues in order to expand her sample. Network sampling is often purposive in this way. Participants are selected because they share a particular characteristic and are likely to know others who share it. Network sampling is a great selection method to use when you want to study members of an under-represented population who may be accessible only through one another.

The fourth non-random selection method is called **quota sampling**, which involves dividing a population into relevant subgroups and then (conveniently or purposively) selecting the desired proportion of people or messages from each group needed to represent the whole population. Quota sampling is useful whenever the characteristics of your population are well known. For example, Friesen, Muise, and Northrup (2009) asked Canadians how they incorporate knowledge of history or the past into their daily lives. To collect data, they solicited roughly 3500 participants and sought to match the demographic profile of their sample to the demographic profile of the entire country. **Demographics** are the general characteristics common to any population, such as age, biological sex, socioeconomic class, ethnicity, and so forth. Friesen et al. created a sample of voluntary participants that represented the population in terms of important categories of personal identity in Canada. These categories included ethnicity, mother tongue, place of residence based on region, and place of residence based on urban and rural differences. Quota sampling provided the research team with the best alternative among the non-random selection methods that could produce a sample that represented the parent population.

Selection Methods for Critical Studies

Critical scholars do not always address the data selection process in their published essays, perhaps because they conceive the process in very different ways. Sometimes academics who adopt a critical approach select data to support a preformulated claim, like discovery researchers. Many times, however, critical scholars gather and analyze evidence until an interesting question emerges. In chapter 2, we noted that critical scholars study the structures of meaning that shape communication and culture. Frequently, these structures are not immediately evident when studying individuals or texts. Hence, even the specific topic may be unknown when beginning a research project because 'the focus of attention often lies in areas at first glance unnoticeable and within data sources possessing mechanisms to conceal, rather than reveal, their secrets' (Thomas, 1993, p. 35).

For researchers who engage in critical studies, 'topic selection usually begins with only a vague idea of some broad question or issue. It may not be narrowed down until well into data collection' (Thomas, 1993, p. 34). For example, you may question the role of gender stereotypes in the way that sport media represent athletes. That particular topic represents a broad issue that encompasses all forms of media (e.g. print, broadcast, digital) and all athletes (e.g. from any sport, male or female, amateur or professional). To explore the topic in detail, you might select a case of 'some typicality, but leaning toward those cases that seem to offer opportunity to learn' (Stake, 1998, p. 101). By 'typicality', Stake means that a case may appear to be representative of the entire population, but its representativeness cannot be identified through any empirical measure. Rather, you believe that the case is representative based on your knowledge of the population. In the case of sport media, perhaps you will examine many different sports until one provides an excellent opportunity to explore the representation of men and women in the same sport at the same venue. Olympic hockey, for example, may provide one such typical case.

Once you have selected a case, the sampling of individuals, events, and texts to observe within the case is another factor you must consider. At the early stages of your critical study, variety rather than representativeness should guide your selection decisions (Stake, 1998). Returning to Olympic hockey, there are many elements that may be sampled. With respect to the athletes, will you look at the representations of individual players, such as team captains, or at the entire teams? With respect to events, will you examine the entire tournament or simply focus on the gold medal games? And when selecting texts, will you look to print or broadcast media for your sources of data? As a critical scholar, you will select the data that provide the most revealing and compelling answer to your question. In doing so, it is possible that you may not use all of the data you collect.

Now that you have some sense of how to approach selection methods for critical studies, and you understand the variety of random and non-random selection methods available, let's consider some specific data collection strategies, beginning with ways to collect observations of communicative interactions.

Capturing Observed Interactions

When studying human interactions, you must devise some systematic means to capture the data you want. Generally, the means we use to capture data emphasize sight and sound. Scholars in the field of performance studies have found ways to capture elements of touch, movement, and scent, but the wide availability of digital devices such as sound and video recorders has only bolstered the prominence of sight- and sound-related data (Lindlof, 1995). Digital devices offer several advantages over other means of capturing observed interactions. For example, when compared to personal memory and hand-written notes, digital devices capture data consistently and accurately while creating a permanent record. Second, these devices allow self-observation and analysis to take place since they enable the researcher to observe his or her own interactions with research participants. Third, if archived digital data is available, the lead researcher can use it to train research assistants before they begin a new project. Last, digital recordings are easily duplicated and distributed, particularly through the use of the Internet. This allows researchers from different universities or even different countries to collaborate efficiently and at a relatively low cost (Amidon, 1971).

Despite these advantages, sound and video recordings do have drawbacks. Even video recorders may be challenged to document every behaviour relevant to your study. For example, a camera lens points in only one direction at a time. By selecting any one angle, you miss data outside the camera's field of vision. All of these considerations must become factors in your research design.

Capturing Self-reports and Other-reports

As we noted earlier in this chapter, there are two common ways to capture self-report and other-report data: through personal interviews or through survey questionnaires, posed orally or in writing. Less frequently, self-report and other-report data are captured by asking people to complete some sort of task, such as rating behaviours, explaining observed behaviours, or sorting written records of observed behaviours into categories (e.g. coding tasks). Table 5.2 shows how particular data collection strategies may be linked to different types of research questions.

Conceptual and Operational Definitions

As already mentioned, there are some aspects of communication data selection that are handled differently,

TABLE 5.2 Linking Typical Data Collection Strategies to Research Claims

DATA COLLECTION STRATEGIES	FOCUS OF RESEARCH CLAIMS
Recorded conversations Written anecdotes of personal experiences Phenomenological literature, such as poetry	Claims exploring the meaning or significance of individual experiences
Unstructured interviews Participant observation Field notes Documents, recordings, images, maps, diagrams	Claims describing group values, beliefs, and practices
Interviews Participant observation Diaries Dialogue (audio- or video-recorded)	Claims plotting experiences that occur through time, especially those that involve changes that occur in stages
Observations Field notes Interviews	Claims regarding verbal interaction and conversational behaviour
Photography Observations Field notes	Claims about macro-level behaviour

Sources: Adapted from Morse (1998) and Lofland, Snow, Anderson, and Lofland (2006).

depending on whether the researchers adopt the discovery or the interpretive or the critical paradigm. If you are conducting discovery research, you must identify both the concepts you want to study and the ways you intend to measure those concepts before you collect data.

When we draft our research claims, we depend on concepts that are informed by experience or theory. To ensure that our concepts are understood by other researchers, it is important to define them. **Conceptual definitions**, then, are similar to the definitions we would find in a dictionary. They specify what a particular concept means, what it describes and what it does not describe. **Variables** are concepts that are defined in measurable ways. Some variables have essential characteristics that are directly observable. For example, observable and measurable characteristics define concepts such as speed, colour, smiling, and biological sex. Many things, however, cannot be directly observed or measured. For instance, we cannot assess

someone's intelligence based on appearances, but we can indirectly observe indicators of his or her problem solving skills or creativity. In fact, the very concept of intelligence is defined only by relating it to other abstract concepts such as these. We use the word **construct** to refer to a phenomenon that is observed only indirectly. Examples of constructs used in published research include 'verbal aggression', 'communication competence', or 'nonverbal immediacy'. The first step in the process of studying a construct is to develop its conceptual definition.

Let's look at verbal aggression as one example of a construct. Verbal aggressiveness was conceptually defined by Infante and others (Infante, 1987, 1989; Infante & Wigley, 1986) as a predisposition to attack the self-concept or self-esteem of another person. The original conceptualization of verbal aggression included behaviours like delivering insults, teasing, employing ridicule, using profanity, and making threats. Notice that all of the terms used to define verbal aggressiveness as a construct are themselves abstractions. What counts as teasing or profanity must be further specified, so those terms alone do not provide a definition that enables empirical measurement of verbal aggression. To measure a construct empirically (i.e. to make it a variable), we need both a conceptual definition and an operational definition.

Operational definitions identify the empirical indicators that allow you to collect data about an intangible construct. We emphasize the term 'empirical' because these indicators must be both observable and measurable. Ideally, the operational definition should also specify an operation, a procedure, or an instrument needed to observe the empirical indicators. Frequently, the indicators are assigned numerical values, or are 'coded', to accelerate the data collection process and allow for statistical analysis. This segment of the research design is known as the **operationalization** of the researcher's ideas or concepts.

For example, Infante and Wigley's (1986) Verbal Aggressiveness Scale (VAS) is an operational definition for the construct of verbal aggression. The VAS is a written survey instrument that consists of 20 statements, each one a statement about how individuals try to get other people to comply with their wishes (e.g. 'If individuals I am trying to influence really deserve it, I attack their character' or 'I refuse to participate in arguments when they involve personal attacks'). Five response choices are provided for each item, from 1 representing 'almost never true' to 5 representing 'almost always true'. You will learn more about this kind of written survey measure, called a Likert scale, in the section about levels of measurement that comes next.

The use of operational definitions is most closely associated with the discovery paradigm, but it is also relevant to researchers who are working from an interpretive or critical perspective. In other words, no matter which paradigm you accept, you must use conceptual and operational definitions when categorizing behaviours and messages. This is true even if you are not using quantitative evidence to support your claims. In the next section, we introduce you to four levels of measurement used in communication and culture research.

Levels of Measurement

To operationalize a concept, variable, or construct, we use one of four different levels of measurement: nominal, ordinal, interval, or ratio. These four levels of measurement are ordered from the least to the most precise empirical indicator.

Nominal and ordinal level measurements yield data that are purely categorical; that is, the numbers generated from these forms of measurement record subjective, and sometimes arbitrary, observations about a case or its characteristics. By contrast, interval and ratio level scales yield data that are measurable against objective scales (i.e. scales that measure size or volume). Interval and ratio level data provide precise measurements that are required for mathematical analysis. Table 5.3 illustrates the characteristics of each of these levels of measurement.

Let's define and consider some examples of each level of measurement, starting with the nominal level.

Nominal Level

Whenever we sort data for a single variable into separate categories, we are dealing with **nominal level measurement**. For example, you may ask survey participants a question with a 'yes' or 'no' response, but you may also allow them to respond 'maybe' or to pass on the question without answering it. No matter how many participants you survey, you can sort their answers into four categories based on these four possible responses. Thus, nominal measures yield categorical data.

Some technical terms are useful to clarify how variables function. When the categories for a single variable are genuinely distinct, and do not overlap, the variable is sometimes called a **discrete variable**. When a discrete variable has only two categories, it may be called a dichotomous variable, as is the case whenever we ask a 'yes' or 'no' question and refuse to accept any other answer. Exhibit 5.1 shows examples of dichotomous variables.

Researchers can create categories in two ways. First, researchers may use **organismic variables**. These variables measure the pre-existing characteristics of a text or participant, the sorts of characteristics

TABLE 5.3 Characteristics of Four Levels of Measurement

LEVEL OF MEASUREMENT	DESCRIPTION	RESULT	DEGREE OF PRECISION OF EMPIRICAL MEASUREMENT
Nominal level	Data are placed into discrete, mutually exclusive categories. The list of categories for any one variable should be exhaustive, but the order of the list does not indicate any value ascribed to any category.	Yields categorical data (see Table 5.2 for examples)	Least precise
Ordinal level	Data have all of the characteristics of nominal level measurement but the list of categories will indicate the relative value ascribed to each category. The list may be ranked in either ascending or descending order.	Yields categorical data (see Table 5.3 for examples)	More precise than nominal, but less precise than interval
Interval level	Data have all of the characteristics of ordinal level measurement plus the difference in value between categories (also known as intervals) is known and equal.	Yields continuous data (see Tables 5.4, 5.5, and 5.6 for examples)	More precise than ordinal, but less precise than ratio
Ratio level	Data have all of the characteristics of interval level measurement plus it is possible to record an absolute zero, meaning that the variable being measured can be entirely absent.	Yields continuous data (e.g. how many hours was your television on today?)	Most precise

with which a text or participant may commonly be identified. For example, demographic characteristics are often sought in survey research because we believe these are important variables in participants' responses (see Exhibit 5.1 for examples). Second, researchers use **researcher-constructed variables**. These variables ask participants to classify themselves using terms informed by the researcher's perspective or theoretical framework. For example, Shoham and Kahle (1996) studied how sports fans most enjoy their favourite sports. One segment of this research asked participants to classify themselves into one of three categories: spectators, television viewers, or readers. The researchers defined each category as follows: spectators enjoy their favourite sports most by attending a live event, viewers do so by watching it on television, and readers do so by consulting print media such as newspapers. It's easy to imagine that most sports fans appreciate all three options when following their favourite sports. Shoham and Kahle (1996), however, theorized that the way an individual most enjoyed a sport indicated something about his or her shopping habits. Hence, they constructed their categories to test their own theory. Notice that both organismic and researcher-constructed categories can be either dichotomous or have more than two categories (see Exhibit 5.1).

All nominal level measurements should satisfy two criteria. First, the list of categories drafted for any one variable should include every possible category required to describe a text or participant. When you draft such a list, you have **exhaustive categories**. If your list omits a category, then participants may not know how to respond, or you will be unable to classify some observations. Many researchers include an 'other' category in their nominal measurements in order to avoid such omissions, as we did in the example of religious preference that appears in Exhibit 5.1.

Second, the list of categories drafted for any one variable should force each response into one, and only one, category. When this occurs, you have **mutually exclusive categories**. In nominal level measurement, participants must choose only one alternative from the list of categorical responses. If, for example, someone indicates that he or she is a member of the New Democractic Party, then presumably he or she is not also a member of the Conservative, Liberal, Green or Bloc Québécois parties.

Researchers frequently assign numbers to their variables and categories in order to make data entry

---

EXHIBIT 5.1   Examples of Nominal Level Measurement

1. **Dichotomous Variables:**
   (a)   Did you eat breakfast today?
   _____ Yes _____ No
   (b)   Indicate your employment status:
   _____ Employed _____ Unemployed

2. **Organismic Variables:**
   (a)   Circle whether you are male or female: M or F
   (b)   Indicate your religious affiliation:
   _____ Buddhism
   _____ Christianity
   _____ Hinduism
   _____ Islam
   _____ Judaism
   _____ Other
   (c)   Indicate your federal political party affiliation:
   _____ Bloc Québécois
   _____ Conservative or Progressive Conservative Party
   _____ Green Party
   _____ Liberal Party
   _____ New Democratic Party
   _____ other political party
   _____ uncommitted

3. **Researcher-Constructed Variables:**
   Indicate how you most appreciate a sport:
   _____ As a spectator at a live event
   _____ As a television viewer
   _____ As a reader of newspapers, magazines, or websites

---

and computer analysis more efficient. For example, we could assign one number to each of the four responses associated with our 'yes' or 'no' question. In this case, it would be quicker for the researcher to record the number 1, 2, 3, or 4 than to record the words 'yes', 'no', 'maybe' or 'no response' for each participant. When assigning numbers in nominal measurement, the order of the categories is unimportant. 'Yes' could be assigned to the number 1, 2, 3, or 4. Indeed, it could be assigned any number you wish. The number serves only as an arbitrary code that is designed to replace a more descriptive name for the category.

Sometimes, variables measured at the nominal level are simply treated as categories, without assigning any numbers to them. This frequently happens in interpretive research when, for example, ethnographers place people in different groups based on their shared cultural norms. Variables are also treated as distinct categories in discovery research when content analysts place texts into categories and then compare how frequently different categories of messages occur. In both cases, empirical observations are placed into discrete categories, and no numbers are needed, unless you want to count the frequency with which responses in each category appear, or determine the percentage of observations in each category. The categories themselves are simply different sets. The categories do not indicate anything about the size or value of the variable. In order to establish categories that accomplish the latter, we need to use ordinal level measurement.

Ordinal Level

Ordinal level measurements allow us to rank the different categories of a variable. Generally, our rankings are based on some scale that estimates or measures a value that is ascribed to each category. Hence, while nominal measures may be assigned to categories arbitrarily, ordinal measures are assigned purposefully in numerical sequence. That said, each ordinal measure may reflect only an approximate value; the mathematical relationship between ordinal measures may not be precise.

Let's consider an example of the use of ordinal measures. Suppose that a media scholar decides to track the relative credibility of news media, such as newspapers, news-related websites, and all-news channels. To measure credibility, the researcher creates a questionnaire that asks survey participants to rank each form of news medium from 1 to 3. The survey goes on to specify that the most credible medium should be ranked '1', and the least credible medium should be ranked '3'. In this example, then, the ordinal measure (i.e. the rank, expressed as a number) expresses a value (i.e. relative credibility) assigned to each category (i.e. each news medium). As a further extension of this example, suppose we asked Alex, Bobbi, and Chris to rank the relative credibility of different media as news sources. Suppose they all responded that newspapers are the most credible medium, that the Internet is the next most credible, and that television is the third most credible news source. Alex's ranking of 1, 2, and 3 may represent a very different estimation of the relative credibility of these media than Bobbi or Chris's rankings (see Exhibit 5.2 for more). How is this possible? Alex may believe that newspapers have far greater credibility than any other medium, and that the Internet- and television-based news sources have much to improve. By contrast, Bobbi may estimate that newspapers have a clear advantage over Internet sources, which in turn have a clear advantage over television sources, while Chris thinks that all three news sources have about the same degree of credibility. Even though all three participants produced the same ranking, Alex's ordinal measures of 1, 2, and 3 do not reflect the same values as those associated with Bobbi's or Chris's measures.

Again, each ordinal measure may reflect only an approximate value; the mathematical relationship between ordinal measures may not be precise. Ordinal level measurement can provide more precise information than nominal level measurement, but ordinal measures are not as precise as the next two levels of measurement, interval and ratio level scales.

Interval Level

Interval level measurements allow us to measure the amount or magnitude of a variable using categories that have precise mathematical relationships to one another. Interval level measurement shares certain characteristics of nominal and ordinal level measures.

All three measurements require categorical responses, and, like ordinal level measurements, interval level measurements must be ordered in numerical sequence. With interval level measurement, however, the distance between categories is known and equal. Two types of interval scales are frequently used in communication research today: the Likert scale and the semantic differential scale. Let's define and consider an example of each scale in turn.

Likert scales measure constructs using a set of statements. Each statement is designed to probe one aspect of the construct (see Tables 5.4 and 5.5 for two examples). Each statement is followed by a range of possible responses. Participants select one response to each statement that most accurately portrays either their conception of themselves (for self-report data)

EXHIBIT 5.2 Examples of Survey Results that Draw on Ordinal Level Measurement

Set out below is the survey results relating to the relative credibility of newspapers, the Internet, and television as sources of news media. The survey participants were Alex, Bobbi, and Chris.

Consider the media sources you use to get news information and rank each source according to its credibility, starting with 1 as the most credible or trusted source of news information:

Alex's response:

1	newspapers, by a wide margin
2	Internet
3	television

Bobbi's response:

1	newspapers have a clear advantage over the Internet
2	Internet
3	television

Chris's response:

1	newspapers have a slight advantage over the Internet and television
2	Internet
3	television

or their perception of a text or another individual (for other-report data). A shortened example of one such scale that is used to measure interpersonal communication appears in Exhibit 5.3.

Constructs measured with Likert scales can be either unidimensional or multidimensional. A **unidimensional variable** cannot be broken down into distinct aspects or subconstructs because all of the items in the measure point to the same uniform conceptual definition. Infante and Wigley's (1986) VAS is a unidimensional measure, since all of the items in the VAS point to the same conceptual definition, a predisposition to attack other people with words.

A **multidimensional variable** has several distinct dimensions or subconstructs. Each subconstruct represents a different aspect of the thing you want to measure. For example, Montgomery and Norton's (1981) measure of Communicator Style contains 11 dimensions that assess if a participant's style is, for example, friendly, relaxed, and/or dominant. Each dimension is measured using three or more statements that ask for Likert-scale responses. Items 3, 6, 38, and 46 correspond to the friendly dimension; items 8, 9, 15, and 16 correspond to the relaxed dimension; and items 28, 35, 41, and 43 correspond to the dominant dimension.

This multidimensional Likert scale is partially illustrated in Exhibit 5.4.

The second type of interval scale is the **semantic differential scale**, which consists of a series of bipolar adjectives placed at either end of a continuum. The adjectives act as anchors for extreme attitudes or beliefs. Respondents are asked to indicate where along the continuum their perceptions lie. Thus, semantic differential scales are used for self-report and other-report data just like Likert scales. Similarly, semantic differential scales may be used to measure unidimensional or multidimensional constructs. An example of a unidimensional semantic differential measure appears in Exhibit 5.5. One multidimensional construct that is often measured with a semantic differential scale is communicator credibility. As we noted earlier, credibility is a construct that has been applied within media studies to news outlets, but it can be applied across several other contexts such as teacher credibility, speaker credibility, and advertiser credibility (McCroskey & Young, 1981). In comparison to use of the ordinal level of measurement, employment of the interval level of measurement using the semantic differential scale would provide a more precise level of measurement when assessing credibility. However,

---

EXHIBIT 5.3   Examples of Interval Level Measurement: Unidimensional Likert Scale

VERBAL AGGRESSIVENESS SCALE (VAS)

The VAS is a research measure developed to identify an individual's tendency, during an interaction, to attack another individual's person rather than his or her arguments. The full VAS uses 20 items to gather data on one dimension. Here we present examples of five items.

Instructions: This survey is concerned with how we try to get people to comply with our wishes. Indicate how often each statement is true for you personally when you try to influence other persons. Use the following scale: 1 = almost never true, 2 = rarely true, 3 = occasionally true, 4 = often true, and 5 = almost always true.

_____ 1. When individuals insult me, I get a lot of pleasure in really telling them off.
_____ 2. When individuals are very stubborn, I use insults to soften their stubbornness.
_____ 3. When I attack persons' ideas, I try not to damage their self concepts.
_____ 4. When others do things I regard as stupid, I try to be extremely gentle with them.
_____ 5. If individuals I am trying to influence really deserve it, I attack their character.

Note: Items 3 and 4 are reverse worded, so scores for those items must be reversed before calculating a summary score on this measure.

Source: Extracted from Infante & Wigley, 1986.

there is one more level of measurement that offers even greater precision, the ratio level.

Ratio Level

Ratio level measurement possesses all the characteristics of interval level measurement plus one additional element. Like nominal, ordinal, and interval scales, the response choices for a ratio scale have different values that represent points along a continuum from one extreme to another (e.g. small to large, or bad to good), separated by equal distances, known as intervals. Unlike interval level measurement, however, a ratio scale has a true or absolute zero point. When a measurement appears as zero on a ratio scale, it means the variable you wish to observe is completely absent; there is nothing to observe or report. Ratio scales are useful when we want to determine the frequency of some behaviour or to measure its duration in time. For example, how many minutes per day do you watch television? That variable should be measured with a ratio scale because it is possible that, on any given day, you may never turn on the television.

Discovery researchers prefer to use interval and ratio level measures because those scales provide the most precise measurement of constructs. Those scales also provide data that can be analyzed in more complex statistical ways than is possible with nominal

---

EXHIBIT 5.4 Examples of Interval Level Measurement: Multidimensional Likert Scale

COMMUNICATOR STYLE SCALE (CSS)

The CSS is a research measure developed to identify an individual's communication style. The full CSS uses 51 items to gather data on 11 dimensions of an individual's style. Here we present examples of 12 items from three dimensions.

Instructions: for each item, please use the following scale to reply to each item:

YES! = strong agreement with the statement
Yes = agreement with the statement
? = neither agreement nor disagreement with the statement
No = disagreement with the statement
NO! = strong disagreement with the statement

Friendly Dimension:

3. I readily express admiration for others.
6. To be friendly, I habitually acknowledge verbally others' contributions.
38. I am always an extremely friendly communicator.
46. Whenever I communicate, I tend to be very encouraging to people.

Relaxed Dimension:

8. I have some nervous mannerisms in my speech.
9. I am a very relaxed communicator.
15. The rhythm or flow of my speech is sometimes affected by my nervousness.
16. Under pressure I come across as a relaxed speaker.

Dominant Dimension:

28. In most social situations I generally speak very frequently.
35. I am dominant in social situations.
41. I try to take charge of things when I am with people.
43. In most social situations I tend to come on strong.

Source: Extracted from Montgomery & Norton, 1981.

EXHIBIT 5.5   Examples of Interval Level Measurement: Semantic Differential Scale

RESPONSES TO JOB REFUSAL LETTERS

These semantic differential scales were used to access business communication students' affective responses to direct and indirect communication styles in refusal letters that follow job interviews.

Instructions: For each item below, please circle the number between each pair of adjectives that best represents your feelings about the content of the letter you have read. Numbers '1' and '7' indicate very strong feelings. Numbers '2' and '6' indicate strong feelings. Numbers '3' and '5' indicate fairly weak feelings. Number '4' indicates that you are undecided, or do not understand the adjectives themselves. Please work quickly. There is no right or wrong answer.

Efficient	1	2	3	4	5	6	7	Inefficient
Insincere	1	2	3	4	5	6	7	Sincere
Concise	1	2	3	4	5	6	7	Wordy
Valuable	1	2	3	4	5	6	7	Worthless
Straightforward	1	2	3	4	5	6	7	Devious
Selfish	1	2	3	4	5	6	7	Unselfish
Persuasive	1	2	3	4	5	6	7	Unconvincing
Timid	1	2	3	4	5	6	7	Bold
Good	1	2	3	4	5	6	7	Bad
Subtle	1	2	3	4	5	6	7	Obvious
Discourteous	1	2	3	4	5	6	7	Courteous
Organized	1	2	3	4	5	6	7	Disorganized
Pleasant	1	2	3	4	5	6	7	Unpleasant
Uninformative	1	2	3	4	5	6	7	Informative
Blunt	1	2	3	4	5	6	7	Tactful
Logical	1	2	3	4	5	6	7	Illogical
Considerate	1	2	3	4	5	6	7	Thoughtless
Unappealing	1	2	3	4	5	6	7	Appealing
Friendly	1	2	3	4	5	6	7	Unfriendly

Source: Extracted from Smith, Nola, & Dai, 1996.

---

or ordinal level measures (note that we shall address statistical analysis in chapters 13 and 14). Because interval and ratio scales require great precision and accuracy, great care goes into the design of every research tool and procedure. We turn our attention to research design in the next section.

Research Design

In its broadest sense, a **research design** is the logical sequence that connects a researcher's claim, data or evidence, and warrants. Still, the term 'research design' is used very differently by different kinds of researchers, as you will see in the sections that follow.

Changing Conceptions of Design

Over the past 40 years, scholars who study communication and culture have greatly expanded the variety of methods they use to conduct research. In so doing, terms associated with one paradigm are now used in quite different ways by scholars working in the other paradigms. Within the discovery paradigm, the term 'research design' encompasses specific strategies that control the selection of texts or participants to be included in a study, the setting in which the data will be collected, and the strategies for capturing those data. Explanatory or predictive claims are best supported by designs that eliminate any competing explanations for a set of observations, and thereby establish a strong argument for causality (see chapter 6, on warrants, for a full explanation of causal arguments).

As we mentioned in chapter 4, however, not all researchers who adopt the discovery paradigm make causal arguments. Sometimes, these types of researchers seek only to explain and predict associations among various characteristics or behaviours. For example, when rhetorical critics categorize messages to determine what message types are associated with particular outcomes (e.g. by linking persuasive speaking strategies to levels of audience applause), the argument is one of association, not causality. Thus, even within the discovery paradigm, the term 'research design' has slightly different meanings, but it is generally understood that it refers to the need to specify all claims, data sources, settings for collection, and strategies for collection before research begins.

By contrast, interpretive research designs are much more likely to change during data collection and analysis (Janesick, 1998). In fact, interpretive researchers typically use the term 'research design' to indicate the unfolding process of collecting and analyzing field data. In interpretive research, design includes the identification and selection of key participants, the development of sampling techniques, and the development of interview questions and/or observation schemes. For example, imagine that you are researching the communication practices of a local business. After a week of observations in the field, you may begin to interpret your data. You may also decide to return to the field to search for counterexamples that would test the validity of your interpretations. This decision to return to the field can only be made after initial data collection and analysis are completed.

Critical scholars often conduct research and report their findings without ever using the words 'research' or 'design'. This tendency provides a clear contrast with discovery and interpretive scholars who may describe their research designs in great detail. Taken altogether, their different approaches to 'research design' underscore the fact that the term itself carries different connotations across the paradigms. Nonetheless, in the most basic sense, a research design can be defined as your plan for exploring a research question or for testing a hypothesis.

Cross-sectional Research Designs

Cross-sectional research designs are the most simple and common form of design used in communication and culture research. In **cross-sectional studies**, a sample of data is collected at one point in time in order to draw inferences about the topic under study. Just as a cross-section of a tree trunk reveals information about the tree's life, a cross-sectional study may reveal information about your research topic. This information provides a single perspective from a single moment in time, which researchers often compare to a snapshot photo. You might design a cross-sectional survey by administering written questionnaires to a sample of volunteers drawn from one population at one point in time. For example, you might poll your classmates to see how many hours of television they watch per day. You could also poll the television-watching behaviours of students in other courses to see how they compare to your own classmates. No matter how many students you poll, however, if your survey is administered only once, then the design of your study is still cross-sectional.

Longitudinal Research Designs

Longitudinal studies collect data at several different points in time, and tend to be more complex and less common than cross-sectional studies. There are three types of longitudinal research designs: trend, cohort, and panel studies (Frey, Botan, & Kreps, 2000, p. 208; Mertens, 1998, p. 108). **Trend studies** are conducted by examining several different representative samples from the same population at two or more points in time. For example, if the market research firm Ipsos Canada conducts a nationwide opinion poll in March, June, and September, the company will select one sample of voters at each point in time to track possible changes in opinion over the course of the year. In **cohort studies**, two or more sets of participants are recruited at two or more points in time. Each set of participants is conceptualized as a distinct sample; that is, the data collected from each set of participants is not combined into a single pool of data. This allows the researcher to track possible changes through time within each set and to compare the experiences of the two sets. For example, Ipsos Canada may track voters in Quebec separately from those in Alberta to see if the Quebec voters respond differently to policy announcements. Finally, **panel studies** examine how one set of participants' attitudes or behaviours may change over time. This type of research is often conducted before and after an important scheduled event, such as a speech or political debate, to assess its impact.

Many of our examples refer to survey research. Even though the vocabulary of research design is most often used in such studies, the concepts of cross-sectional and longitudinal research design can be applied to most communication and culture research. For example, collecting data over a long period of time is one of the defining characteristics of ethnographic and historical research, whereas sampling data from one point in time is more common in content analysis.

Triangulation

The concept of **triangulation** came to the social sciences from the navy. Navigators know that they can pinpoint an object's exact location by using three or more reference points (Newman & Benz, 1998). Since the 1950s, this concept has been adapted to research designs that collect data while using multiple sources, settings, and collection strategies (Denzin, 1978; Janesick, 1998; Lindlof, 1995; Lofland et al., 2006; Miles & Huberman, 1994; Morse, 1998; Newman & Benz, 1998; Seale, 1999; Stage & Russell, 1992).

One basic assumption underlies the use of triangulation in research: that using multiple sources, settings, or strategies will compensate for the weaknesses found in any one source, setting, or strategy. From the perspective of a discovery researcher, then, triangulation may contribute to verification, and the attempt to describe or explain one true reality (Mathison, 1988). From the perspective of the interpretive or critical researchers, however, triangulation is not intended to verify one true reality (Denzin & Lincoln, 1998b). Rather, the critical researcher believes that using more than one source, setting, or strategy can enrich the range of subjective viewpoints available to us. In this way, inconsistencies or 'contradictory findings may actually help to understand the richness of what is being studied' (Stage & Russell, 1992, p. 489).

To build on that point, the advantages of reading and incorporating insights from multiple studies, or even multiple perspectives, simply extends the idea on which triangulation is based (Miles & Huberman, 1994). Insights from the discovery, interpretive, and critical research paradigms have all contributed to our current understandings of, and knowledge about, interpersonal communication, organizational communication, and the mass media. In the sections following, we outline five ways that triangulation can be accomplished within a study. We use Kim, Lujan, and Dixon's (1998) ethnographic study of North American Indian identities to illustrate all five types of triangulation.

Multiple Data Sources

Multiple data source triangulation refers to the method of comparing data from more than one source, such as combining self-report and other-report data, or coupling behavioural observations with textual analysis (Denzin, 1978; Lindlof, 1995). This type of triangulation is quite common in ethnographic research in which researchers observe behaviours over a long time in the field and analyze self-report data gained during in-depth interviews (e.g. Browning & Beyer, 1998; Lindsley, 1999; Tardy & Hale, 1998).

Multiple Data Settings

Besides multiple data sources, another way to use triangulation is to examine a single phenomenon at several distinct settings or data collection sites. Using multiple data collection sites for verification helps increase the generalizability of your findings by reducing the effects of one setting (or one group of participants) on your interpretation of those phenomena (Getis, 1995; Newman & Benz, 1998). In addition, choosing under-researched settings can help to counteract the unique effects of setting on your data and to contribute to a richer description of the phenomena you wish to study (Frey, Botan, & Kreps, 2000; Newman & Benz, 1998). In short, using multiple data settings is a good triangulation strategy whether you adhere to the discovery, interpretive, or critical research paradigm.

Multiple Data Collection Strategies

Recall that data collection strategies determine *how* data for a study are gathered, whereas sources and settings refer to the participants *from whom* we get data and to the places *where* the data are sampled. For example, data about a cultural event such as a music festival can be collected by using your own observations, by conducting oral interviews with attendees, or by consulting written reports describing the event. These are three different methods of collecting data. They may all collect data from the same participants, or from the same setting, but the means with which the data are collected are significantly different. We believe it is good practice to use more than one strategy to collect data in just this way. If you are interested in verifying one knowable reality, then you might combine self-report data (i.e. your observations) with other-report data (i.e. interviews with participants) and existing documents (i.e. magazine articles), and then use only those reports that are confirmed by one or more means of data collection. If you are interested in interpreting multiple realities, then collecting all three sets of data should help you to enrich the range of interpretations you gather from participants at the festival.

Multiple Data Analytic Strategies

Within the scope of a single research design, it is possible to use two or more strategies to analyze data. The most obvious form of analytic triangulation is to combine quantitative with qualitative data analysis. Quantitative data analysis involves the use of numbers or statistics to understand the phenomena observed during your research. Qualitative data analysis involves the use of textual or visual evidence to understand the phenomena observed during your research. Generally, a study using a combination of analytic strategies will rely upon quantitative analysis to establish the context for, and representativeness of, the evidence collected, and it will rely upon qualitative analysis to explore the meaning and significance of the observations.

Multiple Investigators' Viewpoints

The last form of triangulation uses multiple investigator viewpoints. Both discovery researchers and interpretive researchers have incorporated this form of triangulation into their research designs. Discovery researchers triangulate multiple investigators for two reasons: first, to ensure that they achieve consistency in their observations, and second, to reduce the possibility that any individual bias will affect their results (Amidon, 1971; Mathison, 1988). Interpretive and critical researchers use multiple investigator viewpoints for these same reasons, but remain open to individual interventions throughout the course of a study (i.e. during the planning, data collection, and data analysis phases). By remaining open to such interventions, they can take advantage of their individual strengths as researchers when the need arises (Douglas, 1976, as cited in Lindlof, 1995, p. 239). For example, two researchers might collect data together in the same setting, or they might collect data separately in two different settings and then collaborate during data analysis. Through consultation, the utility of a category can be assessed with either a colleague who helped to collect the data or with an expert on the topic. As you can see, collaborative or team research offers several advantages.

Sometimes, more than one type of triangulation is used in a single study. This was the case in Kim et al.'s (1998) study of Native American identity in Oklahoma. During the data collection phase, the researchers employed multiple data collection strategies, sources, and settings. They conducted individual interviews with 182 Native Americans at six different research sites in Oklahoma and, while in the field, collected observational data and testimonials from other community members. During the data analysis phase, the researchers applied two coding schemes. First, they grouped their interview data into thematic clusters that represented Native Americans' different ways of responding to identity dilemmas. Second, the researchers also used statistical analysis, such as measuring the participants' degree of involvement with both Natives and non-Natives. Finally, the study was conducted by multiple investigators: 'The six-member research team consisted of three members who had Indian backgrounds and were long time residents of Oklahoma . . . The other three non-Indian members were of Asian, Black, and Irish backgrounds' (Kim et al., 1998, p. 259). In short, the research team employed all five types of triangulation: multiple data sources, multiple data settings, multiple data collection strategies, multiple analytic strategies, and multiple investigator viewpoints. The result of their triangulations was the accumulation of a dense web of information, whereas the use of any single triangulation method may have left significant gaps in their knowledge.

Summary

In this chapter, we outlined the second component of our *research as argument* model: the data or evidence assembled in support of a research claim. We began by discussing the typical sources, settings, and strategies used by scholars to collect research data. We introduced the practice of sample selection, the means by which participants or texts are selected for study, and we described seven different methods to create samples (three random and four non-random methods).

Throughout this chapter, we have noted the relative value of some data collection sources, settings, and strategies for supporting particular research claims. We also hope that our approach will help you to appreciate the differences in the research conducted by discovery, interpretive, and critical scholars. Table 5.4 recaps some typical uses of data or evidence in each of the three paradigms.

Although we noted in this chapter that researchers across the paradigms deploy terms like 'data' and 'design' in different ways, we described three elements that all research programs share: conceptual and operational definitions, levels of measurement, and research design. The first two elements—definitions and levels of measurement—involve vocabulary and procedures commonly associated with discovery research. As we noted, however, interpretive and critical researchers use these elements as well. The exception is research design. It is frequently discussed in discovery and interpretive studies but rarely in critical studies. Still, whether they are explicitly addressed or not in individual studies, all of these elements are present in all research, regardless of the paradigm from which the researcher approaches the subject. Nevertheless, there is one key difference in how the elements of definition, measurement, and design are deployed. Discovery researchers generally commit to a research design (including conceptual and operational definitions, and levels of measurement) before they collect data. By contrast, interpretive and critical researchers generally develop definitions, measures, and design decisions as their research unfolds. A discussion of all of these research elements leads nicely into the third component of our *research as argument* model, warrants, which we address in the next chapter.

TABLE 5.4 Typical Decisions Affecting Data in the Three Paradigms*

	DISCOVERY PARADIGM	INTERPRETIVE PARADIGM	CRITICAL PARADIGM
Sources	Self-reports, other-report surveys, field observations, and textual analysis	Self-reports, other-report interviews, field observations, and textual analysis	Self-reports, field observations, and textual analysis
Settings	Field, laboratory, archive	Field, archive	Field, archive
Selection Methods	Prefers random selection	Prefers non-random selection, especially purposive selection	Prefers purposive selection
Levels of Measurement	Uses most precise level of measurement possible	Uses nominal and ordinal categories	Uses nominal and ordinal categories
Triangulation	Use to verify one objective perception of reality	Use to enrich understanding of multiple realities	Use to demonstrate hegemonic realities

*Note: This table identifies the data sources, settings, selection methods, and so on that typify communication and cultural research from the perspective of the discovery, interpretive, and critical paradigms but exceptions do exist.

Key Terms

Archive	Nominal level measurement	Sample frame
Bias	Non-random selection method	Sampling
Cohort study	Operational definition	Secondary source
Conceptual definition	Operationalization	Self-report
Construct	Ordinal level measurement	Semantic differential scale
Convenience sampling	Organismic variable	Setting
Cross-sectional study	Other-report	Simple random sampling
Demographics	Panel study	Snowball sampling
Direct observation	Periodicity	Source
Discrete variable	Population	Stratified sampling
Exhaustive categories	Primary source	Systematic sampling with a random start
Field setting	Purposive sampling	Texts
Interval level measurement	Quota sampling	Textual analysis
Laboratory setting	Random selection method	Trend study
Likert scale	Ratio level measurement	Triangulation
Longitudinal study	Representative sample	Unidimensional variable
Multidimensional variable	Research design	Variable
Mutually exclusive categories	Researcher constructed variable	
Network sampling	Sample	

Discussion Questions

1. Academic research is frequently conducted using university students as 'participants'. Considering the random and non-random sampling methods outlined in this chapter, discuss what kinds of research projects in communication or cultural studies could be conducted using students in university classrooms as research samples. When or why should researchers move beyond using university students as participants in communication research?

2. Recall the values of ethical research presented in chapter 2: respect for persons, concern for welfare, and justice. Based on those values, develop a list of some data collection settings or research questions that might raise ethical concerns about the use of random selection methods.

3. What are the differences among the three longitudinal research designs: trend, panel, and cohort studies?

4. Which of the following claims are best studied using a random selection method? Which claims are best studied using a non-random selection method? Give reasons for your answers.

   (a) How do cost and user-friendliness affect the decision of cellphone users to adopt wireless Internet services? (Westlund, 2008).

   (b) Bugs Bunny is often regarded as a 'camp' icon. Warner Brother cartoons used his star position to subvert all manner of power structures in American society, including traditional masculinity (Abel, 1995).

   (c) How effectively are workers in the digital marketing industry able to separate work from home life if they use computers at home? (Ladner, 2008).

   (d) Displays of affection are associated with the human body's ability to handle stress (Floyd, 2006).

   (e) What similarities and differences characterize reports on the Iraq War found in *The Toronto Star* and *The New York Times*? (Ahmad, 2008).

Try It!

1. This is an experiment for triangulation. It works best with three or more people. Depending on the size of your tutorial group, it may also be adapted as a tutorial exercise.

   With your fellow students, gather together three or more accounts of the last lecture given by your professor for this course. It does not matter what format the accounts take; the accounts may be based on memory, hand-written notes, or digital files. Using these accounts, try to answer the following question: 'What was the most important aspect of the last lecture?' Once you arrive at an answer, consider the following issues:

   (a) What kind of data do the accounts provide: texts, direct observation, self-reports, or other-reports?

   (b) Did you define the term 'important aspect' before looking at the accounts?

   (c) How well did the accounts, taken altogether, answer the question? Did each account confirm the others, or did any of them offer contrasting views of the lecture?

   (d) Did any one account offer a more compelling answer to the question? If so, what made it more compelling?

2. This is an experiment for random sampling. It works best with two or more people. Depending on the size of your tutorial group, it may also be adapted as a tutorial exercise.

   (a) Take a standard deck of 52 cards and shuffle it well. With the card faces hidden, have one or more members of the group select 10 cards (any cards!) from the deck. Next, note how many cards of each suit have been selected. Once you have scored the results, return the selected cards to the deck, shuffle it well, and repeat the process. Do this 10 times altogether. At the end of this process, you should have 10 scores for each suit. Tally these scores for each suit and assess the results. The law of averages suggests that each suit will have been selected the same number of times. In this case, with 10 selections of 10 cards each, you should have selected 100 cards altogether and each suit should have appeared 25 times. What did you find? Are the numbers close to the expected average, or greatly different? What does this experiment suggest about random sampling?

   (b) Using the same deck of cards, try an experiment with systematic sampling. Once you have shuffled the deck, start at the top and count through the cards. Pull every fifth card from the deck until you have 10 cards, and then note how many cards of each suit have been selected. Once you have scored the results, return the selected cards to the deck, shuffle it well, and repeat the process. Do this 10 times altogether. At the end of this process, you should have 10 scores for each suit. Tally these scores for each suit and assess the results. Again, the law of averages suggests that each suit should have appeared 25 times. What did you find? Are the numbers close to the expected average, or greatly different? Are the results similar to the previous experiment, or greatly different? What does this experiment suggest about systematic sampling?

   (c) If the deck was new, and the cards had not been shuffled, how might the selections in either experiment have been different?

   (d) If you had wanted to ensure that you selected 25 cards of each suit every time, how would you modify your selection process?

6 Warrants for Research Arguments

Introduction

In this chapter, you will learn about the third element of the *research as argument* model, the warrants and backing. Warrants are the standards used to evaluate whether particular evidence represents an effective way to support a claim. We stress the inherent relationship among the values held by researchers, the forms of argument they prefer, and the standards they use to evaluate evidence in each paradigm (i.e. discovery, interpretive, and critical research). Thus, we first present the values and forms of argument typically associated with each paradigm. Then we show you how to develop the warrants for each type of argument based on those values. We then compare three different views of truth, one for each paradigm. Given the links among values, forms of argument, and standards of evaluating evidence, the process of warranting research is really a process of making ethical choices.

If you look up the noun 'warrant' in the dictionary, you will find that it is 'something that serves as an assurance, or guarantee, of some event or result' (Guralnik, 1986, p. 1602). Similarly, the verb 'to warrant' means to authorize the doing of something, to give formal assurance, or guarantee, to someone for something. Research warrants allow you to state with confidence that your evidence or data supports your research claim (Booth, Colomb, & Williams, 1995).

Each of the paradigms associated with communication and cultural research has slightly different values, so we begin each major section of this chapter with a summary of the values embraced within a particular paradigm. Second, we outline the typical form of argument that researchers operating from each paradigm make. Third, we define the standards used to evaluate evidence in each paradigm, and then provide examples of those standards.

Values guide the way we frame research problems, decide what will count as data, select the strategies to collect and analyze evidence, and estimate the worth of our conclusions. In effect, values inform all of our choices as researchers. You might think of the different paradigm values as being associated with different ethical priorities. We do not mean to imply, however, that any one paradigm is more ethical than the others. In fact, all researchers share certain ethical concerns, such as managing the risks and avoiding harm to research participants, preserving people's right of choice about participating in research, and sharing information ethically (Johannesen, 2001). Likewise, we do not believe that you must adopt any one paradigm and reject the others. To the contrary, we believe all three paradigms should coexist in the world of inquiry. If you want to fully understand any topic, we think you can benefit from knowledge gained via the perspectives of all three paradigms. So, instead of paradigm allegiance, we prefer that you develop methodological awareness, which 'can be acquired by exposure to almost any intelligent methodological discussion' (Seale, 1999, p. 465). Understanding the different ethical priorities and contributions of each of the paradigms will make you a better, more alert practitioner of research methods. Let's begin the discussion by considering the values, form of argument, and warrants that are associated with discovery paradigm research.

Discovery Paradigm Warrants

Recall from chapter 3 that the discovery paradigm has its origins in the philosophical traditions of rationalism and logical positivism. Rationalism emphasizes 'a common reality on which people can agree' (Newman & Benz, 1998, p. 2), whereas logical positivism emphasizes precision. So, the warrants associated with discovery research necessarily address issues of agreement and the values of precision and accuracy. In this section, we describe and illustrate three scientific values, the basic form of scientific argument, and basic attempts to demonstrate causality. We then describe two specific warrants for evaluating evidence, namely, reliability and validity.

Scientific Values: Precision, Power, and Parsimony

You can use alliteration to remember the scientific values embraced within the discovery paradigm. Just remember the three Ps associated with these three words—precision, power, and parsimony. These values guide discovery research at every stage, including how you construct your claim, how you collect and analyze data, and how you establish warrants. **Precision** refers to detailed accuracy when defining and measuring communication variables. Precise definitions specify what the concept is and what it is not. Precise measurements are informative because they show how a variable can

be differentiated from other variables. Precision also connotes agreement among several sources. Let's consider an example. You may think that your professor talks too fast during lectures, but what does that mean, precisely? A rate of speaking that is regarded as too fast for one student may be perceived as ideal for another student. To measure a professor's lecture speed, you could count the number of words spoken in 60 seconds; that would provide you with a precise measure. Then, a group of students could identify a range of words per minute at which point it is no longer possible to follow the professor or to take notes; that would provide you with a precise definition, and the agreement of the students would suggest that you are defining a genuinely shared or objective reality. Our point here is that discovery researchers demand descriptions that are precise and that are compelling to more than one person. Discovery researchers also value precision because they use numerical data, and math demands precision.

The second value embraced by discovery researchers is power. As a value, **power** refers to discovery researchers' preference for **generalizability**; that is, for broadly applicable definitions, data selection techniques, and research findings. The following analogy can help us to explain the value of power. A flashlight is considered powerful when it shines a bright light on a large area of darkness. The more powerful the light, the brighter it shines and the more area it covers. In the same way, conceptual and operational definitions are more powerful when they capture more detail or the broadest aspects of a concept that we are studying. Likewise, data selection techniques are more powerful when they represent the population under study so well that we can generalize from the sample studied to the entire population. Whenever we are able to generalize to larger populations, we can offer more powerful descriptions and explanations of communication and culture.

We should also note the importance of statistical power. In statistical analysis, power refers to a test's ability to detect effects. This use of the word 'power' is related to, but much more specific than, the value of power as associated with the discovery paradigm. The flashlight analogy can help us here again when we consider the following: 'How likely are we to mistake what we see when we look into a dark place?' With the use of a weak flashlight, a dusty floor can be mistaken for a clean floor. If we're looking for dust, the weak flashlight may not detect it! Similarly, if we use a low-power statistical test, a small effect may be mistaken for no effect. This mistake is called a type II error, and you will learn much more about in it chapter 13, on descriptive statistics.

Finally, **parsimony**—an efficient combination of precision and power—is highly valued by discovery researchers. A parsimonious study is both accurate in detail and covers a broad or important concept, but it is also capable of achieving detail and broad coverage in a succinct way. For this reason, discovery researchers are especially keen on the use of statistical techniques that treat the relationships between several variables at once (called 'multivariate statistics'), versus the use of techniques that treat only a few variables at one time. To make further use of the flashlight analogy, this idea of succinctness, or simple elegance, suggests not the use of a standard flashlight but the use of an LED flashlight capable of illuminating a dark area with a concentrated beam of light. Hence, the concept of parsimony involves valuing precise, powerful, and succinct descriptions and explanations of several variables and the relationships among them.

Form of Arguments: Demonstrating Causality

Causal arguments are the basis of discovery research. That said, not all discovery research provides full causal accounts of communication and cultural phenomena. Some researchers, when drafting their reports, argue only that variables are associated with one another. Nonetheless, discovery research is concerned with cause-and-effect reasoning.

As we know from chapter 4, on claims, causal claims are constructed in the form of hypotheses and research questions. Hypotheses are declarative statements that predict what effects a causal variable will have if that variable changes. Research questions, worded in interrogative form, are questions that focus on how variables can be classified or how covariation between variables can be understood. Sometimes, we use scientific notation to express the basic form of a causal claim. The letter X is used to denote the cause, and the letter Y is used to denote the effect. Together

they can express the simple idea that 'X causes Y'. As simple as this appears, however, three types of evidence are needed to demonstrate causality. The three types of evidence are (1) time order, (2) covariation, and (3) control over rival hypotheses (Cook & Campbell, 1979). Exhibit 6.1 defines each type of evidence. We will discuss covariation in chapter 14, on inferential statistics.

There are two basic conditions that must be met in order to establish causal explanations—necessity and sufficiency. In a cause and effect relationship, a cause is necessary if the effect occurs when the cause is present and if the effect cannot occur when the cause is absent. In other words, necessary conditions must be present for the effect to occur. For example, an old saying claims that you can't win the lottery if you don't buy a ticket! Buying a ticket is a necessary condition for winning the lottery. However, a cause is sufficient when it is the best possible explanation for the effect under study. In the case of the lottery, buying a ticket is a necessary condition, but in most cases it is an insufficient condition for winning. Clearly, other necessary conditions must also be met. It is most satisfying to discover a single cause that is both necessary and sufficient—such a discovery would be valued for its parsimony. That said, it is still satisfying to show that a cause is either sufficient or necessary to produce the hypothesized effect.

We evaluate the merit of causal arguments by two standards of evidence: reliability and validity. We

---

EXHIBIT 6.1   Evidence Needed to Support a Causal Argument

Time order: *X* changed or occurred before *Y* changed or occurred.

Covariation: When *X* changed or occurred *Y* also changed or occurred.

Control over rival hyphotheses: A change in or occurrence of *X* is the best possible explanation for the change in or occurrence of, *Y*.

Note: All three types of evidence are required to demonstrate causality.

define and illustrate these types of warrants in the next two sections.

Reliability as a Standard for Evaluating Evidence

Discovery researchers value studies that are replicable. A replicable study is one whose procedures and findings can be verified when they are repeated by another researcher or with different participants or texts in a different setting. For your study to be replicable, your measurements will first have to be reliable.

Reliability refers to consistency of measurement over time, across settings and among participants and texts. Reliable measuring instruments are free from random variations. For example, on a reliable household scale, a 5 kilogram bag of rice will register 5 kilograms every single time. On an unreliable household scale, a 5 kilogram bag of rice might register at 4.5 kilograms the first time you weigh it and 5.3 kilograms the next time you weigh it. If your household scale is unreliable in this way, you should never believe the results when you weigh yourself! Likewise, during research, if your measuring instrument does not produce consistent results over time, settings, and sources, you should not believe the conclusions you are led to draw from that data.

Reliability is an ideal in measurement. In practice, we never achieve perfectly consistent measurement because it is impossible to eliminate random errors completely. Before we spell out all the different ways you can demonstrate measurement reliability, let's take a closer look at the problem of inconsistent measurement due to random error.

Noise: A Threat to Consistent Measurement

Random errors in measurement are sometimes called 'noise' because they attenuate measurement reliability in the same way that static noise attenuates a radio or cellphone signal. When there is too much static noise on your phone, the person you are speaking with is usually difficult to hear. Similarly, when random errors in measurement exist, you'll have trouble capturing the variable you are trying to measure.

Three sources of random error contribute to inconsistent measurement: (1) random individual differences, (2) lack of instrument clarity, and (3) errors in data processing (Smith, 1988). Random individual differences simply mean that every participant, text, or situation is unique. Every day, we all experience transient states of being, such as mood swings, illness, or fatigue. Our settings can also vary, with things as simple as lighting, temperature, and so on. Since random differences in moods and settings cannot be controlled entirely, they threaten our ability to measure a variable across participants or situations consistently.

Research instruments are the tools we use to collect data, such as survey questionnaires, coding schedules for content analysis, or instructions to participants. Random measurement errors also can occur whenever our instruments lack clarity. This happens when our questions are poorly worded or our instructions are too ambiguous. Any lack of clarity or ambiguity can lead participants to respond inconsistently.

Finally, errors in data processing occur when data are translated from one form to another. For instance, an error may be committed when data from hard copies of a survey questionnaire are entered into a computer, or when interview responses are transcribed from an audio recording into written form.

All three of these problems—individual differences, lack of instrument clarity, and errors in data processing—result in inconsistent measurement; that is, they reduce the reliability of your measurements. If your measurements themselves are unreliable, then any conclusions you draw from that pool of data will also be of questionable value. Now that you know how noise can threaten reliable measurement, let's look at some specific ways that you can assess measurement reliability.

Types of Measurement Reliability

Measurement reliability is estimated in different ways depending on the type of consistency you are trying to achieve (i.e. consistency over time, across participants and settings, between two measures, and across scorers). In this section, we introduce you to four ways of assessing measurement reliability: (1) test–retest method, (2) internal consistency, (3) alternate-forms method, and (4) scorer reliability (Anastasi, 1976; Nunnally, 1972).

Stability of measurement over time is achieved using the **test-retest method**. Stability means that the results obtained by one measuring instrument remain consistent when the test is administered to the same group of participants at a later date. Measures with high test-retest reliability are less susceptible to variations caused by random individual or situational differences (Anastasi, 1976). If you want to assess test-retest reliability, you must carefully consider the time interval between the first and second administration of your test. For example, you should think about the experiences participants might have had between tests. Has anything relevant happened to participants since the first test that may have caused them to change their minds? If so, inconsistent scores will be due to the participants' changed attitudes or behaviours, rather than to a problem with the measuring instrument itself. Test-retest reliability is most often used to assess the consistency of behavioural observations and of self-report data (Anastasi, 1976).

The second form of measurement reliability is internal consistency (also known as homogeneity). When we say that a measuring instrument has a high degree of **internal consistency**, we mean that all of its items referring to the same concept yield similar or consistent responses. Look again at Exhibit 5.3 for example. To assess the internal consistency of the Verbal Aggressiveness Scale, you can evaluate whether participants' responses to item 1 are similar to their responses for items 2 and 5. All three items measure the presence of verbal aggression. You can also evaluate whether responses for items 3 and 4 are consistent— these two items measure a lack of verbal aggression. If participants' responses to either set of items were inconsistent or contradictory, then you would need to reconsider the wording or instructions to ensure that they are clear.

Another way to assess internal consistency is to see whether participants whose scores place them at one end of a variable continuum score similarly to one another, and differently from people whose scores place them at the other end of that same continuum. For example, McCroskey's (1982) Personal Report of Communication Apprehension (PRCA) has been shown to have a high degree of internal consistency across participants and settings. People who are highly anxious tend to respond in the same way on each item, and tend to respond differently from people who are only slightly anxious. Attending to internal consistency is an effective way to check the reliability of measurement for self-report and other-report data, especially when we want to measure attitudes and beliefs (also known as psychological trait measures).

The third way to assess measurement reliability is to use the **alternate forms method**, which simply means that we administer two different tests at the same time, and those two tests should yield similar sets of scores. It is important that the two tests be comparable. For instance, they should be about the same length and have the same level of difficulty, and they should employ similar time limits and formats (Anastasi, 1976). Alternate forms method reliability is most often used by researchers who want to find out whether a shorter version of a test will produce results that are consistent with the longer version of the test. For example, the 24-item PRCA test can be compared to a 12-item version of the same test. If the same people are identified as highly anxious on both tests, then we can feel confident about using the shorter version in our research.

Just as we can assess data for its consistency across time, across participants, and across different measuring instruments, we can also assess **scorer reliability**. Scorer reliability refers to the consistency of two or more researchers' judgments about their observations whenever they are working together on a single project. This kind of reliability is especially important whenever the interpretation of data 'leaves a good deal to the judgment of the scorer' (Anastasi, 1976, p. 119). Examples include field research where participant behaviours must be categorized, or content analysis where images must be categorized. In situations like these, we must verify the consistency of judgments by having two researchers independently categorize or 'score' the data. We must then correlate their scores, and estimate the degree of error that should be ascribed due to different scorer judgments. You will encounter three specific kinds of scorer reliability when you read published research: (1) interrater reliability, (2) intercoder reliability, and (3) intertranscriber reliability.

Interrater reliability concerns the degree of agreement among either the researchers or the researcher participants who must categorize or score the characteristics of a single item (e.g. asking participants to rate a person's amount of eye contact as 'too little', 'about right', or 'too much'). **Intercoder reliability** concerns the degree of agreement among two or more researchers who must categorize or score messages (such as how women are represented in advertising). You will learn more about these two kinds of scorer reliability in chapters 7, 8, and 10. Finally, **intertranscriber reliability** concerns the degree of agreement between two or more researchers who must collect data (i.e. transcribe it) from an audio or video recording (Patterson, Neupauer, Burant, Koehn, & Reed, 1996). You will have a chance to practise using this kind of reliability assessment in the 'Try It!' Activities included with chapter 10, on conversation and discourse analysis.

Now that you know these four ways to assess measurement reliability, let's consider the standard of accuracy, or validity, associated with discovery-oriented research.

Validity as a Standard for Evaluating Evidence

Just as reliability is prized by discovery researchers, so too is validity. **Validity** has two aspects. **Internal validity** warrants the precision and factual accuracy of the observations made within a single research study. **External validity** warrants the precision and accuracy of observations made across several studies. By extension, external validity can also warrant the application of one study's findings to individuals, texts, or settings outside of the original study.

Valid measurement is accurate measurement, so to be valid a measuring instrument must measure precisely what it claims to measure. Remember the example we used earlier of the reliable household scale? A valid scale will report the weight of a 5 kilogram bag of rice at precisely 5 kilograms, not 4.5 kilograms or 5.3 kilograms. If the scale is both reliable and valid, it will register precisely 5 kilograms every time that bag of rice is placed on the scale. Effective measuring instruments need to be both reliable and valid, or consistent and accurate. It is possible for a measuring instrument to be reliable but not valid (i.e. consistently inaccurate). If a measuring instrument is accurate, however, it should also be consistent.

Before we look at the different ways to demonstrate internal and external validity, let's consider the problem of inaccurate measurement caused by bias.

Bias: A Threat to Accurate Measurement

Bias is a source of error that occurs frequently when measuring data. When bias is present, it is impossible to measure anything accurately. You are probably familiar with the concept of bias. You may have thought, for example, 'My history professor is biased against communication majors'. If that observation is true, your history professor may be unable to measure accurately your performance in class. In the same way, measuring instruments that are contaminated by bias do not accurately measure research variables. We are trained to guard against several standard biases that are sometimes collectively referred to as 'rival hypotheses'. For example, biased findings may result from selecting only one particular type of research participant (e.g. selecting only women and never men), or bias may emanate from participants who react to the researcher's personal attributes (e.g. an interviewer who wears distracting clothing or accessories). It is crucial to know that any bias, or pattern of constant error, can threaten accuracy of measurement. Let's consider some ways that you can ensure that your measurements are accurate or free of bias.

Types of Measurement Validity

Measurement validity refers to the accuracy of measurement within one study only. In this section, we introduce you to two types of measurement validity: content validity and face validity.

The most basic form of measurement accuracy is **content validity**, which means that the items that make up a measuring instrument cover 'a representative sample of the behavior domain to be measured' (Anastasi, 1976, p. 135). In other words, content validity means that the instrument captures the full richness of the concept it was designed to measure. For example, if you created a measure of professors' persuasive strategies in which you measured only negative teaching strategies (e.g. threats, punishment, and embarrassment) and ignored positive teaching strategies (e.g. praise, encouragement, and rewards), then your measure would lack content validity. Instruments that capture the broadest meanings of a concept are considered richer and more powerful, and enable us to explain a range of weak and strong effects that a variable may have.

One way to foster content validity is to ask experts to review your measuring instrument. You can even submit your measuring instrument to a panel of judges, as Bradford, Meyers, and Kane (1999) did when they asked Latino focus groups to define communication in their own terms. If Bradford et al. had created a measuring instrument based on the group's answers, then the researchers could have made a strong case for content validity as their measure of communication competence within Latino culture would have been informed by a Latino perspective.

Face validity is closely related to content validity, but is significantly different. While content validity addresses what a test actually measures, **face validity** addresses what the test appears to measure (Anastasi, 1976). Face validity answers the question, 'Does this test look valid?' For instance, a test designed for use with very young participants might work with adult participants, and have strong content validity, but if the test's items appear irrelevant or inappropriate to the adults taking it, then the measure lacks face validity for use with adults (Anastasi, 1976). Since 'a test is valid only for some specific functions with specific groups under specific conditions' (Nunnally, 1972, p. 21), you should assess the content and face validity of your measurements in every study. It is simply not sufficient to report that your measure was valid in other research.

These two ways of establishing internal validity refer to the accuracy of the measurements within a single research study. If the results of a study are both valid and reliable, we may wish to generalize the findings or to apply the results to other individuals, texts, or settings outside the study sample. In that case, we must consider the matter of external validity.

External Validity

External validity refers to the accuracy of applying conclusions from a particular research study to people, texts, or settings outside the study. This usually occurs in association with discovery research when discovery researchers apply the results from one sample to an entire population of people or texts. For example, election pollsters survey a few hundred people to predict the likely voting behaviour of millions of people. When you want to generalize the data obtained from one sample to a larger population, establishing external validity is very important.

Researchers sometimes consider **ecological validity**, the degree to which it is accurate to apply the results from one study to the same participants in a different setting. Ecological validity is a special form of external validity that acknowledges the effect of the research itself on the participants. When participants are conscious of their roles in a research program, we know that they may behave differently than they would normally behave. There are ways of controlling important features of the setting, but that control may reduce ecological validity. As a general rule, tighter control over the variables of interest to the researcher will increase internal validity, but usually at the cost of external validity. Hence, even though a study may have excellent internal validity, it could be inaccurate to apply the conclusions from that study to individuals, texts, or settings outside the study. If the data from one study does not represent the larger population because there was some form of bias in the selection of research participants or texts, then external validity is threatened. If the setting in which the data were collected biased the participants' responses, then ecological validity is similarly threatened. In either case, the findings from that study may be accurate, but it would not be accurate to apply those findings to other studies.

In the next section, we turn to describing the values associated with the interpretive paradigm and to discussing the specific warrants that interpretive scholars use to determine the merit of their research claims and data.

Interpretive Paradigm Warrants

As you know from chapter 3, interpretive research is rooted in the philosophy that numerous, equally valid interpretations of reality exist. According to the interpretive paradigm, each reality is best interpreted from the standpoint of the knower, and the most useful ways of knowing are situated, or contextualized, from the participants' perspectives. The purpose of interpretive research is to understand how meanings are created, maintained, or changed by participants in a given context. Therefore, the warrants for interpretive communication research address the researcher's ability to capture and represent multiple realities. Making interpretive warrants also involves the researcher's ability to set aside his or her own understandings to privilege the participants' views.

As you might expect, then, the warrants for interpretive research are quite different from the warrants for discovery research. The discovery researcher's causal argument rests on concerns about validity and reliability. Interpretive research values subjectivity and aims to describe multiple realities, so the warrants for interpretive research shift from reliability and validity to researcher credibility, plausible interpretations, and transferable findings. Before we consider each of these warrants, let's briefly elaborate the values embraced by interpretive researchers.

Interpretive Values: Subjectivity and Rich Description

Just as precision, power, and parsimony guide discovery research, subjectivity and rich description guide interpretive research projects.

The concept of subjectivity acknowledges that human conceptions of the world are fallible. Any time we try to describe the world, we must draw upon sensory experiences that may or may not be accurate, and we must articulate those experiences in language that may or may not be precise. If we further acknowledge that our beliefs, values, and emotions also influence our thoughts, then, as an interpretivist would argue, any discussion of one true reality is fruitless. There is simply no way to confirm that any one interpretation of the world is perfectly reliable and valid. This is why interpretivist researchers emphasize the meaning of human behaviour and texts rather than their functions as they want to know how those behaviours and texts are understood in a particular setting. Furthermore, interpretivists understand that those behaviours and texts may be comprehended in various ways in different settings. Hence, interpretive researchers value subjectivity, whereas discovery researchers value objectivity.

One way that interpretivists demonstrate the value placed on subjectivity is that they study behaviours and texts in their natural settings. Such research may take the form of observations and interviews, such as unstructured conversations between researchers and participants. The reason interpretive researchers tend to prefer naturalistic settings for observation is linked to epistemology as they believe that these settings produce more authentic data relevant to the research context. For example, if a research project involves human participants, then interpretivists believe that face-to-face participation with other humans is needed to acquire relevant social knowledge (Lofland et al., 2006).

Rich description is the other value that characterizes interpretive research (Lofland et al., 2006; Miles & Huberman, 1994). Interpretivists demonstrate the value placed on rich description by the type and amount of data collected, and by the way that data is typically reported. Rich descriptions address every aspect of a social situation or text, including the participants, their actions, their relationships, their roles, and the setting (Geertz, 1973). Rich descriptions are best achieved when the researcher is immersed in a social situation or the analysis of a text for a long time. Therefore, rich description serves at least two purposes. First, it allows the researcher to understand one text or one social situation as fully as possible. Second, rich description helps the researcher to compare one text or social situation to another. Consequently, rich description is important to most interpretive research projects. If you study participants' behaviours in natural settings, then you will use rich description to capture and depict the full range of meaning that participants ascribe to their behaviours. If you analyze texts, you will use rich description to describe multiple readings of the text.

In the next section, we describe the general form of argument used in interpretive research that demonstrates multiple realities. It does this by expressing the points of view associated with either the people under study or the texts to be analyzed.

Form of Argument: Demonstrating Multiple Realities

As we noted above, the philosophical basis of the interpretive paradigm contends that there are multiple valid interpretations of reality. This contention makes it difficult to evaluate the merits of any one interpretive study, since presumably every study may be entitled to multiple interpretations. In the following sections, you will learn more about three specific standards that interpretive researchers use to evaluate claims and data. These are known as researcher credibility, plausible interpretations, and transferable findings.

Researcher Credibility as a Standard for Evaluating Evidence

The term 'researcher credibility' means many things, and it is important to all three of the communication research paradigms. However, for interpretive communication scholars, researcher credibility is an especially important standard because the researcher is the instrument through which data is collected and interpretations are made. In this section, we explore three aspects of researcher credibility: the researcher's training and experience, his or her degree of membership in the social situation under study, and faithfulness.

Training and Experience

Interpretive researchers' instruments for collecting and analyzing data are their own skills and abilities, whether it be their interview skills, their participant observation skills, or their ability to analyze texts (Patton, 1990). For discovery researchers, some measurements may be warranted by an instrument created by another scholar. Interpretive methods, however, rely directly on the researcher's skills and abilities to a greater extent than do discovery methods.

For instance, consider some of the skills you will need as a researcher to be a successful participant observer. You must enter the field of observation in the least intrusive way. You must know when to blend into the social group you are studying, and you must also be adept at taking notes about what you see, hear, feel, touch, and smell. Since interpretive field researchers often triangulate their observations with interviews, you must also have interviewing skills. Of course, if your primary data source is texts rather than participants, then your work as an interpretive researcher will require another, equally comprehensive set of skills (Brock, Scott, & Chesebro, 1990).

Regardless of whether your sources are human subjects or texts, interpretive researchers must have methodological awareness (Seale, 1999) and theoretical sensitivity (Strauss & Corbin, 1998). We addressed methodological awareness at the beginning of this chapter. Theoretical sensitivity is a similar concept that connotes experience with, and knowledge of, communication and cultural theories rather than with research methodologies. Although interpretive researchers often enter the field without hypotheses, and sometimes without explicit research questions, they are not blank slates onto which the lived experience of participants can be written. Strauss and Corbin (1998) emphasized the 'unquestionable fact (and advantage) that trained researchers are theoretically sensitized. Researchers carry into their research the sensitizing possibilities of their training, reading, and research experience, as well as explicit theories that might be useful if played against systematically gathered data' (p. 167). Theoretical sensitivity is also important for interpretive researchers because sometimes 'the method is the theory' (Madison, 2005, p. 18), as is the case with discourse analysis.

As your awareness of method and theory develops, your skills and abilities will also become better developed, and you will likely make better choices as you conduct your research. To illustrate this point, think about one thing that you do very well. Let's say it's riding a bicycle. When you first learned how to ride, you probably needed to concentrate on your balance and steering, and you probably pedalled quite slowly. Once you were comfortable riding on two wheels, however, it probably didn't take you long to gain confidence and gain speed. Effective research skills are obtained in a similar fashion. Researchers who operate from the interpretive framework need some specific knowledge of procedures (which they receive from training) and some practice in context (which they obtain from experience), but once those skills are honed, they are usually able to work quite efficiently.

Degree of Membership

Well-trained, highly experienced, interpretive scholars are not automatically guaranteed researcher credibility. One way that interpretive researchers gain credibility is to study the social groups to which they already belong. A researcher's **degree of membership** in a social group can provide a number of advantages. First, members sometimes gain access to the sites of study more easily than nonmembers (Ellingson, 1998; Lindlof, 1995). Second, members can recognize and participate in a range of behaviours and practices in ways that non-members cannot (Dollar, 1995). Third, members may already understand how social relationships and actions are constructed within the social group. Starting from this point, members can ask more probing questions about a situation than can non-members.

One example may serve here. Baxter-Moore (2010) described the role of music stores in a local music scene, using St. Catharines (Ontario) as a case. His ethnographic observation could have been difficult since he had to gain access to private space and then work in the open among music store staff and customers. His longstanding membership in the local music scene, however, eased store owners' concerns. Store owners and staff trusted Baxter-Moore in his new guise as a researcher, and his musical knowledge and vocabulary meant that he was able to engage everyone in revealing conversations. As he described it, 'For most customers...I was just another patron chatting to the staff, trying out a guitar, asking about the local music scene, or simply "hanging out." Some local musicians...were aware of my research but did not (despite occasional threats) blow my cover' (p. 259). For Baxter-Moore, then, having a high degree of membership in the local music scene was a decided advantage when it came time to conduct his research and to establish his credibility as a researcher.

Not everyone agrees that membership in a social group necessarily confers additional credibility on the interpretive researcher. Sometimes, a greater degree of membership can actually blind the researcher to 'the peculiarities he is supposed to observe' (Newman & Benz, 1998, p. 59). In that case, using multiple observers with varying degrees of membership in the social group can enrich the data and the interpretation of that data.

No matter whether you are an insider or an outsider in a research situation, you should make the familiar unfamiliar and vice versa. Davis (1973) suggested that there are two 'roles' you might adopt, like an actor, when studying data: the Martian and the Convert. The Martian is clearly an alien unfamiliar with the culture and setting who would question every detail in order to understand its significance. The Convert, meanwhile, wishes to embrace the new culture and setting, and tries to make everything seem logical and familiar. These two roles represent two opposing poles of thought about research, and for Davis, these roles also reflect something more profound, as follows:

> . . . They symbolize a tension which many researchers feel *within themselves*. To ask questions of, to 'make problematic', to 'bracket' social life requires distance (Martian). To understand, to answer questions, to make sense of social life requires closeness (Convert). The sensitive investigator wishes not to be one or the other but to be *both* or *either* as the research demands. (Lofland & Lofland, 1984, p. 16)

If you have accrued adequate training and experience to function as a credible researcher, and you have considered your degree of membership in the social group you are studying, you are then ready to apply the third standard used to link interpretive research claims to data: faithfulness.

Faithfulness

In general terms, to be faithful means to remain constant or steadfast. In the context of interpretive research, **faithfulness** means doing things right and doing the right things. A researcher's faithfulness can be demonstrated in a number of ways. Prolonged engagement in the field or topic of study is the hallmark of faithfulness. For instance, Spradley (1980) noted that 'immersion is the time-honoured strategy used by most ethnographers. By cutting oneself off from other interests and concerns, by listening to informants hour on end, by participating in the cultural scene, and by allowing one's mental life to be taken over by the new culture, themes often emerge' (p. 145). Morse (1998) expressed similar sentiments when he observed the following: 'Good qualitative researchers must be prepared to learn to be trusted in the setting; they must be patient and wait until they are accepted by informants; they must be flexible and resilient . . . .' (p. 67). As you can see from the preceding passages, interpretive researchers engage in detailed, patient work, which is another reason why faithfulness is an important warrant. A faithful researcher will stead-fastly do the right things, even when those things are difficult. Doing your own fieldwork, transcription, fil-ing, coding, and writing are some specific and practical ways that you can practice faithfulness (Miller, Creswell, & Olander, 1998). When conducting textual analysis or when identifying your own assumptions about a research topic, a setting, or participants at the outset of your research project, acknowledge your own limita-tions honestly and forthrightly in terms of yourself as a research instrument, show faithfulness.

Plausible Interpretations as a Standard for Evaluating Evidence

Again, interpretive researchers believe that there are multiple legitimate interpretations of any social situ-ation. Because of this belief, our task, as researchers working within the interpretive paradigm, is to develop plausible, rather than strictly correct or accurate, inter-pretations of a situation. In this section, we present three factors to consider when developing plausible interpretations: adequacy of evidence, coherence, and negative case analysis.

Adequacy of Evidence

Adequacy of evidence refers to the amount of data that a researcher must collect to support an interpreta-tion. According to Morse (1998), 'Adequacy is attained when sufficient data have been collected that satura-tion occurs and variation is both accounted for and understood' (p. 76). In interpretive research, it may be necessary to perform data collection and analysis simultaneously to make effective decisions about when adequate evidence has been amassed. You will cease to collect and analyze data when both the data and your interpretations are adequate to support your claim.

There are a couple of ways to determine adequacy. First, with respect to field studies, you may choose to end the data collection stage when everything in that social situation seems routine and nothing sur-prises you anymore. When you arrive at this point, you may also achieve **theoretical saturation**, which occurs when any new data that you collect adds little that is new or useful to the categories or explanations you have already conceived (Snow, 1980). Second,

with respect to textual analysis, you can apply similar criteria: are your understandings of texts in the study challenged by texts outside the study or does another theoretical concept add anything substantive to your analysis? If the answer to these questions is affirma-tive, then you have not yet have achieved adequacy.

Coherence

The concept of **coherence** describes the internally con-sistent logic of an interpretation. In many ways, coher-ence parallels the concept of internal validity used in discovery research. Early interpretive research built upon discovery research, and interpretive researchers assessed the worth of participant observations and tex-tual criticism against internal validity, just as discovery researchers did. However, prompted by the belief that multiple legitimate interpretations of reality exist, inter-pretive researchers rejected the idea of accuracy *per se* and adopted the concept of coherence. Whether you are observing behaviours or reviewing texts, coherent interpretations are supported by clear, reasoned links between the evidence you examine and your claim.

Miles and Huberman (1994) identified some spe-cific techniques you can use to achieve coherent inter-pretations of observational or interview data. These techniques included: clustering similar concepts together; noting patterns or themes that emerge from your data; drawing comparisons or crafting metaphors that serve to convey your data in terms of something you know well; incorporating specific, detailed data into a general interpretation; and building a logical chain of evidence. Each one of these techniques offers a way to synthesize individual pieces of evidence into broader interpretations so that you can convey your detailed understanding of a social situation.

For interpretive textual analysis, coherence is achieved by presenting the totality of the text to read-ers and making logical connections between all aspects of the evidence. For example, in narrative criticism, you must show logical connections among your inter-pretations of the story's characters, setting, and plot development (Fisher, 1987) to achieve coherence. If your interpretations of the evidence are coherent and help your readers to make sense of their own experi-ences (an achievement Fisher, 1987, called **fidelity**), then your interpretations will be warranted.

Coherence, then, refers to the totality of your interpretive study. You must identify a solid claim, select the right kind of evidence, and give effective, logical reasons for the links you make between your evidence and your claim. If you have done these things well, then you are ready to learn about one final means of ensuring plausible interpretations, negative case analysis.

Negative Case Analysis

Negative case analysis is a conscientious search for data that do not fit your categories or interpretations of a social situation or of texts (Lindlof, 1995; Jackson, 1986). We call such data 'counterexamples'. If counterexamples are found, then you must revise your interpretations to accommodate the counterexamples. This process of searching and revising must continue until no further counterexamples are found. When the process is complete, however, 'negative case analysis results in a highly confident statement about a phenomenon' (Lindlof, 1995, p. 240). The search for counterexamples is an intrinsic aspect of inductive analysis, as we described it in chapter 4, on claims.

For researchers engaged in field research, negative case analysis is a way of evaluating the interpretations developed by analyzing participant observations, interviews, and field research. For textual analysis, the search for counterexamples is a central aspect of data collection and not simply a standard used to warrant its worth (Jacobs, 1990; Pomerantz, 1990). For example, a researcher may purposefully gather texts that support interpretations quite different from his or her own interpretations. If so, the researcher will probably report these texts to demonstrate how different interpretations of the same phenomena are warranted.

Transferable Findings as a Standard for Evaluating Evidence

So far, we have considered the interpretive standards of researcher credibility and plausible interpretations. One additional test of the worth of interpretive research is **transferability**—the ability to transfer insights from one study to other participants, texts, or settings. The concept of transferability is related to generalizability as that concept is used in the discovery paradigm. As we noted earlier in this chapter, discovery research is generalizable if a sample selected for study adequately represents the entire population of interest (Kerlinger, 1986). However, because interpretive researchers tend to emphasize the immediate context or specificity of their study subjects, 'the move to generalize in the traditional sense is neither warranted nor particularly desirable' (Lindlof, 1995, p. 238).

Transferability, then, is less direct than generalizability since an interpretive insight cannot be directly applied to other participants, texts, or settings. If you wish to apply an interpretive insight beyond its original context, it must be confirmable in the original study and relevant in its new context. We will describe each of these aspects of transferability in more detail next.

Confirmability

The discovery researcher's quest for valid research findings rests on the assumption that there is only one observable reality. The interpretive researcher's contention that there are multiple, equally legitimate interpretations of reality prompts a desire for confirmability rather than accuracy, *per se*. To establish confirmability, there are two strategies you can pursue: member checks and audit trails.

Member checks are reviews of your data performed by your research participants. Those who perform the checks can be your key informants, but they need not be. For example, you might complete member checks with people who have been insiders to the culture but outsiders to the research project (Lindlof, 1995). You can request that some or all of your data be reviewed, and the checks may be quite informal, even spontaneous. The main idea is that your data be reviewed by individuals with intimate knowledge of your study subject. In this way, you can verify the interpretations that you have attributed to members during fieldwork or analysis (Janesick, 1998; Lindlof, 1995; Miles & Huberman, 1994; Strauss & Corbin, 1998). However, you should also be conscious that, 'no participant is a dispassionate, fully informed member of his or her culture. A person's alliances and passions about certain things, and disinterest about others, surely affect what he or she can authenticate' (Lindlof, 1995, p. 241). Although this complicates the value of a member check, it is consistent with the value ascribed to subjectivity.

One concern in all work with human research subjects is 'fronting'. Douglas (1976) used the term **fronting** to describe participants' attempts to avoid telling the whole truth when being interviewed. Fronting includes telling outright lies and half-truths, and evading questions. The term comes from a theatre metaphor. Those aspects of the story that can be seen by the audience are considered 'front stage'. Other aspects of the story which cannot be seen but which are still important are considered 'backstage'. Fronting behaviours occur most commonly in public settings, with individuals who wish to maintain face in a difficult situation, or who wish to thwart or please the researcher (Lindlof, 1995).

Obviously, fronting is a concern when using research instruments such as interviews and member checks. Interview participants can use fronting to deceive researchers and themselves. Still, if you see it occur, fronting can give you valuable clues about the participant's worldview, and it is not necessarily a threat to your ability to develop plausible interpretations (Van Maanen, 1988). Rather, fronting adds a layer of complexity to your understanding of your participants' subjective realities. You may detect fronting when performing member checks, or you may suspect fronting and log the suspected behaviours into your field notes and then develop the concept as part of an interpretation about the communication that occurred in that setting. Such notes will be useful later if you maintain a careful audit trail.

An **audit trail** is a record that documents the development and progress of an interpretive research study. Audit trails are important because of the massive quantity of data that is generated by interpretive researchers; without an audit trail, you may gather a warehouse of information of which no sense can be made. Notes from participant observations and interviews, plus expanded accounts, journal entries, analysis, and interpretation notes, all need to be retrievable as you write your research report. You may have encountered ethical problems, for example, and want to write about your response to those problems later (Spradley, 1980). Carefully documenting the conceptual development of a project will help you to retrace your steps when reporting how your interpretations were developed.

A well-recorded audit trail also provides evidence that interested parties (like a research partner or research assistants) can use to reconstruct your thought process. An audit trail consists of several types of documentation including: (1) raw data; (2) category lists or classification schemes; (3) notes related to the setting, including permission agreements with participants; (4) materials relating to the researcher's intentions and dispositions, such as a research proposal; and (5) information regarding the development of your research instruments (Lincoln & Guba, 1985; Miles & Huberman, 1994; Morse, 1998). Ethics guidelines also require you to retain all consent forms signed by participants. Your audit trail can also help you to document the relevance of specific interpretations if you later want to transfer their insights to another participant, text, or setting.

Relevance

In interpretive research, **relevance** provides a warrant similar to that of external validity for discovery research. If you wish to apply an insight generated in one research context to a different context, it must be confirmable in its original context and it must also be relevant to the new context. To make an insight relevant in a new context, you must be able to apply it in terms that are meaningful within the new context. Be cautious when assessing how applicable an insight may be as you should not assume that two different contexts are identical even if they have many similarities. Careful researchers imagine that the original and new contexts are two cultures foreign to one another, and hence the process of adapting an insight is similar to translating an idea from one language to another (Spradley, 1980).

In the next section, we turn to describing the values associated with the critical paradigm and to discussing the specific warrants that critical scholars use to assess the merit of their research claims and data.

Critical Paradigm Warrants

When conducting discovery research, the subjective views of the researcher and the participants must be controlled. When conducting interpretive research, the researcher and the participants are a legitimate subject of study. By contrast, when conducting critical research all subjective views are actively embraced. Thus, the warrants for critical research expand upon the warrants for interpretive research.

In making claims of evaluation and ideological reform, your subjective evaluations and criticisms of the evidence are desirable and valuable. If other people disagree with your evaluations, they may ignore them or they may actively resist them. Thus, when you provide an ideological critique, you must warrant your analysis by establishing a coherent argument. To do this, you must demonstrate your credibility as a researcher, show how your interpretations are plausible even though they are subjective, and indicate the degree to which your findings are transferable to other groups, texts, or settings (e.g. Barge, 2004). In this section, we outline some general ways to establish coherence and to acknowledge subjectivity and freedom of choice.

Emancipatory Values: Voice and Liberation

Two values underline the methodology of critical studies: voice and liberation. The *Western Journal of Communication* published a series of essays on **voice** in 1997, essays that 'grapple[d] with the theoretical, personal, social, and political issues related to the voices in which we write and the voices of those we study and about whom we write' (Vande Berg, 1997, p. 87). An individual's 'voice' is crucial to a healthy democratic society. We participate in society by articulating our beliefs and impressions in the public sphere by making our voices heard. To silence an individual is to remove that person's ability to participate in the public sphere. Because critical scholars value voice, then, they ask questions such as: 'Who can and cannot speak here?', 'What is said and not said here?', and 'Who benefits?' (Littlejohn & Foss, 2005).

Making our voices heard is the first step toward **liberation**, which can be defined as the 'securing of equal social and economic rights' (Guralnik, 1986, p. 814). Critical scholars are committed to such social and political action. Critical scholarship aims to give a voice to groups who are underrepresented in current societal discourse and to liberate those groups from the bonds of ideological oppression (i.e. liberation through

awareness). The claims and evidence of critical scholarship are evaluated by considering the researcher's subjective position in relation to the topic, the readers' freedom to disagree, and the coherence of the researcher's argument. The basic form of argument is a demonstration of the need for ideological change.

Form of Argument: Demonstrating Ideological Need for Change

As we've noted many times, critical researchers make evaluative and reformist claims. Most critical studies share the same basic form of argument: that an existing ideology must change in order to stop hegemonic oppression and thereby extend the same rights and privileges to all members of society (Gramsci, 1971; Lears, 1985). **Ideology** is 'a set of ideas that structure a group's reality . . . , a code of meanings governing how individuals and groups see the world' (Littlejohn & Foss, 2005, p. 318). Although any one group's ideology is no less subjective than any other set of ideas, each group's members generally believe their own set is truthful, logical, and consistent. When a single ideology dominates the ways that an entire society operates, we call this hegemony. **Hegemony** occurs 'when events or texts are interpreted in a way that promotes the interests of one group over those of another' (Littlejohn & Foss, 2005, p. 319). Generally, if one group's interests gain an advantage over all other groups' interests, it suggests that the other groups are disadvantaged and may require assistance. To realize that ideological change is needed is the first step toward change itself. It is implicit in the critical scholar's argument, then, that ideological change begins with his or her efforts to expose unjust power relations (e.g. Pearce, 1998; Trethewey, 2001).

The critical form of argument is known as an 'ideological critique'. A critique exposes issues within a particular ideology that may render the ideology less coherent, less logical, and subsequently less acceptable (Deetz, 2005). To argue that ideological change is desirable or needed, critical scholars often highlight the stability of a dominant ideology. If the dominant ideology is very stable, then power relations are heavily entrenched and resistant to change. If competing ideologies are already present, however, change may be more likely (see Dow, 1990, and Shugart, 1997). Grenier's (2001) study of a museum exhibit in Québec provides one example of critical scholarship as an ideological critique. Grenier sought to reveal how the provincial government used the museum exhibit to manage attitudes towards popular music. Essentially, the exhibit championed the notion that Québécois popular music is the dominant form of Québécois culture. In so doing, it privileged particular ways of being Québécois. The exhibit defined certain musical tastes, performances, and histories as genuinely Québécois to the exclusion of other musical tastes, performances, and histories. In effect, this was an act of silencing those alternative tastes. Anyone attending the exhibit may have reacted in multiple ways. As Grenier notes, what attendees remember afterwards 'may well determine where their allegiances lie and whether or not they belong' (2001, p.7) to the collective identity of the province. From a critical perspective, it is troubling to believe that an individual's participation in civic discourse and affairs is framed by his or her taste in music.

Coherence as a Standard for Evaluating Evidence

To make a case for ideological change, you must show that there is a stable and dominant ideology at work in a particular context. This means you must make clear and logical connections between that particular context and your claims. You must also show how a particular ideology fosters hegemony; that is, how the dominant ideology privileges some members in that context and disadvantages other members. Thus, the first standard by which your critical study will be evaluated is **coherence**, the degree to which your arguments are logical, consistent, and intelligible to others. In this sense, coherence serves to warrant interpretive and critical communication research.

That said, there is one small difference in the way we evaluate coherence for interpretive and critical studies. Interpretive researchers focus on making consistent, rational links between their evidence and claims. Critical researchers always ask the question: 'Consistent and rational *for whom*?' Critical researchers always begin with the assumption that hegemony is at work in society, and so what is coherent to the dominant group members will be different than what appears coherent to members of a marginalized group (Lears, 1985).

Let's consider how you achieve coherence in a critical study. Your tactics will depend on your ultimate goal, be that a purely ideological critique or a critique founded upon an empirical study. If you are writing a purely ideological critique, then you will present your own view as a researcher rather than the perspective of the social group that concerns you. You will make clear connections between the existing literature, the theoretical concepts you endorse, and the social context that you wish to critique. If your description and analysis are unclear, others scholars will not understand your argument. If your argument is clear but plagued by internal contradictions, others scholars will not be persuaded by your argument. If your description and analysis are clear and your argument is logical, then other scholars are of course 'free to accept or reject the argument' (Fink & Gantz, 1996, p. 119).

If you are pursuing the second goal by conducting a critique founded upon an empirical study, then you will be inclined to present the perspective of the social group that concerns you. Through your empirical research you will have gathered evidence documenting social relations in that specific context. You will use that evidence to demonstrate how an ideology fosters hegemonic relations. And, once your argument is grounded in empirical evidence, the warrants we described in relation to discovery and interpretive research can be used to evaluate the relationship between your evidence and your claims. For example, if you use a survey to collect data, then you will demonstrate that your questionnaire had content validity, that the sample is representative of the entire population and that all measures are reliable and valid. If you used participant observation to collect data, then you will describe your degree of membership in the social situation you studied and establish your credibility to represent your research participants.

Whether your critical study represents your own views or the views of individuals in the social group under study, your position as a researcher is another important standard for evaluating the worth of your study. Let's consider that standard next.

Researcher Positionality as a Standard for Evaluating Evidence

Critical scholars value voice and liberation, and thus they place great emphasis on their own subjective positions in relation to the topics they select to study. We use the term **researcher positionality** to include both the researcher's standpoint and his or her reflexivity. Let's consider the meaning of each of these terms.

Critical scholars argue that 'the material, social, and symbolic circumstances of a social group shape what members of that group experience, as well as how they think, act, and feel' (Wood, 1997, p. 384). We refer to this combination of circumstance, experience and thought as a **standpoint**. To put this another way, what we see of the world depends on where we are standing as we view it. Your standpoint as a researcher will affect the topics you believe are worthy of study, the aspects of a topic you select for analysis, and the kinds of reforms you support. Further, your standpoint can depend on your membership in various social groups. For example, 'standpoint logic would suggest that whites are less likely than people of color to recognize the continuing legacy of racism and discrimination' (Wood, 1997, p. 255) because people of colour, like Native Canadians, have conscious experiences of being discriminated against, whereas many Canadians of European descent have benefited from racism in ways that are invisible or unexamined.

Kaye (2003), in a study of Western Canadian arts organizations and their use of Native forms of expression, was reluctant to describe Native forms of expression directly. As a white scholar, she made her standpoint explicit, as follows:

> Because I am writing from within the European-descended settler society and with the particular responsibility of being the grandchild of four early Alberta settlers actively engaged in transporting and planting a European cultural tradition designed to overwhelm and bury indigenous cultures, I have focussed . . . on cultures created by those of European descent. . . . I am in no way attempting to speak 'for' Native communities,

who can articulate their own points of view far better than I can. (pp. xxii–xxiii)

Kaye believes that her two identifications—European rather than Native, 'settler' rather than indigenous—contribute to her standpoint, and therefore render her views of Native expression problematic. Her awareness of how each identification contributes to her thoughts, actions, and scholarship is called reflexivity.

Reflexivity is a process by which researchers recognize that they are inseparable from the settings, contexts, and cultures they are attempting to understand and represent. Critical scholars use reflexivity to question their own interpretations and representations of social situations (e.g. May & Pattillo-McCoy, 2000; Nakayama & Krizek, 1995). Quite often, critical scholars examine a social situation or case in which they have some intrinsic interest. When they do, reflexivity becomes doubly important. For instance, you might select a case in which you have a personal stake. Although your familiarity with the case may provide an advantage with respect to access and credibility, it may nevertheless provide a disadvantage if you are unable to consider interpretations separate from your own. As we noted in chapter 5, on data, the primary criterion for your research decisions should be the opportunity to learn (Frey, 1994a; Stake, 1998). Frey (1994a) urged communication researchers to study under-researched populations and groups because they offer an opportunity to learn something that is not represented in existing published communication research.

We can perhaps further illustrate the concept of researcher positionality as a warrant for critical scholarship by considering the method of historical criticism. Historical criticism is primarily accomplished by analyzing existing texts, but some historical critics also employ case studies and interviews (e.g. Carpenter, 1999; Lewis, 1997; McLaughlin, 1991). In either case, 'the interpretation of history varies with the subjective social experience of the historian' (Newman & Benz, 1998, p. 73). Furthermore, historical methods often require the researcher to 'reconstruct the facts from unverifiable sources. These facts are based on their plausibility and can only be inferred' (Mouly [1970] as cited in Newman & Benz, 1998, p. 70). It is at this point that historical criticism bridges the interpretive and critical paradigms. Historical critics' explicit reliance on their subjectivity is consistent with critical scholarship, and the plausibility of inferences is consistent with interpretive scholarship. You will learn more about critical studies in chapter 12.

Three Views of Truth

So far in this chapter, we have looked at the types of warrants used by researchers to evaluate their data. To do so, we discussed each of the three paradigms and isolated three elements of their warrants that make them unique: their values, forms of argument, and standards for evaluating research. Next we examine the backing or support for each warrant. The backing for any warrant depends on the researcher's notion of truth, and we must remember that each paradigm has a different view of truth. In the following sections, we present these three views of truth. Perhaps you will find one paradigm's view of truth compelling and subsequently reject the others. In the hopes of presenting these paradigms even-handedly, we will present all three views through the authors of published research in each paradigm, and we will begin with the discovery paradigm.

Discovery Paradigm

Discovery researchers agree that the notion of 'truth' exists and that it can be objectively verified. Standard ways of designing research and of controlling for rival hypotheses link discovery research questions and evidence to their truth values (Newman & Benz, 1998). As you already know, validity means that the researcher accurately measures variables and makes appropriate attempts to generalize findings from one study to another group of individuals, texts, or settings. To the extent that measurements are reliable and valid, findings are therefore verified empirically or confirmed as *true*. So, for discovery researchers, truth is objectively verifiable.

Newman and Benz (1998) asserted 'science, as reflected in the scientific method, is the only defensible way of locating and verifying truth' (p. 10). Science itself, however, has been the subject of criticism in

recent years. Robert Abelson (1995), a statistician, felt the need to defend the scope and limitations of quantitative research when he wrote the following:

> The field of statistics is misunderstood by students and nonstudents alike. The general public distrusts statistics because media manipulators often attempt to gull them with misleading statistical claims . . . .Suspicion of false advertising is fair enough, but to blame the problem on statistics is unreasonable. . . . Rather than mindlessly trashing any and all statements with numbers in them, a more mature response is to learn enough about statistics to distinguish honest, useful conclusions from skullduggery or foolishness. (p. 1)

The emphasis here is on process. Attention should be paid to proper training in research methods, to careful preparations in every study, and to the accurate interpretation of statistics. Critical scholars argue that individual examples of poor training, inadequate research design, or misuse of data should not be used to condemn the pursuit of truth in general.

Interpretive Paradigm

Interpretive researchers do not believe that an objective 'truth' can be known or verified. That does not mean that truth is a wholly individual conception. Rather, interpretivists believe that some collective truths are held by social agreement and perpetuated through mechanisms like tradition or social authority. Even then, however, such social agreement may be stable or unstable as traditions and authority can both be challenged. In the eyes of interpretivists truth is therefore subject to the interpretations of those individuals who participate in and who conduct academic research. This is one reason why interpretive scholars make every effort to include multiple perspectives in their research. As Strauss and Corbin (1998) pointed out 'Perhaps not every actor's perspectives can be discovered, or need be, but those of actors who sooner or later are judged to be significantly relevant must be incorporated' (p. 172).

May and Pattillo-McCoy (2000) addressed this interpretive view of truth in their collaborative ethnographic description of a neighbourhood community centre. They observed 'most academic writing... requires that there be some suggestion that the author is offering the "truth" about the field he or she studied. What our experience taught us was that there is neither one truth nor one reality' (May & Pattillo-McCoy, 2000, p. 67). These authors emphasized that collaborative ethnography offered them several advantages, such as increasing the amount of detail available in their field notes and revealing each researcher's subjectivity due to background, experience, class, gender, and ethnicity. Yet, May and Pattillo-McCoy cautioned, 'We do not believe that if we just had enough people in the field, then we might have got at some reality that is more true than the one we recorded' (2000, p. 84). Because interpretive researchers view truth as a matter of some social agreement, more agreement does not necessarily equal more truth. Strauss & Corbin (1998) describe the problem of perception in the following terms:

> All interpretations are temporally limited—in a dual sense. First, they are always provisional, they are never established forever; their very nature allows for endless elaboration and partial negation (qualification). Second, like many other kinds of knowledge, theories are limited in time: Researchers and theorists are not gods, but men and women living in certain eras, immersed in certain societies, subject to current ideas and ideologies, and so forth. (p. 171)

Ultimately, what any one researcher or participant sees, at any one moment or in any one setting, is bound to look slightly different at another moment in that same setting. This insight is just as relevant to textual analysis as it is to field research. Hence, the view of truth accepted in the interpretive paradigm is grounded in social agreement and established at particular times and places.

Critical Paradigm

Interpretive and critical researchers tend to agree that nothing is true for all people, at all times, in all places.

However, critical researchers are more likely to emphasize that even socially agreed-upon truths are subjective and intertwined with the exercise of power. Every such truth may privilege certain groups and oppress others. Strauss and Corbin (1998) summarized the relationships among truth, ideology, and power as follows:

> Power certainly affects the ability to convince audiences, including probably oneself, if one takes one's power seriously. Ideologies we all have—we all have political and other positions . . . . The feminist critique of the objective biases of traditional science seems to us correct insofar as some scientists may assume they are just human instruments reporting on nature . . . . Contemporary physical and biological scientists seem to understand quite well the naïveté of such a position. (p. 180)

Denzin and Lincoln (1998a) called the idea that there is no one knowable truth a 'postmodern sensibility' (p. 9).

Within research itself, the debate over truth is more specific than whether one or more knowable truths exist. Every research decision is subject to scrutiny since every concept the researcher uses may be questioned. Thomas (1993), for one, pointed out the multiple complications faced by scholars performing content analysis. It may be a simple matter to count each time a word is used, a colour appears, or a situation is depicted, but even these items may be 'sites of contested meaning' (p. 693). Moreover, even before one begins to count, the particular categories selected for study may be questioned, as may be the very meaning of those categories as understood by the researcher.

The three views of truth that we have outlined in this section correspond to the discovery, interpretive, and critical research paradigms. The standards for evaluating evidence in each paradigm serve to assure readers of its worth, given particular values and forms of argument. When we seek to explain the causes and effects of attitudes or behaviours, it makes sense that we would value precision, power, and parsimony, and as well that we would warrant our research by demonstrating reliable and valid measurement of variables, and that we would show how generalization of our findings to a broader population is warranted. In the same way, when we seek to demonstrate multiple interpretations of reality from the viewpoint of the members of a particular social group, it is practical to value those members' rich, subjective descriptions. It is also practical to emphasize our credibility as researchers, and to call attention to the plausibility and the relevance of our interpretations. Likewise, when we value voice and liberation and, therefore, aim to evaluate and reform ideologies, then warranting our coherence and positionality is an important way to enhance the persuasiveness of our critiques. No matter what paradigm you embrace as a researcher, its conception of truth will be reflected in the methods and warrants that you adopt for your research.

Summary

In this chapter, we outlined the third element of the *research as argument* model, the warrants and backing. We cannot begin to describe all the backing that experienced researchers bring to bear on their assessments of a study's merit. Instead, we described the warrants for each epistemological paradigm by presenting some of the values embraced by researchers associated with that paradigm. We then presented a basic form of argument for each paradigm. Discovery researchers typically seek to demonstrate causality, interpretive

researchers seek to demonstrate multiple realities, and critical researchers seek to demonstrate the need for ideological change. Last, we presented some of the standards used within each paradigm to ensure the value of the data and findings. These standards link particular research claims to evidence, given particular values and forms of argument.

Table 6.1 summarizes the elements of research warrants typically found in the context of each paradigm. If you consult it, you will see that warrants associated with the discovery paradigm ensure consistent and accurate measurement of variables and accurate attempts to apply the results of data analysis from one study to other social groups, texts, or settings. In interpretive research, warrants ensure the researcher's credibility as an interpreter of the data. They also specify when it is, and is not, appropriate to transfer the results of data analysis from one setting to another. Finally, in the critical paradigm, warrants establish the coherence of an ideological critique and reveal the positionality of the researchers. Positionality includes both the researchers' standpoints and the degrees to which they are reflexive (i.e. aware of their own positions). Revealing your own position will allow those who review your research to consider your credibility as a critic and, by extension, to accept or to reject your ideas.

As we said in chapter 3, on the three paradigms, the backing for any argument rests on a large body

TABLE 6.1 Warrants and Backing: Values, Form of Argument, and Standards for Evaluating Evidence

	DISCOVERY PARADIGM	INTERPRETIVE PARADIGM	CRITICAL PARADIGM
Values	Precision Power Parsimony	Subjectivity Rich description	Voice Liberation
Form of Argument	Demonstrate causality	Describe multiple interpretations of reality	Advocate ideological change
Standards for Evaluating Evidence	Measurement reliability Measurement validity External validity	Researcher credibility Plausible interpretations Transferable findings	Coherence Researcher positionality

of information that clarifies how the warrants are to be understood, applied, and trusted. Ultimately, the backing or support for any warrant depends on the researcher's conceptualization of truth. Hence, we compared three views of truth as they are conceived within the three epistemological paradigms

Key Terms

Adequacy	Hegemony	Reflexivity
Alternate forms method	Ideology	Relevance
Audit trail	Intercoder reliability	Reliability
Coherence	Internal consistency	Researcher positionality
Content validity	Interrater reliability	Rich description
Degree of membership	Intertranscriber reliability	Scorer reliability
Ecological validity	Internal validity	Standpoint
External validity	Liberation	Subjectivity
Face validity	Member checks	Test-retest method
Faithfulness	Negative case analysis	Theoretical saturation
Fidelity	Parsimony	Transferability
Fronting	Power	Validity
Generalizability	Precision	Voice

Discussion Questions

1. When you first read chapter 3, we asked you to think of one thing you knew. We also asked you to explain how you knew that thing. Was your argument a causal argument, an argument about your own (or another person's) subjective reality, or an argument about something that needs to be changed?

2. Would a research study be more believable if the researcher used more than one standard to evaluate evidence? Why, or why not?

3. Which paradigm's view of truth seems nearest to your own view of truth? Why?

Try It!

This activity asks you to identify the warrants used in everyday arguments. It can be completed by an individual, but it may be more interesting to work in a group with three or more other members. Depending on the size of your tutorial group, it may also be adapted as a tutorial exercise.

Newspaper editors view themselves as community leaders who can set the agenda for public discussion and sometimes influence the decisions made by both policy makers and citizens. Typically, editors express their own opinions and preferences through editorials. Ideally, an editorial is a concise but reasoned argument addressing an issue of public concern. To be both concise and compelling, an editor must draw upon credible facts and clear logic. Just as importantly, however, the editor must warrant his or her argument in some commonly shared notion of validity, plausibility, or coherence.

1. Select three to five editorials from a local newspaper that were published during the last week. Then, for each editorial, try to answer the following questions:
   (a) What is the main claim or argument of the editorial?
   (b) What evidence is given to support the editor's claim or argument?
   (c) What form of argument does the editorial take?
   (d) What warrants are supplied to back the editor's evidence or argument?
   (e) Do you believe that the editorial is compelling? Why or why not?
   (f) Could the editorial be improved? What would make its argument more compelling?
2. Once you have examined all of your editorials, compare and contrast their claims, data, and warrants. Which editorial do you believe is the most compelling, and why?

Part 2

The How of Communication Research

7 Survey Research

Introduction

In this chapter, you will learn how to conduct survey research. Whereas methods such as content analysis or discourse analysis examine messages (i.e. the content of communication and cultural artefacts), survey research focuses on the characteristics of individuals or groups who send and receive messages or share cultures. The survey process begins when you develop descriptive and explanatory claims about such groups. Next, you will learn about survey data collection sources and strategies, including cross-sectional and longitudinal research designs, sampling techniques, interviews and questionnaires, and instrumentation. Finally, we present three warrants for survey research, including assessment of response rate and measurement reliability and validity.

Survey Research Claims

In chapter 4, we identified the claim as the central assertion or premise on which a research analysis is based. Survey research claims are most frequently framed as research questions or hypotheses. Generally, research questions ask how a concept can be classified, or what relationship exists between variables. Hypotheses make specific predictions about relationships among variables. In chapter 5, we defined the term 'variable' as a measurable construct. By 'measurable', we mean that the elements of a variable can be assigned numerical values according to their magnitudes, categorizations, or scores. For example, the volume of sound is a variable that can be measured in decibels. Biological sex is a variable with two categories: female and male. Because these elements can be assigned numerical values, these concepts can be treated as variables.

There are two general types of claims in survey research: descriptive and explanatory. Descriptive claims define the characteristics of a population based on samples drawn from it (Smith, 1988, p. 219). Explanatory claims in survey research include both associative and causal claims. Recall that in our discussion in chapter 4, on claims, we distinguished between associative claims, which predict phenomena that will occur together, and causal claims, which predict the influence of one phenomenon on another.

Descriptive Claims

Descriptive claims in survey research are often posed as research questions and are used to identify certain characteristics of the individuals or social group under study. For example, Atkin, Smith, Roberto, Fediuk, and Wagner (2002) used a survey to see if they could differentiate between two sets of adolescents, those who are verbally aggressive and those who are victims of verbal aggression. The survey asked all participants to share their experiences of verbal aggression and their demographic information. These two sets of data allowed the research team to categorize each participant and then search for patterns in the results. As you know from chapter 5, on data, demographics are those items that provide telling background information, such as age, sex, education, or socioeconomic class, about each participant.

In some cases, descriptive claims are used in survey research to map out a conceptual territory. You may wish to explore a new concept to find out what types of opinions, attitudes, feelings, or behaviours people identify with a particular communication or cultural variable. For example, Gantz and Wenner (1995) explored the dimensions of sports fanship, particularly those fans who follow professional sports on television. Fanship refers to a level of emotional investment that distinguishes a fan from a casual observer. First, the researchers collected descriptions of fanship from past studies, then integrated these with their own insights to develop a variable with four aspects: an individual's motivations to watch a contest, behaviours before a telecast begins, behaviours during the telecast, and behaviours afterwards. Gantz and Wenner's survey questionnaire contained numerous descriptive statements that they believed reflected the conceptual field of 'fan' (see Exhibit 7.1). In chapter 5, on data, you learned how measurement scales are constructed for variables. Later in this chapter, you will learn how measurement scales are embedded in questionnaires and what warrants are used to evaluate surveys.

Explanatory Claims

Explanatory claims in survey research can be posed as research questions or hypotheses, and are used to explore the relationship between two or more concepts

EXHIBIT 7.1 Descriptive Claims in Survey Research

Descriptive Claims:

RQ1: What are the demographic features that describe adolescents who are verbally aggressive and adolescents who are victims of verbal aggression? (Atkin et al., 2002)

H1: The experience of viewing televised sports varies on the basis of fanship, with fans having qualitatively deeper and more textured responses than nonfans. (Gantz & Wenner, 1995, p. 57)

Note: RQ = research question; H = hypothesis.

or variables. Explanatory claims can be purely associative or can test for causality. Associative claims tested by survey data predict that two or more concepts or variables are related to each other or that changes in one variable are accompanied by changes in the other (this tendency is also known as 'covariance'). Purely associative claims do not satisfy the conditions required for a causal claim. For example, it is commonly perceived that, since 2000, television viewing has fallen while Internet use has climbed. You could test this perception by surveying a sample of Canadians to measure the number of hours they spend watching television and surfing the Web. If the results show that individuals who surf the Web watch less television, then you could make an associative claim that the two variables co-vary. However, simply knowing the number of hours spent participating in each activity does not provide you with a causal explanation. Without knowing the motives of your participants, you will not know why they use each medium as they do.

Associative claims express contingency relationships or correlations, a term you will learn more about in chapter 15. **Correlations** refer to changes in variables that occur together in time. If the variables increase together or decrease together, the type of association is said to be **positive** (see Exhibit 7.2). In the preceding example, Gantz and Wenner (1995) found that fans showed a greater emotional investment in the result of a contest and therefore concluded

---

EXHIBIT 7.2   Two Types of Explanatory Claims in Survey Research

CORRELATIONAL CLAIMS:

(a)   **Positive correlation** (variables change together):

H1: The more a newspaper business reflects a corporate form of organization, the greater the number of editorials written by local staff. (Demers, 1996, p. 864)

(b)   **Negative correlation** (variables change in opposite directions):

H2: The more the newspaper industry adds information technologies to their newsrooms, the less satisfied journalists become with their jobs. (Liu, 2006, p. 695–696)

CAUSAL CLAIMS:

H3: Fearful and dismissive individuals will be rated as less skilled in (a) expressiveness and (b) other-orientation than secure individuals. (Guerrero & Jones, 2005, p. 310)

(In which the independent variable is the attachment style and the dependent variables are expressiveness and other-orientation).

Note: H = hypothesis

---

that there was a positive relationship between a participant's level of pre-game preparation and the duration of his or her post-game emotional state; that is, the more an individual prepares for a game, the longer he or she will experience joy or remorse after the game (p. 59).

If one variable decreases as the other increases, the relationship is identified as a **negative correlation** (see Exhibit 7.2). For example, Gantz and Wenner (1995) found a negative relationship between the emotional commitment of sport viewers and two other variables: the extent to which social interaction was a motivation to watch a game and the tendency of sport viewers to perform household chores while watching. First, fans were motivated to watch solely for the emotional stake they had in the outcome of the game; the fact that family and friends also watched was not important. By contrast, nonfans were more inclined to watch a televised game if others were already watching. Second, fans were willing to ignore chores during and after their viewing, while nonfans were more inclined to do chores while the game was on. Hence, both variables demonstrate a negative correlation. The greater the interest in sport, the less likely a participant was to be motivated by others to watch or to do chores while watching.

Purely associative claims are generally descriptive or exploratory. Causal claims must go several steps

further by showing that a change in one variable precedes and influences a change in the second variable and that the change is not likely to be explained by the influence of any other variable. As we have mentioned in other chapters, the variable that prompts change is called an independent variable; the variable that is changed is called the dependent variable.

Guerrero and Jones (2005) provide a useful example of a causal claim. They used survey research to study courtship behaviours. They believed that an individual's approach to forming intimate relationships (which they called 'attachment styles') predicts that individual's use of conversational skills during courtship. In this claim, attachment styles are the independent variables that prompt changes in conversational skills, the dependent variables. Guerrero and Jones discovered that certain combinations of attachment styles were indeed likely to predict individual conversational skills. For example, those participants who were fearful or dismissive of intimate relationships were less expressive and other-oriented than individuals with secure attachment styles.

Surveys traditionally do not involve any manipulation or controlled change in one of the variables or concepts studied. As Simon has noted, 'the survey takes the world as it comes, without trying to alter it' (Simon as cited in Berger, 1998, p. 35). This may be viewed as a disadvantage because you lack control over all of the variables being measured. However, it can be a decided advantage because the data collected from surveys permit you to test more complex sets of causal relationships as they exist in their natural settings.

One area of research that tests complex patterns of causality is network analysis. The term 'network' here refers to all the component parts of a communication system within an organization or social group. **Network analysis** is both a research method and a theoretical framework (Doerfel & Barnett, 1999). A researcher will describe and explain a network through an analysis of the relationships among its members. As J.R. Lincoln describes it, the analysis focuses upon 'the structure of social relationships . . . , not in the attributions of individual actors (persons, groups, organizations), but in the patterns of ties that relate them to one another' (1990, p. 746). Thus, network studies have claims that are frequently descriptive and explanatory.

Making descriptive and explanatory claims is only the initial step in the survey-oriented research process. Collecting and analyzing the data are the next steps of survey research.

Survey Research Data

Survey research entails a lengthy process of preparation. At each step in the process, you must make some important decisions. Exhibit 7.3 lists the 10 steps typical of most survey research designs. These steps should be conducted before you collect data, analyze it, or interpret the results.

Sources for Data Collection

Surveys usually take the form of questionnaires. As you learned in chapter 5, on data, you can ask participants to supply data about themselves (called self-report data), or to supply data about other individuals or groups (called other-report data). Typically, researchers use surveys to learn about the characteristics of individuals or groups, and to investigate how those characteristics are related to specific issues. These characteristics may be demographic in nature, such as sex or birthplace, or they can be intangible characteristics, such as beliefs, opinions, attitudes, and emotions.

EXHIBIT 7.3 Steps in Collecting Survey Data

Steps in Survey Data Collection
1. Articulate your claim.
2. Identify data sources and settings.
3. Select a general survey design.
4. Select a sampling strategy.
5. Select a collection format, using either questionnaires or interviews.
6. Construct a research instrument (either a questionnaire or interview guide).
7. Develop collection procedures.
8. Pilot the collection procedures and research instrument.
9. Assess the validity and reliability of the procedure and instrument.
10. Assess the generalizability of the sampled data.

Settings for Data Collection

The data collected from surveys can be obtained either in laboratory settings or in field settings. Laboratories in communication and culture research are seldom the sterile environments portrayed in popular culture. They are usually offices, conference rooms, or classrooms at the researcher's university. Generally, a laboratory is used for survey research to facilitate the collection of data or to provide a controlled environment during data collection. Such a setting is most often associated with basic research. Basic research emphasizes investigating theoretical relationships among variables where practical outcomes in specific contexts may be implicit or unknown (Smith, 1988, p. 219).

By contrast, field research is any research that investigates attitudes and behaviours in their most common settings. For this reason, surveys are much more frequently conducted in the field to access groups and contexts that cannot be recreated in a laboratory. For example, Johnston and Ripmeester (2007) approached pedestrians on city sidewalks to conduct a survey designed to assess the impact of historical monuments in urban centres, while Lorimer and Lindsay (2004) used email to recruit volunteers who worked in online publishing. In essence, the data collection setting is generally dependent on the type of analysis you wish to perform.

Applied research may be conducted in a lab or the field, but is commonly conducted at a distance from participants, by phone or by mail. By applied research, we refer to those surveys most frequently associated with political polling, market research, and action research. **Political polling research** assesses popular opinion with respect to political issues, and often tries to predict voter preferences. The major Canadian companies in this field are Compas, Environics, Harris/Decima, Ipsos Canada, and Pollara. Their poll data are a staple of news reports during all federal or provincial election campaigns. **Market research** (sometimes called consumer research) is designed to assess consumer attitudes toward and preferences for various products or services. The Board of Broadcast Measurement, for example, helps media outlets and advertising agencies to assess the characteristics and sizes of audiences who watch each television program or listen to each radio station. In chapter 4, on claims, we described action research as a means to evaluate and change current practices within organizations or institutions.

Whether it is conducted in the field or a laboratory, and whether its purpose is academic or applied, it is important to remember that survey research has the potential to provide important contributions to understanding communication and culture.

Survey Research Design

In chapter 5, on data, you learned that a research design is the plan a researcher creates to test his or her hypothesis or research question. It specifies the procedures for collecting and analyzing data. Recall that there are two general types of designs: cross-sectional and longitudinal. Both of these general designs are relevant to survey research.

Cross-sectional surveys are the more prevalent of the two designs in communication and culture research. They involve the collection of data from participants at one point in time, and provide a 'snapshot' view of the phenomenon you wish to study. For this reason, your findings may be relevant only for a short period of time. Nonetheless, cross-sectional surveys generate detailed insights that are extremely useful to understand an issue of immediate importance.

Longitudinal surveys involve collecting data at more than one point in time. The main advantage of a longitudinal design is its ability to test the durability of findings. Rather than a single snapshot of a phenomenon, longitudinal designs capture a series of snapshots over a long period of time to see which aspects of a phenomenon change and which do not. In practical terms, this type of survey design is more expensive and time consuming than a cross-sectional design, and you risk losing participants as time passes (researchers refer to these losses as **mortality**.) Nonetheless, use of longitudinal designs generates nuanced insights regarding the motivations of your participants and, by tracking the development of trends, may provide predictive insights into future attitudes and behaviours.

There are two types of longitudinal surveys, panel design and trend design. A panel design recruits one group of participants and then revisits them each time the survey is conducted. A trend design recruits a new sample of participants with each new application of the survey. Deciding which type of design is appropriate depends on three key factors: the size of the population, the nature of your claim, and the mortality rate. First, if the size of the population is very large, then the only feasible design is the trend study. It is simply impracticable to survey the same members of a large population, as you would do in a panel study. However, sometimes the claim you wish to test makes a panel study more advantageous. If you want to show, for instance, what types of networks individuals develop online over time, following the same group of individuals will allow you to map out gradual changes in network development. The third consideration in deciding what type of longitudinal study to use concerns the effects of mortality. If your research question or hypothesis poses a claim that is susceptible to this effect, selecting a panel format will be problematic. For example, Bloustein (2004) wanted to understand television fan culture by observing viewers of *Buffy the Vampire Slayer*. The viewers were an informal group of strangers who happened to meet at the same pub to watch the show each week. Although some of them became familiar with one another, no club was established, no membership roll or fees were applied, and new people joined weekly while some regulars stopped coming altogether. As such, Bloustein's sample of television fans was highly fluid in its composition and highly subject to mortality. He could not say that the group he first observed at the start of the season was identical to the group who were watching the show at the end of the season.

Once you have decided which design best matches your claims and population characteristics, you must choose a sampling method to select potential recruits for your survey.

Data Sampling Strategies

Design issues specify how data will be collected, including how your sample will be selected and in what format your data will be recorded. As we stated earlier, the primary purpose of surveys is to examine the characteristics or attributes of interest to our study from a sample that is representative of a larger population. Sample representativeness is, therefore, a key issue in survey research.

In chapter 5, you learned about the general principle of representativeness. When a sample represents its population well, we say it provides a clear picture of what the whole group looks like, even though we have not tested every member. Because representative samples provide such good pictures of the whole population, you can assume that the conclusions you reach about your observations have external validity. External validity is the ability to generalize beyond what you see in your sample to the population at large. With strong external validity, you can say, for example, that your samples of voters, teenagers, women, television audiences, or whatever group you have selected, will allow you to make accurate predictions about what all voters, teenagers, women, or television audiences will do, even though you cannot test or observe every member of the whole group.

The best way to approach representativeness is to have a clear understanding of the entire population you wish to understand. For example, if you wish to survey popular opinion in a specific city, you can review census records from Statistics Canada to uncover the demographic profile of that city. Census data is publicly available and easily accessed on the Internet. If you wish to survey members of an organization, such as a charity group or business, then you might review its membership roll or employee records. Because this kind of data is private and confidential, you must request access to it and—if it is granted—you must follow strict research ethics procedures as you work with it.

Random Selection Methods

The best way to ensure representativeness is to use random selection or another probability sampling method. When you select population members randomly to make up a sample, you are ensuring that every member of the population has an equal chance of being chosen for the sample. Survey researchers may use any of the random sampling methods identified in our chapter on data (see chapter 5). Simple random sampling and stratified sampling are the most frequently chosen. Usually, researchers select the method that is most cost effective and satisfies the goals of obtaining a representative sample

Many telephone survey studies make use of a procedure called **random digit dialing** (RDD). This procedure randomly identifies areas of a region to be sampled with their corresponding area codes and exchanges (i.e., the first three numbers). Then, the last four digits of the telephone number are randomly generated. This procedure enables you to access unlisted numbers. The study by Gantz and Wenner (1995) into the nature of sports fanship used a version of RDD to obtain a representative sample of television viewers who follow sports.

In some cases, survey researchers depend on existing samples and data to produce new studies. For example, Tremblay, Paquet, and Najem (2006) used data from a study conducted by Statistics Canada to assess the impact of telework on corporate employees. The government study, called the Work Employment Survey, had collected information from 6,000 companies and some 23,000 employees. Tremblay and her research partners used demographic analysis to discover who was most likely to perform telework from home, and to assess what impact this work had on private life. Using such data is random in the sense that the researchers have not exercised discretion over the selection of the sample.

If your survey responses are coded for quantitative analysis, then random sampling methods have one clear benefit. Random samples enable you to estimate how far your sample's characteristics may deviate from the population's characteristics. You will learn about this process in more detail in chapters 13 and 14, on statistics.

Nonrandom Selection Methods

Researchers use nonrandom sampling methods in surveys when they cannot afford to use one of the random selection techniques, or when constraints imposed by the setting make random selection impractical (Fink & Gantz, 1996; Stake, 1998). If you want to test a hypothesis, the use of nonrandom sampling weakens your ability to generalize study results. To compensate, you may take steps to boost representativeness in other ways. For example, Nathanson (1999) obtained a sample of elementary school-aged children from two communities outside of the university community to try to increase the variety of participants in her sample. As Nathanson pointed out, samples within the university community were more likely to be 'practiced' research participants and be more educated, two factors the author believed might interfere with her investigation of parent mediation (control of and commentary about their children's television programs) and children's television viewing habits.

In some cases, survey research questions specifically call for a nonrandom sampling method. In organizational communications, network studies emphasize the uniqueness of each network as a whole system. In such studies, the selection method for network analysis is almost always purposive or snowball sampling, rather than random, because the network researcher aims to sample the entire social system. In media effects research, Morton and Duck (2000) wanted to know how gay men's attitudes toward safer sex practices were affected if they were dependent on the media for information. The researchers used a modified snowball sampling technique to recruit gay men to participate. Morton and Duck asked a group of gay men to refer other gay men through personal contact; the researchers also solicited study participation from gay men through university campus groups. If Morton and Duck had recruited their sample through traditional advertising, they may have obtained a sample already biased toward media dependency.

To summarize, the sample selection process for survey research can be accomplished by using either random or nonrandom sampling techniques. If you are interested in obtaining a sample that is a representative subset of its population, then random methods are preferred. If you are not interested in generalizing the study's findings beyond its immediate context, or if you face special constraints on sampling imposed by the context, then you may select a nonrandom method.

Capturing Self-reports and Other-reports

As noted earlier, survey research asks individuals to supply information about themselves, about others, about groups to which they belong, or about whole networks of which they are members. Generally, survey questions address beliefs, attitudes, emotions, behaviours, or demographic characteristics. This information can be gathered through interviews or by administering questionnaires. In the following section, you will learn about the types of interviews you may conduct and how these methods differ from administering questionnaires.

Types of Survey Interviews

When you collect survey data by interviews, you must make several decisions. The first decision concerns the setting for data collection. You can meet participants face-to-face either in a laboratory setting or in the field. If a field setting is selected, you can intercept participants in a public setting, or you can solicit interviews over the telephone. You can meet with individuals, or groups, or conduct extensive interviews throughout whole networks. Second, you must decide what to ask during the interview and how you will format your questions. For example, will the interview be formal or informal? Third, you must also consider your role as the interviewer. In preparing for the interview process, you must decide the degree of participation you will take as the interviewer, and how much training you must receive. Each of these decisions comes with a set of distinctive advantages and disadvantages.

Interviews can be arranged with individual participants, pairs, or groups face-to-face either in a field setting or in a laboratory setting. Natural settings are less likely to foster artificial effects, but they may come with distractions that detract from the interview. Some researchers combine interview questions with other forms of media in order to focus attention on the topic at hand. Participants can be asked to consider any form of text or artefact—be it an audio clip, photograph, video, or anything else relevant—before responding to questions. Other researchers try to compromise on their choice of setting by constructing laboratory settings that resemble the natural environment. Others still use more than one setting for data collection in a single study in order to ameliorate the effects of any one site. For example, Hodson and Vannini (2007) studied residents of Gabriola Island, British Columbia, to see how their dependence on a single ferry affected their concept of time. The researchers interviewed island residents while they were commuting on the ferry and in their homes. Krcmar and Valkenburg (1999) interviewed children to assess their perceptions of whether violence in television programs should be considered justified or unjustified; these interviews took place in the children's homes and in a day care setting.

Face-to-face interviews with individual participants, also called personal interviews, offer unique advantages. It is much easier to establish a climate of trust between the interviewer and the participant if they meet personally than if they talk over the phone or by mailed questionnaire. In a climate of trust, the participant is inclined to respond to all questions, and response rates are typically higher. It is also possible to access more information; the interviewer can probe participants for more in-depth responses, and can monitor participants' nonverbal reactions for further meaning and nuance. This ability is especially important when participants cannot read fluently. This may happen, for example, if English is not the participant's mother tongue, or when the questions are complex and need further explanation (Mertens, 1998).

Sometimes, face-to-face interviews can foster apprehension in participants, especially if a researcher asks to enter a participant's home (Watt & van den Berg, 1995). **Intercept surveys** can overcome this concern. In an intercept survey, you recruit participants in a public place, such as a sidewalk or park. The public setting reassures both participants and researchers about privacy and safety issues, particularly since the setting provides relative anonymity to participants. However, you must remember that spaces such as shopping malls are private spaces; some malls strictly prohibit all research by outsiders and prosecute researchers

as trespassers. More importantly, intercept surveys may lack external validity. You must ensure that your study's purpose is addressed adequately by the individuals found in whatever public space you select.

As an illustration, Feagan and Ripmeester (2001) explored the significance of lawns in residential neighbourhoods. They wanted to know how homeowners conceived the traditional green grass lawn at a time of growing environmental concerns, when native plants were promoted as alternative ground cover. Feagan and Ripmeester recruited their survey sample from two different groups of homeowners: those with traditional green grass lawns and those with alternative lawn coverings. They found participants by driving through residential neighbourhoods until they found an alternative lawn; they then approached the homeowner and the homeowner's neighbours. Taken together, the two groups provided a breadth of data to probe the surprisingly political tension over lawn care, but also the points that both groups shared.

Depending on the nature of the study, it may be easier to interview participants collectively. One such interview strategy is the focus group. A **focus group** is a small group of respondents (between 4 and 10 participants) who are selected by convenience, purposive, or snowball sampling methods. The format of the interview is loosely structured so that a range of information may be collected about a particular subject (Krueger, 1994; Morgan, 1988; Watt & van den Berg, 1995). For example, Hall (2006) used focus groups to explore what young adults value about reality television programming. Hall was interested in identifying attributes of various reality programs, how realism was evaluated, and which attributes were found most enjoyable. Hall (1999) also used focus groups to gather data from professionals regarding their perceptions of gender differences in the workplace as they are manifested in daily interactions and experiences. In this case, focus groups composed of male and female professionals mimicked a small work setting.

Bradford et al. (1999) listed three advantages of using focus groups. First, the 'interactive effects of group settings' help to focus on participants' perceptions, attitudes, and behaviours to explore a specified concept from the perspective of the participants rather than the researcher. Second, focus groups may increase the level of self-disclosure for participants from cultures that are more collective than individualistic. In this case, participants' responses are seen as parts of a whole group discussion rather than singular expressions. The third advantage of focus groups, as identified by Bradford et al., is that focus groups facilitate brainstorming around a specific concept or topic. As Bradford et al. (1999) noted, 'people are more inclined to disclose information amid the security of others similar to themselves' (p. 105).

There are disadvantages to face-to-face interviews and focus groups. If participants are selected using non-random sampling methods, the sample obtained may be less representative and may lack external validity. More practically, both techniques are costly in terms of money and time, since they are more labour intensive than other forms of data collection. By extension, they also require the most intensive form of training to ensure that interviewers are properly prepared. The relative advantages and disadvantages of personal interviews and focus groups are listed in Table 7.1.

The alternative to collecting data via a face-to-face interview or focus group is the mediated interview. **Telephone surveys** provide some distinct advantages. First, you can obtain more representative samples if you use a participant selection method such as the RDD procedure discussed in the previous section. Telephone interviews also eliminate many privacy and safety concerns. Respondents may be more honest since they cannot see the interviewer; that is, the interviewer's appearance and demeanour cannot influence the respondents' answers, and the interviewer cannot confront the respondents personally. Generally, the use of telephones can enhance interviewer consistency. Interviewers are often located at a research centre and may have scripts and computers to aid data collection.

TABLE 7.1 Advantages and Disadvantages of Face-to-Face and Focus Group Interviews

ADVANTAGES	DISADVANTAGES
Face-to-face personal interviews:	**Personal interviews and focus groups:**
1. Easier to establish a rapport and climate of trust.	1. Can lead to hesitancy in participants, especially in response to sensitive questions.
2. More difficult for participants to avoid answering any item.	2. Can foster apprehension in participants, especially when researchers are required to enter participants' homes.
3. Can probe for more in-depth responses.	
4. Can monitor participants' nonverbal reactions.	3. Most expensive form of data collection in terms of labour and time.
5. Can help to clarify any questions participants find unclear.	4. Require the most intensive form of interviewer training.
6. Can combine interview questions with some other form of media as part of the questioning.	5. Samples may not be representative, posing greater threats to external validity.
Focus groups:	6. Some groups may exert conformity pressure over individual responses.
1. Loosely structured format for collecting wide range of information.	
2. May help young children feel at ease with adult interviewers.	
3. Group formats tend to stimulate a greater variety of feedback as a result of brainstorming.	
4. Help to explore a specified concept from the perspective of the participants rather than that of the researcher.	
5. May increase the level of self-disclosure for participants from cultures that are more collective than individualistic.	

The relative advantages and disadvantages of intercept and telephone surveys are listed in Table 7.2.

Technology assists research in many ways. While some telephone surveys also involve the use of computers to help collect data, some computer programs can assist or even conduct complete interviews without human involvement or interference. **Computer-assisted interviews** are programs that provide greater consistency by prompting interviewers with the appropriate questions to ask at every phase of the interview. Some telephone interviews are now entirely conducted by computers, particularly those for consumer surveys and public opinion polls. In these interviews, a computer asks you to indicate your preferences using the touch-tone keypad on your phone or by speaking a simple response clearly. Your response is then converted into digitalized information that is read and measured as part of the same software package.

Some researchers have turned to Internet surveys, which means that every stage of recruiting, data collection, and analysis may occur via technology. Some companies will train individuals to construct online surveys using prefabricated formats. This trend is likely to gain momentum since the Internet makes recruiting remarkably efficient and cost effective. For example, SurveyMonkey started in 1999 and is now one of the major companies collecting data online. Other companies such as Zoomerang produce software for survey design. However, the convenience of prefab survey formats and online recruiting does not remove the need for intelligent research design. Nor does convenience ensure that participants are treated ethically. Moreover, companies like SurveyMonkey may actually interfere with sampling strategies and response rates as individuals and groups become inundated with recruiting appeals.

As survey designs incorporate more digital technology, they face certain disadvantages not associated with face-to-face techniques. For example, respondents may become less willing to disclose information to a machine than to a person. Many respondents distrust any approach conducted by telephone as a veiled marketing pitch, and frequently use call display and answering machines to screen calls. Similarly, online recruiting may be hampered by email programs that filter spam. Even once recruited, participants have no

TABLE 7.2 Advantages and Disadvantages of Intercept and Telephone Surveys

ADVANTAGES	DISADVANTAGES
Intercept surveys:	**Intercept surveys:**
1. Less costly than personal interviews.	1. Participants frequently pressed for time.
2. Provide relative anonymity to participants.	2. Difficult to create representative samples.
3. Public setting reassures both participants and researchers about privacy and safety issues.	3. If out of doors, poor weather can reduce participation.
	4. Some privately owned locations prohibit research (e.g. shopping malls).
Telephone surveys:	
1. Provide more representative samples.	**Telephone surveys:**
2. Eliminate many privacy and safety concerns.	1. Respondents may actually become less willing to disclose information because of the less personal format.
3. Respondents may be more honest if they are not confronted personally by an interviewer.	2. Interviews cannot be as long as those conducted in person.
4. Interviewer's presence cannot influence the way in which questions are answered.	3. Greater distrust of telephone surveys as veiled marketing devices.
5. Interviewers are often located at a research centre where supervisors may be available to answer any questions interviewers may have.	4. Respondents frequently use their call display features or answering machines to screen callers.
	5. Respondents can break off interview at any point simply by hanging up.

loyalty to a machine. This means that the length of an interview cannot be as long or as complicated as those conducted by a person because participants can break off the interview at any point simply by hanging up the phone or logging off the website. That said, recent evidence indicates that digital technology is highly successful in one type of survey design: panel studies with longitudinal analysis. Participants who have committed themselves for the duration of a study find it more convenient to use technology to respond to the same survey over several points in time (Hoppe, 2000). Table 7.3 lists a variety of advantages and disadvantages associated with computer-assisted and computer-mediated interviews.

Formats for Survey Interviews

Once you have decided on the type of survey interview you will conduct, you then need to select a format that will determine how questions are asked and what format their content will take. There are three formats for interview questions: structured, semi-structured, and unstructured. **Structured interviews** have 'schedules' that dictate what questions to ask and when to ask them. They have the following characteristics: (1) The number of questions and their wording must remain identical for all participants; (2) the questions must be presented in the same order; and (3) researchers must not clarify or explain any question at any time during the interview process, even when asked. Researchers who use structured interviews observe these strict requirements in order to preserve the quality of their data. They want to ensure that all variations

in the respondents' answers can be attributed to the respondents and not to the interviewing process itself (Frankfort-Nachmias & Nachmias, 1996).

Most researchers who use structured interviews believe that the interviewer should function as a neutral medium and not affect responses in any way. This belief is based on the assumption that every question will mean exactly the same thing to each participant and that the 'interviewer's presence should not affect a respondent's perception of a question or the answer given' (Babbie, 1995, p. 264). The assumption of complete neutrality on the part of an interviewer necessitates that he or she play the role of detached observer. Even when you ask a respondent to clarify a response, you must be careful not to 'in any way affect the nature of the subsequent response' (Babbie, 1995, p. 267). Watt and van den Berg (1995) have described the following set of rules for interviewers:

> Intrude in the research process as little as possible. This means that the interviewer should never direct the respondent toward an answer, should never be judgmental, [and] should not interpret the respondent's answers according to his or her own beliefs or values. The interviewer must be consistent in his or her communication style and language, so that each respondent is exposed to the same kind of measurement environment. (p. 359)

Clearly, the scheduled interview format establishes very specific guidelines for interviewers. New interviewers

TABLE 7.3 Advantages and Disadvantages of Computer-assisted Interviews

ADVANTAGES	DISADVANTAGES
Computer-assisted interviews:	Computer-assisted interviews:
1. Have all the advantages associated with telephone interviews.	1. Have all the disadvantages associated with telephone surveys.
2. Can provide greater consistency by prompting both interviewers and participants with the appropriate questions to ask at every phase of the interview.	2. Are more likely to be seen as an impersonal intrusion.
3. May be preferred in longitudinal studies in the place of diaries, especially when the same information is repeatedly collected.	

are trained and evaluated before they may contact participants. Sometimes, the interviewer must practise until the lead researcher 'is convinced that the interviewer is sufficiently low-key and consistent and will not bias the results' (Watt & van den Berg, 1995, p. 359).

Semi-structured interviews, which are sometimes called focused interviews (Frankfort-Nachmias & Nachmias, 1996, p. 234), have the following characteristics: (1) the interviewer uses a discussion 'guide' that lists topics of interest rather than a strict interview schedule; (2) the discussion guide refers to experiences or concepts that have been analyzed and defined prior to the interview; (3) the guide focuses on the participants' understanding of each experience or concept; and (4) the experiences or concepts which are discussed will be ones that all participants have in common.

Hodson and Vannini (2007) used semi-structured interviews to study the effects of communication and transportation technology on human perception. As noted earlier, Gabriola Island is accessible only by a single ferry and residents must adjust their lives to its schedule. Hence, these islanders provided an excellent case study to see if they experienced a different sense of time due to their dependence on this one technology, the ferry. Participants were recruited through interception on the ferry itself and through snowball sampling. The questions served only to stimulate discussion during each interview. Five topics were raised: commuting habits, attitudes towards the ferry, life on the island, views of life off the island, and opinions about the ferry's significance for island life (p. 265). They researchers concluded that islanders did share a more casual sense of time which they called 'island time'.

Unstructured interviews have the greatest amount of flexibility. In this type of interview, you will not have any pre-specified set of questions. Instead, you will rely entirely on the participants to identify experiences and concepts that seem significant or meaningful. You may also use initial interviews to help construct questions as probes for subsequent interviews. The purely unstructured approach to interviewing is often associated with interpretive and critical methods such as discourse analysis and ethnography (see chapters 10 and 11). Within these paradigms, you are concerned with

the subjective points of view expressed by your participants. It would not be important to you, therefore, to keep the structure of the interview uniform for every participant. You will learn more about these differences in the last section of this chapter.

As we noted above, researchers who use structured interviews place strict limits on the role of the interviewer. By contrast, researchers who use semi-structured and unstructured interviews do not expect the same precision and consistency of wording from one participant to the next. Nonetheless, if you want to understand an experience or concept from your participant's perspective, then you cannot lead your participant toward certain interpretations; you cannot put words in his or her mouth. At the same time, you may grant yourself more leeway to establish a bond with your participants in order to gain their confidence. This is a fine balance to strike and, hence, the same level of training that applies to structured interviews can be applied to semi-structured and unstructured interviews.

Questionnaires

After interviews, the questionnaire is the next most common way of capturing survey research data. A **questionnaire** is a written form used to collect self-report and other-report data. Questionnaires can be read in structured interview settings with or without telephone and computer mediation, mailed out to participants, or administered through email lists or Internet websites. When using a questionnaire, you must decide upon the structure of the questionnaire and the means to deliver it. As with interviews, every decision you make about a questionnaire has advantages and disadvantages.

The term **questionnaire architecture** was coined to capture the general structure of the questionnaire (Watt & van den Berg, 1995, p. 368). This term focuses very nicely on the care you should invest in the design of the questionnaire. You must consider its length, comprehensibility, and the order of questions. First, length is a critical factor. Questionnaires that are too long will fatigue participants. When that happens, participants choose not to complete certain items, or even the entire questionnaire, because the task is too demanding.

Second, you must consider the clarity of your questionnaire. Because participants often complete questionnaires without a researcher present, both the instructions to participants and the questions themselves should be easy to understand and self-administer. If you have a research team to administer the questionnaire, then it still must be sufficiently clear for them to use without direct supervision. The survey questionnaire should come with a cover letter and/or a set of instructions that identify the basic purpose of the study and how to complete the questionnaire. All three parts—the cover letter, instructions, and questionnaire—should be clearly worded and use a vocabulary appropriate for the age and education level of the respondents. To assess the potential effects of length and clarity, the questionnaire should be pilot tested before it is administered to the study's selected sample.

Third, you must consider the order of your questions. It is critical that questions asked early on will not influence the way participants respond to later questions. These are called **order effects**. For example, you may ask participants to indicate their level of religious devotion early in a questionnaire, and this may affect later questions regarding their attendance at services or the frequency with which they engage in meditations or prayer. Most participants respond in ways that make them appear to be consistent. However, the pattern of order effects isn't always clear. Some researchers have found that asking a specific question first (e.g. like that about attendance at religious services) is just as likely to affect a general response (e.g. like that about religious devotion). Sometimes, researchers randomize the order of questions to eliminate order effects. However, randomizing the order can make the questions appear chaotic if participants must jump from one topic to another, and it still does not guarantee there will be no order effect. You will do well to construct an order that participants find easy, interesting, and topically consistent or logically arranged (Babbie, 1995, p. 151; Berger, 1998, pp. 40–42).

Survey Questions and Their Formats

In this section, we describe three kinds of questions that are categorized by the types of information they seek. We then describe four basic formats for questions used in questionnaires. Each format has its own functions, and these functions can shift depending on the purpose of the research.

Most survey research looks for three different kinds of information: (1) Information that describes participants' social and economic characteristics, which are called demographics; (2) information about participants' beliefs, values, and attitudes; and (3) information about participants' behaviours. First, as a researcher, you may collect descriptive information about the participants' demographics. As we mentioned earlier in this chapter, demographics are common identifying characteristics such as age or ethnicity. You must be sensitive in your handling of these questions (Mertens, 1998, pp. 121–122).

The second type of information you may collect concerns participants' beliefs, values, and attitudes. These lines of thinking or mental state are known as intangibles and can include many things such as ideas, thoughts, goals, preferences, superstitions, fears, and articles of faith. You may also ask participants about their perceptions of these intangibles in other people.

The third type of information you may collect concerns participants' behaviours. Behaviours can include any form of physical activity, though researchers most often explore ritual behaviours. Such behaviours might include television viewing habits, ways of performing work, or daily habits. Questions about behaviours must also be handled with caution. Participants may view behaviours as either threatening or nonthreatening, and this distinction may influence their responses. Nonthreatening behaviours are those that are generally socially acceptable and thus easy to talk about, like the number of times per week a person watches the evening news or how frequently a person emails friends. Threatening behaviours are those that carry some social stigma, and participants may feel defensive when discussing them. As you construct questions, you should avoid using provocative language and make sure your questions are not leading. **Leading questions** direct respondents to answer in a specific way. For example, asking, 'How many times a week do you abuse drugs?' may be provocative *and* leading. It may encourage participants to give you socially desirable responses regardless of their actual behaviours. One way to increase your chances of collecting truthful responses is to assure respondents of complete confidentiality.

All three kinds of questions (i.e. those relating to demographics; those relating to beliefs, values, or attitudes; and those relating to behaviours) can be worded in multiple ways, but they have only two basic formats: open and closed. **Open-ended questions** are those that ask respondents to provide spontaneous answers or to discuss an identified topic in their own words. For example, Mahtani (2008) used focus groups to understand how immigrants to Canada respond to Canadian televised news broadcasts. A premise of the study was that significant demographic differences among audience members can lead to significantly different responses to the same broadcasts. Mahtani asked participants open-ended questions about their opinions of Canadian televised news coverage, and began simply by asking where they looked for news. Hence, participants reported their experiences in their own terms, truly an important factor if researchers were to uncover significantly different perspectives about Canadian televised news broadcasts. Frequently, open-ended questions are used in this way to explore new conceptual territory.

Closed-format questions ask respondents to 'choose from a fixed set of alternatives or to give a single numerical value' (Watt & van den Berg, 1995, p. 366). Examples of closed-format questions include those that ask respondents to identify their biological sex or to indicate their level of agreement with various beliefs or attitudes (i.e. as on a Likert scale). Questions that specify all possible response alternatives are known as scaled items. You will learn more about these types of responses in the next section of this chapter.

Both open-ended and closed-format questions have advantages and disadvantages. Generally speaking, open-ended questions are harder to code and can lead to greater problems with consistency as a result. That said, open-ended questions tend to gather more precise data. They are also helpful when addressing sensitive or provocative issues. If you word a question in such a way that a participant understands its importance, then he or she may be more willing to share personal information. For example, an open question such as, 'Many people complain that tax forms are too complicated to complete accurately. What do

you think?' may elicit more truthful responses than the closed question, 'Do you fudge on your tax form? Yes / No'. Still, closed-format questions generate data that are much easier to handle, although it is acknowledged that this data will reflect the respondents' perceptions and interpretations with less precision. We will encounter these issues again when we consider warrants for survey research.

Questionnaires can also make use of filter and contingency questions. These question formats screen a participant's responses to ensure that only relevant data is collected, which can save time for both the participant and the researcher. **Filter questions** direct participants to respond to specific portions of the questionnaire that are most appropriate for them. **Contingency questions** depend on responses to filter questions. For example, let's say that Question 3 asks, 'Do you own an MP3 player? If no, then skip to question #10.' This is a filter question, since it filters respondents into two groups: those with MP3 players and those without them. By contrast, Question 4 may ask 'How long have you owned an MP3 player?' This is a contingency question. A response to Question 4 is contingent on the participant's response to Question 3. If the participant does not own an MP3 player, then Question 4 is irrelevant.

To summarize, you should follow a few simple guidelines when constructing a questionnaire. These are listed in Exhibit 7.4. In the next two sections of this chapter, you will learn in detail how questionnaire items are constructed as instruments and how their use is validated.

Instrumentation and the Measurement of Survey Data

If you accept the underlying assumptions of the discovery paradigm, you will test your hypotheses by operationalizing your concepts and by statistical analysis. In this section, you will explore operationalization, which addresses how survey data is defined and measured. This section is followed by a brief explanation of which statistical analyses are appropriate in survey research. Note also that a more lengthy discussion of statistical analysis can be found in chapter 14, on inferential statistics.

1. Avoid making the questionnaire too lengthy.
2. Make the instructions and questions clear.
3. Make the instructions and questions easy to understand.
4. Consider the possibility of order effects, test for them, and make adjustments accordingly.
5. Avoid using provocative language.
6. Avoid using leading questions.
7. Use open-ended questions and questions that provide support for answering truthfully when questions are potentially threatening.
8. Be sensitive to diversity issues when asking for demographic information.
9. Pilot the questionnaire with a sample of people who are appropriate to the study.

Operationalization of Variables

Earlier in this chapter, we noted that survey research traditionally relies on descriptive and explanatory claims. Such claims propose that certain variables are related in specific ways. The primary goal of research is to test these proposed relationships by gathering data, or 'empirical indicators'. When researchers identify the empirical indicators of their variables, and create research instruments to take the relevant measurements, the process is called **operationalization**. Even when your research is concerned with intangibles, intangibles usually manifest themselves in a statement, behaviour, or artefact that can be observed and recorded by the researcher.

Recall that you learned about operational definitions and measurement scales in chapter 5, on data. A good operational definition will specify what you need to measure a construct. As you will see in chapters 13 and 14, on statistics, constructs measured with nominal and ordinal scales result in **categorical variables**. By contrast, ratio and interval measurements are called **continuous variables** because they provide information along a continuum. The difference between categorical and continuous scales has serious implications for the types of analyses that you can use to test your hypotheses.

For example, Dupagne (2006) wanted to discover what variables could predict an individual's awareness of digital television. The variables he isolated were an individual's demographic data, current media use, current technology ownership, and perceptions of the technology's complexity and relative advantages. His questionnaire used three of the four measurement scales we have just described. First, Dupagne measured some demographic data, such as gender, with a nominal scale (p. 123). Second, he assessed participant awareness of digital television with an interval scale. He asked participants how familiar they were with digital television and measured their responses across four points ranging from 'not familiar at all' to 'very familiar'. Third, he measured media use through five questions using ratio scales. For example, he asked 'How many days a week, if any, do you read a daily newspaper?' (Dupagne, 2006, p. 122). His use of all three scales is illustrated in Exhibit 7.5.

In the same study, Dupagne (2006) operationalized the perceived complexity of digital television using a Likert scale to measure responses. Participants were given four statements such as 'Learning new technologies is a frustrating experience for me', and 'I find new technologies intimidating'. They were then asked to indicate their level of agreement across a five-point range from 'strongly agree' to 'strongly disagree' (Dupagne, 2006, p. 122).

Once you have operationalized your construct, designed your survey and then administered it, you must analyze your data. Depending on the nature of your data and the scales used to measure each variable, certain statistical tests can be used, which are discussed chapters 13 and 14. Before statistical analyses can be performed, however, you must assess the validity and reliability of the sampling and data collection methods used in your survey to establish the worth of the data as evidence. Validity and reliability assessments are the last topic we consider in this chapter on survey research.

Survey Research Warrants

As you learned in chapter 6, warrants are the standards we use to evaluate whether particular evidence

---

EXHIBIT 7.5   Survey Sample with Multiple Variables and Scales

DIGITAL TV AWARENESS SURVEY

Demographic variables:

Age: Year of birth (interval scale)

Gender: Male or female (nominal scale)

Income: answers ranged on a 5-point scale from 'less than $25,000' to 'more than $100,000' (interval scale)

Digital TV Awareness Variable:

Respondents were asked to indicate their familiarity with digital television by using an interval scale:

'How familiar are you with the new technology known as digital television or DTV?'

Responses ranged along four points from 1 = 'Not familiar at all' to 4 = 'Very familiar'.

Media Use Variable:

Respondents were asked to indicate the frequency of their media use by using ratio scales:

1.   On average, how many days a week, if any, do you read a daily newspaper? (Range: 0–7 days)
2.   On average, how many hours a day, if any, do you watch television? (Range: 0–1,440 minutes)
3.   On average, how many hours a day, if any, do you listen to radio? (Range: 0–1,440 minutes)

Perceived Complexity Variable:

Respondents were asked to indicate their level of agreement with a series of statements describing the complexity of new technology by using an interval scale:

1.   Learning new technologies is a frustrating experience for me.
2.   I often find new technologies intimidating.
3.   I often feel anxious when I use new technologies for the first time.
4.   I am often afraid that new technologies may not work properly.

Responses ranged on 5-point Likert scale from 1 = 'Strongly disagree' to 5 = 'Strongly agree'.

Source: Adapted from Dupagne (2006).

---

is suitable to support a claim. In survey research, our standards focus on validity, a concern for accuracy or precision. Validity has two aspects. First, it refers to the internal validity of a survey study; that is, the ability of the survey to test your claims accurately. In survey research, internal validity is almost synonymous with measurement because surveys generally succeed or fail based on data collection strategies, not on data analysis. This leads us to the second aspect of validity. In survey research, data collection strategies aim to maximize response rates. External validity is the ability to generalize your results from representative samples to larger populations. In this section, we examine validity and reliability and how these are assessed in survey research.

Response Rates

What is an acceptable response rate? There are widely varying answers to that question. Babbie (1995) recommended that survey researchers acquire responses from at least half of the individuals contacted for any one study. This would create a response rate of at least 50%. Babbie (1995) also warned that securing a high response rate is not your only goal when recruiting participants. You should also recruit samples that are not biased by your selection process.

There are two types of response rates: total response rate and item response rate. The **total response rate** refers to the percentage of total surveys successfully completed and collected. The **item response rate** refers to the percentage of completed items on each individual survey. When whole questionnaires or specific items are not answered, this constitutes missing data, and missing data can affect the validity and reliability of any survey. There are many reasons why surveys are not completed. Fear of exposure, or of being singled out, may deter potential recruits from participating at all. Questionnaires that are too long, too complex, too vague, or too provocative may also prompt participants to skip questions.

You can improve your response rate by adjusting the format of the interview or the questionnaire. As we noted earlier in this chapter, each question format has relative advantages and disadvantages. For example, if your survey asks very complex and emotionally sensitive questions, then you may produce a higher response rate by conducting a small number of personal interviews than you would by administering telephone interviews or mailed questionnaires. Interviews of any type can increase response rates because the researcher is present to clarify questions, to monitor respondents' nonverbal reactions, and to probe respondents for more information. In the case of questionnaires, you can contact individuals to follow-up on questionnaires that have not been returned, and this may increase the total response rate. Increasing the amount of information collected usually increases the internal validity and reliability of the responses. Adopting strategies to increase total response rates will also improve external validity.

Establishing Valid Measurement

There are several types of measurement validity, as noted in chapter 6. However, here we will focus on how measurement validity is established in survey research.

Measurement validity requires that you have a clear rationale for your definition of a variable. Remember that your definition does not have to be wholly new. If you have conducted a literature review, you may draw upon existing definitions of the same variable. Ultimately, whatever definition you use should be logical, comprehensive, and defensible. If it is, then your variable should possess content validity. In some cases, when the measurable items of your variable are comprehensive, then the variable may have predictive qualities; in other words, your observations of certain items may allow you to predict certain outcomes.

You may also want to assess construct validity. You'll recall that constructs are variables that describe intangibles. Infante and Wigley's (1986) Verbal Aggressiveness Scale is one example of a construct we have described in this text. You may assess construct validity by evaluating the items identified for measurement and clarifying which are essential and which are not to understand the construct. For example, Levine et al. (2004) conducted two studies of Infante and Wigley's scale. Levine et al. compared aggressively worded items on the scale with other antisocial measures (e.g. narcissism) and the benevolently worded items on the scale with other pro-social measures (e.g. empathy). The researchers then used these comparisons to assess the various dimensions of the scale. They found that the scale might assess two factors or variables instead of just one.

Assessments of validity go hand-in-hand with estimates of reliability. Validity tests establish warrants for the accuracy of a study's measures, whereas reliability estimates establish warrants for the consistency of a study's measures. Babbie (1995) described the relationship between validity and reliability with reference to a bull's-eye. Measures that are valid but not reliable are like shots that scatter around the centre in no particular pattern. The measures have small amounts of error that infiltrate from a variety of sources. This type of error is called **random error** or **noise**. Measures that are high in reliability but are not valid show all of the shots clustered together but off centre. The measures may be consistent, but they are consistently wrong. This type of error is called **constant error** or **bias**. Finally, measures that are valid and reliable are like shots that fall dead centre and cluster closely together. They are not only accurate; they are consistently accurate (Babbie, 1995, p. 128).

Establishing Reliable Measurement

Each type of measurement reliability you learned about in chapter 6 is relevant to survey research. In this section, we briefly explore how researchers establish stability, homogeneity, and equivalence in measurement.

You may recall that test-retest reliability occurs when a survey that has been administered to a group of people is given again, to those same people, on a later occasion. If the same people achieve consistent scores over time, test-retest reliability has been achieved. To demonstrate test-retest reliability, you need to consider what interval of time is appropriate. If your measurement is repeated too soon, participants may recall the items, and their scores may not have changed because of familiarity. If too much time elapses before the second measurement, then real change may have occurred which may affect the variable being measured. Obviously, the appropriate time interval depends on the concept being measured. For example, consider reading ability. For children, reading ability is very likely to change over a six-month span, but for adults it likely will not. For any one variable, then, you must consider how much time is appropriate between your test and retest.

The second way to estimate the reliability of a survey instrument is to assess its internal consistency. Researchers use several methods to check the patterns of response in interval scales, such as Likert scales and semantic differentials. One common technique is called the split-half technique in which one half of the items on a scale are randomly selected and correlated with responses from the other half. As with any correlation, the closer the calculated values are to 1.00, the higher the estimate of consistency. We will consider statistical correlation in more detail in chapter 14.

The final way researchers assess the reliability of variable measurement is to establish equivalence of measurement. Recall that equivalence estimates consistency in two ways. Intercoder agreement verifies the agreement among researchers about how qualitative data are interpreted or categorized, while the alternate forms method verifies the consistency of measurement results yielded by more than one measure of the same construct. Whenever several coders categorize data according to the operational definition of a variable, we expect their decisions to be the same. Intercoder agreement can be expressed as a statistical correlation between the values of +/−.00 and +/−1.00. As we noted above, the closer the value approaches 1.00, the higher the level of agreement.

You should always provide some assessment of reliability and validity of your measures to establish warrants that connect your data to your claims. Measurements that are valid and reliable are not only accurate, they are consistently accurate, and that is a powerful warrant for your research. Having discussed these warrants, and the ways you can highlight the reliability and validity of your measurements, we now turn to the topic of the ethical considerations that need to be taken into account when conducting survey research.

Ethical Issues in Survey Research

Whenever you work with human research participants, you must consider the ethical dimensions of your research design. With surveys, your primary ethical considerations relate to the way data is collected and reported.

First, data collection for surveys must be done with your participants' informed consent. As you will recall from chapter 2, on ethics, all participation in research must be completely voluntary. This means that you have an obligation to inform each potential recruit of every risk that the study might entail. It also means that participants can stop participating at any point. You cannot in any way coerce them to participate or to continue to participate once the study has begun. Obtaining such consent is not always a simple process. If participants are not legally competent to make informed decisions on their own, then informed consent must be obtained from their guardians. When studies address personal issues or 'risky' behaviours, researchers must be very careful not to violate the privacy rights of participants if their guardians want access to the findings. For example, suppose you were examining links between advertising and teen drinking. Even seemingly benign questions about family behaviours surrounding food and drink may foster anxiety in parents who then may force their children to reveal what was told to the researchers.

The second ethical consideration for surveys concerns confidentiality. Most researchers using intercept, telephone, mail, and Internet surveys will guarantee their participants anonymity. That is, the participants' identities will never be revealed. During many

TABLE 7.4 Major Aspects of Survey Research

CLAIMS	DATA	WARRANTS	MANUSCRIPT FORMAT
Describe, explain, and predict	Representative samples from populations of people	• Reliability established through stability, equivalence, and homogeneity • Content, criterion, and construct validity of variable scales • Sample representativeness	Research report

interviews and focus groups, however, anonymity is not possible and instead you must consider how you will protect your participants' confidentiality. One way to reduce concerns for privacy is to guarantee that the findings will not reveal participants' identities without the participants' informed consent. For instance, in our example of advertising and teen drinking, a study could report its findings of drinking behaviours in general without revealing the names of any participants. In this way, parents would gain knowledge from the study without knowing how their own child responded to questions. The researchers' responsibility does not end with a published study, however. As long as the raw data exists researchers must guarantee their safe storage and, usually, their destruction when the analysis has concluded.

A third ethical consideration is distributive justice. Researchers collecting survey data are expected to collect representative samples where possible, and that representation should not misrepresent minorities or socioeconomic groups by selective features. For example, Friesen et al. (2009) were highly sensitive to linguistic, ethnic, and regional variations in opinion when conducting a national survey on perceptions of 'history'. The researchers sought to understand how Canadians think about 'the past' in general. To represent all Canadians fairly, national surveys must recruit participants from each region of Canada and include both francophones and anglophones. Because of the political nature of 'history', however, Friesen and his research partners also recruited three special samples

to ensure that potential minority opinions would be captured; these special samples represented aboriginals, recent immigrants, and Acadians, groups that may have strong historical reasons to perceive the past differently from other Canadians. Failure to include them may have left a significant gap in the survey's findings, and hence reproduced historical inequalities between these groups and the rest of Canada.

Summary

We have shown in this chapter that when surveys are used in communication and cultural research, they require careful preparation and handling. In the preparation of surveys, you must decide if your claims will be descriptive or explanatory. If they are explanatory, they you must decide it they should be associative or causal. Once your claims are identified, you must decide on the sources, settings, and design you will use to collect the data. You must also construct your instrument, be it an interview guide or questionnaire. When operationalizing your constructs, you must decide on the levels of measurement you will use: nominal, ordinal, interval, or ratio. Then, when administering the survey, you must establish warrants for the data collected in support of the study's claims by assessing the survey's validity and reliability. See Table 7.4 for a summary of the major aspects of survey research. You will see in chapters 13 and 14 that the specific tests of survey research questions and hypotheses are statistical analyses that require equal care in interpretation.

Key Terms

Applied research	Item response rate	Positive correlation
Bias	Intercept survey	Questionnaire architecture
Categorical variable	Leading questions	Questionnaire
Closed-format questions	Market research	Random digit dialing
Computer-assisted interviews	Mortality	Random error
Constant error	Negative correlation	Semi-structured interview
Contingency questions	Network analysis	Structured interview
Continuous variable	Noise	Telephone survey
Correlation	Open-ended questions	Total response rate
Face-to-face interview	Operationalization	Unstructured interview
Filter questions	Order effects	
Focus group	Political polling research	

Discussion Questions

1. Why are interviews sometimes conducted 'at random' on a street corner not really random?
2. Why do you think random sampling is essential within the discovery paradigm, but not within the interpretive and critical paradigms?
3. If you wanted to study children's reactions to frightening movies using a survey, would you use interviews or questionnaires? What considerations would affect your decision?
4. Would discovery researchers prefer structured or unstructured interview formats? Explain your answer.
5. Because surveys are traditionally associated with discovery research, how do the warrants of validity and reliability differ from those used in interpretive research or critical research?

Try It!

1. This activity asks you to conduct a simple survey. It can be completed by an individual, but it will be more efficient to work in a group with two or more other members. Depending on the size of your tutorial group, it may also be adapted as a tutorial exercise.

    Some surveys involve long questionnaires that explore highly complex relationships between variables. Not all surveys need to be complex, however. Indeed, public opinion polls that track trends in public opinion are usually quite short and probe very specific issues. For this activity, you are asked to conduct a simple poll of your classmates in your methods course. Your goal is to explore the relationship between three demographic categories and a particular pastime.

    Process
    1. With your research team, select one of the two survey questionnaires provided on the next page, or craft one of your own with your instructor's permission.
    2. Select a method to deliver the survey. It is recommended that you use face-to-face interviews, but you may select telephone or email contact. Your selection should fit with the time available for this activity.
    3. Create a suitable interview schedule or questionnaire for your survey. Remember to be an ethical researcher. Each person you recruit must be given sufficient information to make an informed decision about his or her participation.
    4. Conduct the survey. Try to recruit 20 participants.
    5. Organize the responses. Your first step will be to identify every unique response to items 3, 4 (b), and 5. Your second step will be to count the number of times that each response was given.
    6. Look for patterns in the responses. Ask yourself: do the answers to items 4 and 5 change depending on the age, gender, or hometown or your participants?
    7. Draft a conclusion. What is the strongest relationship you have found between the three demographic items and your two questions about pastimes?

2. This activity asks you to think about your experience conducting your poll. It, too, can be completed by an individual, but it may be more informative to work with your research team, or with members of other research teams from your class who also completed the first activity.

    Post-Poll Debriefing
    1. (a) What ethical concerns surrounded your poll?
       (b) What steps did you take to ensure that the poll was ethical?
    2. Consider the questions used in your poll.
       (a) What kinds of questions were used in this poll?
       (a) Were the questions effective to collect the information you wanted?
       (c) How might you have revised the questions, and how would your revisions have changed the responses?

3. Examine the demographic data.
   (a) How diverse is your sample of your class-mates? Do you believe that your sample is a fair representation of the class?
   (b) How might your findings be different if you had sampled:
     - professors from your university?
     - your parents and their friends?
     - a random selection of pedestrians on a downtown street?
   (c) What could you have done to ensure that your sample was representative?

4. Consider the categories used to organize the responses.
   (a) Did the categories in items 1, 2, and 4 capture all of the responses?
   (b) How did you categorize the responses to items 3, 4(b), and 5? And how did you justify these categories?
   (c) How difficult was it to collate all of the responses? If you conducted another poll or survey, how would you make this process more efficient?

QUESTIONNAIRE 1: MUSIC

Hello, I'm _____. I'm gathering opinion on how students enjoy music, and wonder if you'll volunteer two minutes of your time to answer five questions. These questions involve some personal information, but I will not ask for your name and your answers will remain confidential. If you choose to participate, you may pass on any questions you choose not to answer, and you may withdraw at any time. Completing the questions will be taken as tacit consent that your answers may be used in the research.

1. What is your age? (15–19, 20–24, 25–29, 30+)
2. What is your gender? (M / F)
3. Where is your childhood home?
4. (a) Do you play a musical instrument? (Y / N)
   (b) If yes, what is your favourite genre of music to play on a musical instrument?
5. What is your favourite genre of music to listen to?

Thank you!

QUESTIONNAIRE 2: SPORTS

Hello, I'm _____. I'm gathering opinion on how students enjoy sports, and wonder if you'll volunteer two minutes of your time to answer five questions. These questions involve some personal information, but I will not ask for your name and your answers will remain confidential. If you choose to participate, you may pass on any questions you choose not to answer, and you may withdraw at any time. Completing the questions will be taken as tacit consent that your answers may be used in the research.

1. What is your age? (15–19, 20–24, 25–29, 30+)
2. What is your gender? (M / F)
3. Where is your childhood home?
4. (a) Do you play any sports, either organized or not? (Y / N)
   (b) If yes, what is your favourite sport to play?
5. What is your favourite sport to watch?

Thank you!

8 Content Analysis

Introduction

In this chapter, you will learn how to conduct content analysis. As we noted in the previous chapter, content analysis focuses on messages rather than the individuals or groups who send and receive messages. Following the *research as argument* model, we will begin with claims that describe, explain, or predict specific aspects of messages in particular contexts. We shall consider the appropriate data sources for content analyses, and how you select representative samples from message populations. You will learn to divide textual data into units of analysis and how to place those units into categories according to a predetermined coding scheme. Next, we will discuss warrants for content analysis, including ways to assess the reliability of your coding decisions, the content validity of your coding scheme, and the external validity of your data sample. We conclude the chapter by looking at some ethical issues for content analysis.

Imagine that you want to understand a common type of message, such as gender representation in video games (Ivory, 2006). If you want to use textual data to explore such forms, you will probably use content analysis. **Content analysis** is primarily a quantitative method of describing and categorizing messages in specific contexts (Bereleson, 1952; Krippendorf, 2004; Neuendorf, 2002).

The textual data most commonly studied with content analysis is narrative discourse. **Narrative discourse** occurs when one communicator has greater responsibility for speaking than do others. As Smith notes, such discourse is 'characterized by relatively fixed source-receiver roles' (Smith, 1988, p. 257). For example, public speeches are characterized by fixed roles for the speaker (a.k.a. the source) and the audience (a.k.a. the receivers); the speaker clearly has greater responsibility for speaking while the audience listens. Far more commonly, however, most content analysis examines the texts produced or distributed by the mass media, such as newspaper stories, radio programming, television programs, films, websites, or advertising. By contrast, **interactive discourse**—in which responsibility for speaking is shared among all participants—is usually analyzed using methods such as conversation analysis. You can learn about this method in chapter 10, on conversation and discourse analysis. We note here, however, that content analysis is different from conversation analysis. Where a researcher using content analysis aims to discover the meaning of messages transferred through narrative discourse, a conversation analyst interprets what participants accomplish through their interactive discourses (Sigman, Sullivan, & Wendell, 1988).

Researchers who use content analysis believe that the nature of messages can be discovered through precise, systematic, and repetitive observations. For this reason, researchers using this method have typically followed the epistemological assumptions of the discovery paradigm (see Table 3.2 for a review). The goal of quantitative content analysis is to sort messages into categories and to compare the frequency with which different categories of messages occur. For example, Kubrin (2005) wanted to examine the ways that rap music represents life in inner-city American communities. She collected lyrics from 403 songs sampled from the best-selling rap CDs issued from 1992 to 2000. She then sorted the lyrics into six categories based on the following themes: the search for personal respect, a willingness to fight, the pursuit of material wealth, retaliation against slights or injuries, the objectification of women, and nihilism. Kubrin's analysis fits the discovery paradigm in several ways. First, her hypothesis was based on prior theory and research. Second, she compared the relative frequency with which each theme appeared in her sample. Third, her article is organized as a research report. Kubrin's study also fits the assumption of the discovery paradigm that researchers should produce generalizable conclusions about communication and culture. In her case, she considered how street culture and rap lyrics reinforce a common view of life in inner-city communities.

Before we look more closely at the claims content analysis can be used to support, let's briefly consider the history of this method. Over 300 years ago, in Sweden, a group of scholars and clergy members first used content analysis to examine a collection of 90 hymns called the *Songs of Zion*. The *Songs* were popular but controversial because they were not from the established hymn book of the Swedish church. Critics charged that the *Songs* were blasphemous. To settle the controversy, the scholars and clergy members identified and counted the religious symbols in the *Songs* and compared them to the symbols used in

the state-approved hymnal. When they found no significant differences between the symbols used in the *Songs* and the symbols used in the state-sanctioned hymnal, the researchers concluded that the *Songs of Zion* were acceptable alternatives to the established church music (Krippendorf, 2004).

From this beginning, content analysis was recognized as a legitimate way of analyzing the content of communication and cultural forms. In the early 1900s, as newspaper production and distribution expanded, so did the number of studies using content analysis. Early studies tracked the topics covered in the news and often described the amount of physical space devoted to each topic in terms of the number of column inches devoted to it. These studies were used by journalists, and others, to criticize and improve journalistic practices as well as to identify propaganda or unethical sources of influence. Later in the twentieth century, as movies, radio, and television grew more popular, content analysis was applied to those media as well. Today, the method is used to analyze almost every form of discourse, including those found in digital media.

For over 60 years, then, content analysis has been the primary research methodology used to make quantitative judgments about patterns and trends in the content of communication and cultural forms (e.g. Chang-Hoan & Hongsik, 2005; Druckman, 2005; Haigh et al., 2005, 2006; Ivory, 2006). Again, all of these studies—from song lyrics to radio shows, from trends in news coverage to representations in popular film and television—involve analyzing the content of textual data.

Now that you know something about the history and scope of content analysis, let's look at how you can use this research method to explore your own attempts to describe, explain, and predict the content of communication.

Claims for Content Analysis

Content analysis most commonly tests three types of claims: those that are descriptive, explanatory, and predictive. In this section, we introduce you to these types of claims and we illustrate each type with examples. It is also possible to use content analysis to test evaluative and reformist claims, as Good (2008) did with her study of journalism on climate change. If you wish to test these types of claims about textual data, however, you will need to know more about the analytical methodologies outlined in chapters 10 and 12 of this book. As you read this section, think about the claims you might want to investigate using content analysis.

Descriptive Claims

Perhaps the single most common type of claim for content analysis is description, the attempt to describe messages or their characteristics in particular cultural contexts. Quite a number of different message contexts have been described using content analysis. We've already talked about the prevalence of studies that address mass media content. In addition, there are content analyses of computer-mediated communication (e.g. Stewart, Shields, & Sen, 1998; Chang-Hoan & Hongsik, 2005), health care (e.g. Cegala, McGee, & McNeilis, 1996; Andsager & Smiley, 1998), intercultural communication (e.g. Chen, 1997; Anderson, Martin & Zhong, 1998), interpersonal relationships (e.g. Dainton, 1998), and political communication (e.g. Lasswell, 1927; Barnhurst, 2003).

Describing the characteristics of messages in these contexts is helpful for several reasons. Johnson, Smith, Mitchell, Orrego, and Yun (1999) pointed out some of these reasons in their descriptive analysis of television talk show experts:

> [T]hese findings are designed to inform better those who create the shows, those who watch the shows, and those who critique the shows, as to the content and composition of the show. It also provides evidence for or against many claims made about experts and talk shows . . . . (p. 94)

Thus, the general claim of Johnson et al.'s (1999) study described the content of televised talk shows. That said, the general claim is actually composed of three specific claims regarding (1) the issues covered by television talk show experts (e.g. family relationships, self-improvement, or crime and safety); (2) the qualifications of television talk show experts (e.g. level of education, or official versus self-proclaimed credentials); and (3) the nature of advice given by television talk show experts (e.g. specific or nonspecific suggestions). Table 8.1 shows some descriptive claims from published content analyses.

Content analysis provides an ideal basis for comparative scholarship. If the same research design can be administered to messages found in two or more social settings, then it should produce two or more sets of data that are immediately comparable. Such is the case

TABLE 8.1 Descriptive Claims in Content Analysis

RESEARCH QUESTIONS (RQs)	HYPOTHESES (H)
RQ1: 'Do the behaviors and interaction patterns of online AA groups differ from those of online nonAA support groups?' (Van Lear, Sheehan, Withers, & Walker, 2005, p. 10)	H1: In news magazine stories on the 9/11 terrorist strikes, American magazines discussed revenge more frequently than Canadian magazines. (Deveau & Fouts, 2004, p. 101)
RQ2: 'Is consumer interest in alternative medicine supported by positive media coverage, or do its critics prevail?' (Steuter, 2010, p. 58)	H2: News coverage of famous athletes who contracted HIV/AIDS differed significantly depending on the sexual orientation of each athlete. (Dworkin & Wachs, 1998, p. 5)
RQ3: 'To what extent have *The Toronto Star* and *The New York Times* depended upon official government sources in their coverage of the Iraq War?' (Ahmad, 2008, p. 36)	H3: Hegemonic discourses about Aboriginals and prostitutes framed news coverage of a serial killer's victims in Vancouver. (Jiwani & Young, 2006, pp. 896–897)

with Good's (2008) study of reporting on global climate change. After developing a research design that measured the frequency of climate change stories published in newspapers, she administered it to three different sets of newspapers: leading Canadian papers, leading American papers, and leading international papers. The raw data, grouped into these three categories, allowed her to compare national and international perspectives on the same issue. Comparative studies like Good's can be used to inform explanations and predictions of the outcomes of particular types of messages, or to describe and explain differences in cultures.

Explanatory and Predictive Claims

Researchers using content analysis often seek to understand how messages affect the individuals who receive them. For example, a researcher may try to understand how audiences for television talk shows respond to the shows' content. Do these audience members get angry with guests who are interviewed, or do they laugh at them? Do these audience members change their behaviours to imitate the guests, or do they quickly forget what they have seen once the program ends? Although such studies are common, the actual data needed to understand effects are rarely gathered by using content analysis alone (Rogers, 1994, p. 215). As we noted earlier in this chapter, the focus of content analysis is messages. If we wish to understand effects, then we must use a second research method that collects data from individual audience members. Without audience data, we can only infer the effects of messages, and offer an explanation after the fact.

Similarly, content analysis is used to support predictive claims. For instance, researchers involved in political communication research make predictions about media usage and voting behaviour based on inferences informed by content analyses. Quite often, content analysts make two claims simultaneously, either description and explanation, or explanation and prediction. Table 8.2 shows some explanatory and predictive claims from published content analyses.

Since you now know what kind of claims you can make with content analysis, let's move to the next element of the *research as argument* model, the data.

Data for Content Analysis

The most common means of collecting data for content analysis rely on random selection methods, coding, and quantitative or statistical analysis. These strategies develop descriptions, explanations, and evaluations that can be replicated by other researchers. In this section, you will learn how to define a population of messages and select a representative sample of messages for content analysis. You also will learn how to develop and use coding schemes. In chapter 14, you will learn how to make quantitative or statistical sense of your

TABLE 8.2 Explanatory and Predictive Claims in Content Analysis

RESEARCH QUESTIONS (RQs)	HYPOTHESES (H)
RQ1: 'How did the *Globe and Mail*'s coverage of the 2003 SARS outbreak shift from a discussion of medical risk to a discussion of an economic threat?' (Leslie, 2006, p. 368)	H1: Men swear more often than women do on prime-time television programs. (Sapolsky & Kaye, 2005)
RQ2: 'How do adolescent-to-parent abuse episodes progress and escalate over time?' (Eckstein, 2004, p. 230)	H2: The horoscopes published in magazines that target working women depend more on the women's socioeconomic class than they do on the readers' zodiac signs. (Evans, 1996)
RQ3: 'How did Canadian media coverage of illegal narcotics change while tobacco marketing was increasingly regulated during the 1990s?' (Hathaway & Erickson, 2004, pp. 63–64)	H3: 'Where two or more newspapers competed in the same market, advertising agents placed their clients' ads in the paper that had the greatest circulation, regardless of its political affiliation.' (Johnston, 2007, p. 920)

findings. In the final section of this chapter, however, we show you how to assess the consistency of your coding decisions, which is a primary warrant for content analyses. The sequence of operations for content analysis is outlined in Exhibit 8.1.

Messages, Manifest Content, and Latent Content

When studying communication and culture using textual data, you must pay attention to the fact that there are layers of meaning in every message you encounter. In content analysis, these layers of meaning are divided into two types: manifest content and latent content. The **manifest content** of a message conveys that layer of meaning that will be obvious or apparent to almost anyone who encounters the message. To put this another way, the manifest content is composed of those meanings 'that are evident on the surface' (Clarke, 1999b, p. 63). Consider the typical television advertisement for beer: attractive young people socialize while a voiceover associates the beer with good times. The manifest content of a typical beer advertisement, then, asserts that beer is a refreshing beverage that complements almost any gathering.

By contrast, the **latent content** of a message conveys that layer of meaning that is implied but not expressed directly through the message. Merton (1968) has described this type of content as possessing meaning that lies 'below the threshold of superficial observation' (p. 105). Let's return to our typical beer advertisements. Limitless layers of meaning can be conveyed through the latent content. Advertisers typically use the latent content to convey a brand message that distinguishes an individual brand of beer from all other beers. For example, images of a party outdoors surrounded by maple trees may suggest rustic informality, bonding with friends, or patriotism. Images of a dance club may suggest urban chic, the possibility of new sexual conquests, or a metropolitan or international outlook.

Generally, researchers who use content analysis to test descriptive, explanatory, and predictive claims rely on manifest content. Manifest content can be easily coded and, therefore, is more readily analyzed using statistical techniques. Researchers who use content analysis to test evaluative and reformist claims are more inclined to investigate latent content. The level of interpretation involved in understanding latent content renders latent content much more difficult to code and, by extension, analyze statistically

---

EXHIBIT 8.1   Steps for Conducting Content Analysis

1. Articulate your claim about the characteristics, frequency, structure, or effects of messages. Your claim may be stated as a research question or hypothesis.
2. Identify the unit of analysis into which you will divide textual data.
3. Define the message population.
4. Review the literature, and either identify a coding scheme in the existing published research or develop your own new scheme.
5. Select a representative sample of texts. If your message population is small, you may be able to study all the messages in the population.
6(a). Have two coders unitize a small portion of your data. They should work independently.
  (b). Assess the reliability of the coders' decisions. Do they consistently identify the same units and categories in the same ways, with at least 70% agreement? If so, you may proceed to step 7. If not, revise your units of analysis or retrain your coders.
7. Once you have established the reliability of your coding scheme and your coders, you may code your entire sample.
8. Summarize the frequency with which each unit occurs in your sample. Because frequencies are expressed as numbers, they may be presented in tables, charts, or graphs.
9. Draw inferences from these frequencies, relevant to your original claim.
10. If you want to explore the relationship between two or more frequencies, then you may compare them.

(Neuendorf, 2002). As we noted earlier in this chapter, if your claims are evaluative or reformist, then you will need to know more about the critical methodologies outlined in chapter 12.

Selecting a Representative Sample of Messages

Content analysis begins when you select a representative sample of textual data. To clarify how you might select appropriate texts for content analysis, let's begin by reviewing the concept of random selection. As you already know from chapter 5, a population is a 'comprehensive and well-defined group (a universal set) of the elements pertinent to a given research question or hypothesis' (Smith, 1988, p. 77). A **message population**, then, is a well-defined set of messages pertinent to a given research question or hypothesis. Just as the population of Canada is defined by Statistics Canada, a population of messages must be defined by a researcher. For instance, Barber (2008) believed that perceptions of political bias in television coverage of the 2006 federal election were a concern for Canadian democracy given that television was the most important source of news for Canadian citizens. Barber defined the message population as the news broadcasts of the top three national networks during the last three weeks of the campaign, because those broadcasts were likely to be seen by the greatest number of viewers leading up to election day. Then, she isolated stories that addressed the election, the political parties involved, and the party leaders. Altogether, this produced a message population of 957 texts for analysis (Barber, 2008, pp. 626–627).

A representative sample is a subset of population elements that has been 'selected in such a way that it reflects well the characteristics of its parent population' (Smith, 1988, p. 78). The best way to ensure that a data sample represents the population from which it is selected is to give every element an equal chance to be included in the sample. If you use one of the random selection methods outlined in chapter 5, you will be most likely to select elements that represent the population, and you will decrease the chance of selecting biased elements (i.e. elements that represent some, but not all, of the relevant population characteristics).

You can define a vast array of message populations based on your claim. The two most important considerations when defining a message population are the time frame for your study and the medium in which the messages appear. First, let's consider the time frame. If your claim addresses current issues, then you will want to work with texts that are produced in the present day. However, if your claim addresses issues that are historical or sensitive to specific events, then you will want to work with texts that were produced during the time frame relevant to your topic. For example, Lewis and Neville (1995) wanted to know if popular representations of American women changed during the Second World War. Until then, women had popularly been portrayed as sweethearts and wives who were dependent on men. The researchers wondered if women were portrayed differently after they were drawn into the industrial work force to support the war effort. Hence, the time frame for the study was very specific: Lewis and Neville examined images of women in advertising during the years immediately before and after the United States' entry into the war in 1941.

A second dimension of the time frame that you must consider is the frequency with which new content is produced or distributed. Each source may produce messages according to its own schedule. For example, if your claim addresses an issue pertinent to journalism, it is worth noting that newspapers typically produce new content once per day, many television stations produce newscasts four times daily, and most talk radio stations, all-news cable channels, and Internet sites produce new content continuously, while news magazines produce new content only weekly or monthly. As you select a time frame and medium relevant to your claim, you must take the medium's production schedule into account. To ignore this dimension is to risk an unrepresentative sample.

Along with the time frame, the other important consideration for a representative sample is the medium in which messages appear. Because mass mediated messages are prevalent in our society, they are a common source of data for content analyses. Researchers tend to define their message populations by the medium in which they appear, be that newspapers, magazines, television, radio, film, or the Internet. A population of messages within one medium may be further refined through one of two common strategies. As with the time frame, both of these methods hinge on relevance. You must ensure that the data you collect is relevant to address your claim. First, you may wish to select one or more specific media outlets for study. For example, if your claim addresses newspaper journalism, it would be highly impractical to examine every newspaper in Canada, but you may have reason to select specific titles such as the *Calgary Herald* or *Le Devoir* to represent certain aspects of Canadian newspapers. Similarly, if your claim addresses the play lists at country radio stations located in big cities, you may want to select specific stations such as CJJR-FM Vancouver or CHFX-FM Halifax to represent the entire population of songs played across the country at similar stations.

The second strategy to refine your selection of a medium is to consider a genre or type of content. For example, within any newspaper you may find news stories, feature articles, editorials, advertisements, and cartoons. On television, programs feature news, drama, comedy, and much more, and commercials appear on almost every channel regardless of the program. Even within a genre such as comedy, there are subgenres such as situation comedies, satires, sketch comedies, stand-up monologues, animated series, and comedic variety shows. Again, you need to decide what is relevant for inclusion in your sample.

Content analyses are contributing to our understanding of digital communication and culture, and careful selection in such studies is essential (e.g. Honeycutt, 2001; Rossler, 2001; Weatherby & Scoggins, 2005–06). The Internet has made innumerable kinds of messages available to millions of people. As Krippendorf (2004) observes, 'Newspaper accounts, public opinion polls, corporate reports, files in government archives—all are now linked into networks that can be analyzed from numerous positions' (p. xx). Like other media sources, then, the population of electronic texts can be further defined by type, such as email, listservs, discussion groups, chat rooms, blogs, and websites.

Finally, your topic of study may further delineate the message population by examining only certain kinds of representation within a medium, media outlet, or genre. For example, a researcher may be particularly interested in portrayals of gender, ethnicity, or culture (e.g.

Beasley & Standley, 2002; Billings, Halone, & Denham, 2002). The best way to define your message population is to ask yourself: 'Once this study is complete, where will my findings be applied?' The message population you need to select is the one you hope your findings will address. Again, your decision must allow your sample to be relevant to your claim.

Whether you are interested in analyzing traditional mass media content, computer-mediated communication (CMC) messages, or communication surveys and diaries, there are many sources that may be sampled. Exhibit 8.2 lists a number of message populations used in published content analyses. These examples are grouped according to their sources.

Collecting Texts

Once you have developed your selection method and defined a population of messages from which to draw your data sample, you can collect texts for study. Simply put, to collect texts is to identify specific texts for analysis. If your selection method and your definition of the population are well conceived, then you should construct a representative sample.

There are two ways to collect texts. The traditional means of collecting texts for content analysis involved hands-on work with the original medium. For example, if a researcher sought newspaper articles then he or she would sit down with the selected newspapers published during the selected time frame, and scan each page for relevant articles. Once a relevant article was found, the researcher would take notes directly from it.

Today, most mass-mediated messages are readily available in digital formats. Further, an increasing amount of content produced in the past is being digitized. For example, you can read every page published by *The Toronto Star* from 1892 to 2007 online, in PDF format (see pagesofthepast.ca). For many researchers, then, the task of collecting data has been greatly simplified. If the messages in a selected medium for a selected time period are available in a digital format, then searching for and collecting relevant texts simply entails entering keywords into a database search engine. In this way, computers can eliminate the most tedious work and increase the reliability of decisions that human coders would otherwise make. LexisNexis, for example, is a commonly used search engine for content analysis because it includes newspapers and magazines, two sources that supply important populations of messages. Steuter (2010), for example, used this database to collect newspaper articles on homeopathy, as did Good (2008) for her study on climate change reporting.

The availability of computers and the digitization of all forms of information have changed not just your search for messages. It is now possible to store texts electronically for analysis at a later date. If your data are collected in written form (e.g. either recorded by hand or mechanically printed), then they can be digitized by either typing them or scanning them into a computer. Likewise, if your data are collected as images (e.g. photographs, illustrations, or symbols),

you may either scan them directly or code them as text according to a coding scheme; we will discuss coding schemes in the next section of this chapter. If your messages were gathered from verbal interactions (e.g. conversations or interviews on the radio, film, or video), you may transcribe the data into digital text (e.g. Graham, 1997). **Transcriptions** are verbatim records of the content of narrative or interactive discourse. Transcriptions contain the exact words used in monologues or conversations, but transcriptions may also contain information about the lengths of pauses or a speaker's intonation and nonverbal cues (e.g. behaviours such as winks, shrugs, and facial expressions). Of course, collecting and storing data is only one stage of the research process. Preparing it for analysis requires another set of skills.

EXHIBIT 8.2   Examples of Message Populations Used for Content Analysis

Media sources:
- Newspaper stories (e.g. Hathaway & Erickson, 2004; Ahmad, 2008; Good, 2008)
- Cartoons (e.g. Morris, 1992; Abel, 1995; Niquette & Buxton, 1997)
- Magazine articles (e.g. Evans, 1996; Lenskyj, 1998; Deveau & Fouts, 2004)
- Films (e.g. Weaver, 1991; Ramasubramanian, 2005; Stern, 2005)
- Personal advertisements (e.g. Hatala, Baack, & Parmenter, 1998)
- Song lyrics and music videos (e.g. McKee & Pardun, 2006; Kubrin, 2005)
- Television commercials (e.g. Jones & Cunningham, 2008)
- Television characters (e.g. Lichter, Lichter, & Amundson, 1997; Matabane & Merritt, 1996; Scharrer, 2001)

Surveys completed by participants:
- Open-ended questionnaires (e.g. Chang-Hoan & Hongsik, 2005; Hess, 2000; Fiebig & Kramer, 1998)
- Health-care patients' critical incident descriptions (e.g. Anderson, 2001; Ruben, 1993)
- Interaction diaries (e.g. Dainton, 1998)

Digital messages:
- CMC discussion groups (e.g. Stewart, Shields, & Sen, 1998; Van Lear, Sheehan, Withers, & Walker, 2005)
- Email messages (e.g. Pragg, Wiseman, Cody, & Wendt, 1999)
- Websites (e.g. Chan-Olmstead & Park, 2000; Weatherby & Scoggins, 2005–06)
- Blogs (e.g. Kerbel & Bloom, 2005)
- Online reviews of video games (e.g. Ivory, 2006)

Other sources:
- Jury deliberations (e.g. Sunwolf & Seibold, 1998)
- Audiotaped group discussions of HIV/AIDS (e.g. Pittman & Gallois, 1997)
- Semistructured, open-ended interviews (e.g. Graham, 1997)
- Political communication (e.g. Benoit, 2003).

Coding Texts for Content Analysis

Once you have collected your texts, your content analysis will proceed in two phases: unitizing and categorizing. Both entail reducing the often complex, qualitative information conveyed by individual texts into simplified themes or categories. When you wish to perform statistical analyses of this data, then you will reduce these themes and categories to numerical codes or quantitative information. We refer to this process as **coding**. In the first phase of coding, called **unitizing**, you identify **units of analysis** which are relevant to your claim, such as words, sentences, paragraphs, or thematically coherent phrases or passages. In the second phase of coding, called **categorizing**, you assign each text to its appropriate unit. If you do this work with one or more other researchers, you should assess your ability to code things in the same way, on a consistent basis. This consistency is called 'intercoder reliability', and we will talk more about it in the warrants section of this chapter. Let's consider each step in the coding process in detail.

Unitizing Messages

Your analysis of content begins when you identify your units of analysis. The units you identify allow you to reduce complex messages to simple data by isolating those features of each text that are relevant to your claim. Once a message has been reduced to a simple unit of analysis, it can be grouped or compared with similar units of analysis drawn from other messages. The main question you should ask yourself as you begin to identify your units of analysis is, 'What do I need to know about each message?'

Perhaps the simplest units of analysis to isolate are based on physical distinctions or syntactic distinctions between texts (Krippendorf, 2004). First, physical distinctions define content in terms of some physical medium, such as the amount of space or time given to particular content. Examples of physical units include the number of column inches allotted to a newspaper article, or the amount of time dedicated to a radio phone-in topic. In neither example do we interpret the content of the message, only the size of the message is measured. By itself, the physical distinctions of a message do not reveal anything about its meaning. It may, however, reveal something about the significance of the topic.

Second, syntactical distinctions define content as discrete bits of text. When examining linguistic texts, these discrete bits may be individual words, phrases, or sentences. Visual texts may be divided into individual symbols or colours (Krippendorf, 2004). Like physical distinctions, syntactical distinctions do not require you to interpret the meaning of texts (Krippendorf, 2004). Typically, both physical and syntactical units of analysis can be unitized by coders with consistent reliability. Of course, computers can divide textual data into syntactic units of analysis with perfect reliability.

When you want to describe or explain the meaning of messages, then you must look for other distinctions, and the process of coding becomes more challenging. Krippendorf (2004) identified three further units of analysis that pertain to meaning: categorical distinctions, propositional distinctions, and thematic distinctions. Categorical distinctions divide texts into units that share an important aspect such as the characteristics of their authors, the types of events described, or the types of issues discussed. The importance of any one aspect will depend on your claim. For example, if you believe that authorship is an important factor when interpreting a text, then you will want to know something about the author of each text. Perhaps you will seek the authors' specific names, or perhaps you will seek generic qualities based on demographic data (i.e. the authors' ages or ethnic identities). Your coding scheme would then be a taxonomy (i.e. a classification system) of all the different ways of identifying an author, relevant to your claim.

Propositional distinctions divide texts into units based upon the ways that their conceptual elements are linked semantically through linguistic construction. Put another way, propositional distinctions try to reduce each relevant sentence of a text into its component parts—that is, the subject, verb, and object—so that the meaning of the text can be coded part by part. This type of unitizing can be advantageous for the researcher if rich descriptive data is not required for analysis since each text can be reduced to simple codes.

For example, let's look at humour as a form of linguistic construction. As a form, humour often follows certain patterns of delivery. Anecdotes, shaggy dog stories, and one-liners represent propositional distinctions within humour because the conceptual elements of these linguistic structures have certain, known semantic relationships to one another. For example, the first two turns of a 'knock-knock' joke are recognizable to most speakers of the English language (i.e. 'Knock-knock.'. . . 'Who's there?'). This example also illustrates how important it is to understand the syntax and semantics of language when your unit of analysis is propositional. If you cannot recognize the component parts of a sentence, then you will not be able to unitize your data.

Thematic distinctions divide texts into units based on the topics the texts address. Thematic distinctions afford rich descriptions of textual data. For example, you could analyze parents' emails to their children in university by reviewing the kinds of support the messages contain; perhaps they offer emotional support, or material assistance, or no helpful gestures whatsoever. Because thematic distinctions rely on the subjective meaning of each text and the interpretation of each coder, they are the hardest units to identify consistently and accurately.

Krippendorf (2004) has noted that the five units of analysis for content analysis can be organized from least to most complex, as follows: physical, syntactical, categorical, propositional, and thematic. Physical units are the easiest units to code reliably, but they may be of least interest if you want to explain the meaning of words as they are used in context. The opposite is true of thematic units; they may provide the most substantial data if you want to explore meanings, but it is quite difficult to achieve consistent unitizing decisions.

Depending on your claim, you may need to divide your data into progressively smaller, more specific units of analysis. Let's consider an example. In a study of violence in advertising, Jones and Cunningham (2008) selected five different television channels (CBC, CTV, Global, TSN, and CHCH) and collected every ad broadcasted during primetime hours for two weeks. This produced a population of 7,717 advertisements, of which 232 were unique (i.e. most were repeated several times on more than one channel). The 232 unique ads were coded twice. During the first pass, coders assessed whether or not each advertisement

had violent content. This meant that the coders placed each ad into only one of two categories (i.e. violent or non-violent).

Once this initial pass was complete, the advertisements with violent content were separated from their programs and subjected to a second pass. The coders were then asked to unitize the advertisements by isolating the type of good or service advertised, the number of violent acts portrayed, the type of violence portrayed, and the type of victim portrayed. Each of these units of analysis was further divided into three or more possible categories. For example, the type of product advertised was categorized as a feature film, a television program, or a consumer good or service; the type of victim portrayed in each advertisement was categorized as a person, beast, or object. If the research had wanted greater detail, then even these categories could have been further subdivided into, say, the genres of the films advertised or the gender of the victims portrayed. The level of detail you collect should be guided by your claim.

Once you have identified the units of analysis that will apply to your research, you should have a coding scheme. A **coding scheme** is a coherent set of specific units of analysis, organized into categories, that will collect the data you need from each text in order to address your claim. You may create a coding scheme by drawing inductively upon the data you collect. However, if your literature review reveals that another researcher has already developed a productive coding scheme, then you may draw upon it. Or, you may combine categories from an existing scheme with new ones that you find in your data.

You should always test a coding scheme on a small portion of your sample data before you begin a full content analysis. Such a test can reveal if your units of analysis are appropriate and if your categories address your texts in a comprehensive manner. This is called a 'pilot test', and it is equally worthwhile whether you use another scholar's coding scheme or develop your own. A faulty coding scheme may produce faulty findings. It is far better to discover any faults through a pilot test and to correct these faults before time and energy are invested in a full study. Once the coding scheme is set and has been checked with a pilot test, you can draft a standardized coding sheet. A coding sheet is the research tool you use to collect raw data in content analysis. We will discuss coding sheets in the next section of this chapter.

Categorizing Messages

The next phase of coding is to assign each text, or each unit of analysis, to its relevant category in your coding scheme. You will systematically examine every text in your sample to isolate its units of analysis, identify its relevant categories, and thus group it with similar texts. The process of coding is the same whether you are working with original documents, hard copies, or digitally stored files.

Raw data is recorded with standardized coding sheets. A coding sheet will ask you to identify an individual text drawn from your sample. Then, it will ask you to identify that text's units of analysis and to enter the relevant data. This process is repeated with each text in your sample. It is important that the coding sheets for any one content analysis be standardized to ensure that you collect the same units of analysis from each text. Traditionally, researchers used one coding sheet for each text they included in a study. If the study considered a sample of 1,000 texts, then the researchers required 1,000 coding sheets. Paper coding sheets are still used today, but now it is more common to use computer spreadsheets. Rather than assign one coding sheet per text, a spreadsheet assigns one row to each text. Spreadsheets offer an easy way to organize data, perform simple tasks such as grouping and sorting data, and perform complex tasks such as statistical analysis if the software is designed for that purpose. An example of a traditional, standardized coding sheet is provided in Exhibit 8.3.

Jones and Cunningham's (2008) study of violence in television advertising provided a clear discussion of their coding scheme. The researchers had eight key variables, though they only discussed four of these variables in detail in their report. First, they noted the date and time that each advertisement appeared. Second, they noted the television channel on which the advertisement appeared. Then, they also noted the sponsor's name. These data allowed them to identify each unique ad in the study. Next, they posed a filter question. Did an ad portray violence, or not? They defined 'violence' as any act intended to harm an identifiable victim, be it a person, animal, or object. If the answer was 'No', then no further data was collected from an advertisement. If the answer was 'Yes', then five more variables were measured: the duration of the ad; the type of sponsor; the number of unique violent episodes portrayed; the type of violence portrayed; and the types of victim. Exhibit 8.3 shows what a standardized coding sheet for the study might have looked like, and identifies how we can think about each of the researchers' units of analysis.

This process of entering raw data into a coding scheme is the actual process of coding. By assigning a particular text to a particular category based on its units of analysis, you are reducing its complex message to a single idea—that is, a code. Generally, researchers using content analysis assign a nominal code to each text to signify that they have been assigned to specific categories. For example, if authorship is one of your units of analysis, and you have decided that gender is an important aspect of authorship, then you may code texts with male authors as '1' and texts with female authors as '2'. If your unit of analysis involves a measure such as column length or broadcast duration, then you can code texts with the actual ratio numbers taken during measurement (e.g. number of centimetres, or hours and minutes). Ultimately, the raw data you enter must be relevant to your units of analysis, and should gather the information you need to address your claim.

There are computer software programs that perform the task of coding. One is VBPro, a popular open-source program. If your sample texts exist in digital format, then it is possible to have the program isolate physical and syntactical units of analysis. Although such programs may seem highly advantageous if they can reduce the researcher's workload, they have two drawbacks. The first issue is transparency. The researcher needs to know how the software program makes decisions when isolating and coding each text. If the researcher does not agree with the program's decision-making criteria, then the computer will produce useless data. The second issue is interpretation. At present, programs cannot detect layers of meaning conveyed by a message. Hence, these programs work reliably with only the most mechanical aspects of the language, such as word counts and

| EXHIBIT 8.3 | Assessing the Prevalence and Types of Violence in Canadian Prime-time Television |

Date: _____

Time period: 7:00 _____ 7:30 _____ 8:00 _____ 8:30 _____ 9:00 _____ 9:30 _____ 10:00 _____ 10:30 _____

Television channel: CBC _____ CHCH _____ CTV _____ Global _____ TSN _____

Sponsor name : _____

Violence present in ad? Yes _____ No _____

VARIABLE	UNIT OF ANALYSIS	CATEGORIES
Duration of ad	Physical	_____ in seconds
Type of sponsor	Categorical	_____ product / service _____ upcoming show _____ movie trailer
Number of unique violent episodes	Syntactical	_____ specific number
Type of violence	Propositional / Thematic	_____ degradation _____ physical violence _____ sexual violence _____ threat / verbal violence
Type of victim	Propositional / Categorical	_____ person _____ animal or insect _____ object

Source: Constructed by Johnston based on Jones and Cunningham (2008).

syntax, and provide little interpretive insight on their own (Krippendorf, 2004). For example, Andsager and Smiley (1998) used VBPro to study news coverage of silicone breast implants. The program searched six digitized newspapers for relevant articles, created a sample population of 106 articles, identified the most frequently occurring words in these 106 articles, and then identified clusters of terms that tended to occur closely together across the sample (i.e. 'medical groups', 'patient groups', and 'Dow Corning'). Andsager and Smiley's results suggested that certain groups more than others were able to exert tremendous influence over coverage of the devices (1998, pp. 197–198). This analysis, however, was based purely on the program's

ability to find and count words, not interpret them. This example also indicates the importance of the software's programming and its decision-making criteria. If newspaper reporters use different terms to express the same idea, or if terms are spelled incorrectly, the program can miss them (Krippendorf, 2004, p. 284).

Content Data Analysis

With coded data in hand, you are ready to address your research questions or hypotheses. Content analysis lends itself to statistical analysis. For example, you may want to know the number and percentage of texts that fall into each category of your coding scheme. You may also want to compare the distribution of messages across several categories in your coding scheme, or to compare the distribution you observed against some theoretical distribution you expected to observe. For example, you may predict that the authors of food and drink columns in major newspapers are predominantly women; if you categorize each text in your sample by the biological sex of their authors, then the final distribution of your texts will indicate if your prediction is true or false. Sometimes, however, the answers to such questions are more complex than a simple true or false observation. In chapter 14, you will learn a statistical test called chi-square, which is used to assess how well an observed distribution of messages fits an expected distribution.

As we noted in our discussion of coding, most researchers today use computers and specialized software to complete statistical analyses of raw data. The most popular software packages for researchers in communication and cultural studies are Statistical Package for the Social Sciences (SPSS), Microsoft Excel, or similar programs that can test relationships and differences in data sets. SPSS is the most commonly used statistical program among researchers in our fields, but Excel is sometimes used for small data sets and classroom projects, and it is often used in business environments. You will learn more about such programs in chapters 13 and 14 of this book.

Warrants for Content Analysis

Your ability to develop reliable findings using content analysis depends on three things. First, you must be consistent when unitizing and categorizing your raw data. This is called measurement reliability. Second, the categories you use for coding must be internally valid. Third, your message sample must be representative of the entire population of messages if it is to be externally valid. Since you already know about reliability and validity generally, from chapter 6, let's look at how you can apply these warrants to your content analytic study.

Intercoder Reliability

The results of content analyses depend heavily on measurement reliability, the consistency with which messages have been unitized and categorized. Remember, messages can have layers of meaning. You want to ensure that all coders working on the same project will interpret and code the same text in the same way. In its simplest form, then, **intercoder reliability** is the percentage of coding decisions on which all coders agree (e.g. Johnson et al., 1999). As a rule of thumb, anything over 70% constitutes an acceptable level of reliability for unitizing and categorizing message content. More complicated formulas exist to assess intercoder reliability, such as Scott's (1955) pi or Cohen's (1960) kappa, but we will not discuss them in this text. The main advantage of these more complex measures is that they estimate the degree to which coders' level of agreement differs from the level of agreement likely to occur by chance alone (Krippendorf, 2004; Lombard, Snyder-Duch, & Bracken, 2002).

There are several ways to ensure a high degree of agreement among coders. One way is to train coders especially for each study, so that they understand the nuances of each unit of analysis. Jones and Cunningham (2008), in their study of violence in television advertising, used several techniques to attain intercoder reliability. First, they trained and tested their coders to identify the same units of analysis. With respect to 'violence', this meant that they were given the same definition of violence to guide their decisions. Then, the coders worked independently to prevent either one from dominating the other's decisions. During this time, they could view each advertisement as many times as necessary to be sure of their decisions. Finally, when the two coders did not share the same interpretation of an advertisement, their decision was reconciled by a third coder who had had the same training. Prior to this intervention, however, the two coders achieved a 90% rate of agreement (p. 55).

Generally, it is easier to achieve a high level of agreement among coders when you use physical or syntactical distinctions to unitize your data or when you have relatively few coding categories. Triangulating multiple investigator viewpoints can also increase reliability. Of course, as we have noted, computer software programs can unitize and categorize some data quite reliably, especially when your unit of analysis is physical or syntactical.

Validity of the Coding Scheme

Two factors affect the validity of a coding scheme. The first factor is the content validity of the coding scheme. The second factor is the size of the coding scheme, including the size and content of any 'other' category. We use the term 'parsimony' to refer to this issue. Since we introduced the concepts of content validity and parsimony in chapter 6, we shall focus our discussion here on the ways they apply to content analysis.

Content validity describes the ability of your coding scheme to process, accurately and completely, the messages you want to study. For example, imagine that you want to categorize persuasive messages, and you limit your coding scheme to three categories: threats, promises, and 'other' messages. Such a coding scheme would be too simple to measure all persuasive strategies accurately and completely. If we consider appeals to reason, vanity, envy, or guilt as persuasive techniques, then it is possible that more messages would fall into the 'other' category than the two specific categories. Hence, your coding scheme would lack richness and accuracy.

Coding categories should be mutually exclusive and exhaustive. If you have **mutually exclusive categories**, then each unit of analysis you isolate in a text will fit into one category only. For example, if you are sampling several newspapers to gauge their editorial stances on a cultural issue, then an editorial sampled from the *Calgary Herald* cannot be categorized as an editorial from the Fredericton *Daily Gleaner*. Exclusivity can increase intercoder reliability. By contrast, when categories overlap, it is more difficult to achieve intercoder reliability. Keeping with our example, if an opinion piece is distributed by the Canadian Press news service, then it will appear in several newspapers at once. How would it be categorized? In order to achieve intercoder reliability, you would need to ensure that all coders knew how to deal with wire items. **Exhaustive categories** completely and comprehensively describe a message population. This means that no relevant messages from that population are left out of the coding scheme. Look back at Exhibit 8.3. Can you think of other categories that should be represented in the coding scheme? If not, then you can consider the categories listed there to be exhaustive.

Even as you acknowledge the complexity of the message population that you are studying, you should balance that complexity against the value of parsimony, the preference for a simple, elegant explanation of social phenomena. One of the best ways to evaluate the parsimony of your coding scheme is to look at the presence or absence of the 'other' category. If too much of your data fits into the 'other' category, then your coding scheme may not be adequate to describe the message population. Indeed, your 'other' category may contain valuable but inaccessible details not captured by your study. For this reason, you should always be cautious of the 'other' category in a coding scheme. Analyze the messages placed there to see if they share elements that justify an additional, more meaningful category that has been overlooked, one that should be added to the coding scheme. Remember, however, that while too few categories may result in lost detail or nuance, too many categories will threaten your scheme's parsimony.

External Validity

External validity refers to the accuracy of applying the findings from one study to another setting, group of participants, or messages. It is entirely possible for the results of one study to be internally valid but still not be applicable to other cases. In this section, we look at two factors you should consider to assess the external validity of a study using content analysis: the degree of coder training required for the study, and the representativeness of the sample data.

Coder Training

Many content analyses are premised on the notion that most individuals interpret messages, and by extension units of analysis and categories, in the same ways that trained coders interpret messages. This assumption would be false if, in any given study, the coders require intensive training to achieve an acceptable level of intercoder reliability. Why? If your coders need extensive training to interpret a message, then it is unlikely that most other individuals will interpret those messages in the same way. As such, the study's findings may be internally valid, because the coders share common interpretations, but the findings will be difficult to apply in any other context because other people may not share common interpretations. In other words, they will lack external validity.

Sample Representativeness

To achieve a high degree of external validity, you need to select a representative sample that adequately represents the entire population of messages you wish to study. As you know from chapter 6, the best way to gather a representative sample from a large population is to randomize the selection process. That said, sample selection does not need not to be purely random to be reasonably representative. Sample size also has an impact on the sample's representativeness. Usually, the larger the sample, the better your chances of representing the parent message population. Depending on the nature of your claim, a large stratified sample may be more representative than a small random sample.

To summarize, you will need to pay attention to three things to achieve externally valid conclusions in your content analytic study. First, you must ensure that your coders' interpretive abilities are similar to those of the individuals who live the social setting whose texts you wish to study. Second, you must collect enough relevant messages to represent the entire population of messages you wish to study. Last, you must collect enough messages to ensure you have given the possibility of random error an opportunity to work.

Ethical Issues in Content Analysis

Because researchers using content analysis usually examine messages that are publicly available, their research proposals are generally given expedited status by REBs. There are two reasons for granting this status. First, individuals who voluntarily circulate messages in the public domain have already waived their right to privacy. Hence, researchers do not need to gain the consent of these individuals because their messages are already accessible to the general public. Second, most content analysis aggregates data from hundreds, if not thousands, of messages. The specific identity of individual authors is usually irrelevant to the analysis. Instead, broad demographic identifiers are typically used to describe groups of authors (Palomares & Flanagin, 2005, p. 174).

Even if content analysis of messages in the public domain poses minimal risk to individual authors, it does raise important questions about your motives for research and your responsibility to protect participants' rights. You should never analyze messages simply because those data are conveniently available or because your approval process will be quick and easy. Rather, you should always aim to benefit the producers and/or consumers of the messages you study. Essentially, expediency should never trump beneficence, respect, or justice at any phase of your research project. You must still protect the authors' rights; you must still think about how your study affects the authors' freedom of choice to 'participate' and how the study affects their dignity. For example, if you know or collect their names during your research, will you then use their names when you publish your study? Or will you mask their names to preserve their confidentiality?

When thinking through these ethical issues, it helps to consider how your final report will impact the authors you are studying and their social context. To put this another way, you might consider how your description, explanation, and prediction of messages in that social context might change after your report is circulated. For example, if your research establishes that deceptive messages are more persuasive than truthful messages in that social context, will members of that social group be more likely to use deceptive messages in the future? And what would you do to counter that possibility, if your findings did have potentially antisocial consequences?

Summary

As we found with surveys, we have shown in this chapter that content analysis requires careful preparation and handling. When you begin, you must decide what types of claims you wish to construct: descriptive, explanatory, predictive, interpretive, or reformist. Researchers who make the first three types of claims about messages most often use content analysis, while researchers who make the latter two types of claims about messages more often deploy discourse and conversational analysis. Once your claims are identified, you must decide on the relevant sources, time frame,

TABLE 8.3 Descriptive Claims in Content Analysis

CLAIMS	DATA	WARRANTS	MANUSCRIPT FORMAT
Describe, explain, and predict	Representative samples of texts from message populations (i.e. newspaper articles, songs, chat room postings)	Intercoder reliability, content validity of coding scheme, and sample representativeness	Research report

and selection method you will use to collect the data. You must also construct your research instrument, beginning with your coding scheme. The coding scheme is composed of two elements. First, your units of analysis will isolate within each text the data you need to address your claim. As with surveys, you must decide on the level of measurement you will use with your units of analysis, be they nominal, ordinal, interval, or ratio. Second, your categories will allow you to group your data in a meaningful way for the analysis itself. The coding scheme will then be drafted into a coding schedule, a standardized form that ensures you bring the same set of questions to each message sampled for your study. When administering the coding schedule, you must establish warrants for the data by assessing the survey's validity and reliability. Table 8.3 summarizes the major aspect of content and discourse analysis. You will see in chapters 13 and 14 that certain tests of content analysis claims are statistical analyses that require equal care in interpretation.

Key Terms

Categorizing
Coding
Coding scheme
Content analysis
Exhaustive categories

Interactive discourse
Intercoder reliability
Latent content
Manifest content
Message population

Mutually exclusive categories
Narrative discourse
Transcription
Unitizing
Units of analysis

Discussion Questions

1. Why is content analysis more commonly associated with the discovery paradigm than the interpretive or critical paradigms?
2. What is a message population? Why is it important to define a message population by its source as well as its time frame?
3. Thematic units of analysis can be the most difficult to isolate and code, but they can also be the most informative. Why is this so?

4. What are the advantages of using computers to collect and code data for content analysis? What are the disadvantages of using computers to do this work?
5. What precautions would you develop to ensure that coders achieve a high degree of agreement when coding latent content?

Try It!

1. This activity asks you to define a message population. It can be completed by an individual, but it may be more interesting to work in a group with two or more other members. Depending on the size of your tutorial group, it may also be adapted as a tutorial exercise.

    Review the message samples listed in Exhibit 8.2. For each sample, see if you can describe that message population in one sentence. You can check the precision of your description by answering this question: 'Could your description include any other type of message that would not be included in the study?'

2. This activity asks you to create a research proposal for content analysis. It can be completed by an individual, but it will be more efficient to work in a group with two or more other members. Depending on the size of your tutorial group, it may also be adapted as a tutorial exercise.

Process:

First, brainstorm: create a list of 15 specific message populations. You may define them by their context (e.g. interpersonal or organizational communication, digital culture or mass media); or by their media (e.g. face-to-face, CMC, or mass media); or by their genre (e.g. news, animation, publicity, fiction).

Second, compare: join with another student or pair of students, and review your lists together. Were any of your message populations the same? Which ones were different? Can you describe the characteristics that made them different?

Third, ask questions: working alone or with your original partner, select one message population from all those you discussed in step two. Then, with this message population in mind, develop three research questions (RQs) about it. Be creative! What would you like to know about that type of message? Make sure your RQs address issues related to frequency, degree, magnitude, and similar things which are appropriate for quantitative analysis.

Fourth, Krippendorf: review his five units of analysis (i.e. physical, syntactical, categorical, propositional, and thematic). For each of your three RQs, identify the units of analysis needed to answer that question.

Fifth, hit the books: look for existing research about the message population and units of analysis you want to study. Determine whether or not a coding scheme already exists for this message population. If there isn't, develop your own rough coding scheme.

Sixth, formulate: draft your own standardized coding sheet for your message population. It should be based on the coding scheme you discovered in the existing literature or the coding scheme you developed yourself.

Last, write: describe your plan for acquiring a representative sample of the population of messages. A paragraph should suffice.

You have now completed a research proposal for content analysis.

9 Historical, Policy, and Case Analysis

Introduction

In this chapter, we shall examine three research methods with a similar focus on specific aspects of communication and culture. Where surveys and content analysis tend to examine broad trends that are common to large number of individual people or texts, the three methods to be discussed here tend to examine specific individuals, artefacts, events, or trends.

Historical, policy, and case analysis offer, in some ways, a common approach to empirical data more than a distinct method to gather empirical data. The key to that approach is an ability to synthesize data from many different kinds of sources into a single, compelling argument (Daniels, 1966, p. 7; MacRae & Wilde, 1979, p. 6; Feagin et al., 1991, pp. 19–21; Benjamin, 1991, pp. 13–14; Wieviorka, 1992; Denscombe, 1998, p. 32). Scholars in communication and cultural studies who conduct **historical analysis** can gather data using any of the other methods described in this text. However, they use all data to achieve one of two goals: to understand a topic by reconstructing its historical time period, or to understand a topic by assessing how it developed or changed through time. In both scenarios, researchers seek data to describe and understand a topic by constructing a chronology of events or a rich description of the topic in context.

In **policy analysis**, a researcher either assesses the implications of a proposed new policy or judges the performance of a current or past policy. When assessing a proposed new policy, the research focus falls upon the specific issues addressed by the policy, and detailed, precise information must be gathered to understand the issues, the stakeholders, and the relevant context for its creation. When judging a current or past policy, the research focus falls not only on its development, but also its implementation and enforcement. In either scenario, then, research provides data to assess the performance of a policy. As with historical research, a researcher will present this data through a chronology of events or a rich description of the topic in context (Hansen et al., 1998).

Case study tends to focus on contemporary issues, but it too provides a holistic understanding of a topic by understanding it as one part of a dynamic setting where multiple factors come into play (Feagin et al., 1991). To put this another way, case study allows a researcher to investigate a phenomenon in its real-life context rather than in theoretical terms or in a laboratory setting (Yin, 2002). The precise boundaries of this real-life context can be difficult to draw because so many aspects of life are interconnected, from culture to politics, economics to geography (Gillham, 2000). For case analysis to work well, a researcher must be sensitive to relevant factors while gathering detailed and precise information about a topic. As with historical and policy analysis, this data will be used to construct either a chronology of events or a rich description of the topic in context. This description will then be analyzed for insights on the specific topic as well as general insights that can be applied to other, similar cases.

Because historical, policy, and case analysis share a common approach to data, it is useful to address their common methodological concerns in a single chapter. First, we discuss the five types of claims you are likely to make when using these methods. Next, we explore the major sources of data that are sought to supply primary evidence for analysis. Linked with this discussion of data, we will outline two important aspects of analysis: the need to question the veracity of your sources, and ways of organizing the data you collect. No matter which of the three methods you use, you will most often organize your data by constructing a chronology of events that are documented in that data. Finally, we will outline the warrants typically linked with these research methods, including audit trails, representativeness and adequacy of evidence, and coherence and fidelity.

In the last two chapters, you have learned about survey research and content analysis. Both methods are typically conducted to generate quantitative data, and both methods require careful planning and precise measurement to produce reliable data. Surveys and content analysis were developed during the twentieth century by scholars studying human behaviour who sought methods that mimicked the precision of the natural sciences. We now shift our focus to qualitative methods of analysis. These methods rely on data that are typically gathered, organized, and analyzed in their original formats, and this data is rarely coded numerically. For this reason, there is a very close connection between the claim a researcher advances and the sources chosen for analysis. Typically, evidence is not taken from a random selection of individuals or

texts but is selected for the specific data it provides. Nonetheless, you should remember that careful planning and precise means for collecting evidence are no less important with qualitative research than they are with quantitative research.

As a form of expression, history has an ancient pedigree. As long as people have lived in communities, they have used stories of their gods and ancestors to convey their beliefs and values. Early societies without means of recording their stories shared them orally, and preserved them by passing them from one generation to the next (Benjamin, 1991; Storey & Jones, 2004). With the invention of communication media such as alphabets and writing instruments, storytellers were able to share their stories with wider circles of people and to preserve them through time. The first works of history in the English language were written in the Middle Ages, in roughly 700 CE. During the Victorian period, universities in Europe and North America began to develop scholars who specialized in the research and writing of history. These specialists formed the basis for modern, professional history as it is now understood (Higham, 1983; Berger, 1986).

By contrast, case study and policy analysis are relatively recent innovations if we track them by their current names. Case research first appeared in the work of early French sociologists in the 1800s, and was developed as a critical research tool at the University of Chicago after 1890. Case study use in cultural studies stems from these early applications. By contrast, the use of cases in communication studies, particularly within organizational communication, stems from the method's development in schools of business such as Harvard University and the University of Western Ontario (Sypher, 1997, p. 2; Tompkins, 1997; Leenders et al., 2001, pp. 1–2). Policy analysis took shape in political science departments through the twentieth century as some scholars concerned with public administration turned their attention from ideology and economics to the actual results of policies enacted by local governments. Much early policy analysis was in fact a form of case study, since each policy was treated as a single case examined in isolation (Zelizer, 2004).

As you will see, claims for historical research, policy analysis, and case study can be made about almost anything: individuals and social groups, texts and arte-facts, behaviours and trends, or societies and cultures.

Claims for Historical, Policy, and Case Analysis

Every report of historical research, policy analysis, or case study contains an argument, if only implicitly. It may seem that a journal article, book, or documentary film simply recounts the facts pertaining to a particular individual, event, or culture, and often those facts are recounted in chronological order. However, every decision made when researching and writing shapes the narrative that unfolds in the final report.

For example, imagine that you want to write the story of an influential musician. Where should you begin your research? You have many options: perhaps with her childhood, during her early education in music, at the start of her career, or at a moment of artistic triumph. You have similar options when it comes to methods and sources. You may choose to interview her family, her teachers, her colleagues and fans, or the musician herself. Alternatively, you may only examine texts such as her recordings, reviews of her work, magazine profiles, or broadcast interviews. You have similar options when you decide what facts will be relevant. You may choose to focus strictly on influences and events evoked in her music, or may choose to include intimate material, such as her romances. Each one of these decisions regarding the method and sources, the time frame, and facts, will be influenced by your own beliefs, instincts, or prejudices about what is appropriate for inclusion. By extension, the same is true of those facts you choose to exclude. In the end, all of these decisions will affect your analysis of the musician's story and the conclusions you draw about her life and career.

As such, purely descriptive claims are quite rare in historical, policy, and case analysis that examine communication and culture in Canada. Much more common are interpretive, explanatory, and evaluative claims, and in this respect researchers are more likely to approach their work from the perspective of either the interpretive paradigm or the critical paradigm. As you will recall from chapter 3, on paradigms, interpretive and critical scholars believe that there is no one reality separate from our perceptions. Rather, each person's perceptions and values affect what is seen and understood about the world. Therefore, to be consistent, these scholars must acknowledge that their own values affect their perceptions of reality.

Descriptive and Interpretive Claims

Descriptive and interpretive claims in historical, policy, or case analysis are most often posed as thesis statements when found in critical essays. One of the primary reasons to perform historical research is to understand how specific individuals, social groups, or entire societies may have thought or behaved in the past. With policy and case analysis, we seek to understand specific individuals, social groups, texts, or processes in the present day. Descriptive and interpretive claims, then, seek to identify the particular characteristics that make the object of study worthy of our attention.

The scale of a descriptive claim or interpretive claim can vary greatly from topic to topic. Scholars who study communication and culture can examine the significance of a single individual or artefact, a trend among a particular social group, or the cultural practices of an entire society (Sjoberg et al., 1991, pp. 36–39). For example, Gow (2004) used a single policy process, the CRTC's management of wireless 911 service, as a case to understand the nature of regulatory intervention in technical standards. By contrast, Morris (1978) wrote a large-scale history of the Canadian film industry that was framed by one major question: how did the industry develop in the early years of film? As Morris himself noted, the text was 'essentially descriptive' (p. ix). Because no one else had published an extensive history of Canadian film before the 1930s, the entire time period had to be reconstructed from scratch.

A description or interpretation of the past is useful for many reasons. It is often useful to understand past events for their own sake. Indeed, learning about past civilizations and cultures can be both enjoyable and surprising. In the present day, it is relatively easy to get information about current events. Media organizations circle the globe and compete to bring us news. Typically, we trust journalists, artists, and marketers to report both important and trivial information on a daily basis, to keep us informed about people and things that will affect our lives. For past events, however, we must look elsewhere. As the present fades into the past, our memories often fade as well. The journalist's sources become increasingly difficult to find; the individuals who once participated in important events may change their perspectives, lose their memories, or die. Broadcast news enters the ether and disappears unless someone records it. Similarly, newspapers and magazines get recycled, while new books become old books that few people want. Websites, of course, can change on a daily basis. The loss of such records clearly limits and shapes the choices we make as researchers when we attempt to understand the past. Hence, historical research is often necessary to bring disparate sources together and to reconstruct a view of the past that otherwise may be lost to memory.

For policy and case analyses, which are not primarily focused on historical topics, descriptive claims or interpretive claims are useful to establish an appropriate context to understand their topics. Often, the data will have an historical perspective. Journalists regularly perform this function in relation to current affairs. When significant events happen, stories are written describing the day's events, but stories are also written about related, past events which put the day's events in context. For example, when the movie *Titanic* became a global cultural phenomenon, journalists sought histories of the ill-fated ship to assess the historical accuracy of the movie's narrative. Similarly, with the release of *The Lord of the Rings* trilogy on film, biographies of J. R. R. Tolkien became popular as fans sought to grasp the cultural influences that inspired his writings. Taken together, description, background information and context provide us with a sense of control, or at least comprehension, with unfolding events in our time. When the day's events are seen as the most recent elements of a longer narrative, this can make those events seem less random or threatening because we see them as small parts in a larger pattern (Daniels, 1966, p. 27; Johnson, 1975; Yin, 2003, pp. 4–8).

TABLE 9.1 Descriptive and Interpretive Claims in Historical, Policy, or Case Analysis

RESEARCH QUESTIONS (RQs)	THESES (T)
RQ1: What film activities occurred in Canada before the establishment of the National Film Board? (Morris, 1978, p. ix)	T1: 'The following narrative of how major parties' candidates spent money in the 2006 Canadian general election provides a descriptive inventory of paid promotional and administrative tasks. . . . [It] documents the modernization of constituency campaigning, such as the use of technology and the professionalization of labour services, and sheds light on the tediousness of much electioneering behaviour.' (Marland, 2008, p. 57)
RQ2: 'What kinds of knowledge about human skin colour in the form of racialized imagery are [camera film] manufacturers constructing and defending through . . . their products? What is the corporate stake in investing in or changing a colour aesthetic of Whiteness?' (Roth, 2009, p. 116)	
	T2: 'The paper . . . argues that the Aird commissioners used the public hearings to legitimize their own commitment to the nationalization of Canadian radio by depicting public opinion in its final report as consensual when in fact there was considerable division.' (Gasher, 1998, p. 191)
RQ3: 'How does the state intervene in the development of technical standards, and how effective is this intervention?' (Gow, 2004, p. 66)	T3: 'The cases studied in this paper indicate how unlicensed or licence-exempt spectrum can be deployed by communities and municipalities to develop fairly robust Wi-Fi networks . . . in a local region.' (Middleton & Crow, 2008, p. 420)

Descriptive and interpretive claims are more common in case studies than in historical or policy analyses. Case study, when used as a research method, typically takes one of two forms (Naumes & Naumes, 2006). In the first, researchers assess the utility of a theory by examining a relevant case. During the research process, the researchers gather data and reconstruct their case as faithfully as possible, in as much detail as possible. Then, they present their reading of the theory and demonstrate how it either explains or does not explain the case in a compelling and comprehensive way. If the theory can explain the case in all of its detail, then the theory is judged to be valuable. In the second form of a case study, researchers begin with a case and then seek a compelling and comprehensive explanation of it. We will address this form of case study in the next section. In neither form of case study, however, should the researchers allow their understandings of the case or the theory to influence one another, since this would prejudice a clear analysis of the theory. As such, most claims in these forms of case studies are descriptive (Yin, 2003).

Gow's (2004) case study of wireless 911 services, which we noted earlier, provides a useful example of a descriptive claim. His study first described how the CRTC encouraged private-sector wireless providers to standardize the handling of 911 calls made from mobile phones. To organize his description of the CRTC's policy process, he introduced two theoretical concepts: 'interconnection' and 'the layered model'. Interconnection describes the desire of consumers to access seamless wireless networks, while the layered model is an interpretive framework that shows how various digital technologies can be integrated into a single system. In Gow's hands, a description of a specific case provides data that supports the theory, and the theory provides useful concepts that organize the case data.

Explanatory Claims

Explanatory claims are more common than descriptive or interpretive claims in research programs that centre on historical or policy research. Most scholars in communication and cultural studies are not content simply to describe or interpret the past. They wish to understand why events unfold as they do. Explanatory claims, then, attempt to identify causal relationships between events, or to find the impetus for significant moments or trends (Johnson, 1975; Jenkins, 1978).

Again, the scale of explanatory claims can range as widely as that of descriptive claims. Freeman (2006) provides an example of a small-scale study. She sought to understand how and why the representation of lesbians changed in the pages of *Chatelaine* magazine from 1966 to 2004. She concluded that, until the 1990s, the magazine became more open and politically engaged with lesbian issues, but after that date discussions of their unique issues either disappeared or were integrated into articles about women's issues in general. This research provides important, critical insights into a magazine that was popular, mainstream, and portrayed itself as progressive during the period under study. We may describe this claim as small, however, because the findings apply to a single aspect of a single artefact; it is an historical case study. Until further research is undertaken on other Canadian media outlets, we cannot apply Freeman's insights elsewhere without qualification.

By contrast, Walden (1997) researched the origins of the Canadian National Exhibition in Toronto. He used the exhibition as a lens to focus on the culture of Ontario society as it passed from an agricultural economy to an industrial economy, from 1873 to 1903. As such, his research into the fair's organizers, visitors, and critics provided him with evidence to interpret aspects of their shared beliefs, values, and attitudes as a society. In particular, he tried to explain their notions of individual identity, civic order, the organization of public and private space, and of modern life itself. In so doing, Walden fashioned an argument that attempted to explain an entire society and its culture at the dawn of modernity.

Explanatory claims are useful in two ways. First, if you are concerned about why current events take the shape that they do, then explanatory claims can be highly informative. Just as descriptive claims can provide crucial context or background information on current events, so can explanatory claims. However, explanatory claims can offer a second and potentially

TABLE 9.2 Explanatory Claims in Historical, Policy, and Case Analysis

RESEARCH QUESTIONS (RQs)	THESES (T)
RQ1: 'Why did Alice Peterson call herself a "business girl" rather than . . . an office worker? Why would an office worker's gender have mattered? Was Alice unusual or voicing a common attitude?' (Kwolek-Folland, 1994, p. 1)	T1: '[We] have to see lesbians of any era as they saw themselves . . . and as the media and society regarded them, if we want to understand the historical context for their struggles. An exploration of how the lesbian as subject and her fight for equality have fared in *Chatelaine* will make . . . generational links and lapses more apparent.' (Freeman, 2006, pp. 816–817)
RQ2: '[How] did community radio come to establish itself within Canadian broadcast policy, and what might have instigated or shaped its development?' (Fauteux, 2008, p. 131)	T2: 'This book explores . . . the Toronto Industrial Exhibition and tries to suggest how it contributed, intentionally and unintentionally, to the shaping of understandings of modernity.' 'What made the fair so effective a catalyst in helping people handle new arrangements and possibilities was its ritual quality.' (Walden, 1997, pp. 7–25)
RQ3: 'How do the practices of urban Aboriginal self-authorship at two university radio stations re-situate Aboriginality through media production?' (Buddle, 2005, p. 12)	T3: 'This article focuses on the post-1980 period . . . The analysis seeks to discern the characteristics of the "neoliberal turn" in cultural policy and administration in Ontario and Quebec.' (Gattinger & Saint-Pierre, 2010, p. 280)

more powerful set of insights if their findings are generalizable beyond the specific time period under study. When we examine specific events, either historically or in case studies, we examine how individuals and social groups shaped their society and culture through the decisions they made. If it is possible to learn from those decisions, and apply similar thinking to current issues or proposed endeavours, then that is a powerful insight.

We noted in the previous section that case study typically takes one of two forms. In the first, researchers assess the utility of a theory by examining a relevant case. Such studies most often advance descriptive or interpretive claims. In the second form of a case study, researchers begin with a case and then seek a compelling and comprehensive explanation of it. They may test competing theories, or they may look for an entirely new explanation that fits the data. Once a satisfactory explanation of the case has been found, researchers typically draw inferences from their findings to assess whether this explanation can be applied

to other, similar cases beyond the one used in the study—just as they may be with historical or policy analyses (Yin, 2003).

One case analysis that advances an explanatory claim is Richelieu and Pons's (2008) study of brand identity in the National Hockey League. This study offered a comparative case analysis in which the marketing efforts of three specific franchises (the Montréal Canadiens, Ottawa Senators, and Atlanta Thrashers) were described individually and in detail. Once the cases were described, they were compared for their relative levels of success or failure at achieving a clear identity or brand position in the minds of the hockey audience. The researchers then applied a set of concepts central to brand theory to explain these successes and failures. By examining the entire context in which the franchises exist, and providing a useful conceptual frame for their data, Richelieu and Pons supply an explanatory insight that could be applied to similar small-market franchises in hockey, and perhaps in other team sports as well.

Evaluative and Reformist Claims

Researchers working from the perspective of the critical paradigm will most often use historical, policy, or case analysis to advance claims which are evaluative. Within the areas of policy and case analysis, researchers may also advance reformist claims. Indeed, policy analysis is often designed to find improvement in the design or implementation of a specific, existing policy (Johnson, 1975; Forester, 1993). Although some historical researchers advance reformist claims, most do so only by inference based on their evaluations of their topics. In either scenario, a researcher is not content to describe, interpret, or explain past events. If a researcher advances claims that are evaluative, then that researcher must have a set of criteria against which the topic under study can be assessed or judged (MacRae & Wilde, 1979, 8). If the claims are reformist, then that researcher will also use his or her research to argue for change in the present day.

Babe (1990) detailed the development of the telecommunications industry in Canada in a study that examined both private sector operations and government policy. Babe's historical analysis and policy analysis are inseparable in this study. To understand how the industry developed, you must know how the government regulated it. To understand how the government regulated the industry, you must know how the industry developed. Because much of this story was lost to memory, Babe first had to reconstruct it by interpreting multiple documents and piecing together a coherent description of events. Next, he had to explain why those events unfolded as they did to understand them fully, particularly to understand the motives of both industry and government. Finally, Babe evaluated the various efforts of industry

TABLE 9.3 Evaluative and Reformist Claims in Historical Analysis

RESEARCH QUESTIONS (RQs)	THESES (T)
RQ1: 'Why did the Lincoln Report on Canadian broadcasting, issued in 2003, not receive any substantial coverage in daily newspapers?' (Edge, 2007, pp. 76–78)	T1: '[We] contend that analyses of the processes whereby media "truths" are created can move us beyond simple notions of "the power of the media" to an understanding of how such power is produced and reproduced, by examining coverage of the Westray mine disaster.' (O'Connell & Mills, 2003, p. 324)
RQ2: '[This] paper . . . probes how the colour pink in the breast cancer movement works as a form of public, politicized and frequently contested communication. . . . This article will focus specifically on . . . the ways in which the colour itself has become co-opted and made to signify . . . corporate products and ideologies about women.' (Elliott, 2007, p. 522)	T2: 'This book is an analytical history of telecommunications in Canada . . . emphasizing what is too often omitted in industrial histories— namely, the role of corporate and governmental power in implementing industrial devices and processes. . . . [Our] communications industries took shape and developed through the agency of and the struggle for human power.' (Babe, 1990, pp. 4–5)
RQ3: 'This case study of the television program *Due South* attempts to answer the following questions: (1) What distinctively Canadian elements were integrated into the series?; (2) Were the elements popular with Canadian audiences? and foreign audiences?; (3) Was the series economically viable?, and finally; (4) What impact did the show have upon Canadian culture and Canada's image abroad?' (Tate and Allen, 2003, p. 68)	T3: '[This] paper situates the branding of beef within broader processes of risk communication. To illustrate, I use the Alberta beef industry's branding initiatives . . . .' (Blue, 2009, p. 230)

and government to develop telecommunications in Canada. His standard was public service: were the decisions made by industry leaders and government policy makers the right decisions to serve the communication needs of Canadians? The lessons learned from his explanations and critical judgments led into suggestions for changes that would improve telecommunications policy in the future.

The utility of evaluative and reformist claims is clear: they foster research with actionable outcomes. Where most descriptive, interpretive, and explanatory claims for historical, policy, and case analysis initiate research in which knowledge of the past is an end unto itself, the findings that emerge from evaluative and reformist claims prompt us to action. If we are not urged to change current conditions, then we are at least urged to make judgments that will affect our beliefs or actions in the future.

One example of research that combined policy and case analysis was Blue's (2009) study of Alberta beef marketing. She examined the efforts of the Alberta beef industry to create consumer identification with their product both before and after a local outbreak of bovine spongiform encephalopathy (BSE), a disease more commonly known as 'mad-cow disease'. BSE, when transmitted to humans, can damage the nervous system and can lead to death. The Alberta beef industry, fearful of its complete collapse when consumers subsequently chose to stop eating beef, turned to branding to reassure consumers that the risk of eating BSE-infected meat was low. The marketing pitch targeted women homemakers and portrayed beef as a nourishing part of the family diet. It also portrayed it as an integral part of local agricultural traditions. The pitch did not describe BSE risk or modern beef production on industrial farms. Because agricultural marketing in Canada is regulated and subsidized by the federal government, Blue judged that this branding effort represented a failure of the government's role in protecting public health (2009, pp. 240–241). By implication, her research suggests that the government should review its oversight of agricultural branding practices.

Although there are many types of claims that can be made in historical, policy, and case analysis, the types of data used are quite similar. We shall now turn to a consideration of data.

Data for Historical, Policy, and Case Analysis

When researchers conducting historical, policy, or case, analysis first look for data, they are often met with one of two problems. Both problems are related to the availability of sources that can address their claims: either the researchers will not find enough sources, or they will be overwhelmed by the variety of sources available. If their claims are carefully crafted, however, most researchers can uncover sources that answer their questions, and we will discuss three types of sources in the next section. Once relevant sources have been found, careful researchers must then ask if their sources are relevant and adequate.

With respect to availability, we should remember that finding specific sources can be quite difficult. Researchers who conduct surveys and content analysis on contemporary issues have the luxury of defining their research populations. Generally, their sources of information can number in the thousands and their task is to limit their data to a manageable and representative sample. By contrast, researchers conducting historical analysis may have difficulty simply finding evidence. If an historical fact is part of the public record, then it is already recorded in an easily accessible document, likely a book or journal article. If, however, you wish to answer a question that has never been answered adequately, or indeed has never been asked, then you may be forced to look for sources that have never been used. This is often the case when a researcher wants to understand the motives of individuals or groups during important events or periods in time. When such individuals or group members are no longer living, we must turn to whatever documents or artefacts they left behind; we must hope that these figures recorded their thoughts in some tangible form.

Even when individuals or groups have recorded their thoughts and actions, researchers can still face three problems. First, such documents may not be kept in a publicly accessible repository. When private individuals, businesses, and voluntary organizations maintain their own records, they do so for their own benefit. They are not obliged to share them with researchers. Second, even when documents are

EXHIBIT 9.1   Basic Steps of Historical and Policy Analysis

1. Review the literature on your topic.
2. Articulate your claim that describes, interprets, or explains an artefact, event, trend, policy, or culture, or that evaluates or suggests the reform of a policy, process, or culture. Your claim may be stated as a research question or a hypothesis.
3. Locate relevant primary sources that were used in the secondary literature.
4. Locate additional primary sources through your own search.
5. Gather data by reviewing published documents, interviewing informants, or travelling to archives, museums, and galleries, as necessary.
6. Question your sources for their accuracy and consistency. If needed, confirm the reliability of your sources through data triangulation.
7. Organize your data, either into a single chronology or into discrete thematic clusters. Themes may emerge through your literature review, in a theoretical framework, or through the process of discovery as you gather data.
8. Construct a detailed narrative based upon your chronology, or draft a rich description of your topic. If you have thematic clusters of data, these themes may suggest links between individual facts or reveal patterns in the data. Alternatively, a theoretical framework may inform the way that you link individual facts or see patterns in the data. You should provide an audit trail for every piece of information taken from your sources.
9. Draw conclusions from your narrative or the patterns you identify, relevant to your original claim.
10. Write your critical essay or research report.

EXHIBIT 9.2   Basic Steps of Case Analysis

1. Review the literature on your topic.
2. Articulate your claim that describes, interprets, or explains a specific individual, group, artefact, or trend, or that evaluates or suggests the reform of a policy or process. Your claim may be stated as a research question or a hypothesis.
3. Select a relevant individual, group, artefact, or trend to serve as your case; that is, as the source of your primary data.

Note: steps 1, 2, and 3 may take place simultaneously.

4. Locate additional primary sources relevant to your selected case.
5. Gather data by observing the site of your case, or by consulting relevant individuals, documents, and artefacts, as necessary.
6. Question your sources for their accuracy and consistency. If needed, confirm the reliability of your sources through data triangulation.
7. Organize your data, either into a single chronology or into discrete thematic clusters. Themes may emerge through your literature review, in a theoretical framework, or through the process of discovery as you gather data.
8. Construct a detailed narrative based upon your chronology, or draft a rich description of your case. If you have thematic clusters of data, these themes may suggest links between individual facts or reveal patterns in the data. You should provide an audit trail for every piece of information taken from your sources.
9. Apply an existing theory to the narrative or rich description in order to explain the relationships or patterns that you see in the data. Alternatively, you may draft a new theory or modify an existing theory to explain the relationships or patterns that you see in the data.
10. Draw conclusions from your narrative or rich description, relevant to your original claim.
11. Write your case study in the form of a research report or critical essay.

known to exist in a specific repository, a researcher might not be given access to them. For example, the federal government releases cabinet documents only after 31 years have passed. In the private sector, most sensitive documents may never be released to the public.

Third, as we noted earlier in this chapter, some documents simply disappear over time. What is preserved tends to be what someone with influence, space, and resources considers worthy of collecting (Storey & Jones, 2004, pp. 23–24). Hence, researchers today must rely upon the prescience of librarians, archivists, or collectors in the past to have kept necessary materials for their research. For example, the first major consumer magazine for Canadian women, *Everywoman's World*, appeared in 1914. Its pages might tell us much about how the media and marketers spoke to women during and after the First World War, a time when women fought for the right to vote and modern, urban life was taking hold. Unfortunately, not many issues of this magazine were kept precisely because it was popular culture. Light reading was not considered important enough to be permanently stored. Despite the fact that the magazine sold over 100,000 copies per issue, there are now perhaps 50 individual copies altogether in libraries across Canada.

These three problems with respect to documents can affect researchers conducting historical analysis, policy analysis, and case analysis. Researchers who rely on individual informants to supply data, particularly for policy and case analysis, face two other challenges. First, with respect to policy analysis, those individuals who participate in policy formation do not always want to have their motives and actions examined or critiqued. This point applies in government and in the private sector. Politicians and senior corporate officials may have nothing to gain by sharing information with researchers. At the same time, civil servants and junior staff at private companies may be barred from speaking on behalf of their organizations. If there was any controversy surrounding a policy's development and implementation, it is possible that no one connected with it will want to go on the record by discussing it with you.

Second, researchers studying groups or organizations may face problems when selecting a case for study. Typically, a research question for case analysis is directly tied to a specific case that serves as the source of data. If you are studying a specific group and its culture, then you must have permission to join that group or to observe how it functions. This is an ethical obligation for you as a researcher, and often a legal obligation as well. No matter how carefully you have selected a group for study, and no matter how carefully you have crafted your claims, this work will end abruptly if the group itself does not agree to participate.

We note these problems to underscore the fact that researchers conducting historical, policy, and case analysis generally require specific data to be available in order to address their claims. Whether their sources of data are documents, individuals, or groups (including businesses and other organizations), it can be difficult to find and access the precise data required. That said, finding relevant data is not always difficult. Depending on the topic, the time frame, or the scale of the researchers' claims, relevant sources may be readily available. If a researcher is not primarily concerned with a specific individual, event, policy, or text, but is interested in a general social trend or cultural phenomenon, then the volume of sources may actually be quite daunting. Recently, researchers have begun to assess the legacy of the counter-culture that is associated with rebellious youth in the 1960s. Given that the generation of individuals who participated in that culture are still alive, and may possess souvenirs and other records of their experiences, there is an immeasurable mass of data that may be collected beyond what exists in libraries, archives, and museums. Owram (1996), in his study of Canadian baby boomers, addressed themes as diverse as the advent of teen culture, schooling, pop music, generational politics, and the sexual revolution, among others. In his study, then, the challenge was not to obtain data, but to make sense of the competing voices and formats that were available to craft a single, coherent analysis of the counter-culture.

As a researcher conducting historical, policy, or case analysis, then, you too must be able to find relevant sources. In the following section we will address the forms that sources take and how to locate them in Canada.

Sources of Data

The difficulties faced by researchers using historical, policy, and case analysis have led many to compare their research methods to detective work (Gillham, 2000, p. 32). Like a private investigator, the historian must reconstruct events which he or she did not witness, identify individuals who were present and had a role in those events, and then uncover the motives for those individuals in order to understand why events unfolded as they did. All of these tasks require sources of data. Depending on your topic, the timeframe, or the scale of your claim, there are three basic formats of sources that may be available: traditional documentary evidence, material artefacts, and informants. We will examine each type of format in turn, and then discuss where you can find them.

Documentary Evidence

Documentary evidence is a legal term that describes any written proof that can be supplied to support a fact. In the context of historical research, this is a useful term in so far as it can also describe the most traditional format of sources sought by historians: written or printed records.

Let us recall an important distinction drawn in chapter 5, on data. There we noted that texts can be categorized as either primary or secondary sources: a primary source is one that supplies first-hand, direct, or unmediated facts about the topic you wish to study, while a secondary source is one that supplies second-hand, indirect, or mediated facts about the topic you wish to study. Most scholars conducting historical, policy, and case analysis desire primary sources. They may not believe that a primary source is more trustworthy than a secondary source, but they want to have direct access to their topic; they want an opportunity to assess relevant artefacts for themselves (Benjamin, 1991; Storey & Jones, 2004). This does not mean that secondary sources are ignored. As we noted in chapter 1, the introduction, all research begins by conducting a literature review of the available secondary material on your topic. By reviewing the literature, you can see how other scholars have studied that topic; you can note the methods and sources they used, you can identify the theories they brought to their data, and

you can assess their conclusions. Researchers rely on the work of other scholars, and hence on literature reviews, for two reasons: to supply the facts needed to understand the context for their own research, and to locate important sources that have been used by past scholars. Most new research, however, requires primary sources. We shall describe the kinds of data you are most likely to find in each format, and the kinds of repositories where these formats can be found.

With respect to documentary evidence, there are two types of primary sources: published documents and unpublished documents. Published documents are any texts that are printed and widely distributed. This includes books, newspapers, and magazines. It also includes comic books, booklets, pamphlets, maps, postcards, posters, or any other form of commonly produced paper ephemera. With respect to policy analysis, this includes parliamentary records such as Hansard, the minutes of committees, the Journals of the House of Commons, statutes, legal decisions, and annual department reports, as well as the comparable records of each province, territory, and municipality. Researchers who conduct case studies on organizations will look for comparable corporate records, such as websites, annual reports, technical manuals, advertising, or catalogues. Regardless of the topic, most researchers seeking primary documents look first for published documents. Certainly, if we consider published documents like books, periodicals, and websites, they are the most readily available primary documents since they are intended for a public audience and have wide distribution. Of course, their relevance as primary sources rather than secondary sources is relative to the topic you wish to study.

Earlier, we referred to Walden's (1997) study of the Canadian National Exhibition. Much of the primary evidence he supplied to describe the culture of Toronto during the Victorian period came from contemporary newspapers and magazines published in Ontario. Just as today, newspapers of the Victorian period covered important events in their local areas. Walden found hundreds of stories about the exhibition that detailed the organization and finances of the exhibition, its displays and shows, the crowds that attended, and the problems that occasionally arose when fair-goers were more enthusiastic than the police thought appropriate.

Because the reporters or the individuals they interviewed were participants or witnesses to the events described in the stories, the stories themselves are primary documents. In this case, then, Walden found a primary source of information with an enormous supply of facts and insights about the exhibition.

Similarly, Sims (2000) relied on published reports to reconstruct a case to analyze the ability of managers to change organizational culture. Scholars who study organizations have long debated whether or not managers can actively shape workplace culture. Sims looked at one prominent financial company, Salomon Brothers, after it was rocked by a scandal and then had to rebuild its reputation and clientele. Sims argued that the scandal occurred because the organization's culture prompted its employees to make poor ethical choices. When a new manager arrived, his first task was to remake the culture. To collect data on the company during its fall and rise, Sims relied on contemporary newspaper accounts and business magazines.

Unpublished documents are texts which have never been formally published or which have not had wide, popular circulation. Generally, these kinds of documents fall into three categories: the personal papers of individuals, the corporate records of organizations or companies, and the corporate records of government departments and agencies. Let's discuss each one in turn. First, personal papers can include any documents produced, received, or collected by an individual during his or her lifetime. This can amount to a considerable volume of material. Personal papers are often associated with intimate items such as letters, cards, diaries, and notebooks; administrative items like pay stubs, cheques, receipts and ledgers; or artistic expressions such as unpublished poetry, musical scores, lyrics, manuscripts, photographs, and drawings. This list is not exhaustive. Think of the papers you keep which are personal or financial, whimsical or legal, and you can imagine what anyone else may also keep. Depending on your topic, it may be quite useful to have access to personal papers such as these. Published documents may supply important accounts of events, but they do not always reveal the thoughts or motives of the individuals involved in those events. When the personal papers of participants are available, they can provide invaluable insights into those events

and why they occurred. Indeed, such papers may provide insights that cannot be found anywhere else, particularly if the individual who produced them is dead.

In communication and cultural studies research, personal papers are most often used in one of two areas: to provide data for policy analysis, or to understand better an individual who worked in a cultural industry. With respect to policy analysis, much of the process of government policy formation—such as the work of committees, approval procedures, and enforcement—is publicly documented in the minutes of meetings or in published news reports. Sometimes, however, policy makers make surprising decisions that are not fully explained through the public record. The early years of radio in Canada provide a suitable example, when a Conservative government advocating fiscal restraint nationalized the broadcasting system and established a public broadcasting service (now known as the CBC). Vipond (1992) drew upon the personal papers of several men who were policy makers in the 1930s, including two prime ministers, to understand the personal and political motives behind this decision.

Thousands of people work in cultural industries such as publishing, music, broadcasting, theatre, film, and advertising. The most successful artists and producers can influence millions of people, and so it is not surprising, then, that their work is examined by scholars in communication and cultural studies. Again, when it is possible to access the personal papers of such artists and producers, it can provide insights into their work that cannot be intuited in any other way. This is particularly true when researching biographies, such as Friedrich's (1990) account of pianist Glenn Gould, or Cheney's (1981) study of electrical engineer Nikola Tesla.

After personal papers, the other two categories of unpublished documents are the corporate records of private organizations and companies, and the corporate records of government departments and agencies. By private organizations and companies, we mean any formally organized group of individuals who operate in the private sector or voluntary sector of the economy. Such groups include charities, clubs, religious bodies, and businesses large and small. By government departments and agencies, we mean a range of public sector offices. In Canada, we have three layers of government as jurisdiction over public affairs is divided between the federal, provincial or territorial, and municipal governments. All three levels are of interest to scholars in communication and cultural studies. Within the context of policy studies, for example, the federal government regulates or subsidizes major cultural industries through agencies such as Telefilm Canada and the CRTC, and through crown corporations such as the CBC. Provincial governments have a hand through agencies like the Saskatchewan Arts Board, and municipalities do likewise through agencies like the Edmonton Community Foundation. These kinds of organizations produce records that can reveal corporate decision-making processes and strategies, much like the personal papers of individuals can reveal their thoughts and motives. Such records include publicly available documents like annual reports, financial statements, minutes of annual general meetings, and advertisements. They may also include internal documents like human resource policies, market research reports, product development files, or financial ledgers. Robinson (1999) used the corporate records of several market research and media companies to understand the rise of opinion polling in Canada. He gained access to archives for Gallup Canada and Maclean-Hunter Publishing in Canada, and the Gallup organization and J. Walter Thompson Advertising in the United States. All of these companies were leaders in their fields in their respective countries.

When a researcher gains access to corporate materials, the data can be quite revealing. Martin (1991) gained access to the corporate records of Bell Canada to explore the origins of the telephone system. The records provided the data she needed to describe how A.G. Bell's invention was initially developed and marketed as a business-to-business device. The records also revealed how women's unintended use of the telephone prompted the company to rethink its business model. Subsequently, telephones were marketed as domestic appliances that would improve the lives of women homemakers. Martin's research reveals that corporate records are not only useful to understand the companies themselves; they can also provide evidence of contemporary cultural attitudes and trends.

Once you have exhausted your search for documents, both published and unpublished, you may wish to look for other types of objects that carry meaning or significance in relation to your topic. We shall turn to these next.

Material Artefacts

Material **artefacts** are any physical objects created in relation to the topic of your study. Quite literally anything could be considered a material artefact if it conveys some form of relevant information. This category of sources could include personal effects such as clothing, accessories, jewellery, and cosmetics, household items such as appliances and furniture, works of fine art such as sculpture or pottery, architecture, and landscaping, or industrial machinery and products. Art occupies a grey area with respect to our definitions of documents and material artefacts. Although the fine arts find expression in materials beyond the printed page, many scholars still 'read' them as texts by using analytical perspectives developed in art history and criticism, literature studies, or cultural studies.

A prime example of material artefacts used in communication and cultural research are the technologies we use to communicate, such as printing presses and wireless devices. Scholars who study the early use of these technologies have begun to look at preserved samples of these devices to understand better how they were actually used, both by the individuals who produced books and radio programs, and the audiences who enjoyed them. In one case, a group researching the medieval origins of Gutenberg's invention realized that the press itself had not survived, nor had any plans for it. They then recreated one using descriptions and engravings dating from the century after Gutenberg worked (McGrady, 2008). A close examination of such devices can expose their limitations as well as their possibilities, and hence can reveal aspects of their use that may not be described in contemporary accounts because they were taken for granted.

Currently, few scholars in communication and cultural studies who conduct historical or policy research rely solely on material artefacts as sources of information. Rather, they tend to use material artefacts in addition to conventional published sources or informants, to draw insights they may not have gained from these other sources. There are exceptions. Schiffer (1991) studied portable radio sets of the twentieth century to understand their role in American culture from the 1930s to the 1970s. He found that the designs and features of the sets reflected changing attitudes towards the ideas of mobility, freedom, and youth, much as we might expect changing fashions in clothing or cars to reflect the era's cultural trends.

Research on artefacts is more common in case analyses with a contemporary focus (Gillham, 2000). For example, each new advance in digital technology usually prompts studies examining the utility of a new device or its effect upon existing social groups. Such studies are particularly common in organizational studies that assess how the device affects the morale of organizational members or how the device impacts productivity. Even so, it is unlikely that a researcher will rely on the device alone for data. In a study by Bonneville and Sicotte (2009), the researchers explored the use of laptop computers among home care providers. Although the study was centred on a particular kind of device, the most important data was gathered through interviews with the individuals who used them (in this case, nurses, therapists, and social workers). This example provides a suitable lead into our discussion of the next source.

Informants and Oral History

Informants are any living individuals who have some direct relationship to the topic of your study. Most policy and case analysis is concerned with current conditions. Hence, there may be many individuals with first-hand knowledge of your topic who can provide you with relevant data. Similarly, historical analysis does not focus solely on the distant past. For any event that occurred over the last 70 years there may be individuals still alive who remember it. If you can identify and contact them, then they may provide you with an extremely rewarding set of interviews (Benjamin, 1991, pp. 79–80; Hansen et al., 1998, pp. 74–75). Historians refer to this kind of research as **oral history**, since data is usually collected in person through interview techniques.

Informants may be separated into two groups: participants and witnesses. Participants are those who had a direct hand in the events you wish to study. For

example, if you are studying a particular cultural artefact, then you may want to speak with the artist who created it; if you are studying a specific policy, then you may want to speak with the legislators, civil servants, or lobbyists who helped to draft it. In these situations, you will most likely seek a particular person to interview. In contrast, witnesses are those individuals who did not necessarily affect events but nonetheless were present and have memories of them. For example, if you were studying the excitement surrounding the 1972 hockey series between the Soviet Union and Canada, you might interview anyone who was alive at that time and recalls the events of that September. In cases such as this, there may be a large pool of possible informants with knowledge of your topic.

There is one other group of informants who may be helpful but who have only an indirect relationship to the object of your study. These individuals are relatives or associates of participants and witnesses. While they may not have first-hand experiences of your topic, they may possess knowledge passed to them by those who did have such experiences. Think of the stories that your grandparents have shared with you about their childhood experiences. When they pass away, their stories will remain in your memory, perhaps to be shared with your own grandchildren. A remarkable example of this source of information came to light in 2010, when new information surfaced about the sinking of the R. M. S. Titanic. Louise Patten, the granddaughter of the ship's second officer, revealed that the ship did not hit the iceberg unexpectedly but because of a helmsman's error. Her grandfather, who survived the sinking, knew this but refused to report the truth during his lifetime because of the damage it would have done to his employer, the White Star Line. Patten's grandmother also refused to reveal the facts because she feared it would reflect poorly on her husband (Jack, 2010). Patten herself only made the revelation after the last survivor of the disaster had died one year earlier.

There is no one method to collect data from informants which is unique to historical, policy, or case analysis. Rather, depending on the number of informants who must be contacted, a researcher may use any number of data collection methods linked with other methodologies. When the insights or knowledge of specific individuals are sought, then one-on-one interviews are the most common means of collecting data from them. When a researcher desires the insights or knowledge of a group of people, then focus groups or a survey may be more efficient than interviews. And when the daily routines of a group or organization must be documented, as is sometimes necessary in case analysis, then observational research may be the most efficient way to collect data. Any time researchers use these means to collect data for historical, policy, or case analysis, they then must follow the same procedures we describe in chapters 7 and 11 of this text, on surveys and ethnography.

Penfold (2008) provides an example of how informants aided an oral history project. Penfold sought to document and explain the place of donuts in Canadian culture. To do so, he reconstructed the early history of donut shops through published records such as newspapers, trade publications on the food industry, and relevant government publications. To capture the local character of donut shops, however, and by extension the cultural significance of these places, Penfold collected data from 65 individuals. He specifically sought interviews with owners, employees, and patrons of donut shops who had personal experiences dating back decades. The data collected from these interviews revealed a complex set of personal feelings and motives for those who worked in the business. At the same time these interviews also revealed patterns of experience that allowed him to generalize about the growth of the business and its emergence as an iconic Canadian symbol.

Hanke (2005) and Hodgson and Vannini (2007) provide two examples of how informants aid in case analysis. Hanke (2005) sought to develop a theoretical model that could describe and explain the place of independent media outlets in a media environment that is dominated by national and global conglomerates. To test his theory, he drafted a case around the Ontario Independent Media Centre. Most of his data was collected from publicly available documents. Additional information on organizational matters, however, was from three of the centre's administrators who agreed to help. Hanke collected this information through email questionnaires. By contrast, Hodgson and Vannini (2007) used three different means to

collect data from informants for their project. Their goal was to understand the effects of ferry-commuting on an island's culture by using Gabriola Island, British Columbia, as a case. They observed passengers on the ferry, interviewed selected passengers, and later conducted a focus group with island residents.

Documentary evidence, material artefacts, and informants represent the three main formats of data that are used in historical research, case studies, and policy analysis. Categorizing sources by their format is useful when it comes to locating specific items for a research project. The process of locating sources is the topic of our next section.

Locating Sources

As we have already noted, locating data for historical, policy, and case analysis is akin to detective work. It takes logical thinking, systematic searches, and sometimes a great deal of luck. Some researchers never find the 'missing links' of data that support the claims they wish to make. Others researchers uncover remarkable sources by chance. Hence, we can suggest a series of options that will guide you through a typical search for data but, depending on your topic, you may wish to be selective in the steps you take. The main point to remember is that certain formats of data are collected and maintained by certain types of repositories. We will describe the three steps and five types of repositories.

The three search options are relatively simple. First, you should review the literature on your topic as you prepare for your research project. Chances are, other scholars have already found informative sources about your topic. This information is always contained in the authors' references, regardless of the citation style they use (i.e. endnotes, footnotes, list of references, or bibliographies). If the sources used by past scholars are significant and important, you too should consult them. There is always a chance that you will read them in a different light than past scholars, and thereby generate new insights into your topic.

Second, you can consult relevant reference guides and Internet databases to find sources. The best place to start a search for published documents is the online catalogue of the National Library and Archives of Canada (NLAC) in Ottawa. The mandate of the NLAC is to preserve one copy of every publication ever produced within the present-day borders of Canada, in any language. It also notes where unique or extra copies of publications may be in other libraries across the country. With a single search of the NLAC main catalogue, known as AMICUS, you will discover what books and magazines exist on your topic, and where you can find them.

The NLAC also maintains a second directory for newspapers. As with books, the library has a mandate to acquire a copy of every newspaper ever published in Canada, dating back to the first one published in 1759. The catalogue presently lists over 2300 titles that include First Nation, ethnic, and university newspapers. The vast majority of these newspapers are available in microfilm rather than hard copy. That said, the most popular newspapers used for research have been digitized and are available via the Internet. The digital publishing company ProQuest has digitized every single edition of *The Globe and Mail*, from its earliest edition in 1844 to the present day. These files can be searched online through the ProQuest web portal and the results can be downloaded in PDF format. The ProQuest portal charges fees for access to this material, but most university libraries maintain a subscription to make it available for student use.

It is worth noting that, while the NLAC has a general mandate to collect all things Canadian, there are also provincial and regional institutions that have more focused mandates. For example, the Bibliothèque et Archives nationals du Québec, at the Université Laval in Québec City, has a mandate to collect all works published in French in Canada. If you are searching for specific French-language publications, then, it is worthwhile to visit its online catalogue in addition to AMICUS.

A comparable computer database that lists every collection of unpublished documentary evidence in Canada is in development. The Canadian Archival Information Network (CAIN) links 800 repositories that store collections of unpublished documentary evidence. CAIN maintains a publicly accessible web portal, called Archives Canada, which hosts a search engine, and each repository is gradually uploading its records to it. This engine contains some 50,000 records, which represents only a fraction of all the

collections in Canada. However, these records do represent the most important collections stored at each repository. Often, if a repository has one important collection on a particular topic, it will have other, similar collections.

For material artefacts, there is no reference guide with comparable detail. That said, the Canadian Heritage Information Network, in cooperation with the federal government, maintains a web portal for repositories that store and showcase material artefacts. This portal is known as the Virtual Museum of Canada. It does not have a search engine that will identify individual collections of artefacts, but it does maintain a database of 3000 repositories across the country. This list sorts all repositories by the types of collections they hold and by their locations. If you find

---

EXHIBIT 9.3   Internet Sites

National Library and Archives of Canada
– book and magazine catalogue (AMICUS)
http://amicus.collectionscanada.ca/aaweb/aalogine.htm

Bibliothèque et Archives nationals du Québec
– book and magazine catalogue
http://arianeweb.ulaval.ca/web2/tramp2.exe/log_in?setting_key=french

National Library and Archives of Canada,
– newspaper database and links
http://www.collectionscanada.gc.ca/newspapers-at-lac/

Canada's Heritage from 1844
– digital archive of *The Globe and Mail*
Check with your university library for access to this archive.

Archives Canada
– website of the Canadian Archival Information Network (CAIN)
http://www.archivescanada.ca/

Virtual Museum of Canada
– website of the Canadian Heritage Information Network in cooperation with Heritage Canada
http://www.museevirtuel-virtualmuseum.ca

that a useful collection may be held by a museum listed in its database, you can then contact that museum for more information. For example, if your research interest is early railway transportation, then the database will reveal that there are over 20 museums dedicated to this topic, including the Canadian Museum of Rail Travel in Cranbrook, British Columbia, and the Railway Coastal Museum in St. John's, Newfoundland.

If you cannot identify primary sources through your literature review or available reference guides, then your third option is more challenging. You must start from scratch, using your knowledge of the topic and simple logic. There are four steps. First, try to imagine where the material you want should be. Does your topic have a specific geographic location? If so, you should be able to narrow your search to a specific province, territory, or city. Next, try to imagine the format of your sources. Will they be published documents, unpublished documents, material artefacts, or informants? If you know the format you need, then you will be able to identify an appropriate repository or reference guide to search for your sources. The third step, then, is to look for suitable repositories in the appropriate location. If you do find a promising repository, then the fourth step is to consult its staff, reference guides, or databases to see if it lists the kind of material you need. Throughout this four-step process, online search engines such as Google are extremely helpful.

Let's consider an example. If you wish to understand the role of independent artists in the comic book industry, you might conduct a case study of Dave Sim, an artist from Kitchener, Ontario. Your search for sources might begin in that city. Given that he produced a respected independent comic book, *Cerebus the Aardvark*, one important source of information will be issues of the comic itself. Libraries tend to collect published documents, so the catalogue of the Kitchener Public Library may be useful; if not, the NLAC catalogue should be your next stop. If you want to explore Sim's business operations rather than his art, you have two options. Although the comic ended its run in 2004, the company has a web presence. You could contact it directly to see if an informant is willing to speak with you. Or, if you believe that the company's unpublished documents are available in a public repository, you could contact relevant repositories in the Kitchener area.

To find the right repository for documentary evidence and material artefacts requires knowledge of what each kind of repository does. That is the focus of the next section.

Repositories

There are five types of repositories that collect and maintain documentary evidence and artefacts: research libraries, special collections libraries, archives, museums and galleries, and private collections. Typically, each type of repository collects a single format of material or materials that share a specific theme. The sources found in these repositories are of use to all researchers conducting historical, policy, or case analysis who either study the past or want to reconstruct the context for their topic.

As we have already noted, most published documents are found in libraries. There are three kinds of libraries that handle materials of interest to researchers, and they have very different mandates. These are public libraries, research libraries, and special collections libraries. You are probably familiar with the first two kinds of library. Most cities and towns operate public libraries that maintain collections of books and other materials intended for a general audience. By contrast, most universities operate **research libraries**. These are repositories that collect and maintain scholarly books, journals, and related materials on topics of advanced interest to specialized audiences.

Most libraries acquire books and other materials according to a collection mandate. The collection mandate for any one library identifies the areas of interest that the library must serve, as we noted earlier when discussing the NLAC and Bibliothèque et Archives nationals du Québec. No library on Earth can collect every published document, but each one can specialize in particular areas. The mandate of any one research library will be defined by the subjects taught at its university and by issues of local concern. For example, university libraries in British Columbia, the Maritimes, and Newfoundland are more likely to collect specialized works related to fisheries and oceanography than those in other provinces. Within its mandate, each research library will maintain collections of books, research reports, government documents, and periodicals. It is worth noting that these collections may serve as sources of primary and secondary evidence. How you use these publications will depend on your topic.

The third type of library is a **special collections library**. A special collections library collects and maintains rare publications in their original formats. Such publications are rare for one of two reasons: either very few copies were made or very few have been preserved. Most libraries make copies of their most delicate items so that researchers can study the copies rather than the originals. Copies may be made available in paper formats, microfilm, or digital scans. However, the main task of a special collections library is to ensure that the original itself is preserved. Because their holdings are rare, special collections libraries tend to operate under high security. If you visit, you may be asked for identification as you enter, you may not browse the stacks, you will be asked to wear cotton gloves if you handle an item, you may not use a pen or highlighter at all, you may not borrow any items, and you may have your belongings checked as you exit. All of these rules are enforced to protect the integrity of the holdings. Typically, special collections libraries are established as units attached to a larger library rather than as independent repositories. There are special collections units associated with both public and research libraries in Canada. Those attached to public libraries tend to collect items produced by local citizens or which document local history. Units attached to research libraries tend to collect items connected to the research interests of the university itself or which document local history. One impressive example is the Thomas Fisher Rare Book Library at the University of Toronto. Its holdings include medieval manuscripts (one dating from 1000 CE) and over 200 books published before 1501. Those with an interest in modern media studies will also find almost every magazine ever published by Rogers Publishing. The company's titles include *Maclean's*, *Chatelaine*, and more than 50 business magazines, some of which date from the 1890s.

Archives are repositories that collect and maintain unpublished documents in their original formats. In many ways, they resemble special collections libraries,

with one important difference. Rare books may be few in number, but most unpublished documents are one of a kind and utterly irreplaceable. For example, there may be few remaining copies of *Action Comics* #1, which contains the first appearance of Superman, but there is only one copy of the artist's original conception of Lois Lane. As such, all of the same rules governing the security and integrity of collections in a special collections library are also enforced in an archive.

Further, access to certain archival collections is governed by additional rules regarding their use. The information in some collections can be personally, legally, or politically sensitive. Although donors want to place their records in repositories that can preserve them and provide public access, certain donors are also keen to control how that information is used. There are various levels of control. A donor may place a collection in an archive but ask that the collection remain closed to the public until the last person named in its documents passes away. As we noted above, the NLAC retains the records of federal cabinet meetings but only opens them to the public after 31 years have passed (i.e. the cabinet records from 1980 were opened in 2011). A different tactic for donors is to allow access to a collection but to review how its information is used before it is made available in a public forum. Eaton's was Canada's largest retail chain for much of the twentieth century, and the store donated its records to the Provincial Archives of Ontario. You may consult these records, but if you wish to quote or cite information obtained from certain files then you must get legal clearance from the company that now owns the Eaton brand. When doing historical research, such restrictions threaten a scholar's independence if the donor does not agree with the scholar's findings. Unfortunately, a scholar may not find the same data anywhere else.

As we noted earlier, there are some 800 archives in Canada. Each one has a mandate that governs what it will collect. Each of the federal and provincial governments maintains archives to preserve the public record of government operations, including their administration of communication and cultural matters. In addition, these archives collect personal papers and corporate records from private citizens whose lives, experiences, and work reflect some aspect of our shared culture and heritage. Where the NLAC acquires the papers of prominent artists and entrepreneurs who rose to national prominence, provincial archives acquire similar papers that reflect their regional cultures. For example, the Nova Scotia Archives maintains collections that document the experiences of certain ethnic groups such as the Mi'kmaq, Acadians, Scots, and African Canadians. Most municipalities, universities, and religious organizations maintain archives with similarly structured mandates.

Archival collections contain whatever documents, records, and small artefacts that the donor wishes to include. They can be surprisingly intimate and revealing. Consider the personal papers of former Prime Minister W. L. M. King, held at the NLAC. Among letters to his constituents, memos to his staff, and newspaper clippings, you will also find his diaries, notebooks, letters, photos, drawings, greeting cards, pressed flowers, and locks of hair. More recent donors have provided audio recordings, home movies, and digital files. Again, many such items are never published. They are unique, created by some individual in his or her day-to-day life, or by some group or organization in its day-to-day operations. The fact that such documents are preserved is a wonder; the fact that some individuals and organizations choose to make them available for research is simply an act of civic charity.

You are probably familiar with museums and galleries. These repositories collect and maintain material artefacts. Like special collections libraries and archives, museums and galleries try to preserve artefacts in their original states, and they control the public's access to their holdings to maintain their security and integrity. Typically, museums are repositories for artefacts related to social studies, science, and technology, while galleries are exclusively dedicated to the fine arts. It is worth noting that most museums and galleries have collections of artefacts that are far more extensive than the examples they have on display. Generally, researchers are welcome to consult items in storage on an appointment basis. One example of a museum that caters specifically to communication research is the Military Communications and Electronics Museum in Kingston, Ontario. It houses a massive collection of communication devices used by the Canadian military from its origins to the present day. Part of the collection is displayed in traditional viewing areas open to the public, and the remainder is in storage but accessible for researchers seeking specific items.

There are two final points we should make about repositories. First, it is important to note that almost all repositories contain primary sources in more than one format. Although it is convenient to categorize each type of repository by the things it collects, in reality most repositories perform multiple functions. For example, some archives hold rare books that donors include with their papers and records, while museums and galleries often maintain archival collections associated with their artefacts. A case in point is the National Museum of Technology, which collects telecommunication and broadcasting equipment dating back to the 1800s. Its holdings also include the personal papers of the first civil servant to develop broadcasting policy in Canada. Similarly, the McMichael Canadian Art Collection is a gallery devoted to Canadian art, but it also retains the personal papers of certain Canadian artists. Given that these artists worked in commercial design and advertising as well as the fine arts, their papers could be valuable to researchers in several fields. Hence, if a repository has items that are relevant to your topic, it is always worth asking what else they may have.

Second, it is also important to note that not all collections of publications, documents, and artefacts are in public repositories. Until quite recently, research areas such as popular culture did not fit the general mandate of museums or galleries, and many artefacts related to popular culture were preserved only by private collectors. We have already noted the belated interest in *Everywoman's World* magazine, but the same could be said for pop music recordings, comic books, sports cards, or posters. Thankfully, these areas have now become a target for acquisitions at major repositories, and they should be well represented in public collections in the future. At present, however, it can be rewarding to seek private collectors who are willing to share their passions. Many collectors have knowledge of their subjects that rival professional curators, and they acquire items through the same channels, generally auctions and private sales. One prominent example is Reg Hartt, who has accumulated a massive collection of classic Hollywood animation on film. His collection is not kept in a museum, gallery, or archive, but in private storage. To view his films, you must contact him or attend one of his occasional screenings in Toronto.

Informants

When you seek individuals or groups as sources of information, there is no one way to locate them or contact them. However, there are some guidelines you can follow. First, if you seek specific individuals or groups, then chances are you already know who they are and the names of organizations where they can be located. For example, if you are investigating a policy, and have already found newspaper or government accounts of its development, then you should already know who participated and which stakeholders or organizations they represented. Similarly with case analysis, if you have targeted a specific type of group for study, then you should be familiar with the names and locations of those groups.

It is more difficult to locate specific individuals or groups if your topic is in the distant past. Individuals can change organizations, move, or die. Even if an individual's former organization still exists, current members may not remember him or her. Further, it is possible that a group or organization will have changed its name since the time period you wish to study. Nonetheless, whether you seek an individual or a group, it is best to start at the organizational level and to seek individuals through the organization. When searching for these individuals or groups, basic Internet search engines such as Google and Canada411 are extremely helpful.

Leenders et al. (2001, pp. 43–44) note that there are three ways to approach a recruit and to invite his or her participation: cold calls, intermediaries, or acquaintances. As many researchers have noted, the quality of your initial contact often determines your success at winning recruits and, ultimately, the success of your entire project (Naumes & Naumes, 2006, pp. 43–44). First, the most basic approach is the cold call, delivered either through a letter, an email message, or a telephone call. Typically, traditional letters offer a reliable means to contact potential recruits. If your letter is well written, identifies you as a credible researcher,

and clearly explains the goals of your research, then the individual should give your request serious consideration. Email has similar advantages, although some members of society believe that email correspondence is informal and may not give a request delivered this way the same consideration. Telephone calls, due to their immediacy, may catch potential recruits at an awkward moment or may put undue pressure on them to respond immediately.

The second and third approaches to recruiting require a level of familiarity with individuals who are involved in the area central to your research. If you know relevant intermediaries, then it can be beneficial to ask them for help when recruiting participants. Intermediaries are individuals whom you know who have credibility with the individuals or in the group that you wish to study. If an intermediary is willing to approach potential recruits on your behalf, then that provides you with credibility by association. Acquaintances are actual individuals or members of the group that you wish to study. To know an insider can be a tremendous advantage to any researcher, particularly those who wish to study a specific event, policy process, or group. Of course, it is not always an asset available to student researchers (Leenders et al., 2001, pp. 43–44).

When you do not seek specific individuals or groups, but rather a sample of opinion from the general public, your task is somewhat different. It is possible in this situation to gather participants by following the procedures described in chapter 7, on surveys, and chapter 11, on ethnography. No matter how you recruit your participants, however, you must follow ethical research practices.

Finding relevant primary sources for your research is only one step in the process of historical research or policy analysis. Once you have gathered data from these sources, your next step is to organize them in ways that will produce a meaningful set of evidence addressing your claim.

Strategies for Analysis

There are two common ways to organize historical, policy, and case data for analysis: chronologically and thematically. Before data is organized, however, it is worth asking if the data you have collected can be trusted at face value. In this section, we will briefly discuss the critical eye you should bring to all sources, and then ways to organize your data.

Questioning Your Sources: Triangulation and Resistant Reading

As students of communication and cultural studies, you know that media texts rarely provide unbiased information. Indeed, some scholars argue that all communication is persuasive and that every message you hear throughout the day is intended to reinforce or alter your thoughts and behaviours. For example, we know that fact-based texts such as news stories are shaped by every individual who is involved in their production, from informants, to reporters and videographers, to editors and producers. Each one of these individuals will have a sense of what facts to include, and what facts to leave out. Other texts are more obvious in their use of persuasion. Think of advertisements that try to shape your purchasing decisions, political speeches that seek your vote, corporate annual reports that polish reputations, medical studies that prompt changes in diet or exercise, or any form of artistic expression that affects your moods. When studying such texts, we must remember that individual speakers and authors have motives, and that their messages and texts are tools to accomplish their desires. This does not mean that they are necessarily false or intentionally misleading. It does mean, however, that we must carefully weigh the value of the data all texts provide.

This observation is no less true of the sources used in historical, policy and case analysis. For this reason, **questioning sources** is an important step in analysis. When we question our sources, we assess the extent to which we can trust the data they provide to be accurate. There are three things you can consider when you question your sources: the author, his or her motives, and the intended audience (Daniels, 1966, pp. 93–94; Benjamin, 1991, pp. 7–8; Storey & Jones, 2004, pp. 53–55). First, you should know who the author was, and how he or she may have been connected to your topic. For example, does the author provide you with primary data or secondary data? Was the author an active participant or a witness to the events you are studying? Did the author

have known political leanings, religious beliefs, or other positions that would have informed his or her report? What was the author's reputation among his or her contemporaries? Second, you should know the author's motives when he or she made a report. Did the author have a stake in the events described, and did the author gain or lose anything because of these events? Does the author defend the actions of certain participants, or attack them? Or, was the author a neutral bystander? Alternatively, was the author paid or coerced to provide his or her report? Last, you should consider the intended audience for an author's report. Was the author hoping for a wide and public audience, an audience with specialized technical knowledge, or a restricted audience pledged to secrecy? Or, was the author writing solely for him or herself while producing something like a diary? This is not an exhaustive list of questions, but it is intended to get you thinking about the potential nuances of your sources.

If you can answer such questions, then you should be able to assess the reliability of each source, and arrive at your own conclusions regarding that source's value. Again, you do not have to reject a source's report simply because you believe it is coloured in some way by the author's perspective, motives or intended audience. Even biased information is valuable if it provides an honest report of how an individual or group felt.

Just to be clear, we will state that it is not necessary to question every text that you locate. However, it is worthwhile to question every source. For example, if you locate a government file containing several documents on a single subject, you should be able to perform a single assessment of the file rather than each and every document in the file. Similarly, if one of your sources is the regularly published column of a magazine writer, there is little need to question the character, motives or audience of that writer for each column since these aspects of the column would likely remain the same from issue to issue.

If you have doubts about the accuracy of a source, you can try to verify it by checking it against other sources. In chapter 5, on data, we discussed the practice of triangulation. Ideally, for any topic you study you should locate two or more independent sources that will supply similar information. When two or more sources are genuinely independent of one another, and when they agree on the facts of your topic, then you can feel relatively comfortable that you have found trustworthy information. If you find only a single source, then you must work with the data you have and determine its accuracy for yourself. Similarly, if you find two or more sources but they disagree with one another, then you must weigh the merits of each source and determine which report is more accurate. In these situations, your knowledge of the context surrounding your topic is crucial. The more you know about the individuals, groups, or culture associated with your topic, then the more confident you can be when assessing the value of a source (Naumes & Naumes, 2006, pp. 53–54). Either way, when you make your determination regarding the source and its data, you should be able to explain how you arrived at your conclusion.

One example of this process is resistant reading. **Resistant reading** is an approach to texts that requires you to do two things. First, you must be aware of the author's perspective in his or her report. Second, you must consider the facts presented in the report from an alternative perspective, perhaps even a perspective that would oppose that of the author. For example, in Baum's (1900) novel *The Wizard of Oz*, the character Dorothy spends much of the story fleeing the Wicked Witch of the West. It is clear that the witch is a villain, but her goals and motives are never revealed. A resistant reading would consider the events of the novel from the witch's perspective, rather than Dorothy's, and try to make the witch's statements and behaviours seem rational or sympathetic rather irrational or unsympathetic. One reader has done just this. Maguire (1996), in his novel *Wicked*, recounts the same events told in Baum's novel but from the perspective of the Wicked Witch of the West. Anyone who now reads Maguire's version may feel very differently about the story's ending than they do after reading Baum's tale. Although this example is drawn from works of fiction, it also applies when reading any non-fiction text. Prior to the Victorian era, few women were permitted to express themselves in public. Any scholar who wishes to study communication or culture before 1850, then, must cope with the fact that most reports were authored by men. Hence, scholars have used resistant reading to great effect to introduce an historically situated woman's perspective to analyses of earlier times and cultures (e.g. Landes, 1988; Fraser, 1992).

In our day, there are still many situations in which marginalized groups are prevented from speaking for themselves. Simultaneously, there are many situations in which communications are one-sided, as they are with much government and corporate communications. It can be useful to consider alternative viewpoints to assess the value of what has been said or not said. For this reason, resistant reading can provide powerful insights for policy and case analysis focused on contemporary issues, just as it does for historical analysis. A good example is provided by Blue's (2009) case analysis of branding within the Alberta beef industry. As we noted above, she described the messages conveyed by the industry that emphasized the nutritional value and traditions of beef. At the same time, she also described what was not conveyed by the industry: the risk of BSE infection and the role of modern farming methods in the spread of the disease. We will further discuss this approach to data in chapter 12, on critical studies.

A second way to question sources is to read documents within the parameters of a theoretical model or framework (Jenkins, 1978; Yin, 2003). In chapter 8, on content analysis, we explained the difference between manifest content and latent content. As we noted there, any one message may contain layers of meaning. The manifest content is that layer of meaning which is most evident and directly articulated through the words or images that compose the message. The latent content is that layer of meaning that is not necessarily evident or directly articulated but is implied through the words or images. Many scholars of communication and culture deploy theoretical frameworks to expose and analyze the latent content of the messages that they study. With resistant reading you must imagine how the author's contemporaries would have responded to his or her report, which can be a creative, open-ended process. By contrast, using a theoretical framework, you will isolate specific aspects of the text as identified by the theory. You will then investigate these aspects of the text with questions posed by the theory, or you will assess whether these aspects of the text appear or behave as the theory predicts they will (Hansen et al., 1998).

Marquis's (2009) study of the daily newspaper *L'Action catholique* provides a useful example. *L'Action catholique* was founded in 1907 by the Catholic Church in Québec. It sought to produce a newspaper that would present the day's events while supporting church doctrine. In the 1800s, this practice was common; most newspapers were founded to champion a particular political or religious outlook. After 1900, however, many papers began to offer more objective news reporting. Marquis asked, which type of paper was *L'Action catholique*? To answer her question, she drew upon a set of concepts developed by Mouillard (1968) which distinguished the 'combat press' from the 'information press' by describing how particular elements of a newspaper served either one role or the other. Using these concepts, Marquis isolated these particular elements of *L'Action catholique* and assessed whether the newspaper behaved as Mouillard predicted. She concluded that it did not. Rather, the newspaper found a successful compromise between the role of a combat paper and an information paper.

After questioning your sources, and confirming their relevance and accuracy with respect to your topic, you must then organize your raw data. In the next section, we describe two common ways to perform this task.

Chronology

Most historians agree 'The most distinctive feature of the historical approach . . . is its emphasis on the time dimension' (Daniels, 1966, p. 8). Whether we are locating our topic in its time period, or describing how something changed, we are always aware of the passage of time in the life of individuals, groups, and cultures. When we try to explain the individuals, groups, and cultures we observe, we seek causal links between the events we consider to be the most important. Generally, we assume that events are linked forward through time; that is, that earlier events must affect later events, and not the reverse. Chronological organization is rooted in this assumption. To organize your data in a **chronology** is to arrange all of your data in the order of the events they describe, starting with those that describe the earliest point in time and ending with those that describe the last (Daniels, 1966; Benjamin, 1991, pp. 76–78).

The explanatory power of chronological organization is well understood by policy and case analysts. As Naumes and Naumes point out, 'Writing a case is writing a story—the story of a company or an institution or a situation' (2006, p. xvii). The most common structure adopted for a written case is a narrative that organizes events in chronological order (Feagin et al., 1991, pp. 19–21; Gillham, 2000, p. 96). Similarly, many policy analysts use a chronology to describe several moments in the life of a specific policy. In its simplest form, this chronology has three periods: first, the historical context in which the need for a new policy emerges; second, the process of policy formation as stakeholders debate its shape and goals; and third, the period of its implementation when the policy's implications are projected or its actual performance is measured (Jenkins, 1978).

The most basic form of chronological organization is a time line. If depicted visually, a **time line** is literally a single line with important dates marked along its length, with the earliest date marked at the extreme left and the most recent date marked at its extreme right. As you sift through your data, you can mark important events on the line at the appropriate points. The result should be a graphic representation of how various events are related in time. For example, it should indicate what events happened first, what happened second, and so on. Depending on what information you include, the time line might also show who is involved in events, and in what capacities. It might indicate when new ideas or new technologies become available and, as well, it might depict when disputes arise or when policies are enacted.

Chronological organization has the capacity to impose order on otherwise random sets of data. Simply by fixing your data to points on the line, you are giving them order. By extension, this process should also help you understand the events you have observed. A well constructed chronology can reveal either patterns in events or singular turning points in a series of events. If a pattern emerges in the events you have observed, then chances are that these events share a common trait that is important and worthy of further investigation or explanation. Similarly, if a turning point is apparent, then chances are you have isolated a moment of importance to your topic that is also worthy of investigation or explanation. Either way, you should be able to construct a narrative that links the points in your chronology in a way that makes sense.

There are two ways to conceive of **narratives**. Scholars working from the perspective of the discovery paradigm might argue that their data report a factual account of events and it is their job as researchers to relay this account as accurately as possible. Insofar as a researcher only relays a time line, this is generally true. If you are conducting a study in which historical research is only one part of a larger program, then you may only use historical research to produce a simple chronology to put your topic in context. For example, in case study research, a case may be described in more or less detail, but the researcher's goal is to present the data in clear and precise terms so that it may be analyzed separately. Similarly, in policy analysis, a chronology may establish the historical parameters for a more thorough analysis of contemporary issues. In both of these uses of a chronology, it is implied that the historical information is important to understand the topic, but the researcher's analysis is focused elsewhere.

Scholars working from the perspectives of the interpretive and critical paradigms conceive of narratives much differently. They reject the notion that data can produce a factual account without the influence of the researcher's own values and judgments. For example, every event that you include in your chronology will only be there because you collected the relevant data and judged it to be significant to your topic. If there is a related or parallel set of data that you do not collect or judge to be significant, then those events will not appear in your chronology. In other words, every decision you make while collecting, judging, and organizing your data affects your chronology. This insight is magnified when we consider the task of writing a narrative. By explaining the links between events in your chronology, interpretivist and critical scholars argue that you are actively introducing your own interpretation of events to the raw data. Our earlier comparison of research and detective work is relevant here. A detective may gather many clues from a crime scene, but his or her interpretation of those clues may or may not reflect what actually happened. Similarly, a time line might reveal that one event occurred before a second event, but if you link the two events in a narrative then you are introducing a logic that unites them and explains their relationship. You may or may not be right.

Themes

The second way to organize data for historical, policy, and case analysis is by theme. There are three ways that you may identify relevant themes for your topic: by reviewing the literature, by adopting a theoretical framework, or by discovery (Daniels, 1966). First, before you begin your search from primary data, your literature review may suggest that your topic can be divided into several smaller subtopics. Each one of these subtopics may represent a thematic unit that can be treated individually. Second, if you are working with a particular theory, the theory itself may identify various aspects of your topic that must be examined and understood to explain the topic as a whole. Again, each one of these aspects may represent a thematic unit that can be treated separately. Finally, when sifting through your data you may discover that your sources are particularly rich in detail, and several themes may emerge which are worthy of analysis. When this occurs it is helpful to disentangle each theme to produce a clear analysis of each one. The simplest way to do this is to sort your data by theme into coherent clusters (Gillham, 2000, p. 96). Once the sorting process is complete, you may then create a unique chronology for each theme, and proceed with your analysis as we have just described (Storey & Jones, 2004, p. 63).

As we have already noted in this section, your interpretation of the basic chronology can be affected by many factors, and these factors may affect how readers assess the merits of your research. The best way to enhance the reliability of your findings is to establish the credibility of your data and or your interpretations of them. This will be the main consideration of the next section.

Warrants for Historical, Policy, and Case Analysis

Your ability to develop compelling findings through historical, policy, and case analysis depends on several factors. The most challenging task is locating sources that will address your claim. After that, there are four common warrants for your research data. Using the terminology we introduced in chapter 6, these warrants are audit trails, representativeness, adequacy, and coherence. Let's look at how you can apply each of these warrants to your work.

Audit Trails

As we discussed in chapter 6, on warrants, an audit trail is the best way to document the development and progress of a research study. As you collect each piece of information relevant to your study, you must note its source. This is true no matter what sources or formats supply your data. When the information is drawn from published documents, then you must also ensure that you take all of the information needed to reference them properly in your own research report or critical essay. If your information is drawn from unpublished documents, material artefacts or informants, these too must be referenced properly in any written account of your own research. When you include these references, you should follow the style guidelines expected by your audience (for example, MLA, Chicago, or APA style).

Referencing is required for three reasons. First and foremost, we reference all of our sources in order to give credit to the original authors for their work. Second, the reference establishes that there is a source for any data that you convey. Third, and most important with respect to warrants for historical research, the reference should provide sufficient information about your data for your readers to assess the quality of the source and the data itself. Often, the source of your data affects it credibility as much as the information conveyed by the data itself. If you reference a source that is known to have high degree of credibility, then your readers will likely accept your use of data from that source. If you reference a source that is known to have low credibility, or that is unknown to your readers, then they may question your use of that data. By providing the reference for any source, you are providing your readers with an opportunity to locate and assess the original data for themselves.

Representativeness and Adequacy

In chapter 5, you learned about the general principle of representativeness. When a sample represents its population well, we say it provides a very good picture of what the whole group looks like even though we have not examined every member. We first applied this concept to survey research and content analysis with reference to external validity. Given hundreds, thousands, or perhaps millions of sources of data, you must select a representative sample that adequately represents the entire population of individuals or messages you wish to study. As you know from chapter 6, the best way to gather a representative sample from a large population is to randomize the selection process. Usually, the larger the sample, the better your chances of representing the parent message population. If you are using survey research or content analysis to collect data for an historical study, then these same principles will apply.

Most of the time, however, researchers conducting historical, policy, or case analysis do not have to cope with too much data. Rather, they must cope with too few data for all of the reasons we described in the preceding sections. Case analysis is particularly vulnerable to this problem because a researcher may rely upon a single case to provide all of the required data. For this reason, some quantitative researchers criticize case analysis because they feel no single case can possibly demonstrate a social trend or pattern (Feagin et al., 1991, pp. 15–16). To move forward, then, either with a single case or limited data, you can not dispense with any concern for representativeness. Instead, you must establish that the single case or sources you use are indeed representative of your topic. In effect, topics with limited sources of information demand that you achieve adequacy of data.

The best way to approach adequacy of data is to have a clear understanding of the entire population you wish to understand, and then to explain each case or source in relation to that knowledge. For example, if you wish to understand the development of a particular government policy, then you should be able to find sources which will identify the main stakeholders and their arguments for and against the policy. You may even find that alternative policies were proposed at the same time (MacRae & Wilde, 1979, pp. 9–10). If you wish to understand a group or organization, you should be able to conceive all of the individual interests that compose that group, from those in positions of power to those who are marginalized (Sjoberg et al., 1991, pp. 65–67). Once you understand the outline of your topic in these terms, you can search for sources until you have found at least one primary source to represent each point of view. Doing so, you should be able to argue that you have found a representative sample of opinion on the policy, even if your sample does not include every individual or group who participated.

With respect to case analysis, the best way to achieve adequacy is to select your case really well. This may sound facetious but it is no less true for that. As we noted in a prior section, most researchers conduct case analyses in order to test an existing theory or to develop a new theory. Theories are only useful if they have applications beyond a single case. If you are selecting a case for research, then, it is imperative that your case possess attributes which closely resemble those of every other case to which you would apply the theory (Yin, 2003, pp. 9–13). These attributes will depend on your topic. For example, if your theory is meant to address a specific industry, then you should select a company that operates in that industry. If your theory is meant to address a particular demographic profile within an organization, such as immigrants or women, then you will want to select an organization with members of that demographic group. If your topic is tightly focused, or if your theory is complicated, then the number of relevant attributes may increase. Some researchers use statistical data to compare the general population they wish to understand and the specific case selected for analysis. These statistics are meant to demonstrate that the selected case is adequate, if not representative, of the general population. Most researchers, however, rely upon a compelling description of the selected case and its resemblance to the general population. As Denscombe (1998) notes, 'The most common justification to be offered for the selection of a particular case is that it is typical' (p. 33).

Thus, in historical, policy, or case analysis, you must justify the cases you select or the sources you use. The key is to have a clear understanding of your topic's context and the attributes that are important to your analysis. If you can find sources that possess the necessary attributes while providing a comprehensive range of perspectives on your topic, then you should be able to craft a clear justification for your sources of information.

Coherence

The first two warrants address the credibility of your sources and the extent to which they actually convey information about the topic you are studying. Coherence addresses the extent to which your findings address your claim. The term itself was first developed to assess narrative analyses in the field of rhetorical studies, but as a warrant it is readily applied to the use of chronological narratives to develop claims in historical, policy, and case analysis.

According to Fisher (1987), coherence is a consistency or rationality that can be applied to a narrative. Readers judge a narrative for its ability to present a coherent 'whole' with respect to participants, settings, and the temporal development of your topic. The narrative cannot have gaps, unexplained events, or inconsistencies in logic or chronology (e.g. you cannot say that Event B caused Event A if Event A occurred first). Hence, you must represent individuals in ways that your readers will judge to be well explained and believable, even if surprising. Generally, readers will judge a narrative to be compelling if it rings true with their knowledge of the world. We may refer to this synchronicity of narrative and knowledge as 'fidelity'. That is, if your narrative rings 'true', it may be said to have fidelity. When a narrative demonstrates both coherence and fidelity, it is judged to be an effective and satisfactory argument (Foss, 2004, p. 340). We should note that for a critical scholar, a narrative must also embody worthy values or ethical principles. Critical research, to be considered effective, should demonstrate how undesirable situations have developed and suggest how they can be reformed (Foss, 2004, pp. 339–340).

For most research using data drawn from documents, material artefacts, and informants, the most effective way to achieve coherence and fidelity is through rich description. As we noted in chapter 6, on warrants, rich descriptions address every aspect of a topic in sufficient detail to understand it as fully as possible. Rich descriptions can also help the researcher to compare two or more events by exposing the similarities and differences between them. This capacity is particularly important when pursuing explanatory, interpretive, and critical claims, or when testing theories through case studies. For this reason, most historical, policy, and case analyses are thick with specific details about individuals, artefacts, events, locations, and dates.

We noted at the beginning of this chapter that the methods described here serve as a bridge from quantitative methods of exploring communication and culture (i.e. surveys and content analysis) to qualitative methods. We also noted that the procedures for gathering qualitative data must be just as cautious and precise as are the procedures for quantitative data. Researchers who use qualitative methods do not have mathematical formulas to estimate the possibility of error in their samples, but they must still account for the comprehensiveness and coherence of their findings.

Summary

In this chapter, following our *research as argument* model, we first described the five types of claim made by researchers conducting historical, policy, and case analysis. Scholars who support descriptive claims most often conduct historical or policy research in combination with another method, usually to supply background information on a given topic. In case analysis, descriptive claims most often allow researchers to test the utility of existing theories. More often, however, researchers who focus solely on historical, policy, or case analysis make interpretive, explanatory, evaluative, or reformist claims. Once your claims have been

articulated, you must find evidence that will address them. The process of locating relevant primary sources is a major challenge when specific data is required. We categorized all primary sources into three formats that should help you to think about what kind of information might be available for your topic: documentary evidence (both published and unpublished), material artefacts, and informants. Another challenge is to question these sources, to assess if the data they provide is reliable in the context of your claims. We noted three ways to make this assessment: by questioning the author's character, motives, and audience; by performing a resistant reading; or by introducing theoretical concepts or arguments to the data.

The last challenge is to analyze and explain the data it in a way that others will find sound and compelling. As we noted, researchers conducting historical, policy, and case analysis usually sort data either chronologically or thematically. Once sorted, you may look for patterns or key moments in the data. Through this process of sorting and analysis, you impose an order on the data. By extension, you impart significance and meaning onto the events that the data describe. You may draw links between events that no one else has ever drawn, or conclusions that others will find surprising. If you do, you will want your findings to be well supported by providing a clear audit trail for your sources, by providing evidence and perspectives which are both representative and adequate to support your claims, and by crafting a coherent argument

TABLE 9.4 Major Aspects of Historical, Policy, and Case Analysis

CLAIMS	DATA FORMATS	DATA REPOSITORIES	WARRANTS
Descriptive, interpretive, explanatory, evaluative, and reformist	Published documentary evidence	Libraries (public, research or special collections)	Audit trails, representativeness and adequacy, coherence and fidelity (achieved through rich description)
	Unpublished documentary evidence	Archives	
	Artefacts	Museums and galleries	
	Informants	Individual participants or witnesses, sometimes family or friends	

founded on rich description. Table 9.4 summarizes the major aspects of historical, policy, and case analysis that we have outlined in this chapter. You will see in the chapters that follow that self-discipline, caution, and clear arguments are a necessity in all forms of qualitative research.

Key Terms

Archive	Informants	Research library
Artefact	Narrative	Resistant reading
Case study	Oral history	Special collections library
Chronology	Policy analysis	Time line
Documentary evidence	Questioning sources	Unpublished document
Historical analysis		

Discussion Questions

1. What is the value of historical analysis? Is there a current issue or trend that would be better understood if you placed it in its historical context?
2. Why is historical and policy analysis more commonly associated with the perspective of the interpretive and critical paradigms than that of the discovery paradigm?
3. Why do scholars prefer primary sources over secondary sources when conducting historical research? When performing a policy analysis? When drafting a case study?
4. When we link together events in a chronology and conceive a narrative, we impose an order on those events and give them meaning. How does this happen, and why?
5. Find an article from a communication or cultural studies journal that employs historical, policy, or case analysis. There is a list of suitable journals in the first chapter of this text (Exhibit 1.2). Review the article's notes or references, and identify the sources that the author used to gather data. What format of sources did the author consult? Does the author discuss how they were located in the body of the article? Does the author question the sources or defend their use as trustworthy sources of information? How were these sources used to supply evidence for the author's claims? Ultimately, do you believe that the sources used were relevant and adequate to address the author's claim successfully?

Try It!

1. This is an exercise to find sources for historical, policy, or case analysis. It can be completed by an individual, but it may be more interesting to work in a group with two or more other members. Depending on the size of your tutorial group, it may also be adapted as a tutorial exercise.

Process:

1. Select any topic in communication and cultural studies that can be explored using historical, policy, or case analysis. Then, formulate a claim that you would like to address about your topic. Your professor or teaching assistant can help you to formulate a claim.

2. Try to identify or locate three published sources, three unpublished sources, three artefacts, and three informants that would help to answer your question. Please note: you do not have to obtain the sources. You simply have to know where they are and how you would access them. Do not contact potential informants for this exercise.

3. Once you have a list of 12 sources, consider the following questions:

(a) Which source or sources do you think will be the most valuable to address your claim, and why?

(b) Which source or sources are in the public domain and readily accessible?

(c) Which source or sources require special permission or ethics clearance to use?

(d) Are the most valuable sources also the most readily accessible or easy to obtain?

(e) Do you believe that your sources will represent the entire range of stakeholder perspectives that are relevant to your topic?

(f) Will the information provided by these sources overlap in any way? Will you be able to triangulate the information they provide?

(g) Is there a specific source which you wanted to find, but did not? If yes, what information do you think it would have provided?

2. This is an exercise for writing narratives based on limited information. It can be completed by an individual, but it may be more interesting to

work in a group with two or more other members. Depending on the size of your tutorial group, it may also be adapted as a tutorial exercise.

Process:

1. Select a topic in communication and cultural studies that has been in the news for one year or more (e.g. a policy in development or review, the planning process for a major event, or the fortunes of an artist or sports team).

2. Find one newspaper or magazine article about this topic published during each month over the last year. To find them, try to use an online newspaper or periodical database with full-text articles, such as *The Globe and Mail*'s online archive, *Canada's Heritage from 1844*. When you are done, you should have 12 articles in total.

3. Arrange your articles in chronological order based on their dates of publication. Then, using this chronology as a starting point, try to write a narrative about your topic that is based only on the data provided in your 12 articles. The narrative should be no longer than 250–500 words.

4. When it is completed, consider the following questions about your own narrative. If you are working with a group, exchange your narratives with one another and review each other's work.

   (a) Does your narrative contain adequate data to be coherent, or does it suffer from gaps in information?

   (b) Do you feel that the narrative rings true to the individuals and events it describes? Or do you think that the author has misinterpreted or stretched the facts?

   (c) Do you believe that any relevant stakeholder has not been represented fairly, or at all?

   (d) What new information might you seek to improve the narrative?

   (e) What might this exercise tell you about the search for specific sources?

10 Conversation and Discourse Analysis

Introduction

In this chapter, we will introduce you to two different methods, conversation analysis and discourse analysis. These two methods allow you to analyze textual data closely to support claims of description, explanation, and interpretation. At their core, these methods share a concern for how people use language.

We start by introducing you to **ethnomethodology** (Garfinkel, 1967), a sociological tradition in which the tools of conversation and discourse analysis were first developed. You will learn to develop descriptive and explanatory claims about how conversations are sequentially organized, and interpretive claims about how our use of language shapes our reality in all social situations. You also will learn more about how to collect, transcribe, categorize, and analyze textual data and to protect participants' rights to informed consent and privacy. Finally, you will learn to apply the warrants we use to evaluate conversation and discourse analysis. For conversation analysis, our standards are informed by the discovery paradigm and require you to show that conversational transcriptions are reliable, valid, and detailed. Further, you should be able to show that you analyzed ordinary talk-in-interaction, which is one way of warranting sample representativeness for conversational data. For discourse analysis, our standards are informed by the interpretive and critical paradigms and include your credibility as a researcher, the plausibility of your interpretations, and the degree to which your findings are transferable.

Imagine that you enter an elevator and find that three people already on board are facing the back and staring at the floor. We typically expect people to face the front of an elevator, so this might seem unusual. You will probably look for an explanation. For example, if you see an enormous bug on the floor, you may be able to understand the reason for their behaviour and proceed as usual. If you don't notice anything peculiar, you might ask one of them a question, like, 'What's going on?' Or, you might cock your head to one side and raise an eyebrow, a way of asking, 'What's up?' In all likelihood, one of the people in the elevator will respond to your question or notice your expression and explain what is happening. Until you understand the situation, however, you may feel anxious because their actions do not follow the standards of behaviour you expect from strangers in a public place. You have probably experienced something like this situation, and probably had to make sense of an unusual comment or behaviour in the midst of everyday life experiences. We often encounter such situations when we attend new schools, join new clubs, or visit other cultures where we are not familiar with the local language and social cues.

We offer this scenario to get you thinking about how you might study ordinary language behaviour. When we study the use of language, it is important to remember all of the elements that may compose communication, including body language, social expectations, and, context. Further, it is also possible to integrate language study techniques into other research methods described in this book, such as surveys, content analyses, historical research, and ethnography.

The methods of conversation and discourse analysis arose over the past 50 years from ethnomethodology as it was pioneered by Harold Garfinkel and Erving Goffman (Bode, 1990; Garfinkel, 1967; Maynard & Clayman, 1991; O'Keefe, 1980; Wooffitt, 2005). Ethnomethodology is a sociological tradition that aims to describe, explain, and interpret how members engaged in a social situation go about making sense of their own and others' behaviour. Communication, messages, talk, conversation, and discourse are just one aspect of ethnomethodological research, which also deals with perception, cognition, and embodied behaviour (Garfinkel, 1967; Maynard & Clayman, 1991; O'Keefe, 1980).

Over the last 30 years, scholars in communication and cultural studies have adopted these methods as their own. Within communication studies, the phrase **language and social interaction (LSI)** has been adopted to refer to the following areas of specialization:

> Studies of speech, language, and gesture in human communication; studies of discourse processes, face-to-face interaction, communication competence, and cognitive processing; conversation analytic, ethnographic, microethnographic, ethnomethodological, and sociolinguistic work; dialect and attitude studies, speech act theory, and pragmatics. (LeBaron, Mandelbaum, & Glenn, 2003, p. 2)

LSI emphasizes the study of ordinary social situations and participants' common sense, taken-for-granted

realities (Hopper, 1993; Tracy & Haspel, 2004). However, LSI researchers focus on language use as their only aspect of interest. As such, conversation and discourse analysis are both integral to their work.

By contrast, within cultural studies discourse analysis has taken a pre-eminent role. Indeed, it has become a major component of the researcher's toolbox and is often used in combination with other methods such as content analysis or historical analysis. Where LSI scholars focus on language use alone, cultural studies scholars using discourse analysis believe that any form of data may be relevant to a full understanding of communication and cultural exchange. To understand any one conversation, then, a researcher may need to consider the individual participants, the setting, the time, or any other myriad factors that may influence the participants' use of language, gestures, and symbols.

Let's start by briefly defining each method. **Conversation analysis** is a method associated with the discovery paradigm that aims to describe and explain how people accomplish social actions and events by collaboratively organizing sequences of talk-in-interaction (Schegloff, 2006; Hopper, Koch, & Mandelbaum, 1986). By 'talk-in-interaction', we mean the normal give and take between individuals who take turns to listen and speak with one another. In most research projects, **conversation** usually refers to telephone or face-to-face interactions between two or more participants (Wooffitt, 2005). Think for a minute about all the ways we use language. Only some of those ways involve unscripted or naturally occurring conversation with another person.

Discourse analysis is an umbrella term for research in anthropology, applied linguistics, communication, cultural studies, discursive psychology, and sociology. Discourse analysis can include the more specific method of conversation analysis (LeBaron et al., 2003; Van Dijk, 1997b; Wooffitt, 2005), but it also embraces social constructivist epistemology, which posits that everything we know is made real through language (Berger & Luckmann, 1967; Schutz, 1967; Wittgenstein, 1953). A **discourse** is 'an interrelated set of texts, and the practices of their production, dissemination, and reception, that brings an object into being' (Parker, 1992, as cited in Phillips & Hardy,

2002, p. 3). For example, you are a university student. What is the discourse surrounding the term 'university student' in Canada today? What 'interrelated set of texts' (i.e. written or spoken words, performances, and visual or pictorial symbols) contribute to that social reality? How are those texts produced, distributed, and received? What might it have meant to be a university student in Canada in 1890 or 1968 rather than today? These are the sort of research questions that you can explore using discourse analysis. Researchers in the field aim to describe, explain, and interpret how we construct and maintain our social realities over time through language.

Perhaps you will push your research claim about the term 'university student' further, and you will offer critical or reformist views. If you are concerned with unequal power relations involved in the reality of being a 'university student' at a particular time in history, or in a particular geographical or socioeconomic position, then critical discourse analysis may be a more suitable method for your study. **Critical discourse analysis** (CDA) is 'a form of intervention in social practice and social relationships' (Fairclough & Wodak, 1997, p. 258). Critical discourse analysis evaluates the social construction of reality and suggests how discursive texts and practices should be reformed (Fairclough & Wodak, 1997). If you want to conduct critical discourse analysis, you also should read chapter 12, on critical studies.

It's worth mentioning here that ethnomethodology, conversation analysis, and discourse analysis are all undertaken in English, French, Japanese, Russian, Chinese, Spanish, German, and Italian, among other languages. In any one study, however, researchers usually study social interaction within a single language. Linguistic and cultural limitations prevent most researchers from analyzing social realities across more than one language or culture (Van Dijk, 1997).

In the first section of this chapter, we give you an overview of some of the main ideas of ethnomethodology (Hopper, 1993; Tracy & Haspel, 2004). Specifically, you will learn about the research elements which ethnomethodology has contributed to LSI research. We also outline, in the first section of this chapter, three key differences between conversation analysis and discourse analysis. Then, in the rest

of the chapter, you will learn to conduct both forms of analysis.

The Roots of Conversation and Discourse Analysis in Ethnomethodology

Ethnomethodology literally means 'the people's practices' (Garfinkel, 1967), and ethnomethodologists assume that people are constantly trying to make sense out of a social situation to produce their own appropriate behaviour. In all situations, we have to sort out who we are being, to whom we are speaking, and the topic about which we are communicating to produce seamless interactions (Potter & Wetherall, 1987).

Ethnomethodology relies on three principles: (1) People assume things are as they appear to be unless there is a good reason to believe otherwise; (2) the knowledge held by people is typically incomplete; and (3) whenever people engage in coordinated actions with others, they usually assume that others see things as they do (Schutz, 1967). **Breaching**, or deviating from these three principles, disturbs everyday life, even though some deviations can be interpreted as meaningful (Garfinkel, 1967), as we found with our elevator example at the beginning of this chapter. Just as you were able to proceed once you made sense of the people facing backwards in the elevator, most individuals proceed through everyday actions because social situations are constrained by rules systems. This is true even when our rules systems are unspoken. **Rules** are general prescriptions for behaviour that must be elaborated in context to be applied (Garfinkel, 1967). Because we sometimes deviate from the rules, the reasons we give for such deviations are one important research topic for discourse analytic scholars. Researchers refer to explanations of deviant behaviour as **accounts**, (e.g. Buttny, 1987, 1993; Hewitt & Stokes, 1975; Mongeau, Hale, & Alles, 1994).

The elevator example will also help you to remember three major premises of LSI research, specifically that (1) interactants work together to accomplish sense making; (2) to understand people's methods, we must focus on their everyday life interactions; and (3) language is indexical, which means that 'the understandability of any utterance, rather than being fixed by some abstract definition, depends upon the circumstances in which it appears' (Maynard & Clayman, 1991, p. 397). All three of these premises are important for conversation and discourse analysis, as well as ethnographic research.

In the rest of this section, we outline three important differences between conversation and discourse analysis, namely, their respective (1) paradigm affiliations, (2) levels of analysis, and (3) emphases on context in analysis.

Paradigm Affiliations

Conversation and discourse analysis have come to be affiliated with different epistemological paradigms. Conversation analysis is a discovery paradigm method, often spoken of as a science. Discourse analysis is most often associated with the interpretive paradigm, although CDA is a critical method (Wooffitt, 2005). The paradigm differences between conversation and discourse analysis are most apparent when we compare their respective assumptions, data sources, and selection methods.

Conversation analysis researchers attempt to draw conclusions about their observations using careful, systematic, and repetitive procedures. They endorse the discovery paradigm assumption that any researcher who uses the same definitions and the same procedures will be able to observe the same pattern of results in sampled conversational data. In fact, conversation analysts often work cooperatively in data sessions where they listen to audio recordings or watch videos together and triangulate multiple investigator viewpoints. Some conversation researchers randomly sample conversations to support their arguments that certain interactional practices are organized in generalizable ways across contexts (i.e. across multiple settings, relationships, or participants).

By contrast, discourse analysis researchers are much more likely to embrace subjectivity and, therefore, to assume that there are multiple plausible interpretations of textual data (Van Dijk, 1997; Wooffitt, 2005). Discourse analysis studies may include naturally occurring talk-in-interaction (i.e. conversational data) but also include participant observations; interviews and texts gained from films, novels, or other

print media; as well as pictures or other kinds of symbolic artefacts (i.e. triangulation by multiple data sources). The texts used in discourse analysis are purposively selected for their utility in exploring particular research claims.

Levels of Analysis

A second important difference between conversation and discourse analysis is that they work at different levels of analysis. Conversation analysis studies describe and explain 'sequence organization'. The term **sequence organization** describes 'the ways in which turns-at-talk are ordered and combined to make actions take place in conversation, such as requests, offers, complaints, and announcements' (Schegloff, 2006, p. 1). Thus, conversation analysis emphasizes conversation between two speakers, based on close analysis of transcripts and their audio or video recordings. We refer to this level of analysis as microlevel organization in conversation because it studies the smallest possible units of conversation. It's important to note, however, that conversation analysis can focus on embodied communicative behaviours other than talk, such as the speed one speaks, intonation, facial expression, physical posture, and gestures (e.g. Goodwin & Goodwin, 1986; Sacks, Schegloff, & Jefferson, 1974; Schegloff, 2006).

By contrast, discourse analysis emphasizes macrolevel organization, which incorporates the social practices and ideological structures that are evidenced in the way people talk about things (Duranti, 1997; Van Dijk, 1997; Wooffitt, 2005). This is a major reason why discourse analysis is much more prevalent than conversation analysis in the field of cultural studies. Social practices are broader than the actions or events that we accomplish through talk-in-interaction, although they might include talk. Take debate, for example. The social practice we call debate is key to participation in a democratic society. Debate is used in classrooms, courtrooms, and politics; and it has social, political, and cultural functions (Van Dijk, 1997). Few would call a debate 'conversation', although it is interactive. Furthermore, if we wanted to study how ideas are debated, we might include texts like newspaper editorials and letters to the editor, which are discursive but not interactive.

Even though we introduced the word 'ideology' in part 1 of this book, a brief example of how discourse analysis deals with ideological structures is useful here. You can probably name some of the ideological structures that are evidenced in the ways that we talk about university students. For example, newspaper editors like to remind us that university students are society's future leaders, and that they often earn higher average incomes than those who do not attend university. However, those same editors may argue that university students are irresponsible youths or thoughtless neighbours when discussing life in off-campus housing. To explain the macrolevel social practices and ideological structures that make 'university student' a reality, discourse analysis cannot focus on a single source of textual data, such as conversation (Wooffitt, 2005). Rather, it 'must refer to *bodies* of texts because it is the interrelations between texts, changes in texts, new textual forms, and new systems of distributing texts that constitute a discourse over time' (Phillips & Hardy, 2002, p. 5).

Conversation and discourse analysis scholars share the belief that humans create social realities though our use of language (Berger & Luckmann, 1967). That said, both sets of scholars disagree on how much of an impact talk itself is likely to have on the broad social order. Conversation analysts prioritize talk-in-interaction, *per se*, as the fundamental way we accomplish social order, moment by moment, and turn by turn. Discourse analysts focus on discourses, on the broadest levels, as the best explanation for social structures. These different levels of analysis mean that conversation and discourse analysts (as well as ethnographers) sometimes disagree on the role that their research participants' context should play in data analysis (c.f. Billig & Schegloff, 1999; Hymes, 1974a; Schegloff, 1997).

Emphasis on Context in Analysis

LSI researchers agree that culture is an important context for individual sense making, but they disagree on how the cultural context of texts should be included in their analyses. Essentially, conversation and discourse analysts disagree about which element is the single most important factor to explain human behaviour (c.f. Billig, 1999; LeBaron et al., 1997; Schegloff, 1997,

1999a, 1999b; ten Have, 1999). This is an unfortunate disagreement if you wish to make compelling causal arguments. Conversation analysts typically argue that texts trump culture, while discourse analysts typically argue that culture trumps texts. One ethnographer of communication (Fitch, 1998) has tried to find a compromise by arguing 'text and context form an inseparable analytic unit' (p. 92). For now, just keep in mind the different paradigms and levels of analysis that characterize the two schools of thought as we describe the text-context argument for these methodologies.

Conversation analysts insist upon hard empirical data, which means that they rely only on conversational transcripts as evidence for their claims. They argue that meaningful exchange can be recognized by participants and analysts without considering the context (Schegloff, 2006; Van Dijk, 1997). You may encounter such an exchange in the script of a play with no stage directions, or in an online chat room where every poster remains anonymous. In other words, strictly empiricist conversation analysis does not take into account the local cultural context of research participants unless the participants do so in their conversations (Schegloff, 1997, 1999a, 1999b, 2006). Of course, the researchers' knowledge of the settings or situations they are analyzing may help them to provide a more nuanced account of the interactional practices they are investigating (Maynard, 2003).

Conversely, discourse analysts emphasize local and global **contextual constraints** on discourse (Van Dijk, 1997). Local contextual constraints can include specific or immediate elements such as the time and place of a conversation, or the participants' individual status or goals. Global contextual constraints can include broader, more general elements. First, a participant's membership in a recognized social category or group (e.g. young versus old, inmates versus criminal justice workers) may affect how that participant speaks and is heard by others. Second, the institutional setting for discourse (e.g. the legal system, journalism, health care system, or the financial sector) may affect how a participant speaks and is heard by others. For example, Sillince (2007) identified four dimensions of context in organizational discourse by isolating and examining 'when, where, as whom, and why people speak' (p. 363). He found that a discourse made in one context could easily be transferred to other contexts, with variable effects. Along with discourse analysis, ethnographic studies deal with both local and global contextual constraints on interaction and participant memberships in social categories.

It's fair to say that the role of cultural context in analysis is still debated among conversation, discourse, and critical discourse analysts (c.f. Billig, 1999; Maynard, 2003; Schegloff, 1997, 1999a, 1999b; Wooffitt, 2005). It's equally fair to point out that LSI scholarship benefits from both the insights of conversation analysis and discourse analysis. That said, the tendency of Canadian communication scholars to embrace cultural interpretations of human behaviour means that discourse analysis is much more common than conversation analysis in published research in Canada. Perhaps it goes without saying that the same is true of cultural studies.

In the remainder of this chapter, you will learn to apply the *research as argument* model to the methods of conversation and discourse analysis. We start with conversation analysis claims that describe and explain sequence organization in ordinary conversations and institutional contexts (Drew & Heritage, 1992; Maynard, 2003; Schegloff, 2006).

Conversation Analytic Claims

When you undertake conversation analysis, you examine a conversation by isolating each participant's turn at talk. Typically, you will reduce conversations into a string of individual utterances; that is, the actual messages conveyed throughout the conversation from its beginning to its end. Most importantly, you will consider what each utterance does in relation to the utterances that precede and follow it. You will assume that each speaker's turns at talk prove that he or she is oriented to the previous speaker's turn (Hutchby & Wooffitt, 1998; Schegloff, 2006). To determine how utterances are related, you will focus first on 'turn-taking in conversation—how people get to talk and for how long and with what consequences' (Schegloff, 2006, p. ix).

It is common to study everyday talk-in-interaction. By 'everyday', we mean the kinds of informal, unstructured conversations that occur between individuals

in their daily lives. That said, you might also study talk-in-interaction in formal or structured settings. Many scholars have examined institutional contexts like medical consultations, journalistic interviews, and courtroom interrogations. Exhibit 10.1 illustrates some different types of conversation analysis claims. You might start your project by describing some conversational **units of analysis**, whether those units are utterances, full sentences, or an entire speaking turn (Heritage & Sorjonen, 1994; Maynard, 1997; Raymond, 2000; Sacks et al., 1974; Schegloff, 2006). Notice that Exhibit 10.1 includes claims about several different units of analysis (i.e. adjacency pairs, pre-sequences, and longer action sequences). Remember, however, that the whole endeavour of conversation analysis begins with a focus on turn taking.

Turn Taking

Let's start with some basic terminology. All sequence organizations that are 'accomplished by talking get done in turns-at-talk' (Schegloff, 2006, p. 3). Turns are fashioned out of two related components, the turn-construction unit (TCU) and the turn-allocation unit (TAU) (Sacks et al., 1974). A **turn-construction unit** specifies what counts as a speaking turn. In ordinary conversation, grammar and intonation help speakers negotiate TCUs (Schegloff, 2006). For example, if you are comfortable speaking in your native tongue, then you know when a word, phrase, or sentence counts as a turn. We rely on the rules of grammar, vocal cues like rising or falling intonation, and gestures like eye gaze to indicate when we wish to start or when we have finished speaking. Notice that in this basic sense, turn-taking is 'context independent, because it does not rely on particulars of the circumstance to operate' (Wooffitt, 2005, p. 29).

A **turn-allocation unit** specifies who gets to speak and when. TAUs can be negotiated between interactants, as one speaker recognizes the next speaker's turn by using either words or visual and vocal cues, as we just noted. However, TAUs can be specified before the interaction even begins, especially in institutional contexts such as in a courtroom trial where the order of speakers and even some turn lengths are known at the outset of interaction (Drew, 1992). Interviews,

EXHIBIT 10.1 Conversation Analytic Claims

I. Describing and explaining sequence organization in ordinary conversations

A.   How do interactants accomplish turn taking? (Sack, Schegloff, & Jefferson, 1974; West & Zimmerman, 1983)

B.   How do adjacency pairs work?

   1.   Question-answer (Clayman, 1993; Claymen & Heritage, 2002, 2003; Heritage & Roth, 1995)

   2.   Compliment-response (e.g. Pomerantz, 1978; Valdes & Pino, 1981)

   3.   Greeting-return greeting

C.   How do interactants insert utterances before, during, and after adjacency pair parts to do things with talk? (see Schegloff, 2006)

D.   How are longer action sequences constructed on a turn-by-turn basis?

   1.   Telephone calls (Godard, 1977; Hopper, 1992; Hopper, Doany, Johnson, & Drummond, 1990; Lindstrom, 1994; Park, 2002; Schegloff, 1979)

   2.   Interactions that include quasi-lexical objects (e.g. Heritage, 1984, 1998, on 'oh'; Jefferson, 1983, on 'yeah' and 'mm-hm'; Schegloff, 1982, on 'uh-huh'; Wong, 2000b, on 'yeah' in non-native speakers' English conversations)

   3.   Interactions that integrate vocal and nonvocal activities (e.g. Goodwin, 1980, on achieving mutual eye gaze in turn-beginnings; Goodwin & Goodwin, 1986 on searching for a word)

II. Describing and explaining sequential structures in institutional contexts

A.   How are physician-patient interactions sequenced? (Boyd & Heritage, 2004; Heritage & Robinson, 2006; Robinson, 1998, 2003; Robinson & Stivers, 2001)

B.   How are calls for help sequenced? (Whalen & Zimmerman, 1987)

C.   How are ordinary courtroom interactions sequenced? (Atkinson & Drew, 1979)

Source: Adapted from Adler, Adler, & Fontana (1987).

debates, press conferences, and trials are all examples of institutional contexts in which TCUs and TAUs are enacted differently than they are in ordinary conversation (Duranti, 1997).

Once you orient your research focus to turn taking, you start to notice how sequence is being organized from one speaker to the next.

Adjacency Pairs

A sizeable body of research exists on the two-turn sequence called the adjacency pair. This is arguably the unit on which all other sequence organization is built (Schegloff, 2006). **Adjacency pairs** are two-part conversational structures in which the **first pair part** (FPP) calls for or invites the **second pair part** (SPP). There are several everyday conversational sequences that we recognize as adjacency pairs. Consider the following examples: the question-answer, compliment-response, greeting-return greeting, or invitation-accept/decline.

Questions call for answers, just as compliments invite responses, and so on. Research on adjacency pairs answer descriptive questions like, 'How do speakers construct the parts of the adjacency pair?' or 'What is the preferred SPP for a particular FPP?' The question-answer sequence is the most-researched adjacency pair (e.g. Boyd & Heritage, 2004; Clayman, 1993; Clayman & Heritage, 2002; Drew, 1998; Heritage, 2002; Stivers & Heritage, 2001). Other sample claims about adjacency pairs are shown in Exhibit 10.1.

Preference

Conversation analysts study adjacency pairs because they are used in situations in which there exists some contextual standard for behaviour; in other words, there is a socially recognized and preferred response for each FPP. In the case of questioning, the basic standard is to answer a question truthfully and briefly (Grice, 1975). Similarly, the preferred response to a compliment is modest acceptance (Pomerantz, 1978), the preferred response to a greeting is a return greeting, and so on. Conversation analyses of sequences can explain why common actions like complimenting are accomplished in a particular way (e.g. *X* happens because *Y* culture prefers that behaviour).

In everyday life, of course, we often deviate from preferred standards for SPPs. For example, when asked a question, we can dodge it by changing the topic or by providing only a partial answer. Dispreferred responses are often referred to as 'breaching'. Duranti (1997) makes the following observation about the value of studying such deviations:

> Conversation analysts have shown that in all kinds of situations there are **preferred courses of action** and that the study of both *preferred* and *dispreferred* replies to questions and other first pair parts can give us a sense not only of what social actors are after, but also of what is considered to be normal or expected in any given situation. (p. 260)

Whenever conversational participants have choices of action, the notion of preference becomes important, and this is especially the case when the choices are equivalent (Atkinson & Heritage, 1984). In conversation analysis, then, a claim might address what responses are preferred, how preferred and dispreferred choices are enacted, and what happens to sequence organization when a dispreferred response occurs. Breaching can lead to conversational trouble, usually as interruptions caused by misunderstanding or offence (Schegloff, Jefferson, & Sacks, 1977).

Repair

A considerable number of conversation analyses that deal with the notion of preference address interactants' attempts to resolve conversational trouble, known technically as **repair** (e.g. Drew, 1997, Robinson, 2006; Schegloff, Jefferson, & Sacks, 1977). Conversational trouble can come from a lack of understanding, as happens when one speaker cannot hear the other speaker, does not know the meaning of the other speaker's words, or knows more than one meaning but doesn't

know which one is relevant. Conversational trouble also can arise when a speaker is offended, as happens when you think that another speaker is being impolite, irrelevant, or untruthful. In any case, researchers can stake claims that describe and explain when trouble arises, who initiates the need for repair (e.g. is repair self-initiated by interactants or other-initiated?), how repairs are sequentially accomplished, and how conversation continues after successful repair work (e.g. Robinson, 2004).

Action Sequences

As we mentioned earlier, adjacency pairs are the basic unit of analysis for conversation analysis (Schegloff, 2006). Of course, conversational participants can expand those two-turn sequences by using other conversational units known as 'expansions'. Expansions may occur before a two-turn sequence, during it, or after it (Schegloff, 2006). For example, you have probably realized in advance that a speaker was about to invite you to do something or tell you something (Schegloff, 2006). The more adept we are with language and social graces, the more we can recognize these types of situations.

By combining FPPs and SPPs with expansions, you may describe or explain coherent chunks of interaction. We refer to these chunks as 'action sequences' when they are longer than two sequential turns and accomplish some communicative action such as 'disagreeing, offering, contesting, requesting, teasing, finessing, complying, performing, noticing, promising, and so forth' (Schegloff, 2006, p. 23). Many actions are performed in this way, such as 'being ordinary' (Sacks, 1984), getting ready to ask a question (Schegloff, 1968), or moving from one activity to another in the same interactive context, as physicians and patients move from the diagnostic interview to the medical examination (e.g. Robinson & Stivers, 2001).

As we mentioned earlier, your research claim regarding sequence organization can be based on nonverbal as well as verbal conversational behaviours. Robinson (1998) analyzed 86 audio and video recorded doctor–patient consultations in a British health clinic. He focused on the openings of these visits and analyzed how 'doctors used eye gaze and body orientation to communicate that they are preparing but are not yet ready to deal with' patient complaints (p. 97). These openings were marked by interactional asymmetry because doctors, and not patients, routinely opened the conversations. It is possible that doctors nonverbally controlled the opening of these interactions because they were reproducing social power relationships in which 'doctors are powerful and patients subordinate' (Robinson, 1998, p. 115). Alternatively, the interactions may have been asymmetrical because 'patients are unlikely to know exactly when doctors are ready to deal with the chief complaint and thus wait for and allow doctors to solicit the chief complaint' (Robinson, 1998, p. 115).

We hope that you now have a sense of the kind of descriptive and explanatory claims you might use to explore sequence organization using conversation analysis. Let's turn to the claims of discourse analysis.

Discourse Analytic Claims

Since researchers conducting discourse analysis readily acknowledge the subjectivity of their own interpretations in analyzing spoken and written language, their claims are interpretive and descriptive (Heritage, 1985; Phillips & Hardy, 2002; Wooffitt, 2005). In this section, we consider how you can use discourse analysis to

study interactional performances, that is, communicative functions that are accomplished through embodied interactions between people. Although countless interactional performances can be studied, we will describe 'facework' and 'identity performances' as ways to illustrate such claims. We will also outline how you can use discourse analysis to describe and interpret cultural practices and entities at a societal level of analysis (i.e. beyond individual behaviours). Exhibit 10.2 illustrates some sample claims.

Describing and Interpreting Interactional Performances

Both conversation and discourse analysis are useful research methods to explore how communicative function is accomplished in interaction between people. As we have noted, however, conversation and discourse analysis approach communication function at different levels of analysis:

> In conversational analysis, the functional orientation of language is explored in the design of utterances and their placement within the turn by turn development of interaction. In discourse analysis, the functional character of discourse may be located at a broader level.

EXHIBIT 10.2 Discourse Analysis Claims

I. Describing and interpreting facework

A. How do speakers negotiate power relations in interaction using interruptions, leading questions, and challenges? (e.g. West, 1982; West & Zimmerman, 1983)

B. How do speakers negotiate politeness norms and do facework? (Beck, 1996)

C. How do physicians interact with patients? (Li et al., 2007)

II. Describing and interpreting role/identity performances

A. How did the distinct discourses of fishermen, scientists, and policy makers undermine the cod fishery? (Corbin, 2002)

B. How does the federal government position itself as a 'model user' of digital communication? (Fraser, 2007)

C. How does the term 'victim' empower victims' rights groups? (Rentschler, 2007)

III. Describing and interpreting cultural practices and entities

A. What is the significance of the concept 'pink' in breast cancer awareness campaigns? (Elliott, 2007)

B. How does *The Globe and Mail* downplay or deny the existence of racism in Canada? (Szuchewycz, 2000)

C. What are the policy and programming implications of the CBC's current notions of its 'audience'? (Foster, 2009)

This does not mean that discourse analysts are uninterested in specific conversational activities, or their sequential contexts; rather, their interest is not restricted to that level of action. (Wooffitt, 2005, p. 44)

Studies of communicative function based on conversation and discourse analysis can overlap since 'storytelling may be constitutive of corporate culture, argumentation and rhetoric in parliament may be an inherent part of legislation, and educational discourse may define the social process of schooling' (Van Dijk, 1997, p. 21).

In the first part of this section, we show you how to use discourse analysis to describe and interpret interactional performances. Individuals perform many functions through talk-in-interaction. One common function that is researched through discourse analysis is 'facework'. **Facework** is a term that describes the rituals which individuals perform during conversations that reflect 'each person's want to be respected and not imposed upon, and his/her desire to be seen as competent and likable' (Tracy, 2008, p. 172; Goffman, 1967). Another common area of research is **identity performances**, or the way that we perform particular roles in relation to other individuals and thereby display our social identities. For example, you may adapt your language and behaviours as you move between home, school, work, and private time with friends. Facework and identity performances are just two examples. There are many other functions that people accomplish using talk-in-interaction (for example, see Valdes & Pino, 1981, or Scotton, 1985).

Tracy and Tracy (1998) used discourse analysis to investigate facework. They analyzed two telephone calls to a 911 emergency call centre to understand how individuals indicated that they were being polite, respecting others, or trying not to intrude on another's personal space. These are interactional accomplishments known as 'politeness behaviour' (Brown & Levinson, 1987). Discourse analysis is a good way to study such behaviour, and Tracy and Tracy (1998) explained their project as follows:

In putting these two calls in a category by themselves, we used our everyday knowledge about rudeness. . . . In analyzing the calls, we used action-implicative discourse analysis (Tracy, 1995), a type of discourse analysis that uses ethnographic background knowledge to aid interpretation. (p. 230)

Tracy and Tracy found that an individual's vocal delivery and types of speech acts, as well as the actual messages, conveyed an aggressive stance which was intentionally rude, disrespectful, or insulting (Tracy & Tracy, 1998). This article also provides us with a good point to stress that discourse analysts often start with a theory or concept that can be applied to discourse (e.g. facework, politeness behaviour). By contrast, conversation analysts begin with the talk itself and then seek concepts or structures that will explain their observations of that talk.

A great deal of research has been published on identity performance or how individuals display their social membership categories through language and social interaction (Phillips & Hardy, 2002). Some of the identities you might explore with discourse analysis include cultural membership categories like ethnicity, socioeconomic class, gender, or even gender roles (e.g. Buzzanell, Waymer, Paz Tagle, & Liu, 2007). Of course, discourse analysis can be used to describe and interpret any of these identity performances in a specific social or historical context as well. To illustrate, how do you behave or 'perform' like a 'good student' with your university instructors? How might such a performance have been different at your university 20 or 30 years ago? What texts have contributed to your current ways of performing the 'good student' identity? How were those texts produced and distributed? This is only one example. There is a vast range of identity performances that you might explore using discourse analysis.

Describing and Interpreting Social Practices and Entities

You can use discourse analysis to describe and interpret social practices and entities, and to explain how those phenomena came to exist, how they are maintained, and how they change (Phillips & Hardy, 2002). Essentially, social practices are common behaviours or rituals. Earlier in the chapter, we mentioned the practice of debating as one example of a social practice, but we could add examples like dating, managing, blogging, storytelling, arguing, or spamming to our list of potential social practices. You could study social practices in a specific context, be they business practices in the corporate world, diagnostic practices in a medical clinic, or legal practices in the judicial system. Your discourse analysis claim would describe and interpret how participant meanings are constructed in these contexts. By contrast, conversation analysis of institutional discourse would focus on how ordinary conversations are deployed in those settings.

Entities are individual beings, physical objects, or abstract concepts that are commonly recognized through the language and discourse that describes them. For example, when thinking about individual people we have already noted that we think of them in specific roles, such as men or women, employer or employee, or athlete or coach. Some of the physical objects you might describe include MP3 players, board shorts, sport utility vehicles, or hair styles. Abstract concepts are often used to describe emotions, values, or beliefs with no physical existence, such as sexual preference, 'freedom of speech', or 'faith'. Any of these entities could be described and interpreted using discourse analysis because this method relies on texts for evidence, and 'connects texts to discourses, locating them in a social and historical context' (Phillips & Hardy, 2002, p. 4). Your claim should describe a social practice or entity, and should show how 'incomplete, ambiguous, and contradictory discourses . . . produce a social reality that we experience as solid and real' (Phillips & Hardy, 2002, pp. 1–2).

Now that you have some idea of the range of claims you can support with conversation and discourse analysis, let's consider the evidence you will need to support those claims: the data.

Conversation and Discourse Analytic Data

We begin this section by outlining the procedures for collecting and transcribing talk-in-interaction. This data source is fundamental to conversation analysis and is sometimes used in discourse analysis studies as well. We then elaborate the ways that you can purposively select narrative discourse, and other textual evidence, for discourse analysis. Finally, we discuss two aspects of data analysis strategies. The first aspect addresses how you determine the unit of analysis for your study. The second aspect is the process of analytic induction. Analytic induction is a way of making sense of discursive evidence that starts with particular cases and moves toward general conclusions. Before we take up the procedures for collecting and transcribing conversations, you should review and compare the basic sequence for conducting conversation and discourse analysis, outlined in Table 10.1.

The procedures for collecting and transcribing talk-in-interaction are important for both conversation and discourse analysis, so that's a good place to begin thinking about data sources and collection strategies.

Collecting Interactive Discourse

To describe sequence organization (Schegloff, 2006) in conversation, you will need to accumulate multiple instances of a particular conversational practice and examine each instance as an individual case (Maynard & Heritage, 2005; Wooffitt, 2005). You probably will consider how the words themselves are integrated with other vocal cues, such as laughter or intonation and non-vocal cues, such as pauses or conversational overlaps. Usually, the interactions that comprise data for conversation analysis are captured in real time and in ordinary settings, either by audio or video recording. Then, those interactions are transcribed to written or digital form by the researcher prior to beginning data analysis (Atkinson & Heritage, 1984; Goodwin, 1993; Goodwin & Heritage, 1990; Schegloff, 2006; ten Have, 1999).

A wide range of conversational circumstances have been studied, including home and work settings, situations varying from meals, to arrests, to sales, to therapy and health care. The data for these studies have been collected over the telephone and intercom, in hidden and open microphones, on the Internet, via participant observation and field notes, and so on.

The focus on ordinary conversation and interaction settings is a key aspect of data collection for conversation analysis. For instance, Goodwin (1979) analyzed over

TABLE 10.1 Comparing the Basic Steps for Doing Conversation and Discourse Analysis

BASIC STEPS FOR CONDUCTING CONVERSATION ANALYSIS	BASIC STEPS FOR CONDUCTING DISCOURSE ANALYSIS
1. Notice something analytically interesting about a single case of talk, 'for example, a sequence of turns which seems to display some interesting properties' (Wooffitt, 2005, p. 41). 2. Analyze this one case in detail (i.e. anything you can discern about TCU/TAUs, adjacency, preferences, etc.). 3. Proceed to collect other, similar cases, perhaps from a corpus of archived conversational instances. 4. If you record new conversations, transcribe them at the level of detail required for your analysis. 5. Develop a formal, detailed account of how the cases you have analyzed are sequentially organized (Wooffitt, 2005).	1. Identify the communicative function, social practice, or entity you want to describe and interpret. 2. Purposively select spoken discourse using interviews or participant observations in a natural setting, and/or obtain written texts from archival sources. 3. Look for broad similarities or patterns in the discourse. 4. If there are frequent similarities or patterns, take them at face value, that is, as accurate accounts of what is really going on. 5. Construct a generalized version of participants' accounts of what is going on, and present this as your analytic conclusions (Gilbert & Mulkay, 1984, p. 5, as cited in Wooffitt, 2005, p. 16).

Note: TCU = turn-construction unit; TAU = turn-allocation unit

50 hours of 'actual conversations recorded in a range of natural settings' (p. 113). Goodwin's essay showed how one sentence 'can be shaped and reformed in the process of its utterance' (1979, p. 97). For Goodwin, a sentence was much more than a mere linguistic unit of analysis, or a simple string of words that appeared between a capital letter at the beginning and a punctuation mark at the end. Instead, he showed how a sentence must be interpreted in context. The length and meaning of a sentence emerge as products of a dynamic process, the interaction between speaker and hearer.

Goodwin's (1979) essay focused on a sentence taken from a video recording of a conversation that happened during 'dinner in the home of John and Beth, attended by their friends Ann and Don' (p. 98). John stated that he gave up smoking cigarettes a week earlier. Goodwin showed how John used eye gaze to identify the person being addressed. John oriented to the relationship between himself and the hearers by adding 'A week ago today, actually', as he looked at his wife, Beth. Since the dinner guests, Ann and Don, had only learned of John's decision to quit smoking when he announced it at that moment, John did not need to add the words 'A week ago today, actually', until his gaze moved to his wife, Beth. Beth was the only hearer who knew the precise timing of John's decision to give up cigarettes. In other words, John's turn at talk was mutually constructed between himself and his hearers, as he adapted his word choice and gaze in relation to those individuals listening. This example shows how important the use of verbatim conversations from natural settings is to the conduct of conversation analysis. Without the video recording, Goodwin may never have been able to show how sentences are constructed and understood as a joint production of situation, speaker, and hearers.

As we've already said, interactive discourse is important for both conversation and discourse analysis. Specifically, naturally occurring conversations from ordinary settings are crucial for conversation analysis and are of interest for some discourse analyses. In technical terms, 'conversation' has the element of simultaneous talk, and the potential for overlapping utterances, interruption, and forms of participation that are facilitated by face-to-face or telephone interactions. Discourse analysis uses some interactive discourse that is not conversation. Although discourse analysts collect some interactive discourse through informal interviews, field observation, and transcribed meetings, they also use recorded mediated discourse such as radio call-in shows, chat room talk, and film dialogue.

Audio recordings have been used most to capture interactive discourse for analysis, and they still provide the easiest and most practical method of recording ordinary conversations (Goodwin, 1993). Digital audio recorders produce excellent sound quality. Further, they are typically small and unobtrusive, which enhances their fit with the requirement of naturalness in conversational data acquisition.

Video recordings have a decided advantage over audio recordings, however, because video can capture nonverbal aspects of conversation (Manusov & Trees, 2002; McLaughlin, 1984). The prevalence of digital video technology has greatly increased the potential for conversation analysts to study embodied interactions (LeBaron et al., 2003). As ten Have (1999) has noted, video recording can help you to incorporate how talk is integrated with 'the physical environment, the use of objects, technological artifacts, and/or the body or bodies of one or more of the participants' (p. 52).

Proper use of video depends on your research question, equipment availability, and technical expertise. Its use can be complicated by the intricacies of lighting, camera angles, and so on. It is more expensive and less readily accessible to most researchers, and in most settings it is more intrusive than audio recording. Indeed, video cameras can compromise the naturalness of the conversational data you collect if your participants become self-conscious about their performances. In these situations, video cameras and recording equipment are very intrusive (Wiemann, 1981). Of course, Canadians' increasing familiarity with video cameras is rapidly changing the potential of recorded interaction observations in social settings.

You must consider your participants' rights when using both audio and video recording. Of course, all research involving human participants must be reviewed by a research ethics board that will determine whether your research protocol adequately protects the rights of the participants. In particular, you must consider your participants' rights to privacy and honesty, and their ability to provide informed consent before their conversations are recorded. Of particular concern for conversation analysts is whether participants will permit their conversations to be used in future research; that is, whether their recorded conversations can become part of a pool of data from which other researchers can sample instances of talk. It's one thing to provide anonymous survey data but quite another to be recorded in conversation, knowing that those sounds or images could be published in a research report, shown at a professional association meeting, or studied by other researchers, sometimes years after the original interaction (ten Have, 1999).

This leads us to our last source of data. If another researcher has already collected conversations and archived them for other researchers to use, then you may of course use them when they are relevant to your claim. There are many online archives of audio and video recordings and written transcripts, including TalkBank (http://talkbank.org) and the CHILDES database (http://childes.psy.cmu.edu/data). Once you have accrued an adequate sample of your selected conversational units, you are ready to describe and explain their sequence organization (for conversational analysis) or to interpret their functions (for conversation and discourse analysis).

Regardless of how you gather raw data, if you intend to study interactive discourse then you will want to convert recorded conversations into digital or printed text. Let's look at some basic procedures for transcription next.

Transcribing Interactive Discourse

Transcription is the process of converting audio or video recorded interactions into textual or digital formats. In the past, audio and video recordings were produced in analog formats and then transcribed to print or digital files. Now it is commonplace for audio and video recordings to be produced in digital formats and the task of uploading them to a computer is quite simple. As simple as it is, however, many researchers still desire a textual record of all conversations recorded with audio or video equipment. Textual records, either on a computer or printed on paper, allow the researcher greater time to study the exact words used in each interaction, whereas recordings are generally maintained at speeds reflecting real time.

Speech act theorist Gail Jefferson developed the means of notating and formatting conversational transcripts that most conversation analysts view as standard today (Jefferson, 1983, 1985, 1996, 2004; see also Ochs, 1979; Psathas & Anderson, 1987; Bucholtz, 2000). The standard notation conventions for transcribing natural conversations aim to provide both the exact words of the speakers and their vocal details, such as emphasis and intonation. Exhibit 10.3 contains examples drawn from Jefferson's (2004) glossary of transcript symbols. You will need additional conventions for transcribing the nonverbal aspects of video recorded interactions if you wish to share your transcripts with other scholars in the field (for help, see Goodwin, 1981; Gumperz & Field, 1995; Manusov & Trees, 2002; Wiemann, 1981).

Time is an important factor when doing conversation analysis. Most students are shocked at how slow the work of transcribing conversations is. West and Zimmerman (1983) estimated that it takes an experienced transcriber 8 to 10 hours to transcribe one hour of audio recording; Patterson et al. (1996) estimated a 30:1 ratio for audio transcriptions. The required time would be even more for video recordings. Of course, these estimates depend on what level of detail you need to produce to answer your research question, but conversation analysis usually requires more details, such as paraverbal and phonetic cues, than discourse analysis. Patterson et al. (1996) found that reliable transcription of verbal content was easier to achieve than paraverbal content.

It may be tempting to hire someone to transcribe your recorded conversations. You should bear in mind two important considerations. First, it can be expensive to hire an experienced transcriber. The cost is generally $25 per hour. Given the time involved, a paid transcription for a 10-minute conversation will be quite expensive! Second, if you do not do this work yourself it may affect your analysis of the interactions. Your initial ideas about an interaction will probably emerge as you transcribe the data yourself, while listening to or viewing the recordings many times, and typing out the words and paraverbal behaviours of the speakers (Duranti, 1997; Patterson et al., 1996; Sigman et al., 1988). Staying close to your data is advisable no matter what research method you use.

The level of detail you include in your transcript should reflect how you intend to use the data. First, be sure that you always include in your transcript the time, date, and place of the original recording (ten Have, 1999). Second, think about your research question. Will the words by themselves be enough to answer your question, or will you need to include paraverbal cues like pause length, interruptions, or overlapping segments of talk? Third, consider how your data may be used after your initial analysis is complete. If you are the only researcher who will use these data, and you will use it only once, you can transcribe just as much detail as your initial research question demands. If you think you will be conducting future studies with these data, or if you would like to share your data with other researchers, then you may want to anticipate those needs in the transcription (Preston, 1982). For example, you may transcribe paraverbal details even though they are not the focus of your current research question; doing so will make your transcripts useful for other projects in the future. Another option is to keep your recordings and to enter your discourse into a computer software program so that you can revise your transcripts for each project according to your needs. Indeed, your understanding of the data may change over time, so you may want to revise the transcripts yourself at a later date, even at the original level of detail (Duranti, 1997).

Never attempt to fix participants' talk. For example, it may be tempting to correct their grammar or to misspell words to 'capture the flavour' of a participant's speech (Preston, 2000, p. 614). Attempts to fix participants' talk invariably make them seem less intelligent and could even mask their social practices from analysis (Preston, 2000). Whether you are a conversation analyst describing and explaining sequence organization or a discourse analyst who wants to describe and interpret participants' social realities, you must protect the integrity of the discourse, precisely as it was spoken.

The page layout you use in transcription should ease the tasks of reading your transcript and locating information within the transcript. The way you visually represent verbal and nonverbal interactions on a page or screen is important to consider because 'transcription is a selective process reflecting theoretical goals and definitions' (Ochs, 1979, p. 44). Transcription also has political implications because the way you interpret and represent discourse can enable certain

EXHIBIT 10.3 Sample Notations from Jefferson's (2004) Glossary of Transcript Symbols

[*A left bracket* indicates the point of overlap onset

Kalm: uhv never do anything(.) imprope[r?

Ehrl: [Su:re.

]   *A right bracket* indicates the point at which an utterance or utterance-part terminates vis-à-vis another.

Kalm: en uh [g o for]ward,

Ehrl: [Mmhm,]

=   *Equal signs* indicate no break or gap.

A pair of equal signs, one at the end of one line and one at the beginning of the next, indicate no break between the two lines.

Kalm: Hi:.=

Ehrl: =How'r you:.

A single equal sign shows no break in an ongoing piece of talk where one might otherwise expect it.

Ehrl: A:nd uh so I said I jis'find that hard to ima↓gine.=

Now(0.4).p↑since↓then I've retained coun↓sel.

(0.0)   *Numbers in parentheses* indicate elapsed time by tenths of seconds.

Kalm: kin I git in:dih see you duhmorrow before I go:(.) in there et two?

(0.8)   Ehrl: If you wan'to

(.)   *A dot in parentheses* indicates a tiny 'gap' within or between utterances. Is is probably of no more than one-tenth of a secon's duration.

Kalm: Ehm: I:im uh scheduled för ↑two duhmorrow afternoon;n.

(.)

Ehrl: Aah::whe:re.

⎯⎯⎯
|
(0.0)   *Numbers in parentheses bracketing several lines of transcript* indicate time elapsed between the end of the uteterance or sound in the first bracketed line and the start of the utterance or sound in the last
__|__   bracketed line.

Kalm: He i↓:[s.

Ehrl: _____ [Ya:h.

|

(0.6)

Ehrl: (1.3) .p.k

| (0.3)

Kalm: __|__ °hHe is.°

In this case, then, one- and three-tenths second elapses between Erlichman's "Ya;h.´and Kalmbach's ''°hHe is. °''.

Underscoring indicates some form of stress, via pitch and/or amplitude. A short underscore indicates lighter stress than does a long underscore.

Ehrl: Well Dean has; uh:,h totally coop'rated with the U.S. Attorney

::   *Colons* indicate prolongation of the immediately prior sound. The longer the colon row, the longer the prolongation.

Kalm: The who:::le (.) enchilada?

WORD   *Upper case* indicates especially loud sounds relative to the surrounding talk.

Kalm: I returned it'n went over the:re (.) tih↑da:y, (0.5) A::ND uh (0.8) he said the ↑rea:son thet...

interpretations, advance particular interests, and favour specific speakers (Bucholtz, 2000).

One artefact of page layout is that how you format your transcript will influence what your readers notice and interpret about an interaction. If you place one speaker's turn at talk just below another speaker's turn at talk, readers are likely to view those two utterances as contingent on one another, or at least sequential, which may not have been the case. Ochs (1979) pointed out that certain formats encourage readers to link adjacent utterances, and she argued that such a move would likely be more appropriate when transcribing adult Western speech than when transcribing the speech of language-acquiring children.

In addition to the arrangement of adjacent utterances, we also make meaning of the way pages are spatially organized (Ochs, 1979). In the English language, we read from top-to-bottom and from left-to-right, so things that appear at the top left are attended to first. Given these cautions about formatting pages and cultural biases, it is nonetheless common practice in the English-speaking world to format transcripts so that turns at talk follow one another in sequence, with notation for overlaps, interruptions, and the like. It is also standard practice to number each line of a transcript (i.e. each line on a page), so that the location of an utterance in the total transcript is readily known.

Ultimately, regardless of the specific decisions you make during the transcription process, you must be as explicit as possible in your research report about the conventions you used to notate and format your transcripts (Duranti, 1997).

Collecting Narrative Discourse

As we mentioned earlier, discourse analyses sometimes make use of conversation as well as interactive data that are not conversational, such as interviews or focus group interactions. Discourse analyses also employ narrative discourse like speeches and diaries, and archival texts like print articles, cartoons, films, and novels.

Because discourse analysis will focus on particular interactional accomplishments, social practices, or entities, interactive and narrative discourse are selected for their ability to shed light on what social realities mean, how they came to have those

meanings, and how those meanings are maintained or changed. Thus, in discourse analysis, 'the question of how things work is replaced by the question of what things mean . . . .; we are interested in how and why the social world comes to have the meanings that it does' (Phillips & Hardy, 2002, pp. 13–14). You might start your own project by asking yourself questions like the following:

1. What texts are most important in constructing the object of analysis?
2. What texts are produced by the most powerful actors, transmitted through the most effective channels, and interpreted by the most recipients?
3. Which of the preceding texts are available for analysis? (Phillips & Hardy, 2002, p. 75).

Questions like these should help you focus on the social construction of the reality you aim to describe and interpret. Arguably, texts that are produced by powerful actors and transmitted to many recipients are more likely to change participant realities than are texts produced and transmitted by weak actors or transmitted through ineffective channels. Of course, not all texts are available for analysis, and there may be ethical and practical reasons not to analyze some texts.

By triangulating more than one discursive data source, you can construct a case study, a narrative account of communicative behaviour in some social situation or setting, for your discourse analysis. As we noted in chapter 9, on historical research, case study allows you to describe and interpret how participants understand issues in communication and culture in rich detail, be they facework, social practices, organizations, or whatever else you may wish to study. Let's look at one example in some detail.

Leidner (1991) selected two interactive service jobs for which 'interactions are directly controlled by employers' through scripting, uniforms, rules about proper demeanor and appearance' (p. 156). Leidner used participant observations and interviews to study the workers on a window crew at McDonald's and life insurance agents at Combined Insurance. Leidner attended training classes both for McDonald's and Combined Insurance employees and he also worked at a drive-through window at a McDonald's. Additionally, she interviewed trainers and employees in both companies. Within her research report, Leidner presented an abbreviated case study for each organization. The two case studies contained descriptions of the social situations at these two companies, focusing in each case on the standardized roles proscribed for workers (i.e. scripts, uniforms, rules). The McDonald's window crew members were all women who 'took the division of labor by gender for granted and did not seem to feel any need to account for it' (Leidner, 1991, p. 163). The life insurance agents were men, and even though some aspects of their jobs called for feminine qualities, they reinterpreted or deemphasized those feminine aspects of the job. For example, the men were expected to behave as though congenial and eager to please, which might contradict the unemotional demeanour expected of males in many settings. However, Combined Insurance's trainers and agents interpreted the agent's job as demanding manly attributes. These men assigned a heroic character to the job, framing interactions with customers as contests of will. They believed they required four qualities to succeed: determination, aggressiveness, persistence, and stoicism. Their claims were accurate, but they tended to ignore the importance of other required qualities in which women are said to excel, such as sensitivity to nuance and verbal dexterity (Leidner, 1991, p. 166).

After comparing these two case studies of gender role construction in interactive service jobs, Leidner (1991) concluded that work seen in one setting as natural and appropriate for women was seen in another setting as improbable or even impossible for women. Second, Leidner noted that the actual features of the job did not themselves determine whether the work would be defined as more appropriate for men or women. Instead, she concluded 'these features are communicative resources for interpretation that can be drawn on by workers, their superiors, and other audiences' (Leidner, 1991, p. 174).

Leidner's (1991) case study of gender roles in these two industries also showed the difficulty of categorizing some research studies as clearly fitting one research methodology. Leidner's (1991) study best fits our description of ethnomethodology, how employees make enough sense of the gender segregation in their jobs to keep going on, to 'interpret their jobs as congruent

with proper gender enactment' (p. 159). Even though Leidner's participant observations did capture spontaneous talk among the workers, she did not analyze conversations on a turn-by-turn basis, using transcripts. Rather, Leidner used field notes and interview data to draw her macro-level conclusions about gender role constructions in the two case studies.

Determining the Unit of Analysis

The first step in analyzing discourse is to determine the unit of analysis. Many different units of talk have been identified and studied in conversation analysis, including utterances, turns at talk, gestures, and stories (Ford, 2004; Sacks et al., 1974). Some researchers study the generic context itself, such as interviews or conversations, to be the unit of analysis (Schiffrin, 1997). For example, Mandelbaum (1987) published a conversation analysis of couple's shared stories, a relatively large unit of analysis compared to Sacks et al.'s (1974) study of turn taking in conversations. Of course, your unit of analysis will depend on your research question.

There are two important aspects of interaction that you may consider when determining your unit of analysis. First, it is important to know the function and structure of the talk that you want to describe. A single utterance may serve more than one function. Second, you should decide whether the discursive units that you wish to study are larger or smaller than one sentence. The units typically studied in conversation analyses vary from a single lexical unit (including utterances such as 'uhm' or laughter), to a sentence, a single speaker's turn at talk, or an entire sequence of turns taken by two or more speakers (Schegloff, 2006). Because conversation and discourse analysis are performed in repeated cycles of observation and analysis, it is okay to make an initial decision and then revise your unit of analysis as you work through the transcription and analytic processes.

Several types of units can be identified in a conversational transcript and used as data. For example, the order of talk in a sequence of turns at talk might be examined to support a claim. For example, saying, 'Well, I need to go now', signals the imminent 'Buh-bye', that ends a telephone conversation (Hopper, 1992). Alternatively, you may use unspoken signals or physical gestures as data, if they are captured in digital recordings or written transcripts. Consider that, in response to a cook's comment that 'This dish needs more salt', another individual may wordlessly pass the salt shaker. This action, passing the salt, can be interpreted as a response to the speaker's comment, depending on when it occurs during the meal and on who does it. If a guest says, 'This dish needs more salt', it may be followed with some conversational repair, either because the cook has prepared the dish badly or because the guest has insulted the cook.

In terms of interaction sequences, it is important to remember that one speaker cannot control a sequence. We can initiate what we think is the first part of a sequence, but our interactional partner's response will have as much to do with the coordination of how subsequent talk is sequenced as will our original utterance. For example, Geri may want to compliment Carole on her new haircut:

Geri: 'Hey, Carole. Did you get your hair cut? It looks terrific!'

Carole: 'Are you saying my hair looked terrible before?'

In this situation, Geri may think she is giving Carole a compliment, but the interaction can read as an insult and can potentially lead to an argument. It is likely that some sort of repair sequence needs to ensue with Geri's next turn at talk, a turn that Geri did not likely anticipate when she initiated the interaction. Such examples remind us that conversations can provide wildly unpredictable evidence even when we believe that they normally follow standard patterns.

Analytic Induction

One important strategy for both conversation and discourse analysis is to argue from example. Conversation and discourse analysts refer to this reasoning process as **analytic induction**. Jackson (1986) outlined the process as follows:

The process of analytic induction begins with collection of a set of examples of the

phenomenon being studied. The examples are used to build, inductively, a hypothesis. The hypothesis may be about the properties of a class, the rules that generate a pattern of interaction, the sequential characteristics of a kind of interaction, or some other empirical issue. An initial test of the hypothesis is its adequacy as an account of the examples. But this is only a preliminary step.... The method of analytic induction requires that empirical claims be tested through active, procedurally diverse search for counter-examples. (p. 129)

Hence, arguing from examples should be systematic and careful work (Cappella, 1990; Heritage, 1984; ten Have, 1999).

Review the basic steps for discourse analysis that we presented in Table 10.1. As you argue from examples of discourse, you will try to describe patterns of similar meanings across settings, participants, or texts. It is important that you privilege an insider's perspective by using categories that members apply to themselves rather than imposing categories onto your data (Phillips & Hardy, 2002; ten Have, 1999; Van Dijk, 1997).

Remember, too, that you will not only find and present examples from the data that support your claims. You will also search for counterexamples. Counterexamples are instances of data that do not fit your claim and that might support different, even competing claims (see chapter 11, on ethnography, for more discussion of negative case analysis). It follows that using counterexamples helps to ensure that your examples really do support your claim.

Next, let's consider the warrants for conversation and discourse analysis.

Conversation Analytic Warrants

Conversation analyses are warranted using discovery paradigm standards as outlined in chapter 6. The first two warrants we develop in this section, transcription veracity and detail level, clearly reflect the assumptions and values of the discovery paradigm, especially the value of precision. However, it is important to note that conversation analyses make arguments of association, not full causality. Conversation analysts recognize that there are so many interactional choices in play that researchers cannot predict what people will do in any given conversational turn. Therefore, rather than predicting that some conversational move will happen, conversation analysts look to see what actually happens and seek to explain it by examining its featured regularities. Of course, you will also warrant your inferences about a conversational transcript using your own cultural knowledge of, or experience with, the kinds of conversations you are analyzing (Stokoe & Smithson, 2001).

Conversation analysts must hone their skills at observing details very closely, describing what they observe, and systematically making sense of a myriad of detailed observations (Hutchby & Wooffitt, 1998). For now, let's consider two strategies that are particular to conversation analysis: how you can demonstrate transcription veracity and detail level and how you can assure yourself that the interactions you studied are ordinary, or naturally occurring.

Transcription Veracity

Transcription veracity refers to the degree of correspondence between the words typed on a page (or in a digital document) and those recorded on an audio or video file. Veracity is typically judged as a matter of agreement. If two people write down the same words after listening to one bit of recorded interaction, the transcript is considered to have high veracity.

In this regard, Patterson et al. (1996) conducted an experiment designed to measure **intertranscriber reliability**. Recall that 'reliability' means consistency in measurement. Intertranscriber reliability means that two or more people accomplish consistent transcription of conversation into a written record (Roberts & Robinson, 2004). Patterson et al. (1996) wondered whether written transcripts could be reliably produced by college students who had only about one-half hour's training and who used their own and familiar recording and word-processing equipment. Based on their results, Patterson et al. (1996) concluded 'with a minimum of training, multiple independent transcribers are capable of producing similar transcripts from the same source tape' (p. 87). Even though notation agreement does not guarantee the accuracy of transcription,

Patterson et al. (1996) wrote, 'It does provide corroboration and a greater likelihood of accuracy' (p. 81).

The agreement rates achieved in Patterson et al.'s (1996) study differed depending on the type of communication being notated. The highest level of agreement among the college student transcribers (94%) was for verbal content. Agreement rates were slightly lower for notating speakers' areas of overlapping talk (86%) and for either rising or falling intonations (82%). The lowest agreement rate (49%) was when the students attempted to transcribe pauses in interaction. Interestingly, most of the disagreements occurred because one transcriber failed to notate something that other transcribers did notate. This was categorized as an error by omission rather than by misinterpretation.

Most of the published conversation analyses that you read will not use multiple people to transcribe a recording. Typically, conversation analysts either transcribe their own recordings or hire a person to transcribe the words on the recording and then add details of paraverbal cues themselves. For this reason, most published studies do not assess or report intertranscriber reliability, although other analysts can examine the recorded conversation to verify that the transcript is indeed accurate and that they can agree with the analysis of what happened. Nonetheless, based on Patterson et al.'s (1996) results, it may be a good idea to use more than one transcriber and check the rate of agreement between two or more notations of a recording, especially when your research question implicates paraverbal interaction features like pause length.

Detail Level

For conversation and discourse analysis, both recorded interactions and written transcripts constitute data sources (Patterson et al., 1996; Sigman et al., 1988). As Schenkein (1978) has noted, 'It is, after all, because we can review the recordings and study the transcripts endlessly that we come to see the details of conversational organization hidden by real time and ordinary sensibilities' (p. 3). One warrant for the worth of a researcher's argument is demonstrating that you have recorded and transcribed your raw data with an appropriate level of detail for your claim. For example, if your claim addresses how speakers respond to interruptions, you must demonstrate that your transcription of pauses is sufficiently detailed and accurate before you start interpreting each individual instance of interruption. You may also want to ensure that your transcribers are members of the culture being studied and will therefore understand the verbal practices of the research participants. You can consult our discussion of degree of membership in chapter 6, on warrants, and 11 on ethnography, for more on this issue.

Sample Representativeness

When considering any research program in conversation analysis, scholars may question the extent to which a given sample of conversational behaviour was natural or authentic. We do not want to raise such philosophical abstractions here. Instead, we hope to point out a basic, albeit nonspecific, principle. The samples you select for conversation analysis should, as far as possible, represent talk as it would have occurred if no research project were being conducted. To the extent that talk is contrived or influenced by your presence as a researcher, the natural qualities of a sample will be threatened. Without sample representativeness, all claims of describing and explaining ordinary conversational behaviour and sense making will be suspect.

Discourse Analytic Warrants

Much like historical research, discourse analyses and ethnomethodological research are warranted using standards from the interpretive paradigm, as outlined in chapter 6. Given the interpretive values of subjectivity and rich description, and the processes of triangulation, discourse analysts have various ways of demonstrating their credibility as researchers, the plausibility of their interpretations, and the transferability of their findings. Since you may triangulate evidence from informant interviews or participant observations with archival texts to warrant your interpretations of what is going on in a social situation, you may want to return to the final section of chapter 9, on history, or read chapter 11, on ethnography, in conjunction with the rest of this chapter. We build on the concepts introduced here in the warrants section of that chapter.

Researcher Credibility

If you want to analyze the discourse of any group from a cultural insider's perspective, you should be prepared to demonstrate both that you are a member of that culture yourself and that the talk you analyze was produced by members of that culture. If you hope to interpret the structure or function of these members' turns at talk, you will need to be able to recognize what activities they are engaging in when they interact (Hutchby & Wooffitt, 1998). Interpretive researchers call this work 'building a case' for a particular interpretation (Jackson, 1986).

However, remember that cultural insiders and outsiders make different senses of situations. Even a high degree of membership does not guarantee credible analysis. Keep in mind the advice we gave you in chapter 6 about faithfulness and theoretical sensitivity: the credibility of your discourse analysis depends greatly on you being a good researcher when you are collecting data, be it from participants, from field work, or from the archives. Your dedication to logging detailed notes during your analysis will also contribute to you writing a credible research report because you will be able to specify where, when, and how you arrived at a particular conclusion about the evidence you have analyzed. In other words, good research practices can add to your **researcher credibility**.

Plausible Interpretations

We have already stressed that interpretive research often relies on triangulating multiple data sources, settings, and collection strategies, as well as researcher viewpoints, as a way of ensuring plausible interpretations. A disciplined approach to sampling and describing textual data, in combination with a strong grasp of theoretical concepts, will help to you to create a coherent narrative about the categories or patterns you observe in discourse. You might also use participants' explicit understandings of a situation to show that your interpretations are plausible.

As a case in point, Bastien and Hostager (1992) used a combination of participant observations, interviews, and transcript analysis to examine how jazz musicians cooperatively organized an improvisational concert performance through verbal and nonverbal discourse. The researchers first observed and video recorded a jazz performance. Then they analyzed the recording and transcribed the utterances and actions of all the participants. They interviewed one participant while watching the recording and elicited a blow-by-blow description of all the turns in the interaction. Using their observations, the recording, the transcript of the concert, and the transcript of the interview, Bastien and Hostager interpreted how these musicians accomplished their goals. This study by Bastien and Hostager was similar to Eisenberg's (1990) examination of how basketball players organize 'pick-up' games. In both studies, the research question might be phrased this way: 'How do strangers, who know the rules for a social situation but do not know each other, structure their interactions in ways that accomplish sense making?' Notice that both jazz improvisation and pick-up basketball games are entities, that is, historically and socially situated interactional accomplishments.

You should be cautious with informant data (Sigman et al., 1988; Stokoe & Smithson, 2001). The perspective offered by a participant in an interview may not be the perspective he or she employs when engaged in everyday interaction. Interviews often allow participants time for reflection or encourage face-saving interpretations of their own behaviours. It is also likely that your interview questions will structure what the participant does and does not reveal about a social situation. Questions invite answers, and interview data are always subject to the limitations of questions asked and unasked by the researcher.

Last, when seeking plausibility, you might look for theoretical saturation. Theoretical saturation is the sense, when analyzing discourse, that you understand everything important about the social situation and that analyzing additional texts would not add anything new and important to your analysis. This does not mean that you will reconcile different or competing categories of meaning—in fact, you will allow 'different voices to pervade' your research report in order to provide the richest description your data deserves (Phillips & Hardy, 2002, p. 85).

Transferable Findings

As you know from chapter 6, transferability refers to the ability to transfer insights from one study to other settings, participants, or texts. LSI research contributes to performance studies scholarship in several ways because LSI studies 'invite noticing of poetic and performative features of everyday interaction' (LeBaron et al., 2003, p. 10). First, the findings of conversation and discourse analysis can be reported as research, or used to create plays, novels, or films that more closely resemble everyday life performances. The transcription conventions developed by Gail Jefferson (2004) made it possible for research data to contain detailed descriptions of vocal inflection, overlapping talk, and pausing that would help creative writers produce dialogue that more closely resembles the way people really speak (Stuckey & Daughton, 2003; see also, Jefferson, 1996).

Second, conversational or other everyday life performances (Hopper, 1993; Stuckey & Daughton, 2003) can be used to help practitioners in many endeavours to learn about their contexts, roles, or expected identities. For example, those who train people to do interviews in the medical context, or to provide customer service on the telephone, can use research findings from those settings to construct relevant training scenarios and to train people how to perform those service roles (ten Have, 1999). We don't mean to imply that the findings of all conversation and discourse analyses are generalizable, in the sense that they apply to a whole population. Rather, the insights from those studies may be of benefit to people who are trying to become competent in those contexts or roles. One way that you can make your research more transferable is to anticipate how others might be able to access your recordings and transcripts once your research is complete.

Earlier in this chapter, when we discussed means to collect interactive discourse for conversation and discourse analysis, we stressed that recording talk-in-interaction requires you to protect people's rights to privacy, honesty, and informed consent to participate in research. Similarly, if you are considering the use of video surveillance data for your study, you must remember that the opportunity for informed consent is compromised. This situation puts an even greater ethical burden on you, the researcher. No matter how you collect data, however, you should be able to describe how you will protect participants' rights during data collection, transcription, and analysis, during the presentation of your findings, and in the ways you store your data afterwards. Still, there are two more responsibilities that a researcher must bear beyond protecting participant rights. In this section, we briefly outline them.

First, you already know that researchers conducting conversation and discourse analysis adhere to somewhat different paradigm assumptions (i.e. the discovery paradigm and the interpretive/critical paradigms, respectively). Given our definition of ethics in chapter 2, which stated that ethics translate values into social action, you can be most ethical in your research if you identify your paradigm assumptions and stick to them during the course of any one study. For example, in discourse analyses, the idea of reflexivity includes allowing different voices to pervade the text and acknowledging that all possible voices are not represented in the text (Phillips & Hardy, 2002). Allowing different voices is consistent with the focus of the interpretive paradigm on multiple plausible realities and with the critical paradigm warrant of researcher positionality (including standpoint and reflexivity).

Second, in chapter 8's discussion on content analysis, we pointed out the ethical danger of valuing expediency over beneficence, respect, or justice when unitizing or categorizing messages using computer software. In a similar fashion, you must recognize that simply categorizing messages in a data set for conversation or discourse analysis does not constitute analysis *per se*. Schegloff (2006) addressed this issue when he made the following observations:

> The single most troublesome misunderstanding harbored by those just exposed to conversation analysis, or still coming to terms with it, is that the work of analysis is done when a bit of data is recognized as belonging to some category, and the category term is applied to the data fragment. But that is a taxonomic act, not an analytic one. It locates one possible feature of the event being examined, but not how that event was achieved in its particularity—in *those* words or physical actions, by *that* participant, at *that* point in the interaction, understood in *that* way by co-participants, produced by some *specifiable*

practices of conduct. The formal features do not add up to an analysis until they are filled out by the particulars that constituted that achieved event and relate it to what has come before and what interpretive shadow is cast on what is to follow. (p. 268)

As we said in the content analysis chapter, you can be most ethical by recognizing when you are valuing expedience over beneficence, respect, or justice, at every stage of your research project.

Summary

In this chapter, we have covered two different approaches to the study of messages and language behaviour. In chapter 8, we saw how content analysis looks for patterns and trends in vast numbers of similar messages. By contrast, conversation and discourse analysis look for insights by examining select messages. As with all of the methods we describe in this book, conversation and discourse analysis require careful preparation and handling.

When you begin, you must decide what types of claims you wish to construct. If you are pursuing conversation analysis, then your claims will usually be descriptive and explanatory, and will address everyday talk in interaction. If you are pursuing discourse analysis, then your claims will usually be interpretive, and will address whatever form of communication or culture that interests you. Scholars who engage in critical discourse analysis will usually advance critical claims, but sometimes they will advocate reform as well. The focus of their critiques tends to be messages and language behaviours through which social, cultural, or economic power is justified and maintained.

Once your claims are identified, you must decide on the relevant sources, units of analysis, and selection method you will use to collect the data. Conversation analysts have identified a number of useful sources and units of analysis that provide insights into everyday conversation. In particular, you may choose to examine individual turns at talk or entire action sequences. Discourse analysts have applied their tools to a much wider range of messages, including all forms of recorded texts, artefacts, and language structures.

TABLE 10.2 Major Aspects of Conversation Analysis and Discourse Analysis

METHOD	CLAIMS	DATA	WARRANTS	MANUSCRIPT FORMAT
Conversation Analysis	Describe and explain sequence organization in talk	Audio or video recordings and transcriptions of representative samples of talk-in-interaction, analyzed using the strict empirical requirements	Intercoder reliability (for transcription veracity), content validity of coding scheme (including detail level), and sample representativeness	Research report
Discourse Analysis	Describe and interpret the ways that a discourse constructs social realities over time	Audio or video recordings and transcriptions of purposive samples of discursive texts	Researcher credibility (including degree of membership), plausible interpretations, transferable findings	Research report or critical essay

In both conversation and discourse analysis, your sources may be either historical or contemporary, either archived or collected in person. More often than not, you will not select sources randomly but purposefully. That is, you will select sources for their ability to provide data relevant to your claim.

No matter which sources you use, or how you collect them, you will be careful to collect them, transcribe them, and store them in ways that preserve their fidelity, as much as this is possible. An important warrant for conversation analysis is intertranscriber reliability, which reflects your ability to work with partners and to interpret messages in the same way. An important warrant for discourse analysis is researcher credibility, which reflects your ability to collect and interpret data in ways that others will find to be sound and compelling. In both forms of analysis, you will develop insights through analytic induction. You will work from your specific data and formulate general ideas that may be applied to all similar conversations, texts, artefacts, or behaviours.

As we noted earlier in this chapter, some conversation analysts and most discourse analysts will take the context or culture for communication into account when pursuing their research. Knowledge of this context or culture can be obtained in many ways, though two methods are used more often than not: historical research and ethnographic research. Critical discourse analysts must also have a theoretical framework to shape their judgment of the messages and behaviours they examine. We have already covered historical research in chapter 9; ethnographic research is the subject of the next chapter, and critical studies are addressed in chapter 12.

Key Terms

Accounts
Adjacency pairs
Analytic induction
Breaching
Contextual constraints
Conversation
Conversation analysis
Critical discourse analysis
Discourse

Discourse analysis
Ethnomethodology
Facework
First pair part
Identity performance
Intertranscriber reliability
Language and social interaction
Preferred course of action
Repair

Researcher credibility
Rule
Second pair part
Sequence organization
Transcription
Transcription veracity
Turn-allocation unit
Turn-construction unit
Unit of analysis

Discussion Questions

1. How do the three principles of ethnomethodology apply to the elevator example at the beginning of this chapter? Think of your own example of an everyday social situation where breaching occurs. How do interactants make sense of that reality? What rules and accounts might you study in that situation?

2. Make a list of your identities, such as your gender, class, ethnicity, occupation, or age group.
   (a) What bodies of texts could you draw from if you wanted to describe and interpret how those identities are performed in interaction?
   (b) If you wanted to describe and explain how such an identity came to exist, rather than how it is performed, would you select a different body of texts?

3. Do you agree or disagree with the empirical language requirement of conversation analysis? Recall that this requirement stipulates that claims can be supported by recordings and transcripts alone, without relying on other cultural knowledge of the situation gained from participant observations, interviews, or other data sources.

4. What are the pros and cons of using additional contextual data sources in discourse analysis?

5. What are the ethical implications of studying people's ordinary, natural conversations? Identify at least two ethical dilemmas that might arise, and identify what you might do to resolve those dilemmas. Be sure to consider how your resolution would affect the warrants for your study.

Try It!

1. This is an exercise for collecting conversational data. The first two steps can be completed by an individual, but it may be more interesting to work in a group with two or more other members so that you may complete all four steps. Depending on the size of your tutorial group, it may also be adapted as a tutorial exercise.

Process

(a) Record a brief conversation (i.e. five minutes or less) from your daily interactions. Be sure you get permission from everyone involved in the interaction.

(b) Transcribe your conversation using some of the conventions developed by Jefferson (2004) and outlined in Exhibit 10.3. You might work with a small group of students from your research methods class so that each person transcribes one minute of the interaction. What did you learn from this activity, both the process and the final transcription itself?

(c) Have another student or group in your class transcribe the same recording that you transcribed in the previous activity. Compare your written transcripts. What differences and similarities do you notice? How would you evaluate your own transcription veracity?

(d) Using the transcripts you and your classmates have just developed, determine one unit of analysis that could be applied to your conversational database (i.e. all of your transcribed conversations). Code all the transcripts for that unit of analysis. Based on your knowledge of the transcripts, what tentative hypotheses can you develop about the structure and function of those conversational units in your database?

2. This is an exercise for collecting conversational data. It can be completed by an individual, but it may be more interesting to work in a group with two or more other members so that you may complete all four steps. Depending on the size of your tutorial group, it may also be adapted as a tutorial exercise.

Process

With one other student or a group, choose one popular discourse (e.g. personal ads, yellow pages). Remember that a discourse is an interrelated set of texts that includes information about how the texts are produced, disseminated, and received. Then, on your own or in pairs, write a short paper that outlines some of your initial thoughts about these research questions:

(a) What texts would you use to describe the discourse?

(b) How are those texts interrelated?

(c) To the best of your knowledge, how has this discourse changed over the past 10, 50, or 100 years?

(d) Are there new forms of texts that are relevant to this discourse, based on new styles or technologies?

(e) Do new systems for distributing texts reconstitute this discourse?

(f) If you are working with a larger group, compare your short paper with those of your fellow students. How do your comments agree or disagree, and why? How do the life experiences of individual students play a role in their comments? What can be learned from the insights generated by all of your short papers, considered together?

11 Ethnographic Research

Introduction

In this chapter, you will learn how to do ethnographic studies of communication and culture beginning with research claims of description, interpretation, evaluation, and reform. You will learn to identify and select ethnographic data sources using participant observation, interviews, and archival texts and artefacts. You also will learn how to conduct participant observation and interviews with key informants, record and organize your field notes, and analyze your data. In the last section of this chapter, you will learn to apply the warrants of the interpretive paradigm to your ethnographic research project, including the values of subjectivity and rich description, and the standards for demonstrating your credibility as a researcher, the plausibility of your interpretations, and the transferability of your findings.

Ethnography does not have one universal definition, perhaps because there are several different forms of ethnographic research (Denzin & Lincoln, 2003; Duranti, 1997; Stewart, 1998). In general, ethnography is a method for grasping 'the native's point of view' (Malinowski, 1922, p. 25). There are many forms of ethnography, but Canadian scholars in communication and cultural studies tend to prefer ethnography of communication and autoethnography.

One good place for you to start sorting out these different forms of ethnography is to distinguish between macroethnography and microethnography (Spradley, 1980). The terms 'macro' and 'micro' refer to the scale of the topic addressed by the research. **Macroethnography** is usually focused on a definable community or culture and involves years of field research, whereas **microethnography** is usually focused on a single social situation and requires much less time to complete. Spradley (1980) argued that a microethnographic project, in comparison to macroethnography, is 'no less sophisticated, but only more limited in scope' (p. 47). Otherwise, the general goals are the same, to 'discover the cultural knowledge people are using to organize their behavior and interpret their experience' (Spradley, 1980, p. 31). Since it is a short step from interpreting behaviour and experiences to evaluating them, or thinking about how they might be reformed, ethnographic research bridges the interpretive and critical paradigms for communication research.

Ethnography of communication, autoethnography, and performance are related to grounded theory (Glaser & Strauss, 1967; Strauss & Corbin, 1998) and naturalistic inquiry (Frey, 1994b; Frey et al., 2000; Lincoln & Guba, 1985). Let's look more closely at those two broad terms for field research and consider how they relate to ethnographic research.

Grounded theory is a methodology used to develop theories by systematically gathering and analyzing field data. Rather than starting with an idea about a given topic, grounded theory 'evolves during actual research, and it does this through continuous interplay between analysis and data collection' (Strauss & Corbin, 1998, p. 158). That is, grounded theory begins with evidence gathered through observation and then produces ideas through inductive reasoning. By contrast, most theories begin with researchers' ideas and then those ideas are tested in subsequent data collection and through deductive reasoning. Grounded theory can be used in ways that are quite distinct from the ethnographic desire to grasp the natives' point of view, but grounded theory and ethnography share a preference for starting with data.

In the same way, naturalistic inquiry complements, but is different from, ethnographic research. **Naturalistic inquiry** is 'the study of how people behave when they are absorbed in genuine life experiences in natural settings' (Frey et al., 2000, p. 427). Both grounded theory and naturalistic inquiry are inductive methods. Naturalistic inquiry may be used to test a theory, but it is not necessarily meant for developing theory, which is grounded theory's methodology (e.g. Browning & Beyer, 1998). Ethnographic researchers sometimes make use of grounded theory and naturalistic inquiry, and they usually view those methods as complementary rather than competitive (Strauss & Corbin, 1998).

With this terminology in hand, let's turn now to our three forms of ethnographic research. First, **ethnography of communication** (EOC) focuses on speech communities and assumes that 'the effective communicative resources for creating shared meaning and coordinating action vary across social groups' (Philipsen, 1989, p. 258). Ethnographers do not assume that there is one most effective way to communicate in any social group. Rather, because there are multiple plausible realities, 'there are moments of communicative effectiveness' in which participants 'act as if they express a common sense' (Philipsen, 1989, p. 258). For the interpretive researcher, these moments of acting as if meaning is truly shared suggest ways that participants are able to coordinate their actions and share some of the meanings in their everyday lives.

Furthermore, since interpretive researchers believe that truth is subjective, they take participants' coordinated actions as evidence of their common sense of a situation. As we pointed out in the previous chapter, on conversation and discourse analysis, language and social interaction researchers view social life as a communicative accomplishment. Philipsen (1989) makes the following observation about participants in research studies:

> Participants '. . . coordinate their lines of action in such a way that potentially divergent actions fit together into what the interlocutors perceive to be a harmonious pattern. There is order, at least what the participants sense to be order, in social life. This order consists of the fitting together of potentially divergent lines of action' (p. 259).

The coordination of lines of action is particular to a culture and/or group (Philipsen, 1989). There is a 'community-specific system of resources for making shared sense and for organizing coordinated action' (Philipsen, 1989, p. 260).

In the past decade, there has been a growing use of **autoethnography**, the interpretive or critical analysis of a social setting or situation that connects 'the personal to the cultural' (Ellis & Bochner, 2003). Like EOC, autoethnography relies on systematic gathering and analysis of field data from people involved in genuine life experiences, whether at the microethnographic or macroethnographic level. Autoethnography, however, extends the interpretive values of subjectivity and rich description to include the ethnographer's own sense making in a cultural situation or setting. Thus the key informant is the researcher himself or herself (for example, see

Crawford, 1996; Miller, 2002; Wood & Fassett, 2003). When reading autoethnographic research reports, you will notice a difference from other types of research. As Ellis and Bochner (2003, p. 209) observe, 'Usually written in first-person voice, autoethnographic texts appear in a variety of forms—short stories, poetry, fiction, novels, photographic essays, personal essays, journals, fragmented and layered writing, and social science prose.' Autoethnography can be used in ways that fit the assumptions of the interpretive and/or critical paradigms.

Performance ethnography, sometimes called 'performance (auto)ethnography' (Denzin, 2003), builds on the two previous forms as a way of studying culture and communication by systematically gathering and analyzing field data. That said, 'performance ethnography enters a gendered culture in which nearly invisible boundaries separate everyday theatrical performances from formal theater, dance, music, MTV, video, and film' (Denzin, 2003, p. x). In paradigmatic terms, performance ethnography is explicitly critical because it goes beyond describing and interpreting participants' cultural meanings and uses public performances (and performative writing) to evaluate those meanings and to 'make sites of oppression visible' (Denzin, 2003, p. 14). As you read the rest of this chapter, we give you examples from published studies, starting with the claims you can examine using ethnographic research.

Ethnographic Claims

Ethnographers often '"make problematic" that which is problematic in our lives' (Lofland & Lofland, 1995, p. 13). In other words, ethnographers ask questions about everyday communication and culture that stand out as moments of communicative effectiveness or ineffectiveness (Philipsen, 1989), or about cultural knowledge that is used to organize experiences and coordinate actions. Hence, ethnographic research can support claims of description, interpretation, evaluation, and reform. In the sections following, you will learn how to develop each type of claim whether you are conducting EOC, autoethnography, or performance ethnography.

As we have noted, interpretive ethnographers value subjectivity and aim to privilege participant views. For this reason, they typically use an inductive approach even when crafting their research questions. You might start a research project by specifying a social setting or situation that you wish to study, and then you may collect some initial data without articulating specific research questions. It's necessary to know something about the nature and quality of the relationships in a social context to know what questions can be effectively pursued there (Katriel, 1995). For instance, you need to know if it is acceptable for outsiders to observe and ask questions in any given setting. Of course, if you are doing autoethnographic research, you will already know a great deal about the nature and quality of relationships in the setting or situation you intend to study. With a topic selected and some initial data, you can then start thinking about your specific research questions. You can begin by writing down some general research questions. As you do, your theoretical and methodological assumptions will become clear, and this will help you to make informed decisions about data collection and analysis.

Descriptive Claims

Most ethnographers claim to describe the norms and practices used by the individuals composing a particular group or culture (Philipsen, 1989). Since you already know something about social practices and norms from the last chapter, on conversation and discourse analysis, let's briefly define the terms 'group' and 'culture'. A **group** is a set of '3–12 people who interact regularly over a period of time and conceive of themselves as a social entity' (Lofland & Lofland, 1995, p. 107). By contrast, a **culture** is defined as a system of shared meanings, or 'webs of significance', held in common by group members (Geertz, 1973).

Philipsen (1989) has suggested two kinds of descriptive claims that you might pursue by conducting EOC. First, you may want to describe distinctive **communication resources**—the knowledge shared by members of a culture or group and used to interpret and organize action, such as communication rules. Second, you might want to describe the nature and scope of cultural variation in some communicative conduct. Exhibit 11.1 contains examples of each of these types of descriptive claim.

1. 'How do interactants adapt when the conversational rules identified as essential for successful interaction are repeatedly and consistently violated? In other words, what happens when rule violations become the norm, rather than the exception?' (Braithwaite, 1997a, p. 64).

2. 'How do mobile technologies affect the division between work time and private time for interactive agency workers?' (Ladner, 2008, p. 472)

3. 'The present analysis first explores variations in the identity experiences of Oklahoma Indians . . . . Additional analyses test the linkages between . . . participation in communicative relationships outside one's own ethnic community . . . participation in communication relationships with other Indians . . . [and] development of intercultural identity.' (Kim et al., 1998, p. 259)

4. 'This ethnographic study of a group of sportswriters explores the social world they inhabit, the people with whom they come into contact, and the pressures and constraints under which they labour.' (Lowes, 1999, p. 5)

5. 'In this analysis of my ethnographic fieldwork in a specialized clinic, I describe the reactions of HIV-positive people . . . and their doctor as they work through new medical facts about metabolic issues like cholesterol levels.' (Patton, 2007, p. 337)

Another focus for descriptive claims is a **speech community**, a group of people who share rules for using and interpreting speech (Romaine, 1982). Some of the speech communities that have been represented in published EOC research include street youth (Dollar & Zimmers, 1998), a charismatic church (Sequeira, 1993), a regional symphony (Ruud, 1995), and organizational groups in a television station (Carbaugh, 1988). Each of these studies described the culturally distinct knowledge used by members of a social group to organize and interpret speaking. We refer to this distinct knowledge within a particular speech community as the **communication code**, a set of rules for speaking and interpreting others' speech (Carbaugh, 1993; Dollar, 1999; Philipsen, 1992, 1997). Of course, you also could use autoethnography to describe the communication code used in your own speech community.

Interpretive Claims

So far, you know that EOC studies describe the communication resources or shared knowledge that cultural members use, and you know that those resources vary within a culture or group. A third element of the ethnographic research agenda is to ascertain the relationships between culture and communication (Philipsen, 1989). This is a claim of interpretation. At its broadest level, an interpretive ethnographic claim addresses how culture creates communication and vice versa. Exhibit 11.2 contains several examples of interpretive ethnographic claims from published studies.

Ethnographic methods can also support interpretive claims about specific relationships between culture and communication. A specific relationship that you might study with EOC, autoethnography, or performance ethnography is the ways that communication is used to create and affirm shared identities, what is known as the **communal function** of communication (Philipsen, 1992). Exhibit 11.2 shows several sample claims about the communal function of communication. Note that communication can serve a different communal function for cultural insiders (e.g. Philipsen, 1975; Schely-Newman, 1997) than it does for outsiders (e.g. Murillo, 1996). An interesting focus of some EOC research is **codeswitching**, which happens when the rules of one speech community are mixed with the rules of another. Studies of codeswitching are especially relevant for intercultural communication research (Schely-Newman, 1997).

To study the communal functions of communication, or to study codeswitching in cross-cultural settings, you may stake claims of evaluation and reform as well as description and interpretation. Interpretive ethnographic research stops short of evaluating participants' cultural communication, but critical

EXHIBIT 11.2 Interpretive Ethnographic Claims

1. How do bilingual teachers in Corsica, who speak French and Corsican, use codeswitching to manage their identities? (Jaffe, 2007)

2. 'This paper attempts to show how people use narratives in the process of self-definition based on locale.' (Schely-Newman, 1997, p. 401)

3. 'Drawing upon reflexive, narrative ethnographic data, we aim to contribute to the symbolic interactionist perspective by empirically identifying the role that a medium of communication and daily rituals play in a greater cultural temporal ecology.' (Hudson & Vannini, 2007, p. 263)

4. 'It is not simply the primary text that is important to fan cultures, but the way that the common references facilitate social interactions . . . I shall draw upon one . . . media fan event, the Buffy night at the 'Seven Stars', as a case study to illustrate this phenomenon.' (Bloustein, 2004, p. 149)

5. This study 'explores the contemporary dialogic of one sports subculture—the fan whose desired or acquired site of consumption is a public place. What are the contextualizations of such sports spectatorship that draws these fans out of their homes and into the public setting?' (Eastman & Land, 1997, p. 157)

ethnography is used to support claims of evaluation and reform. Let's consider those claims next.

Evaluative and Reformist Claims

Claims of evaluation are advanced when you judge the worth or value of the communication and cultural practices that you are studying. As we pointed out in the first part of this book, evaluative claims are quickly put to use in support of changing communication practices in particular groups or cultural contexts. It is a short step from evaluating communication practices to reforming them. Around 1990, critical ethnographies (usually EOC, autoethnography, or performance ethnography) began to emerge that showed how norms of communication and power privileged some group members and oppressed others (e.g. Ang, 1990; Conquergood, 1992, 1994; Crawford, 1996; Gordon, 2002; Trujillo, 1993; Witmer, 1997). Critical ethnographers go beyond describing and evaluating cultural variations in speech codes. They also 'attempt to take action against the social inequalities exposed in their research, action aimed at challenging the status quo and calling for a rebalancing of power' (Dollar & Merrigan, 2002, p. 62).

Perhaps the earliest and most well known proponent of critical ethnography in communication is Dwight Conquergood (1991, 1992, 1994, 1995). Conquergood's participatory research with a Chicago Latino gang included actions aimed at helping gang members stay out of jail, learn to read and write, and gain a more empathic voice in the media (Conquergood & Seigel, 1990). Conquergood's (1992, 1994) attempts to understand this cultural group moved well beyond description and interpretation. An equally important goal of that research was the attempt to redress power imbalances experienced by members of the cultures (Conquergood & Seigel, 1990).

When you read critical ethnographic studies, you may notice that some researchers do not entirely separate their scholarly claims from their description or performance of a culture. Goodall (2000) argued that critical ethnographers approach writing as inquiry. In critiquing power relations within a culture, or between cultural groups, writing is not merely something you do after the research is conducted. Instead, writing is the manner of interrogating and exposing power relations within the social situation. It may even be a way of interrogating your own beliefs and participation in an oppressive social system, if you use autoethnographic writing or if you participate in collaborative writing (Trujillo, 1999). Exhibit 11.3 contains several examples of evaluation and reform claims from published ethnographic research.

Furthermore, ethnographers use participant observation, interviews, and textual analyses to create public performances that evaluate cultural communication and suggest how it might be changed

EXHIBIT 11.3 Evaluative and Reformist Ethnographic Claims

1.　'The Internet is not a placeless cyberspace that is distinct and separate from the real world . . . . People in Cybercity are investing as much effort in maintaining relationships in cyberspace as in other social spaces' and 'are widening their relationships, not weakening them.' (Carter, 2005, p. 148)

2.　'Invisibility shapes (and is shaped by) processes of stigmatization, "street smarts" as enacted by youth, and "Mayberry" and "not in my backyard" community discourses . . . . The disappearance of youth without homes simultaneously serves and undermines various stakeholders.' (Harter, Berquist, Titsworth, Novak, & Brokaw, 2005, p. 305)

3.　Autoethnography can extend previous studies that frame 'CMC or computer-aided instruction (CAI) as liberatory without accounting for the cultural and political realities of the classroom' (Wood & Fassett, 2003, p. 287). Second, 'technology is not simply present in the school. Rather, it schools us.' (Wood & Fassett, 2003, p. 287)

4.　Looking at a museum in Niagara-on-the-Lake, Ontario, 'The site is distinguished by its emphasis on material history, by a romantic treatment that enables it . . . , by its simplification of a complex past, and by how interpretation is accessed through consumption. This paper will explore how these factors operate at the Apothecary and how they shape the meaning of the site.' (Litt, 1999, p. 298)

5.　'Artwork themed on the activities of the North American cowboy and the North American west has a marginal status in contemporary art worlds despite its iconic place in popular culture. The expression of such a social distinction is embodied in the performative practices of institutions that collect, legitimate, or exhibit such work.' (Rusted, 2006, p. 115)

(e.g. Jenkins, 1999, 2000). As such, performance ethnographers are always consuming and producing texts, and since both consumption and production are power laden, both activities require reflexivity on the part of the researcher (Bowman & Kirstenberg, 1992). Exhibit 11.3 contains one such sample claim (Rusted, 2006). The use of ethnographic data in performance studies has expanded significantly in the past decade.

Now let's turn our attention to the different sources and strategies for ethnographic data collection and analysis.

Ethnographic Data

In this section, you will learn about the major sources for ethnographic data collection, including participant observation, interviews, and analysis of documentary evidence and material artefacts. We help you consider the procedures you can use to collect these data, from gaining access to selecting key informants, taking field notes, and exiting the field. Finally, you'll learn more about the basic strategies for analyzing ethnographic research data: transcribing interviews, coding and reducing data, applying descriptive frameworks to analyze communication norms and rules of interaction,

and writing case studies. All of these ideas will build on the concepts you learned in chapter 5, on data.

Sources for Data Collection

Two of the defining characteristics of ethnographic research are that 'the investigator goes into the field, instead of bringing the field to the investigator' (Schwartzman, 1993, p. 3) and that data are represented from the view of the participants (Stablein, 1996). **Participant observation** is the process of watching and learning about the setting and participants while participating in the daily realities under study (Lofland & Lofland, 1995; Spradley, 1980). Interviews with key informants are interactions between the researcher and informed, articulate members of the group or culture under study. If any of the key informants are the researchers, then the work is at least partially autoethnographic. And, as we learned in chapter 9 on historical, policy, and case analysis, **documentary evidence** is comprised of written or symbolic records, while **artefacts** are objects used by individuals or groups that can convey symbolic meaning of their own.

In doing ethnography, you will typically triangulate two or more data sources either simultaneously or in alternating sequences. For example, you may follow a period of document analysis and participant observation with some interviews and then do some more observations. Your ethnographic data collection will likely proceed from making broad descriptive observations to making increasingly more selective and focused observations (Spradley, 1980). In this section, we outline how you can proceed to collect each of these four sources of ethnographic data.

Participant Observation

Your level of participation in an ethnographic setting can range from strict observation to complete participation, depending on your research question and the access you have to the setting. In his ethnographic study of Canadian sport journalism, Lowes (1999) used participant observation and interview methods to gather data over several weeks in a single newspaper sports department. His participant observations included a variety of settings, but in terms of roles he was mainly an observer who watched how reporters do their job on a daily basis. Lowes began the process by contacting the sports editor of the newspaper to gain permission for the study (pp. 24–27). Then, for the duration of the study, he followed reporters during their work routines both inside and outside the newspaper's offices. However, in no way did he work for the newspaper himself or assist in the production of daily news.

By contrast, Lindlof et al. (1998) used participant observation to study how American families used television and related video technologies. Although many theories circulated about the ways that individuals watched television, the researchers believed that televisions tend to be household items used by families. Television programs are often watched together; viewing can disrupt family routines or it can become embedded in recognized schedules. To collect data, then, Lindlof and his team had to watch families watch television, and the team had do so in a way that the participating families did not alter their routines and thereby diminish the value of the data collected. Six families volunteered for the study, and only one researcher entered each home. Each researcher then tried to blend into the household dynamic by mimicking the role of a frequent family visitor or domestic helper. The researchers were largely successful, and

each one spent some months with his or her participant family.

Whatever your degree of participation during observations, it is important that you develop and maintain trusting relationships with the group members you study. Your access to participants' knowledge is relative to the kinds of relationships you establish with group members and, in particular, with which group members you establish relationships. The roles that these members play in their local network and their goals in relating to you also influence your degree of participation and the observations you are able to collect. As a case in point, Schely-Newman (1997) observed instances of codeswitching as she interviewed members of her family and friends who all lived in an Israeli *moshav* or cooperative community:

> Members of the older generation speak Arabic, French, and Hebrew with varying degrees of fluency, and codeswitching is an unmarked choice within the community. Nevertheless, because each language has different connotations and prestige, the choice of a dominant language may result from the immediate context (participants), the subject discussed (Israeli politics are discussed in Hebrew; the concerns of women and children, in Arabic), or the image being presented by the narrator (sophistication is marked by French). (p. 405)

Such observations could be made only if Schely-Newman selected informants capable of performing multiple language codes, and if her relationship to the informants allowed them to share stories with her, during which codeswitching occurred naturally.

As these examples suggest, you must possess or develop certain skills and attitudes to be an effective participant observer. These skills involve recognizing and performing communication that is the normal standard in the social group you are studying (Dollar, 1995; Lindlof, 1995). You must also be good at 'creating sharp, detailed, and theoretically informed descriptions' (Lindlof, 1995, p. 135), which involves both analysis and an ability to synthesize your many observations. These skills can be developed through practice.

To be an effective participant observer, though, you also require certain attitudes and sensitivities. You must be capable of and comfortable with fading into the background of a social situation (Lindlof, 1995.) You must be sensitive to all the communication cues that are available in a social setting, both visual and auditory, as well as nonverbal and verbal. As ethnologists, we should 'open up our sensing to the tastes, smells, tempers, touches, colors, lights, shapes, and textures of the cultures we study' (Lindlof, 1995, p. 138). Finally, you must be good at 'giving people the benefit of the doubt, getting along by going along, and not being overly querulous or contentious' (Fine, 1993, as cited in Lindlof, 1995, p. 139). If you are observing yourself, you must use all of these skills and you must develop reflexivity, as Wood and Fassett (2003) contend in this passage:

> A researcher must reflect on their own experiences in order to discern how they are both product and producer of a given cultural phenomenon. . . . [The] researcher must articulate such moments so as to engender similar reflection in the reader, so that the reader might understand how they stand in relation to the same phenomenon. (p. 288)

Participant observation allows you to see what the members of a group or culture do and say in their own setting. By contrast, interviews with key informants allow you to hear how members describe what they do and say, and hear how they make sense of their actions and interactions. Thus, observations provide a different window into the participants' worlds than does participants' talk about their world. Interviews with key informants are one of the ethnographer's methods for uncovering participants' talk about their world.

Interviews with Key Informants

Compared to the individual interviews or focus group interviews that you learned about in chapter 7, on surveys, the **ethnographic interview** is 'the most informal, conversational, and spontaneous form of interview' (Lindlof, 1995, p. 170). Ethnographic interviews take the forms of conversations and storytelling between participants and researchers. The interview

is a way to find out things that you cannot directly observe (Newman & Benz, 1998; Patton, 1990).

Your ethnographic observations will be shaped by every individual you encounter in the field. **Key informants** are notable because they are members of the group under study who are either highly articulate or especially helpful and wise, relative to other participants in that setting (Lofland & Lofland, 1995). Key informants provide information about the relationships, groups, and cultures you seek to describe, interpret, or evaluate.

Just as selecting participants to interview is critical to your participation in and observation of a setting, establishing rapport with informants is essential if you are to gain useful interview data. **Rapport** means that your participants feel comfortable with you and trust you. Just as importantly, it does not mean that they see you as naïve 'or an easy target for deception' (Madison, 2005, p. 32). Your demeanour and appearance, listening skills, and nonverbal style all contribute to your effectiveness as a human research instrument in the interview process. If your research is collaborative ethnography, then you may want to train your fellow researchers to ensure that interviews are conducted consistently; that is, that all interactions and interviews with informants are comparable regardless of which researcher conducts them. We noted this aspect of interviews in chapter 7, on surveys, as well.

There are three main forms of ethnographic interview: (1) 'oral history which is a recounting of a social historical moment reflected in the life or lives of individuals who remember them and/or experienced them', as we noted in chapter 9 when discussing historical, policy, and case analysis; (2) 'personal narrative, which is an individual perspective and expression of an event, experience, or point of view'; and (3) 'topical interview, the point of view given to a particular subject, such as a program, an issue, or a process . . . each type will often and necessarily overlap with the others' (Madison, 2005, p. 26). Each of these types of interview can be structured or unstructured (Spradley, 1980).

If you adopt the discovery paradigm perspective, you will likely use structured interviews. That being the case, you will construct a formal interview schedule. You should ensure that each of its questions and their organization are consistent with your study's purpose and claim. By contrast, if you adopt the interpretive or critical paradigm perspective, you will likely use unstructured, or minimally structured, face-to-face interviews. You may not have any questions written out before beginning to observe the setting and participants because the participants' actions will indicate to you what questions are important to ask (Schwartzman, 1993; Spradley, 1980). That said, a novice should never enter an interview without some interview guide. Even a single page listing your key concerns can maintain your focus during an interview. At the same time, you should not ignore the direction your informants suggest, particularly if they point to issues you have not considered.

As your interview format becomes less structured and more personal, your role will be more interactive. Again, we must emphasize the value of rapport. Whatever degree of structure you plan to incorporate, use these guidelines for a successful ethnographic interview: (1) Respondents must feel that their interactions with you will be pleasant and satisfying; (2) they need to see your study as being worthwhile; and (3) barriers to the interview in their minds need to be overcome (Frankfort-Nachmias & Nachmias, 1996).

Whether your interviews are structured or unstructured, it is worthwhile to develop an introduction, face sheets and post-interview comment sheets. An introduction is important in so far as it sets the tone for the interview and establishes your participants' expectations. What will you say to a participant before you begin the interview? Face sheets and comment sheets are items that will help you to maintain an audit trail, a record of all the data you are about to collect (Lofland & Lofland, 1995). **Face sheets** include details about the interviews such as a code or name for the participant; the date, place, and time of the interviews; and any relevant demographic information about the interviewees. **Comment sheets** are for you to jot down notes after your interviews, perhaps concerning the emotional tone of the interview or your insights and reflections about any difficulties you encountered during the interview.

In some cases, you may want to combine participant observation or interviews with analysis of documents or artefacts. Let's consider these sources of ethnographic evidence next.

Documents and Artefacts

In chapter 9, on historical, policy, and case analysis, you learned about documents and artefacts, and their relative advantages and disadvantages as sources of information. As we noted there, these kinds of sources can provide you with background knowledge needed to reconstruct past events or processes that are not available for you to observe. They can also supplement your ethnographic evidence and help you understand how participants make sense of their situations.

Also in chapter 9, you learned about the kinds of repositories where documents and artefacts are preserved. In ethnographic research, documents are usually written texts that you encounter in the field setting among your participants' private possessions. Participant diaries, memos, newsletters, email messages, and newspaper clippings are all examples of such sources. However, depending on the group or culture you study, you may also find relevant documents in libraries and archives. The same holds true for artefacts. You may want to examine actual objects used by participants in the setting you study to understand the participants' communication rules, meanings, or behaviours. Such artefacts could include obvious things such as media of communication, or less obvious things such as clothing, accessories, and everyday household tools.

Artefacts typically support other kinds of ethnographic evidence, but artefacts can play a central role in critical studies. That is because some sources, particularly those drawn from the media or fine arts, can be considered both documents and artefacts. For example, you may want to incorporate visual media, such as film, video, still photography, or material art such as sculpture in your ethnographic project. As we have noted elsewhere, these are usually considered texts for analysis. In chapter 12, on critical studies, we consider some examples of published research derived from textual interpretation and evaluation of media sources. Ethnographers, however, customarily use documents and artefacts to triangulate evidence gained from observation or interviews.

Strategies for Data Collection

Now that you know about the different sources of data for ethnographic research, let's look at the procedures necessary to collect these data. In the following sections, we briefly describe these procedures. Their sequence can vary across different ethnographic research forms, depending on the participants and the kinds of claims you wish to support (Philipsen, 1982).

When you begin any project, it is important to consider the time necessary to complete your work. As you think about the amount of time needed for an ethnographic study, consider the tasks you must accomplish. You will be conducting a literature review; entering a site of data collection; spending days, weeks, or months at the site; writing up and coding interview transcripts; analyzing data within and across cases; writing up notes from site visits; meeting with other researchers, if necessary; and writing interim and final reports. Trujillo's two-year study of baseball culture involved over 500 hours, or over 60 workdays, 8 hours a day, in just the fieldwork tasks! One issue in planning your timeline is gaining access to the field.

Gaining Access to the Setting

As Schwartzman (1993) has noted, 'Stepping into a setting for the first time is probably the most significant phase of the entire ethnographic process' (p. 49). Ethnographers call the process of getting participants' permissions and approvals for doing research in a particular setting **gaining access** or **entry** (Lindlof, 1995; Spradley, 1980). It is at this stage that you will have the opportunity to make the strange familiar and make the familiar strange (Frey et al., 2000). You should select a role at this point, dependent on the degree of participation you desire in the setting, ranging from pure or even covert observer, to full, overt participant, or somewhere in between these two.

Ethnographers sometimes refer to the period prior to gaining access as 'casing the scene' (Lindlof, 1995). Your initial entry into the setting may be 'simply a matter of walking through the door' (Witmer, 1997, p. 329). While casing the scene, you should collect some initial impressions of the setting and participants, by 'looking, listening, touching, and smelling—*hanging out*' (Lindlof, 1995, p. 82). Then, you may reconsider your choice by asking, 'Is *this* the right project *now, for me*?' (Lindlof, 1995, p. 82). Of course, you should already have some idea that this setting and your timing are appropriate, but your initial observations

may prompt you to change your mind. For example, can you devote the amount of time needed to study this setting? What expenses or risks might you incur while participating as a group member in this setting? Finally, are you competent in the communication or cultural codes needed to function in this setting (Lindlof, 1995; Philipsen, 1997; Spradley, 1980)?

Ethnographers often debate the issue of group membership. Some ethnographers feel it is essential that you be a full member of the culture you study. Others acknowledge that degrees of membership are possible and helpful in data collection and interpretation, especially in gaining access to the setting (Ellingson, 1998; Lindsley, 1999). Not only can you gain access to the setting more easily as a cultural insider, but membership allows you to recognize features of meaning that would be unrecognized by a nonmember. For example, Baxter-Moore's (2010) study of music stores in St. Catharines, Ontario, and their contributions to a local music scene, was facilitated by his background as a local musician. His data collection could have been difficult since he had to gain permission to collect data in the stores among staff and customers. His familiarity with the stores' owners, however, gave him an advantage when he requested their permission. Further, his musical knowledge and vocabulary meant that he was able to engage everyone in revealing conversations and understand the layers of references embedded in their discussions.

Ultimately, then, your degree of cultural membership affects how you enter the setting, how you view the participants and their culture, and how you interpret your data (Dollar, 1995; Dollar & Merrigan, 2002; Spradley, 1980). Your degree of membership will also affect your selection of key informants for ethnographic interviews.

Selecting Key Informants

As we noted above, your ethnographic observations may be shaped most by key informants who can provide highly articulate or especially helpful insights into the social group you wish to study. One way to identify key informants is to look for **gatekeepers**, those participants who have the power to grant or deny your access to the setting. In addition, you might want to identify sponsors. A **sponsor** is a participant who 'takes an active interest in the project, vouches for its goals, and sometimes helps the researcher locate informants or move into participation roles' (Lindlof, 1995, p. 109). In short, you will want to select key informants because you are 'already aware that they know something, or have had some experience, that is important for the project' (Lindlof, 1995, p. 125).

You should select informants who will provide a wide range of qualities that are present in the setting (Lincoln & Guba, 1985). This can be done through a formal sampling method, such as the snowball selection method (e.g. Lindsley, 1999). Alternatively, you can use less formal means of selecting informants such as convenience sampling. Finally, if you are conducting grounded theory, you may want to use **deviant case sampling**, the deliberate search for cases that are different from those you have already collected, to sort out contradictions or inconsistencies in your observations and initial analysis (Janesick, 1998; May & Pattillo-McCoy, 2000).

Once you know who your key informants will be, you should establish the number of contacts or interview opportunities needed to collect data, and the duration of each contact. Then, you should select the best method to record and organize your field notes, appropriate to the setting and culture you are studying.

Taking Field Notes

Since ethnography depends greatly on your prolonged observation of the field setting and its participants, keeping field notes is a crucial aspect of ethnographic data collection. **Data logging** is the ethnographic term for carefully recording various forms of data, including field notes from participant observations, write-ups from interviews, maps, photography, sound recordings, and document collections (Lofland & Lofland, 1995, p. 66). Your ability and motivation to record detailed notes during or shortly after interactions with participants, and to organize these notes effectively to later make sense of them, is vital to doing good ethnographic research.

It is sometimes feasible to make notes quite openly during participant observation. Sometimes, you can incorporate note taking into the roles you are already playing in the field by disguising note taking as some other situationally appropriate behaviour, like doing homework in an educational setting or working on a report in an organizational context (Lindlof, 1995). Trujillo (1992) sometimes posed as a 'reporter' while taking notes in the pre-game dugout and in the baseball locker rooms. As a 'fan', Trujillo carried his notebook inside a game program, where he made brief notes as he observed ballpark employees. He then elaborated these notes during lulls in ballpark action and dictated additional ideas into a voice recorder as he drove home from the games.

When there is no situationally appropriate ploy for taking notes, you can withdraw or be shielded for moments to record notes. You might retreat to a bathroom, your car, or around a corner (Lofland & Lofland, 1995). Tardy and Hale's (1998) participant observations of mother-toddler playgroup meetings were collected when 'the attending researcher sat as unobtrusively as possible near sites of conversations, and essentially, "eavesdropped" (p. 342).

Beyond keeping good field notes, it is also helpful to keep a log of the problems or questions that arise as you plan your study and collect the data. Your log can be used for recording your 'experiences, ideas, fears, mistakes, confusions, breakthroughs, and problems that arise during fieldwork' (Spradley, 1980, p. 71). Such a log can be immensely useful when you are writing up your study since it can remind you of elements of your study you might otherwise take for granted or forget (Lofland & Lofland, 1995; Miles & Huberman, 1994; Miller, Creswell, & Olander, 1998).

Exiting the Field

As you can see by now, ethnographers may be involved with members of a group or culture over months or even years. If you do not already have relationships with group members prior to your study, you are likely to develop relationships with them during the study. These relationships make 'exiting the field' more complicated than just closing your notebook after writing your last field note and then not returning for additional observations or interviews.

Most researchers exit the field through a prolonged process of disengagement rather than an abrupt departure. For example, your observations as a sanctioned researcher may cease on a fixed date, but unofficially you may still have an opportunity to gather new observations in the setting long after that date. Or, you may still interact with some participants, either on related or totally unrelated issues. Or, you may invite group members to read and respond to your interpretations of the group's communication and cultural practices. Ethically, you are required to share your final report with your participants even if you do not share your preliminary notes. Whatever the situation, the way that you exit the field is as important as how you enter the field, and should be handled with care.

Morse (1998) advised that it is time to exit the field when one of two things happens: either you recognize that you are putting other goals ahead of the research, or you realize you have reached theoretical saturation. She explains this sense of completion as follows:

> The researcher may suddenly realize that he or she did not record an event, because it may reflect poorly on the participants, or because it was everyday and not special or interesting enough. . . . If the researcher is not learning anything new, he or she may be reasonably sure that the data are saturated. (Morse, 1998, pp. 78–79)

Of course, you must continually analyze your data to know when you've reached a theoretical saturation point. So, let's consider some strategies for analyzing ethnographic data.

Strategies for Data Analysis

For the ethnographic researcher, 'The analysis of data begins shortly after the data collection commences and continues during data collection and beyond' (Morse, 1998, p. 75). You will amass field notes from observations, interviews, and documents and artefacts, As you do so, Morse (1998) recommends that both 'Transcripts and notes must be easily retrieved, easily cross-referenced, and easily separated from and linked with their original sources' (p. 75). Well-organized notes will help immensely once you begin to reduce and interpret these data to produce a final report.

Strategies for data analysis in ethnographic research typically begin with transcription, when you translate recorded interview conversations with key informants

into textual form. You should integrate the transcripts with your field notes, including your observations of and reflections about the participants, the setting, and relevant artefacts. Just as we discussed with historical research, one way to integrate multiple sources of data is to categorize your many specific observations into general themes. In ethnography, as in survey research and content analysis, this process is called 'coding' the data. At some point, you may apply a descriptive framework that consists of predetermined categories, as you may have with any theoretical framework. Finally, you might write either a narrative account of your experiences in the setting, or a case study of the group's communication practices and culture (Philipsen, 1982). Each of these data analytic processes is outlined in more detail in the following sections.

Transcribing Interviews

At some point, you will need to produce written transcriptions of your interviews with key informants. Ethnographers' transcripts range from verbatim texts of verbal and nonverbal interactions to summaries of what was said at what point. These observations may be combined with the researcher's own tentative ideas, bits of analysis, and notes on methodological difficulties or personal experiences during the work. You already know some elements to consider in formatting transcripts and some of the conventions for notating paraverbal interaction cues from the last chapter.

Your transcripts should reproduce the verbatim verbal interaction between you and each informant, and if possible your transcripts should also include paraverbal indicators such as pause length, word stress, and interruptions. Plan to spend 'as much time *immediately* studying and analyzing the interview material as you spent in the interview itself' (Lofland & Lofland, 1995, p. 87). This means studying transcripts as you go along rather than waiting until your time in the field is complete. Doing so will alert you when you need to collect more data and when you have reached data saturation. It will also help you to classify and file observations, notes, and transcripts. Doing your own transcription is a chore but one of enormous value since it keeps you close to your data.

Next, let's look at the steps you might take to make sense of your collected field notes.

Coding and Reducing Field Notes

Feldman (1995) described the problem of working through massive quantities of field data that included recordings, digital files, documents, field notes, and thousands of pieces of mail and email messages. Feldman (1995) noted that the complexity and ambiguity of this data was at times overwhelming: 'The task at hand is to create an interpretation of the setting or some feature of it that will allow people who have not directly observed the phenomena to have a deeper understanding of them' (p. 2). Ethnographers create interpretations based on participants' meanings. To do so, you have to get away from two kinds of prepackaged interpretation. First, you must avoid creating interpretations that are based only on what you knew about the setting before you began collecting data. Second, you must avoid creating interpretations that are based only on what you know about other similar settings. In other words, your interpretations need to be faithful interpretations of your field notes.

Accordingly, you must be involved in reducing and coding data as you form interpretations and develop theoretical propositions about relationships between concepts in the setting you study. You may impose coding categories onto your data from the outset, as is the case when ethnographers work with pre-existing theories. Alternatively, you could induce categories for coding data after considerable immersion in the setting. This process is used when you develop a grounded theory (Glaser & Strauss, 1967) or when you use analytic induction (Goetz & LeCompte, 1984). For example, Patton (2007) used inductive reasoning to categorize how patients who are HIV-positive understand and explain their diagnoses. Based on data collected through observations of doctor–patient consultations and interviews with medical practitioners, Patton found that each patient's understanding of his or her condition and the options for its treatment, affected how the doctor's message was understood and acted upon.

Descriptive frameworks are favoured by some ethnographers who believe that it is impossible to enter a social scene completely free of any interpretive categories (Philipsen, 1992). A variety of descriptive frameworks may be used to analyze communication within a group or culture. One of the benefits of using the same descriptive framework across many groups is the ability to compare interpretations across more than one group or culture. If your interest is in comparing several groups or cultures, you will probably develop a description of any one social setting as an individual case study. Such is the case with Bloustein's (2004) study of fan cultures. Bloustein sought to test theoretical claims about fan cultures by conducting participant observation of one unofficial fan club of the television show *Buffy the Vampire Slayer*, which met weekly in a pub in Adelaide, Australia. The existing literature on fan cultures suggested that, beyond the text itself, three themes were crucial to an understanding of how individuals engage in the 'serious play' of being a fan: the timing of the activity, its location, and the emotional investment of the individual in the activity (Bloustein, 2004, pp. 155–156). Hence, Bloustein categorized the data gathered from his participant observations and interviews according to these three themes. Initially, his analysis questioned whether the theoretical claims about fan cultures could explain his experience in the one pub. Subsequently, however, he could readily apply the same framework and analysis to other fan clubs in other parts of the world to generate a comparative analysis.

Writing Case Studies

As we noted in chapter 9, on historical, policy, and case analysis, Mitchell (1983) and Philipsen (1982) have argued that theoretically plausible interpretations can be made from one good case (e.g. Bastien & Hostager, 1992; Braithwaite, 1997a; Eisenberg, Murphy, & Andrews, 1998; Hall & Noguchi, 1993; Miller, 1995). A good case is one typical group or culture that 'is similar in *relevant* characteristics to other cases of the same type' (Mitchell, 1983, p. 189). Philipsen (1977, 1982) has advocated that researchers scan a number of cases for familiar concepts that can be analyzed. When the researchers have identified relevant cases, they can then hypothesize links between those cases and particular theories. For ethnography, the data for comparing cases can be gained from participant observations, interviews, documents, artefacts, or some combination of these data sources.

Some Ethical Issues

Recall from chapter 2, on ethics, that research participants have rights to freely choose their participation in research, to privacy, to be treated with honesty, and to be kept free from harm. It is your obligation as a researcher to protect these rights for your participants, and doing so in the field, over a long time, is much more complicated than doing so in a one-shot interview or survey questionnaire (Tinney, 2008). In this section, we stress some of the particular ethical choices you must make in doing ethnographic research.

As you conduct your initial participant observations in the field setting, think about how you might be open and transparent with participants in that setting about your ethnographic project (Madison, 2005). For example, should you share your motivation for selecting that setting and those informants? If your study was funded, should you let participants know? Would you use some of your funding to benefit participants, such as paying participants for interviews or assisting informants who are less fortunate (Dollar & Zimmers, 1998)? How will your interactions with the participants, or your departure from those relationships once you finish data collection, affect them (Tinney, 2008)?

All of these considerations are especially pertinent for researchers who make reform claims (Markham, 1996). All ethnographers affect the lives of their participants, for better or worse. However, Philipsen (1992) reminds us that, 'Just as there are many political ideals which can claim the allegiance of persons of good will, so ethnography leads you to the careful study and appreciation of many discourses, including, on occasions, discourses of power' (p. 329). When studying the structures of power within a group or culture, you must be mindful of how that information will be used after you have completed your study.

As you write your report, consider your participants and the risks they might face when it is made public (Madison, 2005; Miller et al., 1998). What impact will your report have on their safety, dignity, or privacy? Will you offer them any assistance, or reciprocal use of your time, in exchange for their assistance in your data collection? It is not uncommon for communication researchers to offer training workshops, or to volunteer in the community of their ethnographic projects, to compensate participants for their contributions to the research.

Ethnographic data collection solely from computer-mediated communication (CMC) data brings its own ethical issues, whether the data come from email messages, a chat room, or an online social networking site like Facebook or YouTube. CMC interactions are readily observed in a covert fashion, and there are vast 'unsettled distinctions between "public" and "private" behavior across a range of cyberspace contexts' (Lindlof & Schatzer, 1998, p. 186). The processes of gaining participants' informed consent, disclosing research procedures, making agreements with participants, and negotiating access are all impacted by differences between virtual and embodied communities. Further, because the data for such research projects is produced in digital formats, the storage and later use of those data must be approached with particular attention to maintaining participant privacy and assuring freedom from harm.

Deciding when to pursue a review by your research ethics board (REB) for your project is itself an ethical matter. You must get REB approval before you interview participants, but you may want to do some initial observation in a group or culture before you know whom to interview or what questions to ask. Generally, if your group or culture is composed of legally competent adults, in a setting that is observable by anybody, you can conduct your initial observations before pursuing REB approval of your project. With these sobering thoughts in mind, we turn to the warrants for ethnographic research.

Ethnographic Warrants

In chapter 6, on warrants, we explained the standards for good interpretive and critical research. You already know that interpretive researchers illuminate multiple realities by valuing subjectivity and rich description in their data collection, analysis, and reports. In this section, we discuss your credibility as an ethnographer, the plausibility of your interpretations of the field data, and the transferability of the insights you glean from a particular setting. In this context, **transferability** means that interpretations are heuristic or thought provoking, not that they are generalizable in the discovery paradigm sense.

If your ethnographic project includes claims of evaluation and reform, then you must also draw on the values and standards of the critical paradigm values to warrant your project. To make a coherent argument about the need for ideological change, your critical ethnographic research (most likely an autoethnography) should include elements from the interpretive and critical paradigm warrants that we outlined in chapter 6. In the sections following, we bring into play the values of voice and liberation and the standards of coherence and researcher positionality.

Let's start by considering how the interpretive values of subjectivity and rich description are enacted in ethnographic research.

Valuing Subjectivity and Rich Description

As we've noted elsewhere, 'subjectivity' refers to a scholar's acknowledgement that his or her thoughts, feelings, and reasoning affect his or her interpretations of the world. In ethnographic research, this means that your perceptions of the social situation you study, and your ability to represent participants' perceptions in that situation, are as important as any objective reality that may exist independent of your perceptions or the participants' perceptions.

Interpretive researchers value subjective knowledge. In doing ethnographic research, you will act on this value by privileging participant views and field settings for data collection. If you are doing autoethnography, you will privilege your own experiences and feelings in data collection and analysis, even as you remain rigorous and reflexive about your standpoint (Pelias, 2004a). The kinds of ethnographic data you collect, the time you spend immersed in the group or culture, and the level of detail achieved in your interviews and field notes will all be shaped by your judgments. Ultimately, your report will present your subjective understanding of the participants' meanings.

We mentioned earlier in this chapter that triangulation is customary in ethnographic research because this process can enrich your descriptions and help you to flesh out multiple plausible interpretations. One type of triangulation is **collaborative ethnography**, the use of more than one researcher to provide multiple viewpoints on a setting, or on similar settings (Duranti, 1997). May and Pattillo-McCoy (2000) advocated that collaborative ethnographers intentionally induce diversity into their research teams, such

as having researchers from different age groups, races, cultural backgrounds, or disciplines, and that 'collaborative ethnography can be useful for providing a richer description, highlighting perceptual inconsistencies, and recognizing the influence of the ethnographers' personal and intellectual backgrounds on the collection and recording of data' (p. 65). Morse (1998) advocates collaborative ethnography because it 'allows for more complete coverage of the setting and a more rapid period of data collection. . . . The insights of one person trigger new perspectives or insights in other team members. Thus leads may be confirmed or refuted more quickly' (p. 75). Hence, doing collaborative ethnography will complicate your data collection by adding an extra layer of organization, but it will help you to enact the values of subjectivity and rich description.

Whether you are doing solo ethnographic research or collaborating with other researchers, you will need to establish your credibility as an ethnographic researcher. Let's look at how you can do so by considering your training and experiences, your degree of membership in the situation you are studying, and your faithfulness in collecting, analyzing, and reporting evidence.

Researcher Credibility

In chapter 6, on warrants, we said that **researcher credibility** is important in all three paradigms, but that credibility is an explicit standard for evaluating interpretive research because you, the researcher, are the instrument through which subjective interpretations are made, whether you collect and analyze interviews and observations, conversational transcripts, or texts and artefacts.

In all likelihood, you are reading this book as part of your initial training as a researcher. You probably don't have experience collecting and analyzing field data. In this section, we help you to consider two issues related to researcher credibility. First, we ask you to think about your own and your key informants' degree of membership in the culture or group you intend to study. Second, we show you how the issue of **faithfulness**—the steadfastness with which you engage in ethnographic data collection, analysis, and reporting—contributes to researcher credibility.

Degree of Membership

Your credibility as a human measuring instrument in the field is closely related to your degree of membership in the culture or group you seek to understand (Dollar, 1995; Fitch, 1994). You should be 'deeply involved and closely connected to the scene, activity, or group being studied' but you should also 'achieve enough distance from the phenomenon to allow for recording of action and interactions relatively uncolored by what [you] might have had at stake' (Fitch, 1994, p. 36).

You may recognize that these two requirements foster a dialectic tension. Your ability to become deeply involved in a social situation is enhanced by membership, whereas your ability to distance yourself from the interactions you observe may be inhibited by being a member. Remember the Martian and the Convert roles (Davis, 1973) that we described in chapter 6? The Convert makes unfamiliar actions and situations familiar by becoming deeply involved, whereas the Martian tries to make everything strange or unfamiliar, so as not to impose his or her own cultural knowledge on the situation. In any given study, you will want to be 'both or either' of these roles (Lofland & Lofland, 1995, p. 23). Don't expect to always be the Convert or always be the Martian.

Membership is partly a matter of knowing the cultural rules of the situation that you intend to study. If you are a member, you may already know those rules before you begin the study. If you are an outsider, you must learn them as you go. Anthropologists call these emic and etic views of culture, respectively (Anderson, 1987). An **emic view** holds that the participants' understanding of what they are doing in the situation is the most useful or important. An **etic view** prefers the patterns of behaviour that are available to the outside observer. Generally, the emic perspective is preferred when studying culture and communication. Insiders possess at least two kinds of cultural knowledge. First, **explicit cultural knowledge** is used to interpret experience, or to read cultural artefacts, physical environments, and behaviour and events (Spradley, 1980). Second, **tacit cultural knowledge** is used to guide behaviour in culturally appropriate ways, such as how we feel at specific moments or what we wear in certain situations.

Consider Hodson and Vannini's (2007) study that explored perceptions of time among residents of an island accessible only by ferry in British Columbia. Most residents were dependent on the ferry to link them to school, work, hospital care, and basic commodities. The study sought to understand how the ferry's schedule would therefore affect the residents' daily routines and the way that they managed their time. Between them, the two researchers combined the emic and etic perspectives. Hodson was an island resident, and to collect data she drew upon her memories and her daily life. As she described it, having 'natural full member participation conducted over a lifetime of residence' meant 'mundane experiences with the subject matter and . . . being a socialized member of the very culture one is attempting to analyze' (p. 264). By contrast, Vannini was not an island resident but an expert in marine transportation and regional cultures. Their differing perspectives on island culture 'led to an invaluable dialogue throughout the data analysis process, a process that entailed . . . analysis of the data in light of the categories emergent from the data themselves, which were constantly compared to categories existing in the literature' (p. 265).

Many ethnographers feel that the researcher who is a cultural insider is more credible than one who is not. Regardless of your own degree of membership, you will need to evaluate the credibility of your key informants. The people with whom you interact, that is those you observe and interview, must be good representatives of their group or culture. They should represent different types of participants in that setting (i.e. different roles) if you are to capture the full range of subjective meanings available to members.

Both you and your informants enact your degree of membership when you competently recognize and engage in culturally appropriate communication (Dollar, 1995, 1999). Your abilities to recognize and perform a range of practices, to avoid making blunders or mistakes, to recognize violations when they occur, and to be playful with cultural language (e.g. jokes, teasing), all demonstrate your degree of membership (Dollar, 1995, 1999). Of course, recognizing these communication patterns is different from being able to perform competently. If you or your key informants cannot recognize or perform the subtle variations in cultural communication, then the plausibility of your interpretations about the situation or setting will be threatened.

Being honest about your degree of membership and working to locate and build relationships with credible key informants are both related to faithfulness. Even if you and your key informants are members of the culture you study, a lack of faithfulness can threaten your credibility as a researcher. Let's take a look at what you can do to be a faithful researcher.

Faithfulness

No matter how much training and experience you have as a researcher, and no matter what your degree of cultural membership, you will always encounter limits to your credibility. Your memory, hearing, and recognition skills will all influence the credibility of the data you collect and the interpretations you make of those data. Even though some of these limits on your credibility are physical or biological (such as memory or hearing), some are limits of faithfulness, your commitment to represent the participants' meanings fully and fairly. Recognizing and acknowledging these sorts of limitations is part of operating faithfully as an ethnographer.

Faithfulness is further achieved by spending enough time in the field, going over field notes many (rather than a few) times, maintaining close and trusting relationships with key informants, and searching for additional sources of data to corroborate those already considered (Lofland & Lofland, 1995; Miles & Huberman, 1994; Spradley, 1980). Your faithfulness paves the way for you to make plausible interpretations.

Plausible Interpretations

Recall that plausible interpretations are reasonable and likely truths—they are not necessarily 'valid', in the discovery paradigm sense, as one objectively verifiable truth.

After reading this much of the chapter, you should already be able to articulate some ways that ethnographers develop plausible interpretations. First, due to group membership and sustained observation, you can refine your ethnographic interpretations over time; the accuracy of your observations should benefit from your remaining in the field. Second, the everyday settings within which your observations occur should increase the relevance of the behaviours you observe. Third, you can use participants' phrasing and vocabulary whenever possible during interviews with key informants,

and thereby increase your chances of tapping into the emic view of the setting. Fourth, self-reflection during data analysis should continually prompt you to question the data and your interpretations of it. All four of these advantages of ethnographic research were pointed out by LeCompte and Goetz (1982, p. 43) when they argued that ethnographic research had superior internal validity, relative to survey research.

In conducting ethnography, you should triangulate data to ensure plausible interpretations. It can be especially useful to compare meanings across more than one data source, such as self-reports, behavioural observations, archival texts, and material artefacts. Interviews with informants and observations will provide you with instances of verbal and nonverbal communication as practised in the speech community. Documents might also provide such instances but in ways that are more public and verifiable. Artefacts provide additional sources from which you can triangulate interpretations about participant meanings.

When you embrace the idea of multiple subjective realities, you have to consider whether your interpretations are believable and can be supported with arguments (Dollar, 1995; Fitch, 1994). In the remainder of this section, we show you how to make two kinds of arguments about the plausibility of your interpretations. The first is that you have adequate and coherent evidence for making those interpretations. The second is showing that you've thought about alternative interpretations, or 'counterclaims'.

Adequacy and Coherence of Evidence

The evidence you present in support of an ethnographic claim should be based on an adequate selection of the total collection of data (Fitch, 1994). Your argument will necessarily be rooted in the data you amass in interviews, observations, and field notes. However, this data suffers one drawback. Unless you place your notes in a public repository after your report is complete, no other scholar will be able to check your interpretations. Hence, if any segment of your ethnographic data comes from publicly accessible records, that segment will bolster the plausibility of your interpretations because that data can be checked.

In addition, you must include your consideration of 'inferences and interpretations as well as concrete phenomena' when you report your data analysis (Fitch, 1994, p. 36). For example, when you present quotations from interview transcripts to support your interpretations, you allow your readers to see the evidence themselves, and to consider the merits of your analytical inferences. That will allow your readers to 'decide for themselves whether or not to believe [your] account of what it is that a particular group of people are doing at any given time' (McDermott, Gospodinoff, & Aron, 1978, p. 245).

Philipsen (1977) has suggested three questions that you can ask yourself to test 'the adequacy of statements which purport to represent the native's view' (p. 49). These three questions are as follows:

First, does the report use the native's own terms or verbatim description? Second, and failing the first test, do the ethnographer's terms or descriptions refer to something that the native agrees is a recognizable feature of his social world, and if so, can the native person give it a name? Third, does the native person agree that the ethnographer's insight enables him (the native) to better understand his own social world? (Philipsen, 1977, p. 49)

Of course, ethnographers always allow room for more than one plausible interpretation of a situation or phenomenon. Paying attention to other possibly valid interpretations is another way to ensure that your interpretations of ethnographic data are plausible.

Negative Case Analysis

The second way to ensure plausible interpretations in ethnographic research is to deal with other interpretations that could be supported by your data, what we refer to as **counterclaims**. It is especially relevant to consider counterclaims when you are coding data into categories or themes. As you do so, you may find that certain data cannot be easily placed in any of your categories. If that's the case, and they comprise more data than you can ignore, then this may be a signal that you should reconsider your coding, categories, or analytical framework. It is possible that another interpretation—a counterclaim—will in fact make better use of the data (Agar, 1983).

You should also search out disconfirming observations, if they do not readily appear in your analysis of the data, to ensure that your interpretations are plausible. Refer back to our discussion of negative case analysis in chapter 6, on warrants. Consider whether you need to collect more observations using deviant case sampling (Patton, 1990), that is, returning to the field and trying to find instances of data that do not fit the interpretation you have tentatively identified. To the degree that no such instances of data can be located, your interpretations are warranted as plausible.

Now that you have some idea how you might demonstrate the plausibility of your interpretations, you will want to think about the degree to which your findings are transferable, the last warrant for interpretive ethnographies.

Transferable Findings

One goal of interpretive researchers is to produce 'meaning-centered investigations of social life that can be coherently tied to other such investigations' (Fitch, 1994, p. 36). In this section, we help you think about whether the insights from your ethnographic study might be applicable to another group or culture, and how this may be. In addition, we consider how insights from your study might transfer to public performances for performance ethnography. The confirmability, relevance, and generality of your interpretations and inferences all contribute to transferability. Let's look at each of these concepts in turn.

Confirmability means that the findings you posit can be substantiated by another person who had similar access to the same data or evidence. This is somewhat akin to 'agreement among judges', a form of content validity we outlined in chapter 6, and that is used by discovery researchers. When Fitch (1994) argues that researchers should make claims at least partially supported by publicly accessible records, he does so with a desire for confirmability. You can use Carbaugh's (1988) performance tests to establish confirmability. We first mentioned these tests in chapter 6. To use them, you must return to your data collection setting and ask members to confirm the terminology, behaviours, or meanings that you have gleaned from the data. Alternatively, you can try out those interpretations in conversation with members. If they seem to understand your performance, or do not object to your performance, then you have some evidence that your findings are confirmable.

Relevance means that your interpretations are relevant or salient to the people in the group or culture that you are studying. An interpretation or conclusion is only relevant if it matters to the participants. You should be able to show that participants use and invest significance in the terminology and behaviours that you have described, interpreted, or evaluated (McDermott et al., 1978). Your ability to represent these matters in your research report will make your interpretations relevant and potentially more transferable. For example, if you wish to establish that a particular communication or cultural practice is significant to your participants, it is important to provide specific examples of them performing this practice and establishing that it is understood as culturally situated behaviour (Schlegoff, 2006).

By contrast, to establish **generality** means that you try to make interpretations and inferences that apply to more than one participant or moment in the group or culture you studied. One way to do this is by faithfully basing your claims on the total collection of data rather than one or two isolated observations within a data set. Another way is to use the same descriptive framework in more than one study, so that the findings from multiple studies can be compared with one another. In this way, general interpretations about communication in more than one group may be discerned either by you or by other researchers using the same framework you used in your study.

Coherence and Researcher Positionality for Critical Research

As we mentioned at the start of this chapter, ethnographic research bridges the interpretive and critical paradigms. EOC studies nearly always follow the assumptions and values of the interpretive paradigm, but autoethnography and performance ethnography can correspond to either the interpretive or critical paradigm.

If your ethnographic project includes claims of evaluation and reform, you should integrate the values and standards of the interpretive and critical paradigms.

In this section, we give you some examples from published works to show you how the critical paradigm warrants of coherence and researcher positionality can be demonstrated in critical ethnographic research.

Coherence

When you conduct a critical empirical study of communication and cultural practices using ethnographic methods, you evaluate those practices and suggest how they might be changed to interrupt hegemonic power relations. In that case, you must show clear and logical connections between the data you analyzed and the power relations you want to change. A theoretical perspective may help you to make those connections. For example, Kim et al. (1998) began their analysis of communication among Oklahoma Indians with two broad categories of identity, Berry's (1990) identity modes and Kim's (1995a, 1995b) cultural-intercultural continuum. Similarly, Mayer's (2005) essay on the role of whiteness as a concept absent from most ethnographic audience research used poststructuralist theories to argue that ethnographers have essentialized whiteness as either a form of structural dominance or as an individual vulnerability (see chapter 12, on critical studies, for more on poststructuralism). If you read Kim et al. (1998) or Mayer (2005) in full, you will get a better idea how using one or more previously developed theories could help you to establish clear and logical relationships among different forms of evidence in your ethnographic project. Of course, as a critical researcher, you will have to ask yourself, 'For whom is my narrative coherent?' A critical essay or a piece of performative writing like a poem undoubtedly will be more coherent for some audiences than for others.

Researcher Positionality

Carolyn Ellis (2004) is a well-known autoethnographic researcher in communication studies. Ellis's (2004) methodological novel about autoethnography, *The Ethnographic I: The Methodological Novel About Autoethnography*, exemplifies the standard of researcher positionality as a warrant for ethnographic research. Ellis has been applauded and chastised for revealing a great deal about herself in her autoethnographic writing, for making friends with the people she studies, and for fictionalizing characters in the novel based on some of the students in her autoethnography course at the University of South Florida. Each of those choices, and other researchers' freedom to disagree with them, makes Ellis's position as a researcher explicitly relevant in her writing and underscores critical researchers' values of voice and liberation.

In fact, autoethnography demands that you make your positionality as a researcher explicitly available to those who read your critical essays or attend performances based on your data and analysis (Pelias, 2004a). Even if your autoethnographic claims do not include explicit evaluations or suggest reforms of communication, you should disclose your standpoint; that is, the relevant material, social, and symbolic roles you occupy in the situation or group you are studying. For example, Wood and Fassett's (2003) autoethnography of identity, power, and technology in communication classrooms included quotes from student emails, as well as italicized reflections of the authors' thoughts and feelings, in the published research report.

Finally, your ability and willingness to articulate your standpoint will demonstrate your reflexivity as a critical ethnographic researcher. You may want to disclose your reasons for doing a critical ethnographic project as a way of warranting researcher positionality. Alternatively, you may want to justify your decision to collect particular kinds of evidence or to favour certain interpretations of the data over others. Obviously, a good audit trail and faithful, detailed field notes will help you to recover these concepts and represent them in your critical essay or performative writing.

Summary

In this chapter, we have described the research goals and processes associated with ethnographic research. The key element that distinguishes ethnography from other methods is its reliance on first-person data collection. The researcher must have personal knowledge of the group or culture under study. Surveys and oral history interviews may provide a researcher with fleeting glimpses into the lives of participants, while the texts and artefacts used in content analysis and discourse analysis may provide compelling, mediated insights into those same lives. Ethnography, however, requires some measure of engagement with participants in their everyday settings. This requirement shapes every decision you make as a researcher.

As with the other methods which we have discussed, your first task is to identify the type of claim you wish to construct. Descriptive claims are useful when we want to understand the structures and processes in a group, particularly if your focus is that group's communication rules or **cultural resources**. Interpretive claims are more common when you wish to understand the relationship between communication processes and cultural values within a group. Evaluative and reformist claims are made when you wish to expose how the processes, rules, and values within a group may empower some members while oppressing others.

Once your claims are identified, you must decide on the relevant sources and data collection methods you will use to gather the data. As we just noted, the core of an ethnographic study is time spent in the field with your research participants. Surveys of group members, interviews with key informants, or consultation of documentary evidence are generally used to support or triangulate data gathered firsthand in a natural setting. You will not select your group or culture randomly but purposefully because of its ability to provide data relevant to your claim. And before you enter the field, you must make one fundamental decision about your degree of participation: you may choose strictly to observe your research participants or you may choose to participate in their normal activities. Regardless of your degree of participation, you must establish some relationship with them that will encourage mutual respect and trust. A good relationship will enhance your researcher credibility. If you have an intimate link with the group under study, and this affects your positionality as a researcher, then this should be explained as part of your research report.

No matter how you collect your data, it will be wise to review, organize, and reassess your data at the end of each day in the field. This will ensure that you catch interesting or surprising ideas quickly and ensure that you have time to test them while you still have access to the research setting. Rich description, which faithfully reports your observations of the group, supplies two important warrants for ethnography. Through

TABLE 11.1 Major Aspects of Ethnographic Research

CLAIMS	DATA	WARRANTS	MANUSCRIPT FORMAT
Describe and interpret how groups or cultures coordinate social actions and accomplish shared meaning	Participant observations, interviews with key informants, and texts/artefacts collected in a social setting or situation	Researcher credibility, plausible interpretations, transferable findings	Research report, including selected data samples
Describe and evaluate how elements of communication practices and culture enable power relations, and suggest how those relations should be reformed	Participant observations, interviews with key informants, and texts/artefacts collected in a social setting or situation	Coherence, researcher positionality (i.e. standpoint and reflexivity)	Critical essay

inductive analysis, you may then develop findings that are plausible, coherent, and rooted in adequate data to support your claims.

Most ethnographers work within theoretical frameworks that inform their claims, their selection of sources, and their interpretation of the data they collect. In particular, critical ethnographers must have a theoretical framework to shape their judgment of the processes and values they examine. Critical studies are addressed in our next chapter.

Key Terms

Artefact
Autoethnography
Codeswitching
Collaborative ethnography
Comment sheet
Communal function
Communication code
Communication resources
Confirmability
Counterclaim
Cultural resources
Culture
Data logging
Deviant case sampling

Documentary evidence
Emic view
Ethnographic interview
Ethnography
Ethnography of communication
Etic view
Explicit cultural knowledge
Face sheet
Faithfulness
Gaining access (or entry)
Gatekeeper
Generality
Grounded theory
Group

Key informant
Macroethnography
Microethnography
Naturalistic inquiry
Participant observation
Performance ethnography
Rapport
Relevance
Researcher credibility
Speech community
Sponsor
Tacit cultural knowledge
Transferability

Discussion Questions

1. Think about the groups, teams, organizations, or cultures to which you belong. What kinds of beliefs or attitudes are considered 'common sense' for members of those groups?

2. What does it mean to 'make the familiar strange'? If you identified a 'common sense' belief or attitude for the first question, how would you 'make it strange' for ethnographic analysis?

3. What are some of the rules for speaking, and interpreting the speech of others, in one of your groups? Compare your rules with those of your classmates' groups. Are there any commonalities among the rules of your groups? How do they differ?

4. Think about the physical space and material artefacts that one of your group's uses. Is any aspect of that space, or is any one artefact, representative of the beliefs or attitudes of your group? What kinds of messages are conveyed by the space or artefact? How are these messages conveyed?

Try It!

1. This is an exercise for collecting data through observation. It can be completed by an individual, but it may be more interesting to work in a group with two or more other members. Depending on the size of your tutorial group, it may also be adapted as a tutorial exercise.

    Process

    Participate in or simply observe a group, team, or organization for about 30 minutes. When you start, ensure that your observation is welcomed by the participants and is also ethical.
    (a) Write down three research questions that you think might be investigated about the communication or cultural practices in this setting (Spradley, 1980).
    (b) If you are a member of this group, note what processes or artefacts are likely to be misunderstood by an outsider in this situation, or, if you are an outsider to this group, note those things that you do not understand.
    (c) Try to identify one or two people that you suspect might be key informants in that group and explain why you think this of these people.
    (d) What documents or artefacts are available to triangulate your interviews with key informants?
    (e) What would you need to do to gain access to this setting?
2. This is also an exercise for collecting data through observation. However, it is designed to be completed by a group with two or more other members. Depending on the size of your tutorial group, it may also be adapted as a tutorial exercise.

    Process

    With two or more of your classmates, select a setting for observation. Then, working independently of one another, make observations and take field notes for 15 minutes. If there is anyone present in the setting, ensure that your presence is welcome and is also ethical. After 20 minutes, leave the setting and then draft an interpretation of it based on your notes; this may take 10 minutes. When each of you have drafted your interpretations, compare your notes and interpretations with one another.
    (a) How do your observations compare? How are they different?
    (b) Did you use similar vocabularies or concepts to describe the setting? Why, or why not?
    (c) How did the differences in your observations or notes affect your interpretations of the setting?
    (d) Whose interpretation of the setting is the most compelling or thorough? Why? What warrants would support that interpretation?
    (e) Within your notes or your past experiences, is there any evidence that would support a different interpretation than the one you have selected as the best? If so, how might you account for that counterclaim in your research report?

12 Critical Studies

Introduction

In this chapter, you will learn how to conduct critical studies of communication and culture that support claims of description, evaluation, and reform. We have organized this chapter around the distinction between structural and poststructural criticism. The scholars who work within these two schools of thought differ on a fundamental point: structuralists believe that social structures are 'real' while poststructuralists argue that social structures are temporarily constituted in language. You will learn how evidence for critical essays is drawn from mediated and nonmediated texts, including historical and present-day actions and events. Further, your own experiences and beliefs can be analyzed using deconstruction as well as dialectic, speech act, and narrative criticisms. You will also learn to apply the critical paradigm warrants such as subjectivity and coherence.

Critical studies deal with power, oppression, and privilege. More specifically, they deal with how a society's power structures and resources benefit some groups of people and oppress others. As Littlejohn and Foss (2005) have noted about critical discourse analysis, such studies 'look at actual features of texts that manifest these oppressive arrangements, without separating communication from other factors in the overall system of oppressive forces' (p. 47; see also Fairclough & Wodak, 1997). To put this another way, scholars who conduct critical studies try to reveal how our use of language and social practices can perpetuate injustices to members of society.

In chapter 1, the introduction, we mentioned that theories are sometimes quite distinct from the research methodologies associated with them, but that some theories and methods are highly interconnected. With critical studies, theory and method are highly interconnected because the critical paradigm perspective informs both the theory that drives research claims and the analytical techniques used to examine evidence. That said, critical studies do not present a unique set of tools to gather evidence, as we find with survey research and content analysis. There is no equivalent of the questionnaire or coding schedule. Rather, scholars in critical studies have much in common with historians and ethnographers, since all three seek relevant information wherever it can be found and in any format. Indeed, many critical studies involve historical, policy, or case analysis of individual texts or practices.

Scholars in critical studies share one other tendency with some historians and ethnographers: their approach to 'data'. In discovery and interpretive paradigm research, the term 'data' is associated with empiricism, which stipulates that data must be observable and systematically collected. Adherents to those paradigms demand 'intersubjective' agreement about observed events and situations. Intersubjective agreement can be achieved by seeking consensus among researchers (e.g. through interrater reliability, as discussed in chapter 6, on warrants) or among research participants (e.g. through member checks, as discussed in chapter 11 on ethnography). By contrast, critical researchers embrace writing itself as a mode of inquiry (Goodall, 2000). Their positions in society, their language, national or regional affiliations, ethnicity, class, gender, sexuality, and all of their lived experiences and ideological beliefs become the systematic, observable evidence against which they assess the need for social change. For this reason, critical researchers are more likely to refer to the 'evidence' on which their claims are based rather than to 'data'.

In this chapter, then, we introduce you to five types of structural criticism and five types of poststructural criticism, each based on the work of one or two theorists. All 10 types of critical studies make claims of description, evaluation, and reform, and they all draw on the same types of evidence, including actions and events, texts, and the researcher's own experiences and beliefs.

In the third section of this chapter, we show you how to make four analytical moves: deconstruction, dialectical analysis, narrative analysis, and speech act analysis. Some of these analytical moves are shared by interpretive researchers. However, interpretive researchers analyze texts for the purpose of unpacking participant meanings, whereas critical researchers use textual analysis to reveal power-dominance relations, describe consciousness (or a lack of it), and depict 'hegemonic' processes at work. **Hegemony** is the 'process of domination, in which one set of ideas subverts or co-opts another' (Littlejohn & Foss, 2005, pp. 318–319; see also Gramsci, 1971; Lears, 1985). Because critical paradigm research values voice and liberation, it must argue for ideological change when it finds injustice. Hence, the key purpose of critical research is to identify historical, economic, and political sources of power that are rooted in ideology. An **ideology** is 'a set of ideas that structure a group's reality, a system of representations or a code of meanings governing how individuals and groups see the world' (Littlejohn & Foss, 2005, p. 318).

In the last section of this chapter, we show you how to warrant your critical study by establishing coherence, and by disclosing your positionality as a researcher.

Critical Studies Claims

As noted above, this chapter covers structuralist and poststructuralist critical scholarship. When we discussed claims in chapter 4, we mentioned that it is often difficult to classify some studies as exclusively interpretive or critical (Swanson, 1993). The same is true when classifying critical studies as structuralist or poststructuralist. Nonetheless, we categorize them this way because we believe it will help you to grasp the subtle differences between them.

First, structuralist criticism is informed by theories of human behaviour that posit that individual thought and behaviour are constrained, guided, or even determined by some 'structure' in which we live. Each structuralist theory identifies its own key **structure** that unlocks the significance of certain sets of human actions. Some of the structures which have been theorized are physiological, such as the operations of our minds, our material need for food and shelter, or the influence of biological sex. Other structures are culturally conceived, such as the rules of human language or the influence of mythology and religion. Despite the fact that these various theories describe different keys, each one believes that its key is a static or unchanging aspect of human society (Sturrock, 2003). By way of analogy, just as the theory of gravity explains planetary motion throughout the universe, a structuralist theory of sex differences may explain how any individual's biological sex shapes that person's entire life (e.g. Dow, 1990; McLaughlin, 1991).

Second, poststructural criticism is informed by theories of human behaviour that reject the notion that any one key can unlock the mysteries of human behaviour. Indeed, scholars of **poststructuralism** argue that 'there is no objectively real structure or central meaning and that oppressive "structures" are ephemeral' (Littlejohn & Foss, 2005, p. 317). Where structuralists see underlying structures in human behaviour and society, poststructuralists see only webs of meaning constructed by humans through their language and arguments. Researchers engaged in postmodern and **postcolonial** criticism follow this line of thinking, as do critical discourse analysts and semioticians. Much of their research is intent on demonstrating the variety of potential meanings inherent in every utterance, text, and action, such that it undermines the authority of culturally constructed and transient 'structures'.

All critical scholars, whether they are structuralists or poststructuralists, share two values. First, they embrace subjectivity (Peshkin, 1988). They believe that subjective views are impossible to avoid while conducting research, and that subjectivity can be a desirable asset in describing, evaluating, and reforming society. This leads into our second point: all critical scholars are willing to move beyond interpretation to judge the subject of study. Even as they embrace subjectivity, and by extension their own fallibility as researchers, they nonetheless believe that it is everyone's obligation to address social injustice wherever it is found. As a critical scholar, you may study structures and institutions such as the state, the economy, or the media. Alternatively, you may study the ideological beliefs associated with culture, such as those beliefs that define ethnicity, class, and gender. Whatever your topic, your critical studies will aim to liberate oppressed people or groups by making them aware of their own oppression or by reforming structures and symbols in a particular context.

To overcome the subjectivity of their positions, critical researchers must embed their claims in theoretical frames or discourses that are accepted by other members of the society under study. That is, each claim should reference some recognized set of principles that articulate a standard for acceptable behaviour in a just society. By extension, the researcher will judge the research subject against this standard. In most cases, critical scholars rely upon fully articulated theories that describe how society functions or how it could function if individuals were freed from systemic oppression. In the remainder of this section, we provide summaries of 10 such theories that supply perspectives on the just society, and by extension supply theoretical frameworks for critical claims.

Describing, Evaluating, and Reforming Social Structures

The structural criticism models we present here all aim to show how privileged groups oppress marginalized groups based on socioeconomic, cultural, and political structures in a society (e.g. Gilbert, 1997; Wittig, 1990). In Canada, marginalized groups might include First Nations communities, visible minorities, females, people with disabilities, and anyone whose sexual orientation is not heterosexual. Often, members of a numerical minority within a community may comprise an oppressed group.

When you conduct structural criticism, you identify the social arrangements most responsible for unequal power distributions so that they can be changed or adapted, primarily by reforming economic, political, and cultural means of power distribution. Table 12.1 summarizes the key theorists, claims, and research questions of five different types of structural criticism and suggests sample readings that you should pursue if you want to conduct that type of criticism. Let's consider the key concepts of each type of structural criticism in turn.

Marxist Criticism

The writings of Karl Marx, which were first published in English in the late 1800s and early 1900s (i.e. *The Communist Manifesto*, 1888; *Capital*, 1909) have been used widely by scholars in many disciplines to critique dominant social structures. Traditional Marxist criticism focuses on the economic basis of social structures:

> Traditional Marxism separated 'society', the material features of a socioeconomic system, and 'culture', the sense-making processes members of a social collective employ to create meaning of their experiences and context. (Conrad, 1988, p. 180)

For Marx, the economic (or 'material') base of a society was the key to understanding that society.

Political and economic structures are designed to reproduce themselves from generation to generation, while favouring those who are already privileged. Simultaneously, the beliefs, values, and practices associated with specific political and economic structures are also reproduced in cultural forms and artefacts. For example, the legal codes and financial rules that govern a capitalist economy were designed to promote the stability of the system through time, and hence they reproduced the system from generation to generation. Marx argued that the influence of these social structures on individuals was static, overt, deterministic, and unidirectional. In a capitalist economy, this meant that working class groups were inherently oppressed and that their jobs were dependent on investors and managers who controlled their fates. To initiate reform, oppressed individuals had to unite and change the social structure from capitalism to socialism.

TABLE 12.1 Structural Critical Studies

CRITICAL STUDIES APPROACH	CLAIMS DESCRIBE AND EVALUATE SOCIAL STRUCTURES; EVALUATE WHO BENEFITS AND WHO IS OPPRESSED; SUGGEST HOW SUCH STRUCTURES MIGHT BE REFORMED	SAMPLE READINGS
Marxist criticism (Karl Marx)	RQ: What are the means of production (e.g. capitalism)? What are the modes of production (i.e. sources and forms of labour)? Are the workers aware of how the means and modes of production benefit some and oppress others? How is language used to make sense of those experiences?	Smythe (1981) on the political economy of the Canadian mass media; Mosco & McKercher (2006) on how digital convergence has affected media workers.
Feminist criticism (Carole Gilligan, Sonja Foss)	RQ: How do women and men differently participate in and benefit from the means and modes of production? How are gendered experiences reproduced in language (e.g. socialization)? What tensions exist for women in particular contexts?	Martin (1991) on the role of women in the development of the telephone system; Tillotson (1991) on the gendering of the telegraph system; Dawson (1998) on the masculine image of the RCMP.
Psychoanalytic criticism (Sigmund Freud, Jacques Lacan)	RQ: How are the 'self' and 'other' constituted through language? How are our desires hard-wired biologically? What objects of our minds are real, imaginary, and fantasized?	Reyes (2010) on the gendering of film genres.
Universal pragmatics/ critical discourse analysis (Jürgen Habermas)	RQ: In any given discourse, what 'truths' are asserted? Are those 'truths' ever challenged? What attempts at influence are made, such as threats or promises? Are these attempts at influence appropriate or legitimate?	Martin (1998) on nurses and patient advocacy; Cezec-Kecmanovic, Treleaven, and Moodie (2000) on CMC knowledge-sharing in organizational restructuring.
Carnival criticism (Mikhail Bakhtin)	RQ: How can carnival, understood as a temporary release from established order, reveal a critique of dominant structures? What are the divisive forces and the cohering forces in any given situation that may permit carnival?	Lears (1994) on the discourse of abundance in advertising.

Note: RQ = research questions; CMC = Computer Mediated Communication

However, individuals were viewed by Marx as 'passive victims of social forces' (Conrad, 1988, p. 180) who did not realize that they were being dominated by economic and political systems. Some critical scholars believe in '**liberation** through awareness'. They believe that individuals who become aware of their oppressed positions in society can unite to change the systems or can at least withdraw their participation from oppressive social structures.

Withdrawing from oppressive social structures is more complicated than merely collaborating for collective social power. An example can illustrate this point. Imagine that you prefer a small, independently owned coffee shop instead of a large national chain because the small shop is locally owned and buys fair-trade coffee beans. Your preference here may be guided by both political and economic values. Sometimes, however, we recognize that we obtain some benefits from those structures that limit or even harm us. Maybe the national coffee chain has several stores near where you live and work and perhaps their coffee is cheaper, or they offer a wider selection of products. As a consumer, these conveniences can be real benefits when you consider your own time and money. As a citizen, however, these benefits exist in tension with your belief that big national chains compete unfairly with small, local independent stores and oppress the farmers who grow coffee. Hence this situation reveals the importance of collective action. Individuals must sometimes overcome their own short-term interests to achieve long-term social goals.

This example highlights economic structures. Let's look next at a model that highlights a biological structure, feminist criticism.

Feminist Criticism

Some feminist critics follow the structuralist idea that social structures control every individual's potential life experiences (e.g. Ferguson, 1990; Hanmer, 1990; Stoller, 1993). This idea is readily applied to an individual's biological sex, gender, and sexuality. Feminist critics who accept this idea argue that the life experiences of women in a patriarchal society are dictated by the privileged position of males over females in education, the workplace, religion, and all aspects of daily life. This kind of feminist criticism emphasizes the 'gendered nature of institutional structures and practices' (Ashcraft & Pacanowsky, 1996, p. 217). It tries to reveal the impact that accepted norms of behaviour have on individuals and on entire societies.

However, some critical scholars who are sympathetic to feminist criticism argue that gender and sexuality are flexible constructs rather than hard categories. Individuals cannot always be categorized into one of two categories such as male or female, or as straight or queer, as dictated by cultural ideology. This suggests that the ideological structures of gender and sexuality may be laden with social and cultural power, but they cannot entirely determine individual behaviour. Research in this perspective looks not only at the oppression of women but also of men, since both groups are instructed to behave in accordance with gendered norms (e.g. Butler, 1990, 1993; Speer & Potter, 2000). Hence, this research entails critical cultural studies of masculinity as well as femininity (e.g. Collinson & Hearn, 1994; Dawson, 1997; Hanke, 1998). Queer and transgender criticism also works to show how our society's representations of sexuality are power laden rather than neutral, cultural artefacts (e.g. Yep, Lovaas, & Ho, 2001; Yep, Lovaas, & Pagonis, 2002). You may recall our discussion of **resistant reading** in chapter 9, on historical, policy, and case analysis. The types of questions and criticisms posed by feminist scholarship provide one theoretical framework that may guide your resistant reading of texts, artefacts, and practices.

In addition to these strands of feminist scholarship, current feminist criticism incorporates an immense variety of theoretical explanations including liberal, radical, psychoanalytic, socialist, poststructuralist, and postcolonial approaches (Calas & Smircich, 1996). We cannot introduce you to all these approaches here, but later in this chapter we contrast structural with poststructural feminist criticism, and we include poststructural feminist claims and sample readings in Table 12.2.

Psychoanalytic Criticism

Freud agreed with Marx that human life is, essentially, 'a materially grounded struggle to ensure survival' (Reinelt, 1992, p. 384). However, Freud located ideological struggle within the individual rather than within society. Psychoanalytic critics following Freud, such as Lacan, have adopted this insight and critique the notion that each individual exists as a coherent and stable entity, a 'unified self'.

Freud theorized that each individual's identity was, in fact, composed of three related parts: the id, ego, and superego. The 'id' is each human being's drive for pure pleasure, and the 'superego' is our learned rules about what desires are taboo and should be repressed. The id and superego are mediated by the 'ego'. According to Freud, all human development is negotiated within the relationship between these three parts. When an individual denies his or her own id too much, it results in a 'neurosis'; that is, a mental disorder.

Both Freud and Lacan saw psychoanalysis as 'a journey leading to differentiation: first of self from other, then of male from female; finally, the self joins sociality' (Reinelt, 1992, p. 384). In 'sociality' we are connected with but separate from other people. That is, we maintain our individual senses of identity even as we interact with other people and seek our own needs or pleasures through them. For Lacan, our recognition of the 'other' begins while we are still children, when we recognize ourselves in the mirror. Once a child understands the differences between himself or herself and another individual, he or she loses some measure of self knowledge. A child can distinguish between 'me' and 'mommy' or 'daddy', and the child can desire to possess the qualities of the parent, the 'other'. Once this desire is fostered, the child's self-knowledge is bartered for social knowledge. For example, an appreciation of being small is lost in the desire to be big. According to Lacan, that social knowledge is always coercive in its power to shape the individual (Reinelt, 1992).

The identification of 'self' and 'other' is a logical precursor to the argument that social relations benefit some individuals more than others and therefore should be changed. That binary distinction between self and 'other' locates psychoanalytic critics firmly among the structural critics. Unlike Freud, Lacan viewed human needs, desires, and motivations as the outcomes of living in particular social structures. Most importantly, Lacan emphasized the role of linguistic structures in the shaping of cultures and the individual. Use of symbols and language is the path to human development, including our sense of self, our sense of the 'other', and our sense of what is real and imaginary.

Hence, these concepts are not universal to all human beings, as Freud's theory suggests, but culturally oriented. The same observation applies to neuroses.

An emphasis on linguistic structures, and their determining impact on communication and culture, leads scholars in our fields to study linguistic psychology. Similarly, media critics and performance studies scholars, who deal directly with fantasy and desire, make use of psychoanalytic criticism to read popular texts and understand the responses of media audiences. An example can be found in Reyes's (2010) article on the genre characteristics of film noir. Reyes challenges other scholars who view this genre as hypermasculine due to its strong male characters, dark moods, and suspenseful, violent plots. Reyes argues that, in fact, film genre and gender are conceived from the same 'overlapping symbolic economies of control' (2010, p. 87). Whether a film is noir or Gothic romance, the behaviour of male and female characters can be explained with reference to their internal conflicts over their appropriate roles in society. In Lacan's terms, the characters' behaviour indicates neuroses sparked by their failure to achieve sociality according to the norms of their culture. The fact that such movies become entertainment for millions of fans, and by extension reinforce specific notions of femininity and masculinity, makes such a study important for those who wish to challenge dominant cultural structures.

Universal Pragmatics

Jürgen Habermas (1979, 1984) is a leading proponent of the Frankfurt school, which we described in chapter 3, on paradigms. Habermas proposed a theory he called **universal pragmatics** in which he described society and how social interaction occurs. As a critical theorist, his overarching aim was to empower people by making them aware of hidden, oppressive social structures. Habermas saw language as the primary means to achieve emancipation. First, however, individuals require communicative competence to participate in social discourse and to help groups make decisions (Blyler, 1994; Felts, 1992).

Habermas (1979) outlined three types of speech acts that are required to achieve mutual understanding any time people communicate. First, constatives are assertions such as 'X is true'. Second, regulatives are attempts to influence others, such as commands or promises. Finally, avowals describe a speaker's internal state, such as 'I feel happy'. Habermas further proposed three different types of discourse, and each one is a kind of communication that is required when a speaker's statements are challenged. Theoretic discourse is needed to argue the truth of a constative statement. Practical discourse is used to argue the appropriateness of a regulative statement. Finally, metatheoretical discourse is required to argue the sincerity of an avowal. Because universal pragmatics can be used to assess participation in democratic processes, we have included it here as a way of doing structural criticism. That said, it is not commonly used in current communication and cultural research in Canada.

Carnival Criticism

Russian philosopher Mikhail Bakhtin (1981; 1984b) is credited with formulating concepts explaining the 'carnival'. In essence, **carnival** is an approved outburst of abnormal behaviours in spaces where such behaviours are not normally tolerated. If you've ever attended Mardi Gras, then you have a sense of the carnival. It is a ritual spectacle in which the usual order of social life is turned upside down. Bakhtin himself described it in the following terms:

> This temporary suspension, both ideal and real, of hierarchical rank created a special type of communication impossible in everyday life. This led to the creation of special forms of marketplace speech and gesture, frank and free, permitting no distance between those who came in contact with each other and liberating from norms of etiquette and decency imposed at other times. (Bakhtin as cited in Bernstein, 1981, p. 106)

Stemming from this description of the carnival, the 'carnivalesque' is any text, performance, or practice that embodies this sense of social disruption.

Bakhtin divided the 'carnivalesque' into three categories: (1) ritual spectacles like pageants and comic shows; (2) comic verbal compositions like parodies or inversions; and (3) 'various genres of billingsgate' like curses, oaths, and profanity, which he called 'the language of the marketplace' (1984a, p. 5). Janak (2006) used carnival criticism to assess the election campaign of former WWE wrestler Jesse Ventura. In 1998, Ventura was a candidate for the governor's position in the state of Minnesota, and won. As a reformer and an entertainer, Ventura took on 'the carnival fool's role to protest against the prevailing system' (p. 197). Janak showed how Ventura entered the campaign as an outsider, told stories of drinking and vomiting, wore a Jimi Hendrix T-shirt to his inaugural celebration, and used profanity in public, all illustrations of the carnivalesque.

Interpretive scholars and literary critics have also drawn on Bakhtin's distinction between 'polemic' rhetoric and 'parodic' rhetoric. **Polemic rhetoric** is intended to reinforce accepted norms of belief and behaviour within a society. As such, it should convince the listener to act in unison with other members of society. Such rhetoric is often found in texts such as newspaper editorials, sermons, political speeches, and most advertising, and is sanctioned by powerful elites within a society. Its opposite is **parodic rhetoric**, which is intended to undermine accepted norms of belief and behaviour, usually by noting how ridiculous, hypocritical, or simply incorrect those beliefs and behaviours are (Janak, 2006). Parodic rhetoric plays a role in the performance of the carnivalesque. For Bakhtin, there is always a 'dialectic' or struggle between two opposing forces, in language itself. This occurs even in the statements of an individual speaker. Even simple statements can carry depths of meaning and unintended ironies that are not fully conveyed through the words themselves (Hoquist in Bakhtin 1981, p. xx). Nonetheless, these unintended meanings and ironies become targets for parodic response. This kind of rhetoric is the substance of news comedy shows like *The Rick Mercer Report* or *The Daily Show with Jon Stewart*. Both Mercer and Stewart take direct quotes from politicians and other social elites, and then reveal the undesirable implications of these statements.

Again, critical scholars have embraced Bakhtin's concepts for the potentially disruptive insights they provide. Again, recall our discussion of resistant reading in chapter 9, on historical, policy, and case analysis. The search for disruptive insights suggested by Bakhtin offers a second theoretical framework that can guide your resistant reading of texts, artefacts, and practices

TABLE 12.2 Poststructural Critical Studies

CRITICAL STUDIES APPROACH	CLAIMS DESCRIBE THE VALUES, DISCOURSES OR IDEOLOGIES THAT CONTRIBUTE TO UNEQUAL POWER RELATIONS. CLAIMS ALSO SUGGEST HOW REFORM CAN DISTRIBUTE POWER EQUITABLY AMONG ALL SOCIETAL MEMBERS.	SAMPLE READINGS
Poststructural criticism (Michel Foucault) Poststructual feminist criticism (Judith Butler)	RQs: In any given context, how do values, discourses or ideologies privilege one class, gender or ethnicity over another? How can power relations be equalized?	McKay (1997) on the uses of folk culture in Nova Scotia; Lears (1994) on American advertising; Butler (1990) on gender norms; Kendig (1997) on gender scripts.
Postmodern criticism (Jean-François Lyotard, Michel Foucault)	RQs: In any given context, how does discourse function? What do people know, and how is language used to express what they know? How is power manifest in discourse? What competing interests are in play?	Clair & Kunkel (1998) on child abuse; Bradley (2005) on the ideology of open-source software; Zine (2008) on the role of religious schooling in the construction of gendered Islamic identities.
Postcolonial criticism (Edward Said, Homi K. Bhabha, Gloria Anzaldúa)	RQs: In any given context, what are the political relations among the colonized and colonizer? How does colonial oppression intersect with other forms of oppression (e.g. economic, gender, cultural)? Do hybrid categories of colonized and colonizer blur the distinction between them?	Roth (1993) on a Mohawk talk radio station; Clair's (1997) 'Treaty of New Echota'; Buddle (2005) on aboriginal media in urban Ontario.
Cultural criticism (Antonio Gramsci, Raymond Williams, Stuart Hall)	RQs: How are cultural categories such as class, gender and ethnicity produced in the struggle between competing ideologies? What contradictions exist within these ideologies and their categories? How do institutional changes in major structures like the government affect the dominant ideology? How do individuals participate in their own categorization? How can individuals disrupt the power of dominant groups?	Ebanda de B'beri & Middlebrook (2009) on the manipulation of regional identity by *Canadian Idol*; Felczak et al. (2009) on Canadian communication rights.
Semiotic criticism (Roland Barthers, Christian Metz)	RQs: In any given context, how does the selection and presentation of words, sounds, gestures, and images produce meaning? How are these meanings understood by those who receive them? In different contexts, are these meanings understood differently? Whose interests are present, or served, by these meanings? Whose interests are not present, or not served, by these meanings?	Matheson (2006) on notions of good citizenship in Canadian sitcoms; Elliott (2007) on use of the colour pink in breast cancer fundraising.

Note: The categories represented here are provided to help you distinguish these critical methods, but the distinctions represented here collapse easily since poststructuralists resist all structures, including tables like this one.

(as we noted earlier in this chapter, feminist criticism also offers such a framework). If your goal is to undermine social structures, it can be valuable to identify the carnivalesque and the parodic in everyday life.

Evaluating and Reinventing Discourse Processes

Poststructural critics identify ideology and culture, rather than material social structures, as the source of unequal power relations among people. Poststructural criticism evaluates and aims to reform the very ideas that structure a group's reality and the language or code of meanings through which all ideas, values, and beliefs are filtered in that reality. These scholars reject the idea that language has any definite meaning, and they resist assigning explanatory weight to material structures or any fixed categories. In fact, some commentators argue that the poststructuralists' tendency to reject fixed meanings and categories makes it impossible to defend their positions. Any points or arguments that poststructuralists make can themselves be deconstructed. Nonetheless, we sketch out some of the key concepts for five types of poststructural criticism in this section: poststructuralism itself, postmodernism criticism, postcolonialism criticism, cultural criticism, and semiotic criticism. Table 12.2 presents the key theorists, claims, and research questions for each type of poststructural criticism and lists some sample readings you should pursue if you want to conduct a study using one of these approaches.

Poststructural Criticism

Poststructuralism developed as a general reaction against structural theories of language and discourse, like those proposed by Habermas (Littlejohn & Foss, 2005). Poststructural critics frame social structure and individual participation in society as two forces influencing one another. Thus, it is possible for individuals to change the social structures in which they participate by reconstituting language and other symbolic forms of representation (Ely, 1995; Foucault, 1983; Gramsci, 1971; Mumby, 1997b). For example, Judith Butler's (1990, 1993) work has shown how gender norms are at once highly proscribed by cultural logic and yet open to subversion through individual performances. As such, poststructural feminist

deconstruction exposes the ways that the language of society benefits males. For example, it can expose the ways that our use of language is more advantageous for male students than female students in classrooms, through common practices such as being recognized for a turn at talk (Baxter, 2002). To encourage reform, this scholarship introduces a new vocabulary designed to eliminate such benefits (e.g. Kendig, 1997).

Postmodern Criticism

Lyotard (1984) and Foucault (1980, 1983) are the theorists most closely associated with the movement known as postmodern criticism. Lyotard (1984) first coined the term **postmodern turn** to refer to a general movement away from social structure as the explanatory means of domination toward ideology, representation, and discourse as the sites of struggle for social power (e.g. Clair & Kunkel, 1998; Parker, 1992). For the postmodern critic, there is no one rational or correct view of the world. Rather, postmodernists view 'all rationality as relative, or as a product of a given set of historically situated institutional practices' (Mumby & Putnam, 1992, p. 467).

Despite a tendency to dismiss social structures like the economy, or institutions of social control like religious bodies and universities, postmodern critics are still concerned with the structure and function of discourse within specific historical periods of time (Jones, 1992). If we accept Foucault's (1972) insights, it is impossible to separate what we know from the language we use to think about that knowledge. Foucault (1972) called such ways of knowing **discursive formations**, and he argued that power was an inherent part of all discourse. Hence, postmodern scholars invest their research efforts in deconstructing the discourses that surround influential beliefs, practices, and institutions. In deconstructing these discursive formations, they hope to persuade readers that no beliefs and practices are natural or necessary. They argue, rather, that all beliefs and practices can be reconceived and reformed (Bradley, 2005; Zine, 2008).

Postcolonial Criticism

Slemon (1995) described **postcolonialism** as a subset of postmodern and poststructural criticisms. Literally, a colonial society is one whose existing political, economic, and cultural structures have been colonized by another society, just as the First Nations of what became North Amercia were colonized by France and then Great Britain. Taken less literally, the power of any societal system over its individual members may also be seen as 'colonial' (Bhaba, 1990; Said, 1984). By either the metaphorical or literal sense of the term, the basic project of colonial studies is to define colonialism as 'both a set of political relations and as a signifying system, one with ambivalent structural relations' (Slemon, 1995, p. 49).

Carter's (1997) analysis of native imagery is relevant here. The focus of her book was the popular representation of women, and particularly native women, in the late 1800s. At that time in Canada, relations between the First Nations and European immigrants were still unsettled. While the Europeans controlled media and government structures, however, the natives did not. When aboriginal concerns were articulated through the press or official policy, it was through the words and perspectives of Europeans rather than natives themselves. Carter (1997) demonstrated how this situation led to the colonization of aboriginal representations, and that 'late-nineteenth century representations of women . . . bore scant resemblance to the real lives of women' (p. 10). Anyone who tries to understand aboriginal culture today by analyzing the texts and artefacts produced at that time must still cope with this legacy.

It should be noted that categorical opposites are rarely so clear or binary in practice as they are made to appear in language. Clair (1997) reminds us that group memberships are fluid, historic, and partial. In describing her own background, she makes the following observation:

> Being of mixed ancestry which crosses cultural and racial boundaries, and which includes traces of both the oppressor and the marginalized, speaks to the incredible complexity of naming a fractionated identity. I am the colonized. I am the colonizer. I am a reminder that life is not black and white (or red and white). (Clair, 1997, p. 329)

Even so, postcolonial studies often focus on the relations of the oppressor and the oppressed, of the mainstream and the marginal. In doing so, postcolonial scholars also focus on blurred categories such as hybridity or mixed category memberships (e.g. Anzaldua, 1987; Bhaba, 1995; Kraidy, 1999, 2002; Shome, 1998; Yep et al., 2001).

Like feminist criticism and Bakhtin's carnival, postcolonial analysis offers you an established theoretical framework that can guide your resistant reading of texts, artefacts, and practices. Ultimately, postcolonial scholars seek to reveal how colonizing powers marginalize or oppress native cultures, and these scholars hope thereby to foster a desire for positive change.

Cultural Criticism

Scholars who engage in cultural criticism assert that meanings we assign to concepts, objects, and practices are contested rather than fully shared by all members. Hence, cultural criticism investigates the ways that culture is produced through the struggle among dominant ideologies (Hall, 1986). Unlike interpretive cultural analysts who aim only to describe cultures as systems of shared meanings, cultural critics actively evaluate and try to reform cultural meanings and practices. They try to change society by identifying internal contradictions and by providing descriptions that will help people see that change is needed (Littlejohn & Foss, 2005). Paradoxically, the struggles among competing ideologies are always happening, and so, the balance of power is always subject to change.

Cultural critics often point to societal institutions like education, medicine, religion, government, and the media as social structures that work to preserve a dominant ideology. However, unlike traditional Marxists, cultural critics see the relationships among social structures and individual actions as dynamic, bidirectional, and interdependent (Williams, 1977). The chief claims of cultural studies are attempts to expose ways in which the ideologies of powerful groups are perpetuated. Additionally, the goal of cultural studies is to make citizens aware of the ways they can disrupt the power held by society's dominant members. High school and university courses in media literacy are an outgrowth of cultural criticism. Such courses try to make learners aware of how television, the Internet, and other media frame what is good and bad, and who is central or marginal to the society.

Semiotic Criticism

Semiotic criticism attacks our deeply entrenched 'notion that language is *the* medium of representation and communication' (Kress, Leite-Garcia, & van Leeuwen, 1997, p. 257). It does so by reducing communication to a unit of analysis more abstract than words, and this unit of analysis is the 'sign'.

Within **semiotics**, 'A *sign* is anything that can stand for something else' (Griffen, 2006, p. 26). Semioticians refer to this 'something else' as the 'referent'. For example, the sound of thunder is a sign of an approaching storm. Thus the storm is the referent. Or, steam rising from a cup is a sign that the coffee is hot with heat as the referent. As children, we gradually learn those signs which are important to our well-being and which allow us to manage in society. In semiotic theory, words too are signs, but they are qualitatively different from our first examples. Where thunder and steam are natural effects of the causes that precede them, the actual words 'thunder' and 'steam' have no natural relationship to the referents they signify. These words are simply abstractions that have been assigned to those referents within the English language. In French, the same effects are referred to as '*tonnere*' and '*vapeur*'. Rather than calling them 'signs', then, semioticians refer to words as 'symbols'. Visual cues, such as the use of the colour red to signify 'stop' or a logo that signifies a particular product, are similarly referred to as symbols.

This insight reveals a tremendous discontinuity between our experiences of the world, our thoughts, and what we communicate to other people. Whenever you use symbols to communicate, your message is open to multiple interpretations dependent on the referents experienced by your audience. Semioticians refer to this phenomenon as 'multimodality'. **Multimodality** is a term that describes all the different modes of representation that are active in a cultural context. This includes modes of representation in written and spoken language, but it also addresses the material forms in which that language is realized. For example, in the printed word the material form includes font, spacing, and layout. The spoken word may include pauses and physical gestures, as well as visual images. In fact, 'it has become impossible to read texts reliably by paying attention to written language alone' (Kress et al., 1997,

p. 257). This observation is certainly evident in most advertisements and websites.

Semiotic theory, then, provides a theoretical frame that is quite useful in critical studies. Semiotic criticism explores how power is instantiated in multimodal communication. For example, in analyzing websites, a semiotic critic may ask how visual images are used differently than words or sounds, and how they are most often used in combination. That critic may also ask which modes are more valued by advertisers, or by news sites, or in chat rooms. Further, he or she may ask how the use of these signs and symbols on the Internet has affected the production and reception of traditional media such as magazines or radio, or our expectation for other digital devices such as media players and Blackberries. These questions are suitable for semiotic criticism because ideology is a factor in all modes of representation. Hence, when semioticians study communication and culture, they do so by reducing all texts, artefacts, and practices to their signs and symbols in order to 'unpack' all of the possible interpretations of the messages they convey. Knowing how certain ideologies are reinforced through an accepted use of signs can potentially liberate multiple other voices within the same culture, or disrupt an unjust use of power, or reform that culture to achieve some measure of justice.

Now that you have some sense of how structural and poststructural critics stake out claims of description, evaluation, and reform, let's consider what counts as evidence in critical studies.

Evidence in Critical Studies

As we mentioned in part 1 of this book, two types of critical studies have emerged in communication and cultural studies: ideological critiques and critical empirical studies based on ideological critique (Deetz, 2005). Both types of critical studies rely on the emancipatory values we identified in chapter 6, on warrants, and both argue the ideological need for change in a given context. Indeed, the basic method for critical scholarship is to apply 'an ideological perspective to some phenomenon in order to generate a value-based critique' (Fink & Gantz, 1996, p. 118). Essentially, each of the 10 types of criticism is itself an ideological perspective. To develop your own ideological perspective, it is worthwhile to begin by reading some of the primary sources mentioned in the first section of this chapter.

While the two types of critical studies share a common interest in ideology, they nonetheless differ in their use of evidence and warrants. **Ideological criticism** uses textual evidence to evaluate communicative phenomena and to argue the need for change (Deetz, 2005). Ideological critiques are aligned with the more traditional forms of historical, policy, and discourse analysis that you learned about in chapters 9 and 10, and they are usually warranted by coherence and researcher positionality.

Critical empirical studies use some form of empirical data collected from participant observations, self-reports, and other-reports as well as textual evidence to describe and evaluate a particular situation, and to suggest what reforms are needed (Deetz, 2005). Again, the critic's evaluation would be rooted in a particular ideological perspective. Critical empirical studies employ a selection of warrants from the interpretive paradigm, such as researcher credibility, plausible interpretations, and transferability. They also employ a selection of warrants from the critical paradigm, such as coherence and researcher positionality. As always, readers of either type of critical studies are free to disagree with the researcher's interpretations and evaluations.

In the section following, we elaborate on some of the evidence toward which you might turn your attention when conducting structural and poststructural critical studies, in addition to your own beliefs and experiences.

Actions and Events

One way to focus on the lived experience of real people, in context, is to conduct a case study. As you know from chapters 9 and 11, on case analysis and ethnographic research, case studies highlight the actions of individuals and groups. Whether you consider actions and events that occurred in the past or in the present, their historical context will be an important feature of your critical analysis. For example, Ashcraft and Pacanowsky (1996) observed formal company meetings, informal work interactions, and a social function at a small business organization they called Office Inc.

These actions and events formed the basis for their feminist critique of how present-day women participate in their own devaluation in the work setting. Some of the actions and events that Ashcraft and Pacanowsky observed during six months of participant observations at Office Inc. included the president's beginning a maternity leave and the termination of a lawsuit in an 'agreeable settlement' (p. 224). Their case study applied the ideology of feminism to generate value-based critiques of present-day organizational actions and events.

Of course, you might select an action or event from the past for your analysis. Lee (1998) conducted a postcolonial feminist analysis of discourse on an archaic cultural practice in China: footbinding. It was, Lee noted, a 'gendered practice that physically mutilated the feet of Chinese women in the Han ethnicity from middle- and upper-class families' for over 800 years and 'It was a bone-crushing experience in a *literal* sense' (Lee, 1998, pp. 11, 14). For centuries, opposition to the practice of footbinding was silenced, but in the late nineteenth century, a collective movement to speak up brought an end to footbinding for many Chinese girls and women. Lee's (1998) analysis showed how the well-meaning antifootbinding discourse was at once emancipatory and oppressive, a site of identity struggle that implicated the ethnicity, class, and nationality of the dissenters as much as it did the women of the class and ethnicity whose feet were bound. Lee (1998) used the case of footbinding to explore a paradoxical research question, 'How is it possible to foster oppression in the midst of an emancipatory movement?' (p. 16).

Texts

As we have noted throughout this book, 'texts' are discursive representations of the world, and as such, the term 'text' may refer to spoken language (e.g. in a telephone interaction, a film, a television commercial, a musical performance) or to a symbolic representation (e.g. a gesture, a dance movement, architecture). As you can see from these examples, texts can be mediated or nonmediated, and the variety of texts available for analysis is theoretically endless. This includes the stories we tell to represent ourselves and our experiences of the world (e.g. Clair, 1993, 1994, 1997; Clair & Kunkel, 1998; Yep et al., 2002). When we take any source and make it our own through our research, or set it aside for a specific use, we call this 'appropriation'. Rogers (2006) defined cultural **appropriation** as 'the use of another culture's symbols, artifacts, genres, rituals, or technologies by members of another culture' (p. 474).

A number of critical studies have focused on how texts produced by one group have been appropriated by other groups for their own uses. Consider the number of advertisers and sports teams who use native words and imagery to brand themselves. Appropriation does not always entail the powerful using the texts of the marginal, nor does it always involve texts. Roth (1993) and Buddle (2005) both examined the use of radio broadcasting by First Nations communities. In both instances, a group of First Nations cultural producers sought ways to engage other members of their own community, and appropriated European or 'white' technology to achieve their own ends. As Roth (1993) found, a station on the Kahnawake reserve in Quebec was able to cultivate calm during a dispute between Mohawk representatives and the Sûreté de Québec in Oka in 1990. It did so through a talk radio program, broadcast in English, that invited callers from the reserve and from neighbouring non-reserve communities.

Semioticians may also analyze symbolic representations that are entirely nonlinguistic. For example, Drzewiecka and Nakayama (1998) argued that urban geographical spaces could be distinguished as modern or postmodern. San Francisco, California, is a city with a 'stronger modernist influence with their more traditional neighbourhoods that are divided by social divisions' (p. 23). San Francisco has neighbourhoods that are characterized by ethnicity and culture like Chinatown, Japantown, North Beach (Italian), the Castro (Gay), Hunter's Point (African American), and the Mission (Latino/a). During the year 2000, a number of high technology firms rented spaces in the Mission, which created a sort of cultural turf war (Glionna, 2000; Nieves, 2000). Such battles underscore the modernist interpretation of these neighbourhood spaces. By contrast, the complexity and postmodernity of Los Angeles, California, and of Phoenix, Arizona, were reflected in the blurring and fragmenting of traditional neighbourhoods as well as the presence of hybrid areas formed by highly mobile, multicultural groups of people (Drzewiecka & Nakayama, 1998). Hence, the organization of neighbourhood spaces in each city was the text to which Drzewiecka and Nakayama applied their ideological framework.

Of course, more traditional means of collecting texts are also useful in critical empirical studies of communication and culture. Surveys and participant observation are valuable ways to access participants' lived experiences. The responses and field notes that you collect with those methods constitute texts for analysis. As a case in point, Felczak et al. (2009) assessed the federal government's success at protecting the communication rights of Canadian citizens in the digital realm. They triangulated survey responses from Canadians, analysis of existing government policies and reports, and personal observations of contemporary government websites to study the utility and accessibility of government services on the Internet.

Finally, you can collect existing texts in less intrusive ways from archives, as is the case whenever newspapers, films, photographs, television shows, song lyrics, and such are used (e.g. McKay, 1997; Backhouse, 1999, Rutherford, 2000; Dye, 2009). Consistent with the critical paradigm assumption that truth is both personal and political, you will also use your own experiences and beliefs as evidence in making a critical argument.

Researchers' Experiences and Beliefs

Over the last 20 years, interpretive scholars and critical scholars have waged a debate over the question of who has a right to assign meaning to actions, events, texts, and experiences. In brief, we may pose the question as follows: whose perspectives on a social issue should be heard, and who should articulate those perspectives? In critical studies, we refer to this issue as the **politics of representation**. All representations of actions, events, and texts are political because all those representations broach the same questions: whose interpretation is correct? Who says what reforms are needed in a society? And what is the researcher's proper role in any social conflict? At the crux of the debate are the issues of membership in and naming of a social category or group (Lee, 1998). Mumby (1993) asked, 'How can researchers claim to speak for (i.e. construct representations of) social groups to which they do not belong?'

(p. 18). Even if you are a member of the group you want to represent, how legitimate is it for you to represent the voices of research participants, the people whose stories you collect and in whose events you participate?

We raise this question because your own experiences and beliefs are an important source of evidence in critical studies (Foss & Foss, 1994). Your beliefs and experiences are not thought of as biases to be ignored or controlled, as might be the case in discovery research. Your experiences are not just acknowledged as they affect your interpretations, as would be the case in the interpretive paradigm (Peshkin, 1988). Rather, in critical studies, your experiences and beliefs are the basis for your analysis of power, dominance, and the need to reform ideology (Lannamann, 1991; Foss & Foss, 1994).

Analytic Moves in Critical Studies

There is no one method or procedure for conducting critical studies (Sprague, 1992). Instead, there are various ways to collect evidence for analysis, just as there are a series of moves one can make in analyzing that evidence. You already know several nonrandom data selection strategies from chapter 5, on data, so in this section we describe four data analytic moves used in ideological critiques and critical empirical studies. These are dialectical analyses, deconstruction, narrative analyses, and speech act analysis. Each of these analytic forms has a rich history. We cannot do justice to each of them in this short space, but we try to show you what the basic move is in each case.

Dialectic Analyses

Dialectic analysis is the primary analytic move for structural critical studies. The research focus is the **relational dialectic**, a tension between two competing and perhaps contradictory goals in any given relationship (Baxter & Montgomery, 1998). In dialectical analyses, we interpret the tension by identifying the unique goals of each participant in the relationship. We then discern the underlying significance of these goals, and the tension that they produce. Often, this significance is hidden or obscured from the consciousness of the participants themselves (Lannamann, 1991). Through

careful tacking, back and forth, between the whole and the parts of the relationship, and between the whole and the parts of the texts or artefacts that document the relationship, we gradually uncover this meaning.

For example, Bauder's (2010) essay on journalism practice focused on the competing tensions between reporters' position as situated members of society and their role as autonomous observers. Most reporters work in an economic structure that seeks profitability and limits their autonomy (i.e. private sector news organizations). Despite this, reporters generally find news in the frictions that emerge in public and private debates. If they produce balanced reports of these debates, then they are bound to present both sides of every debate. Hence, while reporters generally reinforce existing discourses and social relations through their writing, they also give voice to alternative viewpoints. As Bauder (2010) puts it, 'Dialectical contradiction and juxtaposition are also a way for journalists to *discover* news positions and perspectives' (p. 12). In his estimation, the dialectic of journalism practice is a good thing. Bauder rejects those critics who dismiss reporters as simple stooges of corporate media empires because he is optimistic that reporters use their limited autonomy for the public good. Revealing such insights to others is the point of dialectic analysis.

The shift from interpretive to critical epistemology in dialectic criticism is subtle but distinct. In interpretive dialectic analyses, you begin with emic views, the participants' perspectives about whatever tensions are at play in a given. However, in critical studies, you begin with what Mumby (1993) called the **hermeneutic of suspicion**, an assumption that power is used illegitimately in a specific social situation. As we just noted, Bauder (2010) begins with the assumption that reporters simply reinforce existing discourses through their stories. Given this assumption of domination, you will analyze the struggle among fluid and competing interests in terms of their different ways of representing actions and events (e.g. Mumby & Stohl, 1991; Papa, Auwal, & Singhal, 1997).

Deconstruction

Deconstruction is the critical studies term associated with taking apart, or 'unpacking', the meanings of a text

(Derrida, 1972/1976, 1978, 1981). It is the most basic move for poststructural critical studies. Deconstruction aims to show how texts have hidden dualisms, inner contradictions, or repressed meanings. Mumby & Putnam (1992) described this analysis as follows:

> Meanings are not embedded within a text, but rather they are constructed through dichotomies or binary opposites that are constantly shifting. Derrida reasoned that textual meaning is only apparently stable because it 'privileges' (makes present) one term over the other. (p. 468)

Hence, whenever an author uses a specific word in a text, we can ask why the author believed its connotations were appropriate; we can also ask what connotations were excluded, and what word might have been used in its place. When we do this, we can potentially expose an individual author's prejudices or entire discourses of domination. One simple example may illustrate this move: Mats Sundin was the first captain of the Toronto Maple Leafs who was not born in Canada. Some supporters of the team thought it was inappropriate for a 'foreigner' or 'other' to lead the team. For such individuals, use of the word 'Swede' or 'foreign' was not simply a reference to his background, but an epithet denoting that he was not 'Canadian' or 'one of us'. However, Gunkel (2000) pointed out that any attempt to merely break apart the two halves of a binary opposite (in this case, 'Swede'/'Canadian' or 'foreigner'/'one of us') constitutes only one step of the analytical process for deconstruction. Deconstruction always proceeds in two steps (Gunkel, 2000, p. 52).

The first part of deconstruction is inversion. Two opposite terms are rarely equally valued, and **inversion** is an attempt to describe the qualities evoked by each term such that the value of each term is re-evaluated by the reader. As with carnival or semiotic analysis, this has the ability to upend traditional perspectives, or 'bring low what was high' (Derrida, 1981, p. 42, as cited in Gunkel, 2000). Gunkel (2000) described an episode of an American talk show during which the male host, Phil Donahue, assumed the body posture and facial expression of a centrefold model, while fully clothed, onstage. It was a way of

showing how that physical posture and facial expression functioned to present a nude female model as subservient. The image of an adult white male in that posture, showing that facial expression, fully clothed, made the function of the pose and expression apparent to the audience and resulted in laughter (Gunkel, 2000, p. 52).

In the second phase of deconstruction, **invention**, a new concept emerges that was not readily perceptible in the previous dualism. That is, the scholar introduces a third plausible concept to join the binary opposite terms that were unpacked during inversion. For example, Gunkel's (2000) essay argued that virtual reality is neither real nor simulated but something else that those two terms cannot fully describe. He argued that our experience of virtual reality prompts us to ignore or forget the relationship between 'reality' and its representation in digital media.

The two phases of deconstruction offer us another approach to resistant reading. We have already noted that feminist criticism, Bakhtin's carnival, and postcolonial criticism provide three different theories that can guide our reading of texts, artefacts, and practices. By contrast, deconstruction offers us a specific process to guide your resistant reading. Many scholars in communication and cultural studies combine one or more of these theories with deconstruction and semiotics in order to conduct their research. Generally, a scholar's claim and units of analysis will be rooted in a given theory, while the process of analysis will take place as the scholar deconstructs specific texts, artefacts, or practices. More often than not, the scholar will use semiotic theory to interpret the selected texts, artefacts, and practices. Semiotic theory allows the scholar to 'deconstruct' each text from its apparent whole into its constituent signs and signifiers.

Deconstruction is used as a general strategy for conducting ideological critique, to evaluate dominant meanings, and to propose alternative interpretations that will better serve the interests of formerly marginalized groups (Yep, 1998). If your critique simply inverts the traditional relationship between two binary opposites, then the point may simply be 'to reject one ideology and embrace another' (Parks, 1997, p. 483). In the case of feminist deconstruction, for example, its analysis is geared toward a rejection of traditional, patriarchal conceptions of society and culture, such that a new conception will be fostered to take its place. As Mumby has noted, 'the point of such work is not simply to introduce women into the equation . . . but rather it is to rewrite the equation itself' (Mumby, 1993, p. 23). If the equation is not reinvented by feminist research, perhaps at least such studies function to 'introduce radical doubt' into aspects of traditional social thought (Mumby, 1993, p. 24). Awareness of a need for change is, after all, the starting point for all reform (Mies, 1991; Ramazanoglu, 1992).

Narrative Analyses

We presented some interpretive uses of narrative analysis in chapters 9, on historical, policy, and case analysis, and chapter 11, on ethnographic research. Interpretive narrative analysis focuses on the meanings people make through the stories they tell, whereas critical narrative analyses push those meanings one step farther. Critical narrative analyses seek to expose hegemony (Littlejohn, 2002). Depending on your paradigm perspective, the analysis of such narratives can either raise awareness of the intersections of race, class, gender, and sexuality, or it can obscure knowledge that could and should be gained through systematic observation of categorical relationships and differences (Parks, 1997).

For example, Mumby (1988, 1993) studied the political nature of storytelling in organizations. He has shown how stories told over and over in organizations create and maintain power relations and usually perpetuate the interests of the dominant group, management. Analyzing members' stories is one way that you can access people's lived experiences for critical empirical studies of communication and culture.

The content of the stories we tell is just one feature of narrative analysis. Your critical narrative analysis might also address the situated features of storytelling. You may question who can tell a particular story, and when, and in what location. You may also question what may be accomplished by telling a particular story. The different answers you have for these questions may help you understand that a single story can be subject to 'fluid, competing interests'; a single story can have different significance or levels of meaning relative to the context in which it is told. To illustrate this concept, think of one joke that you find very funny. To whom, and in what times and places, would you tell this joke? In what situations would you avoid telling this joke or mask your true feelings if someone else shared it? If you recognize that the humour of a simple joke is subject to its context, then you are thinking critically about the situated features of narratives.

Speech Act Analyses

Habermas's (1979) critical discourse analysis offers a fourth potential analytical move for critical studies: speech act analysis. For Habermas (1984), the **ideal speech situation** is one that includes free, accessible public discourse and the equal distribution of power to all parts of society. If actions and events, texts, and the researchers' own experiences reveal that these conditions are not being fulfilled in a specific situation, it is unlikely that any discourse can take place that would help to emancipate the oppressed members of that society. We noted earlier in this chapter that Habermas identified three crucial speech acts to be used as units of analysis (i.e. constative, regulative, and practical discourse; see Table 12.1.) By isolating these three speech acts, and the presence or absence of their accompanying forms of discourse, you can assess whether a speaker's statements are being challenged, whose statements are challenged, and with what effects.

If emancipatory discourse does take place within a society, the critical researcher can evaluate its direction and likelihood of equalizing power relations. Because the goal of critical scholarship is to unite theory and action, to actually change existing power relations, criticism of these three linguistic acts and their accompanying forms of discourse can help critical researchers to evaluate social changes already in progress. For example, Martin (1998) showed how nurses can use the ideal speech situation to help them 'be effective advocates for patients without compromising their working identity or facing conflicts of loyalty' (p. 147). Martin sought to foster a more conscientious use of language, and by extension, a new way of thinking about how to equalize power relations within health-care institutions.

Warrants for Critical Studies

The standards for evaluating ideological critiques and critical empirical studies are built on interpretive paradigm warrants, though many poststructural critics resist any form of categorization and standardization. In this section we discuss coherence and researcher positionality with respect to critical claims and evidence.

Establishing Coherence

Deetz (1982) first pointed out that coherence, rather than accuracy, is the most appropriate warrant for critical studies. As we said in chapter 6, on warrants, coherence means that the author's interpretations are logical, consistent, and intelligible. Of course, this raises the question, 'To whom does this understanding of the text appear "maximally reasonable and coherent"?' Fink and Gantz (1996) stated that 'those who share the critical perspective of the researcher are free to accept or reject the argument' (p. 119). Those who disagree with the researcher's ideology, in all likelihood, will not see the researcher's interpretations as coherent. Bochner (1985) called this 'free consensus', which suggests 'verification can only be left to those who agree with that perspective' (as cited in Fink & Gantz, 1996, p. 129).

Ideological critiques typically address an entire social system, though they often do so by examining an individual social structure like ethnicity, gender, social class, political institutions, or the media. They may do so by treating a wide variety of sources, from single texts such as novels or films, to a broad social practice such as dancing or advertising. Such studies may focus on the historical development of such sources, or their positioning at a particular time and place. Either means of achieving focus, the historical or the contextually situated, serve to attain coherence. Even actions that appear unreasonable may be shown to be rational or necessary when their broader historical or social contexts are examined (Ramazanoglu, 1992). Some actions that appear irrational actually are reasonable responses to unreasonable situations (Clair, 1993, 1994; Yep et al., 2002). Knowing this, Deetz (1982) advises 'one should not pass judgment on an individual without understanding the inherent logic which makes his or her actions meaningful' (p. 144). Conquergood's (1991)

critical cultural ethnography of Latino gang members in Chicago showed how young men participated in gangs to fulfill their social needs for inclusion, affection, and control. This was one early example of research that made coherent the seemingly incoherent, even life-threatening behaviour of joining a street gang.

If you are conducting an empirical critical study, you can achieve coherence by becoming intimately familiar with the sources you analyze. In this case, membership in at least one of the social groups under study may be as important a warrant for your critical study as it is in interpretive research. Even as a member of one of the social groups under study, you must stay aware of multiple possible interpretations of the text. You must 'search for the texts which best represent what is thinkable and doable' in that social situation (Deetz, 1982, p. 144). Only when you are intimately familiar with the situation, when you know 'how to get things done, how to avoid unpleasant outcomes, how to recognize critical features', as well as 'with whom to talk, what counts as adequate information', (Deetz, 1982, pp. 140–141), can you achieve a coherent interpretation. Without a coherent interpretation, you cannot possibly evaluate power imbalances or oppression or suggest what actions should be taken to reform those conditions.

Establishing Researcher Positionality

As you know from chapter 6, on warrants, researcher positionality includes both your standpoint and your reflexivity about that standpoint. Van Dijk (1997b) notes that 'critical scholars make their social and political position explicit; they take sides, and actively participate, in order to uncover, demystify, or otherwise challenge dominance' (p. 22). In this section, we elaborate on some of the ways you can demonstrate both aspects of your positionality.

First, the fact that you have a particular standpoint from which you view all evidence is simply common sense to interpretive and critical researchers. Because critical researchers believe it is neither possible nor desirable to eliminate subjectivity or to work around it in doing research, you will want to acknowledge your subjectivity and include it in your analysis. You can begin by learning to know when your own subjectivity has been engaged. You may notice, for instance, that you have positive or negative feelings toward some of the evidence you are analyzing, that there are some experiences you want more of, or some that you want to avoid (Peshkin, 1988). When you are interacting with members of marginalized groups, you may find yourself wanting to advocate for them or take on roles that go beyond your tasks as a researcher. You may notice yourself having a value conflict, such as being completely honest about something you observed in data collection while still wanting to portray your participants in a positive light (Gouldner, 1988). Peshkin (1988) advocated a disciplined, systematic self-monitoring of these cues, 'so that I may avoid the trap of perceiving just that which my own untamed sentiments have sought out and served up as data' (p. 20).

The second part of establishing your positionality as a researcher is to be reflexive about your standpoint. As we said in chapter 6, **reflexivity** refers to your own awareness of the specific ways that you are inseparable from the things you are trying to describe, evaluate, and ultimately change. For example, Tator et al. (1998) wrote about racism in Canadian society. Their approach was to examine the production of six cultural events as individual case studies. They understood that they were challenging certain 'sacred' self-beliefs of Canadians, in particular the notion that Canada is a highly tolerant and open society. As such, they were forthright in describing their own positions and motives:

> The perspective of this book is influenced by many factors, including the following: the ethno-racial backgrounds of the authors; our genders, and our educational and professional backgrounds; our geographic and social locations; our work as academics and our experience as anti-racism practitioners; . . . and finally, our commitment to social change, social action, and social justice. We therefore are neither 'neutral' nor 'objective' observers. (p. 12)

These comments demonstrate that Tator et al. recognize that their positions, and by extension their analysis, may differ from others' locations and experience.

As you read critical studies, you will notice that questioning the correctness of an interpretation receives far less attention than acknowledging multiple, plausible interpretations. This leads us to another way that you can be reflexive, which is to acknowledge your own and your readers' freedom of choice.

As a critical scholar you are free to choose different actions, events, and texts as evidence for your analysis and to support the worth of your analysis with different warrants. You must acknowledge the choices you have made and try to avoid presenting those choices as the only correct ones. Nonetheless, as Deetz (1982) notes, rigour 'is possible in the maintenance of these principles rather than the following of a prescribed method or procedure' (p. 143).

Critical studies essays often contain explicit invitations to readers that they are free to choose another interpretation or to deconstruct the author's interpretation of the actions and events. For example, Ebanda de B'beri and Middlebrook (2009) explored how *Canadian Idol* constructed notions of national and regional identity in Canada. Although the show created a space for Canadian artists separate from *American Idol*, it nonetheless fostered regional rivalries as a means to generate interest in the show by emphasizing each contestant's hometown. Ebanda de B'beri and Middlebrook (2009) concluded that 'the generic structure of the show reinforces systemic ideological practices that produce a fictitious sense of belonging to the nation via selected, dominant regions' (p. 31). However, the researchers also acknowledged that fans of the show responded in a variety of unexpected ways. They described their findings as follows:

> . . . not all viewers internalize, uncritically, the representation of identity as articulated by the show. Indeed, some respondents use the space provided by the *Canadian Idol* message boards to work through these very issues. (p. 37)

In this case, not only the reader's interpretations are welcomed, but the participants' own perspectives offer alternative interpretations of the researchers' findings.

We hope these brief examples give you some idea of how you might warrant your ideological critique by establishing a coherent argument for why ideological reform is needed and acknowledging your positionality as a researcher, as well as your standpoint and your reflexivity. If you are conducting a critical empirical study, you will want to warrant your research with coherence and researcher positionality but you will also pay attention to interpretive paradigm warrants such as researcher credibility, plausible interpretations, and transferability. Such warrants are especially valuable if you use a critical-interpretive method like critical ethnography, critical discourse analysis, or critical content analysis.

Ethical Issues

Critical scholars consider their essays to be 'fictions'. By this, they mean that their scholarship is expressed through rich representations of the actions, events, and texts they study, representations that are inherently biased by their own experiences, values, and purposes. This does not mean that a critical essay will lack rigour or that a critical scholar will intentionally abuse his or her power of representing actions and events through language. In fact, since critical scholarship is characterized by concerns about the politics of representation, every choice about what is said or not said has ramifications that are linked to power and ideology. One way that you can deal with the politics of representation in your writing is by being self-reflexive.

The principle of rigorous self-reflection dictates that you examine your motives, your word choices, and the way you frame an essay with immense care (Allen, 1996). Even then, you should not claim to have captured the true meaning of an act or event. Instead of assuming a false objectivity about the communication and cultures you study, approach your critical essay as an interesting fiction, to be evaluated for its ability to 'read texts in their full variety, rather than to get beneath or behind them' (Deetz, 1982, p. 137). Specify in your essay the criteria by which your research may be evaluated. Make your descriptions of the texts, actions, events, or experiences 'rich and compelling' (Deetz, 1982, p. 147).

Another strategy for ethical critical research is to interrogate yourself about your motives for doing a particular study. Is your purpose really to disrupt hegemonic relations, and if so, will a critical essay be the best tool to accomplish this end? If you are critiquing other people's messages, practices, culture, or ideological choices, what are your ethical obligations to those persons? Just because you disagree with them does not mean that you can violate their right to privacy or their autonomous choice to participate in research. Similarly, you should be concerned with justice. If your work results in a power shift such that the oppressed group becomes the privileged group, and vice versa, is that necessarily just? To be an ethical critical scholar, you cannot just be a crusader against oppression. You must also be a reflective advocate for social change.

Summary

In this chapter, we have described the research goals and theories associated with critical studies. The distinguishing feature of this research is its analytical approach to evidence. The evidence used for critical studies may be taken from any source and may be collected using any of the empirical methods described in this text. When examining this evidence, however, critical scholars interpret and assess their findings in light of particular perspectives on the nature of human communication and culture. Their goal is to reveal how power is exercised in a group or society, and how power is maintained through communication and cultural practices. Hence, their claims can be descriptive, interpretive, or critical, but they always imply critique and reform.

If you conduct critical research, then your perspective and goals will most likely be informed by an established theory. There are many theories that have contributed to the critical perspective, and we have identified two major lines of thought in structuralism and poststructuralism. **Structuralists** argue that individual thought and behaviour are constrained by some material or cultural structure in which we live, such as gender, language, or the economy. These structures are maintained through various ideologies and social practices that tend to distribute power and resources in an unequal fashion. By contrast, poststructuralists

TABLE 12.3 Major Aspects of Critical Studies

CRITICAL ORIENTATION	CLAIMS	DATA	WARRANTS	MANUSCRIPT FORMAT
Structuralism	Describe, evaluate, and reform social structures	Primarily dialectical analyses of actions, events, texts	Coherence, researcher positionality (i.e. standpoint and reflexivity)	Critical essay
Poststructuralism	Describe, evaluate, and reform symbol systems (i.e. discourse)	Deconstruction, paradox, speech act, and narrative analyses of actions, events, texts, and the critic's own experiences	Coherence, researcher positionality (i.e. standpoint and reflexivity)	Critical essay

Note: Critical empirical studies of communicative action are warranted by coherence and researcher positionality in combination with interpretive paradigm warrants.

do not believe that individual thought and behaviour are constrained by such structures, because they do not believe that such structures exist. Rather, they contend that 'structures' such as gender and the economy are purely ideological conceptions with no material reality and that they are ideas conceived by some individuals to exert power over other individuals who accept that these ideas are true. No matter which type of theory you embrace, your own experiences and thoughts will form an important part of your perspective and your motive for conducting the research.

Once your theoretical perspective and claims are known, you must decide on the relevant sources and data collection methods you will use to gather evidence. You will not select your sources randomly but purposefully because of their ability to provide evidence relevant to your claim. After your evidence is gathered, you may select from a number of analytical strategies, such as deconstruction and dialectical and narrative analysis.

No matter how your evidence is collected and analyzed, you will try to ensure that your findings are coherent and supported by adequate facts and arguments. Because your own thoughts and experiences influence your selection of theory, claims, and sources, you must be reflexive in your analysis if you wish to gain researcher credibility with your audience. This includes a consideration of the politics of representation. If you have an intimate link with the group or culture under study, and this link affects your positionality as a researcher, then you must explain this link in your research report. In some situations, it may give you greater credibility because one of your goals may be to give voice to oppressed members of society. However, you should not assert that you speak for all members of that group or culture if, in fact, you do not.

In many ways, the theoretical frameworks associated with critical studies offer a set of analytical strategies for evidence that are primarily qualitative. These analytical strategies offer you ways to move beyond description of a group or societies and to make inferences about their cultural values and their experiences of power. By contrast, statistics offer a set of analytical strategies for data that are quantitative. Statistics, too, can offer tools that both describe data and make inferences about the nature of that data. We discuss statistics in our last two chapters.

Key Terms

Appropriation
Carnival
Critical empirical study
Deconstruction
Discursive formation
Hegemony
Hermeneutic of suspicion
Ideal speech situation
Ideological criticism

Ideology
Invention
Inversion
Liberation
Multimodality
Parodic rhetoric
Polemic rhetoric
Politics of representation
Postcolonialism

Postmodern turn
Poststructuralism
Reflexivity
Relational dialectic
Resistant reading
Semiotics
Structuralism
Structure
Universal pragmatics

Discussion Questions

1. Write a brief description of yourself that you would be willing to share with your classmates and instructor. Would you share the same description with your parents? Your employer? Your significant other? Why or why not? What are the politics of representing yourself? How would those politics affect your thinking if you were trying to represent another person or an event outside your own experience?

2. Hanke (1998) and Dawson (1997) have described the hegemonic nature of masculinity as portrayed in a television sitcom and in stories of the RCMP. What other examples can you think of that show how masculine and feminine roles are portrayed, parodied, and critiqued in the media you encounter in your daily life? Do you consider any of these examples to be role models? Why or why not? How do these portrayals affect the way you think about your own gender?

3. Kaye (2003) studied how the descendants of European settlers in the Canadian West have used elements of First Nation cultures. In the introduction to her book, she commented, 'I am writing from within the European-descended settler society and with the particular responsibility of being the grandchild of four early Alberta settlers . . . .' (p. xxii). How do you think this perspective affected her scholarship? What do you think it means to be rigorously reflective? What perspective do you own? How could you become more reflective about your own position in Canadian society?

4. An important question with respect to acknowledging subjectivity in critical studies concerns the practical problem of conflicting interpretations of the text. Should critical scholars check their interpretations with others, and particularly the participants in their studies? If so, and participants disagree with the scholar, whose interpretation is correct? Whose ideas should be privileged in the scholar's written critical essay?

Try It!

1. This is an exercise for deconstruction. It can be completed by an individual, but it may be more interesting to work in a group with two or more other members. Depending on the size of your tutorial group, it may also be adapted as a tutorial exercise.

    Process

    (a) Select a 30-second commercial appearing either on television or on the Internet, or select a wedding magazine or website (e.g. *Today's Bride*, *Wedding Bells*, or www.CanadianBride.com). The commercial, magazine, or website may be selected by you or your instructor.
    (b) Deconstruct the commercial, magazine, or website. What social structures, events, or actions does your text depict?
    (c) Assess the intentions of the advertiser or the magazine's editor. Do you think the advertiser or the editor wishes to evaluate or reform these structures, events, or actions? Why or why not?
    (d) Does the commercial, magazine, or website reinforce any hegemonic assumptions held in our society? If so, which ones and how are they conveyed??

2. This is an exercise for speech act analysis. It can be completed by an individual, but it may be more interesting to work in a group with two or more other members. Depending on the size of your tutorial group, it may also be adapted as a tutorial exercise.

    Process

    (a) Select a text that represents a segment of dialogue, such as a passage from a film, book, or television show, an exchange via email, or a transcript of a telephone conversation or face-to-face interaction (e.g. the script of a play). The text may be selected by you or your instructor.
    (b) Analyze the text to isolate the three types of speech acts identified by Habermas (1984): constatives, regulatives, and avowals.
    (c) Is there any discourse in this text, as in 'the special kind of communication required when a speaker's statements are challenged' (Littlejohn, 2002, p. 215)? Which types of discourse can you detect?
    (d) Based on the speech acts, and any accompanying discourse you have identified, answer the following questions:

        i. Who has more power in this situation and who is being oppressed?
        ii. Is the discourse present in this situation likely to rectify any power imbalance between/among these participants?
        iii. Do the participants seem to be aware of this power imbalance, or is it hidden from their everyday lived experience?

13 Descriptive Statistics

Introduction

Statistics are used in almost every field of communication and cultural research. They are often used in survey research and content analysis, but they can play a role in other methods as well. In essence, statistics are a branch of mathematics that attempts to find meaning in numbers. Just as the theories associated with critical analysis attempt to find patterns and depths of meaning in qualitative information, statistics try to find patterns and depths of meaning in quantitative information. This is the essence of statistical analysis. **Statistical analysis** is defined as 'the science of describing and reasoning from numerical data' (Smith, 1988, p. 93).

We express many ideas numerically, such as our age, height, and weight. Generally, we value such measurements because we understand how they are taken and they provide us with a sense of scale. The world of sport is filled with numbers that allow us to compare athletic performances, such as record times for track events, 'save' percentages for hockey goaltenders, and efficiency ratings for football quarterbacks. In research, numerical information performs the same tasks, but of course we measure concepts or units of analysis pertinent to communication and culture rather than personal attributes or athletic performances. Further, our research uses scales that are designed especially for our purposes.

In this chapter, we introduce you to the most basic forms of statistical analysis. First, we will introduce you to descriptive statistics, including measures of a distribution's central tendencies, dispersion, and shape. A key component of this discussion will be visual representations of data. Then, we briefly identify three types of distributions: samples, populations, and sampling distributions. We conclude this chapter by introducing you to the logic and steps involved in testing hypotheses and the way that researchers use technology to generate descriptive statistics.

We often associate the term 'statistics' with abstract numbers. However, it is helpful to remember that all numbers and statistics used in communication and cultural research tell us something about very real things. Take film audiences, for example. There are many different kinds of information that we can collect from movie audiences, such as their demographics, the frequency with which they go to movies, or their reasons for attending any one particular film. Some of this information is clearly qualitative, such as an individual's reasons for attending a film and demographic categories such as ethnicity. However, some of this information is clearly quantitative, such as the frequency that individuals go to the movies (e.g. the number of times per month) and demographic categories such as age. Whether qualitative or quantitative, each kind of information tells us about one characteristic of the audience.

Thinking in these terms, we understand that **statistics** provide one way to characterize an aspect of a sample taken from a population we wish to study. We have already encountered the concepts of **sample** and **population**. These terms were explained in chapter 5 and applied to our discussions of surveys and content analyses. In that chapter, you learned the importance of defining a population for study that is relevant to your claim, be it a population of individuals or a population of messages. You also learned how to obtain representative samples from your population to ensure that your findings will be generalizable. Finally, you also learned that the concepts we use to understand a sample are operationalized as variables when we gather numerical data about them. Numerical data is produced using one of the four measurement scales we described in chapter 5, on data: nominal, ordinal, interval, and ratio.

Statistical analyses primarily serve two types of functions: description and inference. In this chapter, you will explore how numerical data gathered from your samples can be described and tested statistically. In the following chapter, you will explore ways to draw inferences from your numerical data.

Descriptive Statistical Analyses

When we use variables as data, we work with them as sets of numbers. **Descriptive statistics** are mathematical tools that allow us to describe a single set of data. The products of these methods are either numbers or visual representations of numbers, such as tables, pie charts, or bar graphs.

Researchers use standard terms to describe their data to each other. Let's start with some basic definitions. In technical terms, when all of the values in a single set of data are organized in a logical way, the set is referred to as a 'distribution'. A **distribution** contains two types of information. The first type of information identifies the thing being measured. We refer to this 'thing' as the **independent variable**. The second type of information is the actual measurement taken. In general, we refer to this measurement as the **dependent variable**, though specific types of measurements are called 'frequencies' or 'scores'.

An example can illustrate these terms. Imagine that you are conducting a survey on daily Internet use. For each participant in the survey, you may collect data day by day, and then calculate the average number of hours spent on the Web. Let's say that we collect data from Participant A for 10 days. The data may be organized into a distribution like that in Table 13.1. The independent variable identifies each unique day sampled for the study. The dependent variable reports the actual amount of time measured in hours for each day. This study lasted 10 days, so we have 10 unique measurements. We can assign a nominal code to identify each unique day (e.g. Day 1, Day, 2, and so on). Then, for each day there is a corresponding score (e.g. the number of hours our participant spent surfing the Web).

When referring to any one matched pair of data, you will always describe the independent variable first. To stay with our Internet example, we can see that on Day 8 our participant spent two hours on the Internet. As a matched pair, this could be expressed as (8, 2). In symbolic terms, independent variables are always denoted x, while dependent variables are denoted y. A matched pair could be expressed (x, y). When data is presented visually, this distinction is maintained. In a table, the independent variables or x-data will normally appear in the first column, while dependent variables or y-data normally appear in columns to the right. We will discuss more visual aids later in this chapter.

These terms are necessary to explain the basic ways we describe the distribution of measurements in a data set, and this is our goal in the next section.

Sample Distribution Characteristics

Sample distributions can be visually represented as we see in Table 13.1. They can also be characterized

TABLE 13.1 Frequency Table with an Example Distribution

SURVEY ON DAILY INTERNET USE—PARTICIPANT A	
DAY (*x*-AXIS)	FREQUENCY OF HOURS SPENT ON INTERNET (*y*-AXIS)
1	1
2	2
3	3
4	3
5	6
6	5
7	3
8	2
9	0
10	1
n = 10	n = 10
	Σ = 26
	Mo = 3

by using descriptive indexes or measures. In the next few sections, you will learn how to interpret three types of descriptive measures: measures of central tendency, measures of dispersion, and **measures of shape**.

Measures of Central Tendency

When we travel, we often rely on signposts to tell us something important about where we are. A signpost may not carry much detailed information, but it can draw your attention to something you might have otherwise missed. Measures of central tendency serve as signposts for statistical data. In technical terms, a **measure of central tendency** is a descriptive statistic that reduces a distribution to one number that best characterizes all of the measurements throughout the sample. There are three measures of centrality: the mode, the median, and the mean.

The **mode** is that measurement which appears most frequently in one distribution. It is coded as 'Mo'. As we know, measurements are reported in the *y* column. Looking at our example in Table 13.1, then, the mode is three because it occurs three times. In other words, on three days our participant reported three

hours of Internet use, and this measurement occurred more frequently than any other in this distribution. A distribution will have no mode if no measurement appears more than once. By the same token, a distribution will have more than one mode if two measurements appear equally frequently, and more than all other measurements in the set. Distributions with two modes are called *bimodal*, and those with three modes are called *trimodal* or *multimodal*.

When a distribution is bimodal, but the two most common measurements are on contiguous points along the **x-axis**, the distribution is still considered to be unimodal or having just one mode (Smith, 1988). Take a look at the first two columns in Table 13.2. The table presents a distribution of measurements taken from Participant B over 11 days. This distribution has two mode values because the numbers 3 and 4 occur equally frequently. Further, they are contiguous when the data are sorted along the *x*-axis. Hence, this distribution is unimodal. When we report the value for this mode, however, we must still report both numbers (Mo = 3, 4).

Modes are most useful when examining the distribution of nominal data. For example, as part of your study of Internet use, perhaps you will ask participants to identify the means they use to connect to the Internet. When collecting the data, you could arbitrarily score dial-up connections as '1', LAN connections as '2', and wireless connections as '3'. Because these scores are nominal and arbitrarily assigned, the scores themselves do not measure anything. However, if any one of these three scores appears more often than the others, then that score would be the mode and it would indicate that one means of connecting to the Internet is more common than the others in your sample. Modes are less useful when examining the distribution of interval or ratio data because modes by themselves are not generally meaningful in these distributions. An exception occurs whenever you wish to show that there are two or more peaks in the data that occur at different points in time.

The second measure of central tendency is called the median, which is denoted as *m* or $\bar{x}$. When all of the *y*-data in a sample are sorted in ascending order, the **median** is the precise midpoint score with half of the scores in the sample appearing above the median

TABLE 13.2 Frequency Table Demonstrating Mode and Median

SURVEY ON DAILY INTERNET USE—PARTICIPANT B			
SORTED BY x-DATA		**SORTED BY y-DATA**	
DAY (x-AXIS)	FREQUENCY OF HOURS SPENT ON INTERNET (y-AXIS)	DAY (x-AXIS)	FREQUENCY OF HOURS SPENT ON INTERNET (y-AXIS)
1	1	9	0
2	2	1	1
3	3	10	1
4	3	2	2
5	4	3	3
6	4	4	3 – median
7	3	7	3
8	4	5	4
9	0	6	4
10	1	8	4
11	6	11	6
$n = 11$	$n = 11$ $\Sigma = 31$ Mo = 3, 4	$n = 11$	$n = 11$ $\Sigma = 31$ $\bar{x} = 3$

and half appearing below it. Look at the second two columns in Table 13.2. We see there are 11 scores ($n = 11$). Because n is an odd number, we know there must be a single midpoint score with an equal number of scores above and below it. When the y-data are sorted in ascending order, they would appear as follows:

0, 1, 1, 2, 3, 3, 3, 4, 4, 4, 6

Hence, the median in this distribution is the sixth score along the **y-axis**, 3. By interpreting this measure, you know that our second participant spent roughly half his days surfing the Web for three hours or less each day, and roughly half his days surfing the Web for three hours or more each day.

When a distribution contains an even number of scores, the median must be calculated. An odd-numbered distribution has a single midpoint score, but an even-numbered set has two scores which share the midpoint. The median in an even-numbered set, then, is the average of the two midpoint scores. We can use

Table 13.1 for our example ($n = 10$). When the y-data are sorted in ascending order, they appear as follows:

0, 1, 1, 2, 2, 3, 3, 3, 5, 6

The two midpoints scores are the fifth and the sixth scores, 2 and 3. The median in this case is obtained by averaging the two scores, as follows:

$$\bar{x} = \frac{(2 + 3)}{2} = 2.5$$

If both midpoint scores are the same value, for example, if they are both 2, then their average, and hence the median, would be self-evident.

Unlike modes, median scores are reported in interval and ratio level measurements of data but not for nominal categories. Typically, median scores are reported along with 'means' to show that distributions do not contain extreme or 'outlying' scores. For example, Hoffman and Heald (2000) used both mean and median score values for frequencies of tobacco advertisements, alcohol advertisements, and frequencies for both types per magazine issue targeted at African Americans. Hoffman and Heald showed that the data was distributed normally in each of the magazines examined because the mean and median values were close together.

The 'mean' is the most sensitive measure of central tendency. A **mean** is the average of all the scores in a distribution. It is represented as M or $\overline{X}$. The mean is considered the most sensitive measure of central tendency in data sets with interval and ratio scores because the equation applies to the values of the scores. To calculate the mean, find the sum of all the scores in a set (denoted by Σ, the Greek symbol referred to as 'capital sigma'), and then divide that sum by the total number of scores (denoted by n). Looking at our example in Table 13.3, we would use the y-data and the equation would look like this:

$$\overline{X} = \frac{\Sigma y}{n} = \frac{34}{11} = 3.09$$

To interpret this statistic, we could say that the mean daily Internet use of Participant C is 3.09 hours. As with median scores, mean scores are reported in interval and ratio level measurements of data but not for nominal categories.

When two or more measures of central tendency are equal or nearly so in a distribution, like they are for Participant C in Table 13.3 ($\overline{x} = 3$, $\overline{X} = 3.09$), then that the distribution is fairly 'normal'. When all three measures have different values, it indicates that 'skew' is present. In skewed distributions, the mode and the median will be closer to the majority of scores (the central tendency) while the mean will be pulled in the direction of the outlying scores. We shall discuss skew in more detail in a later section.

So far, we have introduced you to some basic terms: distribution, x-data, y-data, matched pairs, mode, median, and mean. Before you continue to the next section, ensure that you understand each of these terms. Most of them are applied to figures, which are readily observed if you know where to look. Only three of these terms are applied to calculated figures, and these calculations are fairly simple (e.g. for the median and mean). Chances are, you are already familiar with the calculation for the mean.

To summarize, then, the measures of central tendency are similar to signposts; they draw our attention to important facts about a distribution. Specifically, they are used to characterize an entire sample with one best number or value. By assessing these characteristics of a distribution, we can also ascertain whether error is present. The mean is the most sensitive measure of central tendency, and it is used frequently to describe a distribution. As we shall see later on, the mean is also used in tests of inference.

Measures of Dispersion

Measures of dispersion are assessments of how much variation is present in the scores of any one sample. These measures include the range, the variance, and the standard deviation. As we proceed with this discussion, we would like you to remember one important point: this is an introductory textbook on research methods in communication and cultural studies, not on statistics. Our hope is that you will familiarize yourself with

TABLE 13.3 Frequency Table Demonstrating Median and Mean

SURVEY ON DAILY INTERNET USE—PARTICIPANT C	
DAY (x-AXIS)	FREQUENCY OF HOURS SPENT ON INTERNET (y-AXIS)
1	1
2	2
3	2
4	3
5	4
6	4
7	3
8	6
9	1
10	1
11	8
$n = 11$	$n = 11$
	$\overline{x} = 3$
	$\Sigma = 34$
	$\overline{X} = 3.09$

the basic statistical techniques and formulas described here. We do not expect you to master these techniques and formulas, but to become sufficiently knowledgeable to understand published research reports. If you find the formulas challenging, ask yourself two questions: 'What does this statistic tell me about my topic?' and 'Why is this statistic significant?' The answers to these questions should help you to keep the details of our discussion in perspective.

The most basic way of assessing the amount of variation in a data set is to calculate the **range** of the set. The range is calculated by subtracting the lowest score from the highest score. For Table 13.3, the lowest score is 0 hours and the highest score is 8 hours; since 0 subtracted from 8 is 8, the size of the range is 8 hours. The range is a weak estimate of the total amount of variation present in any data sample. For instance, it does not tell you how frequently any one score appears in the set. It simply tells you the distance between the two most extreme points.

By contrast, variance is a more sensitive **measure of dispersion**. It is also more complicated to calculate because it has a two-step formula. The first step in the formula requires that we know by how much each score in a set differs from the mean. This difference is called 'deviation', and is denoted d. The deviation for any one score in a set is obtained by subtracting the mean from every score. If you want to calculate the deviation for scores on the y-axis, then the equation can be expressed as follows:

$$d = y - \bar{X}$$

By definition, the mean occupies a central position in every set, so there always will be scores higher and lower than the mean. This equation, then, will produce a set of results that are both positive and negative. This set of results is the data used in the formula for variance.

Variance, in technical terms, is 'the average squared deviation of scores about the mean' (Johnson, 1988, p. 88). In plainer language, variance offers us a way to describe and assess the value of the mean. Where the mean indicates the average score in a data set, the variance indicates the average difference between the mean and each score in the set. A

low variance indicates that most of the scores in a set are closely clustered around the mean. A high variance indicates that the scores in a set are widely dispersed throughout the range of the set. With respect to variance, 'low' and 'high' are terms that are used in relation to the range of set. For example, if the range is 100, a variance of 4 is low and suggests that your data is tightly clustered around the mean. If the range is 10, however, a variance of 4 is quite high and suggests that your data is widely dispersed around the mean.

Variance is denoted in one of two ways. If the distribution reports an entire population, then it is denoted as σ^2 (the Greek symbol referred to as *lower-case sigma*, squared); if the distribution reports a sample, then it is denoted as s^2. For the distribution of a sample, then, the equation for variance looks like this:

$$s^2 = \frac{\Sigma d^2}{n-1}$$

This equation asks us to square each deviation score (d^2), and then to sum (Σ) all the squared deviations. Once these calculations are complete, we divide the sum of the squared deviations by the number of scores in the set, minus one ($n-1$).

The data from Table 13.3 is repeated in Table 13.4 to calculate the variance of the distribution. The equation for the variance of this distribution is as follows:

$$s^2 = \frac{\Sigma d^2}{n-1} = \frac{49.7291}{10} = 4.97291$$

Again, variance indicates how the scores in a set are dispersed around the mean. However, we must remember an important fact about our formula: in calculating the variance, each deviation is squared. Squaring the deviations means that our data are no longer in their original measuring units. In our example, all of our measurements were taken in hours, but the variance is not expressed in hours. If you want to obtain the average deviation in your original measuring units, then you must convert the variance back into them. To do this, we calculate the square root of the variance. This result is a new measure called the standard deviation.

TABLE 13.4 Frequency Table Demonstrating Deviation and Variance

SURVEY ON DAILY INTERNET USE—PARTICIPANT C			
DAY (x-AXIS)	**FREQUENCY OF HOURS SPENT ON INTERNET (y-AXIS)**	**DEVIATION ($d = y - \bar{X}$)**	**DEVIATION SQUARED (d^2)**
1	1	$-2.09 = 1 - 3.09$	4.3681
2	2	$-1.09 = 2 - 3.09$	1.1881
3	2	$-1.09 = 2 - 3.09$	1.1881
4	3	$-0.09 = 3 - 3.09$	0.0081
5	4	$0.91 = 4 - 3.09$	0.8281
6	4	$0.91 = 4 - 3.09$	0.8281
7	3	$-0.09 = 3 - 3.09$	0.0081
8	6	$2.91 = 6 - 3.09$	8.4681
9	1	$-2.09 = 1 - 3.09$	4.3681
10	1	$-2.09 = 1 - 3.09$	4.3681
11	8	$4.91 = 8 - 3.09$	24.1081
$n = 11$	$n = 11$ $\Sigma = 34$ $\bar{X} = 3.09$		$\Sigma d^2 = 49.7291$

Variance: $s^2 = \dfrac{\Sigma d^2}{n-1} = \dfrac{49.7291}{11-1} = 4.9729$

Standard Deviation: $s = \sqrt{s^2} = \sqrt{4.9729} = 2.23$

The **standard deviation** is the best indicator of the total amount of variation within a given sample. It is generally used instead of the variance, but once you have calculated the variance then the standard deviation is easy to obtain. Standard deviation is denoted in one of two ways. If the data set is taken from an entire population, then it is denoted as σ (the Greek symbol referred to as *lower-case sigma*). If the data set is taken from a sample, then it is denoted as s. Hence, the formula for a sample would appear as follows:

$$s = \sqrt{s^2} = \sqrt{\frac{\Sigma d^2}{n-1}}$$

Like variance, the standard deviation indicates how the scores in a set are dispersed around the mean but the standard deviation is preferred because it is reported in the original units of measurement. Consider the example of data we have been using in Table 13.4. Our formula, with our example figures, will look like this:

$$s = \sqrt{s^2} = \sqrt{4.9729} = 2.2$$

In this example, we know that our measurements were made in hours, so the standard deviation of this distribution ($s = 2.23$) is also in hours.

Once we know the mean and the standard deviation for a distribution, we can describe it by identifying the centre of its values (the mean) and then noting how tightly the majority of values cluster around that centre (the standard deviation). With respect to our example, we know that the mean of Participant C's daily Internet use is 3.09 hours and the standard deviation is 2.23 hours. Taken together, these two figures tell us that the majority of daily observations fell within 2.23 hours on either side of 3.09 hours. This is a span of 4.46 hours. Given that the range of the distribution is only 8 hours, it suggests that the scores in this set are not tightly clustered around the mean. Rather, the scores are dispersed over much of the range.

Means and standard deviations are the most commonly reported descriptive statistics in communication and cultural research. More often than not, they are reported together. By converting the variance to the standard deviation, you can estimate score distances away from the mean in the same units with which you originally began. We will have more to say about this statistic in the section on various types of distributions. Before you learn about these, we shall introduce the basic forms used to present data visually.

Visual Representations of Variables

Descriptive statistics can be reported in many ways, but it is helpful to present them visually. There are several computer programs that calculate the measures we have just covered, and these programs can also convert data into tables, charts, and graphs. Many researchers in communication and cultural studies rely on Statistical Package for the Social Sciences (SPSS), or basic spreadsheet programs such as Microsoft Excel. Other reliable statistical programs are available as freeware or through the open-source community. Whether you are reading other scholars' work or designing your own visual aids, it is important to understand the conventions governing their use. Generally, each type of visual aid is used for certain types of data, be they nominal, ordinal, interval, or ratio.

Nominal and Ordinal Data

The visual aids most commonly used are frequency tables. **Frequency tables** summarize your data by listing the precise frequencies of all your observations in clearly labelled rows and columns. As we noted earlier in this chapter, independent variables (x) are identified in the left column and the corresponding dependent variables (y) are identified in the next column to the right. If you have two or more dependent variables for each independent variable, then each dependent variable will have its own column. If you perform additional tests or measures on each frequency or score, then these too can be identified in additional columns to the right. For example, in Table 13.4, we have presented x, y, d, and d^2 for each score. In Table 13.5, as you shall see, we have presented x, y, and a percentage share for each score. Tables should provide quick and useful references for readers who want to interpret data for themselves.

When discussing a single set of data, a **pie chart** provides a simple way to depict the relative proportions of each score. The chart does so by using percentages. The sum of all scores in a set of data represents 100% of the scores. Hence, each individual score represents some percentage of the total. If we translate this to the chart, the whole pie represents the sum of all scores (100%) and each slice of the pie represents one independent variable (x) in the set. The size of each slice is determined by the dependent variable (y); more precisely, the size of each slice is determined by the dependent variable's percentage of the sum.

Earlier in this chapter, we noted that a survey on daily Internet use could ask each participant to identify the medium that he or she uses to connect. We suggested that you could nominally code dial-up connections as '1', LAN connections as '2', and wireless connections as '3'. Once the data was collected, you would count the frequency of each response. You could also calculate the percentage share that each medium has of the total responses. Table 13.5 shows how this data might be presented in a table, while Figure 13.1 shows how the same data can be presented in a pie chart.

If you do not need to report precise numbers, or if you want to reinforce a point made in your text with a visual, then pie charts provide graphic representations of the frequencies or proportions of data. Pie charts often serve this purpose in textbooks, popular magazines and newspapers. They are used less frequently in published research, which require greater precision.

When you do want to represent precise numbers visually, then **bar charts** are more effective than pie charts. As with tables and pie charts, bar charts present data in a standard format: x-data is plotted along the horizontal axis of a chart, and y-data is plotted along the vertical axis. Each vertical bar, then, represents the frequency or score of one independent variable. When a set has a second dependent variable (z),

TABLE 13.5 Example of a Frequency Table with Nominal and Ratio Data

SURVEY ON DAILY INTERNET USE—ALL PARTICIPANTS: MEDIUM USED TO CONNECT TO THE INTERNET		
CONNECTING MEDIUM (x-AXIS)	FREQUENCY OF EACH MEDIUM (y-AXIS)	PERCENTAGE USING EACH MEDIUM (y/Σ)
1 — dial-up	9	33.3%
2 — LAN	4	16.7%
3 — wireless	12	50.0%
n = 3	Σ = 24	Σ = 100%

the z-data is plotted on an axis that suggests depth, and the chart will look three-dimensional.

Figure 13.2 provides an example of a bar chart using the same data expressed in Table 13.5 and Figure 13.1. We have used the same data in all three examples so you may note the advantages and disadvantages of each visual aid. Notice that the vertical bars in Figure 13.2 are not connected along the x-axis. The separation between the bars reminds us that these are discrete observations grouped into categories, and in any given chart such groupings may have no mathematical relationship with one another. Indeed, when the x-axis reports nominal data then the order of the units is completely arbitrary. This happens, for example, when we gather demographic data and the x-axis reports categories based on gender or ethnicity (i.e. it makes no difference whether you report data from males first or females first). In the case of Figure 13.2,

the x-axis identifies the medium used to connect to the Internet, and these three media could have been listed in any order without affecting the data. The only numbers with ratio values are on the y-axis, which reports the number of participants who used each medium.

Bar charts can also be used to show how two or more sets of observations compare. In Figure 13.3, for example, we can show data collected from male and female participants in our Internet study side by side. In other studies, we could present data collected from different cities side by side, or data collected from any two media side by side, and so on.

As we noted at the start of this section, most scholars in communication and cultural studies who conduct statistical analyses use frequency tables in their published research. A glance through any recent issue of the *Canadian Journal of Communication*, *Revue Communication*, or *Topia: Canadian Journal of Cultural*

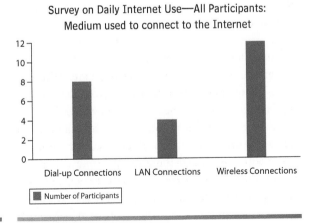

Survey on Daily Internet Use—All Participants: Medium used to connect to the Internet

FIGURE 13.1 Example of a Pie Chart

Survey on Daily Internet Use—All Participants: Medium used to connect to the Internet

FIGURE 13.2 Example of a Bar Chart

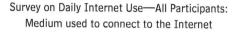

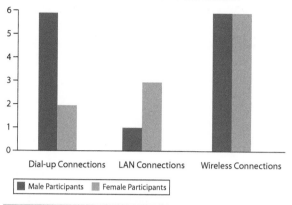

FIGURE 13.3   Example of a Bar Chart with Sub-groupings

Studies will bear this out. The number of scholars using statistical analysis is growing however, and software programs make it easy to produce detailed graphs. As such, you will encounter bar graphs in scholarly publications, but you are still not likely to encounter pie charts in any research report that values precision.

Interval and Ratio Data

When data are measured with interval and ratio scales, their visual representations are more complex than those using nominal and ordinal scales. That said, the basic elements of a visual aid using interval and ratio scales remain the same: independent variables are distributed along the x-axis and dependent variables are distributed along the y-axis. The most precise way to represent this data is with a frequency table, but data can also be represented with histograms and polygons.

There is one key difference that separates the representation of nominal and ordinal data and the representation of interval and ratio data. As we noted in the last section, the first two types of data have no mathematical qualities, and so we gain nothing by subjecting them to statistical analysis. By contrast, interval and ratio data are mathematically meaningful, and it is useful to subject them to statistical analysis. This means that the independent variables marked on the x-axis do not identify categories with arbitrarily assigned names. Rather, the x-axis reports numbers

that lie on a continuum with equal and precise intervals (for example, 1, 2, 3, or 50, 100, 150, or any other sequence of intervals). For this reason, when the x-axis reports interval and ratio scores, we call the x-axis a **frequency distribution**.

Continuous data in a frequency distribution can be represented by a **histogram**. A histogram is essentially a bar chart for data measured with interval or ratio scales. That said, it has one important difference: the bars are connected along the x-axis. This reflects the fact that there is a mathematical relationship between the intervals along the x-axis. Because intervals are equidistant, the numbers report precise values.

Let's return to our example survey on daily Internet use. Imagine that one question in the survey asks participants to state the average daily number of spam emails they receive within the duration of the study. This question will produce a distribution in which the x-data (number of times per day that a participant receives spam) and y-data (number of participants reporting any one number) are both measured in ratio scales. Once the survey is complete, we count the number of times each response occurs, and construct our visuals aids. Table 13.6 and Figure 13.4 present the same example data so that you may compare the relative advantages of frequency tables and histograms.

Occasionally, researchers use frequency polygons to illustrate interval and ratio-level data. Instead of using vertical bars, a **frequency polygon** is formed by connecting the graph coordinates for each matched pair in a data set. For example, if we take the data from Table 13.6, the first matched pair in the data set is (0, 1). This can be plotted as a point on the graph by locating its place on both the x- and y-axes. We can do this for each matched pair. Once all nine matched pairs are plotted to the graph, we can draw a single line connecting them along the frequency distribution—that is, from left to right along the x-axis. The line is rarely straight, and for this reason we call the shape of this line a polygon. A frequency polygon using the example data from Table 13.6 appears in Figure 13.5. Again, you can compare the relative advantages of frequency polygons with tables and histograms.

There are other ways to present interval and ratio data. The relationships between these variables can be described as linear or curvilinear, terms that refer to

TABLE 13.6 Example of a Frequency Table with Ratio Data

SURVEY ON DAILY INTERNET USE—ALL PARTICIPANTS: AVERAGE DAILY NUMBER OF SPAM EMAILS	
AVERAGE DAILY NUMBER RECEIVED (*x*-AXIS)	NUMBER OF PARTICIPANTS REPORTING (*y*-AXIS)
0	1
1	2
2	4
3	5
4	6
5	5
6	4
7	2
8	1
n = 9	Σ = 24

complex patterns of change that are revealed in the shape of a polygon. To explore these relationships you must examine two or more sets of data at once, and that is the goal of the next chapter. In this chapter, we only discuss statistical terms and visual aids that apply to a single data set.

Again, most scholars in communication and cultural studies who conduct statistical analyses use frequency tables in their published research. Histograms

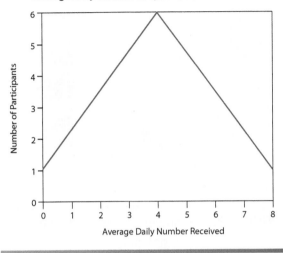

Survey on Daily Internet Use—All Participants: Average daily number of spam emails received

FIGURE 13.5 Example of a Frequency Polygon

and frequency polygons are not generally published. Rather, they are more commonly used in preliminary data analysis to estimate the likelihood of error, a process you will explore in a later chapter section.

Measures of Shape

Once you are comfortable with descriptive statistics and graphs, you can check the shape of a graph to see if error is present in interval or ratio data. Recall from chapter 6, on warrants, that there are two types of error that can enter the measurements of a variable: bias and noise. **Bias** occurs whenever the internal validity of the research design is threatened in some way. **Noise** occurs whenever reliability is threatened by random errors in the data. A frequency distribution that has relatively little error is said to be a normal distribution and its shape is called a **normal curve**. This normal curve is bell-shaped. Any statistical software that can produce graphs can plot a predicted normal curve for your data. In Figure 13.6, the histogram from Figure 13.4 has been redrawn with a normal curve superimposed on it. If your data appear to fit this normal curve, then you may feel confident that your distribution is free of bias or noise.

By contrast, if your data do not appear to fit the normal curve, then you should check your distribution for bias or noise. There are several different shapes

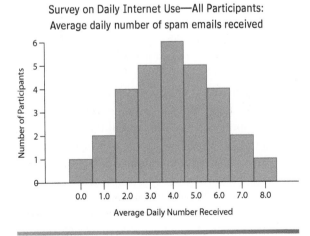

Survey on Daily Internet Use—All Participants: Average daily number of spam emails received

FIGURE 13.4 Example of a Histogram

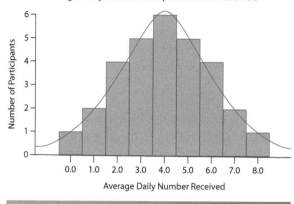

FIGURE 13.6   Example of a Histogram with Normal Curve

that indicate the presence of error, but the most commonly referenced shape is 'skew'. **Skew** occurs when the majority of scores in a frequency distribution are marked to the left or right of the distribution's centre, and skew is apparent when you examine the two ends of the line which forms the curve. When the majority of scores appear to the left, the 'tail' of the line trails off towards the highest numbers on the *x*-axis. Such a distribution is said to be positively skewed (as shown in Figure 13.7). When the majority of scores appear to the right, the tail of the line trails off towards the lowest numbers on the *x*-axis. Such a distribution is said to be negatively skewed (as shown in Figure 13.8). Whether

a skew is positive or negative, it indicates bias in which some measurement resulted in a constant error.

Many of the statistical software packages that are currently available report all three types of measures: central tendency, dispersion, and shape. The visual aids we have described here offer further corroboration that your distribution is normal or that it contains error. The general purpose of calculating descriptive statistics is corroboration numerically and visually that you have obtained normal distributions when collecting your data samples. The assumption of normalcy in the way the data is distributed underlies the logic of hypothesis testing, the main process you will learn about in the second section of this chapter.

Inferential Statistics

Earlier in this chapter, we noted that one function of statistics is to describe our data. A second function of statistics is to infer the characteristics of an entire population from the characteristics of a sample. Before we discuss this process, you must be able to recognize three types of data distributions: sample, population, and sampling.

Three Types of Distributions

Sample Distributions

So far in our discussion of statistics, whenever we have referred to 'distributions' we have talked about sample

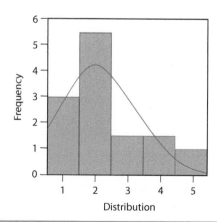

FIGURE 13.7   Example of a Histogram with Positively Skewed Data

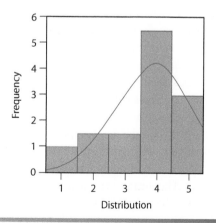

FIGURE 13.8   Example of a Histogram with Negatively Skewed Data

distributions. As we have noted elsewhere, a sample is a subset or group of units taken from an entire population. Put differently, a sample is the actual data set the researcher obtains and examines when conducting a study. A **sample distribution**, then, is the characteristics of a single set of data gathered through sampling and expressed in numbers. The measures of central tendency, dispersion, and shape that we discussed in the last few sections constitute a sample's descriptive statistics.

Population Distributions

In chapters 5 and 6, on data and warrants, you learned about the importance of obtaining a **representative sample**. If you recall, this term means that the characteristics of the sample provide valid and reliable estimates of the characteristics of the population. The term **population distribution** refers to the entire set of data from which a sample is drawn.

Whenever you select a sample for studying some phenomenon, two different conceptions of a population come into play: target populations and survey populations. A **target population** is 'an idealized group representing the totality of target elements that interest a researcher' (Smith, 1988, p. 77), whereas a **sample frame** is the set of individual or elements that can actually be selected for the study. Practically speaking, if you wanted to test gender differences in some aspect of communication or culture, it would be impossible to recruit males and females from the entire target population of men and women. This is an extreme example, but even with a smaller target population you can rarely sample all of its members. As a result, you must make inferences about their characteristics based on the data you obtain through a sample.

When samples are representative, their known characteristics should closely approximate the same known characteristics of the population. For example, if you want a sample of local popular opinion on an issue, you will want the demographics of your survey participants to closely approximate the demographics of your city. These sample characteristics are called **parameters**. The mean of the sample (denoted by $\bar{X}$), should reflect the mean of the population (denoted by μ, the Greek symbol referred to as *lower-case mu*). The variance and standard deviation of the sample, s^2 and s, should be good estimates of the population's variance and standard deviation, σ^2 and σ. Using distinct symbols for sample characteristics and population characteristics helps clarify when and how sample statistics are used as estimates of population parameters. The process of estimation is based on the third type of distribution, the sampling distribution.

Sampling Distributions

A **sampling distribution** is a hypothetical distribution of possible sample values. Whereas a sample distribution reports the actual values in a single sample drawn from a population, a sampling distribution reports the proportions or means for all possible samples drawn from the same population. A sampling distribution is useful because it reports the probable tendencies of a population, and knowing these tendencies allows us to make inferences about the parameters of the population. Most importantly, sampling distributions allow us to estimate how much our sample statistics may resemble the population parameters (Johnson, 1988, p. 284). This estimation of deviance is called 'sampling error' and it is rooted in probability theory.

Estimation and Inference

Probability theory and the mathematical formulas for sampling distributions are complex and we do not need to cover them in this text. As we noted earlier in this chapter, our goal here is to explain their significance for communication and cultural studies so that you will understand them when they are presented in published research.

Smith (1988) identified four assumptions governing sample distributions that are used as a basis for inferential statistics:

(1) All sample data are to be selected randomly, insofar as possible, from some well-defined population; (2) the characteristics of each random sample drawn from a population are related to the true population parameters; (3) multiple random samples drawn from the same population yield statistics that cluster around the population parameters in predictable ways; and (4) we can calculate the sampling error associated with a sample

statistic, estimating how far a population parameter is likely to deviate from a given sample statistic. (p. 106)

As Johnson (1988) noted, 'The purpose of statistical inference is to use sample results to estimate population characteristics and attach probabilities to those estimates' (p. 285). To use a sampling distribution, we must know its mean and its sampling error. **Sampling error** is calculated by taking the standard deviation of your sample statistic (s) and dividing it by the square root of the sample size minus 1 ($n–1$). Because the sampling error is derived from the standard deviation, sampling error is also referred to as 'standard error'.

The Logic of Hypothesis Testing

In hypothesis testing, we begin with a prediction and 'then generate sample data to confirm or disconfirm our a priori assumptions' (Smith, 1988, p. 111). The reasoning process that informs hypothesis testing includes two important concepts: the central limits theorem and the normal curve.

First, **central limits theorem** states that larger samples have a greater chance than smaller samples of approximating the true population distribution (Kerlinger, 1973). It also states that random selection of samples is the chief way of obtaining true statistical estimates of population parameters. Thus, when you cannot obtain either large or random samples, it is especially important to determine whether the sample under investigation is distributed normally before you begin hypothesis testing.

This leads us to our second concept, the normal curve. As we noted in the previous section, the normal curve is a distribution of scores that is shaped like a bell when plotted to a histogram. Normal distributions indicate that there is little error in the data. This means that normally distributed data will yield statistics that are good estimates of the population parameters. Most scholars assume that variables measured with interval and ratio scales have normal distributions. For example, verbal aggressiveness is a variable that you can assume is distributed normally. Most individuals fall in the midsection of a bell-shaped curve for this measure, whereas very few individuals represent the extremes. If a sample group of participants generated

data that produced a differently shaped curve, then that would indicate that there is something wrong with the data or that there is something unique about that group of participants.

Normal curves are so regular that the size of the area under each curve is predictable. The size of this area is measured by using seven intervals along the x-axis, numbering from –3 to 3 (see Figure 13.9). Statisticians refer to these intervals as **confidence intervals**. Each interval is equal to one standard deviation of the sample. When used as a measure in this way, standard deviation allows you to estimate the proportion of scores expected within each interval. According to the **empirical rule** of normal distributions, 68.26% of a sample's scores will fall between plus or minus 1 standard deviation of the sample's mean (this measure can be denoted as ±1s). At the next interval, 95.44% of a sample's scores fall within ±2s, and 99.72% fall between ±3s (Johnson, 1988, pp. 286–290). In practice, if you have an estimated mean for a population, then you can gauge the probability that any one score will be part of the sampling distribution. Again, most statistical software can calculate this figure for you.

Once you understand the normal curve and central limits, you can address the most important characteristic of a sampling distribution: standard error (Johnson, 1988, p. 276). Once again, we will not discuss the formula for this statistic in detail because most software will calculate it for you. You should, however understand what this statistic measures and how it is interpreted.

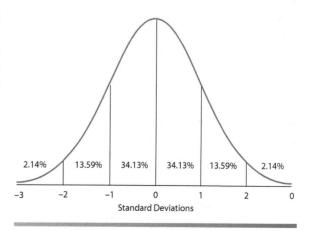

FIGURE 13.9   Areas under the Normal Curve

Standard error is the standard deviation of a sampling distribution. It is denoted $\sigma_{\bar{X}}$, where $\bar{X}$ identifies the distribution being estimated, the sample means. Put in simpler terms, the standard error estimates how far your sample mean is likely to deviate from the true population mean. If the standard error is small, your sample means will be close to the population mean; if the standard error is large, your sample means will be dispersed widely around the population mean. Clearly, this statistic provides a powerful insight for those scholars who want to apply their findings beyond their samples.

Let's consider a research example. Imagine that you conduct a survey and you ask a sample group of participants to score their answers on a 7-point Likert scale. For one of the survey questions, your participants' answers produce a distribution with a mean score of 3.0 and a standard error of 0.5. If the distribution follows a normal curve, then you can estimate that 95.44% of the sample means will fall within $\pm 2s$ of the mean score. We call the percentage of means expected to fall within a specific confidence interval the **confidence level** (Smith, 1988, pp. 106–109). In our example, then, we might claim that we are confident that 95.44% of our sample accurately reflects the entire population.

Most scholars in communication and cultural studies try to achieve confidence levels of 95%. This means that we usually accept a standard error estimate that is roughly $\pm 2s$ away from the sample mean. However we rarely state that we have 95% confidence in our results. Rather, most researchers will claim that the probability of error in their results is 5%. When we present this information, 'probability level' is usually denoted as p and the statistic is denoted as $p < x$, where x represents the specific value calculated for the distribution. In our example, where the confidence level is 95.44%, $p < .05$. When you use statistical software, the reported p level will be expressed as low as it can be. Sometimes, the p level is $< .0001$, which means that your probability of error is less than one/ten-thousandth.

When your sampling error is minimal, your inferences are more accurate. To reduce your sampling error, you must be careful in every step of the research process to ensure that your research instruments are well designed. You must also use what you know about sample statistics to gauge the characteristics of the population you want to study.

Testing Hypotheses

To test a hypothesis, you must complete four steps: (1) formulate a hypothesis; (2) frame your decisions by considering the likelihood of error; (3) calculate the test statistic; and (4) decide whether your hypothesis can be accepted or rejected.

Formulating Hypotheses

There are two basic types of hypotheses in formulating predictions about relationships between variables: the research hypothesis and the null hypothesis.

The research **hypothesis** is the prediction you are trying to test, often predicting 'two or more populations are different in one or more respects' (Smith, 1988, p. 111). For example, Rosenfeld, Richman, and May (2004) hypothesized that office employees and employees in the field would need and receive different amounts and types of information. One of their research questions examined the relationship between the type of employee and the amount of information they received about organizational performance. What they found was that employees in the office ($\bar{X}_1$) received more information than their counterparts in the field ($\bar{X}_2$). This research hypothesis can be expressed as $H_1 : X_1 > X_2$. This hypothesis is **directional** in that one mean is projected to be greater (or less) than the other mean.

Nondirectional hypotheses are those that predict an inequality or difference but do not specify how that difference will occur: $H_1 : \bar{X}_1 \neq \bar{X}_2$. In our study example, a **nondirectional hypothesis** would be expressed by stating that the information received about organizational performance would be significantly different for office employees than for field employees, but the projected difference would not indicate which mean would be greater than the other. We have more to say about testing directional research hypotheses in the next chapter.

The **null hypothesis**, usually expressed as H_0, is 'the antithesis of the research hypothesis', predicting no effects of one variable on another or no relationship between the variables (Smith, 1988, p. 112).

You should assume the null hypothesis is true until enough evidence is accumulated to reject it. As Smith noted, the analogy is like criminal court proceedings where the accused is presumed innocent and the Crown Attorney or Crown Prosecutor must present sufficient evidence to prove otherwise. This concept is sometimes referred to as the **falsification principle** (Popper, 1962).

Framing Decisions Based on the Likelihood of Error

The second step of hypothesis testing is to estimate the probability of error associated with accepting or rejecting the null hypothesis. In the last section, we discussed the sampling error associated with estimation. If you use sampling distributions to test the relationship between the variables, you can project a confidence level with its corresponding interval that will be associated with accepting or rejecting the null hypothesis. Depending on the actual statistics you obtain for your sample data, you can determine the probabilities that certain statistics like the mean are drawn from the same population or a different population. Again, as we explained in the previous section, researchers agree that the probability of error in supporting the research hypothesis should be less than 5%. Put another way, we should be 95% confident that we can reject the null hypothesis.

Calculating the Test Statistic

The third step of hypothesis testing requires that you calculate the actual necessary statistics. There are two basic types of relationships between variables: tests of difference and tests of relationship. The first type of relationship is usually framed as a causal prediction about the effects of an independent variable on a dependent variable, and should address significant differences between the two variables. The second type of relationship is usually framed as a question exploring the degree of association between two or more variables. We explain these statistical tests in detail in the next chapter. Each test yields an obtained value that is associated with the p level of error needed to reject the null hypothesis (i.e. $p < .05$).

Deciding to Accept or Reject the Null Hypothesis

The fourth and final step in the hypothesis-testing process is to make a decision to accept or reject the null hypothesis. Statistical tests of hypotheses usually depend on the sample data we collect during research. In most cases, however, these sample data are used to support or to deny a general claim about the entire population. If your goal is to make a general claim about the entire population, then there are three possible outcomes of your decision, and these outcomes are illustrated in the matrix in Table 13.7. The best outcome, clearly, is to accept the research hypothesis, or reject the null hypothesis, when the sample statistics share significant tendencies with the population parameters. If the sample statistics and population parameters do not share significant tendencies, then your decision will be incorrect.

Incorrect decisions about the null hypothesis result in two types of errors: Type I and Type II errors. A **Type I error** occurs when we decide to reject the null hypothesis when we should not. If you have established a probability level of significance at $p < .05$, the chance of making an error is less than 5%. However, when the error does occur, it is a Type I error.

A **Type II error**, occurs when we decide to accept the null hypothesis when we should not. Failure to reject the null hypothesis results in making an error

TABLE 13.7 Decision Making Matrix for Type I and Type II Errors

SAMPLE STATISTICS	POPULATION PARAMETERS	OUTCOME
No significance	No significance	Correct decision
Significance	No significance	Type I error
Significance	Significance	Correct decision
No significance	Significance	Type II error

in this case. When variable instruments have strong measurement validity and reliability, the chance of committing a Type II error decreases. One good way to maximize the validity and reliability of your measurements is to use larger samples. From the central limits theorem, we know that by increasing the sample size, the closer the sample statistics approximate the true population parameters. By doing so, you decrease the chances that either type of error will occur. Larger samples make statistics more stable generally and the decisions we make about them more accurate (Smith, 1988, p. 117).

The four steps of hypothesis testing appear throughout the next chapter as the 'steps to determine the significance' of the test statistics you will obtain. These steps complete the inferential process of estimation in helping you determine whether your data can support your claims, statistically. You will learn how to complete each of these steps for two types of tests in the next chapter: tests of difference and tests of relationship.

Some Ethical Issues

Before we close, we should note that you have ethical obligations when using quantitative data. You already know that precision is valued in discovery paradigm research. When you are dealing with quantitative data, precision and accuracy go hand in hand with personal integrity and fair dealing with your participants and audience. This principle has a number of practical consequences. With respect to your participants, you should always respect individual privacy concerns. This may mean that you aggregate quantitative data collected from many participants in order to mask recognizable data from any one participant. For example, you might report only the group mean scores from your participants rather than their raw data. With respect to your audience, you should carefully proofread all of the data for your statistical analysis, and never falsify any data to support your predictions (i.e. you should never 'tweak the numbers'). Furthermore, you must disclose the nature and extent of missing or unusable data in your sample. Knowledgeable readers can tell whether or not problems threaten the accuracy of your conclusions.

Summary

This chapter has presented the basic elements of statistical analysis. You will encounter these concepts and tests in quantitative survey research and content analysis, but they can appear in any type of research report that relies upon numerical data. We first introduced

TABLE 13.8 Major Aspects of Survey Research

FUNCTION	TYPE OF STATISTIC	VISUAL AIDS FOR CATEGORICAL VARIABLES	VISUAL AIDS FOR CONTINUOUS VARIABLES
Description	Raw measures	Frequency tables	Frequency tables
	Central tendency (mean, mode, median)	Frequency tables, pie, and bar charts	Frequency tables, histograms, and frequency polygons
	Dispersion (range, variance, standard deviation)	Pie and bar charts	Histograms and frequency polygons
	Shape (normal, skew)	Pie and bar charts	Histograms and frequency polygons
Inference	Hypothesis testing	Frequency tables, pie, and bar charts	Frequency tables, histograms, and frequency polygons
	Estimating error (i.e. when inferring population parameters)	Frequency tables, pie, and bar charts	Frequency tables, histograms, and frequency polygons

you to the concepts that allow us to describe a single set of data, using both numbers and visual aids. We then discussed tests that will allow you to assess the validity and reliability of your descriptions. Table 13.8 provides an overview of the main aspects of descriptive statistics. In the next chapter, we will explore more powerful concepts and tests that allow us to compare two or more data sets.

Key Terms

Bar chart	Inferential statistics	Sample
Bias	Mean	Sample distribution
Central limits theorem	Measures of central tendency	Sample frame
Confidence interval	Measures of dispersion	Sampling distribution
Confidence level	Measures of shape	Sampling error
Dependent variable	Median	Skew
Descriptive statistics	Mode	Standard deviation
Directional hypothesis	Noise	Standard error
Distribution	Nondirectional hypothesis	Statistical analysis
Empirical rule	Normal curve	Statistics
Falsification principle	Null hypothesis	Target population
Frequency distribution	Parameters	Type I error
Frequency polygon	Pie chart	Type II error
Frequency table	Population	Variance
Histogram	Population distribution	x-axis
Hypothesis	Range	y-axis
Independent variable	Representative sample	

Discussion Questions

1. In what ways are the visual descriptions of nominal and ordinal data different than the visual descriptions of interval and ratio data?
2. Why is the mean considered the most sensitive measure of central tendency in a sample distribution?
3. Why is the range considered the weakest measure of dispersion? Why is the standard deviation used more frequently as a measure of dispersion than the variance?
4. How is the sample distribution different from a population distribution and a sampling distribution? Try to come up with examples for each.
5. What is inferred when we do 'statistical inference'?
6. How is a Type I error different than a Type II error? What tells you what chance you have of committing a Type I error? What is one way you can minimize both types of error?

Try It!

1. This exercise asks you to read and understand statistical information presented in a published research article. It can be completed by an individual, but it may be more interesting to work in a group with two or more other members. Depending on the size of your tutorial group, it may also be adapted as a tutorial exercise.

   Over the last 40 years, media conglomeration has become a political issue in democratic countries. As citizens, we depend on timely and reliable news to make important decisions. As the ownership of media outlets becomes concentrated in the hands of fewer and fewer large corporations, however, some commentators warn that our ability to trust news media is diminishing. David Demers conducted research to test this argument using newspapers as his case study. He established two measures, one to assess a newspaper's integration into a conglomerate, and a second to assess a newspaper's editorial quality. Both of these measures rely on concepts that Demers has operationalized as variables by seeking specific indicators about each newspaper, such as the number of employees it retains or the number editorials it publishes on local issues.

   Process

   Read Demers's article (1996), 'Corporate Newspaper Structure, Editorial Page Vigor, and Social Change', in *Journalism & Mass Communication Quarterly*, 73, pp. 857–877. Then, try to answer the following questions:

   1. What are Demers's hypotheses?
   2. How did Demers decide which variables to use in his study?
   3. (a) What variables are used to measure each newspaper's corporate structure?
      (b) How did Demers collect data for the measure of corporate structure?
   4. (a) What variables are used to measure each newspaper's editorial quality?
      (b) How did he collect data for the measure of editorial quality?
   5. Demers presents his data with a visual aid on pp. 866–867.
      (a) What kind of visual aid does he use?
      (b) What statistics does he provide for each variable?
      (c) Using the numbers provided, explain any two variables and their significance within Demers's research. Can you identify what the numbers represent, or what their units of measurement are?
      (d) Is Demers's data easy to understand? Why or why not?
   6. What was the response rate for his survey? Is this a reliable sample?
   7. The second element of Demers's analysis relies on a statistical technique we will examine in the next chapter. Setting this aside, what do you make of his discussion?
      (a) Does he follow the logic of hypothesis testing?
      (b) Has he followed the four steps we have described?
      (c) Does he avoid Type I and Type II errors?
      (d) Ultimately, what do you make of the article?
      (e) Do his measures supply compelling data and evidence?
      (f) Could he have conducted this research without statistical analysis?

2. This is exercise asks you to generate your own statistical information using a set of data provided below. It can be completed by an individual, but it may be more interesting to work in a group with two or more other members. Depending on the size of your tutorial group, it may also be adapted as a tutorial exercise.

   Study Description: A researcher has selected two groups of dating couples to test the effects of training on the couples' interpersonal skills. One of the groups attended workshops on conflict resolution. During these workshops, the researcher stressed the importance of increasing communication with one's partner. The other group did not attend the workshops. In fact, they were not given any instruction at all with respect to interpersonal skills. Following the workshops, the researcher wanted to know how many times individuals in both groups contacted their partners over a five-day period. This information should answer the research question, posed as follows:

RQ: Does interpersonal skills training affect the interpersonal skills of dating couples?

The independent variable is the skills training workshop and it has two categories (i.e. exposure to training / no exposure to training). The dependent variable is the number of contacts made in a five-day period. The data for the two groups are as follows:

GROUP #1: CONTROL GROUP (NO TRAINING)			
0	3	5	7
2	3	4	6
1	3	4	6
1	2	2	4
3	4	5	5

GROUP #2: CONTROL GROUP (TRAINING)			
3	7	6	7
8	6	7	7
3	6	7	7
4	6	5	8
6	7	7	3

Using the sample distributions, calculate the descriptive statistics that will answer the research question. It may be helpful to proceed in this order:

1. How many observations are in each group?
2. What is the mode, median, and mean frequency of each group?
3. What is the range, variance, and standard variation of each group?
4. Create histograms for each group's data. Be sure to label each graph and axis.
5. What do the statistics and visual aids tell you about the two groups?

Use the measures of central tendency and dispersion to contrast the differences between the two groups, and use the visual aids to assess the presence or lack of error. Remember: on their own, visual aids and statistics that describe shape cannot provide evidence to support or to reject the research hypothesis.

Answers

For both groups, $n = 20$.

For the control group, the measures of central tendency are as follows: mos = 3 and 4, $\bar{x} = 3.5$, and $\bar{X} = 3.5$. The measures of dispersion are as follows: range = 7, $s = 1.850$, $s^2 = 3.421$.

For the treatment group, the measures of central tendency are as follows: mo = 7.0, $\bar{x} = 6.5$, and $\bar{X} = 6.0$. The measures of dispersion are as follows: range = 5, $s = 1.589$, and $s^2 = 2.526$.

For the control group, the measures of central tendency are all aligned and the graph shows that the distribution has a fairly normal distribution.

For the treatment group, the measures of central tendency are not aligned and the graph shows that the distribution is negatively skewed. Both of these observations indicate the presence of bias or constant error.

Ultimately, the answer to the research question depends on your interpretation of these results.

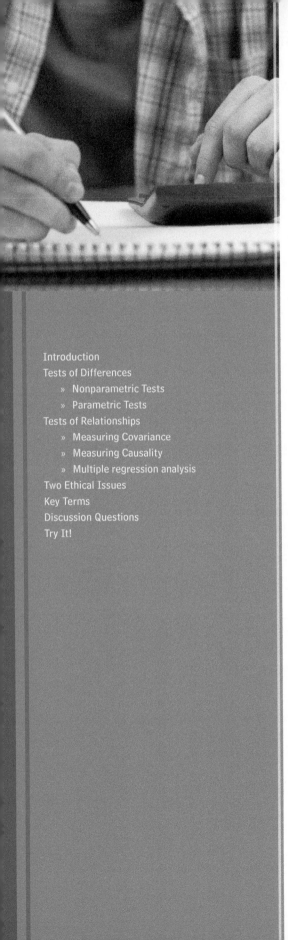

14 Inferential Statistics

Introduction

In this chapter, we will review the four basic steps of testing hypotheses with statistical measures. You will learn how to interpret tests for analyzing group differences, including chi-square, *t*-test, and analysis of variance. You will learn how to interpret the basic statistical test for associative relationships, the correlation. You will also learn to interpret a more complex causal test of linear relationships for multiple variables, called regression. Finally, we will discuss the difference between bivariate and multivariate analyses. Once you have completed this chapter, you will be able to appreciate the purposes of these tests when you read about them in research reports.

In the last chapter, you explored how statistics are used to describe samples and infer population characteristics. To make an inference, you must gather insights from data that you have (i.e. a set of sample statistics) and presume that it applies to data that you don't have (i.e. the parameters of the entire population). By contrast, to test a hypothesis you must predict something about data that you don't have and then test that prediction using data that you acquire.

At the end of the last chapter on descriptive statistics, you learned about the four steps necessary for testing research hypotheses: (1) formulating hypotheses; (2) framing decisions based on the likelihood of error; (3) calculating the test statistic; and (4) deciding whether the null hypothesis can be accepted or rejected. In step 1, a discovery researcher begins by advancing a predictive claim that can be tested statistically. There are generally two types of predictions that can be made: claims of difference and claims of relationship. In this chapter, you will explore both of these types of claims and the statistical analyses used to test them.

Tests of Differences

When we make claims about differences, we generally want to know if two groups of individuals or texts are similar or different. In chapter 4, on claims, we noted that discovery research often tries to identify and categorize things. For example, you may wish to establish that women's magazines discuss environmental issues more than men's magazines. If this was your claim, then you would need a way to measure this difference. Perhaps you would look at a year's worth of each group of magazines, and perhaps you would use content analysis to count the number of pages per issue that cover environmental issues. Once your data were collected, you could then calculate the mean number of pages per issue that cover environmental issues for each group of magazines. A simple comparison of the two group means should indicate whether or not the two groups of magazines cover environmental issues differently. We call this comparison a 'ratio'.

Most statistical tests of difference are variations on the same basic ratio. The ratio compares two numbers. The first number should express the mean differences calculated for your sample or group, using data you have discovered through your research—just as we've noted with our magazine example. The second number should express the estimated mean differences that are due to chance variation, using data from a sampling distribution (which we discussed in the last chapter). Hence, the ratio can be expressed as follows:

$$\frac{\text{Observed group mean differences}}{\text{Chance mean differences}}$$

The calculation of this ratio enables you to estimate the probability that the samples you are comparing are drawn from the same population or different populations.

In the last chapter, we explained that sampling distributions allow you to estimate the probability that any sample statistic came from a given population. Sampling distributions also permit you to compare two statistics, like sample means, to decide whether they are likely to have been drawn from the same or different populations. Thus, the greater the ratio, the greater the likelihood that the means are significantly different. To put this another way, a significant difference between sample means establishes the probability that the sample means are not drawn from the same population. This all sounds pretty abstract, but we will provide examples for each test statistic to show you how the process works.

When deciding how to analyze your data statistically, the first step is to understand the way the data was originally measured. If you understand your variables and their measurement scales, then you will know that different types of data require different statistical tests. Data collected using nominal and ordinal scales are most often analyzed using 'nonparametric tests', while data collected using interval and ratio scales are most often analyzed using 'parametric tests'. In the next two sections, you will learn some of the basic differences between nonparametric and parametric tests.

Nonparametric Tests

Nature of Data and Assumptions

In the last chapter, you learned about the normal curve. We assume that normal distributions are regular and reflect real distributions of interval and ratio data. That is because these measurement scales produce 'continuous variables' (Ferguson, 1981). When we collect interval or ratio data that does not follow the normal curve, then we must check our research for errors or we must conclude that our sample is somehow special.

By contrast, nominal and ordinal data provide 'categorical variables'. You may recall our explanation of this difference in chapter 5, on data. Both survey research and content analysis use categorical variables. Surveys often require participants to answer questions by using fixed categories, such as yes/no or male/female. Similarly, content analysis often organizes texts according to the types of messages conveyed or the types of imagery represented. If we encode these survey responses and textual categories with numbers, we understand that the numbers we assign to each category are arbitrary. Additionally, when data are categorical, they are not distributed in the same way as continuous variables. Hence, we cannot use the normal curve to test this data. Instead, we use nonparametric tests.

Nonparametric tests are useful statistical tools when you have limited knowledge of the parent population for your sample or group. If all of the variables you are testing are categorical, then there are several tests of difference you can use. A common and versatile one is the chi-square, a nonparametric test.

Single-Sample Chi-Square

The **chi-square** test can be used with a single sample or multiple samples. Because it is a nonparametric test, the chi-square follows the basic ratio we described earlier. It expresses a ratio of the observed frequencies within variable categories over expected frequencies within variable categories. That means that we test the actual frequencies we have for each category and compare them to frequencies expected by chance alone to see if there are significant differences between the two. The chi-square score is commonly denoted as x^2, and the formula for chi-square is expressed in the following equation:

$$x^2 = \Sigma \left[\frac{(O - E)^2}{E} \right]$$

where O stands for the observed frequencies of the variable, and E stands for the expected frequencies by chance.

Single-sample chi-square analyses are relatively easy to calculate. For example, let's say that we have a sample of 30 participants, and we want to know which conflict-resolution strategies they will choose in dealing with a given conflict scenario. We hypothesize (H_1) that one conflict-resolution strategy will be more frequently adopted than others. Sillars (1980) developed a typology of conflict-resolution strategies which is commonly used in communication and cultural research. It has three mutually exclusive categories: a confrontational strategy, an avoidant strategy, and a negotiating strategy. Because the three types of strategies are mutually exclusive, each participant's response can be placed in one, and only one, category.

Before we survey our participants, we can calculate the expected frequencies of their responses. The expected frequencies are those due to chance variation among the three types of strategies. The null hypothesis (H_0) for this example is that no one strategy will be used more than the others, so that all three strategy choices will occur with the same frequency. The expected frequencies (E) for each choice, then, are the total number of participants (N) divided by the number of categories (k):

$$E = \frac{N}{k} = \frac{30}{3} = 10$$

Hence, in a group of 30 participants, the laws of chance predict that each strategy will be selected 10 times out of 30.

Now, let's imagine that we have surveyed our sample. The data in Table 14.1 reports that 4 participants chose avoidant strategies, 19 participants chose confrontational strategies, and 7 participants chose negotiating strategies. Just by looking at these values, you can tell that these observed frequencies are different than the expected frequencies. Both the observed and expected frequencies appear in Table 14.1, and as does our chi-square calculation. Using the example data, the chi-square is 12.60.

The chi-square test tells us whether or not the expected frequencies and observed frequencies are significantly different. We always anticipate some difference between the expected and observed frequencies. The value of the chi-square indicates the actual degree of difference. If the two sets of frequencies are not significantly different, this suggests that the observed frequencies could have been generated by chance and thus contain no meaningful information. If the two sets of frequencies are significantly different, however, this suggests that you have discovered a meaningful pattern in your observations. What's more, as the value of the chi-square increases, your findings gain more credence. This is because a high chi-square suggests that the differences between the two sets of frequencies are not due to chance.

To assess the value of your chi-square, it must be measured against the 'critical value', or the expected value of the chi-square distribution. The chi-square value you calculate based on your observations must exceed its critical value as the test of significance. To find the appropriate critical value, there are three steps. First, you must determine the **degrees of freedom** (*df*) in your observations, or the number of frequency categories that are free to vary. In a single-sample chi-square, the number of degrees of freedom is equal to the number of variable categories minus one. The formula is expressed as follows: $df = (k - 1)$. In our example we had three variable categories, so the $df = 3 - 1 = 2$.

Second, we must estimate the probability of error in comparing the critical and obtained values. In the last chapter, we noted that researchers accept a probability of error (p) no greater than 5%, which is usually expressed as $p < .05$ (remember, this estimate is only for a Type I error). When this estimation is applied

TABLE 14.1 Calculation of a Single-Sample Chi-Square

	TYPES OF CONFLICT STRATEGIES		
	AVOIDANT	**CONFRONTATIONAL**	**NEGOTIATING**
Observed frequencies (O)	4	19	7
Expected frequencies (E)	10	10	10
SINGLE-SAMPLE CHI-SQUARE CALCULATION			

$$X^2 = \sum \left[\frac{(O - E)^2}{E} \right] = \frac{(4 - 10)^2}{10} + \frac{(19 - 10)^2}{10} + \frac{(7 - 10)^2}{10}$$

$$X^2 = \frac{(-6)^2}{10} + \frac{(9)^2}{10} = \frac{(-3)^2}{10}$$

$$X^2 = 3.6 + 8.1 + 0.9$$

$$X^2 = 12.60$$

to a chi-square analysis, it means that the researcher is wrong about 5% of the time in claiming that the observed frequencies are significantly different than those predicted by chance variation.

The third step involves a complex formula, which we will not explain. In the past, many researchers did not perform this calculation but instead consulted a table of critical values that cross-indexed each degree of freedom with each level of error and then indicated the appropriate critical value. Today, statistical software programs calculate all three values for us. This is a tremendous convenience and ensures that our calculations are done with great precision. Still, you must know what the values mean if you want to understand their significance for your research.

In most computer analyses, the lowest level for probability of error is reported with each calculation. This means the computer will find the lowest level of p associated with our chi-square value. With respect to our example, then, our software reports that the probability of error associated with 12.60 is less than .05. In fact, it is less than .005. In a research report, we would express this result as $X^2 = 12.60$, $p < .01$. This represents a significantly low possibility of error. If we expressed this p as a percentage, we could say that there is less than 0.5% chance that our sample contains errors, or we could say that there is a 99.5% chance that our sample reflects its population. Hence, our test for significance was confirmed.

Do you remember our hypothesis for this example research? We hypothesized (H_1) that one conflict-resolution strategy would be more frequently adopted than others. The raw data gathered through our survey supported this hypothesis. The chi-square and p-value allow us to reject the null hypothesis (H_0); it claimed that all three strategies would have been selected equally by our 30 participants. Hence, the chi-square provides us with a warrant to conclude that in this sample of 30 people, there were significant differences in frequencies among the various conflict strategy types. The steps to determine the significance of our obtained chi-square are summarized in Exhibit 14.1.

Multiple-sample Chi-Square

A test for **multiple-sample chi-square** is used when you wish to test the relationship between the frequencies of

EXHIBIT 14.1 Steps to Determine the Significance of X^2

1. Calculate the value of the obtained (obt) chi-square: X^2_{obt}
2. Determine the degrees of freedom (df): $df = k - 1$
3. Use a table of critical values or statistical software to calculate the probability of error: p
4. If p is less than .05, the chi-square is significant.

one categorical variable, and when we assume that the categorical variable behaves independently from other variables (Ferguson, 1981). The procedure used is similar to the test for single samples.

To demonstrate how the frequencies of multiple samples are compared using chi-square analysis, let's return to the example of conflict resolution. This time, we will introduce two new considerations. First, let's make a new claim (H_2) and predict that women and men approach conflict resolution in significantly different ways. Second, let's make the size of the two groups different. Our new set of figures appears in Table 14.2.

There is one notable difference between a single-sample chi-square and a two-sample chi-square with unequal groups. We cannot determine the expected frequencies (E) as easily as we could in the single-sample example. We must use a specific formula to calculate the expected frequency of each variable. The formula appears below the rows and columns of data

in Table 14.2. When the data to be tested are organized in a table, the formula asks you to multiply the row sum by the column sum and then to divide that total by the grand sum. The grand sum is calculated by adding all of the column sums (10 + 25 + 15 = 50) or by adding all of the row sums (30 + 20 = 50). The grand sum should be the same no matter which set of figures you use.

Once the expected frequency values have been calculated for each of the observed frequencies, we are ready to calculate the chi-square and determine its significance. The equation for a two-sample chi-square is identical to that used for the single-sample test. The steps for determining its significance are almost the same as well. The one distinction is in the formula for degrees of freedom (df). For multiple sample chi-square, degrees of freedom are calculated by multiplying the number of rows minus one by the number of columns minus one. Our example of

TABLE 14.2 Data for Two-Sample Chi-Square With Expected Frequency Calculation

	TYPES OF CONFLICT STRATEGIES			
	AVOIDANT	CONFRONTATIONAL	NEGOTIATING	ROW SUMS
Males: Observed frequency (O)	5	20	5	30
Expected frequency	$E_1 = 6$	$E_2 = 15$	$E_3 = 9$	
Females: Observed frequency (O)	5	5	10	20
Expected frequency (E)	$E_4 = 4$	$E_5 = 10$	$E_6 = 6$	
				Grand sum
Column sums	10	25	15	50

CALCULATION FOR EXPECTED FREQUENCY

$$E = \frac{\text{row sum} \times \text{column sum}}{\text{grand sum}}$$

$$E_1 = \frac{30(10)}{50} = \frac{300}{50} = 6 \qquad E_2 = \frac{30(25)}{50} = \frac{750}{50} = 15 \qquad E_3 = \frac{30(15)}{50} = \frac{450}{50} = 9$$

$$E_4 = \frac{20(10)}{50} = \frac{200}{50} = 4 \qquad E_5 = \frac{20(25)}{50} = \frac{500}{50} = 10 \qquad E_6 = \frac{20(15)}{50} = \frac{300}{50} = 6$$

a two-sample chi-square calculation is presented in Exhibit 14.2.

With this calculation complete, we can then identify the probability level (*p*) by using a chi-square distribution table. As with single-sample tests, it is important that we select the smallest probability level for a Type I error in determining the significance of chi-square. As we noted above, however, most scholars now use statistical software programs to calculate and report both obtained chi-square and the lowest *p* level associated with it. If the *p* level is lower than .05, your obtained chi-square is significant.

Let's remind ourselves of what this means. The chi-square and *p*-value allow us to assess our actual findings against our projected estimates. If your chi-square has a *p* level of .05 or lower, then your findings report something that is probably significant; that is, there is a measurable relationship between your variables. Note we say 'probably'. There is still a 5% or less chance that your findings are insignificant. In technical terms, a chi-square with a *p* level of .05 or lower allows you to reject the null hypothesis. The null hypothesis always posits that your study's findings are due to chance, or that there is no measurable relationship between your variables. By comparing the frequencies of your obtained data and estimates for that same sample, the chi-square indicates whether or not there are significant differences between them. Hence,

the chi-square provides a warrant for the validity of our findings. The steps to determine the significance of our obtained chi-square for multiple samples are summarized in Exhibit 14.2.

Both single-sample and multiple-sample chi-squares are used to compare the observed frequencies of a category to its expected frequencies. As we have already pointed out, chi-square analysis is fairly common in survey research and content analysis, particularly when variables are coded by categories using nominal scales.

To sum up this section, most tests of nominal or ordinal level data are nonparametric tests. They can be used to test that frequency distributions are significantly different (as predicted by the research hypothesis, H_2), or that frequency distributions are equal (as predicted by the null hypothesis, H_0). Nonparametric tests do not provide much information about the parent population because it is known that the variable distributions under investigation deviate substantially from the normal curve (Ferguson, 1981).

By contrast, most tests of interval and ratio data are parametric tests. **Parametric tests** assume that population distributions have normal distributions. Because population distributions are assumed to be normal, their associated sampling distributions are also assumed to be normal. This means that you can estimate the population parameters from sample

---

EXHIBIT 14.2 Calculation of a Two-Sample Chi-Square With Steps to Determine Significance

$$X^2 = \sum \left[\frac{(O-E)^2}{E} \right]$$

$$X^2 = \frac{(5-6)^2}{6} + \frac{(20-15)^2}{15} = \frac{(5-9)^2}{9} = \frac{(5-4)^2}{4} + \frac{(5-10)^2}{10} = \frac{(10-6)^2}{6}$$

$$X^2 = 0.16 + 1.66 + 1.77 + 0.25 + 2.50 + 2.66$$

$$X^2_{obt} = 9.03$$

STEPS TO DETERMINE THE SIGNIFICANCE OF X^2

1. Find the value of the obtained (obt) chi-square: X^2_{obt}
2. Determine the degrees of freedom (*df*): *df* = (number of rows − 1) (number of columns − 1)
3. Use a table of critical values or statistical software to calculate the probability of error: *p*
4. If *p* is less than .05, the chi-square is significant.

statistics and calculate the sampling error associated with each characteristic. This ability makes parametric tests more powerful than nonparametric tests.

Parametric Tests

Nature of Data and Assumptions

In this section, we consider four parametric tests: two that test differences between group variances and two that test degrees of association between variables. Parametric tests of difference include the **t-test** and the **analysis of variance** (**ANOVA**). The parametric tests of relationship that you will learn about include correlation and regression.

t-test

The *t*-test calculates the probability that two distributions are similar with respect to a given variable. Once again, it follows our basic ratio and compares observed differences with expected differences. As a statistic, *t* expresses a ratio of observed mean differences over chance differences. It is used when the independent variable is measured at the nominal or ordinal level (i.e. with a categorical scale), and the dependent variable is measured at the interval or ratio level (i.e. with a continuous scale). It is best used when a sample is small, or has up to 100 cases (Johnson, 1988, p. 307).

There are two basic types of *t*-test. The first type of *t*-test is called an independent-samples *t*-test. It is used to test the comparison between two groups of the independent variable that are assumed to be not related in any way to see if they exert independent and significantly different influences on the dependent variable. For example, Scharrer, Kim, Lin, and Liu (2006) used content analysis to compare the depictions of women and men doing household chores in television commercials. Their quantitative data suggested that men were portrayed as generally less successful at completing household chores, and that men met with greater disapproval for their efforts. A *t*-test confirmed the probability that their findings were correct.

The second type of *t*-test is called a **paired *t*-test**. It assesses data from samples that are related or matched in some way, as may occur when the same sample is exposed to two different treatments. For example, Miller (2006) wanted to know how television viewers oriented themselves physically to particular types of news stories. A single group of participants was shown a series of news stories which evoked either fear or disgust, and Miller recorded how each participant reacted physically to each story using an interval scale. Her findings suggested that participants spent significantly more time looking at the screen when viewing stories that evoked disgust than those that evoked fear. Again, a *t*-test confirmed the probability that her findings were correct.

Both types of *t*-tests have two variants. The variant you use will be determined by your research hypothesis. In chapter 13, on descriptive statistics, you learned that research hypotheses for tests of difference can be directional or nondirectional. Directional tests of difference look to see if one variable is greater or lesser than another. In technical terms, they are called one-tailed tests; a **one-tailed test** is 'statistical test that takes the probability level required to reject the null hypothesis (typically 5%) from the area under only one tail of the sampling distribution' (Smith, 1988, p. 115).

By contrast, nondirectional tests look to see if two variables differ without assessing that one variable is greater than the other. In technical terms, these tests are called **two-tailed tests** and they use critical rejection regions under both tails of the normal curve distribution (Smith, 1988, p. 115).

It's time to consider an example. In conducting a *t*-test, we test very specific assumptions about the research and null hypotheses. Suppose you wish to discover whether platonic friends and romantic partners differed in the number of contacts they made during a one-week period (e.g. by meeting, texting, calling, or otherwise). The independent variable contains two categories or groups: platonic friends and romantic partners. The dependent variable is the number of contacts measured with a ratio scale.

The research hypothesis in our example (H_3) predicts that platonic friends will make significantly different numbers of contacts than romantic partners. The research hypothesis could be denoted as $H_3 : \overline{X}_1 \neq \overline{X}_2$. In this expression, $\overline{X}_1$ represents the mean frequency for platonic friends and $\overline{X}_2$ represents the mean frequency for romantic partners. Expressed like this, the hypothesis is nondirectional since either platonic friends or romantic partners may make more contact. Let's be more specific, and let's predict that platonic friends will make more contact with their partners than will romantic partners. As such, the hypothesis should be denoted to indicate direction, $H_3 : \overline{X}_1 > \overline{X}_2$. This means that our example will be a one-tailed test.

The null hypothesis (H_0) in any t-test is expressed as random variation between the sample means. Another way of saying this is that the samples are both drawn from the same population, $H_0: \overline{X}_1 = \overline{X}_2$. Applying this to the example, then, the null hypothesis predicts that platonic friends will make the same number of contacts as romantic partners will make. By calculating the t-test statistic, we are able to determine whether we can reject the null hypothesis and support the research hypothesis.

The actual calculation of the t statistic can be completed by statistics software. If you wish to calculate the t statistic manually, there is a formula you may use when the means are derived from random samples that are normally distributed with approximately equal variances. The formula is expressed in this equation:

$$t = \frac{|\overline{X}_1 - \overline{X}_2|}{\sqrt{\left(\frac{\Sigma d_1^2 + \Sigma d_2^2}{n_1 + n_2 - 2}\right)\left(\frac{n_1 + n_2}{n_1 n_2}\right)}}$$

Where $\overline{X}_1 - \overline{X}_2$ is the absolute value of the difference between the means of the independent samples, Σd_1^2 and Σd_2^2 are the sums of the deviation scores from their means squared, and n_1 and n_2 are the sizes of each sample (Smith, 1988, p. 127).

Let us return to our example using the frequency of contacts between platonic friends ($\overline{X}_1$) and romantic couples ($\overline{X}_2$) over the period of one week. The data are expressed in Table 14.3. We expect that the mean for the romantic couples group will be higher than the mean for the platonic friends, or $H_3: \overline{X}_2 > \overline{X}_1$, and so we will conduct a one-tailed test. The calculation of the t-test also appears in Table 14.3.

When statistics software calculates the t statistic, it also identifies the estimate of p associated with the obtained statistic. As we have noted elsewhere, the p level must be less than .05 to reject the null hypothesis (i.e. $p < .05$). If you wish to calculate the p level for the obtained t manually, you must follow the series of steps

identified in Exhibit 14.3. The degrees of freedom for a t-test are determined by calculating $n^1 + n^2 - 2$.

As you can see from Tables 14.5 and 14.6, our obtained t is significant. Table 14.3 shows how the raw data is processed to calculate t, and $t = 5.5249$. When reporting this value, researchers usually round the number to two decimal places (i.e. $t = 5.52$). Exhibit 14.3 shows how the degrees of freedom are calculated, and for our example $df = 18$. With these two statistics in hand, a computer will identify the level of p associated with $t = 5.52$ when $df = 18$. Alternatively, a table of critical values will provide the same information. For a one-tailed test, these results yield a $p < .005$. That means that we have reduced the chance of a Type I error to less than 1% by obtaining such a high t value. According to our hypothesis, then, we have supported the prediction that platonic friends make more frequent contact than do romantic partners.

If our example had been nondirectional, or $H_3 : \overline{X}_1 \neq \overline{X}_2$, then we would have conducted a two-tailed test. Once again, a computer could have automatically calculated the lowest p level associated with our t value, or we could have consulted a table of critical values for the same information. However, this is the point where it is crucial to remember the difference between a one-tail test and a two-tail test. Any given t statistic with a specific df value will always report the same p level for a one-tail test, but the exact same t statistic and df value will report a different p level for a two-tail test. Hence, the significance of the t statistic can differ greatly depending on your hypothesis and its directionality. In order to understand the statistics you calculate or read, you must know what type of test has been conducted.

In the last chapter, you were introduced to the term 'statistical power' to refer to the probability of not making a Type II error. One way to increase the statistical power of the t-test is to increase the sample size. The t formula is dependent on sample size because sample size affects the degrees of freedom. The greater the sample size, the greater the degrees of freedom, which in turn makes it easier to find significance at the .05 level. If the sample size is very large ($n = 500$ or greater), then the t-test becomes less accurate. For samples of that size, other tests of difference such as the z-test are preferred, but we do not discuss them in this text.

TABLE 14.3 Calculation of *t*-test with Data Samples

PLATONIC FRIENDS				ROMANTIC PARTNERS			
X_1	f_1	$d_1 = X_1 = \bar{X}_1$	d_1^2	X_2	f_2	$d_2 = X_2 = \bar{X}_2$	d_1^2
0	1	−3.5	12.25	3	1	−2.5	6.25
1	1	−2.5	6.25	4	1	−1.5	2.25
3		−0.5	0.25	5		−0.5	0.25
3	3	−0.5	0.25	5	4	−0.5	0.25
3		−0.5	0.25	5		−0.5	0.25
4	2	0.5	0.25	5		−0.5	0.25
4		0.5	0.25	6	2	0.5	0.25
5	1	1.5	2.25	6		0.5	0.25
6	2	2.5	6.25	7	1	1.5	2.25
6		2.5	6.25	9	1	3.5	12.25
$\sum X_1 = 35$	$n_1 = \sum f_1 = 10$		$\sum d_1^2 = 34.5$	$\sum X_2 = 55$	$n_2 = \sum f_2 = 10$		$\sum d_2^2 = 24.50$
$\bar{X}_1 = 3.5$				$\bar{X}_2 = 5.5$			

CALCULATION OF *t*

$$t = \frac{|X_1 - X_2|}{\sqrt{\left(\frac{\sum d_1^2 + \sum d_2^2}{n_1 + n_2 - 2}\right)\left(\frac{n_1 + n_2}{n_1 n_2}\right)}}$$

$$t = \frac{|3.5 - 5.5|}{\left(\sqrt{\frac{34.5 + 24.5}{10 + 10 - 2}}\right)\left(\frac{10 + 10}{10(10)}\right)}$$

$$t = \frac{|-2|}{\left(\sqrt{\frac{59}{18}}\right)\left(\frac{20}{100}\right)}$$

$$t = \frac{2}{1.81(0.20)}$$

$$t_{obt} = 5.5249$$

You can see now that *t*-tests are used when you have two groups or categories of data for your independent variable. What happens when we wish to test an independent variable with more than two categories or samples, or if we want to determine the effects of more than one independent variable on the dependent variable? To address either of these possibilities, we will examine the ANOVA.

Analysis of Variance: ANOVAs

We shall discuss two types of ANOVAs in this chapter: single-factor ANOVA and multiple-factors ANOVA. A **single-factor ANOVA** tests the effects of one independent variable with more than two categories on one dependent continuous variable. The term 'factor' refers to the independent variable. By contrast, **multiple-factors ANOVA** tests the effects of more than one independent

1. Calculate the t statistic, t_{obt}.
2. Find the degrees of freedom, $df = n1 + n2 - 2$.
3. Determine whether the test is one-tailed or two-tailed. In the illustration, the test is one-tailed, $\overline{X}_2 > \overline{X}_1$.
4. Use a table of critical values or statistical software to calculate the probability of error: p.
5. If p is less than 0.05, the t statistic is significant.

categorical variable on a continuous dependent variable. Because the ANOVA tests produce a result denoted by F, the tests are sometimes referred to as F tests.

Both ANOVA tests share certain assumptions with t-tests: (1) the distributions of the dependent variables follow the normal curve; (2) the F statistic follows the basic ratio of observed mean differences over chance differences; and (3) as the value of the F ratio increases, the likelihood that the groups were not drawn from the same population also increases.

Let's examine single-factor ANOVAs in detail before we turn to its more complex version. To illustrate how the test works, suppose you wish to test the effects of news stories with three types of endings on listeners' recall levels. The data for this example appears in Table 14.4. Three groups were shown a videotaped news segment on the same story, but each group was shown a segment with a different ending. Group 1 saw a version with a neutral ending, Group 2 saw a positive ending, and Group 3 saw a negative ending. Following the viewings, all three groups were tested to see how many items they recalled from the content of the story. The number of recalled items are reported as the X scores for each of the groups (X_1, X_2, X_3). The means for the three groups are similarly denoted as $\overline{X}_1$, $\overline{X}_2$, and $\overline{X}_3$.

The research hypothesis claims that the group means will be different, and it can be expressed as $H_4 : \overline{X}_1 \neq \overline{X}_2 \neq \overline{X}_3$. The null hypothesis is that the group means are equal, and it can be expressed as $H_0 : \overline{X}_1 = \overline{X}_2 = \overline{X}_3$. If the F statistic has a p value less than .05, then at least two group means are significantly different and are assumed to represent different populations. Notice that the research hypothesis (H_1) stipulates that only one group mean must be significantly different from the

TABLE 14.4   Data Set for Single-Factor ANOVA

GROUP 1 STORIES WITH NEUTRAL ENDS			GROUP 2 STORIES WITH POSITIVE ENDS			GROUP 3 STORIES WITH NEGATIVE ENDS		
X_1	d_1	d_1^2	X_2	d_2	d_2^2	X_3	d_3	d_3^2
6	−3.2	10.24	8	−2.7	7.29	12	−2.2	4.84
7	−2.2	4.84	9	−1.7	2.89	12	−2.2	4.84
8	−1.2	1.44	10	−0.7	0.49	13	−1.2	1.44
8	−1.2	1.44	10	−0.7	0.49	13	−1.2	1.44
9	−0.2	0.04	10	−0.7	0.49	14	−0.2	0.04
9	−0.2	0.04	10	−0.7	0.49	15	0.8	0.64
10	0.8	0.64	12	1.3	1.69	15	0.8	0.64
10	0.8	0.64	12	1.3	1.69	16	1.8	3.24
12	2.8	7.84	13	2.3	5.29	16	1.8	3.24
13	3.8	14.44	13	2.3	5.29	16	1.8	3.24
$\sum X_1 = 92$	$\sum d_1^2 = 41.60$		$\sum X_2 = 107$	$\sum d_2^2 = 26.1$		$\sum X_3 = 142$	$\sum d_3^2 = 23.6$	
$n_1 = 10$			$n_2 = 10$			$n_3 = 10$		
$\overline{X}_1 = 9.2$			$\overline{X}_2 = 10.7$			$\overline{X}_3 = 14.2$		

others for it to be supported. This is true regardless of how many groups or categories the independent variable has. In other words, the F statistic will tell us that one of the contrasts is significant, but it will not identify which or how many of the contrasts are different.

To obtain the F statistic, it is best to rely upon a computer software program. If you wish to find it manually, however, you can follow these steps. First, you must calculate the mean observation for each group, the deviation for each individual observation, and the square of each deviation. These are used to find the **sums of squares for between groups** (denoted as SSb) and the **sums of squares for within groups** (denoted as SSw). The SSb is an estimate of the difference between group means, whereas the SSw is an estimate of chance variation (also known as the sampling error). The calculation of the sums of squares for both between and within groups of the example data appears in Exhibit 14.4.

Continuing your calculation of F, you must identify the degrees of freedom (df) associated with each sum of squares (SS). The df for between groups is the number of groups minus 1 (or $k - 1$). The df for within groups is the total number of scores in all groups minus the number of groups (or $N - k$). With these two statistics in hand, you can calculate the mean for each sum of squares. The mean sum of squares for between groups (MSb) is found by dividing the relevant sum of squares by its relevant df, while the mean sum of squares for within groups (MSw) is found by dividing the relevant sum of squares by its relevant df.

Finally, the F ratio is calculated using the two mean sum of squares. The ratio itself is expressed in the following equation:

$$F = \frac{MS_b}{MS_w}$$

To help clarify our findings, we may report our results for a single-factor ANOVA by using a summary table. An example of a summary table appears in Table 14.5.

EXHIBIT 14.4   Calculation for Between-Group and Within-Group Sums of Squares

Grand Mean Calculation:

$$\overline{X}_g = \frac{\overline{X}_1 + \overline{X}_2 + \overline{X}_3}{n_{\overline{X}}}$$

where n = number of scores per group, and
$\overline{X}_g$ = grand mean

$$\overline{X}_g = \frac{9.2 + 10.7 + 14.2}{3}$$

$$\overline{X}_g = 11.35$$

Between-group SS_b calculation:

$SS_b = \sum n(d^2)$

$SS_b = 10(9.2 - 11.36)^2 + 10(10.7 - 11.36)^2 + (14.2 - 11.36)^2$

$SS_b = 10(-2.16)^2 + 10(-0.66)^2 + (10 - 2.83)^2$

$SS_b = 46.94 + 4.44 + 80.28$

$SS_b = 131.66$

where $\sum d_j^2 = \overline{X}_j - \overline{X}_g$, $\overline{X}_j$ = every group mean,
and $\overline{X}_g$ = the grand mean

Within-group SS_b calculation:

$SS_w = \sum[\sum(d_j)]$

$SS_w = \sum d_1^2 + \sum d_2^2 + \sum d_3^2$

$SS_w = 41.60 + 26.1 + 23.6$

$SS_w = 91.30$

where $\sum d_j^2$ = the sum of the deviation scores
squared for every group

TABLE 14.5 Summary Table and Steps to Determine Significance of F Statistic

SOURCE OF VARIANCE	SS	df	MS	F_{obt}
Between	$\sum n(D^2) = 131.66$	$k - 1 = 3 - 1 = 2$	$\dfrac{SS_b}{k-1} = \dfrac{131.66}{2} = 65.83$	$F_{obt} = \dfrac{MS_b}{MS_w}$
Within	$\sum[\sum d_i] = 91.30$	$N - k = 30 - 3 = 27$	$\dfrac{SS_w}{N-k} = \dfrac{91.30}{27} = 3.38$	$F_{obt} = \dfrac{65.83}{3.38}$
				$F_{obt} = 19.48$

STEPS TO DETERMINE THE SIGNIFICANCE OF F_{OBT}

1. Calculate the F statistic: F_{obt}
2. Determine the degrees of freedom for between groups (df_b) and within groups (df_w):
   $df_b = k - 1$ (numerator df)
   $df_w = k - 1$ (denominator df)
3. Use a table of critical values or statistical software to calculate the probability of error: p
   If p is less than .05, the F statistic is significant.

Note: SS = sums of squares; df = degrees of freedom; MS = mean square.

To determine the probability of error associated with our obtained F (F_{obt}), we would follow the steps that appear in Table 14.5. Once again, it is best to use a computer. However, it is also possible to consult a table of critical values. In our example, the $F_{obt} = 19.48$ at $df = 2$ and 27. This F_{obt} value is associated with a $p < .001$ level. Because $p < .05$, we can assume that the data supports the research hypothesis. If we translate this statistical finding back into the language of our hypothesis (H[4]), we would conclude that there are significant differences among the three news story types and their effects on listeners' recall.

Although single-factor analysis is relatively simple to calculate, it is less commonly used than multiple-factors ANOVA. As we noted earlier, multiple-factors ANOVA is computed for the effects of more than one independent categorical variable on a continuous dependent variable. These designs can be illustrated by using a 2 × 2 research design matrix. A 2 × 2 research design refers to two independent variables with two categories each, and this is the simplest form the test can take. Hence, this would be a two-way ANOVA because there are two independent variables (three-way ANOVAs have three independent variables, and so forth).

Consider the following research conducted by Frymier and Houser (1998). They wished to test the effects of immediacy and topic relevance on students' levels of cognitive learning. Frymier and Houser (1998) defined immediacy as 'the perception of physical and psychological closeness between people' (p. 122). Teachers who express high immediacy nonverbally do so because they smile and nod more in response to their students, have higher levels of eye contact, and move or stand closer to their students than do teachers who express low immediacy nonverbally. Frymier and Houser chose a 2 × 2 design in which high and low levels of immediacy represented the two categories of the first independent variable, and high and low levels of topic relevance represented the two categories of the second independent variable. The dependent variable is the level of learning measured as a continuous variable. The design matrix for this study is presented in Table 14.6. The means within the cells correspond to the sample mean for each cell. The means outside of the matrix are combined averages for each category of the separate factors, or independent variables. Please note, however, that we are using means that are approximate values rather than the exact values reported in the study. We take this liberty for illustration purposes only.

TABLE 14.6 Design Matrix for a 2 × 2 Multiple-Factors ANOVA

	HIGH IMMEDIACY	LOW IMMEDIACY	
High Relevance	$n = 5$ $\overline{X}_2 = 4.0$	$n = 5$ $\overline{X}_4 = 3.0$	$\overline{X}_{HR} = 3.5$
Low Relevance	$n = 5$ $\overline{X}_1 = 4.6$	$n = 5$ $\overline{X}_3 = 3.4$	$\overline{X}_{LR} = 4.0$
	$\overline{X}_{HI} = 4.3$	$\overline{X}_{LI} = 3.2$	

Note: ANOVA = analysis of variance.

As we have done with the previous tests, we recommend that you use a computer to calculate multiple-factors ANOVA. The calculation of the difference among means needed for this 2 × 2 design is very complex. The smallest and easiest examples would take several hours to calculate by hand, while a computer can analyze the same data in seconds. Indeed, the calculation of the various statistics needed to complete multiple-factors ANOVA is beyond the scope of this text. Rather than explain the formula, we shall concentrate on interpreting the summary of this analysis for our study example.

In our example, Frymier and Houser (1998) expected to find two main effects, one for immediacy and one for relevance, as predicted in the research hypotheses:

H₁: Students who are exposed to teachers with higher levels of immediacy will experience significantly greater increases in their cognitive learning than students exposed to teachers with lower levels of immediacy.

H₂: Students who are exposed to teachers expressing higher levels of topical relevance will experience significantly greater increases in their cognitive learning than students exposed to teachers expressing lower levels of topical relevance.

Main effects are the predicted effects of each independent variable (in this case, immediacy and relevance) on the dependent variable (in this case, cognitive learning).

This two-way ANOVA can also test **interaction effects**. The interaction effect is the combined influence of two or more independent variables on the dependent variable. In our example, the interaction effect predicted by Frymier and Houser (1998) was stated in their third hypothesis:

H₃: Students who are exposed to teachers expressing higher levels of both immediacy and topical relevance will experience significantly greater increases in their cognitive learning than students exposed to teachers expressing lower levels of immediacy and topical relevance.

Computer analysis can compute F values associated with the main effects and the interaction effects for multiple-factors ANOVAs. Generally, software programs can provide you with summary tables that will help you to interpret your findings. An example of a summary table appears in Table 14.7.

From the summary table, you can draw the following conclusions. First, H₁ predicted a main effect for immediacy. H₁ was supported because the F_{obt} value associated with immediacy is 7.81 and $p < .05$. This strongly suggests that students who were exposed to teachers expressing higher levels of immediacy experienced significantly greater increases in their cognitive learning than students exposed to teachers expressing lower levels of immediacy. Second, H₂ predicted a main effect for relevance. H₂ was *not* supported because the F_{obt} value associated with relevance is 1.61 and $p > .05$. This suggests that students

TABLE 14.7 Calculating F for a 2 × 2 ANOVA

SOURCE OF VARIANCE	SS	df	MS (VARIANCE)	F_{obt}
Immediacy	6.05	$(k-1)$ 1	6.05	$\dfrac{6.05}{0.775} = 7.81*$
Relevance	1.25	$(k-1)$ 1	1.25	$\dfrac{1.25}{0.775} = 1.61$
Immediacy X Relevance (interaction)	0.05	$(k-1)$ 1	0.05	$\dfrac{0.05}{0.775} = 0.06$
Error	12.4	$(n-k)$ $20 - 4 = 16$	0.775	
		$df_n = 1$ and $df_d = 16$		$*p < .05$

Note: ANOVA = analysis of variance; SS = sum of squares; df = degrees of freedom; MS = mean square.

who were exposed to teachers expressing higher levels of topical relevance did not experience significantly greater increases in their cognitive learning than students exposed to teachers expressing lower levels of topical relevance. Last, H₃ predicted an interaction effect for immediacy and relevance. H₃ was *not* supported because the F_{obt} value associated with the immediacy and relevance factored together is 0.06 and $p > .05$. This suggests there was no significantly different combined effect for immediacy and topical relevance on cognitive learning. Pay special attention to the p level associated with the main effect for relevance and for the interaction affect. The fact that $p > .05$, rather than $p < .05$, is what tells us that the last two results were not significant.

More complex tests of difference are frequent in certain fields of communication and cultural research such as interpersonal communication, audience studies, and marketing. Tests such as analysis of **covariance** allow researchers to clarify main effects by parsing out the variance that can be accounted for by a rival predictor variable. Calculation of these tests is beyond the scope of this textbook, but you can read about them in more advanced discussions (e.g. Pedhazur, 1982). At this point, we consider the second general type of claim made with inferential statistics, the claims of relatedness or association, and the tests of relationships used to assess their significance.

Tests of Relationships

Tests of relationships assess how changes in one continuous variable are associated with or predict changes in one or more other continuous variables. Where tests of differences use measures of central tendency (i.e. means) to examine differences between groups, tests of relationships use all of the information about each variable that is available. This is possible only because the continuous variables are measured with interval or ratio scales. You will begin this section by learning about the general concept of correlation, also called covariance. You will explore ways of interpreting correlations and the types of possible relationships between variables, and you will also examine tests of correlation or covariance.

Measuring Covariance

Nature of Data and Assumptions

When we observe that change in one variable is associated with change in another variable, we believe that there is a **correlation** between the two variables. That is, we assume they 'covary', or systematically share variance. The statistics that estimate the degree of association, however, are not direct tests of causality. Correlation is one condition of causality, but it is not a sufficient condition by itself to prove causality. You may wish to revisit our discussion of necessary and sufficient causes in chapter 6, on warrants.

Many critics of quantitative analysis remind us that we should not assume causality when we find correlations. For example, Ferguson (1981) noted that intelligence and motor abilities may be correlated because of the presence of some third and unacknowledged factor like age. Remove the age factor and the association disappears. Because of the complexity of human communication and culture, there are probably multiple causes for any event, and this event itself is probably composed of many variables. Assuming causality can lead to a **spurious correlation**, or two variables that appear to be associated when they are not causally related. Ferguson (1981) observed that both the birth rate and alcohol consumption rose after the Second World War, though establishing a causal link between the two trends leads to humorous if not dangerous conclusions (p. 138).

Associations of variance between two continuous variables are called **bivariate relationships**. Associations of variance between more than two continuous variables are called **multivariate relationships**. In this section, you will explore calculations and interpretations for statistics based on bivariate relationships.

Zero-order Correlation

For many bivariate relationships, the strength of the association is estimated with a statistic called a **correlation coefficient**. One of the most frequent tests of correlation begins with calculating a statistic, a coefficient that is represented by r for samples, and by ρ (the Greek letter referred to as *lower-case rho*) for populations. The common name of the test statistic is zero-order correlation, though it is formally known as Pearson's product-moment coefficient of correlation.

The test for correlation assumes the variables are normally distributed. The null hypothesis is written as $H_0: r = 0.0$; that is, that there is no correlation between the two variables being studied. The research hypothesis is written symbolically as $H_1: r \neq 0.0$; that is, that there is some relationship between the two variables being studied. As an example, let's say that you wish to measure the magnitude or strength of the association between communication apprehension and level of procrastination when preparing a speech. This topic was studied by Behnke and Sawyer (1999). They predicted that higher levels of communication apprehension would be associated with greater procrastination. We use Behnke and Sawyer's (1999) variables for example data in Table 14.8. The variable X represents communication apprehension scores, and the Y variable represents procrastination scores.

Once again, let us state that it is best to rely upon a computer to calculate the r coefficient. If you wish to do it manually, however, you can follow these steps. First, we must find the deviation scores (d) for both

TABLE 14.8 Data for Correlation Coefficient (R) Calculation

X(CA)	$d_X = (X - \bar{X})$	d_X^2	Y(Pro)	$d_Y = (Y - \bar{Y})$	d_Y^2
60	−10	100	15	−1.5	2.25
65	−5	25	15	−1.5	2.25
65	−5	25	16	−0.5	0.25
70	0	0	16	−0.5	0.25
70	0	0	16	−0.5	0.25
70	0	0	17	+0.5	0.25
70	0	0	17	+0.5	0.25
75	+5	25	17	+0.5	0.25
75	+5	25	18	+1.5	2.25
80	+10	100	18	+1.5	2.25
$\sum X = 700$			$\sum X = 165$		
$n_x = 10$		$\sum d_x^2 = 300$	$n_y = 10$		$\sum d_y^2 = 10.5$
$\bar{X} = 70.0$			$\bar{y} = 16.5$		

Note: CA = communication apprehension.

Note: Pro = procrastination.

X and Y. Then, we multiply every d_x score by every d_y, and sum the results. This produces a sum of the cross products of the deviations, as illustrated in Table 14.9.

It is very important to notice that the deviation scores used to calculate the sum of the cross products are not squared. This column determines the directionality or sign of the correlation coefficient by indicating whether the sum is positive or negative. If the deviation scores were squared, then every sum would be positive. When X and Y scores either increase or decrease together, the sum of the cross products will be a positive number. If X scores increase as Y scores decrease, or vice versa, the sum of the cross products will be a negative number. We will have more to say about the directionality or sign of a correlation coefficient shortly.

Once we have finished calculating the cross products sum, we are now able to calculate r_{xy}. This formula is shown in Exhibit 14.5, where we also show the calculations for our example. To interpret this correlation value further, you will need to examine three of its characteristics: magnitude, sign, and coefficient of determination.

With respect to **magnitude**, the correlation coefficient, r, is expressed as a value between +1.00 and −1.00. The value of r is referred to as its magnitude. The two values +1.00 and −1.00 represent perfect correlations. Perfect correlations happen when the changes in one variable occurs in exactly the same proportion as they occur in the second variable. This

EXHIBIT 14.5 Calculation of the Correlation Coefficient r_{xy}

$$r_{xy} = \frac{\sum(d_x d_y)}{\sqrt{(\sum d_x^2)(\sum d_x^2)}}$$

$$r_{xy} = \frac{50.0}{\sqrt{300(10.5)}}$$

$$r_{xy} = \frac{50}{56.1249}$$

$$r_{xy} = +.89$$

1. Calculate correlation coefficient: r_{xy}
2. Determine the degrees of freedom, $n - 2$, where n is the total number of participants. $n = 10$ and $df = 8$.
3. Use a table of critical values or statistical software to calculate the probability of error for a two-tailed test: p
4. If p is less than .05, then the correlation coefficient is significant.

result does not often occur in practice. Rather, perfect correlations generally represent ideal endpoints rather than actual values. The same is true of the value of 0.0. The value 0.0 means that the variables are not related in any way and are fully independent of each other. This result is as improbable as perfect correlations. In most data sets, you will find random occurrences of covariance in variables which otherwise have no relationship. For example, you might assume that a passion for curling is not related to a passion for soccer. Many Canadians curl and play soccer, but a correlation coefficient would probably report that there is no systematic variance between them; that is, most individuals play only one of these sports. Nonetheless, the existence of people who do play both sports negates the probability of a correlation coefficient of 0.0.

Interpreting the magnitude of r is done using established guidelines. Exhibit 14.6 provides a typical set of ranges. With our example data, then, we obtained $r_{xy} = .89, p < .001$. This suggests that we found very strong relationships among procrastination, communication apprehension, and perceived public speaking competence. In other words, procrastination levels and communication apprehension levels covary more than is predicted by chance or error, and the covariance is significant.

TABLE 14.9 Sum of Cross Products for r_{xy}

$d_x = (X - \bar{X})$	$d_Y = (Y - \bar{Y})$	$d_x d_Y$
−10	−1.5	−10(−1.5) = 15
−5	−1.5	−5(−1.5) = 7.5
−5	−0.5	−5(−0.5) = 2.5
0	−0.5	0(−0.5) = 0.00
0	−0.5	0(−0.5) = 0.00
0	+0.5	0(+0.5) = 0.00
0	+0.5	0(+0.5) = 0.00
+5	+0.5	+5(+0.5) = 2.5
+5	+1.5	+5(+1.5) = 7.5
+10	+1.5	+10(+1.5) = 15
		$\sum d_x d_y = 10.5$

EXHIBIT 14.6 Guidelines for Interpreting Correlation Magnitudes

0.0	No relationship
±.01 – .25	A weak relationship
±.26 – .55	A moderate relationship
±.56 – .75	A strong relationship
±.76 – .99	A very strong relationship
±1.00	A perfect relationship

Source: From *Contemporary Communication Research Methods*, p. 152, by M. J. Smith, 1988, Belmont, CA: Wadsworth, Inc. Copyright 1988 by Wadsworth, Inc.

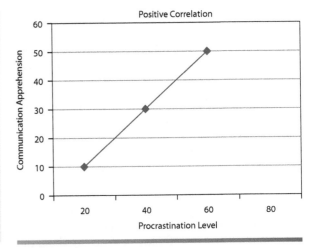

FIGURE 14.1 Graph of Positive Correlation

In addition to the magnitude or strength of the correlation, you also use the positive or negative sign of the correlation to determine the type of relationship that exists between the variables. As we noted earlier, a **positive correlation** describes a relationship between variables that are changing in the same way; they are either increasing or decreasing together. In the example, we calculated a very strong positive correlation between public speaking procrastination and communication apprehension. This is similar to the value reported in the original study, $r = +.70$ (Behnke & Sawyer, 1999). The higher the students' levels of communication apprehension, the more likely they were to procrastinate in preparing their speeches. A positive correlation is graphically represented in Figure 14.1.

When the relationship between the variables is a **negative correlation**, it is called an inverse relationship in which variables change in opposite directions. As one increases, the other decreases, or vice versa. For example, Guerrero and Jones (2005) found a moderate negative correlation between attachment avoidance (discomfort with closeness) and expressiveness (appropriate use of verbal and nonverbal expressions). That is, people who scored higher on the attachment avoidance scale were likely to score lower on the expressiveness measure. The correlation coefficient was $r = -.44$. A negative correlation is graphically represented in Figure 14.2.

Positive and negative correlations express **linear relationships**. Occasionally, associations between variables are more complex and express curvilinear

relationships. The most common forms are the U-shape curve and the inverted U-shape curve. The **U-shaped correlation** occurs when both variables initially decrease together, and then flatten out, and finally increase together. It reflects an association like the one found by Behnke and Sawyer (2000) during the process of preparing a speech. Among their participants, levels of anxiety were high after initially receiving the speech assignment. These dropped off during speech preparation laboratory sessions, and then increased again significantly just before delivering the speech (see Figure 14.3). Curvilinear relationships express patterns between variables that shift in direction at several points across time.

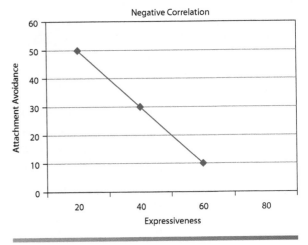

FIGURE 14.2 Graph of Negative Correlation

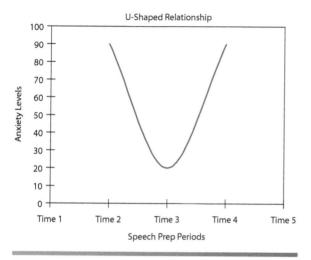

FIGURE 14.3 Graph of U-Shaped Relationship

By contrast, the inverted U-shape follows the opposite path. In a practical example, the inverted U-shape could represent the findings from a study of teacher immediacy and technology use. That study found that student affective learning began lower in the no-technology condition for both high- and low-immediacy teachers, increased with moderate use of technology, and then decreased again when teaching was completely technologized, as it is in distance learning (Witt & Schrodt, 2006). An example of the inverted U-shape appears in Figure 14.4.

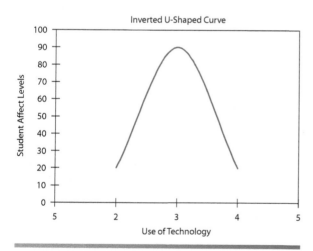

FIGURE 14.4 Graph of Inverted U-Shaped Relationship

The final way to interpret a correlation coefficient is by estimating the actual amount of variance which two (or more) continuous variables have in common. The statistic used for this estimate is called the **coefficient of determination**. This coefficient is found by squaring r_{xy}. If you then multiply the coefficient of determination by 100, you will obtain a percentage. This percentage expresses the proportion of the variation in one variable that can be directly explained by the variation in the second variable. This suggests, then, that as the percentage increases, so too does the strength of the relationship. In the example based on the Behnke and Sawyer (1999) study, the percentage of shared variance between procrastination and communication apprehension was $(.89)^2 \times 100 = 79.21\%$, as depicted in Figure 14.5. In this example, if we knew a student's communication apprehension score, we would have a reasonably good chance (79%) of predicting his or her likelihood of procrastinating on a speech assignment. This percentage of shared variance can be depicted graphically by a diagram known as a Venn diagram (see Figure 14.5).

Magnitude, sign, and estimates of shared variance are attributes of a correlation coefficient that permit us to interpret more accurately the nature of the non-causal relationship between two or more continuous variables. More complex analyses are needed in considering tests of causality.

Measuring Causality

Nature of Data and Assumptions

In bivariate and multiple correlation tests, the researcher is interested in assessing the degree of association between several continuous variables (measured at interval and ratio levels). Regression analysis permits tests of causality among sets of continuous variables.

Linear Regression Analysis

Regression analysis is a common test statistic in communication and cultural research. With regression analysis, the researcher can predict the unknown values of a dependent variable from the obtained value of its independent variable. The variables are expected to covary or share some proportion of variance. The amount of variance in the dependent variable that is

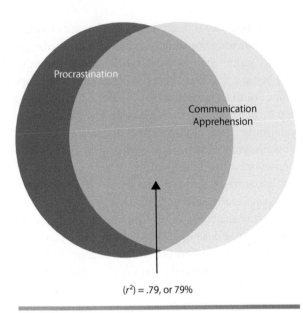

(r²) = .79, or 79%

FIGURE 14.5 Venn Diagram of Shared Variance Estimate in the Behnke and Sawyer (1999) Study

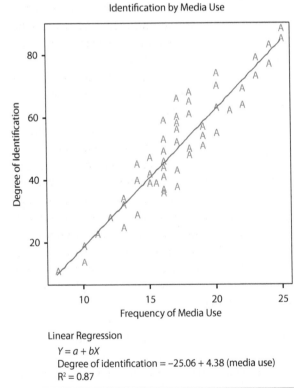

Identification by Media Use

Linear Regression

Y = a + bX
Degree of identification = –25.06 + 4.38 (media use)
R² = 0.87

FIGURE 14.6 Scatter Plot of Two Continuous Variables: Media Use and Identification

explained by the variance in the independent variable is called the estimate of shared variance.

As we have noted with the other statistics we have described, it is best to use statistical software to perform a regression analysis. If you wish to make the calculations yourself, however, you must understand the following formula. Regression analysis is calculated for the relationship between one independent and one dependent variable, and this form is called linear regression. It is expressed by the following equation:

$$Y = a + bX$$

where Y is the dependent variable along the vertical axis, X is the independent variable along the horizontal axis, and a and b are **regression weights** or 'beta coefficients'. If you recall your high school math, you will recognize that this formula is an equation for a line in which a is the intercept (that value where the line intersects the vertical y-axis) and b is the slope of the line estimating how much change should occur in Y based on a single unit of change in X. The line itself is the best estimate of the relationship between Y and X. Another way to perform the same test would be to plot each matched pair of observations (x, y) on a graph, and then to draw a single straight line, from left to right, through the centre of the scatter. The line represents the average distance between each point and the line. However, any line you draw by hand on a scatter plot will simply provide an estimate for the line. By following the formula, you will calculate a precise value for the line. For an example of a scatter plot, see Figure 14.6. We will explain its precise implications below.

Let's consider an example. Suppose we wish to predict the relationship between participants' media use and their sense of identification with a particular social group. A study like this was conducted by Morton and Duck (2000), who examined how gay media use their audience members' personal identification with the gay community. To simplify their study, we shall focus on the relationship between just two variables: the frequency of gay media use as the independent variable and degree of identification as the dependent variable. The researchers determined there was a causal relationship between media use and personal identification with the gay community.

As frequency of gay media use increased, participants reported greater personal identification with the gay community. The scatter plot in Figure 14.6 is a visual representation of the relationship between the two variables.

The regression equation allows researchers to predict unknown values of the dependent variable (in this case, identification) from the known values of the independent variable (media use). Just from examining the graph, you could predict, for instance, that a person who scores a 40 on media use (x-axis) will score about a 15 on the identification measure (y-axis), even though these point coordinates are not among the actual data in the sample.

There is a second point we can take from the graph. As you can see, the two variables X and Y are not perfectly correlated. They are scattered about the regression line. Hence, the regression line is a line that 'best fits' the data. Because the variables are assumed to be normally distributed, and the relationship between them is assumed to be linear, a **standard error** can be calculated for X and Y values that estimates the accuracy of the predictions made by the regression line. From the standard error, we can predict a range of values where X is most likely to be located. Statistical software will provide the standard error for each regression analysis you perform.

Multiple Regression Analysis

In regression analysis, we can examine bivariate relationships and multivariate relationships. We have only discussed bivariate relationships up to this point because we have considered only two variables. Many studies in communication and culture are investigations of multivariate relationships. In these studies, the researcher uses some form of **multiple regression analysis** to explore the relationship between a set of predictor variables and the criterion variable.

Multiple regression analysis derives regression weights from the linear equation so that we can assess how much of the total variance of the criterion variable can be explained by each individual predictor. Two of the more common forms of multiple regression analysis are stepwise regressions and hierarchical regressions. Researchers using **stepwise regression** program their statistical software to try various combinations of

weights until it finds the 'best fit' equation. Using a stepwise regression to test combinations of relationships, Weber (2004) tested the relationships among sets of teacher behaviours and student interest variables. Teacher behaviours were measured as being a positive or negative influence on students' interests, whereas student interest was multidimensional, measured in terms such as impact and competence. The regression analysis showed that different teacher behaviours had varying and complex effects on student interest as the dependent variable.

In a study of parental mediation and children's aggression, Nathanson (2001) used **hierarchical regression**, a form of multiple regression in which the researcher stipulates the order of variables entered into the linear equation based on theory and past research. To isolate the effects of parental mediation and 'coviewing' (that is, parents watching television with their children), Nathanson (2001) first entered control or intervening variables (like violent program content, children's gender, age, and parental education) that she suspected would explain the variance in the children's aggressive tendencies. Past research has shown that each of these variables tends to influence children's expressed aggression.

After removing the control variable effects, Nathanson (2001) found that two types of mediation still explained a significant amount of the remaining variance in children's aggressive tendencies, whereas coviewing did not make a significant contribution. Because she could construct an equation for each predictor, Nathanson (2001) found some evidence that the relationship between parental mediation (such as strict enforcement of viewing rules) and children's expressed aggressive behaviour was curvilinear. In other words, high and low levels of restrictive mediation in the parents were better predictors of aggression in their children than moderate levels of parental restrictive mediation.

Two Ethical Issues

Whenever you conduct statistical analyses and present your findings in a research report or at a meeting of a professional association, you have an ethical obligation to do no harm. In this case, you have an obligation to those who read and use your findings as well as to your participants.

First, you should not use parametric statistics if your sample data is distributed abnormally. You must make every effort to collect data that meets the assumptions of the parametric tests you intend to use to test your hypotheses or research questions. If your data do not meet the assumption of normal distribution, then you may need to collect additional data. Alternatively, you may have to eliminate **outliers**, scores that are above or below three standard deviations from the mean score for your sample. If your data sample is quite skewed, then you must acknowledge that there is a limitation to your findings. It could mean that your findings are less credible than they would be otherwise.

In any case, you must be forthright in acknowledging the limitations of your data as well as your chances of error. Inferential statistics are based on probability. Every single conclusion that you draw from your statistics is subject to error, even if the sample represents the entire population and the measurement is highly reliable. Few studies achieve both of these ideals, however. When you know that your sample selection is biased, or that your measurement is less than reliable, then you must acknowledge those limitations; you must tell your audience how your findings are limited so that other researchers will not replicate the problem.

Summary

In this chapter, we addressed two types of statistical measures: tests of differences and tests of relationships. Both sets of tests provide us with information that allows us to describe our data in rich detail.

When we discussed tests of difference, we noted that they are all modelled on the same basic ratio. In this ratio, observed group mean differences serve as the numerator, and chance mean differences serve as the denominator. The value that is calculated from this ratio indicates the extent to which our observations differ from a perfectly random set of occurrences. If our observations clearly differ from random occurrences, then we can be reasonably certain that we have observed a meaningful pattern. The probability that this observation is significant is indicated by a second measure, the probability of error (p). Social scientists across all disciplines agree that it is important to have a p level of .05 or lower, which indicates that our findings have only a 5% or less chance of being incorrect.

To test measures based on nominal and ordinal scales, we use nonparametric tests such as the chi-square. To test measures based on interval and ratio scales, we use parametric tests such as the t-test and ANOVA. Each of these tests supplies us with a warrant to accept or dismiss a claim by indicating how the data tested differs from a hypothetical random sample. The null hypothesis is crucial here. While our research hypothesis articulates the expected significance of our data, we use the null hypothesis to articulate the alternative, that our data may contain no significance at all.

Tests of relationships do not simply tell us if our data are different or significant in comparison to random data. Tests of relationships such as correlation and regression analysis can indicate the magnitude and strength of the variance shared by two variables. Further, regression analysis can indicate causality; it can indicate how two or more variables covary. Knowing this, we can use past observations to calculate and thus predict future observations. Once again, the statistics we produce through our calculations indicate the strength, direction, and significance of our findings, and thus these statistics provide a warrant to accept or reject our research hypotheses.

In our examples of correlation and simple regression, we examined bivariate relationships. These are defined as associations between just two variables. Often, noncausal and causal tests of correlation in communication and cultural research investigate relationships among whole sets of continuous variables. Researchers use tests of multivariate relationships that permit the researcher to explore how several variables are interrelated through tests of multiple correlations and regressions. In this text, we discussed just one test of a multivariate relationship, regression analysis. If you are interested in more advanced statistical analyses, then we strongly recommend that you take a course specializing in statistics.

TABLE 14.10 Major Aspects of Inferential Statistics

TEST	VARIABLES	HYPOTHESES	EQUATION	TEST TYPE	CAUSAL
chi-square, one sample (X^2)	1 Variable	$H_1 : O \neq E$ $H_0 : O = E$	$\dfrac{\text{Observed frequencies}}{\text{Expected frequencies}}$	Nonparametric	No
chi-square, two samples (X^2)	1 Independent: (2+ Categories) 1 Dependent: (2+ Categories)	$H_1 : O \neq E$ $H_0 : O = E$	$\dfrac{\text{Observed frequencies}}{\text{Expected frequencies}}$	Nonparametric	Yes
t-test (t)	1 Independent: (2 Categories) 1 Dependent: (Interval/Ratio)	$H_1 : \bar{X}_1 \neq \bar{X}_2$ $H_1 : \bar{X}_1 > \bar{X}_2$ $H_1 : \bar{X}_1 < \bar{X}_2$ $H_0 : \bar{X}_1 = \bar{X}_2$	$\dfrac{\text{Observed mean differences}}{\text{Chance mean differences}}$	Parametric	Yes
1-way ANOVA (F)	1 Independent: (3+ Categories) 1 Dependent: (Interval/Ratio)	$H_1 : \bar{X}_1 \neq \bar{X}_2$ $H_0 : \bar{X}_1 = \bar{X}_2$	$\dfrac{\text{Observed mean differences}}{\text{Chance mean differences}}$	Parametric	Yes
2-way ANOVA (F)	2+ Independent: (2+ Categories) 1 Dependent: (Interval/Ratio)	$H_1 : \bar{X}_1 \neq \bar{X}_2$ $H_0 : \bar{X}_1 = \bar{X}_2$	$\dfrac{\text{Observed mean differences}}{\text{Chance mean differences}}$	Parametric	Yes
correlation (r_{xy})	2+ Continuous (Interval/Ratio)	$H_1 : r_{xy} \neq 0$ $H_0 : r_{xy} = 0$	$\dfrac{\text{Cross products}}{\text{Sum of squares}}$	Parametric	No
regression (R)	1+ Independent: Continuous 1 Dependent: Continuous	$H_1 : R \neq 0$ $H_0 : R = 0$	$y = 1 + bx$	Parametric	Yes

Note: ANOVA = analysis of variance; Continuous Data = data measured on an interval or ratio scale.

Key Terms

Analysis of variance (ANOVA)
Bivariate relationship
Chi-square
Coefficient of determination
Correlation
Correlation coefficient
Covariance
Degrees of freedom
Hierarchical regression
Interaction effect
Linear relationship
Magnitude
Main effect

Multiple-factors ANOVA
Multiple regression analysis
Multiple-sample chi-square
Multivariate relationship
Negative correlation
Nonparametric test
One-tailed test
Outlier
Paired t-test
Parametric test
Positive correlation
Regression analysis
Regression weights

Single-factor ANOVA
Single-sample chi-square
Spurious correlation
Standard error
Stepwise regression
Sums of squares between groups
Sums of squares within groups
t-test
Two-tailed test
U-shaped correlation
Zero-order correlation

Discussion Questions

1. Explain the main difference between parametric and nonparametric tests.
2. For tests of difference, explain the main distinctions among t-tests and ANOVAs. In what ways are these tests similar?
3. What is the essential difference between tests of difference and tests of relationship? What are the data requirements for each type of test?
4. Review the underlying assumptions of the discovery paradigm from chapter 3, on the three paradigms. Why is statistical analysis frequently associated with claims and methods informed by this paradigm?

Try It!

1. This exercise asks you to perform a chi-square test. It can be completed by an individual, but it may be more interesting to work in a group with two or more other members. Depending on the size of your tutorial group, it may also be adapted as a tutorial exercise.

   A researcher polled 500 individuals from Western Canada and 500 individuals from Eastern Canada if they were 'for' or 'against' (two categories) the federal gun registry. Among the westerners, 100 participants were 'for', 400 were 'against', and zero had no answer. Among easterners, 300 participants were 'for', 100 were 'against', and 100 had no answer. These numbers are the observed frequencies for each group of responses.

   Using these frequencies, perform a chi-square analysis. You should be able to complete the calculations by hand, though a calculator or computer would be quite helpful. You may use Table 14.2 as a model to guide you through each step in the process. Once you have calculated the expected frequencies for each cell, calculate the chi-square statistic. If you process the data using a spreadsheet or statistical software program, the analysis will provide you with a p value associated with your statistic. What value would it have to have for your test statistic to be significant?

2. This exercise asks you to perform a t-test. It can be completed by an individual, but it may be more interesting to work in a group with two or

more other members. Depending on the size of your tutorial group, it may also be adapted as a tutorial exercise.

A researcher wishes to know whether there are significant differences between romantic partners and close friends in terms of communication frequency. The research hypothesis is $H_1: \overline{X}_1 > \overline{X}_2$. A survey produces the following data reporting the number of times per day that participants communicate with partners and friends. Using this data, calculate the t-test statistic. You should be able to complete the test by hand, but if you enter your data into a spreadsheet or statistical software program, you can determine the p value associated with your t statistic. Either way, remember to round your results to two decimal places. What are the results? Is the hypothesis supported? And if so, what does this mean? If it is not supported, what does that mean?

ROMANTIC PARTNERS X_1	CLOSE FRIENDS X_2
5	2
6	2
7	3
8	3
9	5

3. This exercise asks you to perform a simple correlation test. It can be completed by an individual, but it may be more interesting to work in a group with two or more other members. Depending on the size of your tutorial group, it may also be adapted as a tutorial exercise.

A researcher wishes to measure the degree of association between the circulation of a daily newspaper and the number of advertisements for grocery stores that appear in its pages. Ten daily newspapers

from the Golden Horseshoe region of Ontario are used for the study. Websites provide circulation figures, and a content analysis provides the number of grocery store advertisements in each paper. Both of these variables are measured with ratio scales. It is predicted that as circulation increases, the number of grocery store advertisements will increase. Using the following data, calculate a simple correlation. Then, calculate the coefficient of determination. You should be able to complete the process by hand, but you can also enter your data into a spreadsheet or statistical software program. Either way, remember to round your results to two decimal places. What are the results in terms of the magnitude, sign, and coefficient of determination? Is the hypothesis supported? If so, what does this mean? If it is not supported, what does that mean?

CIRCULATION (in 100,000s)	NUMBER OF GROCERY STORE ADVERTISEMENTS
10	11
4	6
5	2
2	5
3	1
1	3
1	2
2	8
1	7
1	5

Answers

1. Chi-square $(X^2) = 67.5$, $df = 5$, $p < .001$
2. t score $(t_{obt}) = 4.47$, $df = 8$, $p = .001$ for a one-tailed distribution
3. Coefficient of correlation $(r) = 0.50$, coefficient of determination $= 0.25$

Glossary

abstract A single paragraph of roughly 100 words that summarizes an entire research report or critical essay. It should outline the researcher's topic, method, and conclusion.

academic press A publishing company that specializes in books for an audience of trained specialists presenting new, peer-reviewed theory and research.

accounts In conversational analysis, the reasons that communicators give to justify their deviations from the rules.

action research Research that is conducted for the purpose of its practical and applied outcomes rather than for its promise to develop theory or to increase knowledge.

adequacy Occurs when a researcher has collected enough evidence to account for and understand multiple plausible interpretations.

adjacency pairs Two-part conversational structures in which the first pair part calls for or invites the second pair part.

alternate forms method A procedure to discover if there is equivalence in the research findings across different measures of the same variable.

analysis of variance (ANOVA) A statistical test that tests the effects of one or more categorical independent variables on a continuous dependent variable; also called an F test.

analytic induction *See* Inductive reasoning.

anonymity Describes the status of a research participant's identity when a researcher does not collect any information which may identify or single out that participant as a unique individual.

applied research Research that focuses on satisfying practical outcomes by solving specific problems in field settings.

appropriation The use of another culture's symbols, artefacts, gestures, rituals, or technologies by members of another culture (Rogers, 2006, p. 474).

archive A pre-existing collection of textual data or evidence, or a repository where such collections are preserved.

artefact Any object used within a group or culture that conveys some significance. Artefacts can be texts, but they can also be personal items, technologies, or elements of the landscape, among many other things.

associative claim A claim that two phenomena are in some way related, in that a change in one phenomenon is accompanied by a change in the other phenomenon. One change does not necessarily cause the other.

audit trail A record of the development and progress of a research project including the field notes from participant observation, interviews, classification schemes, drafts of data analysis at various stages, permissions/ agreements with participants, and so on.

autoethnography A form of ethnographic research in which the key informant is the researcher himself or herself.

axiom A statement about the relationship among two or more concepts, a relationship that has been demonstrated in previous research.

bar chart A visual aid for quantitative data; uses a standard chart to depict a variable measured with a nominal or ordinal scale, and the frequency of each category of the variable is represented with bars extending up from the horizontal axis.

behaviourism A school of psychology that emphasized observing, manipulating, and measuring human behaviour as empirical tests of hypotheses.

bias *See* Constant error.

bivariate relationship An association of variance between two continuous variables.

breaching In conversation analysis, the act of deviating from the principles that frame social interaction as they are understood within ethnomethodology.

carnival An approved outburst of abnormal behaviours in spaces where such behaviours are not normally tolerated.

case study A research method that provides a holistic understanding of a topic by examining a specific instance in its 'natural' setting.

categorical variable A variable that is measured at the nominal or ordinal level.

categorizing The process of grouping units of data into different categories.

causal claim A claim that predicts that a change in one phenomenon is preceded and influenced by a change in another.

Central Limits Theorem The theory that large and randomly selected samples have greater chances of approximating the true population distribution.

chi-square A statistical comparison of the actual distribution of the sample data (i.e. observed units per category) to the predicted distribution (i.e. expected units per category).

chronology The process of organizing data in the order of the events they describe, from the earliest point in time to the last.

claim The central assertion or premise of an argument. In the *research as argument* model presented in this book, a claim is a central assertion or premise that is argued in a research report or critical essay.

closed-format questions Questions that provide structured or specific response options to research participants (i.e. multiple-choice questions).

codeswitching a process that occurs when members of one speech community mix or integrate their communication rules with those of another speech community.

coding The process of reducing complex, specific observations into simple units of analysis based on themes or categories. When statistical analysis is required, these themes or categories will be coded numerically.

coding scheme A set of categories into which message units are placed.

coefficient of determination In tests of correlation, an estimate of the actual proportion of variance which two continuous variables have in common.

coherence The degree to which a researcher's interpretations of actions, events, or texts are logical, consistent, and intelligible.

cohort study A research design in which data is collected from two or more samples at two or more points in time, and treated as distinct samples to track possible differences between them over time.

collaborative ethnography A form of ethnographic research that employs more than one researcher to provide multiple viewpoints on a single setting, or on similar settings.

comment sheet A record of the researcher's impressions of an interview. It may note the emotional tone of the interview, reflections on difficulties encountered, and so on.

communal function The ways that communication is used to create and affirm shared identities among the members of a group or society.

communication code The set of rules for speaking and interpreting others' speech within a particular speech community.

communication resources The knowledge shared by members of a culture or group and used to interpret and organize their behaviours. Such resources can include communication rules.

computer-assisted interviews A data collection method in which computer software can provide greater consistency by prompting both interviewers and participants with the appropriate questions to ask at every phase of the interview.

conceptual definition A description of a concept that that details the concept's salient features for a research project. Also referred to as a 'working definition'.

confidence interval The interval of distance between various proportions of sample means and the population mean.

confidence level The percentage of sample means associated with each of the confidence intervals.

confidentiality Describes the status of a research participant's identity when the researcher does not share any identifying information about that participant in the transcripts, field notes, and written research reports.

confirmability The degree to which findings that a researcher posits, based on analysis of data, can be confirmed, or echoed by another person who had similar access to those same data sources.

constant error Bias or systematic error in the measurement of a variable. A threat to measurement validity.

construct A phenomenon that can only be observed indirectly.

constructivism A philosophy whose central premise is that there are multiple realities that are socially constructed as groups and societies assign meanings to observations.

content analysis A research method that categorizes and describes communication messages in specific contexts.

content validity A form of measurement validity. The ability of a measuring instrument to represent the full range of the variables that the researcher can observe.

contextual constraints Limitations on conversational participants' choices. Local contextual constraints may include the time and setting, or the participants' roles and goals. Global contextual constraints may include institutional frames or participant memberships in social categories or groups.

contingency questions Questions that follow filter questions. Contingency questions may or may not be answered depending on the research participants' responses to the filter questions.

continuous variable A variable measured with interval or ratio scales.

convenience sampling A nonrandom selection method in which data is selected because it is easily accessible to the researcher.

conversation Interactive discourse that usually occurs through face-to-face interaction or by telephone between two or more participants.

conversation analysis A research method that aims to describe and explain how people accomplish social actions and events by collaboratively organizing sequences of talk-in-interaction.

corrective justice The ethical principle that those who have benefited least in the past, or who have been most harmed by past practices, should be benefited most in present decisions.

correlation An association between two continuous variables, such that a change in one variable is always matched by a change in the other variable, also called 'covariance'.

correlation coefficient An estimate of the strength of the association between two continuous variables, expressed as r_{xy}, showing the degree to which two variables are systematically related to one another or covary.

counterclaim An analytical technique that prompts a researcher to disprove other interpretations that may be supported by his or her data.

covariance *See* Correlation.

critical discourse analysis (CDA) A research method that examines texts to evaluate how they construct reality and to suggest how texts and practices should be reformed.

critical empirical study A research method that draws upon empirical data to describe and evaluate a particular social situation. The researcher will be informed by his or her own ideological standards.

critical essay A manuscript based primarily on textual data sources, whether the text being analyzed is a speech, an artefact, or the researcher's experience as evidence given in support of a claim.

critical theory A philosophy that exposes the ideological structures of power and domination within society, and aims to liberate individuals to make different choices about how they participate in creating, maintaining, and changing those ideologies and structures. Developed as a critique of positivism and modernism.

cross-sectional study A research design where a sample of data collected at one point in time is used to draw inferences about the research question.

cultural resources The knowledge shared by members of a culture or group used to interpret and organize action (e.g. language, iconography, or narratives).

culture A system of shared meanings, composed of beliefs, attitudes, and practices, which are held in common by members of a group or a society.

data The evidence or grounds that support a claim.

data logging The process of recording various forms of data including field notes from participant observations, write-ups from interviews, maps, photography, sound recordings, document collections, and so on.

debriefing The process that occurs after a researcher has completed data collection. The researcher provides the participants with further information on the project's goals and progress, and provides the participants with a chance to withdraw from the study.

deconstruction An analytical process that 'unpacks' or takes apart the meaning of a text.

degree of membership The extent to which a researcher belongs to a social group that he or she is studying.

degrees of freedom When measuring a variable, the number of frequency categories that are free to vary; significant in a chi-square test.

delegated review An ethics review process that is given to proposed studies that are deemed to pose only minimal risk to participants.

demographics The general characteristics common to any group of people such as age, biological sex, socioeconomic class, level of education, and ethnicity.

dependent variable A phenomenon that has been influenced by a change in another phenomenon; sometimes called the frequency or score.

descriptive claim An assertion about how to define a particular phenomenon.

descriptive statistics Quantitative data that describes the characteristics of a sample data or an entire population.

deviant case sampling An analytical technique that prompts a researcher to select sources which are quite different from those already included in an existing sample in order to test his or her observations and analysis.

directional hypothesis In tests of group differences, a hypothesis that predicts that one group mean among two or more group means will be greater or lesser than the other(s).

direct observation A researcher's personal experience and representation of his or her sources of data, but particularly of individuals and their interactions in natural settings.

discrimination The process of grouping or categorizing objects by their differences.

discourse An 'interrelated set of texts, and the practices of their production, dissemination, and reception, that brings an object into being' (Parker, 1992, cited by Phillips & Hardy, 2002, p. 3).

discourse analysis An umbrella term for research methods that examine textual evidence. The theoretical framework for this research is rooted in social constructivist epistemology.

discrete variable A variable with categories which are genuinely unique and do not overlap.

discursive formation The language forms specific to a culture and historical time period that allow members of that culture to think about and express their knowledge.

distribution All of the values in a single set of quantitative data organized in a logical way, usually from the lowest value to the highest.

distributive justice The ethical principle that the costs and benefits of a decision should be distributed fairly.

documentary evidence Any written proof that can be supplied to support a fact (i.e. printed records from individuals, organizations or the mass media, or unpublished records preserved in public or private repositories).

ecological validity See External validity.

emic view (of culture) Occurs when a researcher privileges the ingroup members' understandings of a social situation over an outsider's understandings of the same situation, including his or her own.

empirical method Any research method that relies on measuring observations to gather quantitative or numerical data.

empirical rule The rule of distributions that approximately 68% of the sample's distribution of scores will fall within ±1 standard deviation of the sample's mean, about 95% will fall within ±2 standard deviations, and more than 99% will fall within ±3 standard deviations.

empiricism A philosophy whose central assumption emphasizes that objective reality is known through observing and explaining sensory information.

ethnographic interview A data collection method that involves informal conversations and storytelling between participants and researchers.

ethnography A research method that examines groups, organizations, or cultures that collects data through participant observation, interviews, and/or textual analysis, and that privileges the research participants' interpretations of data.

ethnography of communication A form of ethnographic research that focuses on speech communities.

ethnomethodology An umbrella term for research methods that examine ordinary daily practices.

etic view (of culture) Occurs when a researcher privileges an outsider's understanding of a social situation (perhaps his or her own) over ingroup members' understandings of the same situation.

evaluative claim A claim that establishes a set of criteria and then renders judgments about how well or how poorly a phenomenon meets those standards.

executive summary A brief overview of a research study's purpose, method, and findings. Used to publicize research to audiences who do not regularly read scholarly journals.

exhaustive categories Occur when all possible categories of a variable are available to code data as it is collected (e.g. on a questionnaire or coding schedule).

explanatory claim A claim that explains the relationships between various phenomena, often by identifying reasons or causes for these relationships.

explicit cultural knowledge The form of knowledge used by members of a group or society to interpret their experiences or to read behaviours, events, artefacts, and sites within the context of their own culture.

external validity The ability to apply conclusions from one study to another setting (as in *ecological validity*), or to other samples (sometimes called *generalizability*).

face sheet A record containing details about an interview. It may contain a code or name for the participant as well as the place, date, and time and other relevant demographic information about the interviewee.

face-to-face interview A data collection method that relies on personal contact between the interviewer and the research participant.

face validity The relevance of a measuring instrument for its intended use.

facework The use of politeness behaviours to show respect for and avoid offending other people.

faithfulness The degree to which a researcher remains steadfast in his or her commitment to conduct an important, believable study during ethnographic data collection, analysis, and reporting.

falsification principle The assumption that the null hypothesis is true until enough evidence is accumulated to reject it.

fidelity Occurs when interpretations of the evidence are coherent and help readers make sense of their own experiences (Fisher, 1987).

field setting Any site for data collection where the research topic occurs 'naturally', just as it would when research is not being conducted.

filter questions Questions that, depending on their responses, direct research participants to certain portions of a questionnaire that are most appropriate to them.

first pair part The first half of an adjacency pair.

focus group A data collection method in which a small group of research participants are interviewed, generally with a loose structure, so that a wide range of information may be collected about a particular topic; four to ten participants are considered optimal.

formula A mathematical principle used in the physical and applied sciences (e.g. $y = a + bx$).

frequency distribution A visual aid for quantitative data in which a standard chart depicts interval or ratio scores along the x-axis.

frequency polygon A visual aid for quantitative data. It depicts distributions of continuous variables on a standard chart by connecting the data points with a single line from left to right along the x-axis.

frequency table A visual aid for quantitative data. It lists the precise frequencies of all observations in clearly labelled rows and columns.

fronting A research participant's attempt to avoid telling the whole truth when being interviewed.

gaining access (or entry) The process of getting permission to conduct research in a particular setting.

gatekeeper A research participant who has power to grant or deny access to informants, documents, artefacts, or settings.

generality The ability to apply an interpretation or inference to more than one member or practice in the group or culture studied.

generalizability The ability to apply findings from one sample to other, similar situations because the sample selected adequately represents the population of interest.

generalization The process of grouping or categorizing objects by their similarities.

grounded-theory approach A research method in which the investigator builds theory by systematically and repeatedly gathering and analyzing field data during the data collection process; thus, the theory is grounded inductively in the data.

group A set of '3–12 people who interact regularly over a period of time and conceive of themselves as a social entity' (Lofland & Lofland, 1995, p. 107).

hegemony A form of power that comes from privileging one ideology over another.

hermeneutic of suspicion An analytic technique that prompts the researcher to assume that power is used illegitimately in a specific social situation.

hermeneutics The study of texts and artefacts that seeks to understand their full meaning by examining in detail the embedded historical and cultural contexts in which they were created.

hierarchical regression A form of multiple regression in which the researcher stipulates the order of variables entered into the linear equation based on theory and past research.

histogram A visual aid for quantitative data. It depicts variables measured with interval or ratio scales along the x-axis using bars extending up from the x-axis.

historical analysis A research method that seeks to understand communication and cultural issues of the past by examining them in their historical context, or to understand a contemporary issue by assessing how it developed in the past and up to the present day.

hypothesis A statement that makes specific predictions about relationships between variables.

ideal speech situation The concept of a free, accessible public discourse and equal distribution of power to all parts of society, as described by Habermas (1979).

identity performance The way that an individual performs particular roles in relation to other individuals and thereby displays his or her social identities.

ideological criticism A research method that examines the discourse that emerges from a social group united by an ideology. The researcher assesses that discourse against his or her own ideological standards.

ideology A set of ideas informed by a group or society's system of beliefs and values, which form the cultural basis for that group or society's social system.

independent variable A phenomenon presumed to be the source or cause of change in another phenomenon. It is sometimes called a 'factor'.

inferential statistics Quantitative data that allow the researcher to infer the characteristics of an entire population from the characteristics of a sample.

informant Any living individual who has some direct relationship to the topic of your study, and may have first-hand or unique knowledge of your topic. See also Key informant.

informed consent The ethical principle that all research participants must understand all of the potential risks associated with their participation and must be able to decide for themselves if they wish to participate.

instrument clarity The degree to which a measuring instrument is free from ambiguity.

interaction effect The combined influence of two or more independent variables on a dependent variable. It is measured with two-way ANOVA.

interactive discourse Discourse in which all interactants share responsibility for speaking and listening.

intercept survey A data collection method in which research participants are recruited in public places.

intercoder reliability When coding data, the percentage of coding decisions on which all coders agree; as a rule of thumb, anything over 70% constitutes an acceptable level of reliability.

internal consistency The ability of a measuring instrument's items referring to the same concept to gather similar or consistent data.

internal validity   The ability of a study to accurately test its claim.

interpretive claim   A claim that offers one or more explanations about how individuals, groups, and cultures create and interpret meanings.

interpretive community   A group of people who share rules for how to encode meanings or interpret meanings when decoding others' messages. *See also* Speech community.

interrater reliability   The degree of agreement among either researchers or research participants who categorize or score the characteristics of a single item or source of information.

intertranscriber reliability   Consistent transcription of videotaped or audiotaped conversation into a written record by two or more people.

interval level measurement   Occurs when data are reported in categories that have precise mathematical relationships to one another (e.g. arranged from least to most, or smallest to largest).

introduction   A section of a research report or critical essay that serves as the author's formal opening statement regarding the topic under study, its significance, and the author's approach to it. Usually found in the first section of the report or essay.

invention   The second move in performing deconstruction, in which the researcher disrupts the binary opposite under study by introducing a new concept that was not previously perceptible.

inversion   The first move in performing deconstruction, in which the researcher attempts to show how one half of a binary opposite has been privileged over the other half.

item response rate   The percentage of all items on each individual survey that were completed.

key informant   An individual who is a member of the group, organization, or culture under study and who is either highly articulate or especially helpful and wise, relative to other participants in that setting (Lofland & Lofland, 1995).

knowing by authority   Believing something is true because someone regarded as an expert thinks it is true.

knowing by criticism   The method of knowing by increasing our awareness of the ways in which society or the dominant group constructs our realities, primarily through the processes of privilege and oppression.

knowing by discovery   The method of knowing by discovering objective reality through precise, systematic, and repetitive observations of communication phenomena.

knowing by interpretation   The method of knowing by understanding multiple interpretations people attach to their subjective experiences of the world.

knowing by tenacity   Customary knowledge or believing something is true because it is commonly held to be true.

knowing on *a priori* grounds   Intuitive knowledge; believing something is true based on standards of reasonableness derived from logic, aesthetics, or moral codes.

laboratory setting   Any sites for data collection that are selected and controlled by the researcher.

language and social interaction   An umbrella term for research methods that examine speech, language, gestures and communication competence, conversation analysis, ethnography, and ethnomethodological work.

latent content   The meanings that become apparent with careful analysis and synthesis of messages.

law   An immutable, physical law of nature (e.g. gravity).

leading questions   Questions that direct research participants to answer in a specific way and are considered an adverse effect during data collection.

liberation   The social process of overcoming oppression and gaining equal rights.

Likert scale   An interval scale that allows research participants to indicate varying levels of responses to questions. Typically, the scale asks for varying levels of agreement (i.e. Strongly Agree, Agree, Neutral, Disagree, Strongly Disagree) or frequency (e.g. Always, Sometimes, Never).

linear relationship   A simple association between two continuous variables where they change together proportionately in the same or opposite directions.

literature review   A review of the existing published works that are most closely related to a research topic, or that component of a research report or critical essay that presents the findings from a researcher's review of the literature. It is usually included after the introduction as the second component of a paper or essay.

logical positivism   A philosophy that combines deductive logic with empirical observations to test causal predictions about phenomena.

longitudinal study   A research design that collects data at several points in time to observe possible changes through time.

macroethnography   A form of ethnographic research that examines a defined community or culture, sometimes involving numerous researchers over a period of years.

magnitude   The size or strength of the correlation coefficient.

main effect   The change in a dependent variable that is directly attributable to each separate factor or independent variable.

manifest content   The overt, surface-level meanings of messages.

market research A form of survey research designed to assess consumer desires and preferences and that is often used to create advertising and other marketing materials.

mean Arithmetic average of the value of variables in a sample distribution. It is used as a measure of central tendency.

measures of central tendency Descriptive statistics that reduce a distribution to one number that best characterizes the entire sample (i.e. mean, median, or mode).

measures of dispersion Assessments of how much variation in scores is present in a sample distribution (i.e. range, variance, and standard deviation).

measures of shape Assessments of how much variation is present between a sample and the normal curve; variation indicates the presence of error in a sample distribution.

median The midpoint score in a distribution. It is used as a measure of central tendency.

member checks A procedure in which research participants review, and perhaps verify, research materials developed through observation, interviews, and other means.

message population A well-defined set of messages pertinent to a given research question or hypothesis.

microethnography A form of ethnographic research that examines a single, well-defined social situation and is generally conducted by one researcher in a short time span.

minimal risk The level of risk posed by a research project when the possible harms implied by participation are no greater than those encountered in everyday activities relevant to the research.

mode The most frequently occurring score in a distribution. It is used as a measure of central tendency.

modernism A philosophy that stresses theoretical knowledge based on reasoned action and the technological means for achieving it.

mortality A confounding effect on longitudinal research designs, due to the loss of research participants over time as they withdraw or die. This affects the total change measured through the study.

multidimensional variable A variable that has several distinct aspects that can be measured.

multimodality A concept that describes all the different modes of representation which are active in a given cultural context. It includes modes of representation in written and spoken language, and the material forms in which that language is realized.

multiple-factors ANOVA A form of ANOVA that tests group differences for the effects of more than one independent categorical variable on a dependent continuous variable. It is also called MANOVA.

multiple regression analysis A form of regression analysis that tests the relationship between a set of continuous independent variables (also known as predictors) and a continuous dependent variable (also called the criterion).

multiple-sample chi-square A form of chi-square that tests the relationship between the frequencies of two or more categorical variables that are independent from one another.

multivariate relationship An association of variance between three or more continuous variables.

mutually exclusive categories Occurs when categories prompt each piece of data to be placed in one and only one category.

narrative As a primary document, a narrative is a story recounting symbolic acts that have significant meanings for the individual, group, or society who produces it (e.g. a myth, an origin story, a work of fiction). As an analytical technique, a narrative is a richly described chronology in which the researcher argues (usually implicitly) that distinct events are linked in logical ways.

narrative discourse Discourse in which one participant has greater responsibility for speaking than do other participants.

naturalism principle A professed adherence to studying people in their everyday lives as played out in their natural settings.

naturalistic inquiry A data collection method that emphasizes the study of human behaviour in specific contexts.

negative case analysis A researcher's conscientious search for counterexamples that may disprove his or her claim.

negative correlation An association between two continuous variables where the change in one variable is accompanied by an inverse change in the other (i.e. as one variable increases, the other variable decreases).

network analysis A research design that aims to describe and explain communication processes and structures within a group or organization by collecting data about relationships among people, symbols, or groups.

network sampling A nonrandom selection method in which the research participants are asked to solicit additional participants (perhaps with similar characteristics). It is also called snowball sampling.

noise *See* Random error.

nominal level measurement Occurs when data are reported in unordered categories; the categories may be coded with numbers assigned in an arbitrary fashion.

nondirectional hypothesis In tests of group differences, a hypothesis that predicts that two or more group means will be different but does not predict which one will be greater.

nonparametric tests Statistical tests where all of the variables are categorical (i.e. measured with nominal or ordinal scales) from which no assumptions about populations can be made.

nonrandom selection method A procedure that relies on a justifiable selection of specific data that will represent a population.

normal curve Presumed shape of many continuously measured variables when there is little error present and that provide accurate and reliable estimates of the population parameters; also called a bell curve.

null hypothesis A claim that asserts the logical opposite of the research hypothesis. In statistical analyses, a prediction that there is no relationship between two or more variables.

one-tailed test A statistical test that uses critical rejection regions under only one tail of the normal curve.

open-ended questions Questions that ask research participants to provide unstructured or spontaneous answers or to discuss an identified topic.

operational definition A description of a construct that details every operation, procedure, and instrument needed to measure it.

operationalization The process of specifying the operations, procedures, or instruments used to measure a concept as a variable.

oral history A data collection method that relies upon informants to supply data about individuals, events, or cultures in the recent past (i.e. within the lifetime of the informants).

order effects The adverse effects created during data collection when, during an interview or survey, earlier questions influence the way that research participants respond to later questions.

ordinal level measurement Occurs when data are reported in approximate, rank-ordered categories. The categories may be coded with numbers giving some estimate of a variable's amount, magnitude, or value.

organismic variable A variable that represents organic or natural differences in the characteristics of the concept being measured.

other-report A research participant's perceptions about other people's behaviour, beliefs, and/or characteristics.

outliers Scores that are above or below three standard deviations from the mean score in a sample distribution.

paired *t*-test A statistical test of group differences between an independent variable with two groups that are related or matched in some way and a continuous dependent variable; for example, between pre-test and post-test scores for the same group of participants.

panel study A research design in which data is collected from the same sample over time.

paradigm A way of knowing about communication and culture that is informed by a set of interrelated assumptions about the nature of theory and purpose of research.

parameters The characteristics of a population expressed in quantitative data.

parametric tests Statistical tests where at least one variable is continuous, allowing assumptions to be made about the way populations are distributed.

parodic rhetoric Discourse which is intended to undermine accepted norms of belief and behaviour, usually by noting how ridiculous, hypocritical, or simply incorrect those beliefs and behaviours are, following Bakhtin (1981).

parsimony The combination of precision and power in a research definition, measurement, or finding.

participant observation A data collection method that involves watching and learning about research participants while the researcher participates in their daily activities.

performance ethnography A form of ethnographic research that uses performative writing and public performances of participants' cultural meanings to evaluate those meanings and to expose oppression and injustice.

periodicity Any recurring pattern or arrangement that exists naturally in a sample frame.

personal significance The reasons that a certain topic is uniquely important to the researcher who conducts it.

phenomenology The study of or understanding of our subjective experiences through our conscious attention to these experiences as we live them.

pie chart A visual aid for quantitative data that uses a circle to depict a variable measured with a nominal or ordinal scale. The circle is divided into proportions representing the frequency of each category in the variable.

plagiarism The act of representing another person's words, ideas, or work as your own.

polemic rhetoric A discourse intended to reinforce accepted norms of belief and behaviour within a society, following Bakhtin (1981).

policy analysis A research method that assesses the implications of a new policy, or judges the performance of a current or past policy.

political polling research A form of survey research designed to assess political opinions and attitudes. It is often used to predict voter preferences.

politics of representation The issue of who has a right to name, or to assign meaning to actions, events, texts, or experiences.

popular press   Periodicals publishing news and fiction relevant to the general public, largely without regard to the audiences' occupations or level of education (e.g. newspapers, magazines).

population   The entire set of cases or instances that the researcher is attempting to represent with a data sample. *See also* Survey population and Target population.

population distribution   The entire set of data from which a sample is drawn.

positive correlation   An association between continuous variables that are changing together proportionately and in the same direction (i.e. the variables increase or decrease together).

postcolonialism   A perspective associated with the critical paradigm that claims the Western countries of the 'first world' culturally and racially oppress peoples of the 'third world' through their constructions and representations of third world countries.

postmodernism   A perspective associated with the critical paradigm that claims that all knowledge is discursively formed and historically situated, and that there is no objective reality or organizing structure outside of language. It is a critique of modernism.

postmodern turn   A general movement away from social structure as the explanatory means of domination, toward ideology, representation, and discourse as the sites of struggle for social power.

postpositivism   A perspective associated with the discovery paradigm that argues that human thought may be fallible but that human reason should aspire to map and understand objective reality. It responds to critiques of positivism and logical positivism.

poststructuralism   A perspective associated with the critical paradigm that denies that there is any foundational structure for language, discourse, and society. It is a critique of rationalism and structuralism.

power   The scope and applicability of a definition, measurement, or finding.

precise observation   A research practice in which observations are made carefully for the sake of accuracy.

precision   The detailed and accurate definitions and measurements of communication variables valued in discovery research.

preferred course of action   In conversation analysis, an analytical technique that makes sense of conversational behaviour based on an existing rule or contextual standard for behaviour.

primary source   Any individual, text, or artefact that supplies first-hand, direct, or unmediated facts about the behaviours you wish to study. It may include original research reports or critical essays, written by the researcher, which describe the data and warrants for the study.

principle   A formal guideline within society such as government statutes and regulations.

procedural justice   The principle that a process should be fair, even if some people will benefit more from the outcome of that process than others.

professional association   A dues-paying group of academic, business, or industry practitioners in a particular field of study.

proposition   A statement that predicts what relationships are likely among two or more concepts, given what we already know.

purposive sampling   A nonrandom selection method in which data are selected to test a claim within a specific context.

questioning sources   An analytical technique that assesses the trustworthiness of the data provided by sources. It considers the author, his or her motives, and the original, intended audience for the data.

questionnaire   A data collection instrument for surveys that lists all questions relevant to the study.

questionnaire architecture   The general structure of a questionnaire, outlining its length, comprehensibility, and question order.

quota sampling   A nonrandom selection method for small, well-defined populations in which key population characteristics are proportionally represented in the data sample.

random digit dialing   A random selection method for telephone surveys. The researcher first randomly identifies areas of a region to be sampled with their corresponding area codes and exchanges, and then randomly generates the last four digits of the telephone number.

random error   Measurement error that constitutes noise or interference with the variable's true values. It is a threat to reliability.

random selection method   A procedure that uses some element of chance to select sample data that will represent a population.

range   A measure of dispersion in a sample distribution, obtained by subtracting the lowest score from the highest score.

rapport   A sense of comfort and trust between a researcher and his or her research participant.

ratio level measurement   Occurs when data are reported in precise, ordered categories that have a mathematical relationship to one another and that have a true zero point (i.e. it is possible to observe the absence of the thing being measured).

rationalism A philosophy stressing reliance on the logical processes of the mind for discovery of an objective reality.

realism principle A professed adherence to the importance of accurately distinguishing objective reality from the subjective perspective of the perceiver.

reference list A section of a research report or critical essay that contains the full citations for all the works cited in the manuscript. It appears at the end of the report or essay, and is sometimes titled 'Works Cited'.

reflexivity A process by which researchers recognize that they are inseparable from the settings, contexts, and cultures they are attempting to understand and represent. It is sometimes called *self-reflexivity*.

reformist claim A claim that identifies the negative consequences of an existing phenomenon and advocates for its change.

regression analysis A statistical test of association between continuous variables where one or more independent variables (also known as predictors) are used to assess the values of the dependent variable (also known as the criterion).

regression weights In the formula for linear regression ($Y = a + bX$), the weights are a and b, where a is the intercept (the point at which the line intersects the vertical y-axis) and b is the slope of the line; b estimates how much change should occur in Y based on a unit of change in X. Also called Beta coefficients.

relational dialectic An analytical technique that prompts a researcher to examine the tension between two competing and perhaps contradictory goals of two or more individuals, groups, or concepts in a relationship.

relevance The degree to which interpretations are meaningful or germane to the people in the group or culture being studied.

reliability A consistency in research observations over time, across settings, subjects, and instruments.

repair In conversation analysis, the work done by interlocutors to fix disruptions in interaction.

repetitive observation A research practice in which observations are repeated in various ways for the purpose of verification.

representative sample A sample whose characteristics are good estimates (i.e. valid and reliable estimates) of the population characteristics.

research design The logical sequence used to connect a researcher's claim, data or evidence, warrants, and background reasoning.

researcher constructed variable A variable that has been defined in measurable ways for the purpose of conducting research, usually according to a theoretical framework.

researcher credibility An umbrella term used in field research to cover a number of concerns, including authenticity, training, and experience.

researcher positionality The researcher's standpoint and reflexivity in relation to his or her research topic.

Research Ethics Board (REB) A university committee responsible for the implementation of TCPS standards in all research conducted at the university that involves human research participants. Every Canadian university must have such a committee.

research library A repository that collects and maintains scholarly books, journals, and related materials on topics of advanced interest to specialized audiences.

research question A question that asks how a concept can be classified or that asks what relationship exists between specific variables selected by the researcher.

research report Written summary of a research project that includes some form of data collection from self-reports, other-reports, or observations, or from a combination of those sources, perhaps with textual data as well.

resistant reading An analytical technique that assesses the trustworthiness of the data provided by a source. It identifies the author's perspective and then considers the data from an alternative perspective, usually an opposing perspective.

rich description A description of data or evidence that addresses every aspect of a social situation, text, or artefact.

rule An informal guideline that any individual living in our society would be likely to accept as a basis for some action.

sample A subset or smaller grouping of members from a population.

sample distribution The actual data set the researcher obtains when conducting the study; a small portion, or subset, of the population distribution.

sampling The process of selecting a relatively small number of cases to represent some larger group of cases or instances of phenomena.

sampling distribution An expected, hypothetical distribution of all possible values of any sample statistic from any given population, specifying the probable score associated with each value.

sampling error The standard deviation of a sampling distribution; that is, an estimate of the deviation between a sample statistic and a population parameter. Also known as 'standard error'.

sample frame   A list of all members of the population to be researched.

scholarly journal   A periodical published in a given discipline or field which presents new, peer-reviewed theory and research to a community of scholars with similar interests.

scientific method   A process that tests claims for reasonableness through observation of empirical data, systematic analysis, and logical consistency combined with experience.

scorer reliability   The consistency of two or more researchers' judgments about their observations whenever they are working together on a single project.

secondary source   Any individual, text, or artefact that supplies second-hand, indirect, or mediated facts about the behaviour you wish to study. Such a source may be one scholar's summary and interpretations of another scholar's original research, as appears in a textbook.

second pair part   The second half of an adjacency pair.

self-reflexivity   *See* Reflexivity.

self-report   A research participant's perceptions about his or her own behaviours, beliefs, and/or characteristics.

semantic differential scale   A scale consisting of a series of bipolar adjectives placed at either end of a continuum usually found in survey research. The adjectives act as anchors for extreme responses, and participants indicate where along the continuum between the extremes their perceptions lie.

semiotics   The study of signs and their social significance.

semi-structured interview   An interview format having general, open-ended questions to guide discussion.

sequence organization   'The ways in which turns-at-talk are ordered and combined to make actions take place in conversation, such as requests, offers, complaints, and announcements' (Schegloff, 2006, p. 1).

setting   The location where data are gathered or found.

simple random sampling   A random selection method in which each person (or text) in the population has an equal chance of being selected for inclusion in a study.

single-factor ANOVA   A form of ANOVA that tests the effects of one independent variable with more than two categories on one dependent continuous variable.

single-sample chi-square   A form of chi-square that tests the difference between expected frequencies and obtained frequencies for one categorical variable.

skew   When using a visual aid for quantitative data, the presence of a horizontal shift in the majority of scores either to the right or left of the distribution's centre.

snowball sampling   *See* Network sampling.

social significance   The reasons that a certain topic of study is important to a particular group of people, usually because of an existing problem or injustice.

source   Any individual, text, or artefact that supplies data or evidence which is relevant to your research.

special collections library   A repository that collects and maintains rare publications in their original formats. Such publications are rare because very few copies were made or very few have been preserved.

speech community   A group of people who share rules for using and interpreting speech.

sponsor   A research participant who helps a researcher to establish credibility with other participants, to identify key informants, to arrange interviews, and so on.

spurious correlation   An apparent association between two continuous variables that are not actually related in any way.

standard deviation   A measure of dispersion. It is the most accurate indicator of the total amount of variation within a given sample distribution, obtained by taking the square root of the variance.

standard error   The standard deviation of a sampling distribution. That is, an estimate of the sample mean's probable deviation from the true population mean. *See also* Sampling error.

standpoint   The material, social, and symbolic circumstances of a social group that shape group experience, and by extension how group members think, act, and feel (following Wood, 1997, p. 384).

statistical analysis   'The science of describing and reasoning from numerical data' (Smith, 1988, p. 93).

statistics   The characteristics of any source of information, or a sample taken from it, expressed in numbers, or quantitative data.

status differential   A situation in which one party to an agreement has more power or resources than the other(s).

stepwise regression   A form of regression analysis in which researchers instruct the computer to try various combinations of independent variables until it finds the 'best fit' equation to explain the variation in the dependent variable.

stratified sampling   A random selection method in which the population is first divided into relevant subgroups so that each person or message within each subgroup has an equal chance of being selected for the data sample.

structuralism   A philosophy whose goal is the discovery of embedded rules or laws, forming a permanent structure, that shape human language, communication, and culture.

structure   A theoretical concept describing a fundamental aspect of society that shapes the most significant beliefs, attitudes, and practices associated with human interaction. Depending on the theorist, a structure may be physiological (i.e. as found in certain forms of feminist criticism), psychological (i.e. psychoanalytic claims), cultural (i.e. linguistic theory), or economic (i.e. Marxist philosophy).

structured interview An interview format having protocols or schedules that dictate what questions to ask when.

subjectivity Our human ability to know using our minds, based on our thoughts and feelings.

sums of squares between groups In tests of difference, an estimate of the difference between group means.

sums of squares within groups In tests of difference, an estimate of chance variation, or the sampling error.

symbolic interactionism A school of sociology emphasizing how people construct and interpret the meaning of their experiences in everyday interaction.

systematic observation A research practice in which observations are derived from clear, known procedures.

systematic sampling with a random start A random selection method in which the researcher selects the first element from a sampling frame by chance and thereafter selects each next element systematically (i.e. by selecting each xth element).

tacit cultural knowledge The form of knowledge used by members of a group or society to engage in behaviours that are deemed acceptable or appropriated within the context of their own culture.

target population The complete set of population members forming an 'ideal' population.

taxonomy A categorizing scheme for identifying phenomena that are related theoretically or conceptually.

telephone survey A data collection method in which interviews are conducted by telephone.

test-retest method A procedure to discover if there is equivalence across multiple administrations of the same measure in the same group of subjects.

text Any written or spoken words, performances, and visual symbols used as evidence to support a research claim.

textual analysis Any of several methodologies and techniques, such as discourse analysis or resistant reading, which systematically explore written or spoken words, performances, and visual imagery to be used as evidence in support of research claims.

theoretical saturation The point in data collection when any new data adds little that is new or useful to the explanation or categories that have already been generated.

theoretical significance The reasons that a certain topic of study is important, usually pertaining to the development of a new theory, or the revision of an existing theory by testing its premises.

theory A set of logically consistent statements that describe or explain how a specific thing works, what a specific thing means, or how things ought to work or be interpreted differently.

thesis A declarative sentence found in a research report or critical essay that outlines the researcher's goal for the study. Generally, the researcher's goal is to establish the truth or viability of a particular assertion about the topic.

time line A simplified chronology that provides a visual representation of how events are related in time. It is usually constructed by locating events along a line with important dates marked along its length.

total response rate The percentage of all surveys distributed to potential research participants that were successfully completed and collected for analysis.

trade journal A periodical publishing news relevant to the practitioners in a particular business or industry (e.g. *Playback,* a periodical for the Canadian film and television production industry).

transcription The process of converting audio or video recordings into verbatim textual form, or the actual, verbatim record once the conversion is complete.

transcription veracity The degree of correspondence between the interactions documented by an audio or video recording and the textual transcription made from that recording.

transferability The ability to apply confirmable, relevant insights from one study to other participants, texts, or settings.

trend study A research design in which data is collected from several different representative samples from the same population at different points in time to observe trends.

triangulation The use of several different kinds of evidence to support a research claim.

Tri-Council Policy Statement (TCPS) A formal set of ethical guidelines governing all university research in Canada that involves human research participants.

t-test A statistical test of the effects of one categorical independent variable with two groups or samples on a continuous dependent variable.

turn-allocation unit (TAU) In conversation analysis, a unit of analysis that specifies who gets to speak and when.

turn construction unit (TCU) In conversation analysis, a unit of analysis that specifies what counts as a speaking turn.

two-tailed test A statistical test that uses critical rejection regions under both tails of the normal curve.

type I error An incorrect decision to reject the null hypothesis; that is, identifying a significant difference or relationship in the sample data when no difference or relationship exists in the population.

type II error A failure to reject the null hypothesis when it should have been rejected; that is, overlooking a significant difference or relationship that probably does exist in the population.

unidimensional variable A variable that cannot be broken down into distinct aspects for measurement.

unitizing The process of dividing texts into distinct units of analysis.

unit of analysis The basic element, or part of a thing, to be analyzed.

universal pragmatics Habermas's (1979) theory of social interaction, which describes society as a mix of technical, practical, and emancipatory interests that can be addressed using different speech acts and types of discourses.

unpublished document Any text which has never been formally published or which has not had wide, popular circulation.

unstructured interview An interview format with no pre-specified questions. It relies entirely on the research participants to identify events and experiences that seem significant and meaningful.

U-shaped correlation A curvilinear relationship expressing patterns between continuous variables that change in direction at several points across time, first by decreasing together, then flattening out, and finally by increasing together.

utilitarian ethics An approach to ethical behaviour based on creating the greatest good for the greatest number of people, and for the right of researchers to exercise individual freedoms, so long as no harm is done to another person.

validity Accuracy of measurement, and/or accuracy of applying conclusions from one study to other settings, persons, or situations.

variable A concept with a set of measurable characteristics.

variance A measure of dispersion, obtained by summing the squared deviations of all scores in a distribution, and dividing by one less than the total number of scores (for a sample) or by the total number of scores (for a population).

voice The right to express one's own view, choice, wish, or opinion.

warrant A standard for evaluating the value of the data or evidence provided to support a claim.

x-axis The horizontal axis on a standard graph.

y-axis The vertical axis on a standard graph.

zero-order correlation The simplest test of a linear relationship between two continuously measured variables. Also known as Pearson's product-moment coefficient of correlation.

References

Abel, S. (1995). The rabbit in drag: Camp and gender construction in the American animated cartoon. *Journal of Popular Culture, 29,* 183–202.

Abelman, R., & Atkin, D. (2000). What children watch when they watch TV: Putting theory into practice. *Journal of Broadcasting & Electronic Media, 44,* 143–154.

Abelson, R. P. (1995). *Statistics as principled argument.* Hillsdale, NJ: Lawrence Erlbaum.

Adams, G. R., & Schvaneveldt, J. D. (1991). *Understanding research methods* (2nd ed.). White Plains, NY: Longman.

Adelman, M. B., & Frey, L. R. (1994). The pilgrim must embark: Creating and sustaining community in a residential facility for people with AIDS. In L. R. Frey (Ed.), *Group communication in context: Studies of natural groups* (pp. 3–21). Hillsdale, NJ: Lawrence Erlbaum.

Adelman, R. D., Greene, M. G., Charon, R., & Friedmann, E. (1992). The content of physician and elderly patient interaction in the primary care encounter. *Communication Research, 19,* 370–380.

Adler, P. A., Adler, P., & Fontana, A. (1987). Everyday life sociology. *Annual Review of Sociology, 13,* 217–235.

Afifi, T. D., & Olson, L. (2005). The chilling effect in families and the pressure to conceal secrets. *Communication Monographs, 72,* 192–216.

Agar, M. H. (1983). Ethnographic evidence. *Urban Life, 12,* 32–48.

Ahmad, H. M. (2008). War in Iraq: Comparative coverage of *The Toronto Star* and *The New York Times. Canadian Journal of Media Studies, 3,* 33–56.

Alcoff, L. M. (1995). The problem of speaking for others. In J. Roof & R. Weigman (Eds.), *Who can speak? Authority and critical identity* (pp. 97–119). Urbana, IL: University of Illinois Press.

Alexander, B. K. (2003). Fading, twisting, and weaving: An interpretive ethnography of the Black barbershop as a cultural space. *Qualitative Inquiry, 9,* 105–129.

Allen, B. J. (1996). Feminist standpoint theory: A black woman's (re)-view of organizational socialization. *Communication Studies, 47,* 257–271.

Almeida, E. P. (2004). A discourse analysis of student perceptions of their communication competence. *Communication Education, 53,* 357–364.

Amason, P., Allen, M. W., & Holmes, S. A. (1999). Social support and acculturative stress in the multicultural workplace. *Journal of Applied Communication Research, 27,* 310–334.

American Psychological Association. (2001). *Publication manual of the American Psychological Association* (5th ed.). Washington, DC: Author.

Amidon, P. (1971). Nonverbal interaction analysis coding system. In *Nonverbal interaction analysis* (chapter 4). Minneapolis, MN: Paul S. Amidon & Associates, Inc.

Anastasi, A. (1976). *Psychological testing* (4th ed.). New York, NY: MacMillan.

Andersen, K. E. (2000). Developments in communication ethics: The ethics commission, code of professional responsibilities, credo for ethical communication. *Journal of the Association for Communication Administration, 29,* 131–144.

Anderson, C. M. (2001). Communication in the medical interview team: An analysis of patients' stories in the United States and Hong Kong. *The Howard Journal of Communication, 12,* 61–72.

Anderson, C. M., Martin, M. M., & Zhong, M. (1998). Motives for communicating with family and friends: A Chinese study. *Howard Journal of Communications, 9,* 109–122.

Anderson, J. A. (1987). *Communication research: Issues and methods.* New York, NY: McGraw-Hill.

Andrews, J. R., Leff, M., & Terrill, R. (1998). *Reading rhetorical texts: An introduction to criticism.* Boston, MA: Houghton Mifflin.

Andsager, J., & Smiley, L. (1998). Evaluating the public information: Shaping news coverage of the silicone implant controversy. *Public Relations Review, 24,* 183–201.

Ang, I. (1990). Culture and communication: Towards an ethnographic critique of media consumption in the transnational media system. *European Journal of Communication, 5,* 239–260.

Anzaldua, G. (1987). *Borderlands/La frontera: The new mestiza.* San Francisco, CA: Spinsters/Aunt Lute.

Aoki, E. (2000). Mexican-American ethnicity in Biola, CA: An ethnographic account of hard work, family, and religion. *Howard Journal of Communications, 11,* 207–227.

Ashcraft, K. L., & Mumby, D. K. (2004). Organizing a critical communicology of gender and work. *International Journal of the Sociology of Language, 166*, 19–43.

Ashcraft, K. L., & Pacanowsky, M. E. (1996). A woman's worst enemy: Reflections on a narrative of organizational life and female identity. *Journal of Applied Communication Research, 24*, 217–239.

Atkin, C. K., Smith, S. W., Roberto, A. J., Fediuk, T., & Wagner, T. (2002). Correlates of verbally aggressive communication in adolescents. *Journal of Applied Communication Research, 30*, 251–268.

Atkinson, J. M., & Drew, P. (1979). *Order in the court: The organization of verbal interaction in judicial settings.* London, UK: Macmillan.

Atkinson, J. M., & Heritage, J. (Eds.). (1984). *Structures of social action: Studies in conversation analysis.* Cambridge, UK: Cambridge University Press.

Ayres, J., & Heuett, B. L. (2000). An examination of the long term effect of performance visualization. *Communication Research Reports, 17*, 229–236.

Babbie, E. (1995). *The practice of social research* (7th ed.). Belmont, CA: Wadsworth.

Babbie, E. (2001). *The practice of social research* (9th ed.). Belmont, CA: Wadsworth.

Babe, R. E. (1990). *Telecommunications in Canada: Technology, industry and government.* Toronto, ON: University of Toronto Press.

Babe, R. E. (2000). *Canadian communication thought: Ten foundational writers.* Toronto, ON: University of Toronto Press.

Backhouse, C. (1999). *Colour-coded: A legal history of racism in Canada, 1900–1950.* Toronto, ON: University of Toronto Press.

Bakhtin, M. M. (1981). Forms of time and chronotope in the novel (C. Emerson, Trans.). In M. Holquist (Ed.), *The dialogic imagination: Four essays* (pp. 84–258). Austin, TX: University of Texas Press.

Bakhtin, M. M. (1984a). *Problems of Dostoevsky's poetics* (C. Emerson, Trans. & Ed.). Minneapolis, MN: University of Minnesota Press.

Bakhtin, M. M. (1984b). *Rabelais and his world* (H. Iswolsky, Trans.). Bloomington, IN: Indiana University Press.

Bakhtin, M. M. (1987). *Speech genres and other late essays* (V.W. McGee, Trans., & C. Emerson & M. Holquist, Eds.). Austin, TX: University of Texas Press.

Bales, R. F. (1950). *Interaction process analysis: A method for the study of small groups.* Reading, MA: Addison-Wesley.

Balka, E., Rodje, K., & Bush, C.G. (2007). Rose-coloured glasses: The discourse on information technology in the Romanow Report. *Canadian Journal of Communication, 32*, 475–494.

Barber, M. (2008). Getting the picture: Airtime and lineup bias on Canadian networks during the 2006 federal election. *Canadian Journal of Communication, 33*, 621–637.

Barber, M., & Rauhala, A. (2005). Demographics and political leanings of television decision makers. *Canadian Journal of Communication, 30*, 281–292.

Barge, J. K. (2004). Reflexivity and managerial practice. *Communication Monographs, 71*, 70–96.

Barnhurst, K. G. (2003). The makers of meaning: National Public Radio and the new long journalism, 1980–2000. *Political Communication, 20*, 1–22.

Barrett, M. S., Bornsen, S. E., Erickson, S. L., Markey, V., & Spiering, K. (2005). The personal response system as a teaching aid. *Communication Teacher, 19*, 89–92.

Bastien, D. T., & Hostager, T. J. (1992). Cooperation as a communicative accomplishment: A symbolic interaction analysis of an improvised jazz concert. *Communication Studies, 43*, 92–104.

Bauder, H. (2010). Dialectics of media practice. *Canadian Journal of Media Studies, 6*, 1–27.

Baum, L. F. (1900). *The wonderful wizard of Oz.* Chicago, IL: George M. Hill.

Bavelas, J. B., Black, A., Chovil, N., Lemery, C. R., & Mullett, J. (1988). Form and function in motor mimicry: Topographic evidence that the primary function is communicative. *Human Communication Research, 14*, 275–300.

Baxter, J. (2002). Competing discourses in the classroom: A post-structuralist discourse analysis of girls' and boys' speech in public contexts. *Discourse & Society, 13*, 827–842.

Baxter, L. A., & Goldsmith, D. (1990). Cultural terms for communication events among some American high school adolescents. *Western Journal of Speech Communication, 54*, 377–394.

Baxter, L. A., & Montgomery, B. M. (1998). A guide to dialectical approaches to studying personal relationships. In B. M. Montgomery & L. A. Baxter (Eds.), *Dialectical approaches to studying personal relationships* (pp. 1–15). Mahwah, NJ: Lawrence Erlbaum.

Baxter-Moore, N. (2010). The music store as a community resource. In J. Nicks & B. K. Grant (Eds.), *Covering Niagara: Studies in local popular culture* (pp. 237–261). Waterloo, ON: Wilfrid Laurier University Press.

Beach, W. A. (1989a). Orienting to the phenomenon. In J. A. Anderson (Ed.), *Communication Yearbook* (Vol. 13, pp. 216–234). Newbury Park, CA: Sage.

Beach, W. A. (1989b). Sequential organization of conversational activities. *Western Journal of Speech Communication, 53*, 85–246.

Beach, W. A., & Good, J. S. (2004). Uncertain family trajectories: Interactional consequences of cancer diagnosis, treatment, and prognosis. *Journal of Social & Personal Relationships, 21,* 8–32.

Beasley, B., & Standley, T. C. (2002). Shirts vs. skins: Clothing as an indicator of gender role stereotyping in video games. *Mass Communication & Society, 5,* 279–293.

Beck, C. (1996). 'I've got some points I'd like to make here': The achievement of social face through turn management during the 1992 vice presidential debate. *Political Communication, 13,* 165–180.

Behnke, R. R., & Sawyer, C. R. (1999). Public speaking procrastination as a correlate of public speaking communication apprehension and self-perceived public speaking competence. *Communication Research Reports, 16,* 40–47.

Behnke, R. R., & Sawyer, C. R. (2000). Anticipatory anxiety patterns for male and female public speakers. *Communication Education, 49,* 187–195.

Benjamin, J. R. (1991). *A Student's Guide to History* (5th ed.). New York, NY: St. Martin's Press.

Benoit, W. L. (2003). Presidential campaign discourse as a causal factor in election outcome. *Western Journal of Communication, 67,* 97–112.

Bereleson, B. (1952). *Content analysis in communication research.* New York, NY: Hafner.

Berger, A. A. (1998). *Media research techniques* (2nd ed.). Thousand Oaks, CA: Sage.

Berger, C. (1986). *The writing of Canadian history: Aspects of English-Canadian historical writing since 1900* (2nd ed.). Toronto, ON: University of Toronto Press.

Berger, C. R., & Calabrese, R. J. (1975). Some explorations in initial interaction and beyond: Toward a developmental theory of interpersonal communication. *Human Communication Research, 1,* 99–112.

Berger, P., & Luckmann, T. (1967). *The social construction of reality.* London, UK: Allen Lane.

Bernard, H., & Kilworth, P. (1977). Informant accuracy in social network data II. *Human Communication Research, 4,* 3–18.

Bernard, H., Kilworth, P., & Sailer, L. (1980). Informant accuracy in social network data IV: A comparison of clique-level structure in behavioral and cognitive network data. *Social Networks, 2,* 191–218.

Bernard, H., Kilworth, P., & Sailer, L. (1982). Informant accuracy in social network data V: An experimental attempt to predict actual communication from recall data. *Social Science Research, 11,* 30–66.

Bernstein, M. A. (1981). When the carnival turns bitter: Preliminary reflections upon the abject hero. In G. S. Morson (Ed.), *Bakhtin: Essays and dialogues on his work* (pp. 99–121). Chicago, IL: The University of Chicago Press.

Berry, J. (1990). Psychology of acculturation: Understanding individuals moving between cultures. In R. Brislin (Ed.), *Applied cross-cultural psychology* (pp. 232–253). Newbury Park, CA: Sage.

Berry, M., & Gray, T. (1999). Cutting film violence: Effects of perceptions, enjoyment, and arousal. *Journal of Social Psychology, 139,* 567–583.

Bevan, J. L., Stetzenback, K. A., Batson, E., & Bullo, K. (2006). Factors associated with general partner and relational uncertainty within early adulthood sibling relationships. *Communication Quarterly, 54,* 367–381.

Bhabha, H. K. (1990). The Other question: Difference, discrimination, and the discourse of colonialism. In R. Ferguson, M. Gever, T. T. Minh-Ha, & C. West (Eds.), *Out there: Marginalization and contemporary culture* (pp. 71–88). Cambridge, MA: MIT Press.

Bhabha, H. K. (1995). Cultural diversity and cultural differences. In B. Ashcraft, G. Griffiths, & H. Tiffin (Eds.), *The post-colonial studies reader* (pp. 206–212). London, UK: Routledge.

Billig, M. (1999). Whose terms? Whose ordinariness? Rhetoric and ideology in conversation analysis. *Discourse and Society, 10,* 543–558.

Billig, M., & Schegloff, E. A. (1999). Critical discourse analysis and conversation analysis: An exchange between Michael Billig and Emanuel A Schegloff. *Discourse & Society, 10,* 543–582.

Billings, A. C., Halone, K. K., & Denham, B. E. (2002). 'Man, that was a pretty shot': An analysis of gendered broadcast commentary surrounding the 2000 men's and women's NCAA Final Four Basketball Championships. *Mass Communication & Society, 5,* 295–315.

Bilmes, J. (1976). Rules and rhetoric: Negotiating the social order in a Thai village. *Journal of Anthropological Research, 32,* 44–57.

Blackwell, R. D., Hensel, J. S., & Sternthal, B. (1970). Pupil dilation: What does it measure? *Journal of Advertising Research, 10*(4), 15–18.

Blair, C., Brown, J. R., & Baxter, L. A. (1999). Disciplining the feminine. In J. L. Lucaites, C. M. Condit, & S. Caudill (Eds.), *Contemporary rhetorical theory: A reader* (pp. 563–591). New York, NY: Guilford.

Blanchard, M. E. (1980). *Description: Sign, self, desire.* The Hague, NL: Mouton.

Bloustein, G. (2004). Buffy night at the Seven Stars: A 'subcultural' happening at the 'glocal' level. In A. Bennett and K. Kahn-Harris (Eds.), *After subculture: Critical studies in contemporary youth culture* (pp. 148–161). New York, NY: Palgrave Macmillan.

Blue, G. (2009). Branding Beef: Marketing, food safety and the management of risk. *Canadian Journal of Communication, 34,* 229–244.

Blyler, N. R. (1994). Habermas, empowerment, and professional discourse. *Technical Communication Quarterly, 3,* 125–145.

Boal, A. (1998). *Games for actors and non-actors* (A. Jackson, Trans.). London, UK: Routledge.

Bochner, A. P. (1985). Perspectives on inquiry: Representation, conversation, and reflection. In M. L. Knapp & G. R. Miller (Eds.), *Handbook of interpersonal communication* (pp. 27–58). Beverly Hills, CA: Sage.

Bode, D. (1990). The world as it happens: Ethnomethodology and conversation analysis. In G. Ritzer (Ed.), *Frontiers of social theory: The new synthesis* (pp. 185–213). New York, NY: Columbia University Press.

Bogdan, R. C., & Biklen, S. K. (1982). *Qualitative research for education: An introduction to theory and methods.* Boston, MA: Allyn & Bacon.

Bok, S. (1979). *Lying: Moral choice in public and private life.* New York, NY: Vintage Books.

Bonneville, L., Grosjean, S., & Lagacé, M. (2007). *Introduction aux methods de recherché en communication.* Montréal, QC: Chenelière Éducation.

Bonneville, L., & Sicotte, C. (2009). Les défis posés à la relation soignant-soigné par l'usage de l'ordinateur portable en soins à domicile. *Revue Communication, 26,* 75–107.

Booth, W. C., Colomb, G. G., & Williams, J. M. (1995). *The craft of research.* Chicago, IL: University of Chicago Press.

Bordia, P., & Rosnow, R. L. (1998). Rumor rest stops on the information highway: Transmission patterns in a computer-mediated rumor chain. *Human Communication Research, 25,* 163–179.

Bostdorff, D. M. (2003). George W. Bush's post-September 11 rhetoric of covenant renewal: Upholding the faith of the greatest generation. *Quarterly Journal of Speech, 89,* 293–319.

Bostrom, R. N. (2004). Empiricism, paradigms, and data. *Communication Monographs, 71,* 343–351.

Bouma, G. D., Ling, R., & Wilkinson, L. (2009). *The research process.* Canadian Edition. Don Mills, ON: Oxford University Press.

Bowman, M. S. (1996). Performing literature in the age of textuality. *Communication Education, 45,* 96–101.

Bowman, M. S., & Kistenberg, C. J. (1992). 'Textual power' and the subject of oral interpretation: An alternate approach to performing literature. *Communication Education, 41,* 287–299.

Boyd, E., & Heritage, J. (2004). Talking the patient's medical history: Questioning during comprehensive history taking. In J. Heritage & D. Maynard (Eds.), *Communication in medical care: Talk and action in primary care encounters.* Cambridge, MA: Cambridge University Press.

Bradford, L., Meyers, R. A., & Kane, K. A. (1999). Latino expectations of communicative competence: A focus group interview study. *Communication Quarterly, 47,* 98–117.

Bradley, D. (2005). The divergent anarcho-utopian discourses of the open source software movement. *Canadian Journal of Communication, 4,* 585–611.

Braithwaite, C. (1997a). Blood money: The routine violation of conversational rules. *Communication Reports, 10,* 63–73.

Braithwaite, C. (1997b). Sa'ah naaghai bik'eh hozhoon: An ethnography of Navajo educational communication practices. *Communication Education, 46,* 1–15.

Braithwaite, D. O., Dollar, N. J., Fitch, K. L., & Geist, P. (1996, February). *Case studies for 'ethics in qualitative research'.* Panel presented at the annual meeting of the Western States Communication Association, Pasadena, CA.

Brants, K., & Neijens, P. (1998). The infotainment of politics. *Political Communication, 15,* 149–164.

Brasfield, R. (2006). Rereading: *Sex and the City*: Exposing the hegemonic feminist narrative. *Journal of Popular Film & Television, 34*(3), 130–139.

Bredin, M. (1993). Ethnography and communication: Approaches to Aboriginal media. *Canadian Journal of Communication, 18,* 297–313.

Broad, G., Boyer, S, & Chataway, C. (2006). We are still the Aniishnaabe Nation: Embracing culture and identity in Batchewana First Nation. *Canadian Journal of Communication, 31,* 35–58.

Brock, B. L., Scott, R. L., & Chesebro, J. W. (1990). *Methods of rhetorical criticism: A twentieth-century perspective* (3rd ed.). Detroit, MI: Wayne State University Press.

Brodkey, L. (1987). Writing ethnographic narratives. *Written Communication, 4,* 25–50.

Brookey, R. A., & Westerfelhaus, R. (2002). Hiding homoeroticism in plain view: The *Fight Club* DVD as digital closet. *Critical Studies in Mass Communication, 19,* 21–43.

Brown, P., & Levinson, S. C. (1987). *Politeness: Some universals in language usage.* Cambridge, MA: Cambridge University Press.

Browning, L. D., & Beyer, J. M. (1998). The structuring of shared voluntary standards in the U. S. semiconductor industry: Communicating to reach agreement. *Communication Monographs, 65*, 220–243.

Bruess, C. J. S., & Pearson, J. C. (1997). Interpersonal rituals in marriage and adult friendship. *Communication Monographs, 64*, 25–46.

Bryman, A. (2007). Barriers to integrating quantitative and qualitative research. *Journal of Mixed Methods Research, 1*, 8–22.

Buchmann, M., (1992). Observation: Dilemmas and virtues in research communication. *Curriculum Inquiry, 22*, 313–329.

Bucholtz, M. (2000). The politics of transcription. *Journal of Pragmatics, 32*, 1439–1465.

Buddle, K. (2005). Aboriginal cultural capital creation and radio production in urban Ontario. *Canadian Journal of Communication, 30*, 7–39.

Bulmer, M. (1979). Concepts in the analysis of qualitative data. *Sociological Review, 27*, 651–677.

Burgoon, J. K., Buller, D. B., Guerrero, L. K., & Feldman, C. M. (1994). Interpersonal deception: VI. Effects of pre-interactional and interactional factors on deceiver and observer perceptions of deception success. *Communication Studies, 45*, 263–280.

Burgoon, J. K., Johnson, M. L., & Koch, P. T. (1998). The nature and measurement of interpersonal dominance. *Communication Monographs, 65*, 308–335.

Burgoon, J. K., & Le Poire, B. A. (1999). Nonverbal cues and interpersonal judgments: Participant and observer perceptions of intimacy, dominance, composure, and formality. *Communication Monographs, 66*, 105–124.

Burgoon, J. K., Parrott, R., Le Poire, B. A., Kelley, D. L., Walther, J. B., & Perry, D. (1989). Maintaining and restoring privacy through communication in different types of relationships. *Journal of Social and Personal Relationships, 6*, 131–158.

Burgoon, M., & Bailey, W. (1992). PC at last! PC at last! Thank God almighty, we are PC at last! *Journal of Communication, 42*, 95–104.

Burleson, B. R., Holmstrom, A. J., & Gilstrap, C. M. (2005). 'Guys can't say *that* to guys': Four experiments assessing the normative motivation account for deficiencies in the emotional support provided by men. *Communication Monographs, 72*, 468–501.

Butler, J. (1990). *Gender trouble: Feminism and the subversion of identity*. New York, NY: Routledge.

Butler, J. (1993). *Bodies that matter: On the discursive limits of 'sex'*. New York, NY: Routledge.

Butovsky, J. (2007). Phony populism: The misuse of polls in the National Post. *Canadian Journal of Communication, 32*, 91–102.

Buttny, R. (1987). Sequence and practical reasoning in account episodes. *Communication Quarterly, 35*, 67–83.

Buttny, R. (1993). *Social accountability in communication*. London, UK: Sage.

Buzzanell, P. M., Burrell, N. A., Stafford, S., & Berkowitz, S. (1996). When I call you up and you're not there: Application of communication accommodation theory to telephone answering machine messages. *Western Journal of Communication, 60*, 310–336.

Buzzanell, P. M., & Liu, M. (2005). Struggling with maternity leave policies and practices: A poststructuralist feminist analysis of gendered organizing. *Journal of Applied Communication Research, 33*, 1–25.

Buzzanell, P. M., Waymer, D., Paz Tagle, M., & Liu, M. (2007). Different transitions into working motherhood: Discourses of Asian, Hispanic, and African American women. *Journal of Family Communication, 7*, 195–220.

Cai, X., & Gantz, W. (2000). Online privacy issues associated with Web sites for children. *Journal of Broadcasting & Electronic Media, 44*, 197–214.

Calas, M. B., & Smircich, L. (1996). From 'the Woman's' point of view: Feminist approaches to organization studies. In S. Clegg, C. Hardy, & W. R. Nord (Eds.), *Handbook of organization studies* (pp. 218–257). London, UK: Sage.

Calhoun, L. R. (2005). Will the real Slim Shady please stand up? Masking whiteness, encoding hegemonic masculinity in Eminem's Marshall Mathers LP. *Howard Journal of Communication, 16*, 267–294.

Campbell, D. T., & Fiske, D. W. (1959). Convergent and discrimnant validation by the multitrait-multimethod matrix. *Psychological Bulletin, 56*, 81–105.

Campbell, K. K. (1974). Criticism: Ephemeral and enduring. *Speech Teacher, 23*, 9–14.

Canada Council. (1977). *Ethics: Report of the consultative group on ethics*. Ottawa, ON: Canada Council.

Canadian Institutes of Health Research, Natural Sciences and Engineering Research Council of Canada, and Social Sciences and Humanities Research Council of Canada (2010). *Tri-council policy statement: Ethical conduct for research involving humans*. Ottawa, ON: Interagency Advisory Panel on Research Ethics.

Canary, D. J. (2003). Introductory comments. *Western Journal of Communication, 67*, xi.

Cappella, J. N. (1990). The method of proof by example in interaction analysis. *Communication Monographs, 57*, 236–242.

Capper, C. A. (1992). A feminist poststructural analysis of non-traditional approaches in education administration. *Educational Administration Quarterly, 28*(1), 103–124.

Carbaugh, D. (1988). Cultural terms and tensions in the speech at a television station. *Western Journal of Speech Communication, 52,* 216–237.

Carbaugh, D. (1993). 'Soul' and 'self': Soviet and American cultures in conversation. *Quarterly Journal of Speech, 79,* 182–200.

Carbaugh, D., Berry, M., & Nurmikari-Berry, M. (2006). Coding personhood through cultural terms and practices. *Journal of Language & Social Psychology, 25,* 203–220.

Carpenter, N. (1999). Pictures of prostitutes: The discursive battle of subject position. *Communicate, 28*(2), 21–44.

Carter, D. (2005). Living in virtual communities: An ethnography of human relationships in cyberspace. *Information, Communication, & Society, 8,* 148–167.

Carter, S. (1997). *Capturing women: The manipulation of cultural imagery in Canada's prairie west.* Montreal, QC: McGill-Queen's University Press.

Cegala, D. J., McGee, S., & McNeilis, K. S. (1996). Components of patients' and doctors' perceptions of communication competence during a primary medical care interview. *Health Communication, 8,* 1–27.

Chadwick, S. A. (1999). Teaching virtually via the web: Comparing student performance and attitudes about communication in lecture, virtual web-based, and web-supplemented courses. *Electronic Journal of Communication, 9*(1). Retrieved July 11, 2011, http://www.cios.org/www/ejc/v9n.199.htm

Chandler, D. (1995). *The act of writing: A media theory approach.* Aberystwyth, UK: University of Wales.

Chang, H. J., & Johnson, J. D. (2001). Communication networks as predictors of organizational members' media choices. *Western Journal of Communication, 65,* 349–369.

Chang-Hoan, C., & Hongsik J. C. (2005). Children's exposure to negative Internet content: Effects of family context. *Journal of Broadcasting & Electronic Media, 49,* 488–509.

Chan-Olmstead, S. M., & Park, J. S. (2000). From on-air to online world: Examining the content and structures of broadcast TV stations' web sites. *Journalism & Mass Communication Quarterly, 77,* 321–339.

Chen, L. (1997). Verbal adaptive strategies in U.S. American dyadic interactions with U.S. American or East-Asian partners. *Communication Monographs, 64,* 302–323.

Cheney, G. (2004). Bringing ethics in from the margins. *Australian Journal of Communication, 31*(3), 35–40.

Cheney, M. (1981). *Tesla: Man out of time.* New York, NY: Delta/Dell.

Cheng, H. (1997). Toward an understanding of cultural values manifest in advertising: A content analysis of Chinese television commercials in 1990 and 1995. *Journalism and Mass Communication Quarterly, 74,* 773–796.

Childress, H. (1998). Kinder ethnographic writing. *Qualitative Inquiry, 4,* 249–264.

Christians, C. G. (2003). Ethics and politics in qualitative research. In N. K. Denzin & Y. S. Lincoln (Eds.), *The landscape of qualitative research: Theories and issues* (2nd ed., pp. 208–243). Thousand Oaks, CA: Sage.

Chung, G., & Grimes, S. M. (2005). Data mining the kids: Surveillance and market research strategies in children's online games. *Canadian Journal of Communication, 30,* 527–548.

Chung, L. C., & Ting-Toomey, S. (1999). Ethnic identity and relational expectations among Asian-Americans. *Communication Research Reports, 16,* 157–166.

Clair, R. P. (1993). The use of framing devices to sequester organizational narratives: Hegemony and harassment. *Communication Monographs, 60,* 113–136.

Clair, R. P. (1994). Resistance and oppression as a self-contained opposite: An organizational communication analysis of one man's story of sexual harassment. *Western Journal of Communication, 58,* 235–262.

Clair, R. P. (1997). Organizing silence: Silence as voice and voice as silence in the narrative exploration of the Treaty of New Echota. *Western Journal of Communication, 61,* 315–337.

Clair, R. P., & Kunkel, A. W. (1998). 'Unrealistic realities': Child abuse and the aesthetic resolution. *Communication Monographs, 65,* 24–46.

Clarke, J. N. (1999a). Breast cancer in circulating magazines in the U.S.A. and Canada: 1974–1997. *Women and Health, 28,* 113–130.

Clarke, J. N. (1999b). Prostate cancer's hegemonic masculinity in select print mass media depictions (1974–1995). *Health Communication, 11,* 59–74.

Clay, E., Fisher, R. L., Xie, S., Sawyer, C. R., & Behnke, R. R. (2005). Affect intensity and sensitivity to punishment as predictors of sensitization (arousal) during public speaking. *Communication Reports, 18,* 95–103.

Clayman, S. (1993). Reformulating the question: A device for answering/not answering questions in news interviews and press conferences. *Text, 13*(2), 159–188.

Clayman, S., & Heritage, J. (2002). Questioning Presidents: Journalistic deference and adversarialness in the press conferences of Eisenhower and Reagan. *Journal of Communication, 52*(4), 749–775.

Cleary, R. M. (1993). Rap music and its political connections: An annotated bibliography. *RSR: Reference Service Review, 21*(2), 77–90.

Cohen, J. (1960). A coefficient of agreement for nominal scales. *Educational & Psychological Measurement, 20,* 37–46.

Collinson, D., & Hearn, J. (1994). Naming men as men: Implications for work, organization, and management. *Gender, Work, and Organization, 1,* 2–22.

Conquergood, D. (1991). Rethinking ethnography: Towards a critical cultural politics. *Communication Monographs, 58,* 179–194.

Conquergood, D. (1992). Life in Big Red: Struggles and accommodations in a Chicago polyethnic tenement. In L. Lamphere (Ed.), *Structuring diversity: Ethnographic perspectives on the new immigration* (pp. 94–144). Chicago, IL: University of Chicago Press.

Conquergood, D. (1994). Homeboys and hoods: Gang communication and cultural space. In L. R. Frey (Ed.), *Group communication in cultural context: Studies of natural groups* (pp. 23–55). Hillsdale, NJ: Lawrence Erlbaum.

Conquergood, D. (1995). Between rigor and relevance: Rethinking applied communication. In K. N. Cissna (Ed.), *Applied communication in the 21st century* (pp. 79–96). Mahwah, NJ: Lawrence Erlbaum.

Conquergood, D. (Producer), & Siegel, T. (Producer & Director). (1990). *The heart broken in half* [Motion Picture]. Chicago, IL: Siegel Productions; New York, NY: Filmakers Library.

Conrad, C. (1988). Work songs, hegemony, and illusions of self. *Critical Studies in Mass Communication, 5,* 179–201.

Cook, T. D., & Campbell, D. T. (1979). *Quasi-experimentation: Design and analysis issues for field settings.* Chicago, IL: Rand McNalley.

Cooper, B., & Descutner, D. (1997). Strategic silences and transgressive metaphors in *Out of Africa*: Isak Dinesen's double-voiced rhetoric of complicity and subversion. *Southern Communication Journal, 62,* 333–343.

Cooper, H. M. (1984). *The integrative research review: A systematic review.* Beverly Hills, CA: Sage.

Corbin, C. (2002). How the industrial fishery constrained voices of ecological conservation. *Canadian Journal of Communication, 27,* 7–32.

Corman, S. (2005). Postpositivism. In S. May & D. K. Mumby (Eds.), *Engaging organizational communication theory and research* (pp. 15–34). Thousand Oaks, CA: Sage.

Cosgrave, J.F., & Cormack, P. (2008), Disenchanted wonder: Collecting Canadian identity through the CBC 'Seven Wonders of Canada'. *Topia: Canadian Journal of Cultural Studies, 20,* 5–22.

Couchman, W. (1995). Using video and conversational analysis to train staff working with people with learning disabilities. *Journal of Advanced Nursing, 22,* 1112–1120.

Courtright, J. A. (1984). Methods of integrating observational and traditional data analysis. *Communication Quarterly, 32,* 197–206.

Covarrubias, P. (2007). (Un)biased in Western theory: Generative silence in American Indian communication. *Communication Monographs, 74,* 265–271.

Craig, R. T., Tracy, K., & Spisak, F. (1986). The discourse of requests: Assessment of a politeness approach. *Human Communication Research, 12,* 437–468.

Crawford, L. (1996). Personal ethnography. *Communication Monographs, 63,* 158–170.

Crowell, T. L., & Emmers-Sommer, T. M. (2001). 'If I knew then what I know now': Seropositive individuals' perceptions of partner trust, safety and risk prior to HIV infection. *Communication Studies, 52,* 302–323.

Dainton, M. (1998). Everyday interaction in marital relationships: Variations in relative importance and event duration. *Communication Reports, 11,* 101–109.

Dangle, L. F., & Haussman, A. M., (1963). *Preparing the research paper* (3rd ed.). Fairfield, NJ: Cebco Standard Publishing.

Daniels, G., Gervais, R., & Merchant, S. (Executive Producers). (2005). *The Office* (American version). Universal City, CA: Universal Media Studios.

Daniels, R. V. (1966). *Studying history: How and why.* Englewood Cliffs, NJ: Prentice-Hall.

Davis, F. (1973). The Martian and the convert: Ontological polarities in social research. *Urban Life, 2,* 333–343.

Dawson, M. (1997). 'That nice red coat goes to my head like champagne': Gender, antimodernism and the Mountie image, 1880–1960. *Journal of Canadian Studies, 32,* 119–139.

Deacon, D., Pickering, M., Golding, P., & Murdock, G. (2007). *Research communications: A practical guide to methods in media and cultural analysis* (2 ed.). London, UK: Hodder Arnold.

Deetz, S. A. (1982). Critical interpretive research in organizational communication. *Western Journal of Speech Communication, 46,* 131–149.

Deetz, S. (2005). Critical theory (pp. 85–111). In S. May & D. Mumby (Eds.), *Organizational communication theory and research: Multiple perspectives.* Thousand Oaks, CA: Sage.

De Jong, P. J. (1999). Communicative and remedial effects of social blushing. *Journal of Nonverbal Behavior, 23*(3), 197–217.

Delgado, F. P. (1998a). Chicano ideology revisited: Rap music and the (re)articulation of Chicanoism. *Western Journal of Communication, 62,* 95–113.

Delgado, F. P. (1998b). When the silenced speak: The text-ualization and complications of Latina/o identity. *Western Journal of Communication, 62*, 420–438.

Demers, D. (1996). Corporate newspaper structure, editorial page vigour, and social change. *Journalism & Mass Communication Quarterly, 73*, 857–877.

Denscombe, M. (1998). *The good research guide: For small-scale social research projects.* Birmingham, AL: Open University Press.

Denzin, N. K. (1978). *The research act* (2nd ed.). New York, NY: McGraw Hill.

Denzin, N. K. (1997). *Interpretive ethnography: Ethnographic practices for the 21st century.* Thousand Oaks, CA: Sage.

Denzin, N. K. (1999). Two-stepping in the '90s. *Qualitative Inquiry, 5*, 568–572.

Denzin, N. K. (2003). *Performance ethnography: Critical pedagogy and the politics of culture.* Thousand Oaks, CA: Sage.

Denzin, N. K., & Lincoln, Y. S. (1998a). Introduction: Entering the field of qualitative research. In N. K. Denzin & Y. S. Lincoln (Eds.), *Strategies of qualitative inquiry* (pp. 1–34). Thousand Oaks, CA: Sage.

Denzin, N. K., & Lincoln, Y. S. (Eds.). (1998b). *Strategies of qualitative inquiry.* Thousand Oaks, CA: Sage.

Denzin, N. K., & Lincoln, Y. S. (2003). Introduction: The discipline and practice of qualitative research. In *Collecting and interpreting qualitative methods* (2nd ed., pp. 1–46). Thousand Oaks, CA: Sage.

Derrida, J. (1976). *Of grammatology* (G. Spivak, Trans.). Baltimore, MA: Johns Hopkins University Press. (Original work published 1972).

Derrida, J. (1978). *Writing and difference* (A. Bass, Trans.). Chicago, IL: University of Chicago Press.

Derrida, J. (1981). *Positions* (A. Bass, Trans.). Chicago, IL: University of Chicago.

DeSantis, A. D. (2003). A couple of white guys sitting around talking: The collective rationalization of cigar smokers. *Journal of Contemporary Ethnography, 32*, 432–466.

DeStephen, R. S. (1983). Group interaction differences between high and low consensus groups. *Western Journal of Speech Communication, 47*, 340–363.

Deveau, V., & Fouts, G. (2004). Revenge in U.S. and Canadian news magazines post-9/11. *Canadian Journal of Communication, 29*, 99–109.

Dickinson, G. (2006). The *Pleasantville* effect: Nostalgia and the visual framing of (white) suburbia. *Western Journal of Communication, 70*, 212–231.

Doerfel, M. A., & Barnett, G. A. (1999). A semantic network analysis of the International Communication Association. *Human Communication Research, 25*, 589–603.

Dollar, N. J. (1995, February). *'What a long strange trip it's been': Understanding the expression of cultural identity.* Paper presented at the annual meeting of the Western States Communication Association, Portland, Oregon.

Dollar, N. J. (1999). 'Show talk' and communal identity: An analysis of Deadheads' ways of speaking. *Journal of the Northwestern Communication Association, 26*, 101–120.

Dollar, N. J., & Beck, C. (1997, February). *Advancing and supporting claims in ethnography of communication.* Workshop presented at the annual meeting of the Western States Communication Association in Monterey, California.

Dollar, N. J., & Merrigan, G. (2002). Ethnographic practices in group communication research. In L. Frey (Ed.), *New directions in small group communication research* (pp. 59–78). Mahwah, NJ: Lawrence Erlbaum.

Dollar, N. J., & Zimmers, B. (1998). Social identity and communicative boundaries: An analysis of youth and young adult street speakers in a U. S. American community. *Communication Research, 25*, 596–617.

Douglas, J. (1967). *The social meanings of suicide.* Princeton, NJ: Princeton University Press.

Douglas, J. D. (1976). *Investigative social research: Individual and team field research.* Beverly Hills, CA: Sage.

Dow, B. J. (1990). Hegemony, feminist criticism, and 'The Mary Tyler Moore Show'. *Critical Studies in Mass Communication, 7*, 261–274.

Dragga, S., & Voss, D. (2003). Hiding humanity: Verbal and visual ethics in accident reports. *Technical Communication, 50*, 61–83.

Drew, P. (1992). Contested evidence in courtroom cross-examination: The case of a trial for rape. In P. Drew & J. Heritage (Eds.), *Talk at work: Interaction in institutional settings* (pp. 470–520). Cambridge, UK: Cambridge University Press.

Drew, P. (1997). An 'Open' class of repair initiation in conversation: Sequential sources of troubles in understanding. *Journal of Pragmatics, 28*, 69–102.

Drew, P. (1998). 'Out-of-hours' calls to the doctor: misalignments between callers and doctor during diagnostic questioning. In S. Cmejrková, J. Hoffmannová, O. Müllerová & J. Svetlá (Eds.), *Dialoganalyse VI (Volume 2) Proceedings of the 6th International Congresss of IADA (International Association for Dialog Analysis)* (pp. 65–77). Tübingen, DE: Niemeyer.

Drew, P. & Heritage, J. (Eds.) (1992). *Talk at work: Interaction in institutional settings.* Cambridge, UK: Cambridge University Press.

Druckman, J. N. (2005). Media matter: How newspapers and television news cover campaigns and influence voters. *Political Communication, 22*, 264–481.

Drzewiecka, J. A., & Nakayama, T. K. (1998). City sites: Politics of urban space and communication of identity. *Southern Journal of Communication, 64,* 20–31.

Dupagne, M. (2006). Predictors of consumer digital television awareness in the United States. *Communication Research Reports, 23,* 119–128.

Duranti, A. (1997). *Linguistic anthropology.* Cambridge, UK: Cambridge University Press.

Dworkin, S. L. & Wachs, F. L. (1998). 'Disciplining the body': HIV-positive male athletes, media surveillance, and the policing of sexuality. *Sociology of Sport Journal, 15,* 1–20.

Dye, L. (2009). Consuming constructions: A critique of Dove's campaign for real beauty. *Canadian Journal of Media Studies, 5,* 114–128.

Eastman, S. T., & Land, A. M. (1997). The best of both worlds: Sports fans find good seats at the bar. *Journal of Sport and Social Issues, 21,* 156–178.

Eckstein, N. J. (2004). Emergent issues in families experiencing adolescent-to-parent abuse. *Western Journal of Communication, 68,* 365–388.

Edge, M. (2007). Convergence and the 'Black news hole': Canadian newspaper coverage of the 2003 Lincoln Report. *Canadian Journal of Media Studies, 2,* 76–108.

Ebanda de B'beri, B., & Middlebrook, R. (2009). The paradox of national identity: Region, nation and *Canadian Idol. Canadian Journal of Communication, 34,* 25–40.

Edwards, D., & Fasulo, A. (2006). 'To be honest': Sequential uses of honesty phrases in talk-in-interaction. *Research on Language & Social Interaction, 39,* 343–376.

Eighmey, J., & Sar, S. (2007). Harlow Gale and the origins of the psychology of advertising. *Journal of Advertising, 2007, 36*(4), 147–158.

Eisenberg, E. (1990). Transcendence through organizing. *Communication Research, 17,* 139–164.

Eisenberg, E., Murphy, A., & Andrews, L. (1998). Openness and decision making in the search for a university provost. *Communication Monographs, 65,* 1–23.

Ellingson, L. L. (1998). 'Then you know how I feel': Empathy, identification, and reflexivity in fieldwork. *Qualitative Inquiry, 4,* 492–514.

Elliott, C. (2007). Pink!: Community, contestation, and the colour of breast cancer. *Canadian Journal of Communication, 32,* 521–538.

Elliott, C. D. (2009). Healthy foods look serious: How children interpret packaged food products. *Canadian Journal of Communication, 34,* 359–380.

Ellis, C. (2004). *The ethnographic: I. A methodological novel about autoethnography.* Walnut Creek, CA: Alta Mira Press.

Ellis, C., & Bochner, A. P. (2003). Autoethnography, personal narrative, and reflexivity: Researcher as subject. In *Collecting and interpreting qualitative methods* (2nd ed., pp. 199–258). Thousand Oaks, CA: Sage.

Ellis, D. G. (1976). *An analysis of relational communication in ongoing group systems.* Unpublished doctoral dissertation, Department of Communication, University of Utah, Salt Lake City.

Ely, R. J. (1995). The power in demography: Women's social constructions of gender identity at work. *Academy of Management Journal, 38,* 589–634.

Emmers-Sommer, T. M. (1999). Negative relational events and event responses across relationship-type: Examining and comparing the impact of conflict strategy-use on intimacy in same-sex friendships, opposite-sex friendships and romantic relationships. *Communication Research Reports, 16,* 286–295.

Emmers-Sommer, T. M., & Allen, M. (1999). Surveying the effects of media effects: A meta-analytic summary of the media effects research. *Human Communication Research, 25,* 478–497.

Evans, W. (1996). Divining the social order: Class, gender, and magazine astrology columns. *Journalism and Mass Communication Quarterly, 73,* 389–400.

Eveland, W. P., Jr. & Dunwoody, S. (2001). User control and structural isomorphism or disorientation and cognitive load? Learning from the Web versus print. *Communication Research, 28,* 48–79.

Fairclough, N., & Wodak, R. (1997). Critical discourse analysis. In T. A. Van Dijk (Ed.), *Discourse as social interaction* (pp. 258–284). Thousand Oaks, CA: Sage.

Fauteux, B. (2008). The development of community radio in Quebec: The rise of community broadcasting in late 1960s and early 1970s Canada. *Canadian Journal of Media Studies, 3,* 131–151.

Feagan, R., & Ripmeester, R. (2001). Reading private green space: Competing geographic identities at the level of the lawn. *Philosophy and Geography, 4,* 79–95.

Feagin, J., Orum, A., & Sjoberg, G. (Eds.) (1991). *A case for case study.* Chapel Hill, NC: University of North Carolina Press.

Felczak, M., Smith, R., & Glass, G. (2009). Communicating with some Canadians: communication rights and government online in Canada. *Canadian Journal of Communication, 34,* 435–460.

Feldman, M. S. (1995). Qualitative Research Methods Series No. 33. Strategies for interpreting qualitative data. Thousand Oaks, CA: Sage University Paper.

Felts, A. A. (1992). Organizational communication: A critical perspective. *Administration and Society, 23,* 495–513.

Ferguson, G. A. (1981). *Statistical analysis in psychology and education* (5th ed.). New York, NY: McGraw-Hill.

Ferguson, M. (1990). Images of power and the feminist fallacy. *Critical Studies in Mass Communication, 7*, 215–230.

Fiebig, G. V., & Kramer, M. W. (1998). A framework for the study of emotions in organizational contexts. *Management Communication Quarterly, 11*, 536–572.

Fine, G. A. (1993). Ten lies of ethnography: Moral dilemmas of field research. *Journal of Contemporary Ethnography, 22*, 267–293.

Fink, E. J., & Gantz, W. (1996). A content analysis of three mass communication research traditions: Social science, interpretive studies, and critical analysis. *Journalism & Mass Communication Quarterly, 73*, 114–134.

Fischer, E., & Bristor, J. (1994). A feminist post-structural analysis of the rhetoric of marketing relationships. *International Journal of Research in Marketing, 11*, 317–331.

Fisher, B. A. (1970). The process of decision modification in small groups. *Journal of Communication, 20*, 51–64.

Fisher, W. R. (1987). *Human communication as narration: Toward a philosophy of reason, value, and action.* Columbia: University of South Carolina Press.

Fitch, K. L. (1994). Criteria for evidence in qualitative research. *Western Journal of Communication, 58*, 32–38.

Fitch, K. L. (1998). Text and context: A problematic Distinction for ethnography. *Research on Language & Social Interaction, 31*, 91–108.

Fix, B., & Sias, P. M. (2006). Person-centered communication, leader-member exchange, and employee job satisfaction. *Communication Research Reports, 23*, 35–44.

Flaherty, L. M., Pearce, K. J., & Rubin, R. B. (1998). Internet and face-to-face communication: Not functional alternatives. *Communication Quarterly, 46*, 250–268.

Floyd, C., & Burgoon, J. K. (1999). Reacting to nonverbal expressions of liking: A test of interaction adaptation theory. *Communication Monographs, 66*, 219–239.

Floyd, K. (2006). Human affection exchange XII: Affectionate communication is associated with diurnal variation in salivary free cortisol. *Western Journal of Communication, 70*, 47–63.

Ford, C. E. (2004). Contingency and units in interaction. *Discourse Studies, 6*(1), 27–52.

Forester, J. (1993). *Critical theory, public policy and planning practice: Toward a critical pragmatism.* Albany, NY: State University of New York Press.

Foss, K. A., & Foss, S. K. (1988). Incorporating the feminist perspective in communication scholarship: A research commentary. In C. Spitzack & K. Carter (Eds.), *Doing research on women's communication: Alternative perspectives in theory and method* (pp. 65–92). Norwood, NJ: Ablex.

Foss, K. A., & Foss, S. K. (1994). Personal experience as evidence in feminist scholarship. *Western Journal of Communication, 58*, 39–43.

Foss, K. A., Foss, S. K., & Griffin, C. L. (1999). *Feminist rhetorical theories.* Thousand Oaks, CA: Sage.

Foss, S. K. (1988). *Rhetorical criticism: Exploration and practice.* Prospect Heights, IL: Waveland Press.

Foss, S. K. (2004). *Rhetorical criticism: Exploration and practice* (3rd ed.). Prospect Heights, IL: Waveland Press.

Foster, D. (2002). Cleaning up the city: Squeegee kids and the social purification of urban Canada. In S. D. Ferguson & L. R. Shade (Eds.) *Civic discourse and cultural politics in Canada* (pp. 37–46). Westport, CT: Ablex.

Foster, D. (2009). Chasing the public: The CBC and the debate over factual entertainment on Canadian airwaves. *Canadian Journal of Communication, 34*, 61–77.

Foucault, M. (1972). *The archaeology of knowledge,* (A. M. Sheridan Smith, Trans.). New York, NY: Pantheon Books.

Foucault, M. (1979). *Discipline and punish: The birth of the prison* (A. Sheridan, Trans.). New York, NY: Random House.

Foucault, M. (1980). *Power/knowledge: Selected interviews and other writings, 1927–1977* (C. Gordon et al., Trans., & C. Gordon, Ed.). New York, NY: Pantheon.

Foucault, M. (1983). The subject and power. In H. Dreyfus & P. Rabinow (Eds.), *Michel Foucault: Beyond structuralism and hermeneutics* (2nd ed., pp. 208–226). Chicago, IL: University of Chicago Press.

Frankfort-Nachmias, C., & Nachmias, D. (1996). *Research methods in the social sciences* (5th ed.). New York, NY: St. Martin's Press.

Fraser, N. (1992), Rethinking the Public Sphere. In Craig Calhoun (Ed.) *Habermas and the public sphere* (pp. 109–142). Cambridge, MA: MIT Press.

Fraser, N. (2007). Creating model citizens for the Information Age: Canadian Internet policy as civilizing discourse. *Canadian Journal of Communication, 32*, 210–218.

Freeman, B. (2006). From no go to no logo: Lesbian lives and rights in *Chatelaine. Canadian Journal of Communication, 31*, 815–841.

Frey, L. R. (1994a). The call of the field: Studying communication in natural groups. In L. R. Frey (Ed.), *Group communication in context: Studies of bona fide groups* (2nd ed., pp. ix–xiv). Mahwah, NJ: Lawrence Erlbaum.

Frey, L. R. (1994b). The naturalistic paradigm: Studying small groups in the postmodern era. *Small Group Research, 25*, 551–577.

Frey, L. R., Adelman, M. B., Flint, L. J., & Query, J. L., Jr. (2000). Weaving meanings together in an AIDS residence: Communicative practices, perceived health outcomes, and the symbolic construction of community. *Journal of Health Communication, 5,* 53–73.

Frey, L. R., Botan, C. H., & Kreps, G. L. (2000). *Investigating communication: An introduction to research methods* (2nd ed.). Boston, MA: Allyn & Bacon.

Friedrich, O. (1990). *Glenn Gould: A life and variations.* Toronto, ON: Lester, Orpen, & Dennys.

Friesen, G., Muise, D., & Northrup, D. (2009). Variations on the theme of remembering: A national survey of how Canadians use the past. *Journal of the Canadian Historical Association, 20*(1), 221–248.

Frymier, A. B., & Houser, M. L. (1998). Does making content relevant make a difference in learning? *Communication Research Reports, 15,* 121–129.

Furman, W., & Simon, V. A. (1998). Advice from youth: Some lessons from the study of adolescent relationships. *Journal of Social and Personal Relationships, 15,* 723–739.

Gale, K., & Bunton, K. (2005). Assessing the impact of ethics instruction on advertising and public relations graduates. *Journalism & Mass Communication Educator, 60,* 272–285.

Galvin, J. (1999). *Writing literature reviews: A guide for students of the social and behavioral sciences.* Los Angeles, CA: Pyrczak Publishing.

Gantz, W., & Wenner, L.A. (1995). Fanship and the Television Sports Viewing Experience. *Sociology of Sport Journal, 12,* 56–74.

Garfinkel, H. (1967). *Studies in ethnomethodology.* Englewood Cliffs, NJ: Prentice-Hall.

Gasher, M. (1998). Invoking public support for public broadcasting: The Aird Commission revisited. *Canadian Journal of Communication, 23,* 189–216.

Gattinger, M., & Saint-Pierre, D. (2010). The 'Neoliberal turn' in provincial cultural policy and administration in Québec and Ontario: The emergence of 'quasi-neoliberal' approaches. *Canadian Journal of Communication, 35,* 279–302.

Geary, C. W., Burke, H. M., Neupane, S., Castelnau, L., & Brown, J. (2006). Does MTV reach an appropriate audience for HIV prevention messages? Evidence from MTV viewership data in Nepal and Brasil. *Journal of Health Communication, 11,* 665–681.

Geertz, C. (1973). *The interpretation of cultures: Selected essays.* New York, NY: Basic Books.

Gerbner, G., Gross, L., Morgan, M., & Signorielli, N. (1986). Living with television: The dynamics of the cultivation process. In J. Bryant & D. Zillman (Eds.), *Perspectives on media effects* (pp. 17–40). Hillsdale, NJ: Lawrence Erlbaum.

Gervais, R., and Merchant, S. (Producers). (2001). *The Office.* London, UK: British Broadcasting Corporation.

Getis, A. (1995). *The tyranny of data.* San Diego, CA: San Diego State University Press.

Gibaldi, J. (1995). *MLA handbook for writers of research papers* (4th ed.). New York, NY: Modern Language Association of America.

Gilbert, J. R. (1997). Performing marginality: Comedy, identity, and cultural critique. *Text and Performance Quarterly, 17,* 317–330.

Gill, A. (1994). *Rhetoric and human understanding.* Prospect Heights, IL: Waveland Press.

Gillham, B. (2000). *Case study research methods.* London, UK: Continuum.

Gilligan, C. (1982). *In a different voice: Psychological theory and women's development.* Cambridge, MA: Harvard University Press.

Girardelli, D. (2004). Commodified identities: The myth of Italian food in the United States. *Journal of Communication Inquiry, 28,* 307–324.

Glaser, B. G., & Strauss, A. L. (1967). *The discovery of grounded theory: Strategies for qualitative research.* Chicago, IL: Aldine.

Glionna, J. M. (2000, November 13). Dot-com spurs angry protests: S. F. locals upset over rising land prices in city. *The Los Angeles Times,* p. 02D.

Godard, D. (1977). Same setting, different norms: Phone call beginnings in France and the United States. *Language in Society, 6,* 209–219.

Godley, A. J., Carpenter, B. D., & Werner, C. A. (2007). 'I'll speak in proper slang': Language ideologies in a daily editing activity. *Reading Research Quarterly, 42,* 100–131.

Goetz, J. P., & LeCompte, M. D. (1984). *Ethnography and qualitative design in educational research.* Orlando, FL: Academic.

Goffman, E. (1959). *The presentation of the self in everyday life.* Garden City, NY: Doubleday Anchor.

Goffman, E. (1961). *Encounters: Two Studies in the Sociology of Interaction—Fun in games & role distance.* Indianapolis, MN: Bobbs-Merrill.

Goffman, E. (1967). *Interaction ritual: Essays in face-to-face behavior.* Chicago, IL: Aldine.

Goffman, E. (1971). *Relations in public.* New York, NY: Harper and Row.

Goidel, R. K., Freeman, C. M., & Procopio, S. T. (2006). The impact of television viewing on perceptions of juvenile crime. *Journal of Broadcasting & Electronic Media, 50,* 119–139.

Golish, T. D., & Caughlin, J. P. (2002). 'I'd rather not talk about it': Adolescents' and young adults' use of topic avoidance in stepfamilies. *Journal of Applied Communication Research, 30*, 78–106.

Good, J. (2008). The framing of climate change in Canadian, American and international newspapers: A media propaganda model analysis. *Canadian Journal of Communication, 33*, 233–255.

Goodall, H. L. (2000). *Writing the new ethnography.* Walnut Creek, CA: AltaMira Press.

Goodwin, C. (1979). The interactive construction of a sentence in natural conversation. In G. Psathas (Ed.), *Everyday language: Studies in ethnomethodology* (pp. 97–121). New York, NY: Irvington Publishers.

Goodwin, C. (1980). Restarts, pauses, and the achievement of a state of mutual eye gaze at turn-beginning. *Sociological Inquiry, 50*, 277–302.

Goodwin, C. (1981). *Conversational organization: Interactions between speakers and hearers.* New York, NY: Academic.

Goodwin, C. (1993). Recording interaction in natural settings. *Pragmatics, 3*(2), 181–209.

Goodwin, C., & Heritage, J. (1990). Conversation analysis. *Annual Review of Anthropology, 19*, 283–307.

Goodwin, M. H., & Goodwin, C. (1986). Gesture and co-participation in the activity of searching for a word. *Semiotica, 62*(1–2), 51–75.

Goold, D., & Willis, A. (1997). *The Bre-X fraud.* Toronto, ON: McClelland and Stewart.

Gordon, J. (2002). From gangs to the academy: Scholars emerge by reaching back through critical ethnography. *Social Justice, 29*, 71–82.

Gouldner, A. W. (1988). The sociologist as partisan: Sociology and the welfare state. *American Sociologist, 3*, 103–116.

Gow, G. A. (2004). Public safety telecommunications in Canada: Regulatory intervention in the development of wireless E9-1-1. *Canadian Journal of Communication, 29*, 65–88.

Grabe, M. E. (1999). Television news magazine crime stories: A functionalist perspective. *Critical Studies in Mass Communication, 2*, 155–171.

Grabe, M. E. (2002). Maintaining the moral order: A functional analysis of 'The Jerry Springer Show'. *Critical Studies in Media Communication, 19*, 311–328.

Grabe, M. E., Long, A., Shuhua, Z., & Bolls, P. D. (2000). Cognitive access to negatively arousing news. *Communication Research, 27*, 3–27.

Graham, E. E. (1997). Turning points and commitment in post-divorce relationships. *Communication Monographs, 64*, 350–368.

Gramsci, A. (1971). *Selections from the prison notebooks* (Q. Hoare & G. Nowell Smith, Trans.). New York, NY: International.

Grant, L., & Starks, D. (2001). Screening appropriate teaching materials: Closings from textbooks and television soap operas. *International Review of Applied Linguistics in Language Teaching, 39*, 39–51.

Granzberg, G., & Steinbring, J. (Eds.). (1980). *Television and the Canadian Indian.* Winnipeg, MB: University of Winnipeg/Ottawa, ON: Department of Communications.

Gray, P. H. (1996). The thoroughbred and the four-wheeled cab: Performance beyond literature. *Communication Education, 45*, 102–107.

Grenier, L. (2001). Governing 'National' memories through popular music in Québec. *Topia: Canadian Journal of Cultural Studies, 6*, 11–19.

Grice, H. (1975). Logic and conversation (pp. 41–58). In P. Cole & J. L. Morgan (Eds.), *Syntax and semantics: Vol. 3. Speech acts.* New York, NY: Academic.

Griffen, E. (2006). *A first look at communication theory* (6th ed.). Boston, MA: McGraw-Hill.

Gross, A. G., & Keith, W. M. (Eds.). (1997). *Rhetorical hermeneutics: Invention and interpretation in the age of science.* New York, NY: State University of New York Press.

Guerrero, L. K., & Jones, S. M. (2005). Differences in conversational skills as a function of attachment style: A follow-up study. *Communication Quarterly, 53*, 305–321.

Gumperz, J. J., & Field, M. (1995). Children's discourse and inferential practices in cooperative learning. *Discourse Processes, 19*, 133–147.

Gunkel, D. J. (2000). Rethinking virtual reality: Simulation and the deconstruction of the image. *Critical Studies in Mass Communication, 17*, 45–62.

Gunkel, D. J., & Gunkel, A. H. (1997). Virtual geographies: The new worlds of cyberspace. *Critical Studies in Mass Communication, 14*, 123–137.

Guralnik, D. (Ed.). (1986). *Webster's new world dictionary* (2nd ed.). New York, NY: Simon and Schuster.

Habermas, J. (1979). *Communication and the evolution of society.* Boston, MA: Beacon.

Habermas, J. (1984). *The theory of communicative action: Vol. 2. Lifeworld and system: A critique of functionalist reason* (T. McCarthy, Trans.). Boston, MA: Beacon Press.

Habermas, J. (1989). *The structural transformation of the public sphere* (T. Burger, Trans.). Cambridge, MA: MIT Press.

Haigh, M. M., Logsdon, L., Perrine, C., Baldwin, J. P., Breitenfeldt, R. E., Cesar, J., et al. (2005). Embedded reporting during the invasion and occupation of Iraq: How the embedding of journalists affects television news reports. *Journal of Broadcasting & Electronic Media, 49*, 468–487.

Haigh, M. M., Pfau, M., Danesi, J., Tallmon, R., Bunko, T. Nyberg, S., et al. (2006). A comparison of embedded and nonembedded print coverage of the U. S. invasion and occupation of Iraq. *Harvard International Journal of Press/Politics, 11*, 139–153.

Hall, A. (2006). Viewers' perceptions of reality programs. *Communication Quarterly, 54*, 191–211.

Hall, B. J., & Noguchi, M. (1993). Intercultural conflict: A case study. *International Journal of Intercultural Relations, 17*, 399–413.

Hall, M. (1999). He says, she says: Gender and worklife. *Public Administration Review, 59*, 410–424.

Hall, S. (1986). *Cultural studies: Two paradigms.* London, UK: Sage.

Hallmark, J. R., & Armstrong, R. N. (1999). Gender equity in televised sports: A comparative analysis of men's and women's NCAA Division 1 basketball championship broadcasts, 1991–1995. *Journal of Broadcasting and Electronic Media, 43*, 222–235.

Halloran, J. (1998). Mass communication research: Asking the right questions. In A. Hansen, S. Cottle, R. Negrine, and C. Newbold (Eds.), *Mass Communication Research Methods* (pp. 9–34). New York, NY: New York University Press.

Hamilton, S. N. (2010). Considering critical communication studies in Canada. In L. R. Shade (Ed.). *Mediascapes: New patterns in Canadian communication* (3rd ed, pp. 9–26). Toronto, ON: Nelson.

Hammersley, M. (1992). Deconstructing the qualitative-quantitative divide. In J. Brannen (Ed.), *Mixing methods: Qualitative and quantitative research* (pp. 159–173). Aldershot, UK: Avebury.

Hanke, B. (2005). For a political economy of Indymedia practice. *Canadian Journal of Communication, 30*, 41–64.

Hanke, R. (1998). The 'mock-macho' situation comedy: Hegemonic masculinity and its reiteration. *Western Journal of Communication, 62*, 74–94.

Hanmer, J. (1990). Men, power, and the exploitation of women. *Women's Studies International Forum, 13*, 443–456.

Hansen, A., Cottle, S., Negrine, R., & Newbold, C. (1998). *Mass communication research methods.* New York, NY: New York University Press.

Harter, L. M., Berquist, C., Titsworth, B. S., Novak, D., & Brokaw, T. (2005). The structuring of invisibility among the hidden homeless: The politics of space, stigma, and identity construction. *Journal of Applied Communication Research, 33*, 305–327.

Hatala, M., Baack, D., & Parmenter, R. (1998). Dating with HIV: A content analysis of gay male HIV-positive and HIV-negative personal advertisements. *Journal of Social & Personal Relationships, 15*, 268–276.

Hathaway, A. D., & Erickson, P. G. (2004). A tale of two stimulants: An analysis of newspaper coverage of cocaine and tobacco in Canada. *Canadian Journal of Communication, 29*, 61–80.

Hauser, G. A. (1991). *Introduction to rhetorical theory.* Prospect Heights, IL: Waveland Press.

Henningsen, D. D., Cruz, M. G., & Morr, M. C. (2000). Pattern violations and perceptions of deception. *Communication Reports, 13*, 1–10.

Heritage, J. (1984). *Garfinkel and ethnomethodology.* Oxford, UK: Basil Blackwell.

Heritage, J. (1985). Recent developments in conversation analysis. *Sociolinguistics, 15*, 1–18.

Heritage, J. (1998). *Oh*-prefaced responses to inquiry. *Language in Society, 27*, 291–334.

Heritage, J. (2002). Ad hoc inquiries: Two preferences in the design of 'routine' questions in an open context. In D. Maynard, H. Houtkoop-Steenstra, N. K. Schaeffer & H. van der Zouwen (Eds.), *Standardization and tacit knowledge: interaction and practice in the survey interview* (pp. 313–333). New York, NY: Wiley Interscience.

Heritage, J., & Maynard, D. (2006). *Communication in medical care: Interaction between physicians and patients.* Cambridge, UK: Cambridge University Press.

Heritage, J., & Robinson, J. D. (2006). The structure of patients' presenting concerns: Physicians' opening questions. *Health Communication, 19*, 89–102.

Heritage, J., & Roth, A. (1995). Grammar and institution: Questions and questioning in the broadcast news interview. *Research on Language and Social Interaction, 28(1)*, 1–60.

Heritage, J., & Sorjonen, M. L. (1994). Constituting and maintaining activities across sequences: And-prefacing as a feature of question design. *Language in Society, 23*, 1–29.

Hess, J. A. (2000). Maintaining nonvoluntary relationships with disliked partners: An investigation into the use of distancing behaviors. *Human Communication Research, 26*, 458–488.

Hewitt, J. P., & Stokes, R. (1975). Disclaimers. *American Sociological Review, 40*, 1–11.

Hickson, M., III, Stacks, D. W., & Bodon, J. (1999). The status of research productivity in communication: 1915–1995. *Communication Monographs, 66*, 178–197.

Higham, J. (1983). *History: Professional scholarship in America.* Baltimore, MD: Johns Hopkins University Press.

Hiltz, S. R., Johnson, K., & Turoff, M. (1986). Experiments in group decision making: Communication processes and outcomes in face-to-face versus computerized conferences. *Human Communication Research, 13,* 225–252.

Hinkle, L. (1999). Nonverbal immediacy communication behaviors and liking in marital relationships. *Communication Research Reports, 16,* 81–90.

Hirokawa, R. Y. (1980). A comparative analysis of communication patterns within effective and ineffective decision-making groups. *Communication Monographs, 47,* 312–321.

Ho, E. (2006). Behold the power of Qi: The importance of Qi in the discourse of acupuncture. *Research on Language and Social Interaction, 39,* 411–440.

Hodson, J., and Vannini, P. (2007). Island time: The media logic and ritual of ferry commuting on Gabriola Island, BC. *Canadian Journal of Communication, 32,* 261–275.

Hoffman, E. W., & Heald, G. R. (2000). Tobacco and alcohol advertisements in popular African-American and general audience magazines. *Communication Research Reports, 17,* 415–425.

Hoffman, R., & Ruemper, F. (Eds.) (2010). *Organizational behaviour: Canadian cases and exercises* (7th ed.). Toronto, ON: Captus.

Holling, M. (2006). *El Simpatico* boxer: Underpinning Chicano masculinity with a rhetoric of familia in Resurrection Blvd. *Western Journal of Communication, 70,* 91–114.

Hollingshead, A. B. (1996). Information suppression and status persistence in group decision-making: The effects of communication media. *Human Communication Research, 23,* 193–219.

Honeycutt, L. (2001). Comparing e-mail and synchronous conferencing in online peer response. *Written Communication, 18,* 26–60.

hooks, b. (1989). *Talking back: Thinking feminist, thinking black.* Boston, MA: South End Press.

hooks, b. (1992). *Black looks: Race and representation.* Boston, MA: South End Press.

hooks, b. (1994). *Outlaw culture: Resisting representations.* New York, NY: Routledge.

hooks, b. (2000). *Where we stand: Class matters.* New York, NY: Routledge.

Hoppe, M. J. (2000). The relative costs and benefits of telephone interviews versus self-administered diaries for daily data collection. *Evaluation Review, 24,* 102–117.

Hopper, R. (1992). *Telephone conversation.* Bloomington, IL: Indiana University Press.

Hopper, R. (1993). Conversational dramatism and everyday life performance. *Text & Performance Quarterly, 13,* 181–183.

Hopper, R., Doany, N., Johnson, M., & Drummond, K. (1990/91). Universals and particulars in telephone openings. *Research on Language and Social Interaction, 24,* 369–87.

Hopper, R., Koch, S., & Mandelbaum, J. (1986). Conversation analytic methods. In D. Ellis & W. Donohue (Eds.), *Contemporary issues in language and discourse processes* (pp. 169–200). Hillsdale, NJ: Lawrence Erlbaum.

Houtkoop-Steenstra, H., & Antaki, C. (1997). Creating happy people by asking yes-no questions. *Research on Language and Social Interaction, 30*(4), 285–313.

Hsieh, Y.-C., Hsieh, C.-C., & Lehman, J. A. (2003). Chinese ethics in communication, collaboration, and digitalization in the digital age. *Journal of Mass Media Ethics, 18*(3–4), 268–285.

Hummert, M. L., Shaner, J., Garstka, T. A., & Henry, C. (1998). Communication with older adults: The influence of age stereotypes, context, and communicator age. *Human Communication Research, 25,* 124–151.

Huspek, M. R. (1986). Linguistic variation, context, and meaning: A case of ing/in' variation in North American workers' speech. *Language in Society, 15,* 149–164.

Hutchby, I., & Wooffitt, R. (1998). *Conversation analysis: Principles, practices, and applications.* Cambridge, UK: Polity Press.

Hymes, D. (1962). Models of the interaction of language and social life. In J. J. Gumperz & D. Hymes (Eds.), *Directions in sociolinguistics* (pp. 35–71). New York, NY: Holt, Rinehart, & Winston.

Hymes, D. (1974a). *Foundations in sociolinguistics: An ethnographic approach.* Philadelphia, PA: University of Pennsylvania Press.

Hymes, D. (1974b). Ways of speaking. In *Foundations in sociolinguistics: An ethnographic approach.* Philadelphia, PA: University of Pennsylvania Press.

Infante, D. A. (1987). Enhancing the prediction of response to a communication situation from communication traits. *Communication Quarterly, 35,* 308–316.

Infante, D. A. (1989). Response to high argumentativeness: Message and sex differences. *Southern Communication Journal, 54,* 159–170.

Infante, D. A., & Wigley, C. J., III. (1986). Verbal aggressiveness: An interpersonal model and measure. *Communication Monographs, 53,* 61–69.

Ivory, J. D. (2006). Still a man's game: Gender representation in online reviews of video games. *Mass Communication & Society, 9,* 103–114.

Jack, I. (2010, 25 September). A Titanic mistake we can all learn from. *The Guardian,* p. 27.

Jackson, S. (1986). Building a case for claims about discourse structure. In C. H. Tardy (Ed.), *Contemporary issues in language and discourse processes* (pp. 129–147). Hillsdale, NJ: Lawrence Erlbaum.

Jackson, S., Jacobs, S., Burrell, N., & Allen, M. (1986). Characterizing ordinary argument: Substantive and methodological issues. *Journal of American Forensic Association, 23*, 42–57.

Jacobs, S. (1990). On the especially nice fit between qualitative analysis and the known properties of conversation. *Communication Monographs, 57*, 243–249.

Jaffe, A. (2007). Codeswitching and stance: Issues in interpretation. *Journal of Language, Identity, & Education, 6*, 53–77.

Jaksa, J. A., & Pritchard, M. S. (1994). *Communication ethics: Methods of analysis* (2nd ed.). Belmont, CA: Wadsworth.

Janak, J. A. (2006). The rhetoric of 'The Body': Jesse Ventura & Bakhtin's carnival. *Communication Studies, 57*, 197–214.

Janesick, V. J. (1998). The dance of qualitative research design: Metaphor, methodolatry, and meaning. In N. K. Denzin & Y. S. Lincoln (Eds.), *Strategies of qualitative inquiry* (pp. 35–55). Thousand Oaks, CA: Sage.

Janovicek, N. (2006). Oral history and ethical practice: Towards effective policies and procedures. *Journal of Academic Ethics, 4*, 157–174.

Jansen, H. J., & Koop, R. (2005). Pundits, ideologues and ranters: The British Columbia election online. *Canadian Journal of Communication, 30*, 613–632.

Jarmon, L. (1996). Performance as a resource in the practice of conversation analysis. *Text and Performance Quarterly, 16*, 336–355.

Jefferson, G. (1983). *Issues in the transcription of naturally occurring talk: Caricature versus capturing pronunciational particulars.* Tilburg Papers in Language and Literature 34. Tilburg University, Tilburg, Netherlands.

Jefferson, G. (1985). An exercise in the transcription and analysis of laughter. In T. A. Dijk (Ed.), *Handbook of Discourse Analysis* (Vol. 3, pp. 25–34). New York, NY: Academic Press.

Jefferson, G. (1996). On the poetics of ordinary talk. *Text & Performance Quarterly, 16*, 1–61.

Jefferson, G. (2004). Glossary of transcript symbols with an introduction. In G. H. Lerner (Ed.), *Conversation Analysis: Studies from the first generation* (pp. 13–31). Philadelphia, PA: John Benjamins Publishing Company.

Jenkins, M. (1999). What to do if you find out you have breast cancer. San Francisco State University *Magazine, 17*, 197–201.

Jenkins, M. (Producer) (2000). *A credit to her country* [A staged play based on oral history interviews].

Jenkins, M. (2005). Menopause and desire or 452 positions on love. *Text & Performance Quarterly, 25*, 254–281.

Jenkins, W. I. (1978). *Policy analysis: A political and organizational perspective.* London, UK: Martin Robinson.

Jiwani, Y., & Young, M. L. (2006). Missing and murdered women: reproducing marginality in news discourse. *Canadian Journal of Communication, 31*, 895–917.

Johannesen, R. L. (2001). Communication ethics: Centrality, trends, and controversies. *Communication Yearbook, 25*, 201–235.

Johnson, A. G. (1988). *Statistics.* New York, NY: Harcourt Brace Jovanovich.

Johnson, A. J., Smith, S. W., Mitchell, M. M., Orrego, V. O., & Yun, K. A. (1999). Expert advice on daytime talk television: A beneficial source of information for the general public? *Communication Research Reports, 16*, 91–101.

Johnson, R. W. (1975). Research objectives for policy analysis. In K. M. Dolbeare (Ed.), *Public Policy Evaluation* (pp. 75–92). Beverly Hills, CA: Sage.

Johnston, R. (2007). Partisan politics, market research, and media buying in Canada, 1920. *Journalism & Mass Communication Quarterly, 83*, 917–932.

Johnston, R., & Ripmeester, M. (2007). A monument's work is never done: The Watson monument, memory and forgetting in a small Canadian city. *International Journal of Heritage Studies, 13*, 117–13

Jones, D. (1992). Postmodern perspectives on organisational communication. *Australian Journal of Communication, 19*, 30–37.

Jones, S. (Ed.). (1998a). *Cybersociety 2.0: Revisiting computer-mediated communication and community.* Thousand Oaks, CA: Sage.

Jones, S. (1998b). Understanding micropolis and compunity. *The Electronic Journal of Communication, 8*(3 & 4), 1–8.

Jones, T., & Cunningham, P. (2008). Violent advertising on Canadian primetime television: A frequency analysis and potential impact. *Canadian Journal of Media Studies, 4*, 41–70.

Jorgensen, D. L. (1989). *Participant observation: A methodology for human studies.* Newbury Park, CA: Sage.

Kang, Y., Cappella, J., & Fishbein, M. (2006). The attentional mechanism of message sensation value: Interaction between message sensation value and argument quality on message effectiveness. *Communication Monographs, 73*, 351–378.

Kant, I. (1993). *Grounding for the metaphysics of morals: On a supposed right to lie because of philanthropic concerns* (J. W. Ellington, Trans.). Indianapolis, IN: Hackett. (Original work published 1785).

Kassing, J. W., & Infante, D. A. (1999). Aggressive communication in the coach-athlete relationship. *Communication Research Reports, 16*, 110–120.

Katriel, T. (1995). From 'context' to 'contexts' in intercultural communication research. In R. Wiseman

(Ed.), *Intercultural communication theory* (pp. 271–284). Thousand Oaks, CA: Sage.

Katriel, T., & Philipsen, G. (1981). 'What we need is communication': 'Communication' as a cultural category in some American speech. *Communication Monographs, 48*, 301–317.

Katzer, J., Cook, K. H., & Crouch, W. W. (1998). *Evaluating information: A guide for users of social science research* (4th ed.). Boston, MA: McGraw-Hill.

Kaye. F. W. (2003). *Hiding the audience: Viewing arts and arts institutions on the prairies*. Edmonton, AB: University of Alberta Press.

Kellas, J. K. (2005). Family ties: Communicating identity through jointly told family stories. *Communication Monographs, 72*, 365–389.

Kendig, D. (1997). Transforming gender scripts: Life after You just don't understand. *Text and Performance Quarterly, 17*, 197–210.

Kennamer, D. (2005). What journalists and researchers have in common about ethics. *Journal of Mass Media Ethics, 20*, 77–89.

Kerbel, M. R., & Bloom, J. D. (2005). Blog for America and civic involvement. *Harvard International Journal of Press/Politics, 10*(4), 3–27.

Kerlinger, F. N. (1973). *Foundations of behavioral research* (2nd ed.). New York, NY: Holt, Rinehart, & Winston.

Kerlinger, F. N. (1986). *Foundations of behavioral research* (3rd ed.). New York, NY: Holt, Rinehart, & Winston.

Keshishian, F. (1997). Political bias and nonpolitical news: A content analysis of an Armenian and Iranian earthquake in the New York Times and the Washington Post. *Critical Studies in Mass Communication, 14*, 323–343.

Kessler, R. A. (1995). *Beyond smile sheets: Evaluating a presentation skills training program for industry*. Unpublished master's thesis, San Francisco State University, San Francisco, CA.

Kidder, J. L. (2006). Bike messengers and the really real: Effervescence, reflexivity, and postmodern identity. *Symbolic Interaction, 29*, 349–372.

Kienzler, D. S. (2001). Ethics, critical thinking, and professional communication pedagogy. *Technical Communication Quarterly, 10*, 319–340.

Kienzler, D. S. (2004). Teaching ethics isn't enough. *Journal of Business Communication, 41*, 292–301.

Kim, L. S. (2003). Multiple identities in a multicultural world: A Malaysian perspective. *Journal of Language Identity & Education, 2*, 137–158.

Kim, M. S. (1999). Cross-cultural perspectives on motivations of verbal communication: Review, critique, and a theoretical framework. *Communication Yearbook, 22*, 51–89.

Kim, Y. Y. (1995a). Cross-cultural adaptation: An integrative theory. In R. Wiseman (Ed.), *Intercultural communication theory* (pp. 170–193). Thousand Oaks, CA: Sage.

Kim, Y. Y. (1995b). Identity development: From cultural to intercultural. In H. Mokros (Ed.), *Information and behavior: Vol. 6. Interaction Identity* (pp. 347–369). New Brunswick, NJ: Transaction.

Kim, Y. Y., Lujan, P., & Dixon, L. D. (1998). 'I can walk both ways': Identity integration of American Indians in Oklahoma. *Human Communication Research, 25*, 252–274.

Kirkman, B. L., & Shapiro, D. L. (2000). Understanding why team members won't share. *Small Group Research, 31*, 175–210.

Kitzinger, C. (2005). 'Speaking as a heterosexual': (How) does sexuality matter for talk-in-interaction? *Research on Language and Social Interaction, 38*, 221–265.

Kline, S. L., & Clinton, B. L. (1998). Developments in children's persuasive message practices. *Communication Education, 47*, 120–136.

Koesten, J. (2004). Family communication patterns, sex of subject, and communication competence. *Communication Monographs, 71*, 226–244.

Kraidy, M. M. (1999). The global, the local, and the hybrid: A native ethnography of globalization. *Critical Studies in Mass Communication, 16*, 456–476.

Kraidy, M. M. (2002). Hybridity in cultural globalization. *Communication Theory, 12*, 316–339.

Krcmar, M., & Valkenburg, P. M. (1999). A scale to assess children's interpretations of justified and unjustified violence and its relationship to television viewing. *Communication Research, 26*, 608–634.

Kress, G., Leite-Garcia, R., & van Leeuwen, T. (1997). Discourse semiotics. In T. A. van Dijk (Ed.), *Discourse as structure and process. Discourse Studies: A multidisciplinary introduction* (Vol. 1, pp. 257–291). London, UK: Sage.

Krippendorf, K. (1980). *Content analysis: An introduction to its methodology*. Beverly Hills, CA: Sage.

Krippendorf, K. (2004). *Content analysis: An introduction to its methodology* (2nd ed.). Thousand Oaks, CA: Sage.

Krueger, R. A. (1994). *Focus groups: A practical guide for applied research*. Newbury Park, CA: Sage.

Kubrin, C. (2005). Gangstas, thugs and hustlas: Identity and the code of the street in Rap music. *Social Problems, 52*, 360–378.

Kuhn, T. S. (1970). *The structure of scientific revolutions* (2nd ed.). Chicago, IL: University of Chicago Press.

Kwolek-Folland, A. (1994). *Engendering business: Men and women in the corporate office, 1870–1930*. Baltimore, MD: Johns Hopkins University Press.

Lacroix, J.-G., & Levesque, B. (1985). L'émergence et l'institutionnalisation de la recherché en communication au Québec (1). *Communication Information, 7*, 7–31.

Ladner, S. (2008). Laptops in the living room: Mobile technologies and the divide between work and private time among interactive agency workers. *Canadian Journal of Communication, 33*, 465–489.

Landes, J. (1988). *Women and the public sphere in the age of the French Revolution*. Ithaca, NY: Cornell University Press.

Lannamann, J. W. (1991). Interpersonal communication research as ideological practice. *Communication Theory, 3*, 179–203.

Larson, M. S. (2001). Interactions, activities, and gender in children's television commercials: A content analysis. *Journal of Broadcasting and Electronic Media, 45*, 41–56.

Lasswell, H. D. (1927). *Propaganda techniques in the World War*. New York, NY: Knopf.

Lawes, R. (1999). Marriage: An analysis of discourse. *British Journal of Social Psychology, 38*, 1–20.

Lawrence, S. G. (1999). The preoccupation with problems of understanding in communication research. *Communication Theory, 9*, 265–286.

Lawrence, T. B., Phillips, N. & Hardy, C. (1999). Watching whale-watching: A relational theory of organizational collaboration. *Journal of Applied Behavioral Science, 35*(4), 479–502.

Lears, J. (1994). *Fables of abundance: A cultural history of advertising in America*. New York, NY: Basic Books.

Lears, T. J. (1985). The concept of cultural hegemony: Problems and possibilities. *American Historical Review, 90*, 567–593.

LeBaron, C. D., Mandelbaum, J., & Glenn, P. J. (2003). An overview of language and social interaction research. In P. Glenn, C. D. LeBaron, & J. Mandelbaum (Eds.), *Studies in language & social interaction: In honor of Robert Hopper* (pp. 1–39). Mahwah, NJ: Lawrence Erlbaum.

LeBaron, C. D., & Streeck, J. (1997). Built space and the interactional framing of experience during a murder interrogation. *Human Studies, 20*, 1–25.

Lechte, J. (1994). *Fifty key contemporary thinkers: From structuralism to post-modernity*. London, UK: Routledge.

LeCompte, M. D., & Goetz, J. P. (1982). Problems of reliability and validity in ethnographic research. *Review of Educational Research, 52*, 31–60.

Lee, W. S. (1998). Patriotic breeders or colonized converts: A postcolonial feminist approach to antifootbinding discourse in China. In D. V. Tanno, & A. Gonzalez (Eds.), *Communication and identity across cultures* (pp. 11–33). Thousand Oaks, CA: Sage.

Leenders, M. R., Mauffette-Leenders, L. A., Erskine, J. A. (2001). *Writing cases* (4th ed.). London, ON: Ivey Publishing.

Leidner, R. (1991). Serving hamburgers and selling insurance: Gender, work, and identity in interactive service jobs. *Gender & Society, 5*, 155–177.

Lemke, J. L. (1999). Discourse and organizational dynamics: Website communication and institutional change. *Discourse and Society, 10*, 21–47.

Lenskyj, H. J. (1998). 'Inside sport' or 'On the margins'? Australian Women and the Sport Media. *International Review for the Sociology of Sport, 33*, 19–32.

Le Poire, B. A., & Yoshimura, S. M. (1999). The effects of expectancies and actual communication on nonverbal adaptation and communication outcomes: A test of interaction adaptation theory. *Communication Monographs, 66*, 1–30.

Leslie, M. (2006). Fear and coughing in Toronto: SARS and the uses of risk. *Canadian Journal of Communication, 31*, 367–389.

Levine, T. R., Beatty, M. J., Limon, S., Hamilton, M. A., Buck, R., & Chory-Assad, R. M. (2004). The dimensionality of the verbal aggressiveness scale. *Communication Monographs, 71*, 245–268.

Lewis, C. (1997). Hegemony in the ideal: Wedding photography, consumerism, and patriarchy. *Women's Studies in Communication, 20*, 167–187.

Lewis, C., & Neville, J. (1995). Images of Rosie: A content analysis of women workers in American magazine advertising, 1940–1946. *Journalism & Mass Communication Quarterly, 72*, 216–227.

Li, H. Z., Koehn, C., Desroches, N. G., Yum, Y-O., & Deagle, G. (2007). Asymmetrical talk between physicians and patients: A quantitative discourse analysis. *Canadian Journal of Communication, 32*, 417–433.

Lichter, S. R., Lichter, L. S., & Amundson, D. (1997). Does Hollywood hate business or money? *Journal of Communication, 47*, 68–84.

Lin, C. A. (1997). Beefcake versus cheesecake in the 1990s: Sexist portrayals of both genders in television commercials. *Howard Journal of Communication, 8*, 237–249.

Lincoln, J. R. (1990, December). [Review of the book *Social structures: A network approach*]. *Administrative Science Quarterly* (pp. 746–748).

Lincoln, Y. S., & Guba, E. G. (1985). *Naturalistic inquiry*. Beverly Hills, CA: Sage.

Lindlof, T. R. (1995). *Qualitative communication research methods*. Thousand Oaks, CA: Sage.

Lindlof, T. R., & Shatzer, M. J. (1998). Media ethnography in virtual space: Strategies, limits, and possibilities. *Journal of Broadcasting & Electronic Media, 42,* 170–193.

Lindlof, T. R., Shatzer, M. J., & Wilkinson, D. (1998). Accommodation of video and television in the American family. In J. Lull (Ed.), *World families watch television* (pp. 158–192). Newbury Park, NJ: Sage.

Lindsley, S. L. (1999). A layered model of problematic intercultural communication in U. S.-owned maquiladoras in Mexico. *Communication Monographs, 66,* 145–167.

Lindstrom, A. (1994). Identification and recognition in Swedish telephone conversation openings. *Language in Society, 23,* 231–52.

Litt, P. (1999). The apotheosis of the apothecary: Retailing and consuming the meaning of a historic site. *Journal of the Canadian Historical Association, 10*(1), 297–321.

Littlejohn, S. W. (1996). *Theories of human communication* (5th ed.). Belmont, CA: Wadsworth Thompson.

Littlejohn, S. W. (2000). *Theories of human communication* (6th ed.). Belmont, CA: Wadsworth Thompson.

Littlejohn, S. W. (2002). *Theories of human communication* (7th ed.). Belmont, CA: Wadsworth Thompson.

Littlejohn, S. W., & Foss, K. A. (2005). *Theories of human communication* (8th ed.). Belmont, CA: Thomson Learning.

Liu, C. (2006). De-skilling effects on journalists: ICTs and the labour process of Taiwanese newspaper reporters. *Canadian Journal of Communication, 31,* 695–714.

Lofland, J., & Lofland, L. H. (1984). *Analyzing social settings: A guide to qualitative observation and analysis* (2nd ed.). Belmont, CA: Wadsworth.

Lofland, J., & Lofland, L. H. (1995). *Analyzing social settings: A guide to qualitative observation and analysis* (3rd ed.). Belmont, CA: Wadsworth.

Lofland, J., Snow, D., Anderson, L., & Lofland, L. H. (2006). *Analyzing social settings: A guide to qualitative observation and analysis* (4th ed.). Belmont, CA: Thomson.

Lombard, M., & Reich, R. D. (2000). Presence and television: The role of screen size. *Human Communication Research, 26,* 75–99.

Lombard, M., Snyder-Duch, J., & Bracken, C. C. (2002). Content analysis in mass communication: Assessment and reporting of intercoder reliability. *Human Communication Research, 28,* 587–604.

Lorimer, R., & Lindsay, A. (2004). Canadian scholarly journals at a technological crossroads. *Canadian Journal of Communication, 29,* 253–275.

Lowes, M. D. (1999). *Inside the sport pages: Work routines, professional ideologies, and the manufacture of sport news.* Toronto, ON: University of Toronto Press.

Lowman, J., and Palys, T. (2007). Strict confidentiality: An alternative to PRE's 'Limited confidentiality' doctrine. *Journal of Academic Ethics, 5,* 163–177.

Lyotard, F. (1984). *The postmodern condition: A report on knowledge* (G. Bennington & B. Massumi, Trans.). Minneapolis, MN: University of Minnesota Press.

Mabrito, M. (1995). The e-mail discussion group: An opportunity for discourse analysis. *Business Communication Quarterly, 58,* 10–12.

MacLeod, E. (2002). Ashley MacIsaac: Star image, queer identity, and the politics of outing. *Topia: Canadian Journal of Cultural Studies, 8,* 19–42.

MacRae, D., Jr., & Wilde, J. A. (1979). *Policy analysis for public decisions.* North Scituate, MA: Duxbury Press.

Madison, S. (2005). *Critical ethnography: Method, ethics, & performance.* Thousand Oaks, CA: Sage.

Maguire, G. (1996). *Wicked: The life and times of the wicked witch of the west.* New York, NY: Regan.

Mahtani, M. (2008). Racializing the audience: Immigrant perceptions of mainstream Canadian English Language TV News. *Canadian Journal of Communication, 33,* 639–660.

Malinowski, B. (1922). *Argonauts of the Western Pacific.* London, UK: Routledge.

Mandelbaum, J. (1987). Couples sharing stories. *Communication Quarterly, 35,* 144–170.

Manusov, V., & Trees, A. R. (2002). 'Are you kidding me?': The role of nonverbal cues in the verbal accounting process. *Journal of Communication, 52,* 640–656.

Markham, A. (1996). Designing discourse: A critical analysis of strategic ambiguity and workplace control. *Management Communication Quarterly, 9,* 389–421.

Marland, A. J. (2008). Promotional and other spending by party candidates in the 2006 Canadian federal election campaign. *Canadian Journal of Media Studies, 3,* 57–89.

Marquis, D. (2009). The Catholic press: A challenge to the 'Journalism of information' paradigm (P. Smart, Trans.). In G. Allen & D. Robinson (Eds.), *Communicating in Canada's past: Essays in media history* (pp. 27–46). Toronto: University of Toronto Press.

Marshall, J. (1993). Viewing organizational communication from a feminist perspective: A critique and some offerings. In S. Deetz (Ed.), *Communication Yearbook* (Vol. 16, pp. 122–143). Newbury Park, CA: Sage.

Martin, G. W. (1998). Communication breakdown or ideal speech situation: The problem of nurse advocacy. *Nursing Ethics, 5*(2), 147–157.

Martin, J. (1990). Deconstructing organizational taboos: The suppression of gender conflict in organizations. *Organization Science, 11,* 339–359.

Martin, J. N., & Flores, L. A. (1998). Colloquy: Challenges in contemporary culture and communication research. *Human Communication Research, 25*, 293–299.

Martin, J. N., Hammer, M. R., & Bradford, L. (1994). The influence of cultural and situational context on Hispanic and non-Hispanic communication competence behaviors. *Communication Quarterly, 42*, 160–179.

Martin, M. (1991). *Hello, central? Gender, technology and culture in the formation of telephone systems.* Montreal, QC: McGill-Queen's University Press.

Marx, K. (1888). *The Communist manifesto.* London, UK: Reeves.

Marx, K. (1909). *Capital.* Chicago, IL: Kerr.

Matabane, P., & Merritt, B. (1996). African-Americans on television: 25 years after Kerner. *Howard Journal of Communication, 7*, 329–337.

Matheson, S. (2006). Ruling the inner city: Television, citizenship and *King of Kensington. Canadian Journal of Film Studies, 15*, 46–62.

Mathison, S. (1988). Why triangulate? *Educational Researcher, 17*(2), 13–17.

Mattson, M., & Brann, M. (2002). Managed care and the paradox of patient confidentiality: A case study analysis from a communication boundary management perspective. *Communication Studies, 53*, 337–358.

May, R. A., & Pattillo-McCoy, M. (2000). Do you see what I see? Examining a collaborative ethnography. *Qualitative Inquiry, 6*, 65–87.

Mayer, V. (2005). Research beyond the pale: Whiteness in audience studies and media ethnography. *Communication Theory, 15*, 148–167.

Maynard, D. W. (1997). The news delivery sequence: Bad news and good news in conversational interaction. *Research on Language and Social Interaction, 30*(2), 93–130.

Maynard, D. W. (2003). *Bad news, good news: Conversational order in everyday talk and clinical settings.* Chicago, IL: University of Chicago Press.

Maynard, D. W., & Clayman, S. E. (1991). The diversity of ethnomethodology. *Annual Review of Sociology, 17*, 385–418.

Maynard, D. W., & Heritage, J. (2005). Conversation analysis, doctor-patient interaction and medical communication. *Medical Education, 39*, 428–435.

McCain, G., & Segal, E. M. (1988). *The game of science* (5th ed.). Pacific Grove, CA: Brooks/Cole.

McComas, K., & Shanahan, J. (1999). Telling stories about global climate change: Measuring the impact of narratives on issue cycles. *Communication Research, 26*, 30–57.

McCroskey, J. C. (1982). *An introduction to rhetorical communication* (4th ed.). Englewood Cliffs, NJ: Prentice Hall.

McCroskey, J. C., & Young, T. J. (1981). Ethos and credibility: The construct and its measurement after three decades. *Central States Speech Journal, 32*, 24–34.

McDermott, R. P., Gospodinoff, K., & Aron, J. (1978). Criteria for an ethnographically adequate description of concerted activities and their contexts. *Semiotica, 24*, 245–275.

McGrady, P. (Director) (2008). *The machine that made us.* London, UK: BBC/Norwich, UK: Wavelength Films.

McKay, I. (1997). *The quest of the folk: Antimodernism and cultural selection in twentieth-century Nova Scotia.* Montreal, QC: McGill-Queen's University Press.

McKee, K. B., & Pardun, C. J. (1996). Mixed messages: The relationship between sexual and religious imagery in rock, country, and Christian videos. *Communication Reports, 9*, 163–172.

McLaughlin, L. (1991). Discourses of prostitution/discourses of sexuality. *Critical Studies in Mass Communication, 8*, 249–272.

McLaughlin, M. L. (1984). *Conversation: How talk is organized.* Beverly Hills, CA: Sage.

McLeod, J. M., Scheufele, D. A., Moy, P., Horowitz, E. M., Holbert, R. L., Zhang, W., et al. (1999). Understanding deliberation: The effects of discussion networks on participation in a public forum. *Communication Research, 26*, 743–774.

McLuhan, M. (1964). *Understanding media: The extensions of man.* New York, NY: McGraw-Hill.

McNeil, L. M. (1986). Contradictions of control: School structure and school knowledge. London, UK: Routledge & Kegan.

Mead, G. H. (1934). *Mind, self, and society from the standpoint of a social behaviorist.* Chicago, IL: The University of Chicago Press

Medical Research Council of Canada. (1998). *Tri-council policy statement: Ethical conduct for research involving humans.* Ottawa, ON: Medical Research Council/Public Works Canada.

Medved, C. E., Brogan, S. M., McClanahan, A. M., Morris, J. F., & Shepard, G. J. (2006). Family and work socializing communication: Messages, gender, and ideological implications. *Journal of Family Communication, 6*, 161–180.

Mertens, D. M. (1998). *Research methods in education and psychology: Integrating diversity with quantitative & qualitative approaches.* Thousand Oaks, CA: Sage.

Merton, R. K. (1968). *Social theory and social structure.* New York, NY: Free Press.

Merton, T. (1993). *The courage for truth: Letters to writers* (Selected and edited by Christine M. Bochen). New York, NY: Farrar, Straus, & Giroux.

Meyers, R. A., & Brashers, D. E. (1998). Argument in group decision making: Explicating a process model and investigating the argument-outcome link. *Communication Monographs, 65*, 261–281.

Middleton, C., & Crow, B. (2008). Building Wi-Fi networks for communities: Three Canadian cases. *Canadian Journal of Communication, 33*, 419–441.

Mies, M. (1991). Women's research or feminist research? The debate surrounding feminist science and methodology. In M. M. Fonow & J. A. Cook (Eds.), *Beyond methodology: Feminist scholarship as lived research* (pp. 60–84). Bloomington, IL: Indiana University Press.

Miles, M. B., & Huberman, A. M. (1994). *Qualitative data analysis: An expanded sourcebook* (2nd ed.). Thousand Oaks, CA: Sage.

Miller, A. (2006). Watching viewers watch TV: Processing live, breaking, and emotional news in a naturalistic setting. *Journalism & Mass Communication Quarterly, 83*, 511–529.

Miller, D. L., Creswell, J. W., & Olander, L. S. (1998). Writing and retelling multiple ethnographic tales of a soup kitchen for the homeless. *Qualitative Inquiry, 4*, 469–491.

Miller, G. R. (1970). Research setting: Laboratory studies. In P. Emmert & W. Brooks (Eds.), *Methods of research in communication* (pp. 77–104). Boston, MA: Houghton Mifflin.

Miller, J. M. (2000). Language use, identity, and social interaction: Migrant students in Australia. *Research on Language and Social Interaction, 33*, 69–100.

Miller, K. (2002). The experience of emotion in the workplace: Professing in the midst of tragedy. *Management Communication Quarterly, 15*, 571–600.

Miller, M. (1995). An intergenerational case study of suicidal tradition and mother-daughter communication. *Journal of Applied Communication Research, 23*, 247–270.

Mitchell, C. J. (1983). Case and situation analysis. *Sociological Review, 31*, 187–211.

Mitchell, G. R. (2000). Placebo defense: Operation desert mirage? The rhetoric of Patriot missile accuracy in the 1991 Persian Gulf war. *Quarterly Journal of Speech, 86*, 121–145.

Monge, P. (1987). The network level of analysis. In C. Berger & S. Chaffee (Eds.), *Handbook of communication science* (pp. 239–270). Beverly Hills, CA: Sage.

Mongeau, P. A., Hale, J. L., & Alles, M. (1994). An experimental investigation of accounts and attributions following sexual infidelity. *Communication Monographs, 61*, 326–344.

Mongeau, P. A., Serewicz, M. C. M., & Therrien, L. F. (2004). Goals for cross-sex first dates: Identification, measurement, and the influence of contextual factors. *Communication Monographs, 71*, 121–147.

Montemurro, B. (2005). Add men, don't stir: Reproducing traditional gender roles in modern wedding showers. *Journal of Contemporary Ethnography, 34*, 6–35.

Montgomery, B. M., & Norton, R. W. (1981). Sex differences and similarities in communicator style. *Communication Monographs, 48*, 121–132.

Morgan, D. L. (1988). *Focus groups as qualitative research.* Newbury Park, CA: Sage.

Morris, P. (1978). *Embattled shadows: A history of Canadian cinema, 1895–1939.* Montreal, QC: McGill-Queen's University Press.

Morris, R. N. (1992). Editorial cartoons and the reproduction of capitalist order. In M. Grenier (Ed.), *Critical studies in Canadian mass media* (pp. 145–154). Toronto, ON: Butterworths.

Morse, J. M. (1998). Designing funded qualitative research. In N. Denzin & Y. Lincoln (Eds.), *Strategies of qualitative inquiry* (pp. 56–85). Thousand Oaks, CA: Sage.

Morton, T. A., & Duck, J. M. (2000). Social identity and media dependency in the gay community: The prediction of safe sex attitudes. *Communication Research, 27*, 438–460.

Mosco, V., & McKercher, C. (2006). Convergence bites back: Labour struggles in the Canadian communication industry. *Canadian Journal of Communication, 31*, 733–751.

Mottet, T. P., Parker-Raley, J., Cunningham, C., & Beebe, S. (2005). The relationships between teacher nonverbal immediacy and student course workload and teacher availability expectations. *Communication Research Reports, 22*, 275–282.

Mouillard, M. (1968). Le système des journaux (Théorie et methods pour l'analyse de presse). *Langages, 11*, 61–83.

Mouly, G. J. (1970). *The science of educational research* (2nd ed.). New York, NY: Van Nostrand Reinhold Co.

Mumby, D. K. (1988). *Communication and power in organizations: Discourse, ideology, and domination.* Norwood, NJ: Ablex.

Mumby, D. K. (1993). Critical organizational communication studies: The next 10 years. *Communication Monographs, 60*, 18–25.

Mumby, D. K. (1997a). Modernism, postmodernism, and communication studies: A rereading of an ongoing debate. *Communication Theory, 7*, 1–28.

Mumby, D. K. (1997b). The problem of hegemony: Rereading Gramsci for organizational communication studies. *Western Journal of Communication, 61*, 343–375.

Mumby, D. K., & Putnam, L. L. (1992). The politics of emotion: A feminist reading of bounded rationality. *Academy of Management Review, 17*, 465–486.

Mumby, D. K., & Stohl, C. (1991). Power and discourse in organizational studies: Absence and the dialectic of control. *Discourse & Society, 2*, 313–332.

Munshi, D., & Kurian, P. (2005). Imperializing spin cycles: A postcolonial look at public relations, greenwashing, and the separation of publics. *Public Relations Review, 31*, 513–520.

Murillo, E. G., Jr. (1996, November). *Pedagogy of a Latin-American festival: A mojado ethnography*. Paper presented at the annual meeting of the American Educational Studies Association in Montréal, QC.

Murphy, J. M. (1997). Inventing authority: Bill Clinton, Martin Luther King, Jr., and the orchestration of rhetorical traditions. *Quarterly Journal of Speech, 83*, 71–89.

Myers, S. A. (2002). Perceived aggressive instructor communication and student state motivation, learning, and satisfaction. *Communication Reports, 15*, 113–121.

Nakayama, T. K. (1997). Les voix de l'autre [The voices of the other]. *Western Journal of Communication, 61*, 235–242.

Nakayama, T. K., & Krizek, R. L. (1995). Whiteness: A strategic rhetoric. *Quarterly Journal of Speech, 81*, 291–309.

Nathanson, A. I. (1999). Identifying and explaining the relationship between parental mediation and children's aggression. *Communication Research, 26*, 124–144.

Nathanson, A. I. (2001). Parents versus peers: Exploring the significance of peer mediation of antisocial television. *Communication Research, 28*, 251–274.

National Institute of Health. (2002). *Human participant protections education for research teams*. Washington, DC: U. S. Department of Health & Human Services.

Naumes, W., & Naumes, M. J. (2006). *The art & craft of case writing* (2nd ed.). Armonk, NY: M. E. Sharpe.

Neruda, P. (1972). *New poems: 1968–1970* (B. Belitt, Ed.). New York, NY: Grove Press.

Neuendorf, K. A. (2002). *The content analysis guidebook*. London, UK: Sage.

Neuman, W. L. (1994). *Social research methods*. Boston, MA: Allyn & Bacon.

Newman, I., & Benz, C. R. (1998). *Qualitative-quantitative research methodology: Exploring the interactive continuum*. Carbondale, IL: Southern Illinois University Press.

Nieves, E. (2000, November 5). Mission district fights case of dot-com fever. *The New York Times*, p. 1.27.

Niquette, M., & Buxton, W. J. (1997). Meet me at the fair: Sociability and reflexivity in nineteenth-century world expositions. *Canadian Journal of Communication, 22*, 81–113.

Nozick, R. (1974). *Anarchy, state, and utopia*. Oxford, UK: Basil Blackwell.

Nunnally, J. C. (1972). *Educational measurement and evaluation* (2nd ed.). New York, NY: McGraw Hill.

Ochs, E. (1979). Transcription as theory. In E. Ochs and B. B. Schieffelin (Eds.), *Developmental Pragmatics* (pp. 43–72). New York, NY: Academic Press.

O'Connell, C. J., & Mills, A. J. (2003). Making sense of bad news: The media, sense-making and bad news, *Canadian Journal of Communication, 28*, 323–339.

Office of the Privacy Commissioner of Canada. (2004). *Fact sheets: Protecting your privacy on the Internet*. Retrieved June 17, 2010, from www.priv.gc.ca/fs-fi/02_05_d_13_e.cfm

O'Keefe, D. (1980). Ethnomethodology. *Journal for the Theory of Social Behavior, 9*, 187–219.

Oliver, M. (1992). Changing the social relations of research production? *Disability, Handicap, & Society, 7*, 101–114.

Ono, K. A. (1998). A letter/essay I've been longing to write in my personal/academic voice. *Western Journal of Communication, 61*, 114–125.

Ott, B. L., & Aoki, E. (2001). Popular imagination and identity politics: Reading the future in *Star Trek: The Next Generation*. *Western Journal of Communication, 65*, 392–415.

Owen, M. (2002). Engaging the Humanities? Research ethics in Canada. *Journal of Research Administration, 33*, 5–12.

Owram, D. (1996). *Born at the right time: A history of the Baby Boom generation*. Toronto, ON: University of Toronto Press.

Palmgreen, P. (1984). Uses and gratifications: A theoretical perspective. In R. N. Bostrom (Ed.), *Communication Yearbook* (Vol. 8, pp. 20–55). Beverly Hills, CA: Sage.

Palomares, N. A., & Flanagin, A. J. (2005). The potential of electronic communications and information technologies as research tools: Promise and perils for the future of communication research. *Communication Yearbook, 29*, 147–185.

Papa, M. J., Auwal, M. A., & Singhal, A. (1995). Dialectic of control and emancipation in organizing for social change: A multitheoretic study of the Grameen Bank in Bangladesh. *Communication Theory, 5*, 189–223.

Papa, M. J., Auwal, M. A., & Singhal, A. (1997). Organizing for social change within concertive control systems: Member identification, empowerment, and the masking of discipline. *Communication Monographs, 64*, 219–249.

Park, H. W. (1998). A Gramscian approach to interpreting international communication. *Journal of Communication, 48*, 79–99.

Park, Y. Y. (2002). Recognition and identification in Japanese and Korean telephone conversation openings (pp. 25–47). In K. Kwong Luke and T. S. Pavlidou (Eds.) *Telephone calls: Unity and diversity in conversational structure across languages and cultures*. Amsterdam, NL: John Benjamins.

Parker, M. (1992). Post-modern organizations or postmodern organizational theory? *Organization Studies, 13*, 1–17.

Parks, M. R. (1997). Ideology in interpersonal communication: Beyond the couches, talk shows, and bunkers. *Communication Yearbook, 18*, 480–497.

Patterson, B. R., Neupauer, N. C., Burant, P. A., Koehn, S. C., & Reed, A. T. (1996). A preliminary examination of conversation analytic techniques: Rates of inter-transcriber reliability. *Western Journal of Communication, 60*, 76–91.

Patton, C. (2007). Mobile knowledge: HIV patients' encounter with endocrinology. *Canadian Journal of Communication, 32*, 335–355.

Patton, M. Q. (1990). *Qualitative evaluation and research methods* (2nd ed.). Newbury Park, CA: Sage.

Patton, O. (2004). In the guise of civility: The complications of maintenance of inferential forms of sexism and racism in higher education. *Women's Studies in Communication, 27*, 60–87.

Pavitt, C. (2004). Theory-data interaction from the standpoint of scientific realism: A reaction to Bostrom. *Communication Monographs, 71*, 333–342.

Pearce, W. B. (1998). On putting social justice in the discipline of communication and putting enriched concepts of communication in social justice research and practice. *Journal of Applied Communication Research, 26*, 272–278.

Pedhazur, E. J. (1982). *Multiple regression in behavioral research: Explanation and prediction* (2nd ed.). New York, NY: Holt, Rinehart, & Winston.

Peeples, J. A., & DeLuca, K. M. (2006). The truth of the matter: Motherhood, community, and environmental justice. *Women's Studies in Communication, 29*, 59–87.

Peirce, C. S. (1992). *Reasoning and the logic of things: The Cambridge conference lectures of 1898* (K. L. Ketner, Ed.). Cambridge, MA: Harvard University Press.

Pelias, R. J. (2004a). *A methodology of the heart: Evoking academic and daily life.* Walnut Creek, CA: AltaMira.

Pelias, R. (2004b). The academic tourist: An autoethnography. *Qualitative Inquiry, 9*, 369–373.

Penfold, S. (2008). *The donut: A Canadian history.* Toronto, ON: University of Toronto Press.

Pepper, G. L., & Larson, G. S. (2006). Cultural identity tensions in a post-acquisition organization. *Journal of Applied Communication Research, 34*, 49–71.

Perez, G. J. (1997). Communication ethics in a Latin American context. In C. G. Christians & M. Traber (Eds.), *Communication ethics and universal values* (pp. 159–169). Thousand Oaks, CA: Sage.

Perse, E. M., & Ferguson, D. A. (2000). The benefits and costs of web surfing. *Communication Quarterly, 48*, 343–359.

Peshkin, A. (1988). In search of subjectivity—one's own. *Educational Researcher, 17*, 17–22.

Philipsen, G. (1975). Speaking 'like a man' in Teamsterville: Cultural patterns of role enactment in an urban neighborhood. *Quarterly Journal of Speech, 61*, 13–22.

Philipsen, G. (1976). Places for speaking in Teamsterville. *Quarterly Journal of Speech, 62*, 15–25.

Philipsen, G. (1977). Linearity of research design in ethnographic studies of speaking. *Communication Quarterly, 25*, 42–50.

Philipsen, G. (1982). The qualitative case study as a strategy in communication inquiry. *The Communicator, 12*, 4–17.

Philipsen, G. (1989). An ethnographic approach to communication studies. In B. Dervin, L. Grossberg, B. J. O'Keefe, & E. Wartella (Eds.), *Rethinking communication 2: Paradigm exemplars* (pp. 258–267). Newbury Park, CA: Sage.

Philipsen, G. (1992). *Speaking culturally: Explorations in social communication.* Albany, NY: State University of New York Press.

Philipsen, G. (1997). A theory of speech codes. In G. Philipsen & T. Albrecht (Eds.), *Developing communication theories* (pp. 119–156). Albany, NY: State University of New York Press.

Phillips, N., & Hardy, C. (2002). *Discourse analysis: Investigating processes of social construction.* Thousand Oaks, CA: Sage.

Pittman, J., & Gallois, C. (1997). Language strategies in the attribution of blame for HIV and AIDS. *Communication Monographs, 64*, 201–218.

Pollach, I. (2005). A typology of communicative strategies in online privacy policies: Ethics, power and informed consent. *Journal of Business Ethics, 62*, 221–235.

Pomerantz, A. (1978). Compliment responses: Notes on the co-operation of multiple constraints. In J. Schenkein (Ed.), *Studies in the organization of conversational interaction* (pp. 79–112). New York, NY: Academic.

Pomerantz, A. (1990). Chautauqua: On the validity and generalizability of conversational analysis methods. Conversation analytic claims. *Communication Monographs, 57*, 231–235.

Potter, A. B., McIntyre, N., and Middleton, C. (2008). How usable are wireless networks? *Canadian Journal of Communication, 33*, 511–524.

Potter, J., & Wetherall, M. (1987). *Discourse and social psychology.* Newbury Park, CA: Sage.

Pragg, L., Wiseman, R. L., Cody, M. J., & Wendt, P. F. (1999). Interrogative strategies and information exchange in computer-mediated communication. *Communication Quarterly, 47*, 46–66.

Preston, D. (1982). Mowr and mowr bayud spellin': Confessions of a sociolinguist. *Journal of Sociolinguistics, 4*(4), 615–621.

Preston, D. R. (2000). Three kinds of sociolingusitics and SLA: A psycholinguistic perspective. In B. Swierzbin, F. Morris, M. Anderson, C. Klee & E. Tarone (Eds.), *Social and cognitive factors in second language acquisition: Selected Proceedings fo the 1999 Second Language Research Forum* (pp. 3–30). Somerville, MA: Cascadilla Press.

Psathas, G., & Anderson, W. T. (1987). The 'practices' of transcription in conversation analysis. *Semiotica, 78*, 75–99.

Pyrczak, F., & Bruce, R. R. (1992). *Writing empirical research reports: A basic guide for students of behavioral and social sciences.* Los Angeles, CA: Pyrczak Publishing.

Ralston, S. M. (2000). The 'Veil of ignorance': Exploring ethical issues in the employment interview. *Business Communication Quarterly, 63*, 50–52.

Ramasubramanian, S. (2005). A content analysis of the portrayal of India in films produced in the West. *Howard Journal of Communications, 16*(4), 243–265.

Ramazanoglu, C. (1992). On feminist methodology: Male reason versus female empowerment. *Sociology, 26*, 207–212.

Ramsey, S. (1999). A benchmark study of elaboration and sourcing in science stories for eight American newspapers. *Journalism & Mass Communication Quarterly, 76*, 87–98.

Rasmussen, D. M. (1996). Critical theory and philosophy. In D. M. Rasmussen (Ed.), *The Handbook of Critical Theory* (pp. 11–38). Oxford, UK: Blackwell.

Ray, E. B. (1993). When the links become chains: Considering dysfunctions of supportive communication in the workplace. *Communication Monographs, 60*, 106–111.

Raymond, G. (2000). *The structure of responding: Type-conforming and non-conforming responses to yes/no interrogatives.* Ph. D. dissertation, Department of Sociology, University of California, Los Angeles.

Reich, N. M. (2002). Toward a re-articulation of women as victims: A thematic analysis of the construction of women's identities surrounding gendered violence. *Communication Quarterly, 50*, 292–311.

Reinelt, J. G. (1992). Introduction to psychoanalytic criticism. In J. G. Reinelt & J. R. Roach (Eds.), *Critical theory & performance* (pp. 383–387). Ann Arbor, MI: University of Michigan Press.

Rentschler, C. A. (2007). Victims' rights and the struggle over crime in the media. *Canadian Journal of Communication, 32*, 219–239.

Reyes, C. V. (2010). Film noir's dark secret, or what does the hysteric want? *Canadian Journal of Film Studies, 19*, 75–88.

Richelieu, A., & Pons, F. (2008). Branding sport teams in a competitive context: A look at team branding in the National Hockey League. In S. Chadwick & D. Arthur (Eds.), *International Cases in the Business of Sport.* Oxford, UK: Butterworth-Heinemann. pp. 13–29.

Rinehart, D. (2008). Baby talk: How gender issues affected media coverage of the child-care debate in the last federal election. *Canadian Journal of Media Studies, 4*, 1–40.

Roach, K. D., & Olaniran, B. A. (2001). Intercultural willingness to communicate and communication anxiety in international teaching assistants. *Communication Research Reports, 18*, 26–35.

Roberts, F., & Robinson, J. D. (2004). Interobserver agreement on first-stage conversation analytic transcription. *Human Communication Research, 30*(3), 376–410.

Robinson, D. (1999). *The measure of democracy: Polling, market research, and public life, 1930–1945.* Toronto, ON: University of Toronto Press.

Robinson, G. (2000). Remembering our past: Reconstructing the field of Canadian communication studies. *Canadian Journal of Communication, 25*, 105–125.

Robinson, J. D. (1998). Getting down to business: Talk, gaze, and body orientation during openings of doctor-patient consultations. *Human Communication Research, 25*, 97–123.

Robinson, J. D. (2003). An interactional structure of medical activities during acute visits and its implications for patients' participation. *Health Communication, 15*(1), 27–57.

Robinson, J. D. (2004). The sequential organization of 'explicit' apologies in naturally occurring English. *Research on Language and Social Interaction, 37*, 291–330.

Robinson, J. D. (2006). Managing trouble responsibility and relationships during conversational repair. *Communication Monographs, 73*, 137–161.

Robinson, J. D., & Stivers, T. (2001). Achieving activity transition in physician-patient encounters: From history-taking to physical examination. *Human Communication Research, 27*, 253–298.

Rogers, E. M. (1994). *A history of communication study: A biographical approach.* New York, NY: Free Press.

Rogers, R. A. (2006). From cultural exchange to transculturation: A review and reconceptualization of cultural appropriation. *Communication Theory, 16*, 474–503.

Romaine, S. (1982). What is a speech community? In S. Romaine (Ed.), *Sociolinguistic variation in speech communities* (pp. 13–24). London, UK: Edward Arnold.

Rosenfeld, L. B., Richman, J. M., & May, S. K. (2004). Information adequacy, job satisfaction, and organizational culture in a dispersed-network organization. *Journal of Applied Communication Research, 32*, 28–54.

Rossler, P. (2001). Between online heaven and cyberhell: The framing of 'the Internet' by traditional media coverage in Germany. *New Media & Society, 3,* 49–66.

Roth, L. (1993). Mohawk airwaves and cultural challenges: Some reflections on the politics of recognition and cultural appropriation after the summer of 1990. *Canadian Journal of Communication, 18,* 315–331.

Roth, L. (2009). Looking at Shirley, the ultimate norm: Colour balance, image technologies and cognitive equity. *Canadian Journal of Communication, 34,* 111–136.

Rothman, B. K. (1986). Reflections: On hard work. *Qualitative Sociology, 9,* 48–53.

Rotton, J., & Kelly, I. W. (1985). Much ado about the full moon: A meta-analysis of lunar lunacy research. *Psychological Bulletin, 97,* 286–306.

Roy, A., & Harwood, J. (1997). Underrepresented, positively portrayed: Older adults in television commercials. *Journal of Applied Communication Research, 25,* 39–56.

Ruben, B. D. (1993). What patients remember: A content analysis of critical incidents in health care. *Health Communication, 5,* 99–112.

Rubin, R. B., Palmgreen, P., & Sypher, H. E. (2004). Source credibility scale: 15-item semantic differential. In *Communication research measures: A sourcebook* (pp. 338–339). Mahwah, NJ: Lawrence Erlbaum Associates.

Rubin, R. B., Rubin, A. M., & Jordan, F. F. (1997). Effects of instruction on communication apprehension and communication competence. *Communication Education, 46,* 104–114.

Rusted, B. (2006). Performing visual discourse: Cowboy art and institutional practice. *Text & Performance Quarterly, 26,* 115–137.

Rutherford, P. (2000). *Endless propaganda: The advertising of public goods.* Toronto, ON: University of Toronto Press.

Ruud, G. (1995). The symbolic construction of organizational identities and community in a regional symphony. *Communication Studies, 46,* 201–222.

Sachweh, S. (1998). Granny darling's nappies: Secondary babytalk in German nursing homes for the aged. *Journal of Applied Communication Research, 26,* 52–65.

Sacks, H. (1972). An initial investigation of the usability of conversational data for doing sociology. In D. Sudnow (Ed.), *Studies in social interaction* (pp. 31–74). New York, NY: Free Press.

Sacks, H. (1984). Notes on methodology. In J. Atkinson & J. Heritage (Eds.), *Structures of social action: Studies in conversation analysis* (pp. 21–27). Cambridge, UK: Cambridge University Press.

Sacks, H., Schegloff, E., & Jefferson, G. (1974). A simplest systematic for the organization of turn taking for conversation. *Language, 50,* 696–735.

Said, E. (1984). Permission to narrate. *Journal of Palestine Studies, 13,* 27–48.

Sapolsky, B. S., & Kaye, B. K. (2005). The use of offensive language by men and women in prime time television entertainment. *Atlantic Journal of Communication, 13,* 292–303.

Saunders, C. M. (2008). Forty seven million strong, weak, wrong, or right: Living without health insurance. *Qualitative Inquiry, 14,* 528–545.

Scanlon, J. (1993). Challenging the imbalances of power in feminist oral history: Developing a give-and-take methodology. *Women's Studies International Forum, 16,* 639–645.

Scharrer, E. (2001). From wise to foolish: The portrayal of the sitcom father, 1950s–1990s. *Journal of Broadcasting and Electronic Media, 45,* 23–40.

Scharrer, E., Kim, D. D., Lin, K. M., & Liu, Z. (2006). Working hard or hardly working? Gender, humor, and the performance of domestic chores in television commercials. *Mass Communication & Society, 9,* 215–238.

Schegloff, E. A. (1968). Preliminaries to preliminaries: "Can I ask you a question?" *Sociological Inquiry, 50,* 104–152.

Schegloff, E. A. (1979). Identification and Recognition in Telephone Openings (pp. 23–78). In G. Psathas (Ed.), *Everyday language: Studies in ethnomethodology.* New York, NY: Erlbaum.

Schegloff, E. A. (1980). Preliminaries to preliminaries: 'Can I ask you a question?' *Sociological Inquiry, 50,* 104–152.

Schegloff, E. A. (1982). Discourse as an interactional achievement: Some uses of 'uh huh' and other things that come between sentences. In D. Tannen (Ed.), *Analyzing discourse* (Georgetown University Roundtable on Languages and Linguistics 1981) (pp. 71–93). Washington, D.C.: Georgetown University Press.

Schegloff, E. A. (1997). Whose text? Whose context? *Discourse & Society, 8,* 165–187.

Schegloff, E. A. (1999a). 'Schegloff's texts as Billig's data': A critical reply. *Discourse & Society, 10,* 558–572.

Schegloff, E. A. (1999b). Naivete vs. sophistication or discipline vs. self-indulgence: A rejoinder to Billig. *Discourse & Society, 10,* 577–582.

Schegloff, E. A. (2006). *Sequence organization in interaction: A primer in conversation analysis I.* Cambridge, UK: Cambridge University Press.

Schegloff, E.A., Jefferson, G., & Sacks, H. (1977). The preference for self-correction in the organization of repair in conversation. *Language, 53,* 361-382.

Scheibel, D. (1994). Graffiti and 'film school' culture: Displaying alienation. *Communication Monographs, 61,* 1–18.

Scheibel, D. (1996). Appropriating bodies: Organ(izing) ideology and cultural practice in medical school. *Journal of Applied Communication Research, 24*, 310–331.

Scheibel, D. (1999). 'If your roommate dies, you get a 4.0': Reclaiming rumor with Burke and organizational culture. *Western Journal of Communication, 63*, 169–192.

Schely-Newman, E. (1997). Finding one's place: Locale narratives in an Israeli Moshav. *Quarterly Journal of Speech, 83*, 401–415.

Schenkein, J. (1978). Sketch of an analytic mentality for the study of conversational interaction. In J. Schenkein (Ed.), *Studies in the organization of conversational interaction* (pp. 1–6). New York, NY: Academic.

Schiffer, M. B. (1991). *The portable radio in American life.* Tuscon, AZ: University of Arizona Press.

Schiffrin, D. (1997). Theory and method in discourse analysis: What context for what unit? *Language & Communication, 17*, 75–92.

Schmidt, M. (2005). Individuation: Finding oneself in analysis—Taking risks and making sacrifices. *Journal of Analytical Psychology, 50*, 595–616.

Schneider, B. (2003). Narratives of schizophrenia: Constructing a positive identity. *Canadian Journal of Communication, 28*, 185–201.

Schrøder, K., Drotner, K., Kline, S., & Murray, C. (2003). *Researching audiences.* London, UK: Arnold.

Schrodt, P. (2006). A typological examination of communication competence and mental health in stepchildren. *Communication Monographs, 73*, 309–333.

Schrodt, P., Braithwaite, D. O., Soliz, J., Tye-Williams, S., Miller, A., Normand, E. L., et al. (2007). An examination of everyday talk in stepfamily systems. *Western Journal of Communication, 71*, 216–234.

Schutz, A. (1967). *The phenomenology of the social world* (G. Walsh & F. Lehnert, Trans.). Evanston, IL: Northwestern University Press.

Schwartz, H. S. (1987). [Review of the book *The reflective practitioner: How professionals think in action*]. *Administrative Science Quarterly, 32*, 614–617.

Schwartzman, H. B. (1993). *Ethnography in organizations* [Qualitative Research Methods Series No. 27]. Thousand Oaks, CA: Sage.

Scott, W. A. (1955). Reliability of content analysis: The case of nominal scale coding. *Public Opinion Quarterly, 19*, 321–325.

Scotton, C. M. (1985). What the heck, sir: Style shifting and lexical colouring as features of powerful language. In R. L. Street & J. N. Capella (Eds.), *Sequence and pattern in conversational behavior* (pp. 103–119). Baltimore, MD: E. Arnold.

Seale, C. (1999). Quality in qualitative research. *Qualitative Inquiry, 5*, 465–478.

Searle, J. (1991). Communication at work: An ethnography of checkout operators. *Open Letter, 2*, 28–39.

Sedgwick, P. R. (2001). *Descartes to Derrida: An introduction to European philosophy.* Oxford, UK: Blackwell.

Sequeira, D. L. (1993). Personal address as negotiated meaning in an American church community. *Research on Language and Social Interaction, 26*, 259–285.

Shimanoff, S. B. (1980). *Communication rules.* Beverly Hills, CA: Sage.

Shimanoff, S. B. (1985). Rules governing the verbal expression of emotions between married couples. *Western Journal of Speech Communication, 49*, 147–165.

Shoham, A., & Kahle, L. R. (1996). Spectators, viewers, readers: Communication and consumption communities in sport marketing. *Sport Marketing Quarterly, 5*, 11–19.

Shome, R. (1998). Caught in the term 'post-colonial': Why the 'post-colonial' still matters. *Critical Studies in Mass Communication, 15*, 203–212.

Shome, R. (1999). Postcolonial interventions in the rhetorical canon: An 'other' view. In J. L. Lucaites, C. M. Condit, & S. Caudill (Eds.), *Contemporary rhetorical theory: A reader* (pp. 591–608). New York, NY: Guilford.

Shugart, H. A. (1997). Counterhegemonic acts: Appropriation as a feminist rhetorical strategy. *Quarterly Journal of Speech, 83*, 210–229.

Siebold, D. R., Kudsi, S., & Rude, M. (1993). Does communication training make a difference? Evidence for the effectiveness of a presentation skills training program. *Journal of Applied Communication, 21*, 111–131.

Sigman, S. J. (1985). Some common mistakes students make when learning discourse analysis. *Communication Education, 34*, 119–127.

Sigman, S. J., Sullivan, S. J., & Wendell, M. (1988). Conversation: Data acquisition and analysis. In C. H. Tardy (Ed.), *A handbook for the study of human communication: Methods and instruments for observing, measuring, and assessing communication processes* (pp. 163–192). Norwood, NJ: Ablex.

Sillince, J. A. (2007). Organizational context and the discursive construction of organizing. *Management Communication Quarterly, 20*, 363–394.

Silverman, D. (1993). *Interpreting qualitative data: Methods for analyzing talk, text and interaction.* London, UK: Sage.

Simmerling, M., Schwegler, B., Sieber, J. E., & Lindgren, J. (2007). Introducing a new paradigm for ethical research in the social, behavioral, and biomedical sciences: Part I. *Northwestern University Law Review, 101*, 837–859.

Sims, R. R. (2000). Changing an Organization's Culture Under New Leadership. *Journal of Business Ethics*, 25, 65–78.

Sjoberg, G., Williams, N., Vaughan, T. R., & Sjoberg, A. F. (1991). The case study approach in social research. In J. R. Feagin, A. M. Orum & G. Sjoberg (Eds.), *A Case for the Case Study* (pp. 27–79). Chapel Hill, NC: University of North Carolina Press.

Skovholt, K., & Svennevig, J. (2006). Email copies in workplace interaction. *Journal of Computer-Mediated Communication*, 12, 42–65.

Slemon, J. (1995). 'The scramble for post-colonialism'. In B. Ashcraft, G. Griffiths, & H. Tiffin (Eds.), *The post-colonial studies reader* (pp. 45–52). London, UK: Routledge.

Smart, G. (1998). Mapping conceptual worlds: Using interpretive ethnography to explore knowledge-making in a professional community. *Journal of Business Communication*, 35, 111–127.

Smith, G.N., Nolan, R.F., & Dai, Y. (1996). Job-refusal letters: Readers' affective responses to direct and indirect organizational plans. *Business Communication Quarterly*, 59, 67–73.

Smith, M. J. (1988). *Contemporary communication research methods*. Belmont, CA: Wadsworth.

Smythe, D. W. (1981). *Dependency road: Communications, capitalism, consciousness and Canada*. Norwood, NJ: Ablex.

Snow, D. A. (1980). The disengagement process: A neglected problem in participant-observation research. *Qualitative Sociology*, 3, 100–122.

Snyder, L. (2000). Invitation to transcendence: The *Book of Revelation*. *Quarterly Journal of Speech*, 86, 402–416.

Soukup, C. (2006). Hitching a ride on a star: Celebrity, fandom, and identification on the World Wide Web. *Southern Communication Journal*, 71, 319–337.

Sparks, R., Young, M. L., & Darnell, S. (2006). Convergence, corporate restructuring and Canadian online news, 2000–2003, *Canadian Journal of Communication*, 31, 391–423.

Speer, S. A., & Potter, J. (2000). The management of heterosexist talk: Conversational repairs and prejudiced claims. *Discourse & Society*, 11, 543–572.

Spitzberg, B., & Cupach, W. (1984). *Interpersonal communication competence*. Beverly Hills, CA: Sage.

Spitzberg, B., & Hecht, M. (1984). A component model of relational competence. *Human Communication Research*, 10, 575–599.

Spradley, J. P. (1980). *Participant observation*. New York: Holt, Rinehart, & Winston.

Sprague, J. (1992). Critical perspectives on teacher empowerment. *Communication Education*, 41, 181–203.

Stablein, R. (1996). Data in organization studies. In S. R. Clegg, C. Hardy, & W. R. Nord (Eds.), *Handbook of organization studies* (pp. 347–369). London, UK: Sage.

Stage, F. K., & Russell, R. V. (1992). Using method triangulation in college student research. *Journal of College Student Development*, 33, 485–491.

Stake, R. E. (1998). Case studies. In N. Denzin & Y. Lincoln (Eds.), *Strategies of qualitative inquiry* (pp. 86–109). Thousand Oaks, CA: Sage.

Stamp, G. H. (1999). A qualitatively constructed interpersonal communication model: A grounded theory analysis. *Human Communication Research*, 25, 531–547.

Staton, A., Johnson, G., & Jorgenson-Earp, C. (1995). Communication in the socialization of new university freshmen. *Communication Education*, 44, 334–352.

Steinberg, P. E., & McDowell, S. D. (2003). Mutiny on the bandwidth: The semiotics of statehood in the internet domain name registries of Pitcairn Island and Niue. *New Media & Society*, 5, 47–67.

Stephen, T. (1999). Computer-assisted concept analysis of HCR's first 25 years. *Human Communication Research*, 25, 498–513.

Stephenson, M. T., Palmgreen, P., Hoyle, R. H., Donohew, L., Lorch, E. P., & Colon, S. E. (1999). Short-term effects of an anti-marijuana media campaign targeting high sensation seeking adolescents. *Journal of Applied Communication Research*, 27, 175–195.

Stern, S. R. (2003). Encountering distressing information in online research: A consideration of legal and ethical responsibilities. *New Media & Society*, 5, 249–266.

Stern, S. R. (2005). Messages from teens on the big screen: Smoking, drinking, and drug use in teen-centered films. *Journal of Health Communication*, 10, 331–346.

Steuter, E. (2010). Consumer advocacy or quack attack?: Representations of homeopathy in the media. *Canadian Journal of Media Studies*, 6, 52–71.

Stewart, A. (1998). *The ethnographer's method* [Qualitative Research Methods Series No. 46]. Thousand Oaks, CA: Sage.

Stewart, C. M, Shields, S. F., & Sen, N. (1998). Diversity in on-line discussions: A study of cultural and gender differences in listservs. *Electronic Journal of Communication*, 8(3/4), File Stewart V8N398, 1–15.

Stiles, W. B. (1980). Comparison of dimensions derived from rating versus coding of dialogue. *Journal of Personality and Social Psychology*, 38, 359–374.

Stivers, T., & Heritage, J. (2001). Breaking the sequential

mold: answering 'more than the question' during medical history taking. *Text*, 21(1/2), 151–185.

Stoker, K. (2005). Loyalty in public relations: When does it cross the line between virtue and vice? *Journal of Mass Media Ethics*, 20, 269–287.

Stokoe, E. H., & Smithson, J. (2001). Making gender relevant: Conversational analysis and gender categories in interaction. *Discourse & Society*, 12, 217–244.

Stoller, E. P. (1993). Gender and the organization of lay health care: A socialist-feminist perspective. *Journal of Aging Studies*, 7, 151–170.

Storey, W. H., & Jones, T. (2004). *Writing history: A guide for Canadian students* (2nd. ed.). Don Mills, ON: Oxford University Press.

Strauss, A., & Corbin, J. (1998). Grounded theory methodology: An overview. In N. K. Denzin & Y. Lincoln (Eds.), *Strategies of qualitative inquiry* (pp. 158–183). Newbury Park, CA: Sage.

Stringer Cawyer, C. S., & Smith-Dupre', A. (1995). Communicating social support: Identifying supportive episodes in an HIV/AIDS support group. *Communication Quarterly*, 43, 243–258.

Stroud, S. R. (2001). Technology and mythic narrative: *The Matrix* as technological hero-quest. *Western Journal of Communication*, 65, 416–441.

Stuckey, N. P., & Daughton, S. M. (2003). The body present: Reporting everyday life performance. In P. LeBaron, C. D. LeBaron, & J. Mandelbaum (Eds.), *Studies in language & social interaction* (pp. 479–492). Mahwah, NJ: Lawrence Erlbaum.

Sturrock, J. (2003) *Structuralism* (2nd ed.). Malden, MA: Blackwell

Sunwolf, & Seibold, D. R. (1998). Jurors' intuitive rules for deliberation: A structurational approach to communication in jury decision making. *Communication Monographs*, 65, 282–307.

Suzuki, S. (2006). Gender-linked differences in informal argument: Analyzing arguments in an online newspaper. *Women's Studies in Communication*, 29, 193–219.

Swanson, D. L. (1993). Fragmentation, the field, and the future. *Journal of Communication*, 43, 163–192.

Sypher, B. D. (1997). *Case studies in organizational communication 2: Perpsectives on contemporary work life*. New York, NY: Guilford.

Szuchewycz, B. (2000). Re-pressing racism: The denial of racism in the Canadian press. *Canadian Journal of Communication*, 25, 497–515.

Tardy, R. W., & Hale, C. L. (1998). Getting 'plugged in': A network analysis of health-information seeking among 'stay-at-home moms'. *Communication Monographs*, 65, 336–357.

Tate, E. D., Osler, A., & Siegel, A. (2000). The beginnings of communication studies in Canada: Remembering and narrating the past. *Canadian Journal of Communication*, 25, 61–103.

Tate, M. A., & Allen, V. (2003). Integrating distinctively Canadian elements into television drama: A formula for success or failure? The *Due South* experience, *Canadian Journal of Communication*, 28, 67–83.

Tator, C., Henry, F., & Mattis, W. (1998). *Challenging racism in the arts: Case studies of controversy and conflict*. Toronto, ON: University of Toronto Press.

Taylor, C. R., & Bang, H. (1997). Portrayals of Latinos in magazine advertising. *Journalism and Mass Communication Quarterly*, 74, 285–303.

Taylor, S. J., & Bogdan, R. C. (1998). *Introduction to qualitative research methods: A guidebook and resource* (3rd ed.). New York, NY: Wiley.

ten Have, P. (1999). *Doing conversation analysis: A practical guide*. London, UK: Sage.

Tesch, R. (1990). *Qualitative research: Analysis types and software tools*. New York, NY: Falmer.

Tesch, R. (1991). Computers and qualitative data II [Special issue, Parts 1 & 2]. *Qualitative Sociology*, 14(3 & 4).

Thimm, C., Rademacher, U., & Kruse, L. (1998). Age stereotypes and patronizing messages: Features of age-adapted speech in technical instructions to the elderly. *Journal of Applied Communication Research*, 26, 66–82.

Thomas, J. (1993). *Doing critical ethnography*. Newbury Park, CA: Sage.

Tillotson, S. (1991). 'We may all soon be "first-class men"': Gender and skill in Canada's early twentieth century urban telegraph industry. *Labour / Le Travail*, 27, 97–123.

Tinney, J. (2008). Negotiating boundaries and roles. *Journal of Contemporary Ethnography*, 37(2), 202–225.

Tompkins, P. K. (1997). How to think and talk about organizational communication. In P. Y. Byers (Ed.) *Organizational communication: Theory and behavior* (pp. 361–373). Boston, MA: Allyn & Bacon.

Toulmin, S. E. (1972). *Human understanding*. Oxford, UK: Clarendon Press.

Toulmin, S. E., Rieke, R., & Janik, A. (1984). *An introduction to reasoning* (2nd ed.). New York, NY: Macmillan.

Tracy, K. (1995). Action-implicative discourse analysis. *Journal of Language & Social Psychology*, 14, 195–216.

Tracy, K. (2008). 'Reasonable hostility': Situation-appropriate face-attack. *Journal of Politeness Research*, 4, 169–191.

Tracy, K., & Haspel, K. (2004). Language and social inter-action: its institutional identity, intellectual landscape, and discipline-shifting agenda. *Journal of Communication, 54,* 788–816.

Tracy, K., & Tracy, S. J. (1998). Rudeness at 911: Reconceptualizing face and face attack. *Human Communication Research, 25,* 225–251.

Tracy, S., Myers, K. K., & Scott, C. W. (2006). Cracking jokes and crafting selves: Sensemaking and identity management among human service workers. *Communication Monographs, 73,* 283–308.

Trees, A. R., & Manusov, V. (1998). Managing face concerns in criticism: Integrating nonverbal behaviors as a dimension of politeness in female friendship dyads. *Human Communication Research, 24,* 564–583.

Tremblay, D.-G., Paquet, R, & Najem, E. (2006). A way to balance work and family or an increase in work-family conflict? *Canadian Journal of Communication, 31,* 715–731.

Trethewey, A. (2001). Reproducing and resisting the master narrative of decline: Midlife professional women's experiences of aging. *Management Communication Quarterly, 15,* 183–207.

Trujillo, N. (1991). Hegemonic masculinity on the mound: Media representations of Nolan Ryan and American sports culture. *Critical Studies in Mass Communication, 8,* 290–308.

Trujillo, N. (1992). Interpreting (the work and the talk of) baseball: Perspectives on ballpark culture. *Western Journal of Communication, 56,* 350–371.

Trujillo, N. (1993). Interpreting November 22: A critical ethnography of an assassination site. *Quarterly Journal of Speech, 79,* 447–466.

Trujillo, N. (1999). Teaching ethnography in the twenty-first century using collaborative learning. *Journal of Contemporary Ethnography, 28,* 705–719.

United Nations. (1948). *Universal declaration of human rights.* Retrieved June 15, 2010, from www.ohchr.org.

United States, National Commission for the Protection of Human Subjects of Biomedical and Behavioral Research (1979). *The Belmont report: Ethical principles and guidelines for the protection of human research.* Washington, DC: US Government Printing Office.

Valdes, G., & Pino, C. (1981). *Muy a tus ordenes:* Compliment responses among Mexican-American bilinguals. *Language and Society, 10,* 53–72.

Vande Berg, L. R. (1997). Editor's introduction: Special series on 'voices'. *Western Journal of Communication, 61,* 87–88.

Van Dijk, T. A. (Ed.). (1997a). *Discourse as social interaction.* Thousand Oaks, CA: Sage.

Van Dijk, T. A. (1997b). The study of discourse. In T. A. Van Dijk (Ed.), *Discourse as structure and process* (pp. 1–34). London, UK: Sage.

Van Dijk, T. A. (1998). *Ideology: A multidisciplinary approach.* Thousand Oaks, CA: Sage.

Van Lear, C. A., Sheehan, M., Withers, L. A., & Walker, R. A. (2005). AA Online: The enactment of supportive computer mediated communication. *Western Journal of Communication, 69,* 5–26.

Van Maanen, J. (1988). *Tales of the field: On writing ethnography.* Chicago, IL: University of Chicago Press.

Van Oosting, J. (1996). Acoustic writers and electronic readers: Literature through the back door. *Communication Education, 45,* 108–111.

Veatch, R. M. (1996). From Nuremberg through the 1990s: The priority of autonomy. In H. Y. Vanderpool (Ed.), *The ethics of research involving human subjects: Facing the 21st century* (pp. 45–58). Frederick, MD: University Publishing Group.

Verbeke, W., & Bagozzi, R. P. (2000). Sales call anxiety: Exploring what it means when fear rules a sales encounter. *Journal of Marketing, 64*(3), 88–101.

Vipond, M. (1992). *Listening in: The first decade of Canadian broadcasting.* Montreal, QC: McGill-Queen's University Press.

Walden, K. (1997). *Becoming modern in Toronto: The industrial exhibition and the shaping of a late Victorian culture.* Toronto, ON: University of Toronto Press.

Waldron, V. (1990). Constrained rationality: Situational influences on information acquisition plans and tactics. *Communication Monographs, 57,* 184–201.

Watkins, S. C. (2001). A nation of millions: Hip hop culture and the legacy of black nationalism. *Communication Review, 4,* 373–398.

Watson, G., & Goulet, J. (1998). What can ethnomethodology say about power? *Qualitative Inquiry, 4,* 96–113.

Watt, J. H., & van den Berg, S. A. (1995). *Research methods for communication science.* Boston, MA: Allyn & Bacon.

Weatherby, G. A., & Scoggins, B. (2005–2006). A content analysis of persuasion techniques used on white supremacist Web sites. *Journal of Hate Studies, 4*(1), 9–31.

Weaver, J. B., III. (1991). Are 'slasher' horror films sexually violent? A content analysis. *Journal of Broadcasting and Electronic Media, 35,* 385–392.

Weber, K. (2004). The relationship between student interest and teacher's use of behavior alteration techniques. *Communication Research Reports, 21,* 428–436.

Weick, K. (1989). [Review of the book *Tales of the field: On writing ethnography*]. *Administrative Science Quarterly, 34,* 307–311.

Weick, K. E. (1995). *Sensemaking in organizations.* Thousand Oaks, CA: Sage.

Weitzel, A., & Geist, P. (1998). Parliamentary procedure in a community group: Communication and vigilant decision making. *Communication Monographs, 65,* 244–260.

West, C. (1982). Why can't a woman be more like a man? *Work and Occupations, 9,* 5–29.

West, C., & Zimmerman, D. (1983). Small insults: A study of interruptions in cross-sex conversations between unacquainted persons. In B. Thorne, C. Kramerae, & N. Henley (Eds.), *Language, gender, and society* (pp. 102–117). Rowley, MA: Newbury House.

Westlund, O. (2008). From mobile phone to mobile device: News consumption on the go. *Canadian Journal of Communication, 33,* 443–463.

Whalen, M., & Zimmerman, D. (1987). Sequential and institutional contexts in calls for help. *Social Psychology Quarterly, 50,* 172–185.

White, W. J. (1999). Academic topographies: A network analysis of disciplinarity among communication faculty. *Human Communication Research, 25,* 604–617.

Wiemann, J. M. (1981). Effects of laboratory videotaping procedures on selected conversational behaviors. *Human Communication Research, 7,* 302–311.

Wieviorka, M. (1992). Case studies: history or sociology?. In C. C. Ragin & H. S. Becker (Eds.), *What is a case? Exploring the foundations of social inquiry* (pp. 159–172). Cambridge, MA: Cambridge University Press.

Williams, D. J. (2006). Autoethnography in offender rehabilitation research and practice: Addressing the 'us vs. them' problem. *Contemporary Justice Review, 9,* 23–38.

Williams, R. (1977). *Marxism and literature.* Oxford, UK: Oxford University Press.

Wilson, K. (2008). The last mile: Service tiers versus infrastructure developments and the debate on Internet neutrality. *Canadian Journal of Communication, 33,* 81–100.

Wilson, S. R., Aleman, C. G., & Leatham, G. B. (1998). Identity implications of influence goals: A revised analysis of face-threatening acts and application to seeking compliance with same-sex friends. *Human Communication Research, 25,* 64–96.

Wimmer, R. D., & Dominick, J. R. (1991). Content analysis. In *Mass media research: An introduction* (3rd ed., pp. 156–179). Belmont, CA: Wadsworth.

Witmer, D. F. (1997). Communication and recovery: Structuration as an ontological approach to organizational culture. *Communication Monographs, 64,* 324–349.

Witt, P. L., & Schrodt, P. (2006). The influence of instructional technology use and teacher immediacy on student affect for teacher and course. *Communication Reports, 19,* 1–15.

Wittgenstein, L. (1953). *Philosophical investigations* (G. E. M. Anscombe, Trans.). New York, NY: Macmillian.

Wittig, M. (1990). The straight mind. In R. Ferguson, M. Gever, T. T. Minh-Ha, & C. West (Eds.), *Out there: Marginalization and contemporary culture* (pp. 51–58). Cambridge, MA: MIT Press.

Wong, J. (2000a). Information and responsibility: The case of social kinds. *Canadian Journal of Communication, 25,* 199–210.

Wong, J. (2000b). The token 'yeah' in nonnative speaker English conversation. *Research on Language & Social Interaction, 33,* 39–67.

Wood, A. F., & Fassett, D. L. (2003). Remote control: Identity, power, and technology in the communication classroom. *Communication Education, 52,* 286–296.

Wood, J. T. (1997). *Communication theories in action: An introduction.* Belmont, CA: Wadsworth.

Wood, J. T., & Inman, C. C. (1993). In a different mode: Masculine styles of communicating closeness. *Journal of Applied Communication Research, 21,* 279–295.

Wooffitt, R. (2005). *Conversation analysis and discourse analysis: A comparative and critical introduction.* Thousand Oaks, CA: Sage.

Wright, K. (2002). Social support within an on-line cancer community: An assessment of emotional support, perceptions of advantages and disadvantages, and motives for using the community from a communication perspective. *Journal of Applied Communication Research, 30,* 195–209.

Wright, K. B., & O'Hair, D. (1999). Seeking and resisting compliance: Selection and evaluation of tactics in a simulated college student drinking context. *Communication Research Reports, 16,* 266–275.

Yep, G. (1997). My three cultures: Navigating the multicultural identity landscape. San Francisco State University *Magazine, 15*(2), 43–55.

Yep, G. A. (1998). Freire's conscientization, dialogue, and liberation: Personal reflections on classroom discussions of marginality. *International Journal of Sexuality and Gender Studies, 3,* 159–166.

Yep, G. A., Lovaas, K. E., & Ho, P. C. (2001). Communication in 'Asian American' families with queer members:

A relational dialectics perspective. In M. Bernstein & R. Reimann (Eds.), *Queer families, queer politics: Challenging culture and the state* (pp. 152–172). New York, NY: Columbia University Press.

Yep, G. A., Lovaas, K. E., & Pagonis, A. V. (2002). The case of 'riding bareback': Sexual practices and the paradoxes of identity in the era of AIDS. *Journal of Homosexuality, 42*(4), 1–14.

Yin, R. K. (2002). *Case study research: Design and methods* (3rd ed.). Thousand Oaks, CA: Sage.

Yin, R. K. (2003). *Applications of case study research* (2nd ed.). Newbury Park, CA: Sage.

Zelizer, J. E. (2004). History and political science: Together again? *Journal of Policy History, 16,* 126–136.

Zine, J. (2008). Honour and identity: An ethnographic account of Muslim girls in Canadian Islamic school. *Topia: Canadian Journal of Cultural Studies, 19,* 35–61.

Zoch, L. M., & Turk, J. V. (1998). Women making news: Gender as a variable in source selection and use. *Journalism & Mass Communication Quarterly, 75,* 762–775.

Index

Page numbers in **bold type** indicate illustrations.